CARGO WORK

SECTION DRAWING OF ACL'S 37 000 DWT
THIRD GENERATION RORO CONTAINER SHIP
'ATLANTIC COMPANION'

MAXIMUM CAPACITIES	
CONTAINERS	2 139 teu
CARS	1 697 cars
TRAILERS	2 630 m

CARGO WORK

The Care, Handling and Carriage of Cargoes

Including

The Management of Marine Cargo Transportation

BY

CAPTAIN L. G. TAYLOR (EXTRA MASTER), M.N.

Formerly Training and Education Officer, British Transport Docks Board
Formerly on the Staff of the Sir John Cass Nautical College, London

In Association With
CAPTAIN L. D. CONWAY (MASTER MARINER),
B.Sc., M.B.I.M.

GLASGOW
BROWN, SON & FERGUSON, LTD., NAUTICAL PUBLISHERS
4–10 DARNLEY STREET

First Edition	–	1944
Seventh Edition	–	1970
Eighth Edition	–	1974
Ninth Edition	–	1978
Tenth Edition	–	1981
Eleventh Edition	–	1986
Twelfth Edition	–	1992
Reprinted	–	2008

ISBN 978-0-85174-605-0
ISBN 0 85174 605 5 (Twelfth Edition)

©2008—BROWN, SON & FERGUSON, LTD., GLASGOW, G41 2SD
Printed and Made in Great Britain

PREFACE

This, the 12th edition of this book has been revised only to the extent of illustrating, primarily, the impact of Containerization and the influence of ports, and their activities, upon those, such as Ships' officers and others involved in the maritime environment. Other than that, this book retains much of the 11th Edition insofar as that can be pertinent and useful in a changing international industry covering the widest spectrum of goods and services moving around the world. In this context the text of this book reflects the interest and needs of shippers to obtain the most efficient and profitable means of carriage for their goods and the procedures of cargo handling to that end. While it is appreciated that ships, trades and cargoes have recently indicated the need for different applications none the less there are still ships, both in the UK and abroad, in which, and towards which, older applications can successfully be made: in this respect this 12th Edition can be useful.

In no small way does the Ship Cargo Officer hold a position of high priority in this business for it is he who, in co-ordination and co-operation with associates, enhance the reputation of his ship and of its owners, to be acceptable in the highly competitive 'Transportation Mode' and, by so doing, develops unto his own self a degree of competence and ability in fulfilling his career prospects and ambitions.

This 12th edition aims to foster these ideals. It retains much that is basic in Cargo Handling, without which no meaningful progress is possible but it builds on to those basics the current and envisaged modern developments which trade patterns impose upon ship husbandry. In this respect the edition is aware of the growing international impact in Cargo movement and, where relevant, the text highlights this.

Safety in Cargo Carriage and handling; Cargo Specialisms and the attendent care; Modern ship equipment; Bulk and Dangerous Cargoes are given equal necessary attention alongside General and Unitised Cargoes, all carried in classes of ships designed to effectively meet the trading patterns.

The edition, though understandably primarily with the Cargo Officer in mind, is equally useful to others associated with cargo carriage. The Management of Cargo Control is a facet which requires co-ordination and co-operation at all levels and in most related disciplines, be it the personnel involved in ships, in ports or in shipping business organizations.

This edition benefits from a considerable number of interests who have willingly provided essential and useful material. Thanks and appreciation is hereby made and reference indicated in the acknowledgements at the end of the book.

Sufficient to say that without their help the standard and practical approach aimed for would not have been possible.

L.G.T. 1991

FUNDAMENTAL BASICS OF CARGO WORK
(See also page 469 — A Glossary)

Although the organization of Cargo Work has benefitted from numerous changes and modernization procedures over time ... and more so in recent years, fundamental basics still remain to influence the process of cargo handling. All are covered, in general and specific manner, in the text of this 11th edition.

Some of the more notable, but by no means exhaustive, basics are as follows, each to bear in mind when considering the overall detailed text of this edition.

Bulk Cargoes ... their stowage, safety factors and carriage.
Broken Stowage ... used in two senses ...
    (*a*) Space left in a compartment due to stowage necessities.
    (*b*) 'Small' packages used to fill up empty spaces.
Barrels Containerization ... stowage and security, capacities of different containers insofar as the weights will influence stowage. Similar considerations will apply to drums.
Coal ... its carriage and applicable precautionary considerations.
Cleaning Spaces ... appropriate procedures for different cargoes.
Chilled ... and Frozen carriage for edible commodities.
Dunnaging ... systems and methods for different cargoes and packaging of same. Materials used for dunnaging.
Documentation ... methods of maintaining a record and check of all cargoes. Rules and regulations appropriate to the systems.
Deck cargoes ... related precautions to be taken.
Derrick Rigging ... consideration of modern developments.
Damage to cargo ... precautions and actions to be taken.
Dangerous cargoes.
Hatch openings and Access points. Security factors.
Insulation of compartments relative to the types of cargoes involved.
Load Lines ... influences upon loading.
Lashings ... types and reasons for methods used.
Lifting heavy loads.
Port Speed ... cargo officer's involvement.
Rules ... regulations ... Ministry notices ... Codes of Practice ... observance of.
Safety Factors ... cargoes and personnel.
Species cargoes ... reception and stowage procedures.
Sweat preventation and reduction.
Stowage Factors ... their relevance to cargo stowage.
Tons per Inch and Inch Trim Moments, their influence upon cargo loading and discharge.
Weight and measurement cargoes ... differences in cargo planning.
Stability considerations in the loading, carriage and discharging of cargoes.

CONTENTS

vii

INTRODUCTION

Cargo Handling in Relation to Trade Developments and the Business of Shipping

The Place of the Cargo Officer in the overall pattern

Of recent years, and with current developments, a new dimension has entered into the sphere of Cargo Handling carrying with it new responsibilities. It is that concerned with its relationship towards other associated activities within transportation and has introduced additional basic principles many of which are likely to be influential to a greater and faster degree than previously. Not the least of these are related to TRADE PATTERNS and the Cargo Officer would be wise, and prudent, to consider the implications involved. In doing so he should also seek to understand how all this fits into the BUSINESS OF SHIPPING.

Within the Business of Shipping there are terms and definitions which influence areas of participation and control, be these ships, as such, shipping organizations and companies, ports and docks and servicing transportation/distribution agencies.

Since maritime transportation is highly intermodal, and a ship the major aspect of the integration procedures, it is desirable that ship's officers should be aware of the part they play and the degree to which they can be involved in the overall business, and so thus be able to coordinate effectively with personnel in other related areas dealing with the procedures of cargo handling.

Terms used are numerous and widely appropriate; they have international, national and local origin . . . and application. The following examples, though not exhaustive, are worthy of attention.

(a) Registration.

Ships are registered (or classified) as being suitable for the work they have to do and are designed, built and maintained to that end. Classes of ships, rather than types, is the more appropriate classification in this modern age and it is international in controlling structural, safety and suitability of vessels, in which context shipping companies normally build within the jurisdiction of one or the other classification societies.

1. Lloyds Register of Shipping   Great Britain.
2. The American Bureau of Shipping   U.S.A.
3. Bureau Veritas   France.
4. Registro Italiano   Italy.
5. Germanischer Lloyd   Germany.

6. Norske Veritas   Norway.

7. Polski Registro   Poland.

Within the registration of ships the tonnage measurements are now governed by the I.M.O. (International Maritime Organization) new Convention Rules. There are two main considerations.

  (i) GROSS TONNAGE is based on the volume of all enclosed spaces.

  (ii) NET TONNAGE is the volume of Cargo Space, plus the volume of passenger space, and not less than 30 % of the Gross Tonnage.

Gross and Net Tonnage is now expressed in cubic metres ... no longer is it a case of 100 cu. ft., as hitherto.

(b) Chartering.

Ships, though in the main working for their owners, can be 'hired or lent' to other operators for periods of time. This is known as Chartering. It can be a common practice in all trades and with all cargoes. It can serve a need for all kinds of reasons; it can be profitable business; it can be largely influenced by 'cargo markets' in so far as these can fluctuate. Charters can be ...

1. A Bareboat Charter, where an organization hires a vessel to cover its trading requirements and in so doing is responsible for providing the crew and covering all the costs and charges relative to its usage during the operating period. The owner of the vessel provides only the ship.

2. A Time Charter is where the shipowner provides the ship, together with the crew, and pays the major ship dues.

   The charterer is then responsible for all other charges for the 'whole' time the vessel is on hire to him. If the 'time' is only for one voyage, the period is known as a 'Voyage Charter'.

3. A Gross or Net Charter is where the hirer is responsible for all charges incurred.

   Charters are normally drawn up by Ship Brokers and the document involved is 'The Charter Party'. The broker is the link between Owner and Charterer. It is within the orbit of the Baltic Exchange, in London, where a considerable amount of ship chartering is carried out.

(c) Insurance Cover.

Ships are insured through reputable agencies to cover a variety of major and minor maritime risks. In this context marine insurance is said to be of two forms of 'Average'.

Where a ship, or its cargo, is damaged or lost the term used is 'Average' insurance but if a ship or its cargo is deliberately damaged for the general benefit, then 'General

Average' cover applies. Both arrangements are appropriate forms of indemnity practice in the maritime world.

Maritime insurance...as with all forms of insurance...can be complex and can induce broad litigation. Primarily that part of the issue is that which places a responsibility upon the Cargo Officer towards the safe keeping of the cargo under his care.

There is, however, a specific form of insurance in the Business of Shipping known as P & I (Protection and Indemnity Clubs) which deals with a number of other risks to which ships and owners are subject and these applications can be very wide. Cargo claims, pollution are two cases in point as are injuries to dock workers.

(d) 'Freight' is the term used to denote the charge levied for carrying the goods (cargo).

(e) The Manifest and Bill of Lading.

These documents are probably the most important of all recording systems in the carriage of cargo. Both have direct relationship with the duties of a Cargo Officer. They have close relevance to his preparation and compilation of Cargo Plans.

The former...the Manifest...is the complete list of cargo loaded. It is required by a number of bodies interested in the ship and its cargo, not least being the Customs. It is also needed by the ports and dock authorities in the planning of stevedoring activities and the types of equipment and services to be involved for a ship they are to receive.

The Bill of Lading is, in fact, the receipt for the goods. It is evidence of contract of carriage; it is the document of title to the cargo. Mates Receipts will have important bearing upon this document.

A specific definition relative to the Bill of Lading is the T.B.L. (Through Bill of Lading) which finds application in the European/International/Continental services.

(f) Dwell Time.

This is unnecessary time spent in port. (Ships only earn money when transporting 'cargo' (the term used in the widest sense). It has bearing upon the aspect of 'quick turn round'.

(g) Systems

In many of the highly developed ports of the world the working of Cargo Loads/viz. Ships is highly technically biased. Notably is this the case with the Carriage of Containers.

Fragmentation of cargo operations is overshadowed by computerized methods such that the total operations covering a ship load is planned and programmed into progressive subsequent systems of division covering these loads, their distribution and movement and the labour and equipment needs. Particularly is this approach to be seen in the 'large' container ports and also with the fast moving large ro/ro procedures.

These applications give rise to the term 'Systems' and ship (cargo) officers must be aware of these and become effectively acquainted in so far as ship co-ordination and co-operation with the shore authorities is necessary.

Trade patterns are basic to Cargo Handling, and to its development. They influence the types and classes of vessels used to transport both raw and manufactured commodities and products; they promote the introduction and development of equipment and facilities necessary to the handling of the cargoes, be these in ships, ports or on associated transportation units and they change, progress and/or decline as a result of world economic circumstances.

Whereas hitherto the movement of goods followed, more or less, established patterns, no longer do such restrictions apply nor are ships so consistent in their habits. As markets develop ships quickly follow to benefit from the trade available; conversely, shipping is equally reactive to unprofitable markets with ships, in the ultimate, disappearing from routes previously used, to show up elsewhere later on. Much of this pattern has grown out of new areas where more and newer raw materials have become available and where financial investment in the economy of developing countries has enabled them to compete more widely and require goods and equipment to support their economic progression. Ships have fitted into this need.

This is the real meaning of a Trade Pattern. It is not a static involvement in any insular fashion whatever, indeed it is continuously changing, albeit though doubtless it is only an extension of the past but it is now more 'world' influenced and needs to be interpreted accordingly. For the Cargo Officer the situation presents the desirability for him to be versatile and broad in outlook and conscious of the need to be more adaptable over a reasonably wide sphere of cargo transportation techniques.

In the main, there is need to be aware of:

(a) the technological advances in ship design to meet cargo changes;
(b) the rapid developments and vast increases in the tonnages of bulk cargo carriage;
(c) the considerable impact of unitization, in all its forms;
(d) the fluctuating changes which arise within the oil transportation field;
(e) the new and modern techniques of refrigeration, particularly with container carriage.

Probably, more important than most, is there the need to understand the organizational and operational procedures which the ports of the world, both in the industrial and developing countries, are continually fashioning in order to maintain their capability to receive and handle a variety of different types of cargoes. Fundamentally, a port grows by virtue of the trade it can attract, and maintain. Contiguous with this, the effectiveness of a ship is measured by the 'SPEED OF TURN ROUND' which it can promote. No two ports may require the same services from the ships it receives; likewise no two ships may need similar facilities . . . much depends upon their class and the types and tonnages of cargo they wish to load or discharge. The functions of co-ordination and co-operation loom wide and important in modern cargo handling ports procedures from which the reception and distribution of goods in transit meet the needs of consignors, consignees and transportation carriers.

The cargo officer is no longer isolated from this environment ... he is a part of it and the study of his professional discipline must now contain a wider concern than hitherto applied when cargo matters were less complex. Neither is it sufficient that he should treat the matter in isolation . . . he must encourage a similar broadness of attitude in all those who report, and are responsible, to him.

The Shipping Business is continually concerned in endeavouring to anticipate cycles of prosperity. By the very nature of things these are dependent upon the fluctuations in world trade and, as a result, ships can become both over and under employed both in the short and long term thus creating instability in the business of running ships. It is only by careful and judicious planning, and by balancing the facilities available . . . i.e. types and classes of ships . . . can a shipping company aim to alleviate what otherwise might be a slump period.

In no small measure does the effective running, or operating of a ship in service assist in maintaining an overall 'healthy' company since, as it only earns money (freight) when it is at sea, this ability can be impaired if its reputation to conform to shippers' requirements does not match up to their needs. Indeed, the optimum criterion of effective ship economy is very largely influenced by the manner by which both ship and shore cargo handling procedures are fostered. The shipper . . . as the customer . . . leaves no doubts as to his expectations in these directions.

The range of vessels currently operating, and envisaged to develop over the reasonable future in order to meet the modern marketing patterns is so wide as to prohibit any standard guide as to the extent of a cargo officer's involvement in the philosophy of the business of shipping. Sufficient to say there is a contribution, the influence of which being dependent upon the continued use to which his ship is put, and he, in the planning of procedures by which its use is profitable, being aware of changes taking place in these directions.

The increasing use of computer systems to plan and direct the distribution of cargo within the ship and to facilitate the documentation of cargo, seems to have diminished the direct involvement of the ship's officer with the *raison d'être* of the ship. However, this is more than compensated for by the need for increased vigilance and attention to the many Codes of Practice which must be followed. Knowledge of these Codes is essential and application of them vital if today's cargoes are to be carried safely.

In terms of employment, therefore, the officer must have sufficient breadth of outlook to ensure his suitability for service in shipping companies operating a wide variety of ship types, building on to that breadth a more detailed specialization as his career advances.

This is recognized in the growing number of countries whose maritime administration requires, in addition to standard qualification courses, attendance at specialized courses of instruction before an officer is permitted to serve in a senior capacity on bulk oil carriers or gas carriers. The instruction will extend to the handling and manoeuvring techniques necessary for such vessels.

The United Kingdom requirements are contained in 'M' Notices 771 (September 1976), 952 (December 1980) and 1107 (February 1984).

The mobility of officers between ship types is therefore tending to diminish, nevertheless if a career in any aspect of cargo work is to be meaningful, a study of the features of each category of goods and of the integrated parts in the chain of movement of goods must be regarded as essential.

The following notes, however, indicate a reasonable assessment of ship types and capacities which, normally, could be available in different trades and from which a successful and interesting career in cargo handling can be developed.

Cargo carrying vessels can be classified into a number of groups. In each, modern building tendancy is to provide as wide a versatility of usage as is possible, i.e. relatively fast, both in service and in port working; of a size and design which meets the envisaged marketing trends in trade patterns and with capacity space which can be used in as wide a fashion as circumstances dictate. Restriction on usage is minimized.

The study of cargo handling therefore calls for a comparable breadth of outlook balanced by a need for specialization in some areas in that officers can now expect to move more frequently between different types of vessels in that the major shipping consortiums now control fleets able to cover most, if not all, of the cargo transportation requirements. Shipping groups and consortiums are now the order of the day permitting, as they do, wider and useful diversification of facilities and services both desirable and necessary to profitable business endeavour.

In the context of the foregoing, maritime transportation within the business of shipping and with which cargo officers could be widely involved can cover:

    1. DRY BULKS . . . Coal, Coke, Grains, Ores, Phosphates, Steel, Forest Products.

2. LIQUID BULKS . . . Oil and its By-products. Chemicals, Liquid Gases.
3. GENERAL CARGO . . . Commonly known as 'break bulk' which includes a multitudinous typical selection of manu-factured goods, processed materials, natural edities (tea, cotton, coffee) rubbers, spices. The list could be endless.
4. REFRIGERATED CARGO . . . Meats, Fruits; both in refrigerated and non-refrigerated vessels.
5. Unitized CARGO . . . Commodities which lend themselves to standardized units.
6. CONTAINERS . . . the collection of numerous types of goods stowed into a box, known as a container.
7. Roll on/Roll off Cargo . . . general cargo which can be (or not) unitized, machinery light and heavy, vehicular traffic, cars and all forms of standardized units and palletized loads. Indeed, Ro/Ro cargoes are extensively wide in both type and character.
8. HEAVY LIFTS . . . by Load on/Load off by special lifting gear, indivisible loads shipped on trailers.
9. Automobiles . . . especially in particularly designed vessels.
10. BARGE CARGO . . . In Lash vessels.

While the foregoing list can not be exhaustive, it does indicate that 'Cargo Handling' is more than an 'art, exclusive to the type of goods involved' but also an understanding of the types and classes of ships in which the cargoes are carried, of which the classes indicated below are examples.

1. Break bulk loads of conventional form in:—
   (a) general freighters;
   (b) cargo liners.
2. Unitization and conventional traffic in:—
   (a) general freighters;
   (b) multi-purpose vessels;
   (c) container vessels;
   (d) roll on/roll off vessels.
3. Bulk traffic in:—
   (a) dry bulk carriers;
   (b) O.B.O. (ore, bulk, oil) carriers;
   (c) tankers, including V.L.C.C.s and Natural Gas Carriers;
   (d) lash/barge vessels;
   (e) V.L.C.C.s (very large crude carriers).
4. Heavy lift load traffic in specialized ships.
5. Specialist designs, such as Timber Carriers, Car Transporters.

Within the above outline classiffcation, a general average differen-tiation of trades involvement could be as follows:

	tonnes DW
Cargo vessels (freighters) short sea	3–5000
Cargo vessels, multi-purpose	15–20000

Refrigerated vessels	10–15000
Container vessels, large size	30–40000
Container vessels, general purpose	12–18000
Container vessels, feeder and short sea	2–5000
Roll on/roll off vessels, short sea	Wide tonnage
Roll on/roll off vessels, longer distances	variations
Bulk carriers, general trading	9–12000
Bulk carriers, short sea	3–6000
Bulk carriers, general purpose	25–50000

Bulk carriers known as 'Panamax' are those with
   high deadweight capacity consistent with
   economic usage, and dimensional restraints set
   by ports and waterways.

Bulk ore carriers, wide ranges up to   120–300000

O.B.O. (oil, bulk, ore) carriers, wide ranges from 90 000 and up to
   150–170 000 tonnes DW

Tankers, from 25 000–500 000 tonnes DW (V.L.C.C.s)

Liquefied Natural Gas Carriers 50 000 cu. m. to 125–150 000 cu. m.

(Note: the above list is not intended to be exhaustive nor specific.)

It should therefore be sufficiently clear that a fair degree of ship mobility among sea-going officer personnel is of reasonable assumption albeit particular specialisms will still dictate some need for lesser movement, if at all. If career in cargo handling is to be fully meaningful its study must encompass more than the ship alone; the substance of this book aims to show the relationship of the integrated features.

SECTION 1

The Principles of Cargo Work

See also Section 6, pages 375–388, The Management of Marine Cargo Transportation.

The Cargo Officer's Duties and Responsibilities, Organizing, Administering and Delegating. Procedural Routine, the Code of Safe Working Practices for the Safety of Merchant Seamen.

The Duties of the 'Junior Cargo Officer'. Responsibilities for Cargo Spaces and Gear. The Safety of the Ship, Crew and Cargo. Distinction Between Different Forms of Handling. Check Lists, Hatch Books, Mate's Receipts, Mate's Log Book.

Stowage Principles. Cargo Planning and Distribution. Operating Procedures . . . the Cargo Stow, Accepting Cargo in Different Forms.

Preparation for Cargo Reception. Cleaning Holds and Spaces. Use of Dunnaging. Separation of Cargoes. Port Marking. Special Cargo. Broken Stowage. Voyage Care.

Distribution. Procedures for Discharge and Transportation.

Damage to Cargo. Precautions to be Adopted . . . Slinging, Crushing, Use of Fork Lift Trucks. Strain and Stress on Cargo at Sea.

Modern Developments in Cargo Handling

Relationship with Ports Authorities, Agencies and Transport Facilities. Changing Ship Design and Handling Procedures. Quick Turn Round. Expansion of Unitization and Bulk Carriage. The Effect of Trade Patterns. Ship Design in Relation to Cargo Carriage. Containerization (see Appendix A). Ports Shipping and Cargo Movement (see Appendix B).

The Principles of Cargo Work

1. Cargo Officer

The term 'Cargo Officer' may be defined as one responsible for the safe and efficient handling and stowage of cargo but this responsibility however, does not begin nor end with the actual handling of the cargo. It also entails such aspects as proper preparation beforehand; correct supervision during the time the ship is working cargo; relevant attention when at sea and co-ordination and co-operation with ports authorities while in port or harbour.

1

Cargo handling is an organizational/administrative matter and thus takes its place among all industrial/business activities to which normal management principles can be applied, being no less acceptable to a ship than to any other transport function. It calls for the accepted features of planning; co-ordinating, controlling and motivating . . . fundamental to activities involving the use of physical and human resources.

Within such a system however, certain differences do apply as distinct from manufacturing or processing industry in that for the most part, the cargo officer's involvement is contained in fairly well defined areas having relevance to situations which are never static but may frequently change, as between different ships, different cargoes and different ports. In the main, however, a cargo officer is required to conform to law and legislation which necessitates the carrying out of specific duties as a minimum performance; he is also invariably subject to operating performance contained in manuals published by the shipping company by which he is employed while, at the same time, widely conditioned by well tried and accepted customs and practices. Beyond this there is also the wide, undefined areas of unpredictability peculiar to the shipping industry and the environment in which it works and which, by its own influence, calls for more than moderate initiative to deal with situations as they arise in countries and localities with differing labour and industrial relation practices and equally varied attitudes to working situations. The cargoes may have similarities but the areas of operation can be very different and the facilities not always without the need for improvization.

The term 'Routine' therefore becomes prominent in all functions affecting the care of cargo procedures and this can be both of general and specific application. Generally, the former becomes the more influential towards attitudes and behaviour in cargo work duties although certain features of practice must always remain, irrespective of place or circumstance. As such it is pertinent to point out that although the degree of routine and the extent of its application shall be mainly the responsibility of the Chief Officer or the Senior Cargo Officer, it is desirable that personnel in the more junior positions become familiar with those duties which surely will, at some time, be delegated to them.

In this context, no distinction is therefore made in this book as between major and minor cargo handling duties but only that of drawing attention to effective care, handling and carriage of cargoes, irrespective of the grade of personnel being, at any time, concerned with it.

In considering the principles involved it is wise to bear in mind that whereas of recent years considerable change, progress and development has taken place in the manner of cargo handling, none the less much of basic practice remains and is likely to continue so for some considerable time, based as it is, frequently on long established customs. But the extent to which basic practice will apply will depend upon the type and age of 'the ship' involved and the kind of port in which it will, at any time, be working, acknowledging also the influence upon practice arising from the continuing changes in the types of cargoes which the developing patterns of trade condition. Routine, therefore, should be looked at broadly and by reference to the following.

2. The Duties of the 'Junior' Cargo Officer

It is normal practice for a 'junior officer' to be given charge of the cargo spaces while work is proceeding and be responsible to the Chief or Senior Cargo Officer.

Before loading commences all holds and spaces will be subject to inspection and preparation, 'cleaned' and made ready for the types of cargo to be loaded.

Cargo gear . . . derricks, cranes, wires, pulleys, blocks, ropes, shackles, etc., must be in order and conforming to S.W.L. (Safe Working Load) requirements. Cargo rigging must be set to suit the work in hand. Statutory requirements impose minimum standards but this does not excuse any neglect of daily inspection, or continued supervision during actual cargo working.

Where wooden hatch covers are fitted these should be stowed on deck during working periods in such a place and fashion as not to suffer damage yet be readily accessible for replacement to meet inclement weather. Hatch beams that are not unshipped must be secured against the possibility of being accidentally unshipped. Where power operated steel hatch coverings are fitted attention must be given to their efficient working. See Department of Transport Notice No M524 (and refer page 447).

Hold and space inspection should cover detailed attention to defects of any kind, even where these have been repaired it is not enough to accept completion of the repair without a close inspection. Structural inspection should cover ship plating, access ladders, lighting, guard rails, storm valves and pipes, fire fighting gear and fittings, manhole covers, side port doors and spar ceiling.

Where deep tanks are fitted, inspection of heating coils is necessary and blanks fitted to the bilge lines, if liquids are to be carried.

Much the same general inspection should apply to roll on/roll off vessels, together with attention to the securing arrangements fitted into the ship for vehicular loads and also to the mechanism by which the bow and stern doors are operated . . . as indeed also the operating mechanism of internal deck approaches. See Department of Transport Notice No 542 (and refer page 447).

Of more general nature, a Cargo Officer should become familiar with the specialized equipment and facilities provided by the stevedoring agencies, particularly that related to mechanical handling and mobile carriage; to the types and conditions of pallets which may be used with the loading procedures and to spreaders and sling arrangements. Current cargo handling practice involves a wide variety of unitization with consignments pre-packed into unit loads, ranging from single pallets, pre-slung loads or, to containers. With the former it is good practice to 'sight' the loads arranged in the sheds or warehouses before they are moved to the quay for loading. By so doing possible pre-shipment damage comes to light and the units can be rejected while, also, a general indication of stowage needs is more easily apparent beforehand.

Where isolated pre-packed (stuffed) at quayside containers are carried on conventional vessels it is essential that attention is given to the manner by which the contents of the container are solidly secured inside. (See notes on container handling.)

While cargo work is proceeding the cargo officer should divide his time between the deck and the hold/cargo spaces. In this way he can ensure that the cargo is in all respects carefully handled and stowed. With discharging this practice assists in avoiding over-carriage of cargo.

When work is finished for the day the cargo officer must see that all hatch coverings are in place, secured and made water tight. Derricks should be swung inboard in order that no difficulties will arise if it should be necessary to leave the wharf quickly after completion of work for the day. Cranes should be 'locked' and secured in place; particularly must all electric and electro-hydraulic fittings be safeguarded.

It is usual to keep a record of the amount of cargo worked during the day. An appropriate check on this amount may be obtained from draft comparison with the displacement scale, or curve, for the vessel, taken before cargo work commences and after it is finished.

With bulk liquids of any sort the emphasis changes to ensuring that complex safety precautions are observed and the routines, usually supported by check lists, are strictly followed.

The officer will be conversant with the Chief Officer's loading or discharging orders and will ensure that experienced hands are available to operate the valves in the correct sequence. He must also be aware of the potential sources of ignition and the risks attendant on the concentration of flammable gas on deck.

Instant readiness of all firefighting appliance is required and systems of communication, including means of summoning shore assistance to deal with emergencies beyond the scope of the ship's capacity, must be fully understood. The cargo gear, understandably, consists of lines and valves . . . the officer must become familiar with the pipeline layout and the valve operation for any tank or tanks.

3. Stowage Principles

(a) *Safety of Ship and Crew*

The overriding consideration is for the safety of ship and crew. This implies that the cargo is placed with due regard to the stability characteristics of the ship and in such a way as to avoid excessive bending or shearing stresses in the loaded condition, bearing in mind the intended voyage and likely weather to be experienced.

Furthermore, the total 'weight loaded' must not exceed that which is permitted to meet the appropriate load line indications. Pre-planning calculations will be made with this in mind.

The distribution of cargo must always leave adequate access to crew and navigation spaces, nor must it prevent the correct closure of hatchways and hatches or accommodation doors through which water could enter in adverse weather.

In terms of routine in regard to the safety of ship and crew, attention is drawn to the Code of Safe Working Practices for Merchant Seamen. This code is produced by the Marine Division of the Department of Transport and is concerned with establishing and maintaining safe working conditions on board ships at sea and in port. The code is, in fact, authoritative guidance.

Among the subjects dealt with are the general precautions of cargo handling and working procedures; the operating precautions with winches, cranes and derricks and other forms of mechanical equipment used in cargo work; the care to be exercised with all forms of dangerous substances and the safety requirements with hatches, hatchways and hatch covers. The code is detailed over all the usual activities and functions on board a ship and, as such, provides a good background base for informative study. With cargo work routine procedures particularly can this be useful, and all officers would be advised to make reference to the copies of the code on board their ship. (See also Section 6, page 371.)

Useful guidance is also to be found in the I.L.O. Code 'Accident prevention on board ship at Sea and in Port' in which the basic precautions associated with cargo work are described.

The provision of a copy of this Code for reference on board is strongly recommended. The complementary I.L.O. Code (referred to on pages 439–445) 'Safety & Health in Dock Work' is, likewise an essential document.

(b) *Safety of the Cargo Itself*

Damage to cargo can arise from a considerable number of causes some less obvious than others and precautionary measures need to be applied over broad parameters not the least in respect of the following circumstances—inadequate stowage; uneven distribution; incorrect slinging; careless movement by mechanical handling (fork lift trucks, etc.); insufficient attention to labelling and marking; carelessly packed units; inattention to weight loads and lifting gear; insufficient or incorrect dunnaging; contamination; incorrect ventilation; lack of proper attention to temperature control with refrigerated cargoes, particularly so with container refrigerated cargoes.

Particular preventative measures are necessary with crushing possibilities in compartments where fragile consignments are stowed with heavier loads; with taint from odourous goods, liquids and incorrect mixing of different consignments giving off moisture affect.

Damaged cargo should be placed on one side, recorded as to the extent of the damage, inspected independently and, either rejected if the condition warrants it, or stowed in a more appropriate space after restoring the damage.

Inefficient ventilation procedures are a major cause of damage to cargo and one which can have difficult repercussions with insurance matters. (See Section 3 on Ventilation.)

(c) *The Cargo Stow*

The position of cargo in a hold or space must be such as to assist correct and speedy discharge. Cargo for a port must not be over-stowed by cargo for a succeeding port. This is achieved by the correct use of port marks and is materially assisted by proper labelling by the shipper. Additionally, the quantity of cargo for any port should be divided between a number of hatches so as to minimize working time but there is, of course, a minimum amount of cargo below which it would not be economic to split, since the time spent in rigging gear and the cost of stevedoring would most likely exceed the saving due to reduced time.

Pilferage of cargo parcels must be avoided by stowing them in such a way that they are blocked off by heavier, and less vulnerable packages. With vunerable cargo . . . known as 'Specie' daylight working is preferable. If this is not possible plenty of artificial lighting should be used while with the working of specie cargo in any great amounts makes it advisable to employ a watchman or security guard.

Damage to bulk liquid cargoes is generally from one cause only, that is contamination by mixing. For this to occur there would have to be a mistake in the operating of the valves or in the order of loading which could only occur if the check list and precautions were ignored or misread.

The cargo stow with bulk liquids is predetermined and no major adjustments are possible once loading has commenced.

(d) *During the Voyage*

Apart from refrigerated and oil cargoes, which have their own special requirements, little attention is either necessary or possible once the hatchways have been secured. Some restriction applies with 'general' cargoes, however. Modern ship construction includes points of access to holds and spaces, with entry provisions by ladder/steps arrangements. Through these access points officers can penetrate and view spaces to observe any irregularities in ventilation, dampness/sweat or, indeed, any cargo disturbance. 'See General Arrangements plans included in cover pocket.' One requirement however, is present at sea, particularly on long voyages and more so when this passes through different latitudes with the consequential changes in atmospheric conditions. This is the adequate and constant attention to ventilation, either by the manual trimming of ventilators or the control of air conditioning systems. Ventilation is all important to the safe carriage of cargoes. (See Section 3, page 197.)

In heavy weather there is need to be assured that sea water will not enter the cargo holds or spaces through ventilators or other means and normal appropriate measures must be taken to avoid this.

(e) *Check Lists*

Routine procedures greatly benefit from check lists drawn up to outline those requirements of inspection and attention to which procedure should apply in the preparation of holds and spaces for the reception of cargo. There can be no standard form of check list . . . each will differ according to the type of ship and facilities available but more so will this differ according to the requirements and standards set by the Chief or Senior Cargo Officer.

By way of example the following items could form guide lines against which checking could be made:

Hold/Space Inspection   M.V. ....   Date ....
    Air Pipes.   Sounding Pipes & Striker Plates.
    Scuppers.   Storm Valves & Covers.
    D.B. Manhole Covers.   Locker Doors.
    Spar Ceiling.   Hatch Covers.
    Hatch Rollers.
    Guard Rails & Stanchions.
    Hold Lighting.   Ladders.
    Fire extinguishing systems and detector arrangements.
    Bilges .... inspected .... cleared .... limber boards secured.

Daily Routine   Cargo Working
    Gear Inspection.   Derricks.   Cranes.
    Runners & Guys.   Winches & Power Switches.
    Deck Lighting.   Gangways.
    Hatch Cover Security.   Hatch Beams Security.
    Fire Appliances.   Anti-Rat Precautions.
    Moorings.   Overside Safety Nets.

Special Items
       Lashings Availability.   Lashings Inspected.
       Heavy Lift Spreaders.   Heavy Lift Securing Points.

(f) *The Hatch Book, Mate's Receipt and Mate's Log Book*
The Hatch Book. Most shipping companies require that officers responsible for cargo maintain a hatch notebook, in which can be recorded times of commencing and finishing cargo work, delays due to inclement weather, number of gangs employed, details of any stoppages and the reasons.

Additionally, the hatch notebook should contain reference to the disposition of cargo in a compartment in order to facilitate the compiling of the cargo plan. The use of a hatch notebook can be materially increased by adopting a check list approach and ticking off items as they are covered.

The Mate's Receipt. When a consignment of cargo is delivered to the ship a receipt for that cargo must be given when the goods are on board. This is the mate's receipt, the completion of which being considerably assisted by reference to appropriate information recorded in the hatch notebook.

The Mate's Log Book. This is a record of everything pertaining to the working of the ship, whether the vessel be at sea or in port. In the latter case details of cargo working will be recorded, the substance of which will follow much of the information provided in the hatch notebook.

Some Particular Aspects of Routine

Accepting Cargo. Loads for shipment should be properly packed, i.e. securely and safely, and adequately marked in order to indicate weight, port marks, slinging points and, where necessary, any special precautions. Deficiencies in those directions should be questioned.

Where cargo is pre-slung attention must be given to the system of support which holds the load together as one unit. In stowage, pre-slung loads must be effectively blocked off so as to avoid inter-cargo damage from contact movement or displacement while crushing damage must be avoided by a sufficiency of dunnage/plyboard or synthetic packing between the layers or tiers of the pre-slung units.

Pre-slinging is becoming increasingly adaptable to many types of loads by reason, among other things, of its time, and labour saving advantages.

Bulky Lifts. The position of the centre of gravity of a load should, preferably, be indicated on the outside of the packaging. This allows of correct balancing in slinging, avoids any danger of accident while the load is in suspension while, with fork lift truck movement, permits of equal weight distribution over the machine. Attention in these respects is important and should have regard to the known gross weight of the load being handled and the type of its contents.

Insufficient attention to this procedure can raise difficulties both in lifting and in stowing since it does not follow that the centre of gravity of the 'content', i.e. for example, a machinery unit, coincides with the geometrical centre of the overall package.

Pallets. Where cargo is loaded to be stowed on pallets, these should be in good order and condition and devoid of signs of collapsing under weight stress. Cargo on pallets should be loaded in such a way as to be evenly distributed, not irregular nor overhanging at the sides. The interlocking of the goods on the pallet, known as bonding, is much the preferable method.

Unitization involves a high measure of palletized cargo.

Unit Stowage. All forms of unit stowage require even distribution, to which end 'dunnage' of appropriate form should be sensibly used. Plywood sheets, placed between each layer of a unit stow, is a better system in achieving a level surface and so preventing an otherwise intrusion of damaging causes from other cargo 'pieces'. Indeed, such arrangements are encouraged when loading containers on to the hatchways of 'tween decks as part of a multi-stow.

Containers . . . ex quay. The cargo officer's involvement with cargo stowed in containers is where 'stuffing' is the practice. Stuffing is loading the container, ex quay, prior to shipment, from a variety of relatively small sized consignments.

Stuffing should follow the normally accepted principles of good stowage but, in particular, the following precautions are necessary.

The total load weight should be evenly distributed over the floor of the container such that the centre of gravity is low, and as near to the centre of gravity of the container as is possible.

Lighter cargo should be stowed on top of heavier; precautions against contamination taken and choking off, in order to obtain a tight and solid load is essential.

Particular care should be exercised with goods of a damp or oily texture. This could inhibit a fire risk from spontaneous combustion. Where doubt arises, such goods should be rejected.

Stuffing calls for careful supervision . . . careful in the sense that labour employed may not always be of the usual high standards of normal stevedores nor is the environment of a single box as conducive to 'job satisfaction' as the normal hold/space cargo working operations. Lack of appropriate attention to the loading of the box could well lead to difficulties later, when the vessel would be at sea.

CLEANING AND PREPARATION OF THE HOLDS AND SPACES

Dry Cargoes . . . Basic Aspects

Cleaning. The amount of cleaning with a cargo space will depend upon the nature of the cargo which has been discharged and that which is to be loaded. Generally speaking, a hold which is ready to receive cargo should be clean and dry, well ventilated and free from any odour of the previous cargo.

When discharging is finished, a space in the wings abreast of the hatchway should be cleared and all serviceable dunnage stacked there. Unsuitable dunnage must be sent up on deck to be disposed of. It is a common practice in two deck vessels to shift a quantity of the lower hold dunnage up to the 'tween deck, to be passed down again as required in the lower hold. This saves unnecessary shifting of dunnage when stowing the lower hold.

The hold is then thoroughly swept down and all rubbish is sent up on deck.

Where bilge sections are part of the structure, the limber boards are lifted and the bilges thoroughly cleaned out; particularly, attention must be given to the rose boxes and it is most important to see that all the holes in the boxes are clear. If necessary, the bilges may be cement or lime washed or coated with bitumastic; this tends to prevent corrosion and also disinfects them. After the limber boards are replaced, they should be caulked with oakum and, if the cargo to be loaded requires it, as for instance, a bulk commodity, they must be covered with tarpaulin nailed down with wooden battens. Battens are often more suitable than caulking in order to allow drainage to the bilges. Modern vessels do not have bilge sections, the tank top extends from shell to shell.

To clean a hold from which a coal cargo has just been discharged it is necessary first to sweep it down and then to wash it down with a hose. The bilge suctions and/or rose boxes must be attended to so that the water can be pumped away. After washing down with salt water, the drying of the hold is accelerated if it is wiped down with fresh water. Supplement the ventilation of the hold by wind-sails. Sawdust sprinkled on all ironwork and on the tank top (or ceiling) will help to absorb the damp and may be swept up after a short interval.

When time does not permit the holds being washed down, very satisfactory results may be obtained by sprinkling all ironwork with damp sawdust and sweeping down with stiff brooms.

Preparation . . . Generalities

With a general cargo the holds should be well swept out and any residue of a previous cargo sent up on deck and disposed of. The extent and degree of cleaning will depend upon the nature of the previous cargo. Precautions should be taken to ensure that the space is well ventilated and dry . . . to this end windsails may be rigged and upper hatch covers removed or opened.

Liberal supplies of clean, dry, unstained and appropriately adaptable dunnage to the cargoes to be loaded should be available and handy. Specialized dunnage and packaging of a synthetic nature should be in good condition. With all cargoes which require dunnage it is essential that the latter is clean, dry and free from stain or odour.

Bagged cargo requires widely sized boards for dunnaging, for two main reasons. Firstly in order to provide a reasonable floor between tiers of bags such that sagging will not take place and so that by laying the boards at about four to six inch intervals between edges, air circulation is maintained between the tiers.

Laying dunnage is not a haphazard function. Dunnage has the purpose of assisting in the solidity of stow and also preventing undue damage to cargo in proximity to itself. It must therefore be laid with thought and attention to the purpose for which it is being used and its size and adaptability fitted where this can best serve the total stow.

The main contributory factors towards damage to cargoes whilst in vessels are: crushing; dampness; contact with ironwork of the ship or other cargo; and lack of systems of ventilation specifically suited to the cargoes.

In view of this it is essential to give due attention to dunnaging needs. In terms of the materials which can be used for dunnaging it must be such as will provide protection to and from any or all of the above four factors and could be seasoned wood of different size and shape; pieces of cordwood; bamboos; mats; rattans and plyboard. Modern practices use quantities of blocks of expanded polystyrene and also air filled bags.

In refrigerated compartments permanent steel corrugated dunnage is used with a high degree of success. It allows a sufficiency of air flow and has the strength to carry the load/weight of fork lift trucks.

Double dunnage, that is one layer on top of another, is preferable at all times but particularly so with the bottom layers adjacent to the decks. Modern synthetic dunnaging materials, which serve as packaging as well, tend to lessen the need for an overabundance of other forms of dunnaging, such as wood.

Laying dunnage in preparation for a cargo depends largely upon the type of consignments in the load(s). With most bagged cargoes a complete tier of dunnage is first laid over the floor of the space on to which a complete covering of bags is laid. General cargo, by virtue of its different shapes and sizes, would break up any previously laid dunnage and it is therefore better in such cases to 'dunnage' as the stow goes along.

Sweepings . . . torn or split bags are a common form of damage with bagged cargoes. The extent of the damage depends largely on

the handling of the bags during loading and the care taken to
prevent their coming in contact with projections in the space or
compartment, such as stringers or angle backets. The weight of the
layers of bags also, in some cases, causes those in the lower tiers
to split and the contents seep down to the bottom of the space
where, after discharge, a considerable quantity of the commodity
may be found. It is for this reason that separation cloths, or tarpaulins
should be completely spread over the bottom dunnage in order to
retain this residue on discharge, and to keep it as clean as possible.
Sweepings are part of the consignment, and must be discharged as
such.

Spar Ceiling and its Purposes

Spar ceiling, or cargo battens as they are called in some trades,
comprise portable wooden battens fitted to the inner edges of the
frames of the ship's structure so to form a sheathing to the ship's
side. Normally spar ceiling is made up of $1\frac{1}{2}$ in boards of about 6 in
wide and arranged horizontally in convenient lengths attached to

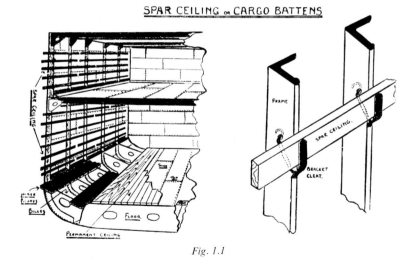

SPAR CEILING or CARGO BATTENS

Fig. 1.1

the frames by angle brackets and spaced about 9 in apart. In some
cases vertical sections are made up to fit in between the frame spaces.

The purpose of this wooden sheathing is to prevent packages of
cargo protruding beyond the inner edges of the frames and so
becoming damaged by moisture which may collect on the side of
the ship. The space so formed between the spar ceiling and the ship's
side helps to provide a complete air space around the cargo and

thereby improves ventilation. The spar ceiling should always be kept in an efficient state of repair.

With a coal cargo it is advisable to remove the spar ceiling before loading, so as to prevent any possibility of 'through ventilation'.

More frequently it is the practice to fit vertical spar ceiling throughout hold and 'tween decks and this usually takes the form of 6-in × 2-in battens, three to each frame space, all of which are bolted to 2-in × $\frac{1}{2}$-in iron brackets.

The advantage of this type of sparring is that it results in less broken stowage than the horizontal battens fitted on the innerside of the frames.

Specialized Arrangements. Spar ceiling fittings in roll on/roll off vessels take on an additional purpose. Cargo is usually loaded quickly into these vessels and can be of considerable variety and size in the main deck/hold stowage. Prevention of movement becomes of paramount importance here and it is necessary to provide this feature as well as ship side condensation effect.

To this end, spar ceiling units are fitted in 15 ft × 15 ft sections, hinged to attachments at the ship side and capable of being pressure-forced to the cargo bulk, thus providing an overall tying effect.

DISTRIBUTION

Separation of Cargo. An efficient system of cargo separation is necessary with most types of cargoes and particularly so with large consignments, if overcarriage is to be avoided and port speed promoted.

With a general cargo separation is not so vital in that the marks and numbers of the cases and packages generally provides easy and quick reference, provided there is an absence of obliteration, in which case some parcels of a general stow do require specific separation.

Cargo loaded for an 'optional' port of discharge will require an efficient discernable method of separation when it is loaded since, at that time, the ship may not be aware of its exact port of discharge. This practice is not unusual with large consignments of edible produce, such as tea, coffee, cocoa or pepper where parcels of possibly 20 to 50 bags or cases are loaded with larger consignments yet have 'optional discharge' for reasons of the trade.

With cargoes of this nature it is possible to evolve a system which permits easy reference and avoidance of overstow. It requires that optional cargo lots be stowed in blocks in the 'tween or upper decks, with small passageways between each parcel, the end of the passageways being blocked off with the first port of discharge cargo. After discharge at the first port it is possible to gain access to any of the remaining parcels. Each parcel is identified with a particular

Chop Mark (which see) suitably stamped on each bag or case and also noted in the cargo hatch notebook and on the cargo plan.

Chop Mark. An example of a chop mark, as used with rubber shipments is shown here.

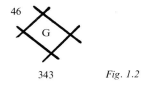

343   *Fig. 1.2*

The chop mark identifies the type and quality of the rubber. *G* represents the type of rubber; 46 the quality and 343 the shipment number.

Rod Iron. Consignments of rod iron are frequently shipped for optional ports of discharge and all stowed in the same compartment. A number of methods of separation are available, three of which are as follows:

1. By laying lengths of old rope on top of each parcel. This also helps to build a compact stow.
2. By lengths of old tarpaulin laid over the top of each parcel.
3. By painting bands across the top of each parcel by a distinctive colour appropriate to the particular port of discharge.

Cargo separation must be used with discretion and, normally, in line with shippers' approval. Some shippers object to 'foreign' markings on their cargo.

Port Marking. Port marking is the name given to a system whereby each port of discharge is allocated a distinctive colour mark, which is stencilled or painted on to each package. The separation of cargo is considerably improved by such a system; the likelihood of overcarriage very much lessened apart from the ease of checking any loading or discharging procedure arising from the familiarity with

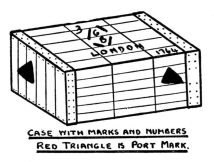

CASE WITH MARKS AND NUMBERS
RED TRIANGLE IS PORT MARK.   *Fig. 1.3*

different colour markings, in that the system can be understood by all persons concerned, irrespective of nationality or education. By way of illustration, Capetown may be given a Blue Triangle; Durban a Red Circle, etc. On other trades, other significant designs may be used but having been established they remain consistent for a trade to which they have been allocated.

Special Cargo. By special cargo is meant any package or parcel which, by reason of its nature or value, calls for special stowage and supervision in order to prevent loss and/or pilfering.

Cases of surgical instruments, drugs, medical supplies, high precision tools, samples of all descriptions, mechanical and mathematical instruments, are but a few items of special cargo, whilst all small packages, though not necessarily of high value, are frequently shipped under this heading.

Cargo classed as SPECIAL is generally shipped at a higher rate of freight and, in consequence, special parts of the vessel are set aside for its stowage. This takes the form of 'special lockers' either built into the structure or part of a deck space separated off by built wooden bulkheads. The advantage of the former type lies in the fact that, being part of the main structure of the vessel, it effectively prevents any attempt at entry provided it is securely locked.

The built wooden section suffers the disadvantage of being reasonably easy of entry and therefore requires careful watching whilst work is proceeding in adjacent compartments; it is frequently left until last when loading and may, in consequence, cause delay.

All special cargo must be carefully checked and tallied into and from the compartment. This is important, for such cargo should never be tallied at the rail or on the quay.

It is preferable that an officer should make a personal tally of this type of cargo and, in addition, whever the compartment is open, ensure that a watcher is in attendance. Hatches in which special lockers are situated should be provided with locking bars and these should be securely locked in place when special cargo is in the locker and the hatch is not working.

It should not be beyond the ingenuity of a Cargo Officer to develop his own system of distribution and relative marking of loaded cargo, provided he supports the interpretation of his arrangements by due references in, and on, his Cargo Plan.

BROKEN STOWAGE

Broken stowage explains space 'lost' in a compartment. This loss of space is due mainly to the variable sizes of packages loaded into a compartment, thus preventing a compact and uniform stow. It is most unlikely that a general cargo will provide many cases or packages of uniform size and, though all due care may be taken in stowing them, it is almost impossible to prevent loss of space between some packages, having regard to the questions of preventing crushing and shifting. This loss of space is increased in those parts of the vessel which are not conducive to compactness of stow and here broken stowage will reach a high ratio. With general cargo stowed in end holds, the triangular shape of these holds will not permit a solid or uniform stow.

Obstructions in holds, such as pillars, ladders, stanchions, large angle brackets and beams, will promote broken stowage though modern construction has minimized this.

Broken stowage can be of considerable magnitude with a general cargo, whilst with most bulk cargoes it may be very small.

Most cargoes require wooden dunnage for their successful carriage, but the inconsiderate use of this dunnage can constitute an element of broken stowage, for unnecessary amounts would involve the use of space, the aggregate of which would represent quite a considerable volume.

Discretion in the utilization of cargo space is important for it must be fully realized that the amount of cargo loaded into a vessel directly affects her freight earning capability.

On most established trades cargo is booked for the vessel before her arrival and unless due attention is given to the stowage factor of cargo and care taken to adhere to that figure as nearly as possible, the vessel may arrive at subsequent ports, unable to take the booked quota owing to lack of space.

On some trades, small cargo of particular type is shipped and carried at a low rate of freight, for the express purpose of filling in the open spaces between the packages and at the ends and sides of the main stow, thus reducing broken stowage.

The term 'Broken Stowage Cargo' covers these commodities, though the term 'Broken Stowage' is more correctly associated with the 'loss of space'.

Attention is drawn to the fact that the amount of broken stowage is related to the cargo and *not* to the space in which it is stowed.

Example— 50 tons of general cargo. Stowage factor 40 cubic feet per ton. Broken stowage 5 per cent. Loaded into a space containing 6000 cubic feet. What is the space remaining?

	cu ft
50 tons at 40 cu ft	2000
+5 per cent broken stowage	100
Space required	2100
Total space	6000
Space remaining	3900

DAMAGE TO CARGO

Causes of Damage and Precautions to be Adopted

Handling. Considerable damage to cargo may result if due care is not paid to handling. The possibility of this source of damage occurs in both loading and discharging and thus devolves on an officer to give efficient attention on all occasions.

Lack of care at port of loading may result in damage such that, though the effect is not immediately apparent, the results may begin to show during the voyage as damage not only to the specific consignment, but also to other cargo with which it is stowed. Bad handling at port of discharge not only spoils a ship's record for efficient carriage, but often lays the ship open to damage claims which could be avoided by careful supervision. The following are some of the more obvious instances of damage through bad handling.

1. *Inefficient and Improper Slinging*. Case goods should be arranged more or less in like sizes before slinging. Heavy cases should not be slung with light cases. Canvas slings should be used for bagged goods in preference to rope slings. For very small packages wire net slings are preferable. With some classes of goods, easily breakable or readily made up into units, the use of trays affords the better methods.

Cargoes, generally, can be classified as being homogeneous or non-homogeneous in character. Non-homogeneous cargoes comprise wide and varied shapes and sizes of loads while the numbers making up a load are equally variable. This class of cargo is 'damage prone' from handling and calls for two distinct and definitie pre-cautions, firstly that the slings to be used should be selected to suit the type and character of the load and, secondly, definite and precise supervision over the stevedoring procedures is essential.

Homogeneous cargoes, by reason of their like characteristics, lend themselves to mechanized handling and this has taken over from slinging where this is possible . . . hence the use of fork lift trucks in the holds and spaces of a vessel. Even so, such cargoes do still remain within the more conventional handling procedures.

In all cases of slinging due attention should be given to the weight of the cargo in the sling. Excessive loads cause undue stress which, apart from deterioration to lifting gear, may also result in crushing packages at the bottom and sides of the sling.

In the well established ports of the world cargo handling pro-cedures follow the modernization of ships' equipment and it is unlikely that facilities and use will be other than up to date but where vessels trade to lesser developed ports there still will remain the need to utilize older fashioned methods to the best advantage. Notably is this the case with the making up of slings. At loading this should be done immediately beneath the head of the outboard derrick or the crane jib. By so doing swinging contact of a load against the ship side is avoided. Similarly, on discharging, a load should be made up in or near to the square of the hatch. Some latitude may be allowed here since experience has shown that no undue damage will result to bagged or baled cargo by slinging in any part of a compartment, and 'breaking out' provided care is exercised in guiding the sling towards the square of the hatch. The practice is not advised, however, with cases, drums or barrels.

Note also 'Pre-slinging' referred to on pages 17, 261.

2. *The Use of Fork Lift Trucks.* The use of these mechanical handling devices can constitute a serious source of cargo damage when working in a ship cargo space, if prudent precautions are not taken . . . albeit, with these, very satisfactory loading and discharging handling and tonnage times can be achieved. However, inattention to 'speed rates' of the F.L.T.s, in relatively confined spaces can lead to collision with the interruption of existing stowage. It is not also unknown for the total load on a F.L.T. to become displaced, or even jettisoned, due to disregard of the elementary principles of load stability with a moving unit. See pages 18, 352 on F.L.T.s.

3. *Cargo Gear.* Much damage to cargo results from slings contacting with hatchcoamings, bulwarks and obstructions within a compartment. This is due, in no small measure, to careless winch or crane work.

Thoughtless acceleration and retardation cause many unnecessary claims for broken packages.

It is most important to urge the necessity of tight guys to derricks. All officers should make the inspection of guys a routine job; by so doing they would not only prevent damage to cargo but would also minimize the stress upon the gear.

All running gear should be kept well greased and lubricated. Wires, swivels, gin blocks and hooks are liable to fail under working stress if neglected in this direction.

4. *Crushing.* Damage to cargo from 'crushing' is mainly due to lack of both thought and care in stowing. Incorrect use of wooden dunnage, unsuitable space allocations to cargo, insufficient attention paid to the type of cargo being loaded and to the order of stowage, are potential factors contributing to damage from this source.

Obviously, heavy bulky packages stowed over and with fragile packages, will produce undue stress upon the latter and, with the motion of the ship, may cause them to collapse. Fragile packages, on the other hand, are considerably less likely to damage from crushing if they are given 'tween deck stowage, where more efficient compactness of stow is possible.

Wooden dunnage, badly laid, is often the cause of crushing

damage, since it is liable to penetrate fragile packages. This is often noticeable with cases of tea and rubber. The plywood cases are easily split and instances are on record of cases having been pierced by the ends of the dunnage battens thus causing loss of tea and damage to rubber, thereby leading to heavy claims. Packages of such nature should be stowed fairly, on top of each other, to form a block, and the wooden dunnage so selected and arranged that the ends will, if possible, coincide with the edges of the cases.

Incompletely filled compartments give rise to damage by crushing if due attention is not given to the security of the cargo. All consignments should be compactly stowed, lashed if necessary, with packages of like size stowed together. 'Stepping down' of cargo may prevent movement when the vessel rolls and pitches, whilst this same motion would aggravate the vibration of cases stowed in end compartments where they are likely to bear against the structural projections in these spaces. It is therefore preferable to reserve the middle holds of the vessel for case goods, leaving the end holds for bagged cargo.

Two obvious methods of preventing crushing damage are worthy of mention: 1. Crates of glass should always be stowed on edges, athwartships, packed solidly together, on a perfectly level floor of dunnage, lashed to prevent movement, and no cargo of any nature stowed on top. 2. Rolls of paper, likewise, should be stowed on their flats. Stowage on the round would very likely result in flattening deformation to such an extent as to render the rolls unsuitable for eventual machine use. See pages 114–123, Newsprint.

STRAIN/STRESS ON CARGO AT SEA

A vessel rolling and pitching heavily in a sea is subject to strain which results in the *build up* of stresses throughout the whole of the structure. These stresses, in the main are of a **VIBRATORY NATURE**.

With cargoes 'correctly' and 'solidly' stowed any resulting damage to the cargo should be minimal . . . if at all . . . accepting that the stability condition of the ship is satisfactory.

But vibratory stresses BUILD UP to have a developing force impact longitudinally with pitching and transversely with rolling, with the result that the maximum stress impact is:—

(*a*) at the end of compartments with pitching (where bulkheads and/or structure fitments oppose the vibratory stress) and at

(*b*) at the port/starboard shell sides with rolling.

See Diagram. Reproduced from 'Safe Packing and Marking of Cargo' booklet, by kind permission of The National Association of Port Employers . . . See page 325.

Where the stow might be loose these stresses could cause damage by cargo movement which, in itself, could cause damage to adjoining stowage.

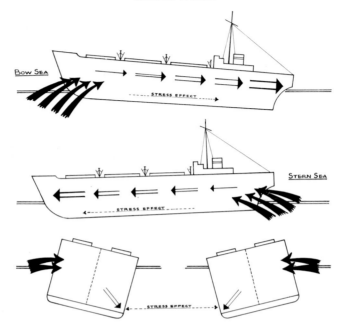

Particularly is this a hazard where cargo, such as that of cylindrical shape and form is stowed on platforms. This is not an uncommon practice where the ship structure suggests this need . . . see notes on Paper Reels . . . pages 120, 122 resulting in movement/shifting of the cargo, probably more noticeable at the ends or outsides of a compartment which, ultimately could lend itself to problems of discharge.

It is the vibratory stresses which have to be taken into account, with appropriate precautions at time of loading necessary of which strapping and lashing is one and another sensible stability (metacentric height) according to the envisaged weather conditions for the voyage.

Cargo in movement when at sea could have extreme problems to overcome . . . if indeed this were possible. Certainly it could be conducive to listing. Therefore, to lessen this possibility and to ensure that the range of stowage requirements for different types of cargoes are appropriate, the vibratory stress effect upon a ship must not be lost sight of.

MODERN DEVELOPMENTS IN CARGO HANDLING

Much of the preceding text in this section is concerned with the basic principles of Cargo Handling. As indicated previously, these

A Modern Twin Hatch General Cargo Vessel

must not be ignored, neglected nor treated lightly since a great deal of basic practice will continue to remain endemic among the various areas of the world to which ships trade, apart from the fact that many applications to effective cargo handling obtain their strength from long tried, and proven, methods.

Recourse to this approach . . . building upon the best of the past to promote progress lies behind most, if not all modern practice. In this context the student and officer is encouraged to digest the observations which now follow.

When the putting together of packages into a unit load which can be handled mechanically and can be moved by any form of transport is reasonably achieved, then we shall have reached a state of efficient and economic transport. The larger the load, and the greater extent of its journey from one place to another, the greater the economies.

This is the fundamental theme behind present and future thinking in terms of the carriage of goods and whereas hitherto the 'ship' was looked at in isolation—one unit transporting goods from port to port—this is no longer the case.

Conditions today, and these are likely to become increasingly so in the future, condition the ship as only one part in the chain of transport, with the movement of goods considered in relation to 'point of origin to point of use'. This involves a variety of transportation areas—land, railways, distribution centres as well as the ship and thus care, handling and carriage of cargoes becomes the responsibility of a number of different agencies working in co-operation and co-ordination than was so pointedly the case with the conventional shipment of goods.

Side Port Loading of Palletized Cargo, Hull

Roll On/Roll Off Services, Southampton

Primarily this new approach is the result of world trade economics and the contiguous increasing competition developing from fast-moving changes in the patterns of trade. New types of cargoes, changing methods of shipping from conventional to bulk methods and revolutionary developments in packaging, together with the need to get goods more quickly to their destination to support viable export needs, are all influencing factors.

As a result, ships are changing in design and size and the ports of the world are no longer looked at as places to store cargo while awaiting ships or for delivery, but as places of quick distribution. Particularly from the shipowner's point of view is this important. He is operating in a capital-intensified industry with increasing costs and charges upon his ship while it is in port adding to the high costs of building and operating. QUICK TURN ROUND is now of paramount importance and is applicable to cargo vessels equally as to tankers and other bulk carriers. This, even in itself, changes the concept of the ship-officer approach to cargo handling.

What, therefore, are some of the main practical issues involved?

(a) Cargoes are becoming more unitized—made up into unit loads.

(b) Palletization, rather than conventional slinging is becoming increasingly the practice.

(c) Cargoes are being 'handled' less but moved by mechanical means.

(d) 'Roll on/Roll off' transportation is developing—the movement of cargo carriers direct into and from the ship.

(e) Containerization—the stowage of goods into a mobile container which itself is placed into the ship is now a common practice.

(f) Side-port loading and discharging, as opposed to conventional hatch work is now usual from the changes in ship design.

(g) Improved methods of packaging are now available, notably with timber and paper products.

(h) Bulk carriage is superceding some forms of otherwise bagged cargoes.

(i) Bulk chemical and mineral cargoes are increasing.

(j) A broader liaison is necessary as between the ship officer and shore staff concerned with cargo handling.

(k) The tendency for larger ships to use only one main port as a feeder, both for loading and discharging, calls for different and broader attention to stowage planning.

(l) A new approach to the stability aspects of loading and discharging is necessary and particularly so with the quicker turn round factor, notably so with containers which frequently are simultaneously loaded and discharged.

Modern Container Terminal with Two 30-ton Capacity Transporters, Grangemouth Docks

30-ton Paceo-Vickers Portainer Cranes, Southampton

Mechanical Handling of Containers, Southampton

Surrounding all of the foregoing is the influence of trade patterns and their effect upon the movement of goods and cargoes. In the training of the ship officer there is now need for him to be aware of these developing factors, since his duties and responsibilities towards cargo are influenced by circumstances frequently beyond his immediate control.

In this respect some useful generalities are as follows:

1. *Trade Patterns*. The trade of Great Britain. Trends suggest that this is likely to develop increasingly in manufactured goods to and from the European Continent. Exports to the continent are showing an increase over those to the rest of the world with the majority made up of manufactured goods. Similarly, imports to Great Britain are showing increasing trends in manufactured goods, with large proportions from Western Europe. Basic materials and fuels are also increasing from hitherto underdeveloped exporting countries.

All this presupposes the expansion of unitized cargoes and the changes in bulk carriage and leads to the desirability of attention to the peculiar problems of 'short sea' routes and the probability of transhipment of bulk cargoes from large to smaller methods of carriage.

With 'foreign' trade of long haul there is every indication of increasing unit packaging, evidenced by the introduction of large-size cellular container vessels.

The carriage of cargoes by conventional methods is likely to still remain for the immediate future years as a result of which a ship officer no longer can devote attention to one aspect of 'cargo care' but must attune his thinking to a variety of methods.

2. *Containerization*. The development of cargo carriage by the use of containers has been said to be a 'container revolution'. The term is a misnomer since containers for bulk stowage are by no means new and have been loaded into and from ships long since. It is the applications and implications of this form of transportation which are significant and which have introduced a new philosophy to the movement of goods over long and short distances. Containerization is developing out of financial/commercial considerations in the need to move goods quickly and safely with minimum disturbance during transit and the economic use of ships in the cost of their running, as the size of ships increases. Out of this philosophy has grown the importance of the 'through transport medium' with technological advancement altering the nature of ports and the facilities provided for the reception of ships, evidenced by specialized cranes and a variety of types of mechanical handling devices. Supporting features are specially designed vessels—the cellular container ship, which leads to quick movement of unit loads and the development of broadly adaptable cranage on other forms of ship construction.

Alongside there has grown the emergence of shipping organizations taking responsibility for moving goods from point of origin to destination, in consequence of which new forms of documentation, as for example 'through coverage' to replace the normal bill of lading.

SHIP DESIGN IN RELATION TO CARGO CARRIAGE

Enclosed in the jacket pocket of this book are two 'general arrangements' plans . . . both of modern vessels:

1. Plan No. . . . is of a multi-purpose vessel.
2. Plan No. . . . is a bulk carrier.

They are included with the kind permission of Austin and Pickerskill Limited, of Sunderland, England, the builders.

Arising from these plans a number of points are worthy of note.

To 'know one's own ship' is a prerequisite to effective and efficient cargo handling. Ships, in the main, are designed for the purpose of trades in which they will be engaged and the cargoes they will carry. Their construction reflects the provisions of space and equipment necessary to that end and the conformities which registration and international regulations and recommendations impose.

In this context 'general arrangements' plans lay out necessary and desirable information to which reference and attention should be given, in order to ensure care and safety to both ship and to cargo.

Aspects to which attention should be given include:—

1. Hatchway layout and Derrick/Crane positioning, the basic factor in the loading and discharging of cargo.
2. Space provisions and capacities for holds/spaces and decks, from which cargo, planning can be determined.
3. Systems of ventilation . . . necessary adjuncts with cargoes of different types.
4. Stability data, in so far as this relates to the cargo loads.
5. Ballasting provisions in so far as this will relate to different cargoes and their positioning.
6. Displacement, Deadweight, Draft, Trim and Load Line information, in so far as this relates to safe loading.

With regard to the plans included with this book, attention is directed to:—

1. Hold and spaces capacities, together with the vertical positions of the Centre of Gravity above base (the keel) in co-ordination with the Deadweight/Displacement particulars. This information provides the basis on which the Stability condition of the ship can be obtained at any stage of draft or loading/discharging of cargo, and thus enabling the calcu-

lation of the value of the **GM** (metacentric height) before leaving or arrival at a port.

These are stability considerations in themselves, but essential important features of cargo handling procedures. Cargo Work cannot be divorced from Stability and reference to stability studies and formulae will be necessary here.

2. The Tons per CM immersion, from the deadweight scale, is important information in the avoidance of overloading to marks.

3. By reason of the dimensional detail included for hold and spaces, this permits the fixing of desirable cargo loads, or special types and forms of cargo relative to Cargo Plan/ Loading Plan preparation, in so far as it is necessary to know the position of the Centre of Gravity for the whole make up of individual cargo loads, viz./viz. the 'final' position of the Centre of Gravity . . . and the resulting value of the GM.

Dimensional detail also provides a guide as to desirable distribution of cargo load in so far as ship structure stress (hogging and sagging) is concerned.

4. Note the points of access to holds and spaces, in respect of internal inspection on voyage, re Cargo solidarity and/or ventilation requirements. All modern vessels have these access provisions.

5. Note also the ballast arrangements, water and oil, in relation to draft restrictions and also for stability requirements (positioning of weight). (See Critical Moment, pages 80, 418).

6. BULK VESSEL.

With regard to the applicable 'general arrangements' note reference to the 'Trim and Stability Booklet' provided for all vessels. Also the references to Allowable heights for Deck Cargoes; Conformity with Rules/Regulations/Recommendations with Bulk Cargoes, for example . . . Grain.

7. Note the saddle tanks provision in respect of heavy, low placed bulk cargoes with low Centres of Gravity, to which end the saddle tanks prevent over stiffness in a vessel, when they are filled with water/ballast.

Information of the type provided in 'General Arrangements' plans is of considerable usefulness in obtaining an overall conception of the extent to which a vessel and its equipment lends itself to cargo handling procedures. Notably would this be so for an officer strange to a vessel in which he is going to be concerned with, and responsible for Cargo Work.

Attention is also drawn to the Cross Section Plan of a V.L.C.C. (Very Large Crude Carrier) . . . pages 306, 307.

SECTION 2

SHIP CARGO WORKING GEAR

Basic Principles

Cargo Gear . . . introductory observations; variety and forms of gear available; principles of lifting and traversing; flexibility of systems.

Cargo Handling Between Ship and Quay . . . dangerous and unhealthy industries, legislation through the Docks Regulations.

The Rigging of Derricks . . . cranes and use of associated gear; inspection and attention to gear; stresses upon gear.

Types of Rigging, Basic Forms . . . union purchase, swinging derrick; heavy derrick (conventional form); doubling up.

Modern Trends in Cargo Gear

Cargo Access Equipment (i.e. Hatch Coverings, etc) . . . precautions with different types; techniques of power operated coverings. Ships involved.

Heavy Lifts . . . range and scope of 'heavy loads'; modern conventional heavy lift rigs. Supply ships heavy lift functions.

Orduna, Furness Group Cargo Vessel

The Stuelcken Mast and Derrick . . . types and applications; operating arrangements. Semi-Submersible Ships.

The Velle and Hallen Derricks   applications and arrangements with normal and heavy lifts; operating procedures. Gearless Ships

Electro-hydraulic Cranes . . . versatility of applications; the Stothert and Pitt range

The Use of Deck Cranes in General . . . tonnage ranges; positioning; siting; hoisting; slewing; luffing. Securing and Lashing Systems.

Forest Products . . . Systems of Carriage . . . types of product.

Newsprint . . . handling, stowage and carriage.

Speciality Craneage . . . forest products, timber, pulp, paper.

Securing and Lashing . . . the safety aspect, types of securing and lashing; applications to different forms of cargoes and types of ships; securing and lashing facilities . . . the Coubro and Scrutton range.

Ship Cargo Working Gear

Loading and Discharging Methods
Cargo Gear—Basic Principles

In the area of cargo gear much remains which is basic to the principles of application and use. On the other hand, considerable development and progress has of recent years been made in the systems employed, and this is reflected in modern ship design and in the handling facilities provided by ports.

This section serves to illustrate the relationship between the two approaches and draws attention to where each, in principle, may support the other.

Sub-Section A is concerned with basic principles; Sub-Section B with modern trends.

Sub Section A

Introductory Observations

At first sight it would appear that the variety of cargo handling gear is endless but in fact there is remarkably little choice although much is now available to provide analysis of suitable application. The purpose of these notes is to examine the loading/discharging operation, and apparatus used, as concisely as possible before considering in detail the merits and demerits of any particular aspect or type of gear.

Loading or discharging a ship can be carried out by two movement cycles:

1. the 'RAISE'; 'TRAVERSE' and 'LOWER METHOD'; or
2. the 'TRAVERSE METHOD'.

The former requires lifting apparatus, either ship or shore based; the latter side doors, access ramps and link spans, together with motive power.

Considering the former method, this can be performed by either:

A. One derrick, crane or hook which must perform each of the three parts of the cycle or by
B. A pair of derricks worked simultaneously.

Method A, the single ship derrick is the oldest form of cargo handling gear and can be rigged in the following ways:

(a) Swinging derrick with guys either manually or power operated.
(b) Swinging derrick with one guy manually or power operated the other led through adjacent derrick headblock to a weight overside, the weight being sufficient to return the derrick outboard. This is known as the 'dead man rig'.
(c) Swinging derrick with doubling gear and powered guys for moderate weights beyond the union purchase tonnage facilities.
(d) As a ship crane, using specialized attachments which virtually turn the single boom into a crane. Examples of this, representative of the modern trend in cargo handling are the Velle Ship Crane; the Hallen Derrick and the Velle Cargospeed Derrick Rig, and other proprietory marketed ship cranes, some of which are considered in detail in Section 5.

The principle of these derrick cranes is important, not only because it is the first significant change in ship's gear for half a century but also because the same principle applies to all modern heavy lift derricks. Whereas the traditional single derrick had, in addition to the cargo fall, a topping lift or span and two guys, the modern versions dispense with the latter and replace them by a device incorporated in the topping lift to control the derrick during the traversing movement. The advantages of this are, apart from the lack of clutter resulting from guys on deck, a complete flexibility of swing to raise and lower the derrick.

This flexibility is achieved at some cost, namely that when the derrick is swung out, careless winch work can set up a swing at the derrick head, particularly where the load is light. Because of the small angle between the two sides of the topping lift/guy arrangement, a limit must be put on the angle to which the derrick can be swung out (75° from the fore and aft line is usual).

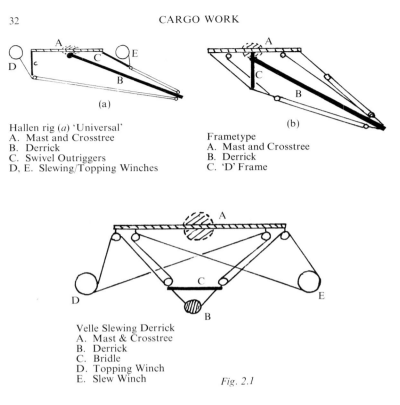

Hallen rig (*a*) 'Universal'
A. Mast and Crosstree
B. Derrick
C. Swivel Outriggers
D, E. Slewing/Topping Winches

Frametype
A. Mast and Crosstree
B. Derrick
C. 'D' Frame

Velle Slewing Derrick
A. Mast & Crosstree
B. Derrick
C. Bridle
D. Topping Winch
E. Slew Winch

Fig. 2.1

These figures illustrate how the devices operate.

The sketches show both Velle and Hallen rigs. The Velle operates by means of a steel bridle attached by means of two short wire pendants to the derrick head. The combined topping lifts/guys are lead to two winches with divided barrels. Both leads to the topping winch pass over the barrel in the same direction, those to the slew winch in opposite directions. Operating the topping winch raises or lowers the derrick; as the slew winch revolves one fall lengthens as the other shortens, thus swinging the derrick outwards or inwards. The function of the bridle is to provide sufficient separation between the guys to enable recovery of the derrick.

There are two forms of Hallen derrick, giving virtually the same operating characteristics as the Velle. The 'Universal' type has a swivel outrigger at each end of the crosstree so designed as to swing over an arc of 90° from the fore-and-aft line outboard. Thus as the derrick moves out the corresponding outrigger maintains a straight line to the derrick head, whilst the other remains fore-and-aft. The 'D' frame type is distinguished by the massive fixed outrigger at the masthead. Two stout pendants shackled to the cross-tree and to each of the topping lifts lead round the curved face of the 'D' frame.to provide separation. With Hallen system the relative speed and direction of the two winches determines whether the derrick raises, lowers or slews.

Instability of Cargo Gear

Instability of cargo gear can occur when the support provided by the guys and/or topping lifts becomes insufficient. This can occur with modern gear or traditional rigs. With the latter, if one derrick is set high and the other quite low (for example, if working the near end of the hatch and dropping far out overside) with union purchase rig, a jerk stress in any part of the rig can cause the high derrick to jack-knife backwards. The propensity to do this depends on design factors such as the distance apart of the derrick heels and the securing points available for the guys.

As the modern derrick is slewed outboard, the pull on the outboard topping lift decreases until, as it approaches zero, the derrick behaves as though unstayed (i.e. with no guys). Stability of the derrick tends to increase if the load is being lowered and vice versa, also if the derrick faces aft stability improves with stern trim. If the outer span tackle becomes slack the gear should be recovered by hauling on the inboard span, and not by attempting to take up slack.

With a pair of derricks the possible rigs are equally limited. The union purchase, universally used, is suitable for light weights at fast speed but it has its drawbacks of additional wear on the gear and of the dangers of working at speed. Skilled winchdrivers are a pre-requisite of this method and frequent inspection of all parts of the rig is vital. Other methods of combining two derricks are either improved union purchase, purpose built and using additional winches, as in the Ebel or Farrell rigs. Alternatively, recourse can be made to *ad hoc* rigging which consists of joining the falls of two derricks or using one fall with a single block in the bight . . . the notorious yo-yo rig. This system can be frowned upon if, indeed considered undesirable and is mentioned here only from the point of view of comparison.

As far as the cargo officer is concerned the gear for his ship is fixed; all he can do is to select that rig appropriate to the cargo to be handled. As he gains experience he should examine critically the shortcomings and the good points of the equipment, assess working cycles, record downtime, either for routine maintenance or for unplanned repairs or replacements as to build up a coherent picture of the operating capability of the gear in varying conditions of service. This is a management task which not only provides the data needed in the planning of successive generations of ships, but it is the best way in which a cargo officer can be completely in control of situations which, often unpredictably, face him.

Some principles which should be considered are:

1. Regular testing, inspection and maintenance of the gear, using the Docks Regulations as a minimum standard.
2. Using the correct rig for the type and weight of the unit to be handled. Dubious rigs should be prohibited.
3. Correct positioning of each derrick to give clear leads at every stage of the cycle.
4. Monitoring load cycles to see whether any improvement can be made . . . but not increases in speed which is a function of operator skill.
5. Recording data (including sketches where appropriate) for future analysis and for design modifications.

In the descriptions which follow the particular shortcomings for each type of gear should be borne in mind.

CARGO HANDLING BETWEEN SHIP AND QUAY

The handling of goods on ship and on quay is classified as being within 'dangerous and unhealthy industries' for which legislative regulations have long applied. There is much uniformity in the safety regulations of many nations since the International Labour Office, as part of UNESCO, acts as an approving agency for the form and nature of tests, examinations and use of cargo gear in affiliated countries. The United Kingdom conforms to these requirements and, as an example of the breadth of application, the following notes are informative.

In the United Kingdom cargo work is regulated by the Docks Regulations 1934 (S.R. & O 1934 No. 279) which were made in pursuance of Section 79 of the 1901 Factory and Workshop Act. The purpose of the regulations was to provide for safe access to ships and quays, to establish safeworking practices and to prescribe for the periodic inspection and testing of cargo gear. Forms were prescribed for recording the tests and inspections.

In more recent times the Factories Act (Section 125/126) extends certain of its provisions to the docks, wharves and ships but these are mainly of general character giving the appropriate Minister powers to make regulations, including those for inspections, the keeping of records and methods of working, etc. The Code of Safe Working Practices for Merchant Seamen—D.o.T., as it relates to cargo work, gives support to this background (see page 431).

Specifically, the Act enables Magistrates' Courts to make orders prohibiting dangerous practices (after an application by an aggrieved person) and any regulation may be extended to any harbour, wet dock, or to the processes of constructing, repairing ships or boilers and cleaning of tanks or bilges where the last cargo was specified as dangerous.

So far, no alterations have changed the general requirements under the 1934 regulations, which, surprisingly, remain up to date. The only area where uncertainty exists is in connection with the gear used in hoisting, lowering or closing ramps, bow and stern doors in roll on/roll off vessels; it has not been specifically declared whether this apparatus is cargo gear, in the accepted sense.

Any person, whether ship's officer or shore supervisor, must make himself familiar with the regulations and their requirements; by way of introduction to this responsibility, a summary follows.

DOCKS REGULATIONS 1934—SUMMARY

Apply to the processes of loading, unloading, moving and handling goods in, on, or at any dock, wharf or quay and the processes of loading, unloading and coaling any ship in any dock, harbour or canal.

PART 1   Safety measures at docks, wharves and quays:

(1) Fencing around dangerous parts, corners, etc., and across bridges, caissons, etc. Height of fence not less than 2 ft 6 ins (0·76 m).
(2) Life saving appliances in readiness at wharf or quay including means of 'holding on' at water level.
(3) Efficient lighting in all places to which people employed have access.
(4) First Aid boxes and ambulance facilities, whereabouts indicated by notices.

PART 2   Access to and from ship and parts of the ship

Alongside quay: accommodation ladder or similar access, properly secured. At least 22 in wide fenced each side to height of 2 ft 9 in with upper and lower rails (accommodation ladder against ship's side needs outboard rail only). Ordinary ladder (secured) may be used if other means not practicable.

Alongside other ship: safe means of access, provided by vessel with the higher freeboard.

Access to holds, etc.: applies where depth of hold exceeds 5 ft. Access by ladder and ladder cleats or cups in the coaming.
Upper and lower ladders in line.
Ladders provide foothold to depth not less than $4\frac{1}{2}$ in for a width of 10 in and a firm handhold. Similar for cleats and cups. Cargo to be stowed so as to leave this clearance.
Room to pass between coaming and any obstruction at the place where ladder leaves the dock.
Ladder may only be recessed sufficiently to keep hatchway clear.
Sloping ladders away from the hatch with separate access may be used provided they offer similar clearances.
Hand- and foot-holds on each side of shaft tunnel.
Efficient lighting in holds, on decks, in access ways and all parts where *persons employed* may go in course of their work.

(b)   Hatch Covers

ALL beams used for hatch covering to have suitable gear for lifting on/off WITHOUT persons having to go upon them to adjust.
All hatch covers to be marked to indicate deck, hatch, and position, unless all covers are interchangeable. This applies to beams similarly adequate handgrips on hatch covers.
If working space around hatch less than 2 ft wide some method of enabling persons to handle beams and hatches must be available.

PART 3　Tests, etc., of lifting machinery

ALL lifting machinery must be tested before being brought into use, and examined by a competent person.
ALL derricks and attachments to mast and deck must be inspected every 12 months and thoroughly examined at least every 4 years. Other lifting machinery thoroughly examined at least every 12 months.

Thorough examination = visual examination + hammer test or similar with dismantling if necessary.

Chains, rings, hooks, shackles, swivels and pulley blocks used in lifting and lowering must be tested and examined before being brought into use.
Annealing or similar treatment—$\frac{1}{2}$ in or smaller at least every 6 months
　　　　　　　　　　　　other　　　　　at least every 12 months.
Gear to be inspected before use unless previously inspected within last 3 months.
Ropes to be suitable quality and free from obvious defect.
Wire rope to be tested before being brought into use, inspected every 3 months and if any wire in the rope is broken, every month. If number of broken wires in a length of 8 diameters exceeds 10% of total wires in rope

THEN THE ROPE MUST NOT BE USED, *NOR IF IT SHOWS SIGNS OF EXCESSIVE WEAR OR CORROSION.*

S.W.L. to be marked on blocks and on disc attached to chain sling. Wire slings may have either disc or notice available giving the S.W.L. Chain slings not to be shortened by tying knots in them.

Machinery to be securely fenced.
Safe access and fencing to crane cabs and driver's platform.
S.W.L.s to be marked on derricks and cranes.
Exhaust steam not to obscure any part of deck or access.
Method of preventing foot of derrick being lifted out of socket.

PART 4　Miscellaneous rules

Means of escape from hold or T/D where coal or bulk cargo is being worked.
S.W.L. of any gear may only occasionally be exceeded and then record must be kept.
No winch drivers or signalmen under 16 allowed.
Walking space around cargo stacked on quay.
If hold depth exceeds 5 ft the hatch must be securely fenced to height of 3 ft unless coaming is 2 ft 6 in or over when the hatch is not in use.
No misuse of hatch covers.
If working cargo is T/D at least one section of hatches to be in place.
If working in hatch square hooks not to be attached to bale bands.
HATCH BEAMS TO BE SECURED.
Signaller to be employed for each fall.

PART 5

No person to interfere with gear, etc., unless authorized.
Only authorized access to be used.
No person to go upon beams to adjust them.

PART 6

If shipowner fails to comply with safe access regulations the duty to do so falls on employer of the persons employed.
Register to be kept available for inspection.

DOCKS REGULATIONS 1934

*TESTS AND EXAMINATION BEFORE TAKING LIFTING
MACHINERY AND GEAR INTO USE*

Every Winch and all Accessories Thereto

TEST   PROOF LOAD IN EXCESS OF S.W.L. AS FOLLOWS:
                S.W.L. UP TO 20 TONS -25% IN EXCESS
                      20–50 TONS $-$S.W.L.$+5$ TONS
                      OVER 50 TONS -10% IN EXCESS

METHOD   *EITHER* WEIGHTS *OR* SPRING/HYDRAULIC
                BALANCE (DERRICK SWUNG OUT AS FAR AS
                POSSIBLE EACH WAY)

Every Crane or Hoisting Machine and all Accessories Thereto

TEST   AS ABOVE

METHOD   WEIGHTS SWUNG AS FAR AS POSSIBLE EACH
                WAY FOR CRANES WITH VARIABLE JIB
                AT MAX. AND MIN. RADII AS WELL

                Loose Gear whether Accessory to a Machine or not

TEST   *PROOF LOAD AS FOLLOWS:*
                Chain, Ring, Hook, Shackle,
                or Swivel $2 \times$ S.W.L.
                Single Sheave Blocks $4 \times$ S.W.L.
                Multiple Sheave Blocks:
                  If S.W.L. up to and including
                  20 tons $2 \times$ S.W.L.
                  Over 20 and up to and including
                  40 tons   S.W.L.$+20$ tons
                Over 40 tons $1\frac{1}{2} \times$ S.W.L.

EXAMINATION   After test of all gear including dismantling blocks to see that
                no damage or deformation has occurred.

WIRE ROPES   Sample tested to destruction.
                S.W.L. not to exceed $\frac{1}{5}$ of the breaking load.

FORMS, AND THE DOCKS REGULATIONS

REQUIREMENTS:

Form 99—*Register of Machinery Chains, etc., and Wire Ropes*

In four sections:
Part 1—4 yearly thorough examinations and annual inspections. Derrick and
        permanent attachments.
Part 2—Annual inspections—cranes, winches and gear other than derricks and
        attachments.

Part 3—Annual thorough examination—gear exempted from annealing (e.g.)
Chains made of malleable cast iron.
Chains, rings, hooks, etc., made of steel.
Rings, hooks, etc., permanently attached to pulley blocks, etc.
Part 4—Record of annealing of chains, rings, hooks, etc.

OTHER FORMS

Form 100   Notice to ship that stevedores have handed over responsibility for the hatches (counterfoil signed on behalf of ship).

TEST CERTIFICATES

Form 86   Chains, rings, hooks, shackles, swivels and pulley blocks before being brought into use.
Form 87   Wire ropes before being brought into use.
Form 1944   Winches, derricks and accessory gear ⎫
Form 1945   Cranes or hoists and accessory gear ⎬ where these tests are carried
Form 1946   Annealing of chains, rings, etc.   ⎭ out by shore firms.

Test certificates must be attached to the back of Form 99, and the Register and all forms and certificates must be kept for at least 4 years.

M. Notices and the Docks Regulations

Certain notices emphasize the need for care in handling hatches:

M 524—Danger with rolling hatch covers—keep men clear after hauling wire has been secured. Particular danger with excessive shear and trim, also where hatch is partly open.

M Notice 992 emphasizes the need for care in securing non-steel hatches with steel locking bars or wire lashings.

M Notice 1007 draws attention to the new U.K. Regulations . . . 'The Merchant Shipping (means of access) Regulations 1981'.

At the time of publication of this book the revision and updating of the Docks Regulations is underway but it must be pointed out that in 1977 The International Labour Office introduced the Code entitled 'Safety and Health in Dock Work' in which the test provisions are substantially the same as in the 1934 Regulations.

This code extends beyond considerations of immediate shipwork and equipment to include information and precautions connected with all forms of lifting devices, fork-lift trucks, dock railways, stacking and handling of goods on the quay and the provisions of first aid and personnel facilities.

A copy of the Code may be regarded as an essential item for all concerned with aspects of port's operations.

The Rigging of Derricks

Despite design and construction development derricks still remain part of conventional cargo handling gear requiring care and attention according to their use for particular types of lift loads.

General cargo of moderately heavy load may be successfully handled by the 'union purchase rig'; lighter loads can be effectively shifted by the 'swinging derrick' whilst heavy cargo, as such, generally needs the 'heavy derrick' . . . possibly the area of derrick design in which the greatest development has taken place.

Each type of rig employed is allied to the degree of stress which the particular type of cargo is likely to impose upon the gear, and all reasonable precautions must be adopted to keep these stresses at a minimum. Generally speaking . . . heavy loads must be handled and swung slowly whilst lighter weights may be handled with more reasonable rapidity. The application of cargo gear in loading and discharging procedures is to a very great extent, influenced and controlled by legislation and all cargo officers should make a point of becoming familiar with the shipping notices which have relevance to the movement of cargoes, some of which are indicated in Section 6, pages 447–449 of this book.

Fundamentally, the underlying fact in the rigging and use of cargo gear is *the safe working load of that gear.* Contravention by default or otherwise in the neglect of this fact is a punishable offence.

In this context the following are some of the more important precautions which must be observed when using and employing all forms of gear in the handling of cargoes:

1. All gear, including derricks and attachments, must be regularly and efficiently greased and lubricated.
2. All wires, chains and ropes must be in good condition, free from breaks or frays and not deformed in any way nor unduly worn. Wires used for purchases and topping lifts should be frequently oiled.
3. All shackles, hooks, blocks and pins should be of the same safe working load as the derrick they serve.
4. With a stationary rig, such as the union purchase, the guys should be led from the derrick at angles as near to 90° as possible and always kept absolutely tight.
5. With a swinging derrick the guys should be led in such a manner as to avoid the derrick taking control and swinging unduly quickly. Considerable stress is imposed upon the gooseneck of the derrick unless these precautions are observed.
6. With a heavy derrick, additional preventer stays are necessary to relieve the stress upon the mast. Unless the structural arrangements in way of the derrick are additionally strengthened, strengthening by means of shores above and below deck will be necessary.
7. In no circumstances should a derrick be overloaded. It is better to have a sling below the recognized weight than to err in the other direction.
8. Careful winch or crane handling is very important. Inconsistent rates of acceleration when heaving up and lowering impose great stress upon all the gear.
   It is worthy of note that a sudden jerk upon a cargo runner,

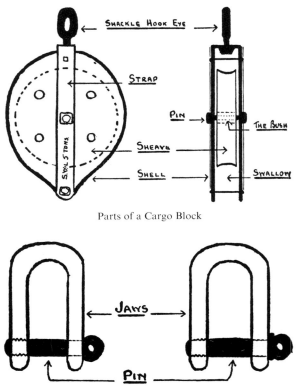

Parts of a Cargo Block

STRAIGHT SHACKLES
Parts of a Shackle. The Collar increases the Rigidity of the Shackle

Fig. 2.2

due to incorrect acceleration, imposes a stress upon all items of gear concerned, perhaps equal to twice the weight being lifted or even more. It can be appreciated that when lifting a sling up to a maximum load allowed, such neglect will impose a stress considerably in excess of the safe working load of the gear.

9. Derricks should be 'topped' to a reasonably high angle, consistent with the distribution of cargo within the hold. The stresses are considerably increased with 'low angled' derricks more so than with those at higher angles.

10. No item of cargo gear should be used unless it is stamped with the 'Safe Working Load' or bears a covering certificate to this effect.

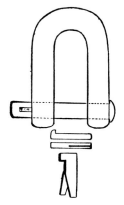

Fig. 2.3 Shackle with a Forelock

When shackles, having forelocks, are used, it is essential to see that the pin is inserted into the jaws of the shackle in such a manner that the forelock is at the bottom, as shown in the illustration.

Such shackles, whilst serving admirably for attaching topping lift blocks to the crosstrees, are apt to be a source of danger with ordinary running gear. There is always the chance of the forelock becoming unplaced and it is not prudent to take chances with cargo gear.

STATUTORY RULES AND ORDERS

Factory and Workshop—Dangerous and Unhealthy Industries
The Docks Regulations (See also pp. 31–34)

The following extracts are taken from the above orders by permission of Her Majesty's Stationery Office.

Lifting Machinery means cranes, winches, hoists, derrick booms, derrick and mast bands, goosenecks, eyebotts, and all other permanent attachments to the derricks and masts used in hoisting or lowering.

Inspection and Testing

All lifting machinery shall have been tested and examined by a competent person before being taken into use.

All derricks and permanent attachments used in hoisting or lowering shall be *inspected once in every twelve months* and be *thoroughly examined once at least in every four years.* All other lifting machinery shall be thoroughly examined once at least every twelve months.

For the purposes of the Regulations thorough examination means a visual examination, supplemented if necessary by other means such as a hammer test, in order to arrive at a reliable conclusion as to the safety of the parts examined.

No chain, ring, hook, shackle, swivel or pulley block shall be used in hoisting or lowering unless it has been tested and examined by a competent person.

Annealing

All chains and all rings, hooks, shackles and swivels used in hoisting or lowering shall be effectually annealed under the supervision of a competent person and at the following intervals:

1. Half inch and smaller chains, rings, hooks, shackles and swivels in general use, once at least in every six months.
2. All other chains, rings, hooks, shackles and swivels in general use once at least in every twelve months.

Periodic Inspection

All chains, rings, hooks, shackles, swivels and pulley blocks shall be inspected by a competent person immediately before each occasion on which they are used in hoisting or lowering, unless they have been inspected within the preceding three months.

No rope shall be used in hoisting and lowering unless:

1. It is of suitable quality and free from patent defect.
2. In the case of wire rope, it has been examined and tested.

Rope and Wire Specifications

No wire rope shall be used in hoisting or lowering if in any length of eight diameters the total number of visible broken wires exceeds 10 per cent of the total number of wires, or the rope shows signs of excessive wear, corrosion or other defect which, in the opinion of the person who inspects it, renders it unfit for use.

Splices

A thimble or loop splice made in any wire rope shall have at least three tucks with a hole strand of the rope and two tucks with one half of the wires cut out of each strand. The strands in all cases shall be tucked against the lay of the rope.

S.W.L. Markings

No pulley block shall be used in hoisting or lowering unless the *safe working load* is clearly stamped on it.

As regards chain slings and wire rope slings, the safe working load shall be marked in plain figures or letters upon the sling or upon a tablet or ring attached thereto.

Every crane and derrick shall have the *safe working load* plainly marked upon it.

Chains shall not be shortened by tying knots in them.

No lifting machinery, chains or lifting appliances shall be loaded beyond the safe working load.

No load shall be left suspended from a crane, winch or other machine unless there is a competent person actually in charge of the machine while the load is so left.

All deck stages and cargo stages shall be firmly constructed and adequately supported. Hatch coverings shall not be used in the construction of deck or cargo stages, or for any purpose which may expose them to damage.

No cargo shall be loaded or unloaded by a fall or sling at any intermediate deck unless either the hatch at that deck is securely covered or a secure landing platform of a width not less than of one section of hatch coverings has been placed across it.

When the working space in a hold is confined to the square of the hatch, hooks shall not be made fast in the bands or fastenings of bales of cotton, wool or other similar goods.

The beams of any hatch in use for the working of cargo, shall, if not removed, be adequately secured to prevent their displacement.

When cargo is being loaded or unloaded by a fall at a hatchway, a signaller shall be employed, and where more than one fall is worked at a hatchway, a separate signaller shall be employed to attend to each fall. (All vessels are required to keep a record of tests and examinations made to cargo gear. Such a record is made on 'Form 99, Register of Cargo Gear'.)

THE USE OF CHAINS AND OTHER LIFTING GEAR

The size of a chain is always stated as the nominal diameter of the bar from which it is made ('d' in the computation of Safe Working Loads).

Short link or close link lifting chains of good quality should have a minimum strength of approximately $27 \, d^2$ tons.

The safe working loads of chain must vary in the manner in which they are used, but provided a definite standard of quality is assured, a standard for maximum safe working loads can be set up.

For close-link welded chain the *safe working load* is $6 \, d^2$ tons and *the proof load* is $12 \, d^2$ tons.

Where there is a special risk to life or limb a maximum safe working load of $5 \, d^2$ tons should be adopted.

The maximum safe working load for a long-link chain should

not exceed two-thirds of that for a short-link chain of the same diameter.

A ring must be sufficiently strong to carry safely a load equal to the sum of the safe loads of all the attached chains.

Cargo Hooks. There is little variation in the general outline of ordinary hooks. The opening or gap of the hook must be sufficiently wide to admit the largest rope, ring or shackle which has to be placed on it.

Various forms of hooks are shown in Figures 1 to 8 (Fig. 2.4).

Fig. 2.4

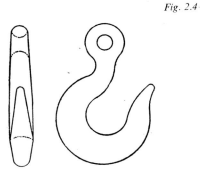 

Fig. 1. Sling hook. Eye rounded for attachment of chain or rope to form a sling.

Fig. 2. Hook with flat eye. Eye made with flat cheeks and drilled hole for use with a shackle.

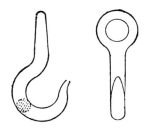 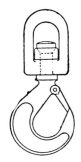

Fig. 3. Cargo hook. Large rounded eye to permit easy attachment of hemp ropes. Type of hook much used in dock processes.

Fig. 4. Swivel spring hook. Spring catch prevents accidental displacement of sling and also prevents hook catching in fixed structure during hoisting. Type commonly used on cranes for loads up to 10 tons.

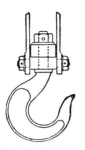

Fig. 5. Ball bearing hook. Ball bearing facilititates the turning of heavy loads, and built-up shackle ensures adequate strength.

Fig. 6. Ramshorn hook. Type used on large cranes. The two hooks prevent overlapping of slings.

Fig. 7. Liverpool hook. The projection over the point prevents the latter catching in any fixture when hoisting, and the incurved point also prevents accidental displacement of sling.

Fig. 8. Hook with handle. Handle obviates risk of slinger's fingers being jammed by slings slipping when handling hook.

The *safe working load* of a cargo hook is found as follows:

B × H tons, where B and H are dimensions in inches.

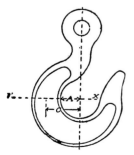

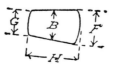

Fig..9.

Fig. 9A. Section at XY.

Shackles. Shackles, according to difference in shape, are known respectively as D or straight-sided shackles and bow or harp shackles.

The best types of shackles have collars on the pin which bear upon the side of the shackle eye and so increase the rigidity of the shackle.

Shackles should be tested to the same proof load as that of the largest chain to which they may be attached. *The safe working load should not exceed half the proof load.*

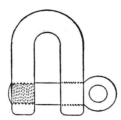

Fig. 10. D shackle. Screwed pin without collar

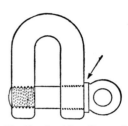

Fig. 11. D shackle. Screwed pin with collar.

Fig. 12. Bow shackle. Screwed pin with collar

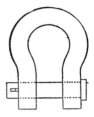

Fig. 13. Bow shackle. Plain pin with collar and split fore lock to hold pin in position.

Chain Slings. Simple types of slings are illustrated in Figures 14 to 22.

The kind of sling to be used will depend largely on the nature and shape of the articles to be lifted.

Marking. It is common practice to stamp each chain, sling, hook and other lifting appliance with some identifying letter or number before putting it into use.

The marks may be stamped on the larger end links or rings, but for smaller sizes various kinds of metal labels are used.

Shackles, loose hooks, swivels and eyebolts should be stamped with identification marks; both parts of a shackle should be marked as the pin is liable to be lost and another pin substituted.

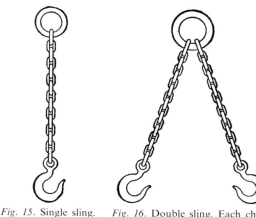

Fig. 14. Collar sling. One end link or a loop of the chain can be passed through the other end link when slinging an article.

Fig. 15. Single sling. Ring can be placed on crane hook and sling hook placed in ring or around chain after passing latter around article to be slung.

Fig. 16. Double sling. Each chain can be placed around article and hooks either hitched on chains or in ring.

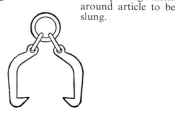

Fig. 17. Timber dogs. The sharpened 'dogs' enter the timber and the pull due to the load tends to increase their grip.

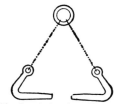

Fig. 18. Lead hooks. The straight portions of the hooks are placed in the ends of a roll of lead and they are kept in position by the pull in the chain legs.

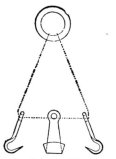

Fig. 19. Can hooks. These are used for lifting bundles of material into which the hooks can penetrate and secure a suitable hold.

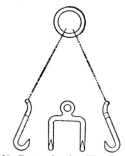

Fig. 20. Cotton hooks. These are used for lifting bales of cotton and similar materials.

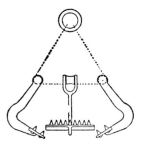

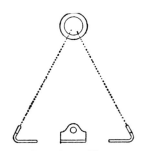

Fig. 21. Case hooks. These are used for lifting wooden cases, the spikes ensuring a proper grip.

Fig. 22. Plate clams. These are used for lifting metal plates.

It is far more essential that the safe working load should be known rather than the test load and hence it is a better and safer practice to have the former only marked on the appliances.

Stresses. A chain will sustain a shock whenever the velocity of a load is suddenly increased or decreased, and the stress in a chain when a load is applied suddenly is twice the stress induced by the same load applied slowly.

Any lifting gear which, after use, exhibits permanent deformation, however slight, should be regarded as having been overloaded, and should not be used again unless annealing or repairing will restore it to its original condition otherwise the gear should be discarded.

UNION PURCHASE

This is the usual type of derrick rig for general cargo handling.

One derrick, called the 'ship derrick' is plumbed over the hatchway in order to allow a direct vertical lead to the cargo within the hold and the other, called the 'off-shore derrick' is plumbed clear of the rail to allow of discharge to the wharf or lighter.

Two guys are shackled to the spider band of each derrick.

The guys from the 'ship derrick' are led, one to each side of the vessel, as widely as possible and with as near a 90° angle of lead from the derrick as is possible.

Guys which approach the vertical impose an additional stress upon the derrick and topping lift.

The guys from the 'off-shore derrick' are led with the inboard one across the vessel and the other forward or aft according to whether the hatch is in the after or forward part of the vessel. Similar angles of lead are advised.

A two fold purchase (2 in manila rope) is attached to the guy

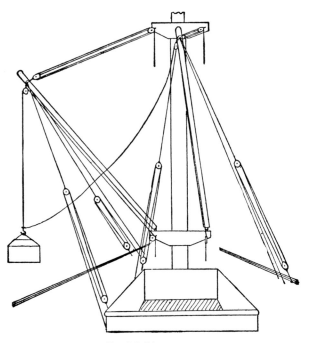

Fig. 2.5 Diagram 'A'

pennants and shackled to ring bolts in the deck or bulwark rail. This permits periodic adjustment to ensure tightness of the guys.

With derricks of a safe working load of 5 or 7 tons, 16 in gin blocks are fitted at the derrick heads and as lead blocks at the heels of the derricks.

Two and a quarter or two and a half inch, 6 stranded wire is used for the runners. Each is rove through the gooseneck lead block and the derrick head blocks and joined together by a shackle passing through their eye splices.

To the shackle is fitted a cargo hook of appropriate design and safe working load.

The wire runners are of sufficient length to reach any part of the lower hold with adequate spare wire on the drum of the winch. Forty fathoms is the usual length of a cargo runner.

Slings up to $1\frac{1}{2}$ tons weight can be safely handled with the union purchase rig.

The topping lift may be either a single wire or chain span, shackled to derrick spider band and to the mast, or a double or treble wire purchase.

The method of application of this type of rig is to lift the weight from the hold by the runner on the ship derrick, and whilst heaving up, to heave in the slack of the outboard runner. As the weight clears the hatch coaming part of its weight is taken by the outboard runner, so that it is suspended at the apex of a span formed by the two runners.

The outboard runner gradually takes more of the weight until it completely holds the sling vertically beneath the outboard derrick, the ship runner being slackened accordingly.

The weight is lowered on the outboard runner, sufficient slack being provided by working back both winches.

When loading, the preceding arrangement is reversed.

SWINGING DERRICK

Opinions differ as to the amount of weight it is advisable to handle with this type of rig. As it is expected to attain a quick rate of work, heavy loads do not seem consistent with safety, to either limb or gear.

Slings of about twenty bags of wheat, baskets of bulk grain or coal and slings of four to six barrels or drums are frequently handled by the swinging derrick, and these loads do not generally exceed one ton. With care, loads up to 30 cwts may be handled.

The advantages of such a system are quick discharge or loading and, with two derricks at each hatch, cargo work is permitted on both sides of the vessel.

The disadvantages may be stated as:

    (a) possibility of undue stress upon all items of cargo gear particularly guys, unless exceptional care is taken, and

    (b) the possibility of the swinging load striking hatch-coamings and rails with consequent damage.

The above observations seem to suggest that careful supervision is essential when using the swinging derrick.

It is usual to lead the outboard guy sufficiently well forward or aft, as the case may be, so as to permit the derricks being hauled over to make wide clearance of the rail. This may be effected by manual or mechanical power. In the latter case, the hauling part of the guy purchase is led through a lead block to a free winch.

The inboard guy is led horizontally from the derrick head to a connection favourably placed on the mast shroud. In some cases this guy is led and attached to the opposite rail, but in both cases some form of heavy weight is attached to the hauling part of the guy. This weight is known as a 'dead man', the object of which is to provide sufficient power to cause the derrick to swing back to the hatch after the load is removed.

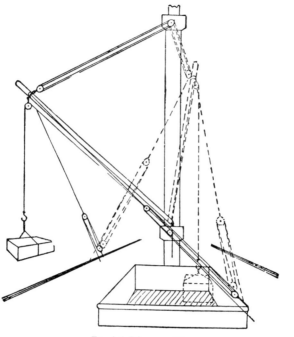

Fig. 2.6 Diagram 'B'

It is imperative that the vessel should be upright. If there is a list towards the discharging side, considerable difficulty will be experienced in bringing the derrick back over the hatch.

Some officers prefer a slight list in the opposite direction. This is certainly conducive to the favourable return of the derrick.

See Part B Velle Swinging Derrick

THE HEAVY DERRICK
(Conventional Design)

In conventional terms a 'heavy derrick' is meant to be a specially fitted derrick capable of handling loads outside of the normal 10–15 ton general cargo loads. In modern tonnage vessels are fitted with derricks to take much greater loads than this, to which reference is made in Sub-Section B, on heavy lifting equipment with modern cargo gear. Some older vessels still operate with 30–50 ton 'heavy derricks' and for this reason Diagram 'C' is included in these considerations.

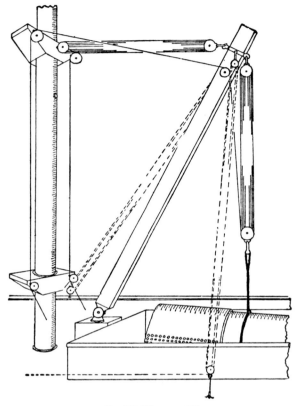

Fig. 2.7 Diagram 'C'

Where this earlier construction still pertains it is usual to fit two heavy derricks, of larger and lesser capacity. The larger derrick is allocated to the largest hold of the vessel, having the foremast for the attachment of the topping lift. The heel of the derrick is stepped into a specially built and strengthened heel piece or shoe.

The smaller derrick, similarly attached to a mast or samson post, serves a smaller hold.

Special multiple sheave blocks of appropriate safe working load are provided for the topping lifts, purchases and guys of both derricks. Wires of larger size, both in circumference and length are provided.

Additional stays are fitted to the mast or samson post and besides the necessary guys, wire pennants are fitted to the derrick to serve as preventer guys.

Unless specially heavy winches are provided, the ordinary winches must be put into double gear when working the heavy derrick.

It is of extreme importance that the vessel should be perfectly upright when working the heavy derrick, and that strict supervision is given so as to ensure that the guys are slowly and rigidly slackened and tightened as required when swinging the derrick.

A measure of 'stiffness' is required as regards the stability of the vessel, for it must be remembered that when such a heavy weight clears the bottom of the hold or the wharf, the effect of that weight is immediately transferred to the derrick head.

As the derrick head may be some 50 ft above the deck, this constitutes a situation which may cause a considerable rise of the centre of gravity of the vessel.

With a tender vessel that situation which brings the centre of gravity above the metacentre might arise and the vessel would then lose positive stability and be liable to take a list. This is known as 'the critical moment' when discharging or loading heavy weights. Attention should therefore be given to ensure that some or all of the double bottom tanks are full. Under no consideration should they be slack.

There are many methods of rigging heavy derricks; all of them equally efficient. The accompanying diagrams illustrate two methods.

WEIGHTS OF MODERATELY HEAVY TONNAGE

It very often happens that a ship is called upon to load a weight which is not sufficiently heavy to warrant the use of the heavy derrick but yet is excessive for the normally rigged derricks.

In such cases it is common practice to double up one derrick, as shown in Diagram E and use it in the form of a specially strengthened swinging derrick.

The weight, under such a rig, is held by two parts of the wire instead of one and, with the winch in double gear, is being lifted at a much slower rate. It can be shown by the principle of the parallelogram of forces that the stresses upon all parts (shackles, derrick and hauling part) is considerably less than with the normally rigged union purchase.

Another interesting and important point, not to be overlooked, is that should a sudden impulse, or load, come upon cargo gear the stress effect is, momentarily, twice that normally carried. Examples of such stresses are those obtained from slings catching on hatch coamings as the load is being drawn from the wings or perhaps, though fortunately very infrequent, a faulty winch gear, which causes slipping.

Derricks which are 'doubled up' minimize these dangerous

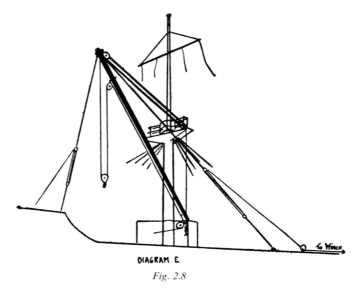

DIAGRAM E.

Fig. 2.8

possibilities and the system finds favour with many experienced cargo officers. As it is a form of single derrick working, the guys may be manhandled or, preferably, led through snatch blocks to vacant winches.

It is the usual type of rig for discharging or loading many forms of light cargo, as for example, baskets of coal, trays of cement in bags and baskets of grain and the application of such a rig is known as 'whipping'.

Note. With all types of cargo rigs it is very essential to ensure that the gooseneck or shoe for the heel of of the derrick is plumb with the shackle of the topping lift. Considerable difficulty will be experienced in swinging the derrick should this not be so. Especially is this necessary when working heavy lifts so that 'the axis of swing' will be in the vertical.

STRESSES ON CARGO GEAR

Whatever the arrangement of cargo gear, it is essential to pre-calculate the loads and tensions imposed at various parts in order to determine that blocks, wires, shackles and all ancillary gear are of adequate *safe working load* before being used.

This involves consideration of the study of mechanics insofar as mechanical advantage and friction are concerned. It also involves vector polygons, i.e. the '*parallelogram of forces*'.

In this latter context the following illustrate the principles:

The Composition and Resolution of Forces. Probably the most elementary principle of mechanics, as it affects cargo work, is the resolving of all the forces acting upon the gear into triangles and parallelograms.

Forces which act in conjunction with or opposition to each other, or parallel to each other, present little or no difficulty, for the total force acting may be computed as the sum or difference of the numerous forces.

When forces are not acting as before mentioned it is a question of resolving those forces into a series of parallelograms, the diagonals of which represent the resultant force.

This principle, known as 'The Parallelogram of Forces' is the basis upon which the stresses on derricks, masts, spans and shackles are computed.

The Parallelogram of Forces may be stated as follows:

'If two forces acting upon a point be represented, both in amount and direction, by two sides of a parallelogram, then the resultant force may be measured as the diagonal of the parallelogram, drawn from the point of application'.

For example: Two forces of 10 tons and 7 tons are acting upon a shackle. One force is vertically downward and the other at a direction of 36 degrees from the vertical. What is the total force upon the shackle?

By laying off the forces as shown and completing the parallelogram it can be seen that the total force upon the shackle is not 17 tons, but $15\frac{1}{2}$ tons, as represented by the diagonal of the parallelogram.

Scale $\frac{1}{2}$ cm = 1 ton.

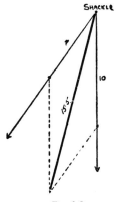

Fig. 2.9

Scale $\frac{1}{10}$ = 1 ton.

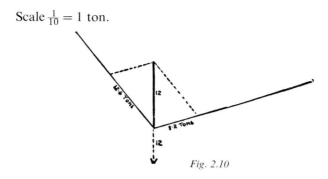

Fig. 2.10

Similarly, if a known weight is suspended from a point, formed by the junction of two spans, it can be shown that this weight now becomes the diagonal, and the forces, or stresses upon the spans are represented as the sides of the parallelogram.

Example: Two spans meet at a point, making an angle of 112°. From this point is suspended a weight of 12 tons. What is the amount of stress upon each span?

The two previous examples are simple, based on first principles and easy to understand. Although some of the following examples are a little more complicated, they are based upon exactly the same principles and study of them will show how important a part they play in the rigging of cargo gear.

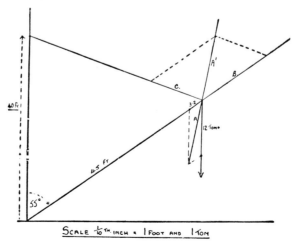

SCALE $\frac{1}{10}$ TH. INCH = 1 FOOT AND 1 TON

Fig. 2.11

A 12 ton weight is to be lifted by a derrick, 45 ft long, rigged at an angle of 55° to a mast. The derrick span is attached to the mast at a point 40 ft above its heel, and a 3 fold purchase is available for lifting the weight. Find the various stresses that are operating.

(a) By referring back to the section on purchases it may be ascertained that the stress on the hauling part, or force required to lift this weight is 3·2 tons.

This force is represented as working along the line of the derrick.

By completing the parallelogram, the following stresses may be determined.

A The diagonal of the parallelogram, represents the stress upon the shackle. 14·8 tons.

A^1 is this force projected to form the resultant of another parallelogram.

B represents the thrust on the derrick. 16·8 tons.

C represents the stress or tension on the span. 10 tons.

It can thus be seen that by the simple process of completing parallelograms, a cargo officer can determine the stresses on the gear and so provide shackles, blocks and spans of the appropriate safe working load.

The following diagrams show how the stresses may be altered by the varying angles to which a derrick is topped.

With the span attached to the mast 20 ft above the heel, the thrust on the derrick is $14\frac{1}{2}$ tons and the tension on the span $9\frac{1}{2}$ tons.

By raising the span to 35 ft above the heel, the respective stresses are $8\frac{1}{2}$ tons and $5\frac{3}{4}$ tons. It follows therefore that the higher the point of attachment of the span, the less are the stresses.

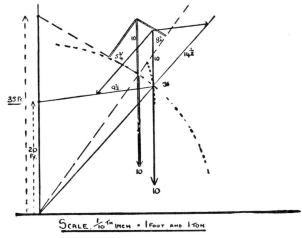

Fig. 2.12

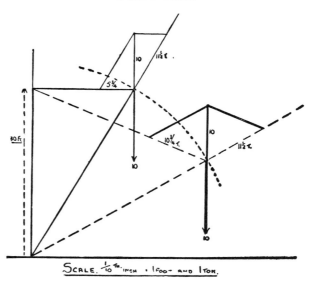

Fig. 2.13. Length of derrick, 30 ft. Length of span, 20 ft. Weight, 10 tons.

On most ships, however, the span, or topping lift is a fixture and usually finds connection at the cross trees of the mast. The question of raising it does not therefore arise, but it is interesting to note how the stresses may be altered by changing the angle of the derrick.

It can be seen that although the thrust on the derrick remains constant, the tension on the span is considerably lessened by raising the derrick. This is an important point when dealing with heavy weights.

The British Standards Institution

For many years the B.S.I. has laid down specifications for cargo working gear, much of which is in accordance with the requirements of the Docks Regulations. Reference to its recommendations should be essential practice by all responsible personnel engaged in cargo handling.

The B.S.I. publish a code of practice, copies of which will invariably be found in ships having conventional gear. The information contained in the code should be studied by cargo officers, relative to the equipment in their ships.

THE BRITISH STANDARD CODE OF PRACTICE, B.S.M.A. 48, 1976, is intended to serve as a guide for the use of ship's officers, stevedores, designers and others connected with the working of cargo. Among other detail it contains definitions of standard application, coefficients for estimating tensions, load diagrams and notes on the testing of derricks and their rigs. Included also are tables setting out the calculation factors for rope tensions.

The illustrations of derrick setting, and its rigging for different purchases are self explanatory. In terms of particular interest the Code uses the letter P as indicative of a force resulting from a load W, both in the diagrams and the tables.

By kind permission of The British Standards Institution extracts from, and reference to the Code are herewith reproduced.

A. Tension on ropes and wires in a purchase Traditionally a simple formula has been used to evaluate the stress on the hauling part of a purchase. This is the quantity required in deciding the size of wire/rope to use and for including in diagrams to find other stresses in the gear.

On the basis of S, representing the stress on the hauling part, P the theoretical power at purchase, W the load and $(N/6)W$ being the frictional allowance on the basis of 6% according to the number of sheaves, the formula was:

$$S \times P = W + \frac{N}{6} W$$

For a luff tackle, lifting 3 tonnes, this would then read:

$$S \times 2 = 3 + \left(\frac{2}{6} 3 \right)$$
$$\therefore S = \frac{3+1}{2}$$
$$= 2 \text{ tonnes.}$$

The B.S.I. Code, however, refines the formula, as shown, and applies reference to its table of tensions, in terms of P. Figure 2.14, page 56, is a reproduction of this table.

Reference to Fig. 2.15, page 57, shows the interpretation of loads and stress points in a conventional derrick rig.

P is the force due to a load of W tonnes from which the stress on each part of rope/wire in the purchase is designated, i.e. P_0, P_1, P_2, according to its location.

Should additional lead blocks be involved, further forces, P_3, P_4 etc., will be taken into account.

By way of nomenclature:

P_0 is the load borne by the 'becket', i.e. at the upper block.

P_1 is the load borne by the las rope/wire, i.e. before the fall passes out of the purchase.

P_2 is the stress on the hauling part.

Reference to Fig. 2.15 indicates P as the force due to the load. This is supported by two parts of 'rope' the stresses on which, P_0 and P_1 together, equals P_2, the stress on the hauling part.

Table 1. Rope tensions in terms of P

Applicable to blocks having sheaves with bushed plain bearings

(An allowance of 6 % per sheave, accumulative, is made for frictional resistance in the blocks)

Number of parts of rope holding the load	Rope tension at specified position (see key diagram, figure 8)									
	P_0		P_1		P_2		P_3		P_4	
	Hoisting	Lowering	Hoisting	Lowering	Hoisting	Lowering	Hoisting	Lowering	Hoisting	Lowering
1	—	—	—	—	1.060 P	0.943 P	1.124 P	0.890 P	1.191 P	0.840 P
2	0.485 P	0.515 P	0.515 P	0.485 P	0.545 P	0.458 P	0.578 P	0.432 P	0.613 P	0.408 P
3	0.314 P	0.353 P	0.353 P	0.314 P	0.374 P	0.296 P	0.396 P	0.280 P	0.420 P	0.264 P
4	0.229 P	0.272 P	0.272 P	0.229 P	0.289 P	0.216 P	0.306 P	0.204 P	0.324 P	0.192 P
5	0.177 P	0.224 P	0.224 P	0.177 P	0.237 P	0.167 P	0.252 P	0.158 P	0.267 P	0.149 P
6	0.143 P	0.192 P	0.192 P	0.143 P	0.203 P	0.135 P	0.216 P	0.128 P	0.228 P	0.120 P
7	0.119 P	0.169 P	0.169 P	0.119 P	0.179 P	0.112 P	0.190 P	0.106 P	0.201 P	0.100 P
8	0.101 P	0.152 P	0.152 P	0.101 P	0.161 P	0.095 P	0.171 P	0.090 P	0.181 P	0.085 P
9	0.087 P	0.139 P	0.139 P	0.087 P	0.147 P	0.082 P	0.156 P	0.077 P	0.165 P	0.073 P
10	0.076 P	0.128 P	0.128 P	0.076 P	0.136 P	0.072 P	0.144 P	0.068 P	0.153 P	0.064 P
11	0.067 P	0.120 P	0.120 P	0.067 P	0.127 P	0.063 P	0.134 P	0.059 P	0.142 P	0.056 P
12	0.059 P	0.112 P	0.112 P	0.059 P	0.119 P	0.056 P	0.126 P	0.053 P	0.134 P	0.050 P
13	0.053 P	0.107 P	0.107 P	0.053 P	0.113 P	0.050 P	0.120 P	0.047 P	0.127 P	0.044 P
14	0.048 P	0.102 P	0.102 P	0.048 P	0.108 P	0.045 P	0.114 P	0.042 P	0.121 P	0.040 P
15	0.043 P	0.097 P	0.097 P	0.043 P	0.103 P	0.040 P	0.109 P	0.038 P	0.116 P	0.036 P
16	0.039 P	0.093 P	0.093 P	0.039 P	0.099 P	0.037 P	0.105 P	0.035 P	0.111 P	0.033 P
17	0.035 P	0.090 P	0.090 P	0.035 P	0.095 P	0.033 P	0.101 P	0.032 P	0.107 P	0.030 P
18	0.032 P	0.087 P	0.087 P	0.032 P	0.092 P	0.030 P	0.098 P	0.029 P	0.104 P	0.027 P

NOTE. No reduction in frictional resistance is made for the angle of lead of the rope to the pulley.

Fig. 2.14

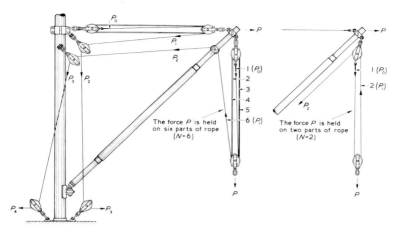

Fig. 2.15

The force acting on each individual purchase is denoted by the symbol P, the value of which must be known in order to apply the coefficients given in tables 1 and 2.

The coefficients for rope tensions in terms of force P are given in tables 1 and 2 at the following positions:

P_0 becket,

P_1 last rope in fall,

P_2, P_3, P_4 after 1st, 2nd and 3rd leads respectively.

Note. The force 'P' is that resulting from the cargo load W.

Extracting from the table, Fig. 2.14 (number of parts of rope holding the load, 2, and rope tension at position $3 - P_2$), the stress factor on the hauling part, for a luff tackle hoisting, is 0.545. P_2 therefore is 3 tonnes $\times 0.545 = 1.635$ tonnes.

Compared with the traditional formula, the latter overstates the stress. While this appears to introduce a safety margin, on the prudent side, greater care is required for purchases of greater power. The rule of thumb 6 % allowance could then be unrealistic.

Figure 2.16, page 58, illustrates diagrammatic representation of the parallelogram of forces appropriate to a ship rig. Applying this to practical cases, the procedure is as follows:

1. Draw diagram to scale, a separate drawing being required for each angle of elevation and for any particular load.
2. For the given load, extract P factors from the tabulated values and multiply by P to obtain stress on the hauling part of each purchase.
3. Complete the parallelograms, the diagonals of which represent the magnitude and direction of the stresses.
4. Ensure that blocks and wires are rated for the correct S.W.L. (Safe Working Load) as indicated by the calculated figures,

always bearing in mind the need for a safe margin if jerk stresses are likely.

It has to be remembered that the stresses represent ordinary conditions and where gear is rigged for Union Purchase general allowance has to be made for unusual stresses. The B.S.I. code deals

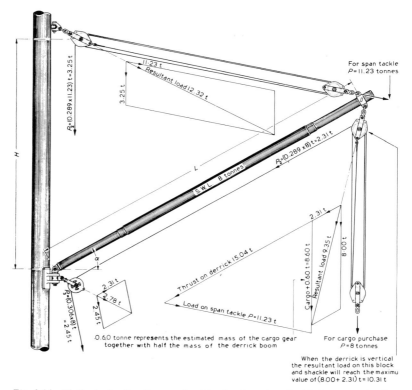

Fig. 2.16 Method of estimating resultant loads when rigged with four parts in the cargo purchase and span tackle (allowing 6 % per sheave, accumulative friction). Safe working load of derrick = 8 tonnes.

When hoisting on four parts, the rope tension is taken as:

$P_2 = 0.289P$
$P_3 = 0.306P$
(See Fig. 2.14.)

$$\frac{L}{H} = 1.48$$

$\alpha = 30°$ (at which angle the resultant loads have been computed. At angles less than 30° some of these resultant loads will be increased).

extensively with these calculations and should be consulted in detail on ships where this rig is used. It is possible to generalise on the factors which are important in any consideration of Union Purchase, and these may be stated as follows. The critical features are:

(a) The tension on each runner which depends on the headroom, i.e. between derrick head and hatch coaming... and thus the angle between the runners when the load is at its greatest height above the deck.
(b) Runners used for Union Purchase must always be of adequate S.W.L.
(c) Tension on standing (preventer) guys requires careful analysis and is dependent both on the angle between the derrick and the guy, and the angle of the guy with the vertical. The smaller these angles the greater is the tension.
(d) The load on the span is generally smaller than when a derrick is used singly. In extreme conditions this can lead to the derrick jack-knifing back against the mast.

THE APPLICATION OF SLINGS TO CARGO HANDLING

Different types of cargoes require different methods of slinging and in different ports of the world different practices apply, largely by reason of custom and tradition although much of the dockers work, certainly in the U.K. and on the Continent, contains a fair degree of similarity in the handling of goods.

In the main, cargo slinging utilizes rope, wire and chain, used either singly or made up into relevant patterns, albeit specialized cargoes, such as containers, bulks, timber and steel, etc., call for particular facilities and do, in fact, use these. Whatever the form, safety of personnel involved is paramount and no lifting gear should be used unless it conforms to regulation standards. Damage to cargo also, i.e. the prevention of crushing by the use of inappropriate slings, must be avoided.

The following list, though not exhaustive, indicates a fair range of slinging requirements with which a cargo officer may become involved:

Type of sling(s)	Cargoes to lift
Automatic grabs	Bulk cargoes
Canvas slings	Bagged cargo
Can hooks	Barrels, drums
Chain slings	Packaged timber, timber logs, beans/girders ex hatch beams
Electro magnets	Iron and steel products, scrap iron
Fibre straps, with	Bales of pulp, where not lifted by
tensioned hooks	hydraulic suction methods
Looped rope slings	Cases, two slings end looped together on the hook

Metal cradles	Loose, round timber
Metal frames	Paper rolls, where not lifted by hydraulic suction methods
Metal stirrups	Pallets
Net slings, wire or rope	Unhomogeneous packages of various 'small' sizes. Pallets with homogeneous loads
Nylon straps	Paper rolls, where not lifted by hydraulic suction methods
Rope slings	Wide applications, including general loads of cases, crates, bagged cargo, packaged unit loads, pallets, packaged timber
Spiked clamps	Heavy cases
Trays	Small cases and packages, cartons, strapped units
Tongs	Log timber for breaking out
Wire slings	Heavy crates/cases, beams/girders, pallets
Wire spreaders	Motor cars (uncrated)
Fork lift trucks	Although not 'slings' as such F.L.T.s have wide application to a variety of cargoes, particularly palletized

The code of safe working practice for the safety of merchant seamen makes reference to slings and their use and draws the attention of officers to their responsibilities in these matters.

A general interpretation of this part of the code indicates the need to be assured that all types of loads are properly put together and properly slung before they are hoisted or lowered.

For example, trays and pallets, widely used in modern practice, should have four legged slings, where nets are unsuitable. Loose goods, such as drums, cannisters, bricks and commodities of comparable small size, should always be lifted in pallets/trays. Loads should be raised and lowered smoothly, avoiding 'jerks' and no winch or crane should be left unattended with a load suspended. Strops and slings should be of adequate size and length. Long metal goods, such as tubes and pipes call for special care. No person should be allowed to stand under, or near a suspended or moving load.

It is in the interest of all personnel concerned with lifting and transportation of cargo to be completely familiar with these contents of the code. (See also pages 431–439, general references to the code.)

SUB SECTION B

MODERN TRENDS IN CARGO GEAR

Although the type of gear fitted to a ship in respect of cargo handling is primarily a matter of ship design related to the trades on which the vessel is likely to be engaged, and the cargoes to be carried, it is interesting to note some of the changes that have taken place in recent years. From the point of view of the ship's officer, he must, of necessity, accept and become familiar with all types of cargo gear fitted to a ship in which he is serving and, to a large degree, must study and understand this application of ship construction. Ship construction is now more of a complex matter than hitherto and the type and distribution of the cargo gear is a major part of the constructional design. In the main it has special regard to the need to turn ships round quickly and cargo handling methods have developed alongside of this.

From the point of view of this book, and its purpose, it would be out of place to devote detailed attention to constructional matters . . . it is a study in ship construction.

However, it is pertinent to comment in terms of hatch covering, heavy lifts, derricks and craneage and securing and lashing, on the basis that within each of these areas all other cargo handling functions are relative.

Cargo Access Equipment in Merchant Ships

The fitting and use of wooden hatch covers are unlikely now to be found in modern vessels; they suffer from three deficiencies . . . safety and security, maintenance and cargo working. While simple in usage, the combination of wooden boards, beams, tarpaulins and wedges, and the time spent in removing and replacing, not to mention personal hazard, does not find acceptance in the modern forms of ship construction and methods of cargo handling.

For these reasons, apart from others, considerable development in the design, construction and application of 'CARGO ACCESS EQUIPMENT' (which is the modern term as distinct from hatch covers) has taken place.

In this the MacGregor Zaire International Group is in the forefront. It is with their kind permission that the notes which follow are included in this book and much of which has reference to an excellent publication, sponsored by that organization, titled 'Cargo Access Equipment for Merchant Ships'. Its authors are Messrs I. L. Buxton, R. P. Daggitt and J. King, each closely having been associated with the Department of Naval Architecture, University of Newcastle upon Tyne.

In this context there is now a wide choice of hatch cover types available to the modern shipowner, carrying designations such as wire/chain/electric/hydraulic operated; end/side/folding/lift off; weather/tween deck; flat/peaked top; single/double skin . . . etc.

In terms of layout for cargo access the type of ship, and the purpose for which it is being used, determines the style of access equipment. These will cover the modern multi-purpose cargo vessel; the roll on/roll off ship; the dry cargo bulk carrier; combination carriers; container/ro/ro vessels; ferries; vehicle carriers and many other different forms of ships . . . not all necessarily concerned with cargo work.

For each class of vessel there is need to provide efficient and effective time saving and secure coverings for weather decks, tween decks, vehicle decks, ro/ro doors, apart from equipment related to the movement of cargo into, from and in spaces.

In the majority of cases the principle behind access points (hatch coverings) is to expose the greatest possible area so that cargo can be lifted into or out of its stowage position with a minimum of horizontal movement. Also, efficient cargo access equipment contributes to the time factor spent in ports by preparing for work and by opening up and battening down cargo spaces.

Access equipment is subject to regulation, the most important being that arising from the 1966 Load Line Convention, which came into force in 1968 and which is concerned, among other things, with adequate and safe freeboard. There is a particular requirement in respect of both 'weathertightness' and 'watertightness'.

Weathertightness must ensure that the tightness of hatch covers can be maintained in any sea condition and watertightness the prevention of the passage of water through the structure, in any direction.

Coaming heights are vital aspects of both weathertightness and watertightness, in which respect the principal determinants of coaming height is the operation of the hatch cover, of which there are a number, such as . . . 'Single Pull' . . . 'Panels' . . . 'Rolltite' . . . 'Hydraulic Folding'.

In terms of hatch covers for vertical loading, as such, there are many types and modes of operation, the principal ones being:—

The classic modern hatch cover is the 'single pull' and is the most common of all the various forms. In simple terms the cover consists of a number of narrow panels which span the hatchway and are linked together by chains.

Folding Covers . . . hydraulic or wire operated may be fitted to weatherdeck and tween deck hatchways. The covers consist of flat topped panels. Folding covers are becoming increasingly fitted for both weather and tween deck use; they lend themselves to a variety of positioning according to the hold/space usage.

Direct Pull Covers can be found in general cargo vessels where multi-panel covers are operated by a wire, actuated by ship gear.

Roll Stowing Covers . . . Rolltite have panels which roll on to a drum for stowage. In itself the cover consists of a number of panels spanning the hatchway. The system is said to have higher standards of reliability and total weathertightness than hitherto has been possible in steel hatch covers.

Side and Rolling Covers consist of two large panels at each hatchway. They are usually fitted to large ships; they are extremely heavy and require hydraulic lifting to raise them into a rolling position.

Lift and Roll Covers . . . (*piggy-back*) are a development of rolling covers. In theory there is no limit to their sizes . . . there can be two 100 tonned panels for a 26 m × 23 m hatchway. They find usage in large specialized forest product carriers.

Sliding 'Tween Deck Covers are made up of a number of 2 section plates which slide under each other to expose the hatchway. When closed they are flush with the surrounding deck thereby facilitating the use of fork lift trucks. They can support normal loads.

Pontoon Covers are the simplest form of steel hatch covers. They are merely lifted on and off the hatch coaming. They have two applications . . .

1. Single piece covers for weather decks on cellular container vessels.
2. Multi-panel covers on 'tween decks of multi deck cargo vessels.

Vessels concerned with 'horizontal loading' are within the roll on/ roll off concept and their access equipment has particular applications, except to point out that vessels with side doors (not ro/ro as such) accepting fork lift truck operations, can be, also horizontal loaders.

In general terms access equipment for the above type of vessels would include Bow Visor and Bow Ramps; Car Ramps, Car Decks; Elevators; Side Doors; Hatch Covers; Bulkheads; Multi-purpose ramps; Stern ramps and doors.

Ramps are externally used to allow vehicular traffic to move between quay and ship . . . internally to provide access from deck to deck for cargo stowage.

External ramps can be:—

(a) axial (centre line) to bow and/or stern.
(b) angled quarter, at offset angles between 30° and 45° to the centre line.
(c) slewing ramps usually mounted on the centre line to be set up to an approximate angle of about 40° from the centre line.

Internal ramps can be:—

(a) fixed.
(b) moveable, serving two or more decks, closing deck openings and providing additional stowage area.

Elevators are used as alternatives to ramps for transferring vehicles and other cargo above and below the main deck level.

There are also, scissor lifts, having a platform supported by levers and hydraulic rams. They are used in 'vehicular vessels' for transporting the loads between decks.

Side Doors (or side ports) are to be found in general cargo and roll on/roll off ships. They augment main cargo access; they are best employed where the draft remains fairly constant or where tidal variations are small. There are various types of side doors, the designs depending upon the type of cargo they are to serve and the handling methods between quay and ship. They are particularly useful for palletized cargo . . . viz. fork lift truck operations.

The types of side doors include:—

1. Inward opening doors . . . opens inward and slides longitudinally along the ship side. Primarily they are suitable for ship's stores and/or small cargo pallets.
2. Side swinging doors, which open outwards to stow along the ship's hull. They are larger than inward sliding doors.
3. Upward folding doors . . . hinged at the upper edges and at the mid length, so that they fold to stow against the hull. A loading platform folds out from the bottom.
4. Side door/hatch cover . . . a two section hatch which folds up and back. It has an adjustable loading platform and is ideally suitable for fork lift truck work.
5. Side port conveyor and Elevator. The system is similar to the side door/hatch cover but has an additional loading platform to facilitate multi-deck transfer of cargo between decks. It is completely automatic.

Car Decks . . . (other than in especially designed car carriers), can be moveable so that they can be stowed away when not required, to give more headroom for other vehicles. They find usage in passenger/vehicle ferries and in ro/ro vessels . . . where they are used during the tourist season for cars but raised at other times to accommodate commercial vehicles.

Portable car decks are hoistable, by wires or hydraulic power.

Other arrangements include Multi-folding car decks, more prominent in larger ships where larger numbers of cars are to be accommodated.

Elevators in 'car carriers' are, in fact, 'lifts' by which cars (and other vehicles) can be transported between decks or deck platforms. There are numerous types, both of simple and detailed design, be they for normal car, as distinct from high tonnage trucks or wagons.

Design Considerations for Access Equipment.

'Access' design, in fact, is not the concern of the ship officer (other than from the point of view of professional interest). However, certain aspects arise to which attention should be given in so far as they have relevance to cargo handling. These are noted below.

(a) Large Bulk Carriers (those of over about 50 000 dwt) are normally loaded by gravity from overhead chutes and discharged by grab. Large hatches are needed. Attention has to be given to longitudinal bending moments and shear forces, from cargo distribution.

(b) 'Smaller' bulk carriers (between 5000–15 000 dwt) call for similar attention.

(c) Ore Carriers (of type over 100 000 dwt) call for care in determining the metacentre height/stability considerations, particularly in avoiding any 'free surface' in the wing water ballast tanks.

(d) Combination Carriers . . . ore/oil or ore/bulk/oil, being multi-purpose ships call for attention in ensuring the spaces are 'clean' viz. the different loads and also towards anti pollution regulations.

(e) Forest Product carriers are of special design of large 'open hatch' type, presenting in themselves few, if any, loading/discharging problems other than the correct use of fork lift trucks operating in the holds. In so far as these ships are designed to carry a wide range of products . . . newsprint . . . pulp and packaged timber, etc. the solidarity of stow is a matter of attention.

(f) Conventional break-bulk vessels . . . classed as cargo liners of the 10 000–15 000 dwt range, with multi-decks, provide wide variations of cargo handling. Attention to appropriate handling gear . . . derricks, cranes, conveyors, fork lift trucks, etc. must always concern the ship's officer. The uses to which the gear is put raises the important matter of maintenance. Important also is sensible cargo planning, taking into account the deck spaces available . . . which has relevance to stability care.

Modern cargo liners are now designed around the 'container module' such that correct height stowage and efficient safeguards are provided . . . lashings for example.

(g) Container Vessels . . . Cellular are designed to 'open up' the weather deck to the maximum extent compatible with ship strength, in order to provide vertical access to the container cells.

(h) Roll on/Roll off ships are designed with access equipment providing wide facilities for most forms of cargo, though mainly unitized and/or indivisible. Deadweight and draft rarely limits a ro/ro ship's capacity unless a lot of water ballast is required for stability or trim purposes.

Considerations, however, need to be given to distribution of cargo, fuel and ballast, not only to assist cargo operations but also to give a satisfactory GM . . . giving easy rolling. Above all else, is the attention needed to be given to safeguard vehicular loads from movement for which purpose, design provides adequate provision.

There is a further point of cargo handling considerations with ro/ro vessels which has relevance to the wide clear space which the design of these vessels provide and the matter of quick turn round, for which these ships are suitable. Both of these aspects can encourage overzealousness and hurried loading activities . . . which calls for strict supervision on the part of ship's officers to ensure that the vessel is safely loaded.

Refrigerated Ships . . . Reefers are of special design, frequently three of four deck ships, this multi-arrangement providing a number of compartments capable of being maintained at different temperatures, with the fitted access equipment arrangements such as to minimize heat transfer into cargo spaces.

The major cargo handling attention is to use this equipment correctly. However, hatchway sizes are restricted, their comparatively 'small size' limiting direct sunlight into the cargo spaces during loading in hot climates. Partial opening of hatch covers may at times be desirable but with weather decks the rapid operation of covering in inclement weather is essential. Particularly is this so with Banana carriers.

———

The 'correct' type of ship, by design or by access equipment is not an easy matter, nor can it be clearly defined. The principal factors involved include:—
1. Cargo type and quantity.
2. Voyage distances and route characteristics (canals etc.).
3. Ports facilities . . . cargo handling methods and costs.
4. Infrastructure of countries served, in terms of national economy and inland transport facilities.
5. Frequency of service and commercial competition considerations.

Summary of Cargo Access Equipment
(Types of ships)

Rolling hatch covers	For bulk carriers, OBO carriers, combination carriers.
Rolltite hatch covers	For general cargo and bulk carriers weather deck installations.
Hydraulic Folding hatch covers	For general cargo vessels, refrigerated ships, multi-purpose container vessels, ro/ro ships.
Single Pull hatch covers	For weather deck hatches on most carriers.
Flush Sliding hatch covers	For all types of cargo ships, ro/ro vessels and vehicle ferries.
Direct Pull hatch covers	For geared vessels.
Pontoon covers	ro/ro, lo/lo, container and heavy lift ships.

Piggy-back covers   For combination carriers, bulk
                                     carriers, container ships, multi-
                                     purpose vessels.

Sincere appreciation is here afforded to the MacGregor Navire
International and to the MacGregor Cargo Access Equipment Ltd.
of MacGregor House, 86/90 Front Street, Whitley Bay, Tyne and
Wear, England in the compilation of this section.

ASPECTS OF DESIGN REQUIREMENTS
FOR ACCESS EQUIPMENT
(Points to consider)

Hatch Covers consist, in essence, of steel beams or girders spanning
the shorter hatchway dimension, plated over on top and completed
by steel side and end plates.

Structural Regulations are governed by the 1966 Load Line Convention (LLC).

Cleats are required by the 1966 LLC to be satisfactory means for
securing weathertightness.

Loads. Hatch loadings are laid down by the 1966 LLC and take
account of the forces exerted on exposed covers by heavy sea
breaking over the deck. These are mandatory values subject to
Classification Societies approval.

Deck Cargo. Where containers or additional cargoes are to be
carried on exposed hatch covers, the actual loads expected must be
used for design purposes.

Wheel Loads. Tween-deck and flush weather deck hatch covers are
usually designed to take fork lift trucks wheel loads, now commonly
used for general cargo.

Containers. Hatch covers on which containers are stowed must be
designed to withstand point loads transmitted through the container
corner fittings.

Liquid Cargoes. Combination carriers are built with large, heavy
oiltight covers which, apart from keeping the sea out, must keep the
cargo in. Both *Hydrostatic* and *Hydrodynamic* forces may be exerted
on the interior surface of the cover.

Hydrostatic forces occur when a ship is rolling and pitching and the
liquid cargo may press intermittently against the internal surfaces of
the hatch covers.

Hydrodynamic Forces are caused by liquid cargo moving within the
hold and sloshing against the hatch covers.

Deformation. As ships become larger and hatchways take up a greater percentage of the deck area, so the question of hatchway deformation becomes more important. Compensation, in the form of thickened plating or box girders may be required.

Longitudinal Deformation of the top of the coaming is due to the hogging and sagging of the vessel. It depends upon the hatchway length. It is compensated by the fitting the ends of the hatch cover with wide gaskets whose rubber absorbs the relative movement of the compression bars as the ship works.

Transverse Deformation is caused mainly by a vessel's changes in draft as the cargo is worked.

Horizontal Loading Ships

At the present time ro/ro vessels are regarded as ferries or cargo ships by the Classification Societies. The 1966 LLC treats bow, stern and side doors in ro/ro vessels as access openings into an enclosed superstructure.

They are required to be framed, fitted and stiffened so that the whole structure is of equivalent strength to the unpierced shell or bulkhead, and watertight when closed.

Hull deformation is not usually a serious problem in ro/ro ships so far as access equipment is concerned.

Access equipment in Service. Relative to Cargo Loading.
Seaworthiness of a ship . . . its structure, equipment and manning is of extreme importance.

There must be an express warranty of seaworthiness contained in a contract of affreightment or a contract of marine insurance. Breach of statute is a criminal offence. In this respect warranties must be given by the shipowner every time he undertakes to carry cargo.

The interpretation of the principles of law varies from one country to another. In English common law there is an absolute warranty of seaworthiness in contracts of affreightment. Cargoworthiness is also an essential element of seaworthiness.

As a general rule, steps must be taken at the outset of a voyage, to ensure that all cargo spaces are fit to receive the goods placed in them and to ensure, also, that the goods will be maintained in a satisfactory condition in the face of the ordinary perils of the sea.

In particular this is important relative to the prevention of sea water entry through hatches and other access openings.

The increasing use of steel instead of wood for hatch covers will decrease any possible claims arising.

Cargoes vary in the extent to which they can be damaged if not kept dry. Materials such as newsprint, tobacco and cement are *Hydroscopic* and can deteriorate in transit if not kept dry . . . the absorption of even small quantities of water can give rise to substantial claims.

It has been noticed that damage arising from the entry of sea water is more likely in bulk carriers and multi-deckers. The problem is less serious in container ships where each item of cargo is protected by its own container.

Sea water damage is also relatively uncommon in ro/ro vessels where there access equipment is usually sheltered.

Attention is drawn to the Department of Trade and Industry Shipping Notices concerning all forms of hatch coverings.

Notice M992 draws attention to the necessity of ensuring that all hatchways are properly closed and secured, correctly battened down and adequately covered, before a vessel proceeds into open water.

Where, in special circumstances at sea, in providing draught or ventilation for particular cargoes, such as coal, the same responsibility falls on the ship to correctly re-close when the weather conditions indicate the necessity.

Particularly is it necessary to ensure that hatchways are securely and correctly closed and covered where deck cargo is to be stowed over them. Neglect of this precaution will quickly highlight carelessness in insecurity in that, with inclement weather considerable difficulty would arise in remedying any arising dangers.

Notice M524 points out the dangers to life and limb where ineffective pulling, rolling and securing devices would result in accidents to men working on, or near the hatchways to which steel covers are fitted. It is the duty of the ship to ensure that all such arrangements are in perfect maintenance order.

Some examples of the more usual types of access equipment

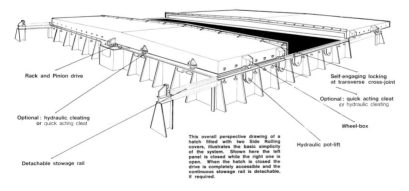

Rolling Covers

Piggy-back Hatch Covers

Side Loading Systems

Pontoon Covers for Weather Deck Hatches

Cargospeed Equipment. See pages 75–96

Another organization prominent in the manufacture and supply of power operated steel hatch covers is Cargospeed Equipment Limited, of Greenock, Scotland. This company produces both wire pulled and hydraulically operated hatch coverings, which are fitted into ships as wide apart in size and design as trawlers and large ocean liners.

A feature of all steel type hatch coverings is the watertight sealing necessary on closure. Cargospeed hatch covers incorporate the Velle twin chamber neoprene packings in the provision of water-tightness. Planned supervision and maintenance with the sealing provisions of steel hatch covers is necessary; indeed the matter is of such importance that where deficiencies become apparent it is preferable to 'renew' the packing units rather than endeavour to remedy any defect.

Heavy Lifts

The term 'heavy lift' in modern cargo carriage can extend to loads of over 1000 tonnes; 500–700 tonnes can be commonplace. As a result ship design had developed in specialized degree with lifting equipment following this trend. And it is not confined, as hitherto, to what might be termed 'large ships'. Conventional ship tonnage is now extensively fitted with heavy lift facilities of wide application, apart from those vessels especially built to carry exceptional loads requiring particular handling and ballasting functions.

The range of 'heavy lift' cargo can well be of the order of 100–800 tonnes.

Heavy lift carriage is also served by smaller vessels of low draft which can enjoy unrestricted port entrance and, for example, meet trades to the lesser developed parts of the world where investment in industrial equipment requires heavy units, yet have ports insufficiently equipped to handle such loads by shore gear. To meet this need vessels are in service capable of handling lifts of 500–600 tonnes, some with Stuelcken derrick facilities.

The 'Small' Heavy Lift Vessel—Specialized Heavy Lift Ships

Trade Features. A specialized trade exists, and is growing, which calls for specialized lifting and carrying facilities, the demand for which arising from the need to transport heavy indivisible load units from point of manufacture to place of installation, with the least amount of interruption in their passage.

Loads such as refinery, chemical, electrical, mechanical and transportation units, for example, cover some of the cargoes involved. All are of extremely high tonnage and size; most are in a stage of construction as will permit direct installation, at site; all require transportation applicable to their design.

The trade is therefore competitive, primarily because the site installations are in countries and areas which are developing their industrial capacities, not only quickly, but, frequently, away from deep water ports without suitable connecting land routes. For this reason, alone, the transportation of these heavy units, while possible by conventional purpose built heavy lift ships, creates economic and carrying problems which the smaller vessel can reduce, or overcome by transporting 'direct'. Indeed, the trade, in some circumstances, is introducing a completely integrated consortium of road and maritime transport, the former 'rolling' on to, and off the latter, the ship being an incorporated part of the exercise. In other cases, the ship operates within the market demands and offers facilities of its design acceptable to shippers' needs.

Carrying Features. Whatever the form, the 'carriage' is highly specialized, demanding of the cargo officer complete adoption of the practicalities involved and strict attention to the operating manuals provided by the owners, particularly where these relate to stability needs and ballasting procedures.

Type of Ship. For the reasons for which this trade is developing, draft of these vessels is 'small', thus overcoming any water restrictions; their ballasting facilities sophisticated; but their lifting equipment and stowage availability of high capacity. By no means are these vessels restricted to short sea work—on the contrary, some continental owners operate numerous types of ships.

Within this field of maritime transportation a British company, 'Starman Shipping', an associate of the Blue Star Line, Limited, operates an 1585 dwt vessel *Starman* (with additional tonnage on order), its uniqueness of bow and stern ramps, independent of link span facilities, a clear 'drive through' roadway and an ability to beach, making it an extremely versatile heavy, or large load, carrying vessel.

Notes on 'Starman'. The later following notes, and illustration (Illus. p. 79), are included with the kind permission of Starman Shipping and indicate the manner of operation. Apart from the cargo load stowed into the hatchway, some of the deck loads have been of the order of 130, 150, 180 and over 200 tons. Furthermore, attention is drawn to the siting of the 152 tonnes Stuelcken mast/derrick on the port side, permitting clear lifting off, or on to, the upper deck, to and from the starboard side, utilizing ballast pumping to offset any adverse or negative stability situations, and to assist in the provision of lifting/lowering power.

Attention is drawn to the general arrangements plan, Figure 2.17, some detail of which is as follows:

L(OA), 93·6 m; L(BP), 83·5 m; B (moulded), 15·25 m
Deadweight, 1585 tonnes
Gross tonnage, 1629–2515 tonnes
Nett tonnage, 681–1247 tonnes
Deck space, 717 m^2
Roadway clear width, 9·12 m
Deck capacity load, 1016 tonnes
Service speed, 12 knots, at 3·65 m draft.

'Starman Shipping' Notes

Starman has been built for classification by Lloyd's Register of Shipping ✣ 100A1 ✣ LMC Ice Class 2, and complies with DTI requirements for a class VII vessel.

As can be seen from the accompanying general arrangement drawing and photographs, the ship has an unusual appearance in that Stuelcken derrick legs are mounted in the longitudinal

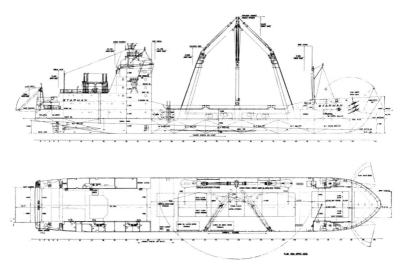

Fig. 2.17 General Arrangement Plan *Starman* Heavy Lift Ship

direction and are offset to port. In addition the superstructure is split into two tall, narrow houses, port and starboard, to allow a clear roadway through the vessel having an unrestricted height. A walkway joining the two houses just below bridge level is removable.

Stern Access. Access to the deck over the stern is via a stern door/ ramp which is raised and lowered by means of two Clarke Chapman-John Thompson Ltd. single drum electric winches situated on the after deck. The permissible deck loading is at present 10 tonnes/m² to cater for heavy axle and crawler track loadings, but provision has been made so that if necessary at a later stage a lattice work steel structure could be welded on under the deck to give a 30 tonnes/m² permissible loading. The stern ramp itself can take 330 tonnes.

Bow Access. The bow opening is formed when the two box con- struction half sections of the bow, which can be lifted off if required, swing outwards on hinges to allow the rigging of a 660-tonne capacity ramp. This ramp is held on arms either side and as the arms swing up and forward, hinging about deck level, so the ramp moves forward between them and drops into place. The ramp is a substantial structure, and when stowed on deck takes up almost a fifth of the available upper deck space forward of the superstructure. It is of course possible to load cargo on to the ramp using the Stuelcken derrick when the ramp is in its stowed position. Bow door and ramp movements are hydraulically activated by means of

Specialized Heavy Lift Ship *Starman*

equipment supplied by Dolphin Hydraulics Limited. The upper deck can take large indivisible loads of up to 1016 tonnes.

The large hatch on the upper deck is closed by a flush WT pontoon cover in seven sections supplied by MacGregor & Co. The non-WT 'tween deck covers of the same make can be left off to allow the carriage of tall pieces of cargo. Four of the 'tween deck pillars unbolt to enable wide pieces to be taken if necessary.

Under the Stuelcken derrick, situated in the 'tween deck space, are the four Clarke Chapman 14/5 ton single drum electric winches for operating the derrick.

Apart from these exceptions, and in more general terms, weights of 80, 150, 250, and 400 tonnes, notably units of machinery and industrial equipment, form the more usual loads carried on modern conventional ships with lifting equipment, either by heavy derrick or craneage, adequately provided.

With heavy lift handling stability considerations become paramount and, irrespective of the ballasting systems which may be built into ships engaged in this form of traffic, prudent attention to weight distribution and metacentric height is essential. Heavy lift carriage also requires pre-planning with the arrangements determined and set out beforehand. A form of critical path analysis is not out of place in order to ensure that all the precautionary measures involved when moving such weights are covered at the right time (See Critical Moment, Heavy Lift, Stability Notes, page 418.)

A Modern Conventional Heavy Lift Rig

By way of illustration one well known British shipping company, long experienced in the carriage of heavy cargoes, has two of its vessels fitted with 125 ton derricks, serving main hatch lengths of 50 ft capable of receiving rolling stock of heavy design.

The overall rig is supported by adequate and comprehensive eye plates within the cargo spaces to which can be attached heaving in gear and to assist in efficient securing.

Heavy lift rigs of the nature outlined require the disposition of winch control to be particularly adaptable. While the winches themselves may be situated at the base of the derrick, it is preferable for the controller to be housed at a higher level thus permitting a clear view of the work in hand. This is essential planning for heavy lift work.

By way of example, gear to serve the rig illustrated would be of the following order:

Mast 80–90 ft long, 3 ft 6 in diameter and stepped on to double bottom tank.

Derrick 70 ft long, 2 ft 3 in diameter, with a single sheave at the top end.

Topping lift of two four-sheave blocks and led to 20 ton winch.

Cargo runner utilizing two, four-sheave blocks in association with the sheave at the top of the derrick and down to a hauling winch.

The lifting equipment includes a 25 ft lifting span beam, giving a total weight lift of 110 tons.

Allowing for friction the minimum pull on the winch barrel is about 20 tons.

The Stuelcken Mast and Derrick

Prominent in the area of heavy lifts is the Stuelcken mast and derrick arrangement, a patent of Blohm & Voss A.G. of Hamburg, West Germany, by whose kind permission the following notes and diagrams are included.

The late 1960s and the early 1970s have seen a considerable number of these masts and derricks fitted into ships of varying tonnage and nationality, with S.W.L. capacities ranging from 25 tons (100 kg) to 350 tons (1000 kg). The ranges between 60–80–100 tons indicate the tendancies towards conventional tonnage; those upwards of 350 tons being illustrative of the now usual exceptional heavy lifts which some vessels can handle. The Stuelcken arrangements are also prominent in vessels handling containers by the LO/LO procedures; a container type derrick is, in fact, fitted with S.W.L. capacities of 20–50 tons.

The Stuelcken mast/derrick-crane arrangement is available to different forms of application, the appropriate types being shown on pages, 84–89.

The manufacturers, Blohm & Voss A.G., claim the following main advantages in the Stuelcken mast/derrick-crane cargo fittings.

The main advantages of the Stuelcken Mast compared with other cargo gear are:

(a) Absence of all guys and preventers for slewing the derrick;

(b) no tackle work, even when swinging the derrick through the posts or when changing to smaller loads;

(c) swinging the derrick through the post allows hatchways, both forward and aft of the mast to be served;

(d) the winches—and hence also the derrick—can be operated by one man by means of controllers or by remote control;

(e) the whole derrick installation is largely maintenance-free;

(f) The speed of cargo handling can be susbstantially increased by using suitable powered winches;

(g) ordinary light cargo gear (union purchase) can be attached to the posts and operated on one side simultaneously with the heavy lift derrick operating on the other side;

(h) Stuelcken container masts can transship payloads of 3–5 tons in less than 2 minutes, thus replacing a pair of light derricks, so that only one pair of the latter for swinging through between the posts needs to be arranged to serve the hold away from the container mast. Such an arrangement yields important economies without limiting the cargo handling rate;

(i) so far the Stuelcken mast is built from 15 tons S.W.L. up to 525 tons S.W.L., but there is no limit to the capacity of this cargo gear, provided, however, that the vessel has sufficient loading stability;

(j) when installing two Stuelcken masts, for example to handle

M.V. *Trifels*/Stuelcken

260 ton loads with two equal 130 ton derricks, it is not necessary to use a traverse. The biggest two Stuelcken masts installed on board of one ship are of 350 ton capacity each, i.e. loads up to 700 tons may be lifted.

One of the advantages of the Stuelcken container mast is that light derricks can be fitted to the posts and work simultaneously

over the hatch opposing the heavy derrick. Therefore almost all Stuelcken masts use at each side one pair of light derricks.

Today Blohm and Voss presents an improvement to the effect that the light derricks are designed in a way to also swing, like the heavy derrick, from the hatch forward of the Stuelcken mast to that aft or vice versa and only one pair of light derricks is fitted.

This arrangement reduces the investment by an amount equivalent to two light derricks, the corresponding winches and its installation, without affecting the capability of the cargo gear at all. Furthermore this results in less maintenance work.

1. The heavy derrick of the Stuelcken container mast which is usually built for a safe working load of 22 tons for the 20 ft container and of 35 tons for the 40 ft container can operate over the hatches fore and aft of the Stuelcken con-

Figs 2.18 (1–7)

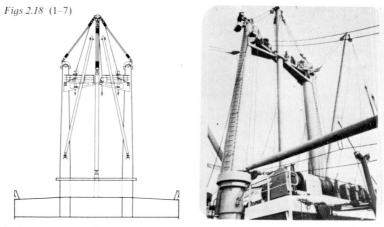

1. *Rotary Type.* The cargo tackle is brought from fore to aft or vice versa by rotating the boom through 180° when in vertical position. This is the first patented design and has been installed on 15 ships for working loads of up to 60 tons. Today this type is occasionally used when existing cargo gear has to be converted.

2. *Pendulum Type.* The cargo tackle is arranged at one side of the boom and passes automatically from fore to aft position or vice versa, when the boom is swung through.

This is the first patented design of the 'pendulum type' and has been built about 80 times for working loads of 30–130 tons.

The photograph shows the earlier arrangement with controller stands at the posts, whereas the drawing represents the modern design with mobile remote control of the boom. The same applies to the illustration of the 'double pendulum type'.

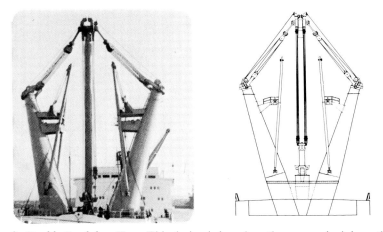

3. *Double Pendulum Type*. This design is based on the same principle as the 'pendulum type', but the cargo tackle is suspended on either side of the boom head. After the crossbar on the lower cargo blocks is disconnected, the cargo tackles automatically swing from fore to aft hatch and vice versa with the boom in the same way as those of the 'pendulum type'. The cargo tackle can also be used on one side in which case the other side is fastened to the boom, thus allowing double the hook speed at half load. Up to now about 75 units of this type have been built for working loads of 80–320 tons.

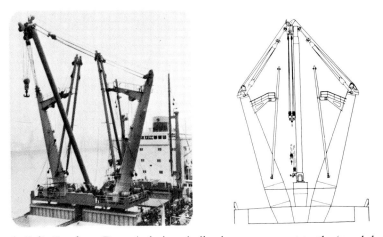

4. *Split Purchase Type*. A design similar in arrangement to the 'pendulum type', but in this case the cargo tackle itself is split. Depending on the arrangement used when splitting, the hook speed is increased when the load is reduced. This design can be employed for working loads of 50–130 tons, and up to now 30 units have been built.

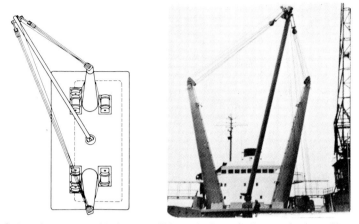

5. *High Speed Version.* This is a possible variation of all types by installing a second disconnectable drum on either of the two topping winches. Thereby the reeving of the span tackle is halved and the swinging speed doubled under half of the working load. Up to now 18 units of this type have been built.

The illustration shows the design for a cellular container vessel without light cargo booms, however, these may be added if required.

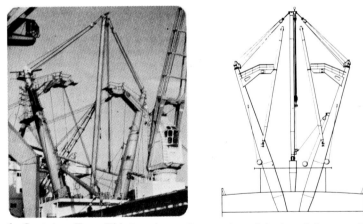

6. *Container Type.* This type is another version of the 'pendulum type' with unsplit cargo tackle. By guiding the hauling part of the cargo tackle down the boom to the gooseneck bearing the span forces are not reduced, which fact provides a high stability of the gear in the outboard position. This is of advantage for operations at rapid swinging speeds, i.e. container handling. When swinging through the cargo tackle passes at the side of the boom and simultaneously turns by 180°. Eighty units of this type have been built up to now.

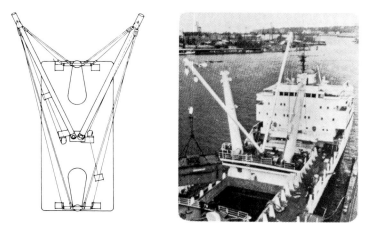

7. *Log/Lumber Type.* For simultaneous operation on both sides this type is equipped with two cargo booms which may have different working loads.

Particularly, because of the high speeds and the stable design of the Stuelcken Cranes this type has proved very satisfactory for handling logs. This crane has developed from the 15 ton cargo boom 'System Stuelcken' fitted aboard M.S. *Lichtenfels* in 1953 and is supplied upon request either with posts or mast and large outrigger.

Approximately 35 units of this type have been delivered up to now.

      tainer mast with three 4-pole changeable, 50 hp 8 ton winches mechanically changeable to 4 tons being the standard winch equipment.

2. Assuming a Ship's breadth of 20 m and an outreach of the derrick of 6 m beyond the ship's side the 22 ton type achieves a load cycle time below two minutes when switched to 2 tons S.W.L. and the 35 ton type of three minutes when switched to 3 tons S.W.L.

3. These high speeds of the Stuelcken container mast when handling smaller loads perfectly justify to only use one pair of light derricks and let the heavy derrick work simultaneously also for small loads.

4. The light derricks swing outside of the Stuelcken posts without rigging work being necessary and can operate in union purchase or as swinging derricks on either side of the Stuelcken container mast.

A more recent improvement in the container type has been the fitting of only one pair of light derricks—as distinct from two pairs—one on each side supported on, and operating from a trunion stool at the near outside position of the mast. (See Figure A–B, page 89.)

General Working Arrangements

The general working procedures with the Stuelcken facilities are best illustrated by the following notes covering the M.V. *S.A. Vergelegen*, which have been extracted from the instructional manual provided by Blohm and Voss for the ship personnel and the owners. They are included with the full permission of the manufacturers.

M.V. 'S.A. Vergelegen'
250 ton Stuelcken Mast
Description

1. Safe Working Load: 250 tons
2. Building Year: 1970

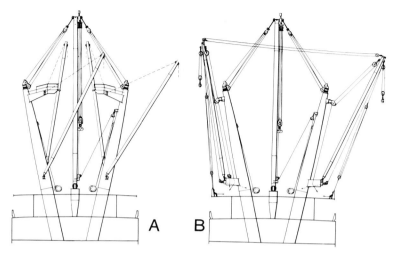

3. Rules and Regulations of Lloyd's Register of Shipping and Board of Trade have been complied with.
4. General Conditions:
    maximum list of the vessel: 14°
    maximum trim of the vessel: ±2°
    maximum outreach beyond the ship's side: 6 m
    maximum top angle: 75°
    minimum top angle: 25°
5. Ropes:
    (a) Span Tackle:
        Construction Seal Compound,
        39 mm in diameter,
        $6 \times 55 + 7 \times 7 = 379$ wires
        Effective breaking load: minimum 105 tons
        Length of each tackle: 560 m
    (b) Cargo Tackle:
        Construction Seal Compound,
        39 mm in diameter,
        $6 \times 55 + 7 \times 7 = 379$ wires
        Effective breaking load: minimum 105 tons
        Length of tackle: 600 m

General Explanations

1. The head of the derrick is held and moved by two spread span tackles, each span winch (heavy cargo winch) working one of these tackles.

2. The cargo tackle is endless rove. It consists of two upper and two lower cargo blocks. Each end of the tackles is led over the corresponding guide sheave of its pendulum block fitting to a heavy cargo winch.

3. Maximum pull of the cargo winches: 25·5 tons for 250 tons lift.
   Maximum pull of the span winches: 25·5 tons for 250 tons lift.

4. Each of the two span tackles is capable of carrying the total safe working load of the heavy derrick alone, the stress on the material in this ultimate position always being within required regulations. In all other cases the stress on the derrick and posts is less.

5. All lowering and hoisting of the span tackles means a movement of the derrick.

6. From the lubricating plan can be seen which joints are arranged in ball bearings or friction bearings.

Method of Operation

The following movements of the derrick can be carried out by the span tackles:

(*a*) Both span tackles lower together evenly and at the same time—the derrick lowers without swinging.

(*b*) Both span tackles hoist together evenly and at the same time—the derrick tops without swinging.

(*c*) The port span tackle lowers alone—the derrick swings to starboard and lowers slowly.

(*d*) The port span tackle hoists alone—the derrick swings to port and tops slowly.

(*e*) The port span tackle lowers and the starboard span tackle hoists—the derrick swings quickly over to starboard and keeps at about the same height.

(*f*) The port span tackle hoists and the starboard span tackle lowers—the derrick makes the same movement as under (*e*), but to port.

(*g*) With both span winches working the same way but at different speeds, when hoisting the derrick will swing towards the winch running faster and will top; when lowering, the derrick will lower and turn away from the side of the winch running faster.

The operations under (*c*) and (*d*) can, of course, also be carried out with the starboard span tackle.

With the ship on an even keel, with regard to list, the pull on the two span tackles will be equal if the derrick stands in midship position.

In case of topping angle exceeding 80° please move the derrick only in centreline.

Trim and list and also the position of the derrick govern the distribution of the pull on the span tackles.

When the derrick swings outboard, the pull on the outboard tackle lessens and that on the inner tackle increases. In order that the derrick may never collapse, the pull on the outboard tackle must never be zero.

Any reduction in the pull on the outboard tackle will be clearly shown by the tackle's slackening and starting to sag. This sagging of the outboard tackle is shown still more plainly by the relatively heavy span blocks twisting as the tackle slackens.

In the case of heavy cargo gears that, under full load, noticeably affect the list of the vessel the outboard span tackle requires special watching. Any visible sagging is an automatic indication of the gear itself, that the position of the derrick is nearing its limit position.

The cargo tackle can be served by both winches and the hoisting and lowering speeds will then be doubled. If served by only one cargo winch and when hoisting, the pull on the working and hauling part is greater by the friction of the sheaves and rope than in the outer stationary part. Under these circumstances, when hoisting or lowering there is an additional rotating moment round the gooseneck pin, which can be of importance when the derrick is in a limit position.

A further increase of the lowering and hoisting speed can be obtained by locking one half of the cargo tackle (with the endless rove rope) to the derrick heel. By this measure the number of the suspended parts will be halved and the speed will be doubled.

By utilizing the mechanical reversibility of the winches from low speed to high speed the following safe working loads can be handled:

1. Total cargo tackle—all winches at low speed = 250 tons.
2. Total cargo tackle—all winches at high speed = 120 tons.
3. Half the cargo tackle—cargo winches at low speed = 120 tons
   span winches at high speed = 120 tons
4. Half the cargo tackle—all winches at high speed = 60 tons.

When operating a load of 60 tons (half the cargo tackle, winches at high speed) the hook speed will be fourfold as against 250 tons (total cargo tackle, winches at low speed). Please see operation manuals regarding changing of speed from low speed to high speed and vice versa. (Operation Manuals of Bröhl Winches.)

Swing-through of the Derrick

There are two possibilities to swing through the derrick:

1. Either by means of the own cargo tackle or

2. by means of the pendant being fixed on the boom.

(*a*) The boom is arranged in approximately vertical position (85–86°) in the centre line by means of the span winches. Thereby the support for the connecting traverse being arranged on the side to which the boom is to be swung through will be connected with the cargo tackle (lower cargo block) by means of a sling. The boom is automatically swung through its dead centre by tightening the cargo tackle. Without fixing one of the lower cargo blocks on the boom the swinging-through of the two cargo tackles will only be possible if the two lower cargo blocks are empty (same weight). The sling to the support must then be fixed on the two blocks. If the connecting traverse and the Flemish hook are to be swung through together, the empty block will have to be fixed on the boom.

(*b*) The derrick is in the midship plane having a top angle of about 80°, the fore or aft pendant must be led on to one winch according to which direction the derrick shall be swung through.

After having belaid the pendant on one winch the derrick will be pulled by means of both span tackles nearly into the vertical position between the posts. Then the derrick will be pulled by the pendant and simultaneous slow lowering of both span tackles over the dead centre.

The cargo tackle is swung sidewards the boom. As in the first case the empty block has to be fixed on the boom, excluding, however, the case of equally heavy lower cargo blocks. It has only to be paid attention that elements being attached thereto go free off the winches and other parts on the winch deck.

Working Instructions

The derrick can be moved into each working position by both span tackles.

If the two cargo winches work together, evenly, the speed of the hook will be doubled.

1. *If the span tackle (outboard tackle) should slacken when swinging the derrick with load, no further outboard movement must be allowed. Slackness will clearly be shown by sagging of the span block at the head of the derrick.*

2. *The slack outboard tackle must not be tightened.*

3. The derrick must be swung in by the inner tackle so as to lessen the list of the ship by reducing the inclination moment whereby the outboard span tightens again. This movement can be assisted by slow lowering of the outboard tackle.

4. The pull on the span tackles becomes less as the derrick is topped, the outboard tackle of a fully topped derrick shows slackness, i.e. the lowered derrick is more stable in relation to the steadiness of the gear.
5. When swinging out the derrick under load the steadiness of the gear decreases as the list and swinging increases. Therefore, swinging-out should always be done very slowly.
6. If the stability of the ship is uncertain a heavy load being swung out should be stopped several times so as to watch and to check the movement of the ship.
7. If there are free surfaces of liquid in the ship's tanks, which should be avoided in any case with heavy loads, the swinging-out movement should be interrupted in order to give time for the liquid to run over, in order that the ship may come to rest and the list to be expected may be judged.
8. If the head of the derrick is towards the lighter draft end of the ship, the limit positions of the gear, indicated by the outboard span tackle slackening, will be reached sooner. In other words, the range of action of the derrick is less in this position than the opposite case, i.e. when the head of the derrick is towards the deeper and draft end of the ship.
9. *The boom must always be swung out at its lowest speed, but can be swung in as rapidly as desired.*
10. The limit position of the gear is reached when the lower span block of the lea tackle sags and thus indicates that the tackle slackens. In this case the derrick must not be swung out any further in the same direction. This limit position depends on the list and trim of the vessel.
11. Deadreach of the gear, with attached connecting traverse and Flemish hook is 5·9 m. The upper and the lower cargo blocks must have a clear distance of at least 1 m.
12. The boom must never be slewed if the topping is more than 80°.

Semi-Submersible Vessels

Modern development of heavy lift vessels include semi-submersible ships. These are capable of being submerged horizontally to load and/or discharge heavy floating objects. Weights of 20 000 tons are envisaged.

The Deadweight tonnage of these vessels is of the order of 25 000 tons and their particular suitability is for the transportation of a variety of large dimensioned modules, as for example, off shore drilling equipment.

Craneage capacity can be of the order of 250 tons while there is, also, combined in the construction, improved ro/ro facilities.

By size these submersible vessels are of the order of L.O.A. 160 m Beam 140 m, with a submerged draft of 20 m. Specialized ports/docks facilities will be necessary.

Sealashing

During a voyage the derrick is standing approximately at an inclination of 9° from the upright between the posts in forward direction. The 250 tons Flemish hook is loosened from the connecting traverse of the cargo tackles and lashed in the support being provided for this. The connecting traverse is fixed in the foundation being provided therefore by means of a bolt.

The execution of the sealashing is strong enough to take up a pull of about 250 tons.

The boom is lashed by tightening the cargo tackle with the span tackles and the cargo tackle as well as the pendants which are to be arranged additionally.

Craneage

Craneage in ships, and in ports, has been one of the more outstanding developments in transportation technology in an endeavour to increase handling facilities through improved lifting and speed capacities. In this connection, the average 5 ton crane in use in ships at the end of the Second World War has now been overtaken by capacities of up to 25–30 tons, the higher loads with unitization and 8/10/15 loads for normal cargoes being usual. Specialized cranes, for particular classes of loads, and ships, can handle up to 40 tons of general character; when 'twinned' or 'teamed' load lifting of up to 160 tons is possible.

International regulations now set more stringent tests in crane construction, covering drums, wires and sheaves; necessary safety equipment and control devices. Included also are provisions to meet environmental considerations in minimizing noise, which can have more than disturbing effects upon crane drivers, loading supervisors and stevedores working in the holds. As the size of the crane increases, so can the noise be more pronounced. It is interesting therefore to note that the I.S.O. (International Organization for Standardization) has issued ratings for noise levels to be observed and crane manufacturers take these into account. In one instance alone, this conditions the fitting of enclosed, insulated driver cabins . . . without loss of visibility . . . on to modern cranes.

Furthermore, distinctions are made between general cargo cranes, grab cranes and heavy unit cranes, since the dynamic forces activating on these different handling/lifting procedures, require different constructional considerations.

Lifting facilities are now far advanced on the earlier conventional ship derrick systems. Even so, their rigging and setting continues to follow the basic principles outlined in pages 44–50.

Derrick systems, as such, are unlikely, if at all, to pass out of maritime lifting equipment in that ports on some trades remain dependent upon the methods of handling which derricks encourage, mainly by reason of the type of labour employed, to which they are acceptable.

The derrick, appropriately rigged, is a very adaptable piece of equipment, flexible and versatile in its application. Furthermore, derricks have low centres of gravity, as distinct from cranes, and are said, in some quarters, to be more acceptable as a result. Crane-age, on the other hand, has developed into various sophisticated forms, albeit the deck crane of 15 tons capacity, and relatively high speed action, is a popular fitting to modern tonnage.

Numerous manufacturers in the market offer systems which will lift over the 5–10 ton areas to the 25–40 and 50 ton range, thus permitting their use for containers and other 'heavier' bulk loads, especially where twinning (or doubling up) on a synchronized Master and Slave arrangement pertains with electric and electric-hydraulic cranes.

Indeed, deck cranes now are mostly of these types and can be manufactured to have adaptable attachments applicable to the lifting of special types of cargoes by grabs, clamps and other fit-ments, as for example with forest products and associated bulk commodities.

Furthermore, the Master and Slave arrangement, with two cranes situated at opposite ends of the hatch opening, provides more effective working visibility, a wide span of operation and, by reason of the system, one man operator in the 'Master'. There is also more efficient weight/lifting strain movement control and steady non-swinging movement of the load where spreader beam arrange-ments between the two runners are fitted. This procedure is highly desirable with container lifting and other lifts of up to 180 tons are not out of place with these facilities. Indeed, twinning provides flexibility in lifting planning, particularly for heavier loads. The Hagglund Organization, A. B. Hagglund and Soner Deck Machinery Division, of Ornskoldsvik, Sweden, has, in fact, intro-duced a variant of the Master and Slave arrangement which they term the 'Team' crane. This is a system in which two deck cranes for one hatch are not located on a common base, but mounted independently, usually on opposite sides of the ship, serving the same hatch (see Fig. 2.20). The 'Team' cranes operate with syn-chronized winches for lowering and hoisting and can be manoeuvred by the driver, by electric remote control, either from one of the cabs, or from the deck. The synchronized operations permits of the lifting hooks, on each crane, remaining on the same level at all times, thus allowing for a load to remain parallel with the ship's fore and aft line. With bulky and/or irregular loads this can have many advantages.

Modern craneage, however, requires positive attention to planned maintenance and to this end the Cargo Officer should work closely with engineering staff. Control systems in electric and electric-hydraulic cranes should have high priority in routine. (See

Chapters 15/15. Code of Safe Working Practices for Merchant
Seamen. M.S. Notice M 584.)

Of the many types of ships' cranes available, the following are
some interesting examples, the notes on which being included with
the kind permission of the manufacturers referred to:

Cargo Speed Equipment Ltd., Greenock, Scotland, manufactures
and supplies the now established 'Velle' derrick crane. Of simple
but rugged design the 'Velle' has high performance, versatility and
reliability for loads up to 26 tons, as shown fitted to the M.V.
Orduna, illustrated on page 26. Heavier lift Velle cranes can
handle 100 ton loads.

The general arrangement of a Velle crane is as follows: the topping
lift falls act on four short steel wire hanger ropes connected to the
derrick head. The arrangement makes possible very wide slewing
angles since the topping lift falls act in such a manner that the
recovery movement is maintained when the derrick is slewed outboard, even when the vessel has a severe adverse list.

The load hook is operated by a cargo winch of standard design
controlled from a standard lever remote controller. Luffing and
slewing motions of the derrick are powered by two winches each
equipped with divided barrels, to which the ends of the falls are
secured. On the luffing winch the falls are laid onto the half barrels
in the same direction, so that both falls will shorten or lengthen
together upon rotation of the barrel, to effect upwards or down-
wards luffing respectively of the derrick.

The falls to the slewing winch are laid onto the half barrels in
opposite directions, thus one fall shortens while the other fall pays
out when the barrel rotates. The slewing winch controls are
arranged to give identical heaving characteristics in both directions
of rotation, giving the derrick slewing motion to port or to starboard.

The luffing and slewing winches are operated by a joystick type
duplex remote controller. Forward and aft movements of the
joystick motivate only the luffing winch and movements to port
or to starboard of the joystick activate the slewing winch.

Since cargospeed is essential to every ship operator, both luffing
and slewing motions (in any combination of steps) are possible at
the same time with the *derrick under full load*.

The crane operator can combine hoist, luff and slew motions
simultaneously using his left hand to control the cargo hoist and
his right hand to work the joystick controller. The levers on both
controllers return automatically to the neutral position on being
released.

Load Stabilization

The attainment of fast hook cycles on most cranes is dependent

'Velle' Diagram 'A'

upon skilful control by an experienced crane operator in avoiding pendulous swinging of the load, and in restricting rotation of the load about a vertical axis.

Diagram B shows the Velle 'T' shaped derrick which allows sympathetic motion between the load on the hook and the derrick head, via the diverging cargo runners. This arrangement is remarkably effective in damping out both pendulation and rotation of the load.

Elimination of the bridle bars, characteristic of earlier Velle cranes, is made possible by the inclusion of special heel bearings. in the 'T' shaped derricks. One of the several benefits of this type of derrick is improved steadiness where working at maximum outreach overside.

'Velle' Diagram 'B'

Working cycles with the Velle range are of the order of:

Heavy range	26 tons	32 ft p/m	11 cycles per hour
Medium range	13 tons	64 ft p/m	20 cycles per hour
Light range	8 tons	104 ft p/m	26 cycles per hour

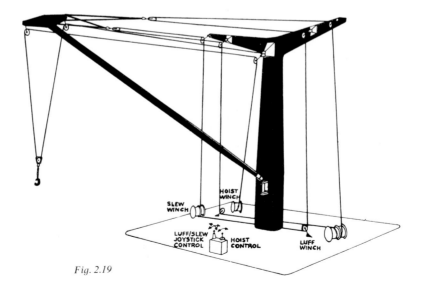

Fig. 2.19

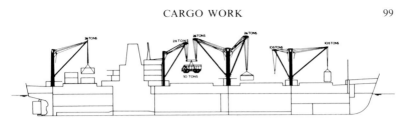

Fig. 2.20 Master and Slave Derrick Arrangement

Stothert & Pitt Limited, of Bath, England, have designed, manufactured and fitted numerous ships with their electro-hydraulic
deck cranes, a most recent range being in the 5 to 25 ton capacity,
both as single and twin units.

Of particular note is the 10 ton capacity crane illustrated on
page 99.

The crane rotates on a totally enclosed high capacity slewing rig
giving smooth and precise control. It has the 10 ton capacity over
a radius of 60 ft. The slewing, luffing and hoisting is through

Fig. 2.21

electro-hydraulic transmission, without the need for luffing ropes, which are replaced by the two hydraulic luffing rams. The jib movement is also by ram arrangement.

The cranes can be fixtures to the structure or be mounted on travelling carriages running on rails fixed to the deck or hatch between working positions, when it is then clamped to the structure.

Deck Cranes in General

Electro-hydraulic single deck cranes range, generally, over hoisting capacities of 3, 5, 8, 10, 12, 15, 20, 25, 40 tons.

Twin cranes are designed to have hoisting capacities of 2×12; 2×20; 2×25 tons, but they can operate either singly or in concert. Heavier hoisting capacities are also available for specialized ships and cargoes, even up to the extent of 150 tons or more (see pp. 68–81.

These crane types are suitable for relatively fast moving general, bulk and container cargoes.

The positioning of deck cranes is a matter of importance. The siting of deck cranes on mountings along a mid-transverse position between double hatch openings greatly assists both speed and radius of operation. Where the crane fittings are mobile, i.e. on carriages or portals permitting fore and aft movement, greater flexibility of operation is available. The crane is locked, stationery, during actual operations.

Cranes fitted as 'fixed' benefit from mountings which provide height visibility well above the hatch openings, illustrations of which can be seen in types where the crane, itself, is mounted on a vertical pillar structure, from the deck. Visibility and line of vision is important, if not vital, to crane cab operators.

Effective hoisting, slewing and luffing are the three essentials of good crane work and are the activities needful of attention by Cargo Officers, depending upon the type of labour employed as cab operators. Unnecessary acceleration, retardation, sudden and rapid restriction increases the normal stresses provided by a load upon the cargo gear, apart from its effect upon the mechanism of the crane, however robust this may be.

Modern deck cranes incorporate these three functions by automatic lever controls in the operator's cab.

Gearless Vessels: Dry Cargo Vessels and large bulk carriers, do not necessarily now require their own cargo handling gear (derricks, etc.), although the arrangement is more likely to be related to the large 'bulkers' and where influence from the trades in which these vessels are to be employed, have affect.

Where this is so the ship acquires the nomenclature of 'Gearless Vessel'.

Modern Forest Products Carrier
By kind permission of Handford Photography, Croydon, England.

Forest Products

A. *The Trade*

Forest Products is a collective term by which the harvesting of treelogs is such that numerous varieties of wood or wood products make up maritime shipments for numerous marketing needs and manufacturing processes, with the result that a wide range of 'terms' designate types of forest product shipments.

'Lumber' include timbers and framing suitable for the constructional industries, while 'Plywood' serves numerous uses for both internal and external needs.

'Panels' and Panelboard are produced to a wide range of applications, industrial and domestic.

'Pulp' is a substantial part of wood conversion which lends itself to fine paper ... 'Newsprint'.

'Kraft Pulp' is a further development of pulp, suitable for tougher paper needs and packaging.

The industry is highly sophisticated and technological, strongly based on research and development ... the by-products of a tree can be extremely broad.

Forest products has become an increasingly progressive trading pattern, developing from conventional carriers, utilizing manual labour and basic techniques of handling, to technologically designed large size bulk carriers where specialized handling is the more prominent.

Not particularly does the trade lend itself to containerization. Shippers find it more advantageous and profitable to use appropriately designed ships. Roll on/Roll off vessels, with both stern and side loading can be suitable, especially for newsprint rolls.

The older, traditional conventional systems are quickly falling out of the trade.

The trade is wide, with shipments from the East and West coasts of America, the Gulf Ports, Europe, which includes Scandinavia and from the Far East. Shipments are truly international, from the producing areas to industrial European centres, to South East Asia and to Australia and New Zealand.

In the case of the MacMillan Bloedel Meyer organization, of British Columbia, Canada, from whom kind permission has been given to refer to published information, large vessels and specialized terminals cover the transportation of timber and its by-products from producer to user to terminals now internationally situated. They are to be found widespread in many key European ports and in Great Britain primarily at Newport, Gwent and at Tilbury in Essex. In all of these terminal environments the objective is cost effective services. Indeed, the linking of sophisticated ships to modern terminals provides exceptional handling rates and tonnages, apart from the conveniences of distribution, which acts to the benefit of importers.

The ships normally used vary from specialized forest product carriers, for specific trades, to bulk carriers serving a variety of ports.

In terms of carriage the modern trade has developed from vessels fitted with Munck Transporter Cranes, through conventional bulk carriers to the 25 ton self releasing Cranston Units. The Munck and the Cranston carriage operates by self releasing heads handling multiple lifts of pre-slung timber as also do they serve unitized pulp bales and also liner board. On the conventional bulk carriers pre-slung loads are prominent.

Additionally, further new types of vessels are coming into use.

Other vessel types handle unitized pulp bales and newsprint (see also page 112) by clamping methods, where core probes are not applicable.

Quayside handling can be by either 35 ton trailers hauled by tractors or 15 ton fork lift trucks to service multiple lifts.

Operations on these terminals in Canada and in Great Britain are carried out by MacMillan Bloedel trained personnel; it is unlikely therefore that ship's officers would be greatly involved, short, of course of retaining a professional interest in the activities involved.

By way of comparison, Forest Products carriers can be large 'Open Hatch' vessels, such as:—

(a) 18 ton Munck Transporter Unit vessels of 21/22 000 tons gross and deadweight 28 000 tons.

(b) 20 ton Cranston Type Craneage Vessels of 30 000 tons gross and deadweight of 48 000 tons.

(c) Conventional Bulk Carriers of from 16 000 to 27 000 tons gross and deadweight of from 24 000 to 46 000 tons respectively.

(d) Very large 'OPEN HATCH' carriers of up to 44 000 dwt.

(e) 'LASH' barge vessels serving trades from the U.S. Gulf ports to Europe.

(f) Roll on/Roll off vessels, known in the trade as 'StoRo' ships now trading being of the order of 6000 dwt for the inter-European voyages to those of 13 000 dwt, known as 'Jumbo Ro/Ro', and a new generation of superships of 35 000 dwt for international long distance work. Indeed the use of Ro/Ro for forest products is encouraged by shippers by reason of economic advantages.

Invariably packaged timber boards are Pre-Slung; Plywood boards unitized into packs, kraft liner boards in reels, pulp in bales and newsprint in reels.

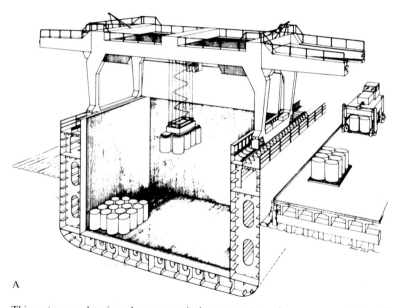

A

This cut-away drawing shows a typical cross-section of an open or 'all-hatch' forest products carrier. The gantry crane is being used for loading paper reels. End-folding hatch covers are shown, but lift and roll covers could also have been fitted. Cargo can also be stowed on top of the covers. This type of ship, which can also be used to carry containers, was pioneered by R. N. Herbert with the 9300 tdw *Besseggen* in 1963.

B Discharging Forest Products

C   Discharging Forest Products

D   Side Port Conveyor System. Newsprint.

Newsprint can also be shipped (vertically stowed) on Pallets, 8 reels per pallet, the total load of approx 5 tons and being discharge by ship gear.

Maritime transportation of timber is broadly governed by international and national regulations, an interesting feature of which being consideration of reduction in ship freeboard by reason, for example, the protection which deck loads give to hatch coverings, albeit the I.M.O. (International Maritime Organization) set stringent safety standards for timber on deck. (See Section 4, pages 184–193). The Codes of Practice for Ships carrying Timber Deck Cargoes.

B. *Modern Carriage Systems*

Figs A to E illustrate systems applicable to the carriage of Forest Products.

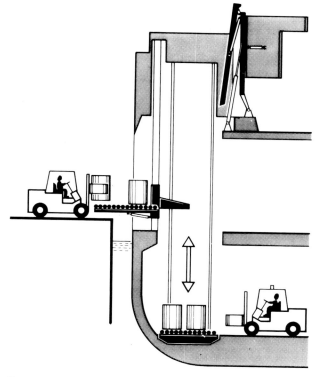

E　　　　　　　　　Side Loading Newsprint.

Fig. A, page 103, denotes a cross section rail mounted gantry craned 'open hatch' carrier, as fitted in vessels of about 18 000 dwt. This type of vessel is ideally appropriate for newsprint.

Pulp pales or packaged timber can equally be stowed and lifted by this arrangement.

Fig. D, page 106, illustrates Side Port Conveyor systems.

Each of these diagrams are included by kind permission of the MacGregor Navire International.

(By the gantry cranes each can lift 16 reels in a single lift, each reel being of the order of 1 metre in diameter and of a weight of 700 kgs).

Photograph E . . . page 107 and the accompanying profile is of a smaller 5500 dwt newsprint carrier, for shorter trades. The two side loaders automatically convey the cargo (paper reels) or palletized pulp and lumber from the quay and elevate them to the deck on which they are to travel on voyage. Once there, irrespective of deck, the movement of stowage is facilitated by fork lift truck operations.

Each side loading unit comprises a combined side door/top hatch, a loading platform and twin pallet lifts, embodying integral conveyors.

The loading/discharging rate can be of the order of 400–700 tonnes/hour, depending upon the unit weight of the packages handled.

A full cargo can be stowed/discharged in about 18 hours. The system is technological but, to the cargo officer, simple in application and suitability.

Product Types

In the trades concerned with forest products highly sophisticated craneage systems are fitted to vessels engaged in the carriage of these commodities.

Paper pulp is a highly developed commodity now shipped in high tonnages and with ships trading direct from source to discharge terminals (see reference to Newport and Tilbury Timber Terminals, p. 102), heavy constructional equipment is used, in the form of gantry cranes, as part of the structure.

The paper pulp is packed at mill source into 8 steel taped or wire strapped bale units and lifted by automatic pneumatic electro-controlled arrangements by basket clamps, the term indicating a system whereby 8 lifting heads in the 'basket' magnetically grip the steel banded bales and, through tension, securely lifts the load. The equipment is of the 16 tons S.W.L. range for the handling of 8 × 8 strapped bales.

Multi-grabs and wire clamp arrangements are also used in the handling of paper pulp. The MultiGrab is a mechanical hydraulic device which lifts a unit of 8 bales, up to 2 tons weight, and is invariably fitted to luffing cranes on a 6–12 S.W.L. range. The wire clamp is a relatively simple arrangement which grips the steel tape, or wire, by which the bales are made up.

Paper pulp bales are also palletized, generally 36 to a unit and transported to the vessel by straddle carrier for roll on/roll off transportation where they are stacked by fork lift trucks. A pulp bale, normally, is of standard size 750 × 720 × 700 mm (30 × 29 × 18 in).

Improvements on this system include straddle carriers which pick up palletized loads and deliver these direct into the vessel, on to the loading deck.

These forms of carriage involve numerous port callings, with quick dispatch required at each.

Reels of paper are also handled by similar methods on gantry crane equipment. Vacuum power clamps fitted to the lifting unit engage the reels geometrically concentric to the clam and, on a multi unit, lift, simultaneously, 6 to 12 reels of paper. Vacuum handling is accepted as the most dependable damage free method of moving reels of paper; it is also fast moving but does incorporate a 'danger factor' . . . by reason of the method . . . and no personnel should be allowed within range of the crane during a handling operation. The operations are remote controlled from a crane cab and much of the efficiency of the system depends upon the effectiveness of the controlling systems.

Vacuum handling for reels of paper is also available by attachments to luffing cranes, subject to the necessary additional power cable fittings.

Newsprint. Rolls of newsprint by conventional handling can be subject to irreparable damage . . . a distorted roll is unsuitable for paper printing machinery. It should therefore, be slung, and stowed in a manner avoiding such distortion.

Of the modern systems achieving this is that of a 'probe' form of lifting which fits into the hollow centre of the roll and, on lift-strain, exerts pressure by expansion on to the top, thus providing the lifting force. These probes can be mechanically fitted to ship's lifting gear, and systems available include 'spreaders', permitting the lifting of 6 rolls at a time, each of about 2250 kilos in weight. Vacuum attachment systems of handling is also now a common form of operation which can be adapted to either conventional or container carriage.

Purpose-built vessels covering the Canadian/U.K. trade handle all of the paper-roll load by 'Hyster' straddle trucks, fitted with clamp attachments adjustable to the size of the roll and capable of tilting it over any angle necessary to its carriage and placement. The handling is into and out of the vessel through side-loading doors and on to intermediate decks by structurally built-in lifts. See also, Section 4, page 106, 'Reels of Paper'.

Packaged timber. Gantry crane units are also used in the handling of packaged timber, where lumber clamps are fitted to the lifting unit designed to lift a load of approximately 5–6 tons within a S.W.L. range of 16 tons.

The clamps fit beneath the steel tapes or wire by which the packaged unit is bound and, by tension, grip and lock the load while it is in suspension. On landing the clamps are automatically released.

Smaller timber clamps fit on to luffing cranes and are used mainly with lighter cargoes while lumber forks, also fitted to luffing cranes, handle packaged timber where there are variations in the size of the packages. Three standards of packaged timber can be handled by a lumber fork . . . up to 2 tons weight. As distinct from clamps, the 'fork' acts independently of the securing tapes of the package and grip the load through its forks.

Logs are now extensively carried as a bulk cargo and loaded/discharged by log grapple equipment.

The grapple is an electro-hydraulic unit, insensitive to water submersion and thus is able to lift the logs direct from the 'ponds'.

It grips the uppermost logs in a bundle, the total weight of which being within $1\frac{1}{2}$–4 tons.

Log grabs, also electro-hydraulically operated, handle heavier and larger dimensioned log units (6 tons). With these methods a total log load is encompassed in the grab.

Examples of cargo handling systems for forest products are as follows:

'Hagglunds' A. B. Hagglund & Soner, Ornskoldsvik, Sweden. 5. 89101.

Acknowledgement and thanks is here conveyed to the Deck Machinery Division of the above organization, for its kind permission to refer to its own literature on handling systems for forest products, which it manufactures and markets, as part of its world wide reputation as a leader in the design and supply of craneage systems. Figs 2.22 A to J.

A. *The Vacuum Clamp.* Used for the loading and discharging of paper reels. Considered to be the most dependable method for damage free handling of this form of cargo, the automatic vacuum clamp may be used with either gantry or luffing cranes. The system lifts from 6–12 reels of paper, entirely by vacuum action. It is entirely electrically powered and is operated from the panel in the crane cab. There is a safety element in that no people shall be allowed within the cargo handling area (see diagram).

B. *The Probe Clamp.* A semi-automatic equipment yielding high handling rates, designed to lift paper reels in pairs. The probe inserts into the centre holes of the reels and a crank adjusts to the reel diameter. When the reels are landed, and the lifting wire slackened, the probes automatically release (see diagram).

C. *The Core Probe.* This equipment is independent of the diameter and height of the paper reel and can be operated by one man. The probe inserts into the centre hole of the reel and grips by expanded force. It has particular application to single reels (see diagram).

D. *The Bale Clamp.* A fully automatic lifting implement designed to handle units of up to 8×8 strapped pulp bales. Basically designed for use with gantry cranes it can also be applied to luffing cranes. The head of the clamp picks up the steel tapes of the bales by magnetic means, to permit the insertion of grips which lock the tapes securely, and these are then tensioned by the widening action of the lifting head (see diagram).

E. *The MultiGrab.* A mechanical-hydraulic clamp device for the handling of steel tape or wire bound bales of pulp, in multiple units, primarily intended for use with luffing

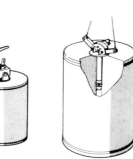

'A' Vacuum Clamp   'B' Probe Clamp   'C' Core Probe

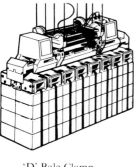

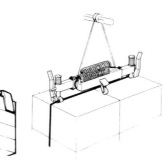

'D' Bale Clamp   'E' MultiGrab   'F' Wire Clamp

Fig. 2.22

cranes. The grab is an automatic, self-locking tool, like a
mechanical shears-type clamp, dependent only on the
tension in the cargo runner. The clamping device acts on
the uppermost bales in each eight-bale block (see diagram).
F. *The Wire Clamp.* A semi-automatic tool for handling
   unitized pulp bales without baskets. The tool has two
   locating tongues, one at each end, which pluck the steel
   tape or wire, and firmly secured so that it cannot slip off.
   The weight of the load acts on an expanded linkage so that
   the steel tape or wire is tensioned. When the load is landed
   springs cause retraction of the linkage so that the tongues
   release the tape or wire, allowing removal of the tool (see
   diagram).
G. *The Lumber Clamp* (1). Designed to lift cargo units comprising timber packages of approximately one standard
   each, assembled by strapping with steel tape or wire, four
   packages to one lifting unit. The tool has two lifting heads,

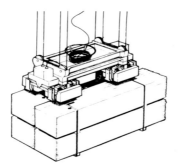

'G' Lumber Clamp (1)

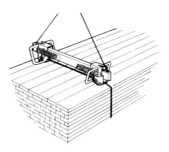

'H' Lumber Clamp (2)

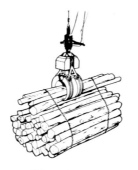

'I' Log Grapple

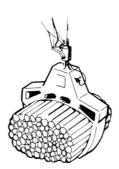

'J' Log Grab

Fig. 2.22 (cont'd)

each equipped with two clamps. A tongue on each clamp slides on top of the package with light pressure and picks up the steel tape or wire. After gripping, the clamps automatically widen towards the ends of the package, thus tensioning the tape or wire. When landing the load, the tongues are automatically released and the clamps return to a neutral position. The entire process is controlled from the crane cab. The lumber clamp is adaptable to both gantry and luffing cranes (see diagram).

H. *The Lumber Clamp* (2). This type of clamp activates in pairs, each pair lifting a unit of two packages. When the cargo is lifted the tool grips the securing tape or wire and lifts by means of the latter. It is a simple, straightforward system. When lifting commences the weight causes the carriages to be drawn apart, towards the sides of the package, tensioning the steel tape or wire. When the cargo is landed springs bring the moving carriages together again and the locking devices release the steel tape from the tool and it can then be lifted free from the cargo (see diagram).

I. *The Log Grapple.* This is an electro-hydraulic grapple for handling logs in bundles. It grips only the uppermost logs in the bundle and is unaffected by submersion in water (see diagram).

J. *The Log Grab.* This is an electro-hydraulic tool with fully enclosed hydraulic equipment. Oval in shape, it is intended for the lifting of bundled logs from the water. A rectangular form operates with logs from trucks, wagons or piles. The grab arms are manipulated by hydraulic cylinders and can be arrested and restarted from any position. They are controlled by the crane driver, from his cab panel. On luffing cranes a cable winder is required to carry the power and control cables (see diagram).

Newsprint—The Handling

The carriage of reels of paper is a major part of forest products transportation, with systems now outstandingly progressive. Whereas formerly reels were loaded into and discharged from conventional ship hold spaces by normal handling gear the practice now is increasing to the use of specially designed ships, and ro/ro vessels employing sophisticated handling methods, the use of the clamp lift truck being prominent. (See also lifting diagrams pages 103–107). Even so, though the slinging of the reels may be by conventional means, in older ships, their handling within the cargo spaces will doubtless be by clamp truck methods.

However, certain precautions are necessary and certain knowledge desirable, in which connection we are indebted to Overland Freight Forwarders Ltd. of Sheerness Docks, Sheerness, Kent, England for permission to include notes to follow.

Within the trade the cargo handling activities of this organization are of high reputation.

(The notes are mainly concerned with the Swedish and Finnish trades, but have relevance and similarity to other trades practices.)

————

Newsprint (the end product of a reel of paper) is used under conditions of stress; the demands on the paper as it runs through the printing presses are high. It is important, therefore, to remember that the paper reel should arrive at the stage of printing with NO, or a minimum of damage or deformation. To this end the reels of paper are usually wound and wrapped to protect them from physical damage and/or distortion, as well as from moisture, water and/or dirt damage . . . as well as from handling. (See Fig. 1–3, Diagram A).

Good winding, wrapping and careful handling are the three essentials in the transportation of paper reels.

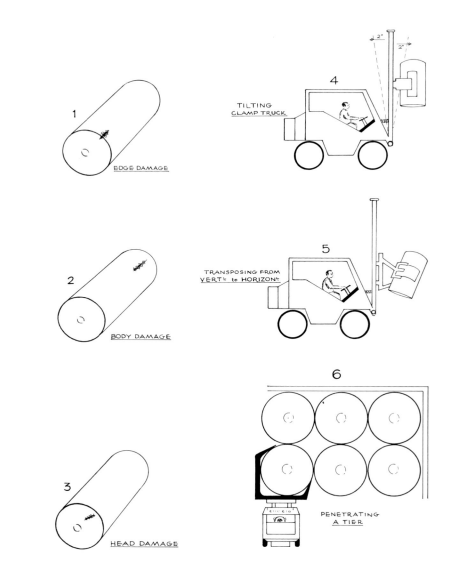

Diagram A   Methods of Fork Lift Truck Handling (Paper Reels)

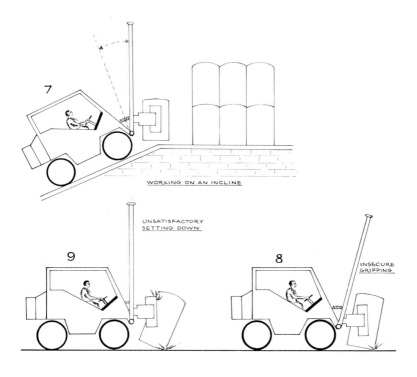

7

WORKING ON AN INCLINE

UNSATISFACTORY
SETTING DOWN

9

8

INSECURE
GRIPPING

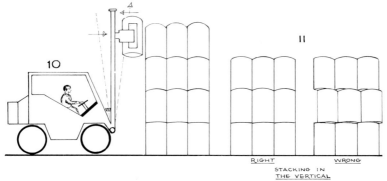

10

11

RIGHT

WRONG

STACKING IN
THE VERTICAL

Cranston Derrick Handling

Clamp Lifting—Paper Reels

Low Loader Transportation—Paper Reels

A. HANDLING

1. In terms of handling the ends of a reel of paper are protected by an inner and an outer paper disc, which overlaps the reel wrapping paper. The paper itself is wound on to the core, the ends of which are plugged in order to make it more rigid during handling.

   (With this kind of protection signs of chafing . . . assuming the rolls are in good condition at the time of loading . . . can only come from the movement or the shifting of the roll. Stowage, therefore, must be such as to prevent this, by adequate chocking and the effective positioning of the rolls in the make up of a secure full load).

2. Possible areas of damage can be edge damage (cuts or bruises) caused by the reel edge being subjected to striking or heavy pressure . . . the edges are the most vulnerable parts of a paper reel. (See Fig. 1, Diagram A, Edge Damage).

3. Body damage (gauges on the surface) can be caused by the belly of the reel striking or scraping against obstructions. (See Fig. 2, Diagram A, Body Damage).

4. Head damage (indentations in the ends of the reel) can result from reels being stowed on or scraped across rough surfaces . . . apart from the more obvious unsatisfactory handling. (See Fig. 3, Diagram A, Head Damage).

5. Out of roundness . . . this can result if the reel of paper:—
   (*a*) is handled with excessive clamping pressure.
   (*b*) is incorrectly gripped.
   (*c*) is dropped on to a hard surface or landing unevenly
         when manually removed from a stack.
   (*d*) is subjected to high pressure if stowed horizontally.
         (Note . . . It is preferable for reels of paper to be
         stowed ON END).
6. Water damage can result from the reel being subjected to
   rain, snow or condensation (hence hold ventilation). The
   ends are the parts of the reel most vulnerable to water
   damage.
7. Wrapper damage can result from rough handling by a
   F.L.T. Clamp Truck . . . i.e. improper gripping of the reel
   or insufficient clamping pressure, or even defective clamp
   plates.

B. FORK LIFT TRUCK CLAMPING

1. Clamp trucks must be of the correct type and be properly
   equipped for their purpose . . . the stowage/discharging of a
   ship.
2. Trucks should be chosen relative to their usage. They can
   have semi-solid or pneumatic wheels and these should be
   determined by the area over which the truck is working and
   the type of the 'floor' surface on which it works.

   Trucks used for the handling of reels must have 'tiltable'
   masts so that the clamp plates and the longitudinal axis of
   the reels can be kept parallel when the reel is gripped. A
   'tilting' angle of 2° forward and backward is the usual pattern.
   (See Fig. 4, Diagram A, Truck Tilting).

   Note:—a further aspect of the use of a F.L.T. Clamp truck
   relates to a ventilating issue. Trucks can be diesel, petrol,
   propane gas or electric battery power. In the case of the
   former three types, these should only be used where
   ventilating provisions are adequate and satisfactory.
3. The attachment of Clamping in the handling of paper reels
   is of the utmost importance.
4. Trucks used for the handling of printing paper can be of
   three main types . . . fixed, rotating and tippling.

   With paper reels by seaboard transportation these will, in
   all probability be stowed in a vertical standing position, in
   which case FIXED clamping attachments will be those used.

   Where, however, it is necessary to lift reels from the
   vertical and transpose them to the horizontal (for purposes
   of slinging for discharge) a TIPPLING clamp attachment
   will be needed. (See Fig. 5, Diagram A).

   There is a definite responsibility on those concerned with

the use of lifting trucks and their attachments, be they ports
stevedore personnel or ship's officers. In this connection
certain specific areas of attention must be fulfilled.

(a) The gripping arms attachment must be of appropriate
    and correct length such that they do not touch the paper
    reel when it is gripped.

(b) Clamp plates are vital parts of the equipment and must
    be so designed (curved) to conform to the circumference
    of a reel. Neglect of this can prevent secure gripping and
    could well cause damage to the reel. Clamp plates should
    frequently be inspected. Broken or bent edges can cause
    serious damage to the reels during handling.

(c) A particular clamping force is required for a paper reel
    to be transported without risk of dropping.

    The clamping force required depends upon the weight
    of the reel and the friction between the reel and the
    clamp plate. Any doubt that the clamping is inadequate
    should give rise to checking and testing, for which
    applicable test equipment is available. Indeed, it is good
    practice to regularly check the clamping force.

C. HANDLING PAPER REELS...GENERALITIES

1. All truck attachments must be aligned correctly before
   lifting a paper reel.

2. Gripping arm attachments (two) can be of similar lengths or
   one arm longer than the other.
   Working from a 'bulk of reels' it is preferable to have
   tippling or rotating clamps such that the *short arm* penetrates
   between reels in a stack and the *longer arm* being on the
   exposed side. Indeed, working from or with a vertical stack
   of reels, this approach should apply. See Fig. 6, Diagram A.

3. Clamp plates must be parallel with the longitudinal axis of
   the reel. If the truck is being used on an inclined surface
   (as may be present in ship deck design and form, or across
   ro/ro ramps) then, to ensure this, the truck must be tilted in
   order to obtain the correct grip. See Fig. 7, Diagram A.

4. A paper reel should not be lifted before it is securely
   gripped. See Fig. 8, Diagram A.

5. Reels must be set down flat so that they land evenly on
   their ends. Considerable damage can arise from uneven
   setting down. See Fig. 9, Diagram A.

6. Never 'drive' a truck with a high load, otherwise the truck is
   liable to tip over. (Stability considerations).

7. In the stacking of reels they must be lifted sufficiently high
   so that they do not foul reels below. Lifting to upper tiers
   necessitates some slight tilting (1–2°) backwards, for better
   stability. When setting the reel down the mast is tilted

forward again, so that the reel lands and sets vertically and directly above the reel below, *with no overlap.*

    The reverse procedure applies when removing reels from a stack. See Fig. 10, Diagram A.

8. Paper reels can be stacked in one or another of two systems . . . staggered honeycomb fashion, sometimes referred to as cantlined, or in straight columns. Whatever the system the vertical columns must be stable and straight. *Uneven stacking* is on of the most common causes of edge damage. See Fig. 11, Diagram A.

9. Effective supervision is essential in overseeing the correct methods and procedures of loading/discharging paper reels.

    This includes the operations of the clamp truck operator . . . for which he, himself, has particular responsibility and duty in respect of the clamp truck and its attachments.

    None the less, ship officers cannot be absolved.

10. By reason of the overall normal height of a reel of paper (and to avoid crushing damage) it is good practice to consider a vertical stow of 4 reels high. This will, normally, entail a stacking height of about 6.5 metres.

Attention is also drawn to Section 2 pages 88/93 where reference is made to methods of slinging paper reels, as per the 'Hagglunds A. B. Hagglund & Soner, Ormskoldsvik, Sweden 5. 89101. Organization.

––––––––

Developments in Paper Handling

Research has established that a reel of newsprint can pass through a dozen or more handling practices, from mill to paper user, and with the tendency towards larger reels methods of handling calls for examination. In this the 'Clamp' is of critical importance.

If the clamp is weak the reel can slip out; if the clamping force is too great it can cause 'out of roundness' or ovality damage.

It is the friction between the clamp pad and the paper wrapping which is the key element. The higher the friction the less clamping force required but where clamp pads may wear down, more clamping force is needed to hold the reel.

Developments in flexible pads, rubber covered bands, as distinct from steel plates and vacuum clamps are now in being.

Vacuum clamps have proved to be ideal for newsprint reels, albeit considerations need to be given to the grades of paper.

Conventional Carriage of Paper Reels

While it is only infrequently that the older conventional traditional vessel will be worked with newsprint rolls (and, in the future much

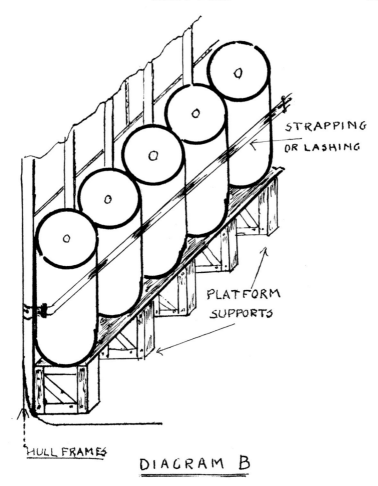

STRAPPING
OR LASHING

PLATFORM
SUPPORTS

HULL FRAMES

DIAGRAM B

less, if at all) there could be occasions where the reels may be stowed
on platforms. This could arise to overcome the difficulty of stacking
vertically at the turn of the bilge or where angle brackets from the
ship side to tank top create difficulties.

Two systems can be adopted:—

1. A Vertical Stow . . . see Diagram B.
2 A Horizontal Stow . . . see Diagram C, p. 122.

In either case the platform must be adequate in size and strength
to accommodate the diameter dimensions and the weights of the

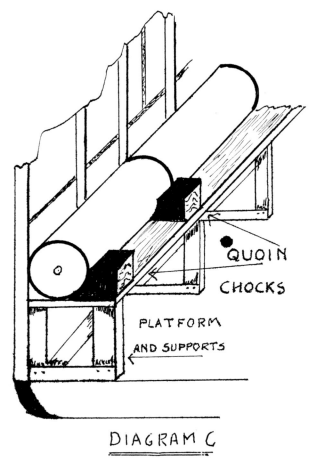

DIAGRAM C

reels. In terms of the diameter of the reel it is highly desirable that
the width of the platform is no less than this, where vertical stow is
used. It is also essential that suitable strapping/lashing arrangements
are made to ensure rigidity in the stow and to avoid the possibility
of the reels moving/shifting on the platform as a result of dynamic
stress within the vessel when at sea.

    With horizontal stow wood chocks, or quoins should be fitted to
the outside edge of the platform and butting against the reels. This is
considered by some, experienced in the trade, to be the better of the
two systems, in so far as the reels, lying horizontally, will react less, if
at all, to the dynamic stresses, their centres of gravity being lower
and nearer to the platform, than those stowed vertically.

Modern Carriage of Paper Reels

As distinct from the foregoing, diagram A, page 103, indicates the methods employed in the open or 'all-hatch' forest products carrier.

Roll on/Roll off Carriage of Newsprint Reels

Considerable development is now in being with the transportation of Newsprint Reels . . . and the similar reels of Craft Liner Board . . . by roll on/roll off vessels. This is particularly so in the trade with Finland, with vessels purpose built to accommodate the services.

Pre-loading is on to trailers with little or no broken stowage in the loading operations. The reels are lashed in sets of four by horizontal nylon web banding with additional vertical plywood separators inserted at irregular intervals, these having the dual function of separating marks and providing improved vertical stability to the stow.

The arrangement ensures that the reels are stowed exclusively on a rigid flat surface care being taken to avoid the possibility of the reels being stowed on top of one another moving out of a common line.

The trailers are discharged from ship to shore intact and then 'broken down' by dock labour for distribution by road vehicles, etc. The breaking down is done by tilting fork lift clamp trucks, in which context it is essential that the loads on the trailer are upright, otherwise there would be difficulty in the F.L.T. correctly picking up the reels.

SECURING AND LASHING

'Securing and lashing' is a complimentary term relating to the use of cargo gear. To effectively ensure that a cargo stow is 'safe' it needs the application of a variety of safeguarding equipment, according to its type, bulk, method of packaging and disposition in the ship. There is no one single method; each cargo load needs to be considered individually be it general break bulk or unitized, while with container and roll on/roll off systems a variety of forms of securing and lashing has been introduced, and continue to develop.

It is a statement of the obvious that with the sizes and weights involved, the need to provide complete security of movement is paramount, but the systems involved are, of necessity, far in excess of normal conventional lashings and thus they call for knowledge of the types and methods of operation. It is unlikely that the conventional systems of wire rope and chain lashings will remain dominant, in, for example, the container and roll on/roll off forms of carriage, albeit it is here that the emphasis on securing and lashing has played a major part.

Furthermore, by virtue of the different types of vessels employed in this type of carriage, flexibility and interchangeability of securing and lashing systems is now a part of the policies of manufacture. As a result, the 'earlier' securing systems have been developed to include more sophisticated and adaptable arrangements. On the other hand, the use of wire and chain will in many cases not become obsolete and may well be, with relatively small consignments of containers carried in conventional ships, the more preferable, provided all the other safety requirements are met, as required by legislation. (See page 383, M/Shipping Notice No. 624.) Normally, lashings in general, apart from the steel fittings, comprise, chain, wire and belt; web strapping is used with the carriage of cars.

Securing and lashing systems have relevance to the type of ship and its particular problems of cargo safety. These differ according to the service in which it is normally engaged and thus these flexibility provisions dictate the need for ship officers to be familiar with the various designs and adaptability functions. Basically, securing and lashing has regards to the forces acting upon a ship, and on to its cargo . . . mainly consequent upon rolling and pitching. Accepting this premise, the question then arises as to the comparative needs of supporting elasticity or rigidity; strength loads; load heights involved, i.e. containers; deck security attachments, both for containers and for vehicular traffic and the prevention of distortion in the cargo load. Such a view adds strength to the considered opinion that containers stowed 'on deck', for example, provided the securing facilities in purpose built ships are fully utilized, constitute no unreasonable insurance risk.

Particularly, in the roll on/roll off trades, is the foregoing relevant where cargo loads can be disposed in blocks or remain in or on vehicular carriage during the voyage. Block stowage, frequently mostly unitized, will require dunnaging, lashing and blocking off of reasonable conventional form such as will afford easy fork lift truck loading and discharging. Vehicular stow, however, will not only require that the load itself is protected from movement, either in itself or within/on its carrier, but that, also, the trailer on which it is carried is secured to the deck of the vessel. In these cases the use of wires, chains and web strapping, together with steel solid rod attachments will all play a part.

The disposition of cargo in roll on/roll off vessels also has a bearing upon its security. Where it is customary to load vehicular traffic in 'lanes', in line with the ship fore and aft line, this is encouragingly more acceptable to port working, being conducive to quicker movement and handling. As such, being less cumbersome, it tends to promote and attract more effective attention to cargo securing. A block, or tight stowage by which it is sometimes referred, is more labour intensive and thus calls for more prudent supervision in order to be assured of correct blocking off and lashing, although where trailer carriage is loaded this way, each does support the other.

A further point arises with loads on trailers. Their form, design and weight may be such as to carry a *centre of gravity* well above the base of the trailer on which the load is carried. Bearing in mind that momentum is the result of force and weight, acting through the centre of gravity, the acceleration and retardation of forces arising from ship movement in heavy weather could well inhibit the cargo load itself to move away from the trailer . . . its centre of gravity being much lower . . . which, in turn, could force the trailer to move against its own lashings.

The remedy is to completely arrange the lashings to pass over the top of the load and encompass both it, and the trailer together. This ensures that:

(*a*) the load itself is secure;
(*b*) the trailer is secure to the deck . . . by virtue of built-in structural arrangements; and
(*c*) (*a*) and (*b*) are secured together.

By adopting this procedure any movement possibility is considerably lessened.

Vehicular loads into roll on/roll off vessels encourage the adaption of numerous securing and lashing systems. These range over the chain, wire and rod applications, suitably tensioned by bottle screws, to twist locking fittings built into the deck and side structure over the area in and on which the vehicular traffic is placed.

With container stowage, particularly on deck, the stresses upon the load, arising from wind and weather, can be considerable. Modern practice, on purpose built ships, is to utilize twistlocking arrangements as between the containers with iron/steel rod and hook supports, fitted to deck attachments, covering the overall load. Smaller consignments, carried on the deck of conventional/ multi-purpose vessels, though not subject to equally sophisticated methods, nonetheless must conform to comparable rigid systems of securing and lashing.

NOTE: Cargo Officer's attention is drawn to the Merchant Shipping Notice M 624 which relates to the need for effective and efficient securing and lashing requirements with container carriage. Particularly does this notice point out that without fitted appropriate securing devices a ship should not carry containers more than one high; two or more only where proper securing provisions apply. It is also important to have accurate information of weight distribution, in the form of a stowage plan.

No one rule can be applied as a base for lashing/securing arrangements. Much depends upon the size, weight and configuration of the load; the securing provisions fitted into the ship structure and the expected voyage sea/weather conditions.

The general approach is the consideration of longitudinal and transverse stress effect on loads placed in and on a moving body; dynamic acceleration and deceleration forces arising from ship movement in a seaway and the overriding necessity of solidarity in

stow. To a large extent, experience with cargoes of the nature involved
is the only safe guide.

Experiments have been carried out with a view to determining
guide lines but with conclusions only to the extent of drawing
attention to the need for overall securing at all the corners of a
heavy load, as for example, a 40 ft trailer, transversely over the
load and adequately attached by tensioned chain to deck structure
fittings.

In the larger established container terminals the operating
personnel working with, or associated to the ship owner, are
especially trained in securing and lashing techniques and they
cover the operations exclusive of ship personnel. Irrespective, it
must not be forgotten that ultimate responsibility rests with the
ship, and the cargo officer, to ensure that the operations are
satisfactorily carried out. Insurance claims on the ship, arising
from damage due to ineffective securing, can be high.

An interesting feature of securing and lashing, be it for container
or roll on/roll off traffic, is that different ship designs and layout
may require different patterns by which the lashings are arranged.
It is for this reason that the manufacturers of appropriate equipment
have set up special divisions to research and design, by which their
investigations can offer a variety of systems appropriate to the
type of cargo carriage for which a ship has been built.

Of a number, a U.K. organization, namely, Coubro & Scrutton
(M. & I.) Ltd., of Barking Road, London, E.13, has widely-
developed methods for all types of vessels and with whose kind
permission the following notes are included:

Securing and Lashing Systems Cover

Permanent fitted container-locating equipment, such as cone locators
and locking-pins, corner guide brackets to lock against a container
corner or to lock two adjoining containers, stool fittings for deck
and hatch cover clearance, insert and shoe fittings for use on hatches,
decks and tank tops and hatch cover lifting sockets.

Removal location equipment, including insert fittings, shoe fittings,
corner and intermediate guide fittings.

Container stacking fittings include stacking adaptors of a variety
of design to suit a vessel's container stowage, by which the boxes
can be locked into position and/or lashed.

Container top tier fittings include clamps for locking top tiers of
containers together, for securing those stowed close together, or
for attaching adjacent containers, and coaming lashing devices to
assist with under-deck stowage in conventional vessels.

Lashing terminals are such as provide for fixtures serving lashing
attachments, and vary from single- and double-cup fittings, according to the type of deck. There are also star domes, star fittings,

recessed terminals and bracket terminals, appropriate to securing in roll on/roll off vessels.

Container lashings range from straightforward chain systems, with screw attachments to lashing rods and wires adaptable to 2-, 3- and 4-tier container lashing. Lashing facilities vary widely both in design and strength and, invariably, are manufactured to meet the special needs of a particular ship.

Lashing fittings include hooks of different types and design to fit on to single or adjacent containers, together with attachable bottle-screws and tensioners. For roll on/roll off securing, the lashing systems range from tensioned chain attached to deck terminals, load binders and lever type, long link chain fittings. Components include bulb hooks, load binders, trailer jacks and wheel chocks.

The range of equipment is extremely wide and comprehensive to meet any anticipated or known load/stress situation. Familiarity only comes with experience in operational use, but it is important and valuable, to have a general, all-round knowledge of the principles behind lashing and securing systems prior to service in vessels where such equipment is likely to be used. To some extent this can be obtained from technical data, normally published in brochure form by the manufacturers.

Internal lashing (containers). It is important to remember that lashing and securing is not a practice exclusive to the container, as such, itself. Similar precautions are necessary with the load(s) inside the box.

While a solidly-stowed container should in itself produce restraining influences, experience indicates that this may not be altogether complete, and for this reason containers can be fitted, and are indeed fitted, with lashing fixtures, both to the sides and the floor, on to which strapping devices are attached.

An illustrated leaflet of securing systems, manufactured by Coubro & Scrutton Ltd., is printed on pages 128–131.

Particular Handling Practice for Roll-on/Roll-off Carriage

Whereas the general observations contained in pages 93–101 (securing and lashing) have relevance, attention is drawn to particular precautions to which emphasis should be given.

Vehicles and Loads presented for shipment should be in *acceptable satisfactory condition* (ship officer responsibility to be satisfied on this)... structurally, loaded, secured and with adequate protection to offset the particular stresses which can be imposed upon them by reason of ship movement in possible heavy weather. Furthermore, ship provision for the 'securing' and for the placement distribution within the vessel (e.g. dangerous commodities) should meet all the recommended requirements.

It is the duty of ship's officers, and other personnel involved, to ensure the above is met, and maintained.

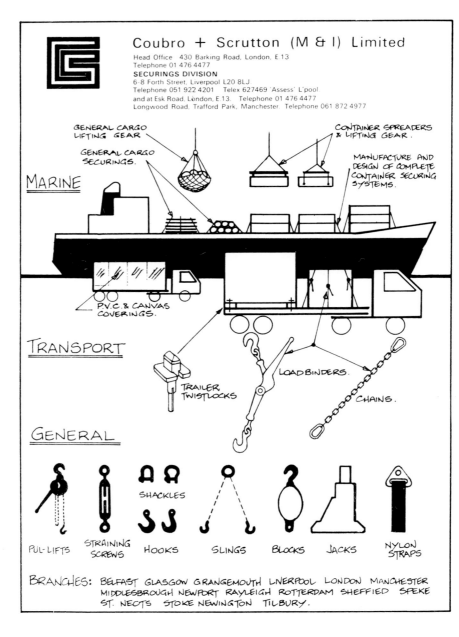

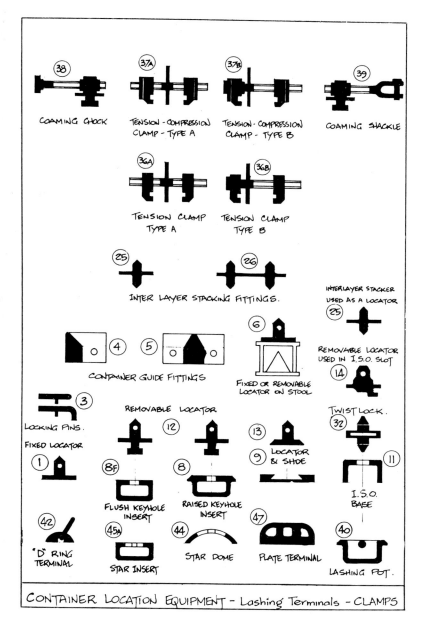

CONTAINER LOCATION EQUIPMENT – Lashing Terminals – CLAMPS

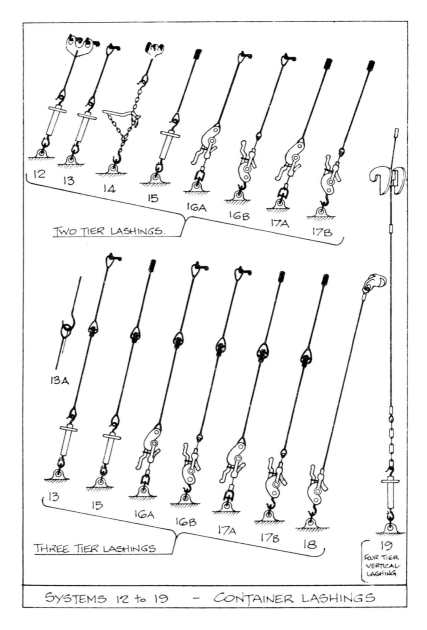

12
13
14
15
16A
16B
17A
17B

TWO TIER LASHINGS.

13A

13
15
16A
16B
17A
17B
18
19

FOUR TIER
VERTICAL
LASHING

THREE TIER LASHINGS

SYSTEMS 12 to 19 — CONTAINER LASHINGS

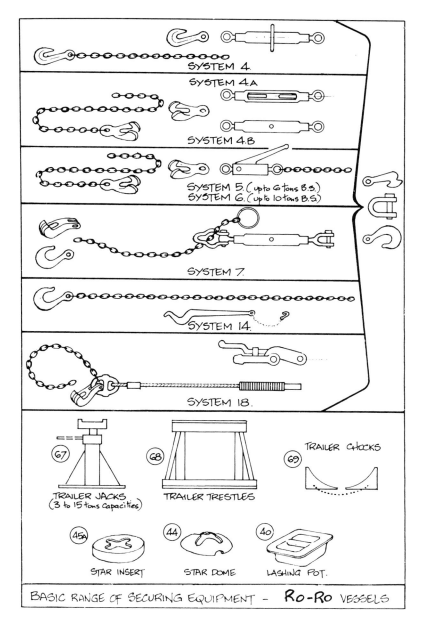

SYSTEM 4.

SYSTEM 4·A

SYSTEM 4·B

SYSTEM 5. (up to 6 tons B.S.)
SYSTEM 6. (up to 10 tons B.S.)

SYSTEM 7.

SYSTEM 14.

SYSTEM 18.

67 TRAILER JACKS
(3 to 15 tons capacities)

68 TRAILER TRESTLES

69 TRAILER CHOCKS

45A STAR INSERT

44 STAR DOME

40 LASHING POT.

BASIC RANGE OF SECURING EQUIPMENT — Ro-Ro VESSELS

In this connection not only is it important that Ro/Ro ships are adequately fitted with securing devices but that:

(a) the vehicle and/or load is similarly secure and appropriately 'fitted';

(b) the decks of the loading areas are not wet, greasy or slippery;

(c) access to vulnerable parts within a loading area is not obstructed, i.e. bow, stern or side doors, firefighting provisions, drainage outlets etc. and that, also, those parts are adequately protected against damage, should any failure of securing provisions arise during the voyage;

(d) with particularly heavy vehicles it may well be necessary to add to the normal securing devices jacking arrangements or other frictional resistance material placed beneath the unit, on to the deck;

(e) vehicles carrying dangerous goods should be segregated from other vulnerable cargoes and closely available to firefighting provisions;

(f) vehicles with flats...open sided bogies or trailers...must be so loaded and secured that the contained cargoes should not move, or slip, against the movement of the vessel;

(g) as indicated earlier, fore and aft (lane stowage) is the more desirable procedure with vehicles, with brakes on and the engine in gear. Where thwartship stowage is unpreventable, this calls for especial lashing security;

(h) tall-high vehicles...so loaded that their centre of gravity is relatively high, require a particular degree of security and lashing provisions.

Roll-on/Roll-off ships, obviously, also carry considerable tonnages and varieties of 'general cargo'. By reason of the 'fast moving' procedures inherent in this form of traffic, particular supervision is required of ship officers, in the ensurance of a 'solid stow'. In this connection 'parcels' of steel, in any form, pipes, cylindrical packages, paint drums and other liquid containers, call for special care.

It is as well to bear in mind that shippers of vehicles and goods on Ro/Ro vessels also have responsibilities to ensure their shipments comply to service conditions to which these types of vessels are subject, not the least of which is the provision of relevant documentation and the marking of goods and their labelling, apropos weight and precautions to be observed. Dangerous goods are cases in point and it behoves the Chief (Officer or Cargo Officer) to liaise with the shipping agent(s) in these matters. DoT Merchant Shipping Notice No. M 673 also covers regulations appertaining to petrol in vehicles on Ro/Ro ships, notably applicable with 'ferries'.

The particular attention of ship personnel is drawn to the Department of Transport Merchant Shipping Notice No. M 849, which, in some detail, covers observations on, and recommendations for the correct safe procedures to be adopted with the traffic outlined in the foregoing.

SECTION 3

Cargo on Passage . . . Ventilation

Ventilation and sweat . . . generalizations; prevention of temperature extremes; evolution of gases; use of ventilators in the circulation of air with different forms of cargo Moisture Migration.

Sweat . . . types of sweat; trades on which it is likely to occur; moisture content of air; condensation factors; hygroscopic and non-hygroscopic cargoes; temperature and dew point.

Rules of hold ventilation . . . natural and unassisted systems; practical guide lines.

Modern ventilation procedures . . . the Hall-Thermotank International Limited systems of 'marine air conditioning'.

Prince Line Cargo Vessel

VENTILATION AND SWEAT
(Generalizations)

Most cargoes, particularly those of a raw nature, are liable to suffer considerable damage if they are subjected to extreme ranges or fluctuations of temperature.

It is easy to appreciate that cargo is loaded at the temperature prevailing at the port of loading and, during its transit, may experi-

ence climates and temperatures varying considerably from the
original, with consequent effects due to heating and cooling.

Excessive overheating of a cargo leads to severe deterioration;
rapid cooling leads to the presence of much condensation in the
holds and a consequent effect on the cargo, whilst sweat, or condensation, may also result when passing from cold to warmer
climates. Warmer outside air, by the process of through ventilation,
will in all probability, deposit its moisture on the cooler cargo
within the ship. In such cases it might be advisable to prohibit
through ventilation.

Condensation can also occur when passing from cold to warmer
climates, for if the temperature of the cargo is below the dewpoint
of the external atmosphere, and air is admitted to the holds—condensation on the cargo will result.

Under these conditions it would be better to keep the ventilators
closed and this practice is employed by a number of cargo vessels
which load in U.K. ports during winter months and proceed directly
into the latitude of the trades.

It should be the aim of every deck officer to arrange the ventilation of the holds in such a way that the original temperature of
loading is changed slowly as the ship passes into other climates, so

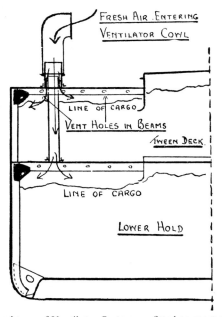

Fig. 3.1 The general type of Ventilator System, as fitted to most cargo vessels. The
diagram shows how one ventilator cowl serves both 'tween deck and lower hold.

that there is little or no difference between the temperatures inside the holds and that of the outside air.

Another important factor which must not be overlooked is evolution of gases and odours by the cargo which, if not dispersed into the open air, may be absorbed by other cargo within the hold. Even though deterioration may not occur to a very large extent, a cargo may suffer a depreciation of market value as the result of a 'foreign smell'.

If it can be shown that inefficient ventilations is the cause of damage to a cargo, the ship is held absolutely responsible and the claims can be very heavy.

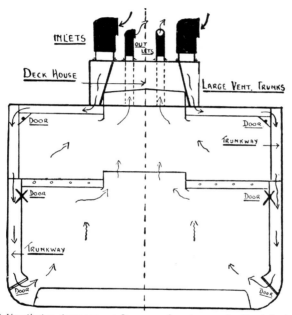

Fig. 3.2 A Ventilation Arrangement. Large cowl vents serve to direct fresh air down and along trunkways within the holds. The trunkways are situated at the ends of a compartment (port and starboard corners) and formed by plating over one frame space. Doors are fitted, as shown, to allow air circulation to be adjusted to the type of cargo. The small vents serve as outlets or uptakes.

The general system adopted, from a constructional point of view, is to arrange the ventilators so that, with a knowledge of air circulation, they can be trimmed so as to obtain constant circulation of air within the hold. Cool and dry air is sent into the hold through one set of ventilators; this will dilute the warm moisture laden air and any gases or odours from the cargo and by virtue of the circulation, transfer them to the outer atmosphere, via the exit ventilators.

In modern ship construction many elaborate systems of ventilation are introduced but the main point is that there should be constant circulation through or over the cargo according to its nature.

With regard to the carriage of coal, 'through ventilation' can be dangerous, for the contact of excess of air with the coal cargo is liable to cause increasing risk of fire and explosion. It is the practice with coal cargoes to prevent any 'through ventilation' by blocking those ventilators which lead to the bottom of the hold and so allow the coal gas to rise naturally to the surface where it may be dispersed into the outside air, either by the top ventilators or by removing the wooden hatch covers. (See section on Bulk Cargoes—Coal.)

A full cargo of rice, on the other hand, due to its damp nature and capacity of evolving carbonic acid gas, requires a very elaborate system of ventilators built within the cargo to increase the air circulation. (See section on Bulk Cargoes.)

To promote 'through ventilation' the ventilators are trimmed as shown. 'Lee' vents are downtakes, 'weather' vents are uptakes.

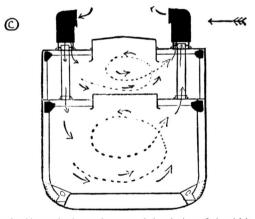

Fig. 3.3 This method is conducive to the natural circulation of air within the compartment, i.e. opposed to the outside air.

Air Circulation to Ventilation

Warm air, like any other gas that has been heated, tends to expand and rise. Cool air is heavier than warm air and therefore tends to fall and take the place of the lighter rising warm air. This difference in the densities of air at different temperatures produce a circulation within a cargo hold. The air in the lower portions of the space is relatively warmer than in the higher portions and will rise in conformity with the natural laws of air circulation.

The air in a ship's hold will move in a direction contrary to that of the outside air. The establishment of a circulatory system of air ventilation can be achieved by leading to the lower parts of the hold, those ventilator shafts which serve as 'intakes'. The cool air thus entering will dilute the warm air rising through the cargo and disperse it via the upper ventilators ('out-takes') into the outer atmosphere. Further improvement is effected by making the lee ventilators 'intakes' and the weather ventilators 'out-takes'. This will aid the circulation within the hold already established by the ventilator system. This will involve the trimming of the ventilators (cowl direction); the lee cowls will face the wind and the weather cowls will back on to the wind. Steady circulation of air in the holds will disperse any pockets of warm air and prevent possible deterioration of portions of the cargo.

Ventilation with Specific Cargoes

The ventilation of cargoes is a matter of very special significance. Natural and artificial products are legion, and it is certain that sooner or later each one will have to be transported as a ship's cargo.

It is not a mere matter of receipt and consequent delivery—there is the question as to what will happen to the cargo during the interim period.

With some cargoes chemical reactions are constantly proceeding; sometimes slowly—but in other cases rapidly—and where these occur there will be inevitable products of reaction. These products if allowed to remain *in situ*, may constitute a source of danger from fire and explosion, or perhaps contaminate or deteriorate other susceptible cargo.

Even though chemical reactions may be so slow that the reaction products are regarded as producing no obvious risk, there is still the question of the variable content of water vapour in air—a quantity dependent upon temperature. This latter point links up with the 'sweating' of cargoes and condensation of moisture in cargo spaces and on metal structures. Obviously, all reaction products viz, water vapour, gases, fumes, odours, etc. must be removed by the only practical method—ventilation.

Coal Cargoes. Coal cargoes evolve methane gas, which in admixture with certain proportions of air will ignite with a spark, just as in a coal mine under certain conditions. The methane which is set free, rises up through the bulk owing to its low density (0·55 that of air) and is then diluted with the continuous air current at the surface, being finally swept out via the weather uptake. (See diagram showing ventilators trimmed to ensure *surface ventilation* for coal cargoes.)

Bulk coal is also subject to spontaneous combustion, a reaction due to contact with excess oxygen. The risk of spontaneous combustion will therefore be reduced by *avoiding through ventilation.* Coal subjected to oxidation or weathering develops a caustic soda

soluble portion termed 'ulmins'. These do not occur to any extent
in freshly mined coal, and any quantity found in any given sample
of coal will show how far storage has impaired the coal. Tests carried
out to determine the rate of development of ulmins in an average
sample using standardized conditions of oxidation, will therefore
afford information as to the risks of spontaneous combustion in
the sampled bulk.

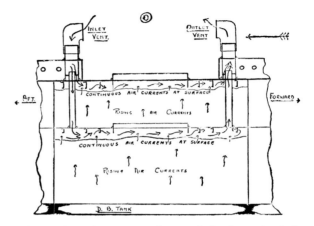

Fig. 3.4 Ventilators trimmed to ensure surface ventilation for coal or bulk cargoes

Grain Cargoes are subject to germination, which will depend
upon temperature and the presence of moisture.

Through ventilation will therefore be essential.

The air between the grains will be saturated with water vapour
which can only be removed by a through current of drier air. Should
a sudden fall of temperature take place, then condensation will
occur. If care is not taken, the water will lead to germination of the
grain, and this will be accompanied by a rise of temperature and
evolution of gas.

*In ventilation, therefore, it will be important to adjust the hold
temperature to that of the outside air.*

Rice (New) is particularly likely to suffer from moisture effects.
It heats up quickly and evolves odours likely to affect other cargo.
Under ordinary conditions, it gives off carbon dioxide. With the
matured grain less ventilation is required.

Green Sugar. Contains molasses since it has been crystallized
from concentrated sugar juices. Molasses is fermentable by air
borne or plant borne spores, and when it is fermented as a commercial
process in alcohol production, yeast extracts are used. Zymase,
a substance contained in yeast cells, can induce fermentation in

sugar liquids if phosphates are present. Fermentation is a chemical process which causes a rise in temperature. The major products are *ethyl alcohol* and *carbon dioxide*, the former increasing up to a definite strength beyond which the Zymase activity falls off, and the latter amounting to over 500 lbs in weight for every ton of molasses converted. Other products are also formed at the same time and include other alcohols (including a mixture of the two amyl alcohols called fusel oil) glycerol, aldehydes and various acids. The last named section includes formic and acetic acids which are capable of *corroding iron* and this fact must be borne in mind in dealing with raw sugar cargoes in iron ships. Thus raw sugar cargoes under special conditions of temperature and moisture will evolve alcoholic vapours and carbon dioxide and also produce acidic substances. Volatile substances evolved by such cargoes are capable of producing deleterious effects upon workers and hence *through ventilation* will be imperative.

A Fruit Cargo will require an accurate control of temperature otherwise considerable deterioration will occur. Ventilation in this case will be devoted to maintaining the required temperature. Such control will require a cooling system placed in the path of the circulating air current, and fans will be utilized for maintaining circulation.

Unique systems of ventilation have been introduced into a number of vessels which carry citrus fruits on relatively short voyages.

A battery system of brine pipes has been fitted in an enclosed section of each hold or compartment and fans draw in fresh air from the atmosphere and pass it over the chilled pipes, after which it is then blown into the cargo spaces.

The holds are not insulated and the brine delivery only operates for short periods when the vessel may be passing through relatively warm temperatures.

Extractor fans are also fitted and these draw off the gas laden air from the compartments, freshly precooled air being automatically circulated to complete the cycle.

The system is adaptable to ordinary general cargo, for in such cases, the brine circulation is stopped, thus allowing the fans to keep the air within the holds in a constant state of circulation. It will be appreciated how such a ventilating system maintains temperatures within the holds similar to those of the outside air.

The above instances give a slight indication of the problems involved in the ventilation of cargoes.

Speaking generally, ventilation consists of the dilution of deleterious gases, fumes and odours and their expulsion from a required space by air circulation. *The current movement within the ventilated space will be in the opposite direction to that of the outside air* (see diagram).

The Moisture Content of Air is illustrated by the following figures:

Weight of water vapour in *grams* in
1000 litres of saturated air.

Temp.		Weight
0°C	32°F	4·8
5°C	41°F	6·8
10°C	50°F	9·4
15°C	59°F	12·8
20°C	68°F	17·3
25°C	77°F	23·0
30°C	86°F	30·3

Note that the weights of water vapour correspond very roughly to the numerical values of the centigrade temperatures (for the range 0°–30°C). The same relationship exists between the pressures of water vapour (reckoned in mm of mercury) and the centigrade temperatures for the same range.

It is obvious from this, that any concentration of saturated air must be prevented, otherwise any fall of temperature, due to outside weather temperature or badly adjusted introduction of cooler air, will result in *condensation.*

SWEAT

Trades on which it is likely to occur and the usual procedure adopted to counteract it

Sweat is condensation which forms on all surfaces and on all goods in a compartment or hold due to the inability of cooled air to hold in suspension as much water vapour as warm air.

It will be appreciated that the air in all compartments of a vessel loading in tropical climates is warm, and that the cargoes loaded are also warm. This warm air contains much water vapour which is not visible to the eye. On passing into temperate latitudes the colder sea water and air cools the structure of the vessel, which in turn causes a drop of temperature within the cargo spaces. This cooling, particularly if sudden, causes much condensation and water drops will be observed forming on deckheads and frames, whilst all goods within the spaces will be subject to considerable moisture deposit. This deposit is termed 'sweat'. The possibility of this condition will arise, irrespective of trade, with cargoes, which by virtue of their nature, are damp and moist and so give rise to moisture saturated air in their vicinity.

If precautions are not taken to reduce sweat to a minimum considerable damage to cargo is likely to result. Claims for damage through sweat can be high and if it can be shown that all reasonable precautions have not been taken, the ship is held responsible. Although intelligent use of dunnage will minimize damage from sweat it is better to approach the problem from the point of prevention at source. Using natural processes of air circulation and trimming the ventilators to suit these, enables through ventilation to be achieved such as to assist in bringing the air temperature in a compartment to approximate more nearly to that of the outside air. It is better to eliminate the possibilities of damage from sweat by efficient ventilation.

Some Practical Observations on Sweat and Ventilation

1. *Sweat* is of two kinds:
   (a) Ship's sweat . . . condensation on the ship's structure.
   (b) Cargo sweat . . . condensation directly on to the cargo.
       Ship sweat takes place when the 'dew point' in a cargo space exceeds the temperature of the structural parts of the ship. It is minimized, or eradicated, by passing adequate volumes of outside air over the cargo, more particularly necessary in a vessel passing from warm to colder atmospheric conditions.
       Cargo sweat can arise when passing from cold to warmer climatic conditions since the cause is from the warmer moisture laden air condensing on the cargo. Its prevention is by sealing off the ventilating facilities, although extraction fans will be necessary to offset any moisture effects emanating from the cargo itself, or its dunnaging materials.

2. *Cargo Effect.* Cargoes are mainly of two kinds:
   (a) *Hygroscopic*, mainly of vegetable origin such as grain, flour, cotton, tobacco, wood and the like, all of which are affected by the humidity of the atmosphere attracting, retaining and giving off moisture. Hygroscopic cargoes cause ship sweat by virtue of changes in temperature, particularly when passing from warm loading areas to cooler conditions. Especially can this be so with sudden falls in outside temperature.
   (b) *Non-hygroscopic* consist of materials of solid nature, such as steel products, machinery, earthenware, canned goods and the like, which can be subject to damage from cargo sweat . . . condensation . . . in the form of rusting, staining or discolouration. Particularly is this so if loading has taken place in cold climates and the cargo later subjected to warm climatic conditions, when internal condensation is likely to be more applicable.

3. *Temperature change* in cargoes need not be more than one or two degrees a day to activate sweat, irrespective of larger outside temperature fluctuations. When passing from cold to warm regions it may be advisable to seal off ventilators in order to avoid problems of sweat which may arise.

4. *Hygrometry/sweat/dew point.* A knowledge of hygrometry is essential to the understanding of sweat and its problems since it is concerned with the retention of water vapour in

concentrations of air. The controlling factor is the relationship between the temperature and the humidity of the air. Air having 100 per cent humidity is said to be 'saturated'. Generally, sea air is of the order of 75 per cent humidity, requiring only that amount of moisture to cause saturation.

Where unsaturated air is cooled it ultimately reaches a temperature at which it becomes saturated ... this temperature is known as the 'dew point' of the air ... and is entirely dependent upon the amount of water vapour in the air.

Any cold surface having a temperature at, or below the dew point of the air on contact with it, becomes a condensing surface and sweating takes place on that surface.

The dew point is normally obtained by the use of the wet/dry bulb thermometer readings, by reference to conversion tables, as indicated in Figure 3.5.

HUMIDITY.		DRY BULB TEMPERATURE.						
		32°	40°	50°	60°	70°	80°	90°
100%	WET BULB TEMP.		40°	50°	60°	70°	80°	90°
	DEW POINT.	32°	40°	50°	60°	70°	80°	90°
	WT. OF MOISTURE lb. PER 1,000 cu.ft.	0·303	0·41	0·58	0·829	1·15	1·58	2·17
90%	WET BULB TEMP.		39°	48·5°	58°	68°	78°	88°
	DEW POINT.	30°	37·5°	47°	57°	67°	77°	87°
	WT. of MOISTURE lb. PER 1,000 cu.ft.	0·274	0·37	0·52	0·74	1·03	1·43	1·95
80%	WET BULB TEMP.		37·5°	47°	56·5°	66°	75°	85°
	DEW POINT.	28°	34°	44°	54°	64°	74°	84°
	WT. OF MOISTURE lb. PER 1,000 cu.ft.	0·243	0·33	0·46	0·66	0·92	1·27	1·74
70%	WET BULB TEMP.		36°	45·5°	54·5°	63·5°	72·5°	82°
	DEW POINT.	24°	30°	41°	50°	60°	70°	79°
	WT. OF MOISTURE lb. PER 1,000 cu.ft.	0·215	0·28	0·41	0·58	0·825	1·1	1·52
60%	WET BULB TEMP.		35°	44°	54°	61°	70°	79°
	DEW POINT.	21°	27°	36°	46°	55°	65°	74·5°
	WT. OF MOISTURE lb. PER 1,000 cu.ft.	0·182	0·245	0·35	0·49	0·69	0·96	1·3

Fig. 3.5

THE 'RULES' OF HOLD VENTILATION— PRACTICAL GUIDE LINE EXAMPLES

Natural and Unassisted Systems

In ventilating practice the ship officer can collect only limited evidence of hold atmospheric conditions through the use of wet and dry bulb temperature readings in a few locations in the holds and on the open deck. If there is any circulation of air in the hold it can be assumed that the former will be representative of overall hold conditions unless the thermometers are placed close to ventilator inlets. Comparing the dew points of the hold air and the outside air enables decisions to be taken as to whether or not to continue ventilating. The following basic rule provides relevant guidance:

(a) If the dew point outside is lower or equal to that of the hold dew point . . . *continue ventilation.*

(b) If the dew point outside is higher than the hold dew point . . . *do not ventilate with outside air.*

Considering the two basic categories of cargo, i.e. hygroscopic and non-hygroscopic, then a further extension of the basic rule can be made. Any voyage will involve one or more stages during which the outside air and the sea temperatures will either progressively rise or fall, or where there is little change.

As an example, the west coast of Africa/United Kingdom trade is illustrative and the effects of the outside changes on the two basic categories of goods can be summarized as follows:

Hygroscopic Cargo	Cold to warm voyage	Not critical, therefore ventilation not essential. On opening hatches at destination immediate condensation may form a surface but will dry off when cargo is discharged.
	Warm to cold voyage	Ventilation should be as vigorous as possible during the early stages but eventually the outside D.P. will be too low. This is the most difficult voyage situation in which to arrange satisfactory ventilation.
Non-hygroscopic Cargo	Cold to warm voyage	No ventilation; cargo sweat would occur on the surface of the stow if relatively warmer moisture laden air was admitted. Example . . . steel exports U.K. to tropical ports.
	Warm to cold voyage	Ship sweat inevitable but cargo unaffected unless condensation drips back on to the stow.

It is emphasized that the above guide lines are only basic. The proximity of both types of cargo in the same space will cause modifications to achieve a satisfactory balance of ventilation effectiveness.

MOISTURE MIGRATION

We can replace the basic rules by more detailed consideration of the physical conditions in the hold and outside. There are six temperatures which are relevant, Outside Air Temperature and Dew Point, Hold Temperature and Dew Point, Sea Temperature and the Temperature of the cargo mass. The last two named are slow changing and exercise a considerable control over the conditions of the hold, and in particular the cargo temperature is crucial.

Because sweat represents a source of moisture, it is relevant to consider that moisture in the hold may exert in several forms as vapour in atmospheric air, as free moisture in the cargo and packaging, or as hygroscopic moisture which is combined in the cargo but which cannot be released without affecting the nature of the goods. Free moisture will tend to evaporate in contact with unsaturated air at or near the same temperature and the rate of evaporation depends on the relative humidity of the air and the speed at which it passes over the cargo surface. Thus in arranging ventilation, the state of the cargo 'free' moisture content is a further essential quantity. The hygroscopic moisture, on the other hand is not readily released but does tend to affect the surrounding air and sets up an environment within the cargo which does not significantly change during the normal length of the voyage.

As the ship proceeds on her voyage there will be some transfer of moisture through the stowed cargo, a phenomenon known as moisture migration. The direction and rate of this depends on the vapour pressure of the air at various points in the stow, for example, in a large consignment of grain there will be a migration of moisture towards the outer parts of the stow if the latter is subject to cooling under the influence of the ship's steelwork, which is cooled by falling air and sea temperatures. In these conditions, the vapour pressure at the edges becomes lower than at the centre and the moisture moves in response to this pressure gradient. In a mixed cargo of course the movement is not so clearly defined, but it is shown that moisture migration coupled with ship sweat could result in damage to cooler parts of the cargo unless the excess moisture can be removed. Adequate dunnage to protect cargo from contact with the steelwork is vital.

The one factor not mentioned so far is time. The rate at which temperatures change will greatly affect the application of the basic rules given above. Consider a vessel making a ten day voyage from, say, West Africa to Europe. If temperatures are plotted daily on a graph, a pattern such as that indicated below, Fig. 3.6, will emerge, and this representation often indicates with greater clarity the periods when ventilation may or may not be carried out and, more important, those days on which the situation is critical. Days on which ship sweat will occur are also indicated. Clearly, the critical time is when the outside and inside conditions are not greatly different and to guard against this it is often suggested that when the difference between the dew points outside and in the hold is within the range ±3°C, no ventilation should take place with outside air.

One last variation must be mentioned. Since it is often difficult to ascertain hold dewpoints in the absence of proper instruments, we must consider whether it is sufficient to modify the rules using data which is available, for example, the cargo temperature. Provided the surface of the cargo is at a temperature above the dew point of outside air, ventilation may proceed without condensation forming.

However, it would be possible (at the critical times mentioned above) for the outside dew point to be below the hold temperatures, yet *above* the hold dew point, for example, outside D.P. 13°C, hold temperature 14°C, hold D.P. 12°C. In such a case condensation on

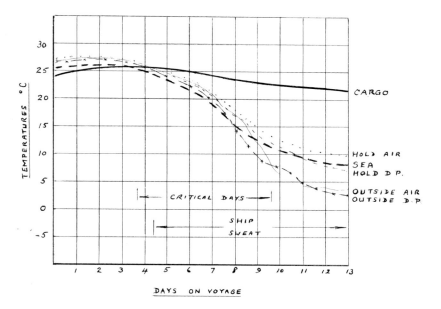

Fig. 3.6. Diagram showing possible changes of temperature during a voyage from tropical to temperate climate.

the cargo would occur where ventilation was carried out, and the ± 3° limit already mentioned should apply.

The only satisfactory method of preventing sweat damage is, therefore, to adopt apparatus for controlling hold conditions and these systems are now described.

MODERN VENTILATION PROCEDURES
(Mechanical Systems)

Modern vessels of all types invariably are now fitted with systems of mechanically activated air conditioning and ventilation facilities, some more elaborate than others, depending upon the class of vessel, types of cargoes carried and trades in which they are involved.

Modern air conditioning and ventilation is very much a 'science' backed by considerable experience and research. The systems involved require of all those associated with them, due attention to the methods of operation and also to the control functions. While it would be unreasonable to expect understanding of all of the systems available to the maritime industry, those which are operating successfully and which are based on proven need, are worthy of attention and study.

In this context the following material has been kindly supplied by Hall Thermotank International Limited, of Dartford, Kent, England, an organization with a wealth of background applications to appropriate ventilation and air conditioning systems in many types of ships. The text which follows is taken from the publications of this company, with its full permission.

Halltherm Marine Air Conditioning

Air conditioning in its true sense covers the complete process of controlling the physical and chemical properties of an enclosed atmosphere within the limits required for human comfort. In the context of this brochure it is restricted to filtration and the control of temperature, humidity and air movement by the proper regulation of heating, cooling and air distribution.

The Shipboard Environment

Climatic Variation. The world map indicates the wide changes in average climatic conditions that are encountered in the sea routes of the world. Supplementary to these variations are the local fluctuations of temperature and humidity that can occur within a short time and which affect the shipboard environment of passengers, crew and cargo.

The fact that dry bulb temperatures alone cannot be considered as a basis for comparison is readily evident. However, the term 'relative humidity', expressed as a percentage, is a definitive factor when used in association with the dry bulb temperature. It represents the ratio of the water vapour pressure in the particular air sample to that in saturated air at the same dry bulb temperature. It can readily be determined by references to a psychometric chart after measuring the corresponding dry and wet bulb temperatures of the air sample. The fact that more water can be absorbed as air is warmed, and less when air is cooled provides the basis on which air conditioning designs are formulated.

The injection of hot or cold air into a given space to achieve a desired temperature/humidity combination may necessitate procedures for the addition or extraction of moisture at the air processing unit as well as the use of simple heating and cooling devices.

The term 'effective temperature', although empirical, has been introduced to provide a single reference appropriate to a given air condition. It may be defined as the temperature of still, saturated

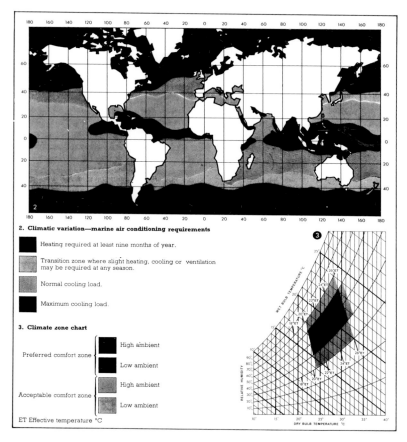

2. Climatic variation—marine air conditioning requirements

Heating required at least nine months of year.

Transition zone where slight heating, cooling or ventilation may be required at any season.

Normal cooling load.

Maximum cooling load.

3. Climate zone chart

Preferred comfort zone { High ambient / Low ambient

Acceptable comfort zone { High ambient / Low ambient

ET Effective temperature °C

air which would induce a sensation of warmth or cold identical to that caused by the actual temperature, humidity and air movement then prevailing. The basic 'still air' figure for effective temperature is reduced proportionally by approximately 1 °C for each metre/second air flow up to a maximum of 1·5 m/s (300 ft/min).

Other factors associated with the proper design of a ship's air conditioning system are the proximity of heat sources (e.g. boilers, uptakes and galleys) and exposure of windows, deckheads, etc. to direct sunlight, sea or weather as well as the degree of insulation provided.

Ventilation and Statutory Requirements. The basic need for ventilation on board any ship with closed decks was evident in Roman times, but the shipboard introduction of forced draught fans in the

latter half of the nineteenth century was a significant factor in the
increased number and size of passenger ships that became evident
before the First World War. Such ventilation systems not only had
to provide the fresh air needed where any member of the crew might
be working or passenger accommodated, but also to allow in warm
climates for the hot air within the ship to be replaced by cooler air
from outside.

The cooling effect of air movement was also not overlooked. As
previously indicated, Hall-Thermotank International Ltd., and its
predecessors were pioneers in the introduction of heated air supplies
for ships operating in colder climates. With the increasing desire of
governments and shipowners to ensure high standards of working
conditions on board ship, strict minimal standards for air changes
and other factors have been introduced for all working and accommodation areas. Likewise statutory regulations covering air conditioning have been introduced by many countries.

Fresh Air and Recirculation. Whilst the simplest ventilation system
operates with 100 per cent fresh air, the use of air processing,
whether heating or cooling, introduces economic and other factors
which often justify the introduction of recirculation procedures.
Such arrangements must take into account the function of the
space concerned and the grouping of spaces within a single ventilation system; although recirculation is not applicable to galleys and
sanitary spaces, it is advantageous for public rooms and accommodation.

It is usual and often obligatory for all processing units involving
recirculation arrangements to have the facility for circulating 100
per cent fresh air should the need arise.

Systems—Air Conditioning

General Ventilation. The previous section outlines the essential need
for mechanical ventilation in all classes of ships and the varying
requirements of different spaces within. The simplest of such
systems comprises a fan of appropriate size delivering air into a
given space with used air discharged to atmosphere through natural
exhaust ventilators fitted with adequate weather protection. Such
an exhaust arrangement rarely proves satisfactory for accommodation and galley areas but may be acceptable for sanitary spaces
and cargo storage areas.

It is therefore current practice for modern ships to incorporate
one or more properly balanced mechanical delivery and exhaust
systems, each associated with the correct location of air entry and
exit terminals within the relevant space or spaces to ensure good
air distribution.

Where cross-tainting problems do not arise, it is obviously
advantageous to utilize a single ventilation system for as large an

area as possible, commensurate with the size of installation and ducting required.

Whereas the desire for personal adjustment of air delivery into cabins is almost always provided for—the 'Punkah Louvre' having been invented by Thermotank Ltd. for that purpose—it is usual to accept a common exhaust facility for the area, utilizing door jalousies and passageways accordingly. For public rooms a pre-set balanced distribution for both delivery and exhaust is usually installed.

The proper location and size of fan rooms as well as the economical design of trunking layout is an important feature of good ship design. With its considerable experience of all classes of ships, Hall-Thermotank International Ltd. is often consulted by shipbuilders and shipowners to advise in this respect.

Air Conditioning—General. The basic requirements of air conditioning have already been defined in the introduction. Due consideration must also be given to the filtration and removal of dust, smoke and other unwelcome odours from the processed air. Likewise, the quantity of fresh air to be introduced must meet statutory requirements for the relevant spaces and ensure that carbon dioxide is kept at minimal level.

It will be appreciated that a greater degree of air treatment must be provided in air conditioning systems, as compared with the air heating procedures previously described, if these conditions are to be met. The removal of moisture from air under humid conditions necessitates air being cooled below its dew point, with resultant precipitation which must not be allowed to enter the ducting system. Reheating procedures may also need to be introduced to raise the delivery air temperature to acceptable levels.

Facilities for humidifying air by the addition of water or steam may be included in the air processing unit should the ship's operating area warrant it.

From their many years experience, Hall-Thermotank International Ltd. have developed alternative systems of air treatment, ducting and distribution arrangements with appropriate control of temperature and humidity to suit every type of space combination and economic consideration.

Factors taken into account when designing the most suitable installation include the number and location of air treatment units to serve relevant groups of spaces to be air conditioned; the siting of refrigerating plant and the position of heating equipment associated therewith; the size and layout of ducting connecting the air treatment unit to and from the various spaces. It is only after such basic design points have been considered that the theoretical design calculations and plant selection can be finalized.

By 1956 Thermotank Ltd. had introduced into their designs the use of high velocity systems, where warranted, for the conveyance

of treated air to the air conditioned spaces. Such systems are
associated with duct velocities around 23 m/s (4500 ft/min) and
their chief advantage lies in the reduction of ducting cross-sectional
area as compared with the larger rectangular ductwork associated
with conventional velocity systems. This reduction in size is usually
of great benefit to the ship designer since the volume of ducting,
often to be accommodated below deckheads, can be reduced

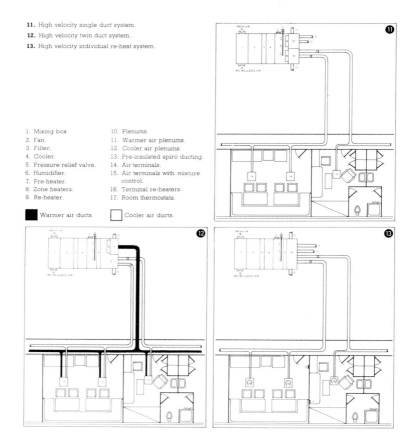

11. High velocity single duct system.

12. High velocity twin duct system.

13. High velocity individual re-heat system.

1. Mixing box.
2. Fan.
3. Filter.
4. Cooler.
5. Pressure relief valve.
6. Humidifier.
7. Pre-heater.
8. Zone heaters.
9. Re-heater.

10. Plenums.
11. Warmer air plenums.
12. Cooler air plenums.
13. Pre-insulated spiro ducting.
14. Air terminals.
15. Air terminals with mixture control.
16. Terminal re-heaters.
17. Room thermostats.

■ Warmer air ducts.   □ Cooler air ducts.

drastically. The cost of such trunking and the simplicity of manufacturing spiral-wound ductwork, including insulation, generally
offsets the disadvantages of higher powered fans and increased
sound generation. It is in this specialized design field that Hall-
Thermotank International Ltd. has devoted much research to the
benefit of shipowners and shipbuilders generally.

A general description of the three main types of marine high velocity air conditioning systems is given below. It should be appreciated that for large public rooms in passenger ships and ferries the well established low velocity systems may well prove acceptable and more economical. This similarly applies to other areas such as engine rooms, cargo spaces and the simpler installations fitted in vessels. Due to space restructions and the larger air volumes involved, conventional rectangular ducting is often used in preference to spirally wound.

High Velocity Single Duct (Zoned) Systems. Still the most widely used systems for tankers and cargo ships, this is based on one or more air processing units, with appropriate refrigerating plant, being sited strategically throughout the ship. From each unit air is delivered at high velocity through small diameter pre-insulated ducts to the groups of spaces to be conditioned. These groups are 'zoned' on a basis of proximity and similarity of heated air temperature requirement.

In colder conditions a mixture of fresh and return air is warmed and, if necessary, humidified using thermostatically controlled zone heaters fitted within the air processing unit (see Fig. opposite).

In warmer climates the air is cooled and dehumidified whilst passing over the refrigerated heat exchanger operating on a direct expansion or chilled water system.

Heating of the air is achieved by steam, hot water or electric elements as required. Air treatment, both temperature and humidity, is controlled automatically within predetermined limits at the central unit; this incorporates a sound absorbing plenum through which the air passes before distribution.

At the end of each branch duct an attenuator/diffuser reduces the pressure and noise level of the air being delivered and controls its supply and distribution to the space served. Adjustment of temperature within each space is effected by volume control at the delivery point. The air from the relevant spaces is either recirculated into the air conditioning system or discharged to atmosphere.

Special Requirements for Shipboard Spaces. In designing and supplying air conditioning installations for ships, it has already been emphasized that the overall project must conform to appropriate statutory requirements of the country of registration, to the basic standards of materials and manufacture specified by Lloyds or other relevant classification society and to such international design criteria as are applicable to the working conditions and accommodation standards for the crew.

Having supplied and installed air conditioning plant in ships built for owners in all parts of the world, H-TI Ltd., is well acquainted with such disciplines and its designs are based accordingly.

CARGO HOLDS. The degree of mechanical ventilation required is dependent on the type of cargo carried. With hygroscopic cargoes

such as grain, wound pulp or cotton, the need for humidity control
is important. H-TI Ltd., has established the Dri-hold cargo ventilation system which includes both dehumidification and recirculation
facilities.

VEHICLE SPACES. Regulations are usually applicable regarding
minimum air changes related both to the space and to the number
of vehicles carried. Flame and explosion proof fan motors are
normally obligatory.

LIVESTOCK SPACES. Statutory requirements are usually applicable
for spaces in which cattle, sheep and other livestock are carried.
These include air distribution arrangements as well as minimum
air changes dependent on type and number of animals carried.
Where the space is also used on occasions for other purposes, such
as vehicle ferrying, the minimum standards for both functions
must be met.

Equipment—Air Conditioning

General. Air conditioning equipment for marine applications needs
to be of special design to meet the exceptional conditions likely to
be experienced as compared with similar plants in fixed locations
on land. Previous sections of this brochure have indicated the
varied technical requirements involved and it must be realized that
the physical disciplines are equally important. On board ship space
is always at a premium and height limitations between decks
present a major problem. The corrosive effects of seawater spray
must be countered and rugged construction generally must be
adopted.

To minimize shipboard work H-TI Ltd. has devoted much attention to the establishment of a full range of factory tested packaged
air conditioning and refrigerating units. Similarly the use of spirally
wound ducting associated with high velocity systems has greatly
reduced the time required for manufacturing and installing complex
ductwork systems.

In the following pages examples are given of typical designs in
the wide range of equipment available. Research and development
is constantly in progress to ensure further improvements and new
designs being made available for the clients of H-TI Ltd.

Central Type Air Conditioning Unit. Fundamentally, the basic
essential of all air conditioning systems is the central air processing
unit in which the air, fresh or recirculated, is delivered by an appropriate fan via a filter to the cooling and heating coils, and thence
to the plenum chamber where it is discharged through one or more
ducts to the relevant spaces.

Within the assembly may be fitted appropriate supplementary
humidifying or heating units to process part or all of the air supply,
depending on the type of air conditioning system being employed.

With 75 years of experience in the design and building of such equipment, H-TI Ltd. manufacture central type units with pro-cessed air supplies ranging from 2500 m³/hr to 17 000 m³/hr. A suitable design is, therefore, available for any type of air condi-tioning system using local or remote refrigerating plant as preferred.

Normally installed in an appropriate fan room, such a unit usually incorporates a centrifugal fan, direct or V-belt driven by a marine type electric motor. The unit casing is acoustically and thermally insulated and contains an air filter screen of the nylon fibrous type, cooling and heating coils plus automatic air pressure relief valves. Humidification equipment can also be incorporated.

The unit can equally be cooled by direct expansion or chilled water refrigeration. Heating equipment can operate from steam, hot water, thermal fluid or electricity.

Halltherm Seapak (Combined air conditioning and refrigeration plant). Each assembly in this range is a fully packaged unit com-prising both air processing section and refrigerating plant on a common framework with anti-vibration mountings. The air pro-cessing section comprises a mixed flow type fan, driven by a marine type electric motor, with cooler and heater contained in an acous-tically and thermally insulated mild steel casing. Also incorporated within the casing is a removable air filter screen of the nylon fibrous type, direct expansion evaporator coil, heating coils and automatic pressure relief valves for the ventilation system.

Heating is by means of steam, hot water, thermal fluid or electricity.

The refrigerating plant consists of an open type compressor, V-belt driven by a marine type electric motor, supplied with seawater cooled condenser and necessary operational and safety controls. All refrigerant piping is fitted, tested and the unit charged with appropriate refrigerant. Before leaving the factory all necessary electric wiring is fitted and the refrigerating plant fully insulated. A composite starter is supplied for remote mounting. To give auto-matic capacity control for maximum variation in cooling load a hot gas bypass system is incorporated in the refrigeration system.

The three basic sizes of Halltherm Seapak provide air circulation ranging from 5000 m³/hr to 13 500 m³/hr. (Cooling capacities range from 50 000 to 160 000 Kcal/hr using R12 or R22 refrigerant as appropriate.)

Fans. The importance of good fan design for air conditioning systems was realized by the founders of Thermotank Ltd.; since the beginning of the century the design and manufacture of specialist fans for shipboard ventilation and air conditioning has been continued. Of recent years, H-TI Ltd., has, in the interests of its clients also utilized fans from other leading manufacturers to ensure maximum efficiency of the particular ventilation or air conditioning project.

Centrifugal fans are usually selected for the central type air conditioning units and for normal mechanical supply and exhaust systems. A number of marine fan designs are available to cover all sizes of shipboard installation, it being usual for fan impellers of the backward curve type to be incorporated for high velocity systems and forward curve impellers for low velocity installations. All impellers are statically and dynamically balanced for good performance with special attention given to motor design and mounting for minimum noise generation.

Axial flow type fans provide an economic and efficient alternative to the centrifugal fan for mechanical supply and exhaust systems. With the integral motor construction such fans are incorporated within the ductwork. Impellers are of aerofoil section manufactured in plastic, steel or cast aluminium.

Mixed flow fans with their special suitability for high velocity systems are fitted in the Halltherm Seapak units and used on other special applications. In addition to their excellent characteristics at high pressures, they benefit from compactness and flexibility, particularly when belt driven. Direct coupled designs are also available.

SECTION 4

SPECIFIC CARGO TYPES

Characteristics of different forms of cargoes, care and attention in handling. Methods of loading and discharging. Legislation and control.

A. Bulk Cargo—General
Conventional carriage, roll on/roll off carriage, indivisible loads. part bulk loads . . . I.B.C.s (Intermediate Bulk Carriers). Iron and steel cargoes, solid ballast. Mineral products in bulk.

B. Coal Cargoes
Hazards and precautions with carriage. Hot Coal. Pond Coal. Specific 'Long Haul' precautions. Safe Temperatures. Coal Trimming.

C. Dangerous Cargoes
Regulations governing the carriage of Dangerous Cargoes . . . Ministry of Transport and I.M.O., I.M.D.G. Code. Responsibilities of Master and Officers. Definition of dangerous cargoes. Departmental committee on the carriage of dangerous goods and explosives in ships . . . The Blue Book. Types of dangerous goods. I.M.O. . . . International Maritime Organization recommendations for the packing and marking of dangerous goods (and their hazards). Dangerous chemicals in bulk. Merchant Shipping Notices . . . recommendations and regulations. Petrol in fuel tanks . . . ferry transport. Packaging and marking (labelling) of dangerous goods.

D. Forest Products and Timber
The Code of Practice for ships carrying timber deck cargoes. The I.M.O. recommendations. Stability references. Merchant Shipping Notices . . . loading and securing provisions. Wood pulp . . . precautionary measures. The economics of timber transportation . . . packaged and loose handling procedures. Special timber terminals.

E. Grain
Comparisons of methods of loading, carriage and discharge. The Merchant Shipping Grain Regulations (1980) and I.M.O. recommendations on the carriage of grain in bulk. Ventilation of grain. Stability considerations with bulk grain cargoes.

F. Liquids in Bulk
Vegetable and edible liquids, their composition and properties affecting bulk carriage. The cleaning and preparation of tanks, heating arrangements. Latex . . . particular provisions. Molasses . . . care after discharge.

G. Ores and Similar Derivitives
Categories of Bulk Cargoes. Modern ore carriage . . . quantities and types of vessels. Basic conventional carriage and comparisons with modern ship design. The Code of Practice for bulk cargoes . . . I.M.O. document on hazards in carriage, movement/shifting precautions . . . densities and structural disposition. 'Dry' and 'wet' ores . . . trimming. Merchant Shipping Notices . . . systems of stowage and trimming. Precautions prior, to loading bulk ore. Safe carriage of bulk cargoes . . . precautions with moisture content.

H. Refrigerated Cargoes
Basic principles of refrigerated cargoes, preparation of compartments, cooling and temperature control, basic systems of refrigerated commodities . . . frozen and chilled cargoes, fruit, CO_2 gas control. Containers . . . refrigerated cargoes. Non-insulated holds, systems applying. Modern marine cargo refrigeration . . . The Hall-Thermotank International Limited arrangements.

I. Unitized Cargoes
Containerization . . . its influence upon handling procedures. Lifting containers . . . loading and discharging. Carriage below and on deck. Sizes of containers. Systems of handling methods. Use of spreaders. Stuffing and stripping. Palletization . . . types of pallets and methods of handling, loading, securing and moving. The concept of unitized cargoes. The multi-purpose and roll on/roll off vessel. The indivisible heavy load.

J. Miscellaneous and Conventional
General . . . sugar, cotton, rice, barrels, casks, motor cars, deck cargoes . . . coke.

K. Petroleum

Tanker fleets, their growth and development. Cleaning of tanker compartments, including 'crude oil' processes. Pollution. General observations on petroleum carriage. Oil and oil products. Loading and discharging systems. Guide lines for tanker personnel . . . operating procedures. Tanker International Safety Guide. Liquefied natural gases . . . L.P.G. and L.N.G.

A Bulk Carrier

'A' BULK CARGOES—GENERAL

Bulk cargoes (in the main) comprise Iron and other Ores, Coal, Grain, Bauxite, Phosphates.

1. *Bulk Cargo, Conventional Vessels.*

The loading and discharging of bulk cargo can be cumbersome, not particularly a clean process and accompanied with various factors of delay with vessels not 'purpose built' as bulk carriers, of which the modern tendency is to find more applicable to the increasing tonnages and types of raw/bulk cargoes now available. There still will remain for some time the need to serve ports where the handling facilities are not highly sophisticated, and in these cases the carriage of quantities of bulk cargo will remain available to conventional vessels.

Where the 'bulk' is of a type to respond to suction loading and discharging, systems are now available whereby mobile hydraulic suction facilities, as part of a complete working unit, feed into and out of the hold or compartment by remote control. The mobile suction portion is capable of moving along the berth side, as work in the hold(s) dictate.

2. *Bulk Handling, Roll on/Roll off Systems*

In order to maintain the quick-turn-round reputation of roll on/ roll off vessels, it is essential that the cargo load is into and away from the ship with least delay. Where, in a fast-moving transport arrangement there is wide variations of light, moderate and heavy loads, the last must not be such as to introduce unnecessary delay, at the expense of the others. This is fundamental to the economics of ro-ro, and with normal working presents little, if any, difficulties, but the increase in the size and capacity of these vessels, and the type of loads they can carry, does raise problems of loading to take full advantage of space availability and those of discharge as will proceed quickly, without unanticipated restrictive delays.

This aspect of large-size roll on/roll off working can be seen from the introduction and development of large-size vehicular unit frames on to which unitized cargo of high tonnage and capacity can be placed, and moved into and out of the vessel through the ramp access.

Loads of up to 100 tons are possible on these lifting units. They are popularly known as 'LUF', and are of trailer construction on 32 wheels of special rubber manufacture, the mobility being provided by a tractor unit. In effect they are a further form of pallet, since a load is made up on to the trailer to form a compact load.

Experimentation with this system is being promoted on the North Sea Ferry Services with the vehicular unit moving four containers at a 2-high stack, in order to stow 2-high in the ship space without removal from the transport unit. The operators contend that 10 units can completely discharge a vessel and that it can be loaded again by replacement units in a matter of hours. It could be said that this is an adaption of the 'indivisible load' procedure, to which reference is made earlier in this book. It is, however, not restricted to container movement but can be equally useful for loads of packaged timber, paper rolls and large-size palletized goods.

3. *Part Bulk Loads . . . Intermediate Carriers*

Developments in the carriage of cargo in bulk form has moved towards 'part' as distinct from 'full' loads (bulk carriers) and has also changed the pattern of bagged or drummed bulk. forms of cargo, hitherto a common feature of conventional ship cargoes. Particularly, however, are these developments attractive to shippers who look for a method of moving relatively large tonnages, but not of sufficient quantity to warrant bulk carriage as such, and which can be more economical throughout transit by virtue of lesser damage risk, frequently a case with paper bags.

These 'so called' part bulk loads are now being carried in specially manufactured bags of cylindrical form of about 100 cm (girth and height) size and of such fabric material suitable to the use to which the bag is to be put. Capacities can be of the order of 1200 kilos and the bag can be lifted either by normal slinging, through lifting loops attached to its top, or it can be palletized. The system is a cleaner form of carriage from that of normal bags in that the tearing and splitting factor is less; solidarity of load is more compact and, where palletization is employed, the use of mechanical handling is possible. Furthermore, these bags lend themselves to container stowage.

The material of manufacture is appropriate to temperature variations in that different classes of bags can meet the sub-zero or high tropical ranges, thus providing for carriage which otherwise might well suffer damage if carried in hitherto conventional methods.

The bags are known as 'intermediate bulk containers', the term having obvious definition. Some of the types of bags are disposal; they are all filled, and emptied by, and through, inserted arrangements and all fit into the through transport context in that their form is readily changeable from one type of carriage to another, source to destination.

The development also includes non-collapsible rigid 'containers' built into a supporting framework and forming a unit in itself which is easily transportable by fork lift truck and stowed in the vessels on unitized pattern.

INTERMEDIATE BULK CARRIERS (I.B.C.s)

Intermediate bulk carriers take on a number of forms but in each the object is to provide a means of transportation easily adaptable to modern handling transportation techniques, convenient to the shipper in terms of quantities distribution; cargo protectiveness and versatility of use. Normally in bag form, I.B.C.s are also available in tank and bin design, the former extensively used for chemical commodities.

One type of I.B.C. used for dry goods and being widely applied to maritime transport is the 'mini bulk' carrier, manufactured and marketed by Pertwee Industrial Limited, Harbour House, Colchester, Essex, England, with whose kind permission the following notes are included.

1. The range of 'mini bulk' carriers cover:

   mini Bulk Standard Single Lift: comprising a 2000 denier woven polypropylene container with a single lifting harness attached to four paired sub-loops, a discharge chute with tie cord and document pocket.

   mini Bulk Standard 4 Loop Lift: comprising a 2000 denier woven polypropylene container with 4 lifting loops a discharge chute with tie cord.

   mini Bulk Landforce: comprising a 2000 denier woven polypropylene container with 4 lifting loops. A seamed discharge hole is cut in the base. One polypropylene base cover insert.

   mini Bulk 1 Trip: comprising a 2000 denier woven polypropylene container with 4 lifting loops.

   Safe working load for all mini Bulk containers is 1 tonne.

   The above product range is available in the following sizes:

   Size Code 1 29 in × 29 in × 54 in—26 cu ft capacity
   Size Code 2 35 in × 35 in × 48 in—34 cu ft capacity
   Size Code 3 35 in × 35 in × 57 in—42 cu ft capacity
   Size Code 4 35 in × 35 in × 66 in—49 cu ft capacity

2. Illustration (p. 129) shows 'mini bulk' handling by fork lift truck.

3. In terms of ship carriage and cargo handling the following is an extract from research carried out by the manufacturers.
   mini Bulk is our trade name for a system of 1 tonne flexible containers which are made from 2000 denier woven polypropylene. Our container is based on a top loop lift principle which simply means we have developed a flexible container which will carry 1 tonne of dry free flowing material and it is lifted by either using a single lift or 4 lifting loops attached to the top of the container, the lifting loops being manufactured from nylon or terylene webbing. In our range we have 4 types and 4 sizes of container each designed to carry a tonne with a 5:1 safety factor, the different sizes are to enable customers to carry 1 tonne of varying densities of materials.

   To date mini Bulk has been used to ship materials from ports in the U.K. to locations in Europe, South Africa and the U.S.A. and this field of activity should shortly be extended to cover ports throughout the world. We are now selling mini Bulk to companies in 17 countries and they are being used to carry such materials as clay, plastics/P.V.C., fertilizers, base ore materials, food stuffs and powders of varying types.

To date the ships carrying mini Bulk have been of a small tonnage carrying from 500–2000 tonnes. mini Bulk is ideally suited for movement by sea because it can be easily loaded and off loaded with conventional dock side gear. No pallets are required as the lifting loops are utilized,

Intermediate Bulk Carrier

two loops being used to each hook on a two point lifting mechanism. When four lifting hooks are available on a crane two containers can be lifted as per attached photocopy. Storing in a ships hold presents no problem as long as the hatch openings leave clear access to complete storage compartment. When a cantilever effect is left because hatch openings are small a fork lift truck can be lowered to ensure that maximum storage capacity is used. The containers can be stored up to 5 high and again pallets are not used. mini Bulk does represent a major breakthrough in the handling of ships cargoes because loading and unloading can be reduced by more than 30 per cent and the labour force required at docks can be reduced accordingly to the facilities available. There is a tremendous reduction in the amount of waste materials due to split sacks on pallets and unloading of granular material is virtually dust free. The high factor of safety built into mini Bulk means that the system has been accepted by dockers in all ports so far used and when required safety certificates can be supplied.

The intermediate bulk carrier caters for the amounts larger than can be carried in conventional bags or sacks but less than is profitable for normal bulk carriage. One ton disposal units seem to be the more usual but capacities of up to 3 tons are available for multi-trip use. The difference is largely one of cost. An overriding advantage claimed is the aspect of 'one operation' . . . filled and lifted for loading and/or lifted and discharged, avoiding numerous otherwise handling procedures involving package contamination and breakage. The I.B.C. can be mechanically handled by fork lift truck, can be palletized and is ideal for container stowage. Environmentally, these methods are favourably acceptable to labour where fertilizer, cements and chemical products are being handled.

Tank I.B.C.s are now being used extensively for fruit emulsion derivatives.

An interesting feature of bulk carriage is the tendency to process bulk commodities at source. The method has acceptance with some 'ore' products, some chemicals and also edible foodstuffs and thus permits a unitized cargo form . . . suitable for containers, rather than would be otherwise a break bulk cargo activity. This promotes less time in port (quick turn round) and a reduction in cargo handling, as such.

IRON AND STEEL CARGOES

Iron and steel cargoes can comprise pig iron, steel billets, steel coils, round bars, pipes and iron and steel swarf. Each contains a danger risk of shifting, if not secured effectively and cases are on record of mishaps to ships by reason of insecure stowage. In general terms these cargoes not only need to have individual securing arrangements, such as lashings and/or interlocking but, preferably, should be overstowed with other suitable cargo.

The Department of Trade and Industry Shipping Notice M 813, 1978, points to specific cases.

Pig Iron

    (*a*) Only the smallest necessary weight load should be carried in 'tween decks as to prevent undue stiffness in a vessel. A vessel is 'safer' with a reasonably large GM, should there be a shift of the pig iron, than being in a tender state.

    (*b*) The pig iron should be trimmed level, both in lower hold and in 'tween deck stowage.

    (*c*) Where the above is not the case, nor is it possible to overstow, the pig iron should be stowed in bins, formed by the bulkheads, the ship's sides, hatch coamings and either fore and aft, or transverse shifting boards of robust form and dimension, not less than 3 in thick, supported by uprights 5 ft apart and rising above the level of the pig iron.

        The maximum height of a pig iron cargo in an 8 ft 'tween deck must be such as not to cause structural distortion. Compared with normal cargo stowage of about 50 cu ft per ton, the height for pig iron stowing at about 11 cu ft per ton, should be $11/50 \times 8$, i.e. $1\frac{3}{4}$ ft.

    (*d*) 'Glossy finished' pig iron, which has a smooth finish, should be loaded on to a wooden ceiling or wood dunnage, well levelled out and into the wings of holds. In 'tween decks it should conform to the recommendations contained in (*c*).

Steel Billets. These must be effectively overstowed, especially if carried in 'tween decks. Where possible, it is better to load them into holds where tunnels, or other obstructions, will restrict movement. Tomming and/or other securing provisions are desirable with these cargoes.

Steel Coils. Great care is needed in stowing and securing cargoes of steel coils. Wherever possible, they should be stowed in regular tiers from side to side of the vessel, making full use of pillars, stantions and centre line bulkheads, and the like. It is preferable for the coils to be stowed 'on the round' each coil hard up against its neighbour, with wedges of dunnage driven well home under the rounds. Ample 'small timber' should be available to block off and secure a solid stow, as it settles.

Round Bars and Pipes. Levelling out is not sufficient. Additional precautions are necessary, in the form of strong wires, adequately set up and by careful 'tomming'.

Steel Plates. Wherever it is not possible to stow steel plates where they cannot be locked by the boundaries of timber spacing, they should be independently secured by chain or wire lashings, as well as by 'tomming'. Steel plates are prone to slip over decks, other cargoes or their own surfaces and constitute a high risk, likely to be impossible to overcome by restowage at sea.

The notice sites 8 examples in the Appendix of dangerous circumstances following non-observance of the above precautions. Officers are recommended to study these in full.

The notice also draws particular attention to the precautions where these cargoes form only a part of the deadweight cargo of a vessel such as would be the case in first loading the 'iron and steel' commodities at one port before proceeding to another to complete, not an unusual practice on the coasts of the U.K. and the continent.

Attention is drawn to D.o.T. Merchant Shipping Notice No. M 831, which indicates possible sources of danger which can arise from inadequate stowage with the foregoing cargoes.

Iron and Steel Swarf. This cargo is liable to overheating and spontaneous combustion if, loaded as a bulk, it is wet or contaminated with materials such as unsaturated cutting oils, oily rags or paper known to be liable to over heating. The finer the turnings, cuttings or grindings, the more liable they are to heat.

D.o.T. Shipping Notice M 909—1979, draws attention to these hazards and recommends:

> (*a*) that bilges strums and rose boxes are free and clear before commencement of loading;
> (*b*) fire appliances and pumps are in order;
> (*c*) any water which may enter the space is pumped out immediately; and
> (*d*) thermometers are available for watching the temperature of the swarf.

Surface temperatures of swarf may reach 48°C (120°F) immediately after loading and then quickly fall. Further loading should not continue until the temperatures show a decided downward trend. Should a rise go above 38°C (100°F), the area around the pocket should be raked, or agitated, to a depth of about 30 cm (12 in).

Discretion must be observed in turning back the hatch covers (in dry weather only) to allow heat to disperse. Should the temperature rise above 65°C (150°F) the Master should make for the nearest port.

The Carriage of Dangerous Goods in Ships (the 'Blue Book') recommends that iron and steel swarf should be carried in effectively closed steel drums. It recommends, also, that its shipment should be within home trade limits. Outside of these limits this should be only after consultation with the appropriate Ministry.

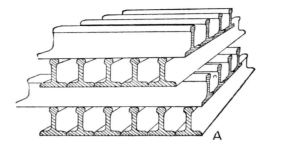

Fig. 4.1

Steel Rails. This cargo needs great care in stowage to prevent its movement during the voyages and also to avoid an unduly stiff ship.

Considerable heavy wood dunnage will be required in order to build a floor on which to stow the rails, and also to shore off at the ends and sides of the compartment.

For loading in the lower holds, two methods of stowage are suitable.

1. Successive tiers interlocked ('rail up' and 'rail down') as shown in diagram B.
2. The first 3 or 4 tiers stowed flat, with the remaining tiers grating fashion, as shown in diagram A.

The weight of a full cargo of steel rails will not permit its entire stowage in the lower holds and part of the consignment will have to be given 'tween deck stowage in order to raise the weight.

Heavy planks should be arranged at the bulkheads to avoid damage to them and also to prevent the rails moving in a fore and aft direction with the pitching of the vessel, whilst chocking with timber is necessary at the sides of the compartment.

Part of the consignment of rails, appropriately stowed, may be used in place of timber to prevent damage to the ship's side and the bulkheads.

It is advisable to provide efficient chain and wire lashings, whilst lengths of old rope laid between tiers help to provide a compact stow.

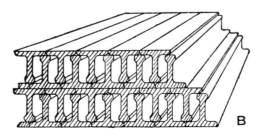

Fig. 4.2

Tomming from the deck head beams may be necessary, but if heavy cases are available they be stowed on top of the rails to prevent movement.

THE CARRIAGE OF SOLID BALLAST

While ballast, in itself, is not strictly a cargo, it presents similar problems as regards safety and seaworthiness and, it is the responsibility of the Master and Officers to take all reasonable precautions to ensure that a vessel in ballast is seaworthy.

As seaworthiness is largely dependent upon stowage, it is as well that all officers should apply to ballast stowage the same principles of care as they do to normal cargoes.

Types of solid ballast with which care must be taken include, shale—mainly mine refuse; colliery stones—brittle and slatey; slag; sand, shingle and Thames ballast—a mixture of sand and stone, all of which have angles of repose liable to cause shifting in heavy weather, added to which, as they are usually shipped in varying degrees of wetness, dry out during the voyage and become even more liable to shift.

It would appear that the critical angle of rolling is around 30° and that the usual prudent measures most effective are:

1. The ballast should be well spread out and trimmed level.
2. Stiffeners and shifting boards of adequate strength and stiffness should be fitted.
3. A reasonable quantity—approximately about one-third of the total—should be distributed over the after lower holds on either side of the shaft tunnel. Ballast carried in the holds is less liable to shift than that carried in the 'tween decks.
4. Stability should be such as results in a reasonably active metacentric height. With some ships a GM of 5–6 ft is not unreasonable for ample stability has an important effect in minimizing a resulting list and also provides a measure of reserve against wind and weather.

Shifting boards are recommended for the carriage of solid ballast in the holds, 'tween decks and on deck and the notice referred to tabulates their sizes, disposition and strengthening in relation to the amount of ballast carried.

It is considered necessary to include detail of the Ministry requirements and it strongly urges all officers to study the above principles and substantiate such by reference to the appropriate Ministry notice.

Briefly, however, the following Ministry observations are worthy of thought and study:

(a) Strength and stiffness is necessary in the rigging of shifting boards if these are to be really effective.

(b) Solid ballast may be carried on deck, in the 'tween decks or in the lower holds, but shifting is less likely when it is carried in the holds and undue stiffness should not arise with the lower hold distribution about one-third of the total ballast, loaded into the afterholds on either side of the tunnel or tunnels.

(c) Fore and aft distribution also requires attention, particularly in regard to the normal weight distribution of the vessel in order to avoid undue stress on the structure.

Fore and aft distribution should be well spread out and trimmed reasonably level.

(d) Shifting boards are recommended for hold, 'tween deck or deck stowage of solid ballast. In the holds there should be at least two rows of shifting boards; in 'tween decks not less than two rows, so that the deck space is divided into three compartments, bearing in mind the greater tendency for shifting with 'tween deck stowage.

MINERAL PRODUCTS IN BULK

Cargo Constituents. Mineral products, such as mineral concentrates and their similar associates like metallic residues, phosphates or industrial ash; fine coals and coal slurries and anthracite duff constitutes a hazard when carried in bulk and although the I.M.O. Code of Safe Practice for Bulk Cargoes draws attention to this, the U.K. Department of Transport considers it necessary to provide more detailed advice on the precautions necessary with such cargoes. This it does in Merchant Shipping Notice No. M746, 1976.

In general terms it is necessary:

1. For the Master of a ship contemplating the carriage of such cargoes to be given, by the shipper, beforehand, in approved certificate form, certain precise information of the major influencing constituents of the cargo, as will support his responsibilities in safely transporting the cargo.
2. Desirable that the Master of the ship having carried such cargoes, to report to the U.K. Marine Division of the Department of Transport, information gathered from experiences of carriage.

Both the former, and the latter requirements are aimed at providing the best guidance available in the prevention of hazard development with cargoes of this nature which, in the main, are subject to shifting by reason of wetness or moisture which may aggravate a solid state to become fluid, because of ship movement and vibration.

The carriage of cargoes of this nature require that certain 'states and conditions' are understood. For example, a mineral concentrate is a fine granule extracted by crushing and processing from the products of ore bearing rock.

Coal slurry is fine particles of coal, generally under 1 mm in size, containing a large proportion of inerts, i.e. moisture and mineral matter. Other fine coals, mainly below 6 mm in size, also fall within these characteristics, such as anthracite duff.

Influences upon the safe carriage of these 'fine mineral products' include the *moisture content* which, by definition, is the amount of moisture present in a sample, expressed as a percentage of the total wet weight. The 'average moisture content', which is the moisture content of a complete cargo, is, in fact, one of the criteria by which the safety of the cargo is assessed. The *flow moisture point* or *critical moisture point* (to which it is sometimes referred), is the moisture content at which a fluid state could occur. As such, it is vitally important for this 'state' to be ascertained, and is, in fact, laid down in the I.M.O. code. Indeed, the safe carriage of these cargoes is limited to the 'material' having a moisture content nine-tenths the flow moisture point; known as *the transportable moisture* limit.

The inclination properties of these cargoes, in stow, is also important and gives rise to the term *angle of repose* . . . that being between the horizontal plane and the cone shape which forms when the bulk is loaded on to a horizontal plane surface.

Principles of Stowage and Carriage.

1. In view of the foregoing it will be appreciated that the information to be provided for the Master contains:
   (*a*) The flow moisture point.
   (*b*) The average moisture content.
   (*c*) The angle of repose.
   (*d*) General aspects on the physical properties of the cargo.

2. Bulk cargoes having a low angle of repose are liable to shift and the I.M.O. code draws distinction between cargoes having such characteristics greater than 35°, or equal to or less than 35°. Notices of this is essential in loading procedures, particularly so in small coasters.

3. Desirably, these cargoes should be loaded into lower holds. 'Tween deck stowage is permitted, but only if the information provided on the cargo is considered to adequately indicate acceptable safety limits.

4. These are cargoes which necessitate precise and careful attention to clean and clear bilges, strums/rose boxes and tight limber boards. The bilges should be regularly pumped out.

5. Trimming of the cargo should, as far as is reasonable and practicable, be into the wings and to the ends of a compartment.

6. Prevention of any water or wetness entering any compartment so loaded is essential, which points to the closing and/or covering of any openings during wet weather, or before proceeding to sea.
7. Certain types of these cargoes may emit flammable or toxic fumes. This fact must be recognized, and ascertained beforehand and no personnel be permitted to enter any compartment before it is adequately ventilated.

Testing. Arrangements are provided for the testing of these commodities before shipment. Approved centres are in being for this purpose and the procedures to be followed are laid down in the I.M.O. Code. It is vitally important that the *average moisture content* is determined.

Ideally, the most satisfactory time for testing for moisture content is immediately before the cargo is loaded into the ship, bearing in mind the possibilities of wetness accruing from the various forms of transportation (lorries, wagons, etc.) by which the bulk may reach the vessel.

Stability. Irrespective of the importance which should be attached to any type of cargo, in any type of ship, relative to stability qualities and conditions, it has particular relevance to bulk carriage and even more so with the carriage of concentrates. In the case of these mineral products under review, and relevant to the stability requirements under the 'Survey of Load Line Ships . . . Instructions for the Guidance of Surveyors', specific factors of 'stability condition' must be met before loading.

General. Experience of vessels foundering as a result of inadequate attention to these outline notes points to the need for all cargo officers being involved with mineral concentrates in bulk, fully studying the Merchant Shipping Notice 972.

'B' COAL CARGOES

Coal remains a bulk cargo commodity internationally transported; Japan, for example, imports high tonnages of metalurgical coal for its steel industry while, of recent years, modern loading facilities have been built at Immingham, England, for the export of coal from the U.K.

Considerable risk attaches to coal cargoes. Coal, under certain conditions, evolves *methane*, known as marsh gas or fire damp.

In methane-air mixtures, in proportions ranging from 5·3 to 13·87 per cent, by volume of methane, a spark will produce explosion.

Apart from the explosion risk, there is the risk due to spontaneous combustion. This is due to causes other than those leading to explosion.

The risk of explosion becomes greater with broken coal, in either transit or loading, or when the coal has been freshly worked and stowed in a compartment where older coal yet remains. This is a risk attached to bunkering.

It is considered that spontaneous combustion is the cause of 14 per cent of the fires in coal cargoes and to reduce this possibility to the minimum, two precautions stand out prominently from those generally taken with all cargoes. These are that the coal shall be

(a) kept as cool as possible, and
(b) free from any suggestion of through ventilation.

In considering the carriage of a coal cargo, the outstanding question is 'surface ventilation' of the gases which are given off by the coal as from the introduction of quantities of air into the bulk of the cargo which promotes spontaneous combustion.

It should, therefore, be appreciated that only surface ventilation be given to any mass of coal. Ventilation into a mass of coal is dangerous.

Where it is possible to use ventilators which project well above the upper deck, as for example, those which are fitted through deck houses, these should be devoted to coal ventilation. These ventilators are less liable to damage from heavy seas which might fracture less protected coamings and so allow water to enter the holds. Masts and derrick posts fitted as ventilators are ideal in this respect.

Generally speaking, each compartment in which coal is stowed, should be provided with at least two ventilators, one at each end of the compartment.

These shall be so arranged that one shall be an 'inlet' and the other an 'outlet' so that a continuous and unrestricted flow of air passes over the surface of the coal. During fine weather it is advisable to open up hatch coverings in order to facilitate the 'surface ventilation'.

Before coal is loaded the ship's hold should be well swept, the cargo battens (or spar ceiling) removed (if left in place they would allow air to circulate between the cargo and the ship's side) and the bilges thoroughly cleaned. After the limber boards have been replaced, the seams should be caulked or the boards covered with old tarpaulins, secured by wooden battens. With some varieties of coal, such as those shipped as 'peas and beans' and those of the anthracite and smaller types, it is considered advisable to rig fore and aft bulkheads to serve as shifting boards.

These boards should be covered with some impervious material, such as cloth or thick brown paper, to prevent any flow of air through the spaces between the boards.

When the coal is carried in both lower holds and 'tween decks, the ventilators should be independent. That is to say, each compartment should have its own 'inlet' and 'outlet' ventilators in order to promote independent surface ventilation. When a cargo of coal is destined for a far distant port, it is prudent that 'for the first five days after loading, all ventilators should be used for removing the gases, after which, the ventilators to the lower holds should be plugged and only opened for about six hours every two days'.

All reasonable means should be taken to keep the compartments cool; awnings can be used to great advantage in tropical latitudes, while the covering of the whole of the upper deck with wooden dunnage would considerably lessen heating from the sun's rays.

Any temperature over $77°F$ is considered critical with a mass of coal. Spontaneous heating is accelerated at $100°F$ with some varieties of coal.

In order to keep a check on the heating of the cargo during the voyage, means should be provided whereby the temperatures may be taken regularly. Pipes led into the cargo, provided due care is taken to prevent air circulation, allow temperatures to be taken at intermediate depths of a compartment.

Naked lights should never be allowed in a coal compartment; any inspection should be made with the aid of torches or Davy lamps; a number of the latter should be carried in all coal carrying vessels.

Due regard should be paid to the discharge of the coal. The compartments need to be well ventilated before men can safely enter them, and it should be realized that the sudden influx of air to coal compartments immediately before discharge may have disastrous results. Careful ventilation should be directed towards removing the gases from both 'tween decks and lower holds before the ship arrives.

Explosion from flammable gas is present where this accumulates and is unable to escape . . . adequate ventilation for this escape of gas must be provided. Furthermore, naked lights must be prohibited near to spaces in which coal is carried. Artificial lighting must be of an approved type in vessels normally engaged in coal cargoes, otherwise power and supplies should be discontinued.

Coal slurry is a cargo which contains moisture and there is a tendency for this to rise to the surface. As a result, the upper portions of the cargo is loosened, becomes mobile and its possible movement is accentuated by ship vibration. The need therefore arises to provide adequate and efficient means to prevent this movement while, also, the prevention of water gaining access to such a cargo is important.

Hot Coal

Since coal is becoming an increasing bulk cargo, and being shipped over long distances, it is as well that Cargo Officers should be aware of certain hazards to which particular attention is necessary.

To some extent this essential care results from recent shipments of coal, termed Pond Coal, left over from earlier mining and dumped into ponds and lakes, to be later reclaimed for shipment. The situation was peculiar to coal shipped from the southern U.S.A. (lower Mississippi ports) for transportation to Europe and the Far

East. It took on the name of 'Hot Coal' since so shipped, with a high water content, it was highly dangerous and also was not free of a high sulphur condition. It was a type of coal giving rise to high temperatures from self heating during a long voyage, such that, in the absence of preventative measures, 220° F being not uncommon, against a safety level of 130°F.

Where this type of coal may still form shipments particularly, are safety considerations necessary with voyages passing through the tropics.

Much depends, with a coal cargo, upon its type and content, be it of high water content, sulphuric or the size of the coal particles and the amount of volatiles present. The methods of loading are also important.

As a result of the problems involved certain conclusions have arisen and are worthy of consideration, not only for the trades indicated above, but also towards 'all' coal cargoes.

High quality coals generate a high methane gas content and thus are more likely to induce explosive reaction. Lower grade coals lose their gas content more quickly since they are of a more porous nature.

Trimming of 'long haul' coal cargoes has been found to be a safer procedure than with a hold of coal solidly into a conical mass from being tipped from a height. The coal, in effect, by trimming, can be spread out more evenly so that the coarser heavier content can be to the sides and bottom of the pile, where more opportunity for gas freeing for the finer granules towards the top can pertain. Ships (and the ports involved) must be aware of these potential dangers.

While the distances of transportation do allow for the gaseous element to diminish (or disappear) the spontaneous factor remains.

Apart from the accepted procedures of keeping coal as cool as possible, and avoiding any question of through ventilation, (see page 169) attention is drawn to the I.M.C.O. (now known as I.M.O. International Maritime Organization) Code relating to safety measures to avoid fires from overheating in coal cargoes.

Doubtless influences from the experience of the U.S.A. southern states have had bearing upon this code none the less, its guide lines are strict. Apart from the continuous necessary attention to be given to temperature checking in the holds containing coal, it points out that where hold temperatures reach 55°C and are showing rapidly rising tendencies, the cargo spaces should be closed down.

An interesting feature of coal carriage development as a bulk shipment is an overall design of vessel which, irrespective of a d.w. tonnage of 100 000 tons, permits a stowage factor of 46 cu. ft. per ton, as against the normal of 42/44 with conventional bulk carriers and, at the same time, the vessel has shallow draft of 12·6 m, permitting the better use of ports water facilities. The vessel is of Japanese design with a L.O.A. of 240 m and a beam of 50 m. (Note—this is one example of the influence of Patterns of Trade).

Official Guide Lines

Official recognition of the hazards attendent upon the carriage of coal is contained in Department of Transport M Notices 970 and 971.

Although the general provisions of the I.M.O. (International Maritime Organization) Bulk Cargo Code will be followed for coal cargoes it is pointed out that with small coal, slurry, duff and coke, the danger of liquefaction of the cargo is considerable and that careful attention to testing and sampling procedures is vital. (See page 216).

For single cargoes tests for moisture content and transportable moisture limit should be carried out before shipment, but with consignments regularly and frequently shipped from the same source, it is generally recognized that regular testing will establish a set of values which may be accepted, provided that the interval between tests does not exceed 4 months.

The Master's duties are to ensure he has proper information, that the tests are recent and that the stability condition of the ship is satisfactory for the intended cargo.

In M971 the main hazard discussed is the emission of flammable gas. It is necessary to ensure that bulkheads at the boundaries and decks of spaces utilization are gas tight, so that accommodation and stores, and machinery spaces, are not affected by gas. Electrical equipment in the holds must be safe or disconnected . . . the aim being to prevent sources of ignition wherever gas is likely to be present.

Combined with Notice M970, these guide lines summarize the situation and amplify the I.M.O. Code in respect of coal cargoes.

'C' DANGEROUS CARGOES

The growth of the chemical and petrochemical industries and the increasing industrialization of many nations with consequent increases in the demands for complex materials for processing has resulted in an enormous growth in the carriage of hazardous materials by sea, be they solids, liquids or gases. It is essential for all concerned with the carriage of these materials to appreciate fully the extent to which they are regulated by official requirements. In outlining the regulations and giving a general explanation, it must be emphasized that in every case where dangerous goods are carried, the regulations must be consulted for proper information, and that neither shipper, handler nor ship's officer should rely on memory, nor assume knowledge of any consignment.

There are three publications relating to the carriage of dangerous goods by sea. These are, firstly, the Merchant Shipping (Dangerous Goods) Rules 1981 (S.I. 1981, No. 1747). Secondly, the I.M.O. (formerly I.M.C.O.) Dangerous Goods Code (generally known as the I.M.D.G. Code). The third publication is the Report of the Standing Advisory Committee of the Department of Trade, which is usually referred to as 'the Blue Book'. This is often confused with the Dangerous Goods Rules, but in fact is not part of the latter except in so far as its requirements are mandatory under the rules.

(i) *The Merchant Shipping (Dangerous Goods) Rules*
The rules apply to United Kingdom ships and to other ships whilst they are working cargo or embarking or disembarking passengers or bunkering or discharging fuel within the United Kingdom or in U.K. Territorial Waters. Where these ships have loaded in accordance with the laws of their own country, being a member of the 1978 Protocol relating to the 1974 SOLAS Convention, the U.K. requirements are deemed to have been compiled with.

An important section of the rules imposes duties on Master, shipowner or employer of persons (Master in the case of non-U.K. ships) to ensure the health and safety of any person likely to be affected by the handling and carriage of dangerous goods. This includes attention to the condition and suitability of the cargo gear, the method of stowage and, a point not previously included, the proper instruction and delivery of information regarding the specific hazards of the cargo, to the crew. At the same time, each employee is required to take reasonable care in the course of his time aboard the ship not only of himself but of other persons who may be aboard. Misconduct by any person in this regard is now an offence.

However, the main purpose of the 1981 rules is to set out specific requirements as to the labelling, handling, stowage and documentation of dangerous goods. For packaged goods and bulk materials, the following outline of the requirements indicates the general scope of the rules:

Goods are divided by reason of their hazard, into the following categories:—

Class 1 — Explosives.
Class 2 — Gases compressed, liquefied or dissolved under pressure, subdivided into three categories:
    2.1— Flammable gases;
    2.2— Non-flammable gases, being compressed, liquefied or dissolved, but neither flammable nor poisonous;
    2.3— Poisonous gases.
Class 3 — Flammable liquids, subdivided into three categories:
    3.1— Low flashpoint group of liquids having a flashpoint below $-18°C$ ($10°F$), closed cup test;
    3.2— Intermediate flashpoint group of liquids having a flashpoint of $-18°C$ ($10°F$) up to, but not including, $23°C$ ($73°F$), closed cup test;
    3.3— High flashpoint group of liquids having a flashpoint of $23°C$ ($73°F$) up to and including $61°C$ ($141°F$), closed cup test.

Class 4.1 — Flammable solids.
Class 4.2 — Substances liable to spontaneous combustion.
Class 4.3 — Substances which in contact with water emit flammable gases.
Class 5.1 — Oxidizing substances (agents).
Class 5.2 — Organic peroxides.
Class 6.1 — Poisonous (toxic) substances.
Class 6.2 — Infectious substances.
Class 7   — Radioactive substances.
Class 8   — Corrosives.
Class 9   — Miscellaneous dangerous substances which present a danger not covered by other classes.

Before shipment, the shipper must declare in writing the nature and class of the goods, together with information on the number and type of packages, weight, flashpoint (if appropriate) and the total quantity of goods, and if the goods are packed in a container or vehicle, the person packing them must also certify as to the condition of the container or vehicle and the efficacy of the stowage within it. In all cases the correct labelling must be attached. It is the duty of the Master to set out a plan or separate manifest indicating where goods are stowed on board the ship, whether stowed as general cargo, or in a container modular stow, or in a vehicle on ro/ro ship. Packaging of all dangerous goods is subject to strict standards. Apart from being well-made and in good condition, the nature of the package must be such as not to react with the contents, and in the case of liquids be sufficient to absorb the contents should the receptacle break. It is an overriding requirement that goods shall not be taken on board if the shipowner or his employees or agents know or ought to know that packaging is insufficient to withstand the ordinary rigours of carriage by sea.

The marking of packages or containers, or road tank vehicles as appropriate, is equally strict. Labels must be attached to all packages or containers indicating the Class of goods and their hazard, according to the designs specified in the Blue Book, or the I.M.D.G. Code (there is in fact no difference between them). The quality of the marking is important. On the outer package the marking must be capable of surviving at least three months' immersion in the sea, or if the package itself will not survive that period then the durable marking must be on the inner receptacle. On road tank vehicles or tanks and containers suitable for road transport, the marking and labelling must be, not only durable as described above, but on each side and at each end (tanks and containers) or on the rear end (vehicles). There is a code of practice for the construction of such tanks and vehicles as part of the Blue Book contents.

With regard to stowage the rules are, of necessity, general. Goods must be stowed in a safe and proper manner, for goods of the class, and with adequate ventilation. Where reaction or interaction between two different parcels of cargo is likely, these must be kept effectively segregated, and similar provisions apply to goods stowed in containers.

Explosives must be stowed either in a magazine or in a compartment which is electrically safe, and with certain limited exceptions, must not be carried on passenger ships.

It must be remembered that certain commodities classified as dangerous may be carried as bulk shipments and in such cases the rules refer to the appropriate I.M.O. Code for Bulk Dangerous Chemicals or Bulk Liquefied Gases; provided the provisions of these codes are followed in the case of any particular shipment, then the Dangerous Goods Rules are deemed to have been complied with.

(ii) *The Blue Book (1984 Edition)*

The place of the Blue Book is expressed in the Book itself where the Standing Advisory Committee reports that ... 'in general, the recommendations of the Blue Book and the I.M.O Dangerous Goods Code are in harmony'. The differences found in the Blue Book are those relating to the carriage of explosives and certain other substances where the I.M.D.G. Code states that packaging or other requirements are to be in accordance with national standards. The Blue Book details these standards for the United Kingdom, and with regard to explosives, details the recommendations for military explosives, which have different requirements from commercial. The former would be loaded under the control of H.M. Government or of a visiting army representative. The remainder of the book details the design and constructional features required for portable tanks and road tank vehicles for the carriage of liquid dangerous goods in ships, and a list of tank requirements for such liquids.

(iii) *The I.M.D.G. Code*

The I.M.O. Dangerous Goods Code results from a resolution embodied in the 1960 International Convention for the Safety of Life at Sea. The code is now in six volumes, and obviously to present any summary in a book of this nature is merely to reinforce the caution that the code must always be referred to before accepting any shipment of dangerous goods, so that the provisions of the code are always adhered to.

The code appears as six volumes. Volume 1 contains a general introduction, and the remaining five volumes consist of the full list of known dangerous goods, arranged in the same nine categories as are listed in the 1981 regulations referred to above.

The purpose of the introduction is to describe the classes of goods, the label designs and colours, and the general requirements for stowage. In this connection the guiding principle is the need to segregate most consignments from others likely to interact, or to provide safeguards where leakage of cargo would be injurious to the health and safety of crew and passengers. For example, flammable or explosive substances must be effectively segregated from possible sources of ignition, or a substance liable to emit toxic fumes or gas must not be stowed where such emission could penetrate any part of the accommodation. To facilitate stowage planning the code provides a segregation table or matrix in which all classes of goods are tabulated according to four categories of stowage requirement. These requirements are (1) *Stow 'away from'*, that is separated by a minimum distance of 3 m between the two consignments, but may be carried in the same hold or compartment. (2) *Separated from*, where the two consignments must be in separate holds, or in the same hold provided an intervening fire resistant deck intervenes, (3) separated by a complete compartment or hold, which is self explanatory and (4) separated longitudinally by an intervening complete compartment or hold, which means that vertical separation alone will not suffice. Stowage on deck means the upper deck or main deck, not a shelter deck or tween deck compartment. In the main body of the code these expressions occur in respect of every item. It must be pointed out that when dangerous goods are packed in containers, the segregation expressions described above are still valid.

In the case of goods carried on vehicles in a ro/ro ship, stowage and segregation are effected by separation of vehicles carrying incompatible loads, but care has to be taken that no sources of ignition (e.g. power units of temperature controlled container vehicles) are allowed where there is any possibility of the emission of flammable gases from other loads.

In the specimen pages from the Blue Book and the I.M.D.G. Code, reproduced below, it can be seen that the format and information are often identical and the numbered arrows form the basis of a checklist which should be developed by any cargo officer on a ship where dangerous consignments are offered, so that he is fully conversant with the nature of the goods and the requirements for this safe carriage and stowage. He should never rely on memory, but always refer to the codes, and make a careful study of the introductory sections for full detailed guidance.

Dangerous Goods in Bulk

In other parts of this book, reference was made to bulk cargoes and it is important to establish the link between the requirements for dangerous goods and these cargoes. Many substances listed in the I.M.D.G. Code are carried in bulk and therefore are also treated in the I.M.O. Bulk Cargo Code. It is not sufficient to refer only to the latter, since this considers problems of weight distribution, fluidity and movement but not necessarily the hazards of flammability, toxicity or reactivity. For dangerous liquid chemicals these may only be carried on ships having a certificate of fitness, so that the hazards listed in the I.M.D.G. Code are continually in view. The Code of Practice for the construction of ships carrying bulk liquid chemicals lists substances which can only be carried in specially constructed vessels, and any requirements of the I.M.D.G. Code will automatically be met by such ships.

Chemical cargoes in bulk present their own hazards. Among others, these can be poisonous, irritating and reactively dangerous by contact with other materials, and by water. Also, they can be flammable and/or spontaneously combustionable.

Chemical carriage in the modern industrial world can include coal and tar derivatives, animal and vegetable oils, carbohydrates derivatives as well as petrochemicals.

Ships for the carriage of chemical cargoes have to meet specialized designs standards while the I.M.O. (International Maritime Organization . . . formerly I.M.C.O.) Codes of Carriages are very strict in their application. Apart from general health safeguards, attention is drawn to the problems of fire, water and air pollution. Ship's officers, in co-ordination with ports personnel . . . and the facilities available . . . must constantly be aware of chemical cargo hazards.

THE CARRIAGE OF DANGEROUS CHEMICALS IN BULK

Merchant Shipping Notice M576
The carriage of dangerous chemicals give rise to danger from asphyxiation and/or effects of toxic or other harmful vapours on entry into tanks and other enclosed spaces.

This is the substance of the above notice and indicates clearly the responsibilities incumbent upon officers where work with tanks and spaces in which certain chemicals have been carried involve personnel.

In this context reference to Notice M576 is probably of special interest since it indicates the provisions encouraged since 1971 whereby the construction of vessels intended for the carriage of dangerous chemicals in bulk should meet certain standards; indeed, as with other pertinent recommendations relating to safety of ships and crew, the Inter-Governmental Maritime Consultative Organization adopted and approved a code, since when considerable acceptance of the requirements have been carried out. Vessels intending to carry such dangerous chemicals require to have certificates of fitness and the notice lists some 50 or more substances for which a certificate is appropriate and some 40 or more where this is not so, but it does not follow that these lists can, or will remain exhaustive and the attention of cargo officers is drawn to the necessity of keeping up to date with relevant information where their duties involve them with these form of substances.

The general precautions outlined in Notice M576 restrict the entry of personnel into tanks, void spaces and other cargo handling spaces where dangerous chemicals are, or have been carried, unless authorized by a responsible officer. Even so, any suspect that any such spaces are not free of toxic vapours must be first checked and that, as major precautionary measures, the space is effectively ventilated, approved breathing apparatus and lifelines are ready for immediate use and a competent person is available at the entrance to any such space into which personnel go, to summon assistance if necessary.

Furthermore, the notice goes on to point out, in:

para 2—the requirement of supervision associated with the emergency entry into any enclosed space.

para 3—the use of gas indicators to check the atmospheric vapour before entry.

para 4—the vacating of all spaces likely to have been affected by liquid or vapour.

para 5—the wearing of breathing apparatus.

para 6—the display of warning notices.

para 7—the wearing of protective clothing.

para 8—the danger of explosion and fire hazard.

These notices should be studied in detail and familiarity with the requirements determined. While the contents are not concerned with the actual stowage or handling of such dangerous chemicals in bulk, they are very relevant to 'safety measures' important to the work of personnel in contact with these forms of cargo. The hazards arise from the ambient, i.e. surrounding temperatures within the atmospheric pressures existing at any time. Indeed, the carriage of dangerous goods by sea involves such high danger hazards that careful attention must be given to the various notices and amendments published from time to time by the Department of Trade and Industry.

M.S.N. M807 relates to the need for approval of portable tanks and tank vehicles intended for carriage by sea, be this either for short sea, or ocean routes. Letters of approval by the D.T. must be provided by shippers when offering cargoes for shipment and be sighted by Masters, Agents and/or Officers before acceptance of these 'tanks' is allowed.

The intention is that, following I.M.O. recommendation these 'tanks/vehicles' should be issued with a metal identification plate or certificate, indicating that it meets the appropriate standards for the carriage of dangerous goods by sea It is pointed out that such tanks and vehicles are of far greater capacity than traditional packaging for dangerous goods and thus any hazard incident can have far more serious consequences.

M.S.N. M673 is concerned with petrol in the fuel tanks of motor vehicles in roll on/roll off ferries. This notice has very pertinent relevance to intercontinental transportation. The notice recommends that:

(a) the tank should not be so full as to create a possibility of spillage;

(b) the ignition should be switched off.

and places responsibility upon the ship staff to ensure that:

1. Spot checks should be made to ensure tanks are not overloaded.
2. Passengers do not have access to vehicles stowed under deck.
3. No smoking notices are clearly visible.
4. A fire patrol system is maintained on vehicle decks.
5. Vehicles should not be stowed across water spraying fire curtains.

M.S.N. M527, 1968, draws attention to fire fighting arrangements in ships carrying explosives. It points out that explosives packed and stowed in accordance with the recommendations contained in the 'Blue Book' should offer no more risk to a ship during the course of a voyage than any other dangerous goods. The risk, however, arises if a fire starts in any other cargo and is in danger of spreading to explosives.

As such, the notice lays out acceptable provisions for fire detecting and fire fighting.

In short, these should be fitted in any compartment containing explosives and in any adjacent compartments fire detecting system, but it goes on to detail acceptable systems and methods of handling relating situations which may arise.

In view of the detail officers are advised to study the requirements of M.S.O. No. 527. Since this also draws upon the International Conference on the Safety of Life at Sea, 1960, and also the Merchant Shipping (Fire Appliances) Rules, 1965, it requires more than cursory consideration.

The current I.M.O. Code 'International Code for the Construction and Equipment of Ships Carrying Dangerous Chemicals in Bulk' cover all aspects of construction of tanks within the hull of a ship, pipe line arrangements, ventilation and temperature control of cargo, gauging arrangements and vapour detecting systems.

The entire emphasis is on safe operation. On ships covered by the code there is little left to discretionary loading under the direction of the Cargo Officer. His whole consideration is directed to strict adherence to carefully regulated procedures for cargo handling, and to the safety of personnel at all times.

As referred to earlier (page 177) special training is mandatory specifically directed to a particular class of ship.

EXTRACT FROM SOLAS, 1974.

INTERNATIONAL CONFERENCE ON SAFETY OF LIFE AT SEA

Included by kind permission of

The Inter-Governmental Maritime Consultative Organization now known as The International Maritime Organization, 4 Albert Embankment, London SE1 7SR, ENGLAND.

CHAPTER VII
CARRIAGE OF DANGEROUS GOODS

Regulation 1

Application

(a) Unless expressly provided otherwise, this Chapter applies to the carriage of dangerous goods in all ships to which the present Regulations apply.

(b) The provisions of this Chapter do not apply to ship's stores and equipment or to particular cargoes carried in ships specially built or converted as a whole for that purpose, such as tankers.

(c) The carriage of dangerous goods is prohibited except in accordance with the provisions of this Chapter.

(d) To supplement the provisions of this Chapter each Contracting Government shall issue, or cause to be issued, detailed instructions on the safe packing and stowage of specific dangerous goods or categories of dangerous goods which shall include any precautions necessary in their relation to other cargo.

Regulation 2

Classification

Dangerous goods shall be divided into the following classes:

Class 1 —Explosives.
Class 2 —Gases: compressed, liquefied or dissolved under pressure.
Class 3 —Inflammable* liquids.
Class 4·1—Inflammable solids.
Class 4·2—Inflammable solids, or substances, liable to spontaneous combustion.
Class 4·3—Inflammable solids, or substances, which in contact with water emit inflammable gases.
Class 5·1—Oxidizing substances.
Class 5·2—Organic peroxides.
Class 6·1—Poisonous (toxic) substances.
Class 6·2—Infectious substances.
Class 7 —Radioactive substances.
Class 8 —Corrosives.

MMM—43

Class 9 —Miscellaneous dangerous substances, that is any other substance which experience has shown, or may show, to be of such a dangerous character that the provisions of this Chapter should apply to it.

---

* 'Inflammable' has the same meaning as 'flammable'.

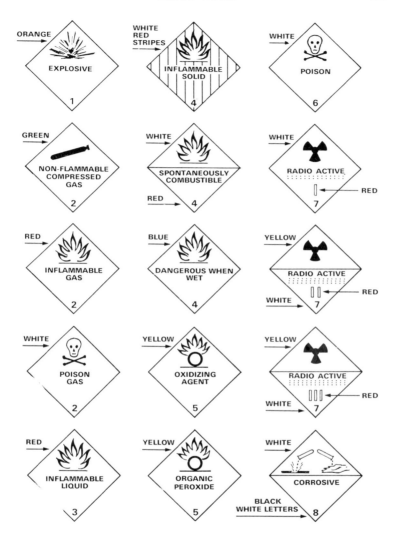

ORANGE → EXPLOSIVE 1

WHITE RED STRIPES → INFLAMMABLE SOLID 4

WHITE → POISON 6

GREEN → NON-FLAMMABLE COMPRESSED GAS 2

WHITE → SPONTANEOUSLY COMBUSTIBLE RED → 4

WHITE → RADIO ACTIVE RED → 7

RED → INFLAMMABLE GAS 2

BLUE → DANGEROUS WHEN WET 4

YELLOW → RADIO ACTIVE RED → WHITE → 7

WHITE → POISON GAS 2

YELLOW → OXIDIZING AGENT 5

YELLOW → RADIO ACTIVE RED → WHITE → 7

RED → INFLAMMABLE LIQUID 3

YELLOW → ORGANIC PEROXIDE 5

WHITE → CORROSIVE BLACK WHITE LETTERS → 8

ALL LETTERING BLACK

INTERNATIONAL MARITIME DANGEROUS GOODS CODE

UNITED NATIONS LABELLING

Numbers 1-8 indicate classification.

Regulation 3

Packing

(a) The packing of dangerous goods shall be:
- (i) well made and in good condition;
- (ii) of such a character that any interior surface with which the contents may come in contact is not dangerously affected by the substance being conveyed; and
- (iii) capable of withstanding the ordinary risks of handling and carriage by sea.

(b) Where the use of absorbent or cushioning material is customary in the packing of liquids in receptacles that material shall be:
- (i) capable of minimizing the dangers to which the liquid may give rise;
- (ii) so disposed as to prevent movement and ensure that the receptacle remains surrounded; and
- (iii) where reasonably possible of sufficient quantity to absorb the liquid in the event of breakage of the receptacle.

(c) Receptacles containing dangerous liquids shall have an ullage at the filling temperature sufficient to allow for the highest temperature during the course of normal carriage.

(d) Cylinders or receptacles for gases under pressure shall be adequately constructed, tested, maintained and correctly filled.

(e) Empty receptacles which have been used previously for the carriage of dangerous goods shall themselves be treated as dangerous goods unless they have been cleaned and dried or, when the nature of the former contents permit with safety, have been closed securely.

Regulation 4

Marking and Labelling

Each receptacle containing dangerous goods shall be marked with the correct technical name (trade names shall not be used) and identified with a distinctive label or stencil of the label so as to make clear the dangerous character. Each receptacle shall be so labelled except receptacles containing chemicals packed in limited quantities and large shipments which can be stowed, handled and identified as a unit.

Regulation 5

Documents

(a) In all documents relating to the carriage of dangerous goods by sea where the goods are named the correct technical name of the goods shall be used (trade names shall not be used) and the correct description given in accordance with the classification set out in Regulation 2 of this Chapter.

(b) The shipping documents prepared by the shipper shall include, or be accompanied by, a certificate or declaration that the shipment offered for carriage is properly packed, marked and labelled and in proper condition for carriage.

(c) Each ship carrying dangerous goods shall have a special list or manifest setting forth, in accordance with Regulation 2 of this Chapter, the dangerous goods on board and the location thereof. A detailed stowage plan which identifies by class and sets out the location of all dangerous goods on board may be used in place of such special list or manifest.

Regulation 6

Stowage Requirements

(a) Dangerous goods shall be stowed safely and appropriately according to the nature of the goods. Incompatible goods shall be segregated from one another.

(b) Explosives (except ammunition) which present a serious risk shall be stowed in a magazine which shall be kept securely closed while at sea. Such explosives shall be segregated from detonators. Electrical apparatus and cables in any compartment in which explosives are carried shall be designed and used so as to minimize the risk of fire or explosion.

(c) Goods which give off dangerous vapour shall be stowed in a well ventilated space or on deck.

(d) In ships carrying inflammable liquids or gases special precautions shall be taken where necessary against fire or explosion.

(e) Substances which are liable to spontaneous heating or combustion shall not be carried unless adequate precautions have been taken to prevent the outbreak of fire.

Regulation 7

Explosives in Passenger Ships

(a) In passenger ships the following explosives only may be carried:
  (i) safety cartridges and safety fuses;
  (ii) small quantities of explosives not exceeding 9 kilogrammes (20 pounds) total net weight;
  (iii) distress signals for use in ships or aircraft, if the total weight of such signals does not exceed 1,016 kilogrammes (2,240 pounds);

MMM—39

(iv) except in ships carrying unberthed passengers, fireworks which are unlikely to explode violently.

(b) Notwithstanding the provisions of paragraph (a) of this Regulation additional quantities or types of explosives may be carried in passenger ships in which there are special safety measures approved by the Administration.

'D' FOREST PRODUCTS—THE CARRIAGE OF TIMBER

The Code of Practice for Ships Carrying Timber Deck Cargoes

Considerable tonnages of timber form extensive proportions of world trading patterns and are of such varied types that far wider reaching considerations than hitherto are necessary for the safety of both ship and cargo.

Timber is defined as being loose or packaged, though the latter forms by far the greater amounts now carried. Loose timber can be individual planks, cubic units, logs or pit props. Packaged timber is bundles of sawn timber and can be regular or irregular, in terms of size and packaging. Carried as a deck cargo, timber requires attention to the provisions contained in the I.M.O. Code of Practice for Ships Carrying Timber Deck Cargoes; the Regulations of the International Convention on Load Lines and various relevant Merchant Shipping Notices, published from time to time.

Introduction

The carriage of timber, as a deck cargo, inhibits the possibilities of shifting and the consequences of not only loss of cargo but, more important, damage to the ship particularly, in the latter case, where navigational control is incautiously carried out. As such, a considerable duty rests on those responsible for the loading and stowage of a deck cargo of timber, the essential requirement being that it should be compactly stowed, rather than stacked and with adequate appropriate securing lashings. *This is a fundamental requirement.*

Since deck timber cargoes are mostly in packaged form there is need to promote certain basic handling procedures, such that:

(*a*) the packages are securely bound such that they are in 'solid' form;

(*b*) a level surface of dunnage provides a secure foundation to evenly spread the load over the ship structure;

(*c*) each tier, within the stow, is equally firm by the use of loose chocking material to fill up any gaps, such as would arise in and around hatch coamings and deck structures;

(*d*) the extremities of the stow do not obstruct provisions for the attachments of lashings;

Bulk 'Packaged' Timber Carrier

(e) prudent separation of heavy boards and square units is such as to prevent any movement at sea as would cause compacting damage or loosening of the lashings;

(f) in general, stowage is in a fore and aft direction in order to assist proper and adequate athwartship lashing arrangements;

(g) provisions are made providing for the tightening of the lashings where this may, at times during the voyage, be necessary;

(h) random, irregular packaged lengths should, preferably, not be loaded on deck.

Specifics

1. SHIP SIZES. The Code of Practice for ships carrying timber deck cargoes recommends that its provisions apply to all ships of 79 ft (24 m) or more, in length.

2. STOWAGE. The stowage shall be compactly stowed and chocked and arranged in such a way as not to interfere with, or impede, the normal navigational requirements; allow access to accommodation and machinery spaces; enable freedom of approach in the event of temporary steering arrangements arising and not endangering, in general, the overall safety of the crew in their normal duties.

Where the nature of the height stow of the timber requires it, uprights of adequate strength must be provided and spaced at intervals not exceeding 9·8 ft (3 m). It is not unusual for arrangements within and part of the structure to serve as permanent upright facilities.

The arrangement of the uprights however, whatever their form, must be such as to extend above the outboard top edge of the cargo; be fitted with securing and/or locking devices in their housings and arranged such that each port/starboard pair can be effectively linked with athwartship lashings.

3. LASHINGS. The deck must be covered by an overall independent athwartships lashing arrangement, each lashing secured to eye plates or similar provisions in the structure, with stretching devices capable of providing adequate tensioning, and subsequent adjustment, as may be required. The lashings, $\frac{3}{4}$ in (19 mm) close link chain or flexible wire rope, must show certificates of testing and should be examined at intervals not exceeding 12 months. The lashings should be fitted with sliphooks and turnbuckles, while wire provisions should have a short length of long link chain, enabling the wire lengths to be regulated.

4. COMPACTNESS. Compactness of stow can be achieved by a combination of level surfacing and adequate lashings, conditioned by the height of the stow. It is recommended that a maximum 19·6 ft (6 m) height above the weather deck calls for lashing spacings of 4·9 ft (1·5 m) whereas with 13 ft (4 m) and below, the spacings should be 9·8 ft (3 m). Intermediate height loading can be covered

by linear interpolation, while packaged timber in lengths of 11·8 ft (3·6 m) allows for lesser lashing spacings. Furthermore, an important aspect of lashing arrangements is that at the ends of the athwartship stow, the fitments should be as near to the ends as is practicably possible.

5. LOGS, PIT PROPS, WOOD PULP. Timber of 'log' form should be uniformly and compactly stowed in a fore and aft direction with a level or crowned top surface such that the total stow interlocks and can be effectively restrained by lashings, attached to uprights, in similar fashion to that recommended for packaged timber.

Wood pulp stowage invariably conforms to local practice (see page 108) concerned with craneage with timber loads. Pit prop stowage enjoys a similar reputation.

6. HEIGHT OF A TIMBER DECK STOW. The height to which a deck load of timber should be taken is conditioned in the main by its weight effect upon the structure of the vessel and also by reason of a voyage which passes through a seasonal winter zone (load line marks), and Masters should be provided with sufficient information as will permit them to judge accordingly. The height should not impede navigational visibility in any way; it should not, viz a *winter zone, exceed one-third of the extreme beam of the vessel.*

7. SAFETY OF CREW. The code provides detailed recommendations covering the satisfactory and safe access to crew accommodation, with guard lines or rails on each side of the deck cargo spaced not more than 13 in (33 cm) apart vertically and to a height of at least 3·3 ft (1 m) above the walking surface. Furthermore, an additional life line, along the centre line of the vessel, should be provided. Masters and Officers are recommended to study in depth these requirements as set out in the code.

Stability

Timber deck stowage requires prudent reference to the stability characteristics of the vessel on and in which it is being loaded. Merchant Shipping Notice M687 refers particularly to this (see page 448).

Suitable information must be available to Masters and Officers by which they can prejudge the stability characteristics desirable with deck loads under all conditions to which the vessel may be subject in voyage weather circumstances. Indeed, these requirements . . . as outlined in Notice M687 . . . suggest the need for some deep study of stability characteristics relative to ship design and weight distribution, which go beyond the general purpose of the text content of this book.

In this context doubtless the major key point in Notice M687 is that in para f in which it is pointed out that 'the quantity of timber carried on deck has a significant bearing upon the ultimate safety of the ship' and 'as a general rule not more than one-third of the weight of timber carried should be stowed on the open deck'.

Merchant Shipping Notices
Merchant Shipping Notices relevant to the foregoing summary of
the code are as follows, and to which attention should be given:

M.S.N. No. 687 emphasizes the need to be aware of those timber
   cargoes with which special care is necessary, viz.:
   1. loose, individual planks of sawn timber, logs or pit props;
   2. regular packaged timber;
   3. irregular packaged timber.
   It further emphasizes that hazards to ships carrying a cargo
   of timber, though doubtless from a shift of the stowed load,
   the dangerous effects are more the results of:
   1. inadequate stability standards;
   2. imprudent stowage or unsecured deck openings which
      permit the ingress of water.
   While it is recognized that to completely eliminate the
   possibility of a shift of a timber cargo is impracticable, it is
   vitally important to:
   1. Observe the guidance information contained in the Stability
      Booklet. The information so contained . . . from the Depart-
      ment of Trade . . . instructions for the guidance of Sur-
      veyors . . . refers to allowances for buoyancy with deck
      cargoes of irregular packaging insofar as these relate to the
      cross curves of stability for the vessel; the quantities of
      timber which can be safely carried on deck and the regard
      to be given to inappropriate reliance upon timber load
      lines. In the preparation of a Stability Booklet for the
      guidance of Masters and Officers the above, and other
      points must be duly observed.
         The notice also draws attention to the need for an
      adequate initial standard of stability and its maintenance
      during the voyage by calculations based upon probable
      envisaged weather conditions and consequent absorption
      of water, ice or snow, for example, upon the timber deck
      cargo.
         Security of stowage, compactness, height of the timber
      on an open deck and its weight are other matters to which
      the notice draws attention, as well as to the provisions
      whereby all weather tight doors, pipes and ventilators
      within the area surrounded by the timber, are in place
      and secure.
M.S.N. No. 1110 draws attention to the necessity to be assured that
   'slip hooks' with timber lashings are of a type and design
   which in no way can release or unlock under tension on the
   lashings. A case is recorded where neglect of this resulted in
   loss of timber overboard. Serious consequences can result
   from inadequate/deficient slip hooks; they should be maintained in good order.

TIMBER DECK CARGOES
Cargo Lashings—Slip Hooks

The carriage of timber 'on deck' must conform to two situations, both contained in the Department of Transport Merchant Shipping (Load Lines) (Deck Cargo) Regulations of 1968.

Either the vessel will be allocated *Timber Load Lines*, or it will not be so marked.

In the first instance loading will be permitted to deeper draft, by reason of stowage and security provisions contained in the regulations, bearing in mind, also, Zones, Areas and Seasonal periods which condition load drafts. Information, in booklet form, indicating these constraints, is available from the Department of Trade.

However, a particular feature arises with deck loaded timber, i.e. the use of effective lashings and slip hooks.

Slip hooks must be adequately designed and fitted, such that jamming is unlikely to occur. In the event of unforseen circumstances, pointing to danger with the cargo, i.e. the possibility of jettisoning cargo, pre-arrangements should be taken to enable this to be done without danger to ship personnel.

Attention is drawn to the Department of Transport Merchant Shipping Notice No. M1110.

MSN. No. M1051 refers to the dangers with the carriage of wood pulp in holds and confined spaces, where water can inadvertently enter. Saturated wood pulp bales of the air-dried chemical variety can expand considerably to the extent of exerting considerable pressure sufficient to rupture the boundaries of a compartment and associated structural fittings. Fifty per cent free expansion of a wood pulp bale is not exceptional.

In this context all proper precautions must be taken to prevent water entering any such compartments and pipes, ventilators, etc., efficiently closed and protected from damage which could accentuate this hazard.

Some General Observations on the Carriage of Timber

The economics of timber transportation lend themselves less now to conventional ship handling and carriage. Loose timber has almost given way to packaged loads, which are less cumbersome and, economically, more easily transportable by mechanical means. Logs, in particular, now have influenced the design and construction of purpose built carriers having their own craneage for loading and discharging, both under and on deck. On the Far Eastern/European trades vessels of 30 000 tons and over serve this pattern. Even so, it should be mentioned that within the equatorial belt the ports involved still accept logs from producing areas into floating ponds where they are appropriately designated for export with loading, ex-ship gear alongside or from warehouses/quay space if the timber is unsuitable for water storage. On the continent of Europe discharge may also be off ship into water, the logs then being transported by tug towage through the water/canal systems. See, however, the later notes on terminals especially built for timber reception.

Loose timber, as distinct from packaged, is wasteful of labour, involves high costs in handling and assorting the loads and certainly not conducive to quick movement, particularly with conventional ships. Indeed, it is interesting to observe that conventional ships, by virtue of their design, do not lend themselves to compact timber stowage which the modern producing consignors look for.

By comparison, Canadian loose timber of 14 in × 14 in baulks to 1 in boards of 24 ft lengths, discharged by chain slings, either by ship derrick/cranes, or quayside cranes, can utilize four or five gangs at a rate of 25 standards (165 cu ft) per day. A vessel carrying 2000 standards could take 14–16 days to discharge and this rate is unlikely to remain, or be acceptable as economic, either to the consignee or to the ship operator. Canadian packaged timber in standard unit loads of 36 in × 26 in × 28 ft lengths, utilizing fork lift trucks, can work 80 standards per day, per gang over a total of four gang employment. Similar comparisons can be made with Baltic and Scandinavian timber.

Rates of discharge with packaged timber require the support of quick movement on the quay. The timber has a tendancy to dry on the surface with the interior remaining moist and this is likely to encourage fungi growth . . . another reason which makes it desirable to clear packages quickly at their destination.

Overall, the advantages of packaged timber are:

1. Increased efficiency of handling.
2. Reduction in manpower loading/discharging.
3. Quicker ship turn round.
4. Less damage and breakage.

In the study of bulk carriage probably no area has greater significance than that of timber. Where most commodities are assisted by a variety of sophisticated equipment, timber requires somewhat less but still retains a wide and broad influence upon manually assisted movement and effectively deployed facilities, albeit the trend in the increasing tonnages of timber being traded internationally suggests that the unitization of timber handling is not far short of approaching the systems adopted with other unit loads. Indeed, purpose built vessels for the carriage of timber, with their own craneage and packaged timber quickly overshadowing loose, indicates this trend. It is for these reasons that practical attention to, and observance of the recommendations in the Code of Practice is significantly important.

New Developments in the Carriage of Timber

Far reaching trends in the carriage of timber are rapidly developing, particularly with soft woods. The significant feature is the concentration of producers and shippers, notably seen on the North Pacific and Scandinavia, merging with U.K. importers such that

Modern Bulk Timber Vessel alongside Timber Distribution Area, Newport (Gwent)

larger cargoes are moving in specially designed vessels with the timber 'unit loaded' or packaged, each vessel capable of carrying some 20000–30000 tons, or more, to selected terminals (20·321–30·481 metric tons).

In Newport, Gwent, U.K., one such terminal provides an area for the discharge of packaged timber in 2 ft × 4 ft × 20 ft (0·61 × 1·219 × 6096 m) units of 2 ton weight (2·032 metric tons) or more by specially designed ship craneage and associated mechanical handling equipment of straddle carriers and fork lift trucks.

Similar developments are taking place in other British ports, such as Tilbury, London, where $\frac{1}{4}$ of the tonnage of cargo discharged in the London docks is in forest products. The terminal facilities include a straightforward quay; large areas and transit sheds for certain types of materials and the discharging operating procedures are by ship's own gear. Indeed, the absence of cranes with forest products berths is characteristic of this now fast growing trade.

The Newport terminal covers over 40 acres to accommodate increasing Far Eastern timber trades, including the hardwoods carried as bulk cargoes from Malaysia and Indonesia, additional to the established North American shipments. Softwood, pre-slung packaged timber is discharged by high capacity ship gear and 650 standards in 7 hours is not unusual. Full underdeck stowage of prepackaged timber units, together with deck loads, comprises most of the full loads now carried on the timber trades.

A type of 'bulk' vessel now operating is that designed for the carriage of multi-bulk dry cargoes below deck and is used for grain and/or timber, either as separate or multi-cargo. Figure 4.3 illustrates one such vessel and attention is drawn to the design arrangements to protect the stability conditions of the ship.

Reference to the illustration of the Newport timber terminal will show the gantry crane equipment of a vessel alongside for discharging the timber.

The pattern of handling on terminals such as those referred to provides for cargo distribution direct from the discharging areas . . . hence the space involved . . . with different timber consignments according to the manifest requirements and speedy mobile moving equipment. The aim is not for stacking, but quick clearance, either by transportation or from 'buying' off site.

Timber is measured in standards. In the European trades a standard contains 165 cu ft whilst on the North American trade 192 cu ft is the average. It is usual to compute the weight of the cargo from the average weights given by the shipper and since the Code of Practice for Ships Carrying Timber Deck Cargoes concerns itself, among other things, with weight distribution, stability and effective lashings, it is pertinent for the Cargo Officer to be aware of the sources from which he can obtain his loading guide lines.

In some trades the amount of timber is computed in fathoms; one fathom of timber containing 216 cu ft, i.e. a cube 6 ft × 6 ft × 6 ft.

Some timber shipping terms include:

A Shipping Ton	42 cu ft
A Load	50 cu ft
A Load (untrimmed)	60 cu ft
A Stack	108 cu ft
A St Petersburg and Baltic Standard	165 cu ft

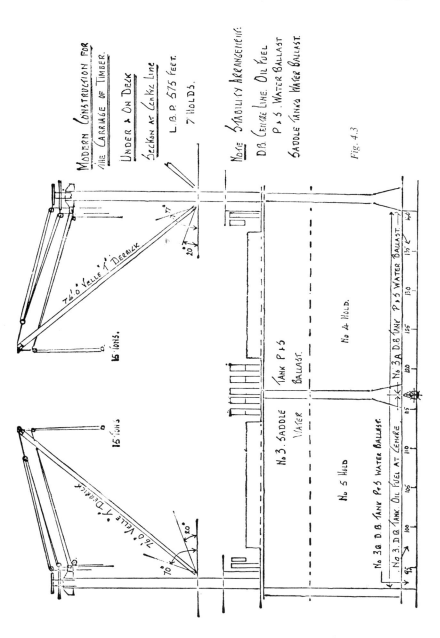

MODERN CONSTRUCTION FOR THE CARRIAGE OF TIMBER.

UNDER & ON DECK

SECTION AT CENTRE LINE

L.B.P. 575 FEET.

7 HOLDS.

NOTE STABILITY ARRANGEMENTS:
D.B. CENTRE LINE. OIL FUEL
P & S. WATER BALLAST
SADDLE TANKS WATER BALLAST.

Fig. 4.3

'E' GRAIN CARGOES

Introductory Notes

Grain remains a prominent bulk commodity and of recent years has influenced the introduction of more sophisticated forms of loading, carriage and discharge than hitherto. Notably is this so in the availability of mechanical and mechanical/pneumatic equipment, as distinct from graps, although these are still used.

In terms of 'ships' carriers of multi-purpose design, adaptable to ore, oil and similar commodities, also load grain shipments in bulk. These vessels are of upwards of 150 000 D.W.T. but the lower deadweight tonnage of 30 000–40 000 are the more common. Ship sizes are largely dominated by the trade patterns and the ports used.

The handling of grain is usually of one of three systems. Each, however, is usually the prerogative of the port, rather than that of the ship, in that the type of equipment available reflects the requirements best suited to the volume and distribution needs of the trade which the port covers.

Grabs are versatile units and can cover high tonnages and capacities not affected by the type of the grain. The mechanical conveyor systems have high capacities but suffer some restrictions in accessibility to hold spaces, but with the introduction and fitting of closed screw functions, as they are termed, large discharge rates can be achieved by relatively easy access to any part of a hold or space. The closed screw function is capable of 'breaking up' 'solidified' grain configurations and thus serves better the heavier grain derivative products, which can be of a more sticky nature.

By comparison, the pneumatic suction systems are said to be preferable for free flowing grains of low density and also have the advantage of being relatively dust free. These suction systems, capable of penetrating to otherwise inaccessible parts of the hold, can have normal capacities of 500–700 tons per hour, although figures of 10 000–15 000 tons per hour, though exceptional, are not out of place in some ports.

The Carriage of Grain

Grain in bulk is carried in accordance with either the Merchant Shipping (Grain) regulations 1980, for ships loading in the United Kingdom, or the I.M.O. Grain Rules for other vessels.

In practice any differences between the two are confined to the acceptance in the U.K. of documents of authorization carried by a ship indicating that loading complies with the 1974 Solas Convention, chapter VI, or with approved equivalent arrangements.

If there is no authorization document the Master must demonstrate to the satisfaction of a Department of Transport Surveyor that the vessel can be loaded to the requirements of chapter VI (Solas).

The principles on which the rules are based reflect the capability of modern loading methods and the design of modern ships and may be briefly summarized as follows:—

1. Modern loading methods enable grain to be blown into the extremities of the holds so that initially there is very little void space. Even after the grain settles the voids will be small.
2. The amount of grain which can shift is thus limited by the size of the voids, and any movement will impose a moment, causing the vessel to heel to one side.
3. The amount of heel can be calculated, and if it is within suitable limits the vessel will be safe.
4. The vessel must have a residual dynamical stability after grain shift has occurred, and a minimum initial G.M.
5. If the vessel complies with the requirements, shifting boards are not required and the grain surface in partly filled holds can be secured physically by strapping or overstowing. Grain surfaces in way of the hatches may likewise be secured. Feeders are then not necessary.

The rules centre around a calculation when the vessel is under construction, showing the effect of grain shift. This consists of an assessment of void spaces above the grain, using this as a volume which can be translated into an expression from which the angle of heel, due to grain shift, can be determined.

Grain loading countries require a good standard of preparation for the cargo, as outlined below.

General Practicalities of Grain Carriage
Two features have particular relevance:

1.
(*a*) The space in which it is carried should be perfectly clean and free from objectionable odour.
(*b*) The bilges should be free and clean, particular attention being given to the strum boxes. A coating of lime and cement wash is advisable.
(*c*) The limber boards should be in good condition and repair, seams caulked and boards covered with pieces of clean tarpaulin, secured by wooden lathes.
(*d*) The tank top ceiling, if fitted, should be clean and dry and free from any stains. If the ceiling is damp or stained, sprinkle lime all over and leave for a while before sweeping.
(*e*) All cement chocks and frame fillings should be in perfect condition.
(*f*) A liberal supply of mats, separation cloths or tarpaulins should be available. With a bagged cargo such provisions will assist in the collection of 'sweepings' whereas, where bagged or other means are used to support a 'loose' load

the surface must first be completely covered with tarpaulin or separation.

2. *Ventilation.* Grain is a cargo which is subject to heating and condensation effects, particularly if shipped at the beginning of the season. It is a cargo which absorbs moisture very easily and this is not always openly apparent.

In view of the above, grain will deteriorate in quality very quickly unless all reasonable means are provided for efficient ventilation. Cases have been recorded where germination has occurred in grain bulk interiors owing to insufficient ventilation. General 'through' ventilation should be provided. With bagged cargo this is comparatively easy, with intake air directed towards the bottom of the stow and out take air cleared from the top. The introduction of 'intermediate bulk' carriers, superceding to some extent bag carriage, largely eliminates these ventilation problems, since the material of which the carriers are made safeguard the contents against condensation effects. With bulk carriage ventilation must follow devices similar to those for coal cargoes, by providing a continuous flow of air over the surface of the grain to remove the warm air currents arising from the bulk.

THE I.M.O. RECOMMENDATIONS (SUMMARY)

The Carriage of Bulk Grain

In any compartment filled with grain there will exist a void space between the grain cargo surface and the crown, or deck head of the compartment. It is this 'void space' aspect which needs to be uppermost in mind, since it has bearing upon any grain shifting tendancy, and conditions the need to ensure that adequate stability remains with the vessel so loaded, such that heeling moments will not adversely affect the grain behaviour in those void spaces.

The need to provide shifting boards or other temporary grain fittings, in order to reduce the effects of grain shifting depends upon the stability qualities of the vessel, i.e. metacentric height; angle of heel and residual dynamical stability. Furthermore, feeders do not necessarily reduce grain voids and thus should not, in themselves, be regarded as a heeling precautionary factor.

Recommendations (Appendix to the Code)
Grain, by definition, includes wheat, maize, oats, rye, barley, rice pulses and seeds. A 'filled' compartment is meant to be that in which, after trimming, the bulk grain is as high as possible. A 'partly filled' compartment does not meet these provisions.

Trimming, by definition, means that all spaces under the decks and hatch covers are full to maximum extent and is intended to minimize the effect of grain shifting. In partly filled compartments trimming means a level surface, with the ship upright.

The stability characteristics of a vessel loaded with bulk grain should be such that:

(a) any angle of heel due to a shift should not exceed 12°;
(b) the initial metacentric height (GM), after correction for any free surface effect, should not be less than 0·30 m;
(c) the statical stability conditioning the residual area between heeling moment and righting moment should take account of the stability characteristics indicated by the design curves of stability and dynamical stability.

Longitudinal divisions, which must be grain tight, may be fitted in both filled and partly filled compartments. In filled compartments they must extend downwards from the underside of the deck, or hatchcovers, to a distance below the deck line of at least one-eighth the breadth of the compartment. In a partly filled compartment the division, if fitted, will extend both above and below the level of the grain, to a distance of one-eighth the breadth of the compartment.

Bagged grain, or other suitable cargo, may be stowed in the wings and ends of a compartment as a means of reducing grain shift but these arrangements must be adequately secured and are detailed in Part 2 of Schedule 2 of the Shipping Notice M599.

Schedule 1 of the Code
This is concerned with determining the stability requirements of a vessel carrying grain in bulk and concerns itself with void depths, volumetric centres of gravity of the whole cargo space; heeling moments due to a shift of grain and righting arm counteracting effects. The schedule is detailed and positive and thus beyond any attempt to generalize on it; it should be studied with care. Essentially it is stability orientated and emphasizes the extent to which stability considerations influence grain carrying regulations more so than was the case hitherto, doubtless due to the considerable increases in grain carriage of recent years; the size of vessels carrying it and the very modern, fast operating loading terminals.

Schedule 2 of the Code
This is concerned with the strength of grain fittings (Part 1) and the securing of partly filled compartments (Part 2). There is some differentiation of interpretation as between horizontal divisions loaded on both or on one side only.

Some of the highlights of Part 1 are as follows:

1. All timber used for grain fittings should be of sound quality and proven satisfactory for the purpose for which it is

intended. Suitably grained and bonded plyboard can be acceptable, provided its strength is equivalent to solid timber. Materials other than wood or steel may also be approved.

2. Uprights must be of sound construction and adequately secured against displacement from their end sockets. Where there is no securing at the top then the uppermost shore, or stay, must be fitted as near thereto as is practicable.

3. Shifting boards should have thicknesses of not less than 50 mm, be grain tight and, where necessary, supported by uprights.

Additional to the foregoing obvious basic requirements, Part 1, of Schedule 2 details standards of effectiveness, methods of calculation of sizes of uprights, shores, stays and load maximums permitted on longitudinal divisions and their securing.

Wood shores, for example, must be single piece timber, securely fixed at each end and heeled against the permanent structure of the ship but not abutting on to the side plating. Shores of 7 m or more in length must be bridged, at approximately mid length.

Shores must not exceed an angle of 45° to the horizontal; where the angle of the shore exceeds 10° then its size must be increased. Where stays are used to support divisions loaded on both sides they must be of steel wire rope, fitted horizontally and well secured at each end.

Part 2 relates to the securing of partly filled compartments by reason of strapping or lashing. The grain should be levelled in partly filled compartments but *slightly crowned* and the surface covered with separation cloths or tarpaulin which overlaps at least 1·83 m. Two solid floors of 25 mm timber should be laid longitudinally and athwartships over the surface of the grain and steel wire or chain used as strapping lashings which should be attached at their ends on to shackle or beam attachments at a point approximately 450 mm below the anticipated final grain surface. This is to permit of tensioning arrangements to operate. The lashings, in themselves, should not be spaced more than 2·44 m apart.

Where bagged grain, or other suitable cargo, is used for securing partly filled compartments, the free grain surface must be covered with separation/or equivalent cloth and/or by a suitable platform laid on to bearers. Bagged grain must be carried in sound bags, well filled and securely closed.

Some Points of Detail Relative to the Differentiation of Interpretation of Divisions Loaded on Both or on One Side

1. LOADED ON BOTH SIDES.

The minimum thickness of 50 mm for shifting boards applies. Maximum unsupported spans for shifting boards of various thickness range from 50 mm–2·5 m; 60 mm–3 m; 70 mm–3·5 m; 80 mm–4 m.

The ends of all shifting boards should be securely housed with a minimum bearing length of 75 mm.

Where stays are used to support divisions they should be fitted horizontally, well secured at each end and of steel wire rope.

2. LOADED ON ONE SIDE ONLY.

Tabular detail indicates the loads permitted, in kg per metre lengths.

The recommendations covering the carriage of grain in bulk are so comprehensive that effective stowage and handling procedures can only be promoted by officers studying their applications to the ship(s) on which they would be serving. A general understanding of the code, as outlined in these notes is essential, but it would be wrong to ignore these in any other way than by relating the requirements to vessels in which an officer is serving.

'F' BULK LIQUIDS

Vegetable Oils

The fats and fatty oils derived from seeds and animal sources consist of mixtures of 'triglycerides', as distinct from the 'hydrocarbons' which are the essential constituents of mineral oils. Some fats and fatty oils are used in the manufacture of food products, and others allocated to soap, paint and varnish manufacture.

A 'triglyceride' is a reaction product of a glycerol group and three fatty acid groups. These latter may be identical or dissimilar. If dissimilar, the triglyceride belongs to the *mixed* class. Mixed triglycerides are of very frequent occurrence in fats and fatty oils. It must be noted that some fatty acids which occur in vegetable oils and fats, occur also in animal oils and fats.

An arbitrary distinction between oils and fats is made by calling those substances *fats* which are solid at ordinary temperature in this country, e.g. 15°C, and applying the name *fatty oils* to those which are liquid at that temperature. Fatty oils differ from fats in that the fatty acid groups of the former are more chemically reactive than those of the fats. Thus we should expect a divergence of properties between the two classes. The *iodine value* is a measure of the ability of a triglyceride to enter into chemical reactions, and will therefore be related (with reservations) to such subjects as 'spontaneous combustion', 'drying properties' and 'hydrogenation'. The reactive fatty oils in the presence of a catalyst and under pressure will join with hydrogen producing what are essentially new fats. The process is called 'hydrogenation' and the oils are said to be 'hardened'. The triglyceride composition has been modified by this hardening, producing substances of higher melting points which are edible after refining. With very moderate cooling, fatty oils often show sedimentary deposits or cloudiness, but they all become solid if cooled to $-20°C$. The temperature required to solidify a fatty oil would be decided by the properties and proportions of the various triglycerides present. Some common triclycerides are:

Stearin   —melting point 71°C (small amounts in beef-tallow)
Palmitin—melting point 65·5°C (occurs up to 10 per cent in Palm Oil)
Olein   —melting point $-6°C$ (occurs in Olive Oil)

The mixed triglycerides, an important and numerous class, have melting points which vary according to the dissimilarity of their fatty acid groups, and also according to the order of their arrangement in the molecules of the substance. Palmito-distearin (melting point 63°C) occurs in lard and beef-tallow, and the latter substance also contains Oleo-dipalmitin (melting point 48°C).

Oil from seeds grown in any special locality varies very little in composition, but any individual variety of oil might show considerable variation in composition according to the geographical region of production.

The '*drying property*' of a fatty oil is associated (roughly and with reservations) with the Iodine value. The higher the Iodine value, the greater the facility with which a thin layer of oil exposed to the air at standard temperature will form a tough elastic coating. The oil absorbs oxygen in the process, and the rate of absorption is increased by previous treatment of the oil with certain oxides using heat, e.g. the drying of linseed oil is hastened by boiling it previously with 'driers' such as manganese dioxide and lead oxide.

Common Name	Class	Specific Gravity 15°C (average values)	Solidifying Point °C	Iodine Value
Coconut	Vegetable fat	0·926	22 to 23·5	8 to 10
Cocoa butter		0·969	25 to 27	33 to 41
Palm		0·923	23 to 27	44 to 58
Linseed	Vegetable drying oil	0·934	-19 to -20	180 to 190+
China wood		0·942	2 to 3	160 to 170
Soya bean		0·925	-8 to -16	131 to 135
Cottonseed	Vegetable semi-drying oil	0·924	4 to -5	103 to 116
Sesame		0·923	-4 to -6	103 to 117
Olive	Vegetable non-drying oil	0·91·7	-6	79 to 88
Groundnut		0·917	3	88 to 98
Rapeseed		0·915	-10 to -12	94 to 105

Linseed oil is the most important drying oil, with Chinese wood oil (Tung) second.

The figures indicated refer to some physical and chemical characteristics of certain vegetable fats and oils·

Rancidity. The ordinary unrefined commercial fatty oils and fats contain certain products imparting strong flavours and odours. These are developed by the action of light, moisture and air, and constitute the state of rancidity. These three agents set up complicated chemical reactions whereby the triglycerides are split up into *fatty acids* and *glycerol*. The fatty acids suffer further decomposition resulting in the formation of other compounds with strong odour and flavour. Temperature increase will accelerate the change. Fatty acids are useful for soap manufacture, but their presence to any extent in a commercial fatty oil means so much less quantity of refined oil obtainable.

Free fatty acidity per cent (F.F.A. per cent) is a familiar statement on technical documents relating to vegetable oils. The fatty acids are called *free* because they exist as free acids, i.e. uncombined, whereas *combined* with glycerol they constitute the triglycerides which make up the fatty oil or fat.

Spontaneous Combustion. In Model Rules for Ensuring Safety in Chemical Works (Association of British Chemical Manufacturers, 1938) Section 36 refers to inflammable and combustible material including oily waste, which must not be kept in contact with or near to steam pipes and radiators. Section 42 contains a warning about accumulation of such material except in lidded metal containers. Spontaneous combustion might occur whenever oily materials are distributed over suitable fibrous materials of inflammable character, and an increased risk would result from a higher temperature. In the case of vegetable oils, the risk of spontaneous combustion might be ascertained (roughly) from the iodine values, e.g. fabric saturated or splashed with linseed oil would be more dangerous than if treated with palm oil or olive oil. It is also possible that the presence of water in or on oil-splashed material might contribute considerably to the risk of spontaneous combustion when the subsequent drying process followed. Compared with mineral oils, the vegetable oils are relatively less flammable, but once well alight are difficult to deal with owing to the nature of the fumes evolved.

The Carriage of Vegetable Oils. Coconut oil, palm oil, wood oil, cottonseed oil, olive oil, soya bean oil, peanut oil and rapeseed.

The carriage of vegetable oils has, of recent years, grown to such a large extent that many modern cargo vessels are fitted with a number of deep tanks suitable for the bulk carriage of these liquids.

These tanks vary in capacity from 500–1000 tons and are subdivided by longitudinal bulkheads, which provide for the carriage of different types of oil, in separate tanks, during the same voyage.

The carriage of an edible oil involves a strict standard of cleanliness and cargo officers should pay due attention to this very important point. In all trades the cleanliness and tightness of the tanks are subject to supervision and final surveying by both Lloyd's and Shipper's surveyors. Appropriate certificates as to seaworthiness and cleanliness are necessary before ship and shippers should take their respective responsibility.

To avoid any possibility of foreign matter entering the tanks, the ventilators serving the deep tanks should be fitted with portable sections, preferably in the 'tween deck spaces immediately above the deep tanks and blank flanges fitted to the ventilator pipe line. Most shippers will not permit these blank flanges to be fitted at the upper extremity of the air vent in view of the possibility of damage to the pipe from the weather or from cargo working within the 'tween deck space.

The sounding pipe extensions to the tanks should be removed and the remainder of the pipe blanked off and any steam or gas fire extinguishing pipes, which enter the tanks, should also be plugged or disconnected at the deck. It is advisable to ensure that provision has been made for blanking off the bilge suction pipes if they are not fitted with non-return valves.

There is no objection to the carriage of any of these vegetable oils in tanks which, on a previous voyage, have been filled with dirty oils such as lubricating oils or fuel oils. However, particularly with the latter oil, the tanks will need exceedingly careful attention to ensure that they are scrupulously clean. Any trace of a bitumen content will dissolve in the vegetable oil with consequent contamination. Claims for contamination of vegetable oils are very high.

Cleaning of Tanks. Assuming that fuel oil has been carried in a deep tank, preliminary cleaning of the tank will be necessary in order to remove as much of the oil as possible, after which the tank should be steamed out for at least twenty-four hours. On completion of the steaming and whilst the tank is still warm, it is necessary to wash the tank down with a hose under pressure.

This early cleaning should be completed either at sea before the vessel arrives at the port of loading or at a specified anchorage so that the discharge of the residue will not contaminate the harbour.

The tank is now filled with water and tested for tightness, to the satisfaction of the surveyor. Some shippers require a further steaming of the tank to ensure complete removal of any traces of oil fuel, but in some ports the tanks are subject, after water testing, to a very thorough cleaning with caustic soda and steam. In Manila very satisfactory results have been obtained by cleaning down with caustic soda and sand, using scrapers and stiff coir broom heads; this latter operation for an 800 ton tank takes the better part of twenty-four hours.

The surveyors will then inspect the tank and if satisfied as to cleanliness will issue the certificate 'that the tank is in fit condition to carry oil in bulk'. No master should allow loading to commence before receipt of this certificate, duly signed. It is very unlikely that any question in this direction will arise, for the shippers are very particular in ensuring that the tanks are fit before delivering the oil. It is usual to wipe down the whole of the interior of the tank with oil of the type to be carried.

Arrangements for Heating the Oil. As has already been pointed out, certain vegetable oils are liable to solidify at normal temperatures and provision needs to be made in order to facilitate easy and quick discharge of the oil.

Heating elements, in the form of steam coils, are fitted in the bilges of the tanks and on the tank tops. These coils are arranged in sections so that they may be easily and quickly removed when loading general cargoes. They are of $2\frac{1}{2}$ in diameter and raised off the tank top by brackets to a distance of about 2 in.

In many vessels it has been found to be of great advantage to fit independent heating coils in the upper part of the tanks, as for example, at the deck head.

Very frequently, with only a lower heating coil system, the upper layers of the oil remain in a state of solidity, leaving large fatty deposits on the top portions of the tank beams and frames as the oil level recedes in the tank during discharge.

The upper coils warm the upper layers of oil so that as the level falls it leaves a comparatively clean tank. This certainly results in a better discharge and considerably reduces cleaning costs.

The heating arrangement for the lower part of the tank should be such that the steam enters first the coils situated in the bilges. In this way the maximum heat will be given to that part of the tank which is naturally colder as a result of contact with the cold outside water.

The carrying temperatures of vegetable oils differ somewhat with the class of oil. It is usual for the shippers to specify the temperature at which they require the oil to be kept and the temperatures allowed for discharge.

Palm nut oil and palm kernel oil may be successfully carried at temperatures of 78–86°F, whilst palm oil suffers no deterioration at temperatures of 75–105°F. The maximum temperature, however, will be stipulated by the shipper and the oil should only be brought to this temperature about four days prior to discharge. Experience in the carriage of these oils teaches that due regard must be given to the season of the year during which the vessel arrives at port of discharge, winter months necessitating a gradual rise of the maximum temperature, possibly more than the four days above mentioned.

Discharge of the oil is effected by shore plants either in the form of independent steam pumps operating at the tank top flat or by a combined suction and discharge pump which may be lowered into the tank.

Before discharging commences, it is a requirement that official forms be completed showing ullages, temperatures, specific gravities, draughts of the vessel fore and aft, and list, if any.

Latex

Trees of *Hevea Braziliensis* are grown in large numbers on Malayan and East Indian plantations. On incising the bark to a certain depth, a milky fluid exudes called 'Latex'. It is of a viscid character and is an emulsion containing up to 40 per cent of a hydrocarbon *caoutchouc*, the remainder being water with small amounts of other substances which serve to stabilize the emulsion. Changes occur in the latex from the time of tapping and the chemical reactions produce an acidity which results in ultimate coagulation.

The latex can be kept fluid by adding ammonia. The addition of this gas can be carried out by using ammonia gas from cylinders or by adding concentrated ammonia solution. M. W. Philpot in Rubber Research Scheme (Ceylon) 1936, recommends 7 lb ammonia gas per 100 gallons latex, which would correspond to $2\frac{1}{2}$–3 gallons of liquid ammonia (Liq. Ammon. Fortis).

Since ammonia is used to preserve the latex, it is essential that tank fittings should contain no metal likely to be attacked by ammonia, e.g. brass fittings would introduce copper into the latex. In addition, the iron tanks holding bulk latex must be given an internal coating of some protective medium such as wax or a chemically resistant paint. This will prevent contamination of the latex with iron impurities which might considerably affect its subsequent history. The tanks must be fitted with a suitable device for allowing the escape of superfluous gas and at the same time be capable of excluding air. It is to be noted that preserved latex will stand low natural temperatures. It can be coagulated by adding acids and rubber obtained thereby.

Rubber (caoutchouc) is classified chemically as a 'Polyterpene' and may be represented by the formula $(C_5H_8)_n$, which indicates its hydrocarbon character. Industrial chemistry affords instances of synthetic products displacing natural products and it should therefore be mentioned at this stage that synthetic rubber production is becoming more prominent. For example buna rubber (S) made from the products resulting from the 'cracking' of petroleum is reputed to be 15–30 per cent better than natural rubber for average purposes. In 1943 the U.S.A. produced 250 000 tons of synthetic rubber. This form of manufacture is now international.

The caoutchouc particles in the latex are very small and have diameters up to four-thousandths of a millimetre. They are charged with negative electricity and electrical methods can be used to deposit them as rubber on fabrics or on objects.

Pure rubber (unvulcanized rubber) softens considerably on

warming and disintegrates with cooling to 0°C. It is therefore not suitable for practical purposes. To obtain the desired qualities of maintaining elasticity over a wide range of temperature and of durability, the pure rubber must be *vulcanized.* Sulphur is the agent employed in vulcanization and can be added or incorporated by various methods. The vulcanized rubber can also be reinforced by adding such materials as zinc oxide, carbon black and silica.

Transportation. The carriage of bulk latex is now becoming universal. Very careful preparation is necessary with regard to the cleaning of the tanks. It is said that a surveyor should be able to enter a tank cleaned for latex, wearing white gloves and complete his examination without dirtying his gloves. This may be somewhat of an exaggeration, but it serves to point out the state of cleanliness required.

It is suggested that tanks in which latex is to be carried should never be given over to fuel oil, for this commodity leaves a tank in such a condition as to prevent quick cleaning. In any case, a period of at least six months should elapse between cargoes of fuel oil and latex in the same tank.

To obtain the proper degree of cleanliness, a tank will need to be steamed out several times, the number of operations depending upon the type of oil last carried.

Each steaming operation should be followed by efficient wiping down with caustic or other similar solution.

Attention is drawn to the manner in which tanks are cleaned for the reception of vegetable oils: such methods lend themselves very satisfactorily to preparation for latex reception.

After cleaning the tanks will need to be filled with water and proven tight to the satisfaction of the surveyor, after which they are emptied and subjected to a final cleaning and drying.

After satisfactory cleaning, the whole of the interior of the tank is covered over with a solution of wax which, on cooling, forms a thin but impervious white coating.

Notes on the Preparation of Tanks for Latex.
>Remove sounding pipe extensions and blank off remaining pipes.
>Remove bilge suction pipes and plug remaining pipes.
>Remove steam pipe coils.
>Remove all brass, copper and galvanized fittings.
>Ensure that all fire extinguishing pipes are plugged.
>Ensure that all ordinary vents are blanked off, and that special ventilators with relief valves are properly fitted.

Notes on the Carriage of Bulk Oils. Providing the longitudinal bulkhead between the port and starboard tanks has been tested and proved tight to the satisfaction of the surveyors, coconut oil, palm oil and wood oil may be carried in adjacent tanks, but no oil, such as kapok seed oil, which is liable to deterioration or discoloration by exposure to the degree of heat necessary to liquefy adjacent oils, should be loaded thus.

Latex, vegetable oils or water may be carried in adjacent tanks, but only on the written authority of the shipper. This precaution is necessary because of:

1. The affinity of the ammonia in the latex for water.
2. The danger of contaminating vegetable oils by ammonia leaks.
3. The deterioration of latex by the heating of adjacent compartments.

The Preparation of Tanks for Molasses

After the completion of the discharge of an oil cargo, windsails should be rigged to promote ventilation and the tanks hosed down from the tank hatch, in order to get rid of as much sediment as possible before steaming down. The ballast pump is kept going during this hosing down, in order to remove all sediment and residue.

In some vessels a caustic boiler is fitted in the poop space into which about 4 cwt of flaked caustic is added and a special steam pipe line is fitted to carry the caustic steam to all tanks. The pressure on the line is about 65 lb per sq in and the time taken to complete the first steaming is about 4–5 hours.

Experience shows that the caustic merely removes the oily smell and it frequently happens that a tank might pass the 'odour' test after the first steaming and washing down and yet still be far from clean enough for molasses.

Masters on this trade have expressed the opinion that, on inspection of a tank for cleanliness, they would be guided in their decision by the fact that, if they could run their hands along shell plates and longitudinals without soiling, they would pass the tank as satisfactory. The inside of a tank may look quite black but as long as everything is perfectly dry, there is little chance of contamination to the molasses cargo.

The part of the tank most difficult to clean seems to be that part of the shell from the curve of the bilge to the light load line and this will often need to be swabbed with tank cloths and diesel oil before the final steaming down.

With some previous cargoes, such as heavy fuel, four operations of steaming down are necessary before the tanks are fit for the molasses.

Experience shows that contamination of a molasses cargo is due to dirty pipe lines, or, possibly, to not cleaning the ballast tanks. It is advisable to discharge all dirty ballast water and to steam and clean the tanks as well, so that when the ballast is discharged at the loading port, there is no fear of dirty, oily water passing through the ballast pipe lines.

Twenty-four hours should be given to the cleaning of the pipe lines after the cleaning of the tanks, pumping in all directions so that an efficient state of cleanliness is attained.

Following clean oil, the main work, after washing down, is directed towards removing the smell; caustic steam and windsails seem to do this very well. Four to five days will suffice to prepare a vessel for loading molasses after a cargo of light oils; but after heavy oils, cases are on record of the whole of a 30-day passage being given over to tank cleaning and then it was found necessary to employ shore labour to wipe down some of the tanks.

The ideal method appears to be to carry a cargo of gas oil after a cargo of heavy oil before changing over to molasses.

The use of a caustic boiler seems to be the most satisfactory method of cleaning, but many vessels employ the method of slinging a drum filled with caustic inside the tank and then administering steam, washing down afterwards with hot salt water.

The carriage of bulk liquids 'has now moved into the container field with tanks fitted into steel-framed container units, of 20 ft × 8 ft × 8 ft (6·096 m × 2·438 m × 2·438 m). Other types enclose glass reinforced plastic tanks.

The tank capacities are of the order of 4000 gallons (18 184 litres) with the total weight of the unit about 3–4 tons (3·048–4·064 metric tons). The container units are self-stacking in that each can be interlocked with another and lifting is by 'four-leg' chain sling arrangements fitted into the four corners of the unit.

'G' ORES AND SIMILAR DERIVATIVES

The production of iron and steel is a principal basic industry; there will ever be an increasing demand not only of iron and steel but also for associated metals used in the preparation of special steels and ferro alloys and to meet this need, increasingly new 'ore' mining areas are being developed, both in the U.K. and abroad, though more extensively in the latter.

Ore carriers of up to 90–100,000 D.W. tons and above are anticipated developments, supported by loading and discharging capacities of 20 000–30 000 tons per hour from sophisticated multi-conveyor systems covering different grades of ore simultaneously. Trades on which these cargoes are based include Norway, Sweden, Spain, South Africa, Newfoundland, Canada, U.S.A., Brazil, Australia...See Section 5, page 275, on loading and discharging facilities.

Types of Ore. The more important ores are the oxides and a carbonate of iron. The oxide minerals are magnetite and haematite and the carbonate mineral is spathic iron ore. The desirability of working a deposit is decided not merely on the percentage of iron, but also by the proportion of other substances present which might hinder or improve the smelting process. Magnetite is an important iron ore and it is so called on account of the permanently magnetic character of some specimens. This variety occurs in Norway and Sweden, Saxony, Canada, U.S.A., Mexico, the Urals, Siberia, Elba and in the West of England. If it were pure it would contain 72·4 per cent of iron, but other substances are often present and the value then varies from 5·4–61 per cent. Haematite occurs in various shades of colour ranging from deep red to steel gray. Red haematite shows 60–66 per cent iron and, like magnetite, is practically free from sulphur and phosphorus compounds. This variety can be found in Spain, Canada, U.S.A. and Northern England. Brown haematite (limonite) is found in England, France, Germany and Spain. It may contain 40–43 per cent iron and varies in phosphorus content and proportion of water. The ore, if pure, would contain about 60 per cent of iron.

Spathic ore (siderite) if pure would contain about 48 per cent of metallic iron. Actual specimens from the British Isles show 34–35 per cent iron. The ore is a carbonate mineral and is available in the British Isles and on the Continent. If mixed with clay, it is called ironstone, and if associated with coaly matters it is called blackstone ironstone.

Pig iron arises from the primary process of converting iron ore into pig iron, for commercial purposes. This involves heating the calcined ore with coke and limestone in a blast furnace and an alloy of iron and carbon is obtained.

Ore Cargoes. The carriage of ore cargoes require very special and individual care; they are naturally heavy cargoes and their deadweight nature precludes their stowage unless due consideration is given to structural stresses upon the vessel and on its stability characteristics. Most vessels carrying ore cargoes tend to be stiff and thus are prone to heavy rolling and pitching so that loading methods must be adopted to reduce this to a minimum. Currently, the majority of vessels in the ore trades are especially built to conform to the particular requirements of the cargo but where, in possible isolated cases, a general conventional trader may be chartered for an ore cargo, a number of necessary precautions must be adopted.

Where special carrying facilities are not available loading arrangements may take the form as illustrated in diagrams A and B but it emphasized that these are exceptional and are only included here

Diagram 'A'   Figs 4.4

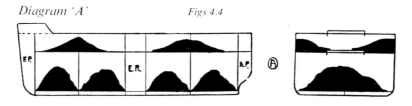

Diagram 'B'

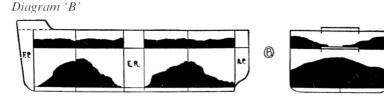

for the purpose of comparison between hitherto systems and the now, more sophisticated and applicable recommended practices. Indeed, the carriage of bulk cargoes, which includes ores and their derivatives, is now covered by 'The Code of Practice for Bulk Cargoes' sponsored by I.M.O. (International Maritime Organization) and supported by Ministry of Shipping Notices.

In this case the ore in the lower holds is built into pyramid fashion in the middle of the hold, with about one-third of the weight distributed at the bulkheads in the 'tween decks and out into the wings.

Numbers 2 and 3 holds have the greater proportion of weight. (See Structural Stresses when loading cargo.)

A summary of these recommendations, and references to ministry notices follows at the end of these notes.

Modern Ore Carriage. Figure 4.5 illustrates, in profile a British built standard bulk carrier suitable for the carriage of ore cargoes. Attention is drawn to the upper deck saddle water ballast tanks which are embodied in the construction to offset bottom weight and so

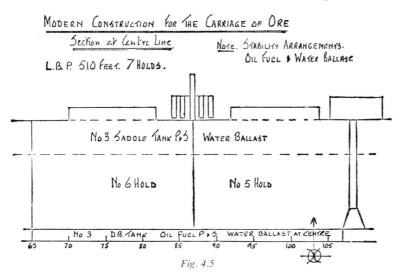

Fig. 4.5

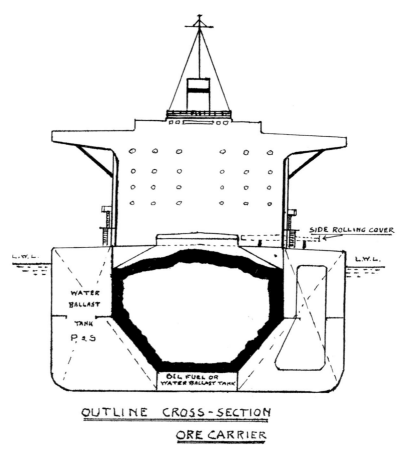

OUTLINE CROSS-SECTION

ORE CARRIER

improve the stability factor. No cargo gear is fitted since loading and discharging is by mechanical means. This diagram should be studied in relation to the provisions recommended in the Code, which follows. See also 'General Arrangements'—Bulk Vessel, in jacket pocket.

STOWAGE OF STEEL, ORES OR OTHER HEAVY CARGOES IN TWEEN DECKS

Heavy cargoes of the above types, as stowed, can induce excessive structural stress. Restrictions, therefore, are indicated by which the intensity and distribution of loading must be contained to the extent to which the 'tween decks' stowage is designed, on the basis of a stowage factor of 50 cu. ft. per ton.

For example, bulk ore, stowing at 19 cu. ft. per ton should be distributed to a depth of $\frac{19}{50}$ of the height of the tween deck.

Some vessels engaged in the carriage of these types of cargoes may well be designed to meet the intensity of load, in which case reference to the ship's capacity plan will provide the relevant information and guide lines.

Detail of these precautions is contained in The Department of Transport Merchant Shipping Notice No. M899, to which reference should be made.

THE CODE OF PRACTICE FOR BULK CARGOES

Introduction

The carriage of bulk cargoes is conditioned by 'The Code of Practice for Bulk Cargoes', a document of recommendation arising out of the 1960 International Conference on the Safety of Life at Sea. At that conference a study was made of the factors inherent in, and with, bulk cargoes and detailed consideration recommended as being appropriate to the influence and sponsorship of the International Maritime Organization (I.M.O.) The code is the result of studies since that time and now forms the basis on which the international maritime world advises its governments, ship operators and ship masters to follow, where responsibilities for these forms of cargoes arise.

The code is a document of intelligent and positive application now internationally accepted as a method of dealing with hazards which can be encountered with bulk cargoes. The summary which follows is included with the kind permission of I.M.O.; it draws attention to the main features involved; it indicates the wisdom of careful attention to the full contents of the code; it behoves all associated personnel, and particularly Cargo Officers, to study its implications to the full. Copies of the code can be obtained from I.M.O. (4 Albert Embankment, London SE1 7SR).

Summary

In this context the following notes are not related to the carriage of grain in bulk, for which particular recommendations are available (see section on the Carriage of Grain, pages 194–199), but are concerned with 'dry' bulk cargoes and 'wet' bulk cargoes, normally referred to as 'ore concentrates'. Generally speaking, a bulk load is considered to be that which forms a considerable part of the total cargo for a voyage, normally more than one-third of the cargo deadweight of the vessel. Less than this amount, except with concentrates, which even with small loads calls for special consideration, permits some prudent decisions on the part of the Master, as to the amount he may wish to carry.

Hazards. Bulk carriage involves three main hazards:

1. Structural stress upon the vessel due to improper weight distribution.
2. Lack of initial stability of sufficient amount at time of loading or by its reduction during the voyage.

(With 1 and 2 both can have some interrelationship, particularly 2 over 1, by reason of stresses set up from excessive motion where the GM (metacentric height) and the GZ (righting moment) accentuate this.)

3. The possibility of spontaneous heating within the bulk, toxic or explosive gases and, also, corrosive effect.

Movement. Bulk cargoes are liable to inclination, or shifting, and this largely depends upon their constituent make up. They are said to have 'an angle of repose', the angular inclination between a horizontal plane and the cone slope which results from a bulk load being loaded on to a horizontal plane.

A 'low' angle of repose characterizes a bulk cargo which is prone to dry surface movement. For this reason the code differentiates between bulk cargoes having angles of repose more than and less than $35°$ (see later notes).

Concentrates. A 'concentrate' bulk cargo is of material which having undergone some form of purification or physical separation of undesirable ingredients, renders it more liable to movement, or shifting. In this context attention is drawn to the term 'transportable moisture limit' which defines the maximum amount of moisture concentrate considered safe for carriage by sea, *in normal cargo vessels.* The 'moisture content' is the percentage water/liquid present in the bulk which, at some point, known as the 'flow moisture point' a flow state develops.

Vessels specially built for the carriage of bulk cargoes and sufficiently internally subdivided are not so highly restricted in their loading procedures with concentrates, as normal cargo vessels would be (see later notes).

Densities. Bulk cargoes with which the code is concerned are, in the main, of high density. A 20 cu ft per ton (0·56 cu m per metre ton) density cargo imposes far greater structural stresses upon a vessel than is usual with normal cargoes stowing at 50–60 cu ft per ton (1·39–1·67 cu m per metre ton). Prudent precautions on weight distribution is therefore obvious.

Normally it would be expected that ship masters would be provided with information data by which adequate load distribution can be determined.

Generally this information is available in the ship's stability information booklet. Additionally, the vessel might be equipped with loading calculator systems, i.e. Load Meters/Load Masters.

Where this is not the case a formula is recommended in the I.M.O. (1981) Bulk Cargo Code:

The maximum number of tonnes of cargo loaded in any cargo space should not exceed:

$$0.9 \, LBD \text{ tonnes,}$$

where L = length of the hold in metres
B = average breadth of hold in metres
D = summer load draught in metres.

Where cargo is untrimmed or only partially trimmed the corresponding height of cargo pile peak above the cargo space floor should not exceed:

$$1.1 \times D \times \text{stowage factor,}$$

where the stowage factor is given in cubic metres per tonne.

Furthermore, high density loads of the types under consideration can result in high metacentric heights (GM) from which, by reason of the stiff condition of the vessel, heavy rolling in a seaway could well result. By and large such a condition need not be of undue concern since the resistance to listing is greater should a shift of cargo occur. Nonetheless, regard must be given to Regulation 19a of the International Convention on Safety of Life at Sea, 1974, whereby stability information, in the stability booklet, is available to ship masters from which calculations can be made on both desirable initial stability conditions and that which could arise in the event of unfavourable conditions arising during the voyage.

Trimming. Preferably, bulk cargoes should be trimmed entirely level. Where this is not so, and a corresponding pile peak arises, this should be restricted as follows:

ANGLES OF REPOSE GREATER THAN 35°

High density cargo should be loaded entirely into lower holds, due regard being given to excessive stiffness and structural stress. It should be trimmed well out across the bottom and out to the ship's side. Acceptable trimming can be accomplished by bringing the load within the hatch square and levelling off, with the remainder of the load gradually sloped towards the sides of the lower hold. Where any peak remains above the hatch centre it should be sufficiently clear of the edges as will allow it to slide into the lower hold.

High density bulk is not recommended for 'tween deck stowage, bearing in mind the lessening of GM which would result (see p. 356 on Stiffness and Resistance to Shifting). Where such loading cannot be avoided this should be the least amount necessary to prevent undue stiffness. Furthermore, with bulk loaded in the 'tween decks, the hatchway should be closed; the load trimmed reasonably level from side to side and bulkhead to bulkhead, or it should be stowed in bins.

ANGLES OF REPOSE LESS THAN OR EQUAL TO 35°

It is essential that these cargoes are properly and effectively trimmed and that the load, as far as is practicable, fill the space into which it is loaded, due regard being given to structural stress.

'Tween deck stowage calls for level trimming and, where the possibility of heeling could give rise to shifting, adequate shifting boards, or bins should be provided. Indeed, in any compartment, partly filled with bulk having this lesser angle of repose, shifting boards, bins or other securing provisions should be made.

Free flowing dry bulk cargoes should be treated in like manner to the provisions applicable to grain cargoes (see p. 182).

Hazards with Concentrates. The risks with concentrates arise from the possibility of the moisture content being below the transportable moisture content, which can then introduce a dry movement hazard, albeit this can, at the time of loading, be latent yet arise later from the stimulus of compaction or of vibration during the voyage.

Where such a viscous state arises the bulk may move with the ship in rolling, but does not completely return as the period of rolling moves from port to starboard, or vice versa. Herein lies the risk, from which the ship may take on a dangerous heel.

General cargo vessels, as such, should not carry concentrates having a T.M.L. above the defined limit. Where they are above the limit, and so permissible, no other liquid container cargoes should be stowed in the same compartment; all adequate precautions must be taken to avoid liquids of any form from entering the space and, if any cooling of the concentrate becomes necessary, this should be done by 'spraying' with water.

General cargo vessels which have specially designed arrangements to restrain cargo movement may load concentrates with a T.M.L. above the limit but these arrangements must be completely adequate to meet any possible envisaged situations and be approved by the country of origin of the ship's registry.

Specially constructed bulk carriers are not so restricted, by virtue of their structural arrangements but, even so, in these cases the vessel must be in possession of evidence, in the form of structural design and stability conditions, that it is suitable for this type of cargo carriage.

The Categories of Bulk Cargoes

The greater part of the I.M.O. Code lists the substances to which it refers. It is important to stress that the list is not exhaustive. In case of doubt advice should be sought by the Master as to whether the cargo offered possesses the characteristics likely to merit its inclusion.

The categories are:—

1. Cargoes which may liquefy, generally all concentrates,

palletized ores and slurries, but including any fine particuled substances.

2. Bulk materials possessing chemical hazards. These are, for the most part, included in the I.M.D.G. Code.

3. Substances possessing neither of the above properties. For these it is necessary to seek up to date information from the shipper, re their physical and/or chemical properties, before the shipment is made.

A fourth category, not specifically listed is that of material hazardous only in bulk. They may not be listed in the I.M.D.G. Code and are not listed in the Bulk code.

However, a substance which, through internal reaction, depletes the oxygen content of the cargo space would be included . . .

Department of Trade M Notice 613 points out the dangers associated with heavy density bulks of quarried products, such as ores, granular salt and other similar commodities, when carried in small coasters.

It can well be that without careful and adequate level trimming heavy density cargoes may leave considerable void spaces in the holds which, by reason of the ship's motion, could result in the cargo shifting into the void, and producing a list. In severe weather this list could progressively increase, until the vessel capsizes.

Where good trimming cannot be carried out, Notice 613 strongly recommends the fitting of a centre line division.

Attention should also be given to likely weather conditions with small single deck vessels and attention also be given to official weather forecasts before deciding upon the course to take and/or where 'shelter' if necessary, can be found.

The Safe Carriage of Bulk Cargoes

There is an M Notice . . . No. 970, under the above title, which supplements the requirements of the I.M.O. Code by emphasizing the necessity of ascertaining the moisture content and T.M.L. of all bulk cargoes, whether or no the substances are listed in the code.

The M notice points out that there are three possible sources of moisture in bulk cargoes of which two, exposure to the elements and stockpiling on wet ground, are likely to dominate. (See pages 170, 171, cargoes from ponds) . . . over the natural moisture content. Thus, care is necessary to protect the cargo prior to shipment.

Since such care may well be impractical, check lists must be carried out to verify the moisture content. It is the Master's duty to decide whether a cargo is safe to carry, by reference to the information given by the shipper.

This will call for careful scrutiny, looking for suspect details . . . particularly test values not of recent date.

Further attention will centre on the assessment of the vessel's stability condition in the loaded state, the proper trimming of the cargo and any inclement weather conditions (rain) having taken place during loading.

The Department of Trade encourages voluntary reports by shippers, owners and Masters on cargo conditions and ship's behaviours with bulk loads, the purpose being to enable information to be analysed with a view to improving the standard of safety on bulk cargo voyages.

Sampling Test Procedures with Concentrates and Similar Materials

It is unlikely that Cargo Officers would be involved with the procedures whereby samples of concentrates intended for carriage by sea would be carried out since these are of chemical analysis under laboratory conditions, either at the point of production of the concentrate or at an intervening interval between point of production and shipment at the loading terminal.

Sufficient to say that the Code fully details the requirements covering sampling procedures and the facilities whereby Masters of ships can be aware of the outcome. It is more than likely that at any reputable loading terminal these facilities are available and unlikely that any difficulties would prevent a Cargo Officer from seeing the manner in which the tests are carried out.

General Precautions Prior to Loading a Bulk Cargo

Prior to and during the loading operations with a bulk cargo certain general routines are both desirable and advantageous.

All the normal safety precautions for ship personnel and others working on the vessel at the time must be taken and these, particularly, would ensure minimum contact with any moving machinery relevant to the loading procedures.

Of necessity, all hold and spaces for the reception of cargo should be inspected beforehand and be in a proper state for the reception of the cargo, with particular attention given to bilge wells and lines, sounding pipes and other service units, with protective coverings checked or, indeed, strengthened if necessary, bearing in mind the velocity with which heavy density cargoes can enter into the hold or space.

Dust is another factor and protective measures should be taken to prevent this coming in contact with moving parts of deck machinery though it can be pointed out that modern ore loading plants, for example, are fitted with extensive dust protective facilities.

At the completion of loading it is seamanlike practice to sound the bilges.

'H' REFRIGERATED CARGOES

Where, in this section, temperatures are given in Fahrenheit notation, they should, for comparison, be interpolated to show Centigrade notation.

Considerable development has taken place in recent years with regard to the carriage of edible goods in the refrigerated state.

In the field of development, some modifications and changes, but much progress has accompanied a highly complicated science, not the least of which is the introduction of refrigerated produce to containerization. Even so, much of the present is based upon earlier refrigerated practices, adapted to new knowledge and research, with vessels such as the *Afric Star* illustrated on page 238 with the kind permission of The Blue Star Line, Limited, designed as a fully refrigerated cargo ship.

Additionally, the text 'Shipboard Cargo Refrigeration', included by kind permission of Hall-Thermotank International, Limited of Dartford, Kent, England, illustrates the modern approach to refrigerated carriage and the kind of research and manufacture which now forms a large part of the science.

It is desirable that cargo officers should not lose sight of the earlier basic thinking, by so doing it provides a constructive base for comparison and it is, therefore, a pre-requisite that officers look closely at the systems of refrigeration in the ships in which they serve in order to ensure an adaptability to whatever forms of refrigeration with which they may be involved. It is for these reasons that this section contains 'two' sides of a major part of cargo carriage and handling.

By virtue of the fact that some countries have a surplus of meat, fruit, provisions, etc., whilst others, of necessity, must rely upon imports to supplement their own production, large trades have developed utilizing fast cargo vessels having all or part of their cargo space given over to refrigerated cargoes.

The success of a 'refrigerated' trade depends principally upon the condition in which the cargo arrives at the port of discharge, and this success is not attained solely by the efficiency of the refrigerating machinery or the high standard of the insulation. To ensure that such cargoes arrive in the best possible condition considerable responsibility rests with cargo officers in the discharge of their duties. It is essential that proper methods of stowage are employed and that all proper precautions are taken both prior to and during the reception of the cargo, and also that the cargo is kept at proper temperatures during the voyage.

Any departure, however slight, from the highest standard of efficiency in these respects may result in deterioration of part or all of the cargo, in which case the loss of value and the extent of the claims may be very large.

Most shipping companies engaged on the refrigerated trades issue to their officers their own official regulations. These differ only in regard to the type of cargo carried; essentially they are the same and stress the importance of precautions under the following headings:

1. The preparation of the compartments.
2. The precooling of the compartments.
3. The loading, which includes the methods of handling and stowage.
4. The carriage, which includes the maintaining of proper temperatures and the precautions to be adopted to prevent undue accumulation of CO_2.
5. Precautions to be adopted during discharge.

Refrigeration transport may be divided into three main classes:
1. The carriage of goods in the frozen state.
2. The carriage of goods in the chilled state.
3. The use of air cooled systems.

In the first class such commodities as beef, mutton, lamb, offal, butter and fish comprise most of the shipments. Beef is also extensively carried in the chilled state, as also are cheese, eggs and fresh vegetables whilst most cargoes of fruit (apples, pears, citrus fruits and grapes) are best carried in spaces which are served by air cooled systems.

'Frozen' compartments may be either lower hold or 'tween deck spaces which are served by a system of 'grids' or 2 in pipes, fitted to the inboard side of the insulation, through which the brine is pumped at the required temperature.

The 'grid' system is more usually employed in modern vessels, in preference to continuous piping, because each grid or section of piping has its own independent supply and return direct to the evaporator and brine tank. The advantage lies in the fact that should one grid become choked the temperature may be maintained by increasing the brine supply through the other grids.

'Chilled' compartments differ very little in construction from those used for frozen cargoes, except that more extensive coils or grids are fitted. The carriage of chilled meat needs even greater care than that of frozen meat, because a definite uniformity of temperature must be maintained for the successful carriage of such cargoes.

Air cooled compartments are not fitted with grids or pipes, but have their temperatures maintained by air circulation. The system of air circulation is maintained by supply fans which force precooled air along trunks and through ducts to the compartment, while extractor fans withdraw the air from the compartment when it becomes overcharged by heat or moisture or carbonic acid gas.

The interest of the deck officer in refrigerated cargoes must be directed primarily towards loading, carriage and delivery and it is proposed to discuss the salient features as they affect the officer from loading to discharging port.

The question regarding the methods of refrigeration or the construction and operation of the refrigerating machinery; though equally important, is outside the scope of this book, such information may be found in any good book on engineering.

A. The Preparation of the Compartments

All compartments intended for the carriage of refrigerated goods must be thoroughly clean, dry and free from any odour or taint.

If it is usual on the outward passage to carry general cargo in refrigerated spaces, after discharging, the spaces will require to be thoroughly cleaned out, leaving no dunnage of any kind. Particular attention must be given to the sides of the insulation and to the floor of the space to ensure that there are no remaining traces of stains of previous cargoes. In some vessels the compartments are washed down with a mild solution of carbolocene, but in most ships today the major operation of disinfecting the space is accomplished by means of patent deodorizers.

Particular attention will be needed to ensure that the bilges, if fitted, are clean and free from any foreign odour; they should be deodorized if necessary. Care must be taken to see that strum boxes are free and tank top drains, if fitted, sealed with brine, also that all valves on drain pipes are working easily and closing tightly.

Limber hatches and tank manhole plugs must be inspected to ensure that they are free from damage. They should then be carefully fitted in place and their joints sealed by caulking and/or papering.

With 'battery' compartments, i.e. brine batteries over which clean air is passed to be pre-cooled before circulation, the battery scuppers and fittings and water courses are to be examined for freeness and cleanliness to ensure that the moisture shall have free and easy access to the bilges or wells when thawing off.

Complete and thorough inspection of the insulation must be made and any defects, however slight, remedied, and all insulated ventilator plugs (unless previous instructions require otherwise), must be closely fitted in place, wedged tightly and sealed with sawdust.

All portable trunks in the holds of 'battery' compartments must be assembled in place and all necessary dunnage battens, suitable to the type of cargo to be loaded must be in place.

In 'grid' compartments the brine circuits will have to be tested to ensure that they are running freely, that no leaks occur at the joints and that all fastenings and connections are perfectly secure.

In 'tween deck compartments attention must be given to the deck scuppers; the traps or U-bends must be efficiently sealed to prevent the possibility of warm air or taint odours rising from the bilges.

Brine pipes are tested to $1\frac{1}{2}$ times the normal working pressure.

In all spaces the thermometer tubes must be in place and lengthened, if necessary, by wooden extensions, to enable temperatures to be taken from both the top and bottom of the space. (See notes on Thermometers.)

In all ships, unless otherwise directed, special precautions should be adopted to prevent the possibility of conduction of heat between adjacent spaces in the same hold, carrying cargoes whose temperatures differ considerably, as in the case of frozen cargo over chilled cargo.

Reinforcing of the insulation between the spaces is necessary and usually takes the form of a layer of clean, dry, inodorous sawdust, laid over the floor insulation to a depth of about 6 in.

This precaution is very necessary when carrying frozen meat and chilled cheese in adjacent compartments in the same hold.

It is advisable, and particularly so with frozen cargo, to have all the dunnage battens necessary for the stowage, in the compartments before pre-cooling commences. Such a procedure ensures that the dunnage acquires the same temperature as the compartment.

Although considerable quantities of new dunnage battens are generally necessary for each cargo, the use of previously used dunnage is not prohibited for consecutive voyages. Discretion must be used, however, in choosing dunnage for re-use, because, apart from the obvious necessity of clean and dry battens, it would be injurious, for example, to use for butter or eggs, dunnage which had been used previously with a fruit cargo.

Indiscretion in the use of dunnage may be the cause of damage resulting from taint.

All spaces intended for the carriage of refrigerated goods must be cooled down before loading. The pre-cooling temperatures depend upon the type of cargo to be loaded, but in every case they are considerably lower than the transit temperatures, to allow for fluctuations, whilst loading.

The pre-cooling is frequently regulated by the requirements of the port regulations and a knowledge of the current regulations is necessary in order to avoid delay. Usually the pre-cooling of the compartments commences from 48 to 24 hours before loading is to commence.

Frozen compartments are pre-cooled to about	10°F
Chilled compartments (meat)	22°F
Apples, pears, peaches and grapes	28°F
Citrus fruits (oranges, lemons, grapefruit)	36°F
Cheese	40°F

By virtue of their small stowage factor, ingots of tin, lead or copper find ideal bottom stowage in refrigerated compartments. These are loaded before pre-cooling and it is very important that all surplus heat should be extracted from them before commencing to load the refrigerated cargo. It is impossible to state any hard and fast rule as to the length of time required to accomplish this, for much depends upon the weight and specific heat of the ingots. It is advised, however, that spaces so loaded should be maintained at the transit temperature for a chilled cargo and at 14°F for a frozen cargo, for about 6 hours for each whole floor tier of ingots. Battens of 3 in × 3 in will be necessary before overstowing with refrigerated cargo. On no account must the lead, tin or copper touch the meat.

After the cleaning preparation and cooling, the spaces must be inspected by a Lloyd's or other approved surveyor and a loading certificate granted before any cargo is stowed in the spaces.

B. The Loading and Handling

It is very important that ships' officers should be fully conversant with all local loading regulations. These regulations are designed to ensure quick delivery and the avoidance of friction between ship and stevedores. Considerable delay to the ship may result should a vessel be unaware of the various regulations as to opening and closing of compartments and the accepted working temperatures of the spaces.

The successful carriage of a refrigerated cargo is, in no small way, dependent upon close co-operation between engine and deck departments. This point cannot be too strongly stressed, and during loading the officers should, as far as possible, carry out a careful and continuous supervision of the stowage.

The maintaining of proper temperatures in the spaces, appropriate to the type of cargo to be loaded, is very important. It is not always possible to advise beforehand which compartments may be needed first and, when loading in the 'tween decks, it must not be overlooked that the lower hold may suddenly be required. The temperatures should be such that no delay is encountered by having to wait whilst the loading temperature is achieved; this should always be at the required degree.

It frequently happens that cargo, not necessarily refrigerated, has to be loaded into a lower hold through a 'tween deck in which there is refrigerated cargo.

To prevent the ingress of warm air to the 'tween decks temporary screens of clean tarpaulins should be hung round the sides of the hatchway.

When loading a general cargo into compartments above or below those containing refrigerated cargoes precautions must be taken to prevent the possibility of condensate forming in the 'general' spaces. It can be appreciated that excessive condensation results in much moisture liable to damage general cargo and it is usual to lay at least 3 in of dunnage on the floors, filled in with sawdust. On top of this a further 2 in of dunnage should form the 'bedding' for the cargo.

It has been pointed out that the maintaining of proper temperatures is particularly important in 'battery' compartments. Every reasonable opportunity should be taken to run the refrigerating plant, as for example, during stoppages for meals, etc., and deck officers should be aware of this fact in order to advise the engineers when it will be necessary to operate the plant in order to maintain the required temperature.

During loading and discharging, it sometimes happens that snow forms on the brine pipes and may be knocked on to the cargo.

This is very injurious, for it melts and causes damage by wetting, resulting in a deterioration of the value of the cargo. Every effort should be made to avoid such damage by carefully brushing the snow from the pipes on to tarpaulins and removing same.

The necessity of proper unimpeded circulation of air in all compartments cannot be too strongly impressed upon all officers and no cargo should be stowed in such a way as to impede the circulation over the top of the cargo, or in air channels provided by dunnage battens, or in the way of air trunks. Particular care is necessary in the laying of floor battens and side battens whilst a clear space of about 6 in should be kept between the top insulation and air ducts of battery compartments and at least 3 in between the top of the cargo and the undersides of grids.

Upon the temporary completion of a compartment the insulated doors are to be firmly closed and fastened. Greater efficiency in this respect will be achieved if the lower screw fastener is tightened first thereby allowing the door to plug itself firmly in place.

When the loading is finally completed, all insulated hatches and doors must be firmly shipped in place and effectively sealed. Insulated hatches are satisfactorily sealed by caulking the seams with burlap over which is placed a layer of sawdust, whilst insulated doors may be made air tight by pasting layers of thick paper over the seams.

Very strict supervision on the part of officers is necessary to enforce careful handling of refrigerated cargo. As a rule little or no trouble is experienced at loading ports, for the stevedores are continuously employed in the handling of such cargoes and strict regulations are issued and enforced by loading port authorities. Most of the trouble in this direction results from inefficient supervision at port of discharge; but the following points are worthy of note as applicable in all cases.

1. No workman should be permitted to walk on meat unless his boots are covered with clean material such as matting or burlap.
2. Slings should be 'broken out' or 'made up' in the hatchway, just clear of the square, and running boards employed to facilitate stowage in the wings.
3. No heaving out or dragging should be allowed when discharging; running boards and/or chutes should be provided to pass the cargo from all parts of the space to the sling.
4. Canvas nets should be used for the slinging of meat. Trays should be used for crates of cheese, cases of butter and cases of fruit.
5. Because of the fragile nature of cases of fruit, walking boards should be provided to facilitate the building of a compact stow. Walking on the cases would inevitably result in their being crushed.

C. Reception of Cargo

Considerable care and attention is necessary when receiving refrigerated cargo. Cargo which is in any way unfit for carriage will not only deteriorate in value itself, but will cause damage to adjacent cargo. Frozen cargo, for example, must be frozen hard and free from any sign of mould; the coverings and wrappings of carcasses must be undamaged. Any fruit shipped in an advanced state of ripeness is a prolific source of damage.

The general precautions to be adopted are dealt with in greater detail under the heading of Individual Commodities.

D. Notes on Individual Commodities

Frozen Meat. All compartments are to be thoroughly cleaned and sterilized.

Before pre-cooling is commenced the appropriate dunnage battens are to be laid in place. In lower holds 3 in × 3 in floor battens are necessary, laid athwartships at about a 12 in spacing, centre to centre, whilst in 'tween deck compartments 2 in × 2 in battens suffice, laid similarly to those in the lower holds.

Great care must be taken to ensure that these battens are not displaced during loading, or that the cargo is allowed to extend between them, for such would destroy the efficiency of the air circulation.

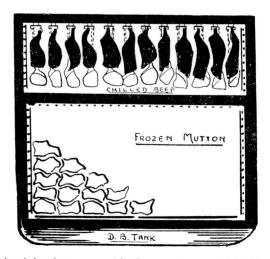

Fig. 4.6 Insulated chambers arranged for frozen mutton and chilled beef. Note how the chilled beef is hung from hooks and chains, whilst the frozen mutton is stowed fore and aft, in the block.

If stowing bagged meat or offal, the bottom battens are to be supplemented with a fore and aft tier of 3 in × 3 in battens, both in the lower holds and 'tween decks.

Pre-cooling should commence at least 24 hours before loading commences, though vessels must be guided by local regulations in this respect, and the temperatures of the compartments reduced to 10°F. During loading the temperatures must be kept as low as possible, and should not be allowed to rise above 25°F.

Strict supervision must be maintained during loading to ensure that all meat is hard frozen and in good condition; any soft, mis-shapen, soiled or damaged meat should be rejected. Frozen meat, particularly lamb and mutton, is subject to mould damage which shows itself as light yellow markings. This is usually the result of meat having been subjected to temperature fluctuations.

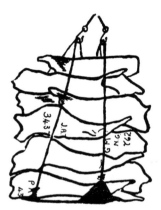

Fig. 4.7 The Correct Method of Slinging Frozen Carcasses.

Beef, lamb and mutton may be stowed in the same compartment, but lamb and mutton carcasses must not be overstowed with beef in view of its heavier weight which might cause crushing damage to the lamb or mutton.

Frozen fore and hind quarters of beef are stowed on their edges, fore and aft, but lamb and mutton stow better by placing the lower tier on their backs and subsequent tiers belly to belly, all carcasses being laid fore and aft.

Bagged meat and offal is frequently very uneven in stowage and will require to be covered with a double tier of battens when stowing other cargo on top of it.

The carrying temperature during the voyage should be maintained as near to 15°F as is possible and never allowed to rise above 17°F.

Offal. Offal is now carried packed in frozen individual containers, palletized into refrigerated containers. It is thus cleaner, easier of stow and ready for distribution at port of discharge. The New Zealand trade is a case in point.

Chilled Meat. All compartments are to be thoroughly clean, dry and sterilized before loading commences. The cleaning of a chilled compartment will include the sterilizing of the meat chains, hooks and runways. In some ports meat hooks are cleaned and disinfected at the factory and hooked in the quarters of beef ready for shipment.

The carriage of chilled meat is an even more specialized trade than the carriage of frozen meat and definite markets require this cargo in preference to frozen. Opinion suggests that the tissues of beef may be damaged as a result of being frozen, thus lowering its value.

The necessity of maintaining a uniform temperature with chilled meat demands that all precautions are taken to ensure that recording thermometers are examined and tested before loading commences.

The introduction of certain amounts of CO_2 gas and its control are important factors to the successful carriage of chilled meat. The fans, the motors, the CO_2 charging plant and the CO_2 recorders must be thoroughly examined and put in reliable condition prior to loading. (See notes on CO_2 Recorders.)

No dunnage is required other than the permanent baffle boards which serve to keep the meat off the brine pipes.

Compartments should be pre-cooled to about 22°F and opened up at a temperature of about 26°F.

Chilled beef is hung from the overhead rails and on chains. In 'tween deck compartments the hind quarters are hung direct from the rail and two fore quarters immediately below, on chains, 12 in apart. Lower hold compartments, of course, permit more carcasses (see diagram).

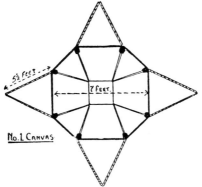

Fig. 4.8 Canvas Meat Net.

The carcasses are stowed reasonably tightly to prevent movement, but not so tightly as to impede the circulation of air, and all precautions must be taken to prevent any contact with the brine pipes.

The carrying temperature of chilled meat is generally advised by the shippers whose instructions should be carefully followed, but such temperatures are usually within the range 28–29·5°F.

The nature of the damage prevalent in chilled beef includes mould, taint in fat, loss of bloom, slime, bacteria and frost. Close watch must be kept on the condition of the meat during loading and any carcasses which show signs of the above damage should be rejected.

When the compartments are fully loaded, closed and sealed, the fans may be started in order to change the air frequently. This does not damage the beef in any way and it is recommended that the air should be changed from 20–25 times an hour.

With compartments which are charged with CO_2 gas, the charging is commenced as soon as the spaces are sealed. About 14 lb of CO_2 gas is introduced for every 1000 cu ft of air space and such circulation is aimed at as will maintain a concentration of not more than 8 per cent.

One very well known shipping company, engaged in the refrigerated trade, requires the following information from their officers when chilled meat is carried.

Ship Chambers	*Air Circulation*
When sterilized	When commenced
Disinfectant used	Approximate air changes per
When loaded	hour, first few days
When discharged	Approximate air changes per
Opening temperatures	hour, subsequent period
Closing temperatures	CO_2
Beef temperatures	Quantity used
Carrying temperatures	When first applied
Stowage	Minimum concentration
Number of Hinds and	Maximum concentration
Weight	Average concentration
Number of Crops and	Dates and times at which
Weight	readings are taken

Butter. Butter is carried as a frozen cargo, and may be stowed by itself or with frozen meat. Due to its weight it is preferably stowed in lower compartments in order to achieve a reasonably satisfactory condition of stability, this being always of prime consideration with refrigerated vessels having several separate compartments.

The compartment in which butter is to be stowed will require to be cleaned, prepared and pre-cooled as for frozen meat and similar precautions must be adopted as to the maintaining of proper temperatures during the voyage.

Butter is shipped in boxes and may be satisfactorily carried as block stowage, provided the butter is well frozen when received. The boxes may have $\frac{1}{4}$–$\frac{1}{2}$ in battens fitted to them, or, if not so fitted, $\frac{1}{4}$ in laths must be laid, athwartships between every other tier.

Battens of 3 in × 3 in are placed on the floor of the compartment athwartships, spaced about 9 in (centres) apart, and if meat is to be stowed in the same compartment, it is necessary to have 3 in × 3 in battens placed athwartships, 9 in apart, between the boxes of butter and the meat.

Butter must not be stowed in the same hatch as fruit, for it is easily contaminated by the gases and odours given off by the fruit.

Cheese. The carriage of cheese as a cargo requires certain precautions. It is easily tainted and requires very consistent temperatures because fluctuations in the temperature of a compartment will cause serious damaging effects. The local dairy board at port of loading will specify the loading and carrying temperatures; the former being approximately atmospheric and the latter 40–50°F according to the quality of the cheese. In some cases a carrying temperature of 55°F is specified; in such cases strict supervision is necessary to ensure that the temperatures *never* rise above this figure.

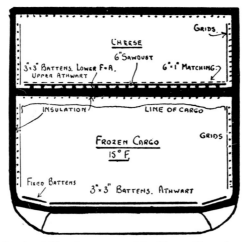

Fig. 4.9 Insulated Chambers arranged for Frozen Cargo Lower Hold. CHEESE in 'Tween Decks.

It follows therefore that cheese is carried in chilled compartments, on either the grid or battery system and in consequence of the importance of correct temperature control, all thermometer tubes should be correctly in place.

Cheese is shipped in boxes or crates and may be given either lower hold or 'tween deck stowage. It is advisable however that adjacent spaces in the same hatch should contain chilled cargo, if cheese is stowed in one of them.

If, however, with adjacent spaces, there is no alternative to carrying frozen cargo over cheese, then in grid ships, drip trays should be fitted under the grids in the lower holds and in all ships the separating insulation should be reinforced on the deck with 9 in of sawdust kept in place by a treble tier of 3 in × 3 in battens. The lowest tier of battens should be laid fore and aft and the remaining tiers alternatively athwartships and fore and aft, and it is usual to lay a further tier of battens athwartships at 12 in centres on which to stow the frozen cargo.

The dunnage for the cheese itself in the lower hold should consist of a bottom layer of 3 in × 3 in battens, laid athwartships at about 12 in centres apart and a top tier of 6 in × 1 in matching, laid fore and aft at about 9 in centres apart.

The boxes or crates should be arranged so that their ends rest squarely on a batten with an intermediate batten below the middle of the box or crate, and the stowage so arranged that the tiers are immediately over each other.

Where frozen cargo is carried in the lower hold and cheese in the 'tween decks above, the floor of the 'tween deck compartment will require similar sawdust reinforcing, but in this case a 6 in layer of sawdust will suffice, with two tiers of battens, upper tier athwartships, lower tier, fore and aft.

Special precautions will be required, in the form of sawdust box frames, to prevent interchange of heat through adjoining hatchways (see diagram).

Fig. 4.10 Insulated Chambers arranged for Frozen Cargo Lower Hold. EGGS in 'Tween Decks.

The compartments to be used for cheese should be pre-cooled to about 40°F and whether it be carried in 'grid' or 'battery' compartments, strict supervision is necessary in regulating the brine supply or air circulation in order to keep the uniform temperatures specified.

Eggs. Eggs are shipped in light, fragile crates, suitably packed with shavings, straw or bran to prevent breakage of the shells. They readily absorb moisture and taint and must not, on any account, be stowed in the same hatch as odorous cargo, such as fruit. It is preferable that eggs be stowed in a separate compartment.

Very careful handling of the crates is necessary; trays should be used for loading and discharging and walking over the crates is to be strongly deprecated. Because of the fragile nature of the crates it is advisable to limit the height of stowage to about 12 ft.

Shell eggs must not be frozen and all reasonable precautions must be adopted with the dunnaging to prevent the crates coming in contact with possible points where freezing might occur, such as brine grid leads or cold air delivery trunks.

Similar precautions to those adopted with cheese are necessary when eggs are stowed in a compartment adjacent to one in which frozen cargo is stowed. It is most important, however, to ensure that the sawdust is completely free from any odour.

Drip trays will be necessary with overhead grids, for eggs quickly tend to become mouldy from drippings.

Before loading eggs the compartment should be pre-cooled to about 32°F and during transit the temperatures should be maintained at about 33–34°F.

The bottom dunnage should consist of 3 in × 3 in battens, laid athwartships, suitably spaced to allow the ends and middles of the crates to rest on battens and between each tier 1 in laths must be laid to promote air circulation.

Eggs are sometimes shipped in tins and may be carried at 'frozen' temperatures as for meat. Carried in a compartment alone, they suffer no damage from temperatures as low as 10°F.

Fruit. For relatively short voyages, fruit may be successfully carried in ordinary cargo compartments, and during the late autumn Great Britain receives many cargoes of apples from Canada and the U.S.A. without any form of refrigeration being employed. A very considerable and successful trade has been built up by the carriage of oranges in ordinary cargo vessels from Palestine, the voyage taking some 12–15 days.

For longer passages, however, and also with such fruits as peaches and grapes, it is necessary to make use of refrigerated vessels and the carriage of fruit in chilled compartments forms a very large proportion of the cargoes carried from Australia, New Zealand, U.S.A. and the Argentine.

The successful carriage of fruit in refrigerated vessels depends mainly upon four important factors and all precautions taken and attention given are related to these four factors, which are:

(*a*) The thorough and careful inspection. of the fruit at the time of loading.

(*b*) The rapid reduction of temperatures after loading.

(*c*) The maintenance of even and proper temperatures during transit.

(*d*) The efficient control of CO_2 gas.

Fig. 4.11 Insulated Chambers arranged for Frozen Cargo Lower Hold. FRUIT in 'Tween Decks.

Fruit may be carried in both grid-cooled spaces and battery compartments, but in both cases it is important that the spaces should be perfectly clean, disinfected and free from any foreign odour. Pre-cooling is necessary and should be commenced at least 24 hours before loading is to commence. With 'grid' spaces it is usual to fill all pipes with cold brine in order to reduce the temperatures to about 28°F, whilst in 'air' cooled spaces the air delivery to the compartments varies with the type of fruit and its carrying temperatures. Delivery may be as low as 28°F and strict attention must be given to the shipper's requirements.

In grid-cooled spaces, 2 in × 2 in battens must be secured vertically at about 12 in (centres) along the sides and bulkheads leaving a space of from 4–6 in from the brine pipes.

Floor dunnage should consist of 3 in × 3 in battens in lower holds and 2 in × 2 in battens in 'tween deck spaces, laid athwartships at approximately 24 in (centres) apart. On top of the battens in both lower hold and 'tween decks 6 in × 1 in boards should be laid fore and aft, at about 12 in (centres) apart.

In air cooled spaces the side battens will not be necessary but along the sides of the compartments $\frac{1}{2}$ in battens are sometimes fitted vertically in order to promote complete air circulation. In some vessels the sides and ends of air cooled compartments are fitted with 2 in $\times$ 2 in battens spaced about 12 in apart, both fore and aft athwartships, arranged vertically and horizontally.

Fruit accepted for shipment must be in good condition and the greatest care must be exercised to ensure that fruit which is over-ripe, affected with skin discoloration or internal browning is not shipped.

With all kinds of fruit, samples should be picked indiscriminately from boxes offered for shipment and cut open for inspection. This is a very important precaution for fruit which is over-ripe generates heat and carbon dioxide gas to the detriment of the other fruit in the compartment.

Fruit should be shipped in such a state of maturity as will permit of its being ready for the market on arrival. It follows therefore that pre-shipment inspection, efficient cooling down, and due attention to the shippers' requirements as to temperatures, are of paramount importance.

Considerable quantities of fruit are shipped at atmospheric temperatures and under these conditions rapid cooling is necessary in order to avoid unsatisfactory discharge. Even though proper attention may be given to the temperatures during the voyage the damage will have already been done if the cooling down of the fruit is unnecessarily delayed.

It cannot be too strongly emphasized that attention must be given to shippers' requirements, but experience has shown that a satisfactory state of affairs will be achieved if the time limit does not exceed 4 or 5 days in order to bring the fruit to the carrying temperatures.

Fruit is, of course, offered for shipment at various temperatures and thus it is important that all temperatures at the time of shipment are recorded in the cargo book.

Apples, Pears, Grapes, Peaches, Plums. These fruits are shipped in boxes, with or without battens attached, and the method of stowage will depend upon whether the boxes are of the former or latter type.

It is not advisable that spaces be solidly filled, for this would prevent a continuous air circulation. A modern method of stowage with boxes of apples and pears utilizes what is known as the 'Tower' system of fruit stowage, i.e. a series of open airways or shafts formed by leaving out a fruit box at each tier, distributed in symmetrical positions throughout the stowage.

A space of about 9–12 in should be left above the top tier of boxes, and, with pears, it is advisable that they be stowed in compartments which allow of not more than about 10 tiers. 'Tween deck compartments are therefore preferable to lower holds.

The more general method of stowage is to lay battens between the tiers of boxes, unless these are already fitted to the boxes. These take the form of 2 in laths, popularly known as 'apple battens', and are so laid as to support the ends of the boxes, each of which is stowed immediately above the one below.

The battens must be placed parallel with the air flow and in air cooled compartments they should be laid fore and aft in the main body of the compartment and athwartships at the ends. If the battens are badly arranged they will obstruct the natural flow of air, with the result that undue pressures will be set up, perhaps causing damage to insulation and consequent leakage of air.

Fruit in Cardboard Cartons

Considerable quantities of fruit, particularly apples, are now shipped in cardboard cartons, each of which has a number of perforated holes for ventilation. Block stowage of such a cargo can so easily prevent air circulation through the cartons if fruit battens and adequate dunnage is not provided to counteract this.

Carriage temperatures are as follows:

Apples, carried alone	34–37°F
Apples and pears together	33–35°F
Pears, carried alone	31–33°F
Grapes, carried alone	33–35°F

Peaches and plums may be carried with apples and/or pears at their respective temperatures.

CO_2 *Gas.* As fruit ripens it evolves heat and carbon dioxide gas, which, if not controlled, will become excessive and cause rapid deterioration of the fruit.

The amount of gas permissible in a fruit compartment is still a debatable point. Small quantities do not cause any appreciable damage, but experiments have shown that a high gas content is definitely dangerous. It is well to bear in mind the findings of the Food Investigation Department on this point.

These findings state that: *'Until more is known of the effects of various concentrations of carbon dioxide on the different fruits it is clearly desirable that ventilation should be sufficient to keep the concentration in a ship's hold from rising above 5 per cent'.*

In order to ensure this, it is advisable that a lower concentration be aimed at, and a well known shipping company issues instructions to officers to the effect that the delivery and extractor fans be operated in order to achieve circulation of air such that the CO_2 gas content does not exceed 3 per cent.

The gas concentration of a compartment should be determined at least daily, using results from various parts of the space, particularly at the bottom and all officers should be familiar with the CO_2 recorders provided for this purpose.

Citrus Fruits (Oranges and Lemons). When carrying and stowing citrus fruits, regard must be paid to the other refrigerated cargo to be loaded. They should never be stowed in compartments with or adjacent to such cargoes as butter or eggs otherwise the latter will suffer considerably from taint.

The risk of damage to cargo by fruit, and particularly citrus fruit, is more acute in air cooled ships than in grid ships, due primarily to the use of forced air circulation in the former, as against natural air circulation in the latter.

Bottom dunnage is necessary in the compartments in the form of 3 in × 3 in battens laid athwartships and between each second tier 2 in battens should be laid athwartships. To facilitate complete air circulation $\frac{3}{4}$ in battens should be arranged vertically between each tier.

The compartments allocated to citrus fruits should be pre-cooled to about 36°F and a temperature of about 39–42°F maintained during transit.

Dunnage used with citrus fruit should not, on any account, be used with other refrigerated or taintable cargo on a subsequent voyage.

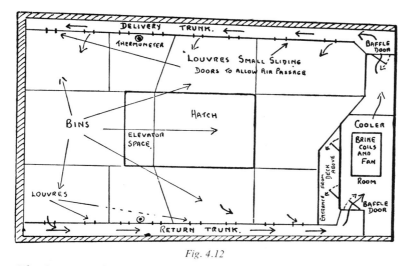

Fig. 4.12

The Carriage of Bananas (Conventional Systems)

After cutting to a schedule so that the shortest time elapses from cutting to loading, the fruit is transported to the vessel by methods which vary according to the particular port. In Jamaica, trucks are used between plantation and port, and lighters complete the transport to the vessel. In some cases, there is direct rail transport to the pier alongside which the vessel is lying. All loading is done by hand, and at Kingston over 18 000 stems can be loaded in 1 hour. Central American ports use elevators for loading.

The vessel carrying the fruit is divided into decks, approximately 8 ft in height, which are subdivided into 'bins', each of average deck area 100 sq ft. This area will vary according to the vessel. As each bin is loaded, bin boards are fitted. These are 5 in × 2 in in section and spaced about 1 ft apart, thus allowing a suitable circulation of air for cooling. Stems are loaded one or two upright and the remainder flat with the big end out, so that the bananas are not stripped from the stem when getting them out at the port of discharge. Stems are stowed very firmly so that movement at sea is prevented. It is found however that a certain amount of settling occurs after a few days at sea. During stowage, the handling of the fruit appears to be rough, but it must be realized that as the fruit is still green and unripe, it is not easily bruised. The cooling systems of different vessels are essentially the same in principle, and importance is attached to proper insulation. The diagram illustrates a popular system.

Temperature of Carriage. This may vary with the vessel, but usually a temperature is 53°F. Before loading, the vessel is cooled to a temperature well below carrying temperature. The introduction of warm fruit into the holds may raise the temperature to over 90°, therefore after each deck is completed and plugged up the temperature must be reduced to carrying temperature. The time taken for this is a matter on which opinions differ. Some consider that too quick a reduction, viz. anything less than 36 hours, is apt to impair the fruit and affect the ripening, others approve of very quick reduction. However, once the carrying temperature is reached, *it must be maintained constant if the fruit is to arrive in good condition.* In modern vessels, the variation of temperature does not exceed half of one degree.

Ventilation. The gases evolved by the fruit must be removed at least once per day, twice being usual. This means that the air in the holds must be completely changed. This is done by blanking off the return side of the deck, and opening ventilators so that fresh air is drawn in by the fan and blown across the deck. The clearing of the foul air may take up to half an hour. Provided that the temperature of the atmosphere is suitable, the holds are also on continuous fresh air, i.e. two small vents are opened, one on the delivery side and one on the return side to allow a small amount of air in and out respectively while the deck circulation is operating.

Discharge. This is usually carried out with elevators into rail transport, the fruit being sent to various centres for ripening as required. The ideal cargo will be discharged in the same condition as loaded. The normal banana carrier is loaded in about 20–24 hours, and is discharged in the same time.

Terminology. Various terms are used in connection with bananas.

Full fruit is fruit which has been cut late. Owing to the shorter passage, fruit for American ports can be 'fuller' than that shipped to markets in Great Britain. Fruit which is too 'full' should be rejected and not loaded.

A *bunch* is a stem of nine hands or over: eights, sevens or sixes are stems of the corresponding number of hands. The stems are graded under these headings as they are tallied whilst loading.

Turners are stems which ripen during the passage.

(b) *Bananas* (Modern Systems)

New vessels, recently introduced to the banana trades, are of the order of $43\frac{1}{2}$ thousand cubic feet capacity reefer space constructed into a number of temperature zones, permitting flexible carriage of refrigerated produce, which may call for different storage methods.

Cardboard cartons enclose the fruit and transportation (loading and discharging) is by fork lift trucks, all part of the ship equipment.

A full load of bananas (approx. 3500 tons) will cool from a loading temperature of 28°C to a carrying temperature of 12°C, within a time factor of 36 hours. Cooling is by forced air and calculated to have changing periods of 80 per each hour.

CO_2 CONTROL

One of the greatest assets to the successful carriage of refrigerated produce is a system of accurate and easily operated CO_2 gas recorders.

In the early days of refrigerated transportation the methods adopted to obtain the gas content of the compartments were very primitive. With care, and in small ships, the efficiency maintained did not result in any undue deterioration of the produce, but it is hardly to be expected that with numerous compartments officers can give the attention that is necessary without the use of proper instruments.

Litmus cartridges, which could be lowered into insulated compartments in a like manner to thermometers, served the purpose of CO_2 reading in many vessels. The degree of discolouration in the litmus could be measured in terms of CO_2 gas content.

The degree of CO_2 gas in insulated compartments is of paramount importance; it must be constant in amount and suited, in quantity, to the type of cargo. It can be appreciated, therefore, that in modern vessels, having numerous compartments, the need for quick and accurate readings in this respect is closely associated with the successful carriage of refrigerated produce.

One method by which the percentage of CO_2 gas may be ascertained is by the use of the Thermoscope, the principle of which is as follows:

When carbonic acid gas, either pure or in admixture with air is brought in contact with caustic soda, a chemical reaction takes place and heat is evolved, the amount of which is proportional to the quantity of CO_2.

If, therefore, a measured quantity of the gas mixture to be analysed is brought into contact with excess caustic soda, it is only necessary to measure the heat evolved to obtain a measure of the CO_2 in the mixture.

The thermoscope has three essential parts, viz:

A cylinder into which is drawn by means of a plunger, a sample of the air mixture within a chamber from which the mixture is passed to a cartridge shaped receptacle containing caustic soda.

A thermometer, the bulb of which surrounds the cartridge, measures the heat of reaction imparted to the mercury and thence the CO_2 percentage.

A length of rubber tubing of about $\frac{1}{4}$ in bore is attachable to the thermoscope in order that this tubing may be lowered through one of the thermometer pipes into the hold or 'tween deck spaces.

The modern tendency is to fit 'Distance CO_2 Recorders'.

The accompanying illustration 'A' is of a Thermoscope in section.

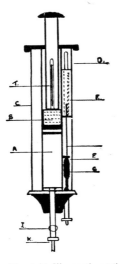

THE THERMOSCOPE
(SHOWN IN SECTION)

'A'   The cylinder fitted with a piston.

'B'   Thermometer suitably mounted on cylinder.

'C'   Outer metal jacket enclosing the whole.

'D'   The stem of the thermometer.

'E'   A movable scale, graduated in CO_2 per cent.

'G'   Cartridge of thin sheet metal containing caustic soda, surrounded by

'F'   The thermometer bulb.

'T' and 'S' are thermometer and piston rod, graduated to control the volume of gas into the cylinder. Connection is made between cylinder and cartridge by a rubber tube K and a tap I.

Fig. 4.13 Illustration 'A'
Reproduced by permission of the New Zealand Shipping Co., Ltd.

Refrigerated Cargoes—Containers

While the carriage of edible products by conventional refrigeration is likely to be maintained, the growth of refrigerated containers shows all the trends of increasing, both in number and importance. Particularly is this likely to be so in the deep sea, European/Antipodes; European/West Indian; European/South African and the Australian/U.S.A. trades. Vessels are planned to operate with capacities of up to 2500–3000 units available for refrigerated cargo carried at temperatures as low as −29°C.

In this context the governmental bodies involved are introducing stricter regulations for the control and care of edible produce carried in containers. Apart from the normal and usual prevention of damage and contamination, insulation by itself is now considered insufficient, but that continual refrigeration in transport must apply, both on ship and in the methods of distribution to the vessel and to the consignee.

Cold storage containers, to coin a phrase, are mostly of two types, those with a built in integral diesel or electric refrigeration unit, which are popularly termed 'reefer containers' or those which connect to a separate refrigeration source, as for example the ship unit. The term 'port hole' is given to the latter type and they find favour in those trades where refrigerated cargo is of high proportion and where purpose built vessels are available. The integral type would more reasonably apply to conventional ships carrying a 'small' number of containers, over shorter distances.

The 'port hole' type of refrigerated container is usually of 20 ft design with the 40 ft type mainly of the 'integral' form.

As with all forms of refrigerated carriage, control of temperature in containers is of paramount importance and this is achieved by the installation of recorder-controlling instrument units. (See text on the Hall-Thermotank International provisions.)

The fully insulated container is well suited to the carriage of edible goods which do not call for extreme low temperature refrigeration. 'Heat' does build up in insulated containers but over longer periods of time, as compared with the conventional non-insulated type, and condensation problems can be relatively minimal. To some extent, the construction of the insulated container adds to these advantages.

It is because of these considerations that markets destined for relatively short distances attract the use of insulated containers for such products as, for example, chocolate and other confectionery substances from the U.K. to the Middle East.

An important aspect of 'care' however, arises with insulated containers. They must not be left exposed to high, or rising temperatures, for any length of time after discharge or, indeed, be subject to sunshine/heat exposure during a discharging process. Critical changes of temperature within the container, and resulting commodity damage, could well occur by reason of this neglect.

Non-Insulated Holds. An interesting development in the carriage of refrigerated products in containers is that which covers their stowage in non-insulated holds. Research has proved this method to be acceptable, given appropriate safeguards in the provision of a cold air supply and temperature control.

The systems available operate from a refrigerated air supply, frequently on the Freon-Brine circulatory system, through vertical ducts serving a stack of containers, thus obviating the need for the units to have integrated, individual supplies. Different stacks of containers can be kept at different temperatures thus providing for ship capacities over a mixed type of cargoes.

Experiments have shown that ambient, and hold temperatures do not unduly, if at all, affect the performance of refrigerated containers during a voyage. Fresh fruit in containers in non-insulated holds is a developing aspect of the Australian/U.S.A. and the West Indian/South African trades.

Modern Marine Cargo Refrigeration

The notes which follow are included by kind permission of Hall-Thermotank International Limited, of Dartford, England.

Blue Star Line's *Afric Star*, a modern fully refrigerated cargo ship.

Shipboard Cargo Refrigeration

The specialization of Hall-Thermotank International Limited in the design, supply and installation of all types of cargo refrigeration systems is based on almost a century of experience with ships and the world-wide carriage of meat and other perishables. Starting with the introduction of the 'cold air' machine in 1877 J. & E. Hall Limited as the company was then called, developed the marine application of refrigeration for transporting meat, fruit and dairy produce on the long voyages from Australasia and South America to the European markets.

The first of the Hall range of CO_2 compressors and brine cooling systems was installed on board *Highland Chief* in 1890 and, before the turn of the century, the carriage of refrigerated cargoes in ships had rapidly expanded. It was J. & E. Hall Limited that first overcame the special refrigeration problems associated with the carriage of chilled rather than frozen meat and the close temperature tolerances required; also the transport of citrus and deciduous fruits with the control of CO_2 percentage as well as temperature, and the many factors associated with the shipment of bananas and their controlled ripening en route.

It is no idle boast to state that the historical development of trade between the primary producing areas and their remote markets is due in no small measure to the technical designs standards and general reliability of the Hall marine refrigerating plants. It is interesting to note that, despite increasing competition, over half of the world's marine refrigerated cargo capacity registered with Lloyd's, has been cooled by plant supplied and installed by Hall-Thermotank International Limited and its predecessors.

Until the late 1950s the refrigerated cargo ship, often with over fifty separately cooled compartments, relied primarily on manual temperature regulation for each space. However, within the past twenty years the company has introduced many improvements to the automatic operation of its refrigerating plants and has also developed reliable systems for the recording of temperatures, both space and refrigerant. The Halltherm Redicon system described later, provides at a central location an accurate temperature control, measurement and if required, print-out facility; it meets Lloyd's requirements for cargo temperature indication to an accuracy of $\pm 0.15°C$ and can control to $\pm 0.25°C$.

During this period Hall-Thermotank International Limited has also expanded the range of high speed reciprocating compressors for use with the fluorinated refrigerants R12, R22 and R502, and also introduced the screw compressor in various sizes for use with the larger marine cargo plants.

As well as participating in the supply of refrigeration installations for the carriage of liquefied gas, the company has made a major contribution to the development of the refrigerated containership, a significant number of which now operate with Halltherm refrigeration systems.

For cargo installations it is usual for the designs to conform fully to the stringent regulations of Lloyd's or other approved classification societies. Having worked with the world's leading societies for many years, the company has established duly approved designs of all major components. It is a normal discipline to supply them with full particulars and drawings of each new plant and to provide inspection facilities both during manufacture and for the comprehensive shipboard trials which follow its installation on board ship.

Due regard is also taken of statutory and other national and international requirements appropriate to the particular types of cargo, trading area and ownership of the vessel. For example Hall-Thermotank International Limited duly observes and meets as appropriate the special rules of, amongst others, the United States Department of Agriculture and the Perishable Products Export Control Board of South Africa concerning the carriage of fruit cargoes.

The dependence of an efficient marine refrigeration plant on the proper insulation of each cargo space is obvious. With the complex shape and structure of all classes of ship, the company has throughout its history devoted much research to the theory and practice of shipboard insulation; in this and other studies, it has worked in close association with the Shipowners Refrigerated Cargo Research Association since its foundation in 1946.

This is but one example of the company's recognition of the mutual benefits that result from close consultation and co-operation with owners and shipbuilders. Comprehensive records on each plant are maintained and special attention has been given to the establishment of an efficient spares replacement facility.

From Dartford, a world-wide network of installation, commissioning and service engineers is controlled. Group companies operate in five continents, supported by experienced service agents in most maritime countries.

Refrigeration Systems

Whilst certain marine cargo installations may be restricted to the cooling of a single insulated locker, it is more usual for multi-space cooling to be involved, with cargo temperatures varying from fruit at $12°C$ ($54°F$) to frozen produce at $-30°C$ ($-22°F$) or below.

To give the degree of flexibility required and yet provide a relatively simple installation, Halltherm systems generally utilize the air cooler method of space temperature control refrigerating plant.

The modern brine circuit indicates the methods by which brine at differing temperatures can be circulated to any given space by the use of brine injection, circulating pumps and appropriate brine headers. Whilst temperature control was for many years effected by manual restriction of brine flow, this is now achieved automatically by the use of modulating valves.

It was in 1890 that J. & E. Hall Ltd. introduced a brine circulation system for the shipboard carriage of frozen cargo. Cooled by the first marine CO_2 refrigerating plant, the *Highland Chief* successfully transported frozen meat from the Argentine for a period of over 20 years. Hall's invention of the continuous welded steel grid, through which the cold brine circulated in the cargo space, led to the rapid extension of the safe and reliable CO_2 brine cooling system to all types of refrigerated cargo ship.

This quickly gained popularity over the more toxic ammonia systems then in use on many ships. It should be noted, however, that refrigerating plants using ammonia have been manufactured at the company's Dartford works for over 75 years but these are primarily used for land applications. CO_2 plants continued to meet shipowner's requirements until the marine introduction of the first Hall range of 'freon' compressors in the early 1950s for use with the fluorinated refrigerants, which had then become more generally available. In the meantime improvements in the design of fans for refrigerated spaces had led to the air cooler supplanting the use of brine grids, firstly for all spaces where fruit or chilled meat was to be carried, and subsequently for almost all low temperature spaces. Initially the air coolers were constructed from plain steel piping, hot dip galvanized as before, but in recent years these have been superseded by smaller and more efficient galvanized steel coolers with spiral or plate fins to improve heat transfer.

By using properly designed air coolers with their associated fans and air circulation arrangements, Hall-Thermotank International has been able to reduce the number and size of brine circuits and make other improvements in space temperature control as referred to later. Hot brine defrosting arrangements are also handled with greater efficiency.

The duplication of expansion facilities for the brine chiller is another example of the protective design features incorporated by the company in its marine installations; it is also designed to meet classification society requirements that facilities for cooling should continue to be provided even if failure occurs in one circuit. Halltherm plants are always provided with appropriate protective controls to shut down the plant in an emergency should an abnormal oil, seawater or brine flow condition arise. Recent improvements in the design of brine cooling evaporators have greatly reduced both size and weight of the heat exchanger. As compared with earlier shell and tube evaporator designs where brine flowed through the tubes, the present design with primary refrigerant evaporating within rather than outside the tubes, obviates problems of oil return to the compressor and reduces the gas charge required.

For the medium size or smaller cargo installation, where the refrigerated spaces are relatively few and close to the machinery site, direct expansion cooling systems may well be preferred. In recent years the company has incorporated many new features to improve the flexibility of such plants.

A typical direct expansion system for use with multi-temperature cargo spaces is suitable for carrying fruit or frozen produce. The use of two sets of refrigerant controls for each cooler enables optimum operating conditions to be provided for the alternative types of cargo carried. Where the cargo rooms are situated well above the machinery site it is usual to improve efficiency by fitting a liquid cooler. Automatic space temperature control is provided both by thermostat or other sensing device within the space and by the relevant pilot operated back pressure regulating valve. The compressor in use, or the stand-by compressor usually required would normally incorporate automatic cylinder unloading to meet fluctuations in demand associated with climate and cargo.

Cargo Space Cooling
As previously stated, during the early part of the century the great majority of cargo spaces were cooled by steel pipe grids using brine as the secondary refrigerant. Direct expansion grids were often used for the smaller cargo spaces as well as in provision room installations. Grids are still standard equipment in trawlers and other ships engaged in the fishing industry; they are also used for special purpose cargo installations such as in the carriage of horticultural produce where blooms might be damaged by forced air circulation.

The introduction of air coolers greatly increased the flexibility of the basic refrigeration plant design, enabling shipowners to carry a greater variety of cargoes. Hall-Thermotank International played a considerable part in the pioneer work associated with the design of air cooling and distribution systems for use with all types of refrigerated cargo.

Due to various economic and political factors the historic chilled meat carriers, averaging 400 000 cu ft capacity built for the South American trade and incorporating Hall refrigeration plant, have largely been phased out. However, other classes of specialist refrigerated cargo ships fitted with Halltherm installations are very much in evidence. These include vessels primarily designed for Europe/Australasia trading. In the past these ships operated on the basis of a 15°F general storage temperature for frozen produce with a reduced facility for 0°F storage; ducted air cooling systems were provided both for the deep insulated holds and for the 'tween deck spaces with their port and starboard lockers.

In recent years the modern reefer ship must cater for cargo of all types, using palletized or conventional stowage, and have refrigerating plant capable of maintaining storage temperatures varying from 12°C (54°F) for bananas to −25°C (−13°F) for deep frozen cargoes or below. A diagramatic illustration of a modern air trunking and cooler arrangement is given in Diagram 12. Using multiple fans, the cooled air is delivered to the refrigerated cargo space through side ducting and deck gratings.

After rising through the cargo the air returns to the fan suction via openings in the cooler bulkhead and special return ducts adjacent to the hatch access. Depending on the type of cargo and owner's requirements, such air circulation may include two-speed fans with or without reversible feature. With properly designed ducting arrangements the reversing of air flow is of particular benefit during temperature stabilization after loading.

Hall-Thermotank International has supplied and fitted refrigerating installations for banana carrying vessels since the turn of the

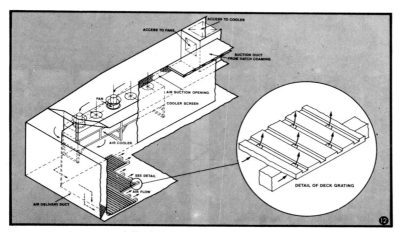

A Typical Reefer Air Duct System

century. The refrigeration factors associated with the respiration and heat generation of this fruit during transit have been given special study.

Coupled with a high loading temperature such vessels have always required above average air circulation within the space to accelerate cooling and ensure minimum temperature variation. Recently 70 or even 90 air changes per hour have been specified; this has been considered necessary by some owners to eliminate local 'hot spots' within the space. The company's design engineers have given special consideration to the properly integrated design of fan, cooler, ducting and air distribution arrangements which often enable efficient cooling to be achieved at lower air circulation rates.

Similar design considerations need to be given to the carriage of citrus and deciduous fruits on the South African and similar trades. Whilst conventional air changes of 35 or so are applicable, the concentration of CO_2 within each refrigerated space can become a critical factor. The company has well established procedures for monitoring the percentage of CO_2 present and providing the necessary induction of fresh air to control same.

With the increasing competition in marine trading, shipowners now require great flexibility in their refrigerated cargo installations. Hall-Thermotank International has designed and supplied hold and 'tween deck space air cooling arrangements of many types; these include deckhead delivery trunking (using buried air trunks or false deckheads), side-to-side circulation, the Robson system of balanced distribution and the so-called 'ductless' arrangement.

The close relationships established over many years by the company with leading shipbuilders and owners' Naval Architects and Superintendents, help to ensure that the complete installation shall prove fully appropriate to each ship's trading and operational needs. With this in view, comprehensive drawings are provided giving ducting and other relevant data for the use of shipbuilders and insulators.

Container Ships

The second half of the 20th century has seen the rapid expansion of containerized transport of goods both by land and sea. From the refrigerated container aspect, the initial problem was associated with the incorporation in each container of reliable refrigerating plant that would maintain the cargo at the desired temperature and condition throughout the transport period involved. Commencing in the mid-fifties the company designed and supplied a variety of shipboard containers, each fitted with refrigerating plant driven by electric motor or with its own fully independent power unit. Tested and approved by Lloyds or other classification society for the carriage of refrigerated cargo, they provided excellent service and many are still in use today.

The introduction and universal acceptance of I.S.O. standard container dimensions and the extension of the portable clip-on refrigerating unit to containers for shipboard use, led to a rapid increase in the demand for reefer containers. The early sixties saw the worldwide expansion of port facilities for the handling and storage of all types of containers and the planning of the first centrally refrigerated container ships.

When the British container ship consortia were formed at this time, Hall-Thermotank International assisted with the initial design studies that have since resulted in the sophisticated refrigerated container ships currently operating on the trade routes of the world.

The establishment of the 20 ft I.S.O. insulated container with appropriate circular inlet/outlet air connections as the agreed basic design, enabled both port installations and shipboard facilities to be co-ordinated, with clip-on units only needed for land distribution from the container base to client site, and vice versa.

With their great experience of refrigerated cargo installations, Hall-Thermotank International has established a flexible system of container ship refrigeration utilizing cooled brine circulation to the air coolers from a central refrigerating plant similar to that described for cargo ships. This is often considered preferable to the multi-unit direct expansion systems sometimes incorporated in certain Continental designs. The Halltherm system is designed for use with a large number of containers stowed in tiers within insulated holds approximating to the full depth hatch spaces of conventional ships. To provide maximum choice of temperatures for mixed cargoes, multiple independent air cooling units are provided for each hold (Pat. No. 1126270).

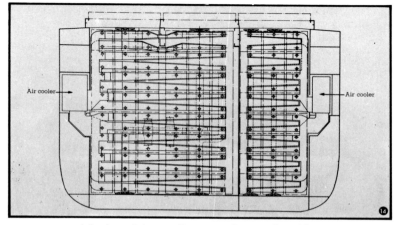

A horizontal duct cooling system for container ship.

Diagram 14 and the associated illustration shows a typical hold space with horizontal delivery and return ducts to each tier of containers; this hold accommodates up to 144 refrigerated containers at varying temperatures using 4 coolers sited in wing compartments as shown. The company also supplies corresponding designs using vertical rather than horizontal ducting. Such an arrangement as shown in diagram 16 enables a greater temperature selection, based on 8 coolers, to be made with the containers connected in stacks instead of tiers. Prefabricated preinsulated vertical ducting of this type is the basis of the Halltherm Searod design.

A typical hold arrangement.

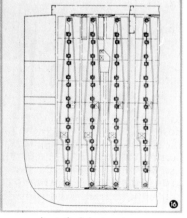

A vertical duct system.

By a combination of brine temperature selection from the central plant and automatic air temperature control and fan operation at the hold cooler, the correct supply of refrigerated air is circulated to each container. To compensate for partial loading of any hold, each pneumatically operated container coupling can readily be blanked off by the shutter mechanism incorporated in the assembly.

It is a unique feature of the Halltherm design to include one or more 'conditioners' within each hold so that the environmental temperature surrounding the insulated containers shall also be controlled by a forced air distribution system (Pat. No. 1160391).

These conditioners incorporate both heating and cooling facilities, with appropriate ductwork to ensure that an even hold temperature is maintained under both high and low ambient conditions. Such units facilitate the stabilizing of temperatures associated with loading or unloading procedures and also prevent ultra-low temperatures occurring in the vicinity of ship's structural steelwork with consequent damage or need for expensive material specification.

Typical of the designs now being supplied by Hall-Thermotank International are the systems for a number of refrigerated container ships under construction in Germany for the Australasian trade. These vessels have net cargo capacities of 33 000 m^3 (1,168 000 ft^3) and facilities for carrying up to 1226 reefer containers. The company designs such plants to meet the owner's specified container cooling requirements, often ranging from fruit storage at 12°C (54°F) to frozen cargoes at −30°C (−22°F).

These ships inherit the successful operational characteristics of the various 'generations' of refrigerated container ships fitted with Halltherm designs; these include the eight 'ACT' class vessels and the *Remuera*, which when commissioned was the largest refrigerated container ship afloat.

It should be noted that Hall-Thermotank International Limited has also been involved in the design and supply of major refrigeration installations for multiple container cooling at port facilities both in the United Kingdom and abroad. The modular Halltherm Unicore system, primarily designed for open marshalling sites, has proved very popular and its marine application is rapidly developing.

Control and Instrumentation
In the last twenty years the company has devoted much research to the design of fully automatic marine refrigerating plants and improved monitoring/control of cargo space temperatures. This has been in line with the modern desire of shipowners to operate their vessels with minimum personnel and yet ensure that all items of machinery shall function correctly and within both their own safety limits and those laid down by the classification societies.

Up until this time, it had been the accepted practice for watch keeping attendance to be provided for all but the smaller cargo installations whilst the plant was in use. Additional personnel were often involved in routine maintenance and also, on board the larger refrigerated cargo ships, with the regular logging of up to 300 individual space and air stream temperatures. The modern cargo and container ship installation now operates virtually un-manned with sophisticated automatic control, electric and pneu-matic, of both primary and secondary refrigerating systems.

Direct expansion systems for provision room and small cargo installations have for many years been supplied with fully automatic facilities combined with appropriate safety devices. Progress in the design of refrigerant controls suitable for shipboard use has been rapid and Hall-Thermotank International, with its own Systems Design Department, has made a special study of the functions and reliability of components currently available from the world's manufacturers for its various marine applications. As a matter of policy, designs are kept as simple as possible commensurate with using components of proved efficiency and ease of replacement.

Where a wide range of space temperatures are required, use is often made of supplementary valves to meet the exceptional plant operating conditions. This ensures that the automatic controls shall not be expected to operate outside their design parameters.

Such conditions apply equally to the automatic brine control valves which in recent years have been successfully energized by pneumatic systems, thus providing an alternative to the use of motorized or other electrically energized valves.

The need for a marine refrigeration plant to operate satis-factorily, with wide variations in refrigeration load, is a funda-mental reason for ensuring that shipboard installations are properly engineered. Various alternative unloading procedures are available to suit the requirements of a client's particular application. Com-pressor cylinder unloading, which has been in use for many years, can now be supplemented or replaced by automatic hot gas bypass systems; the company's designs ensure that such equipment can provide infinitely variable unloading down to 10 per cent of specified duty, this being applicable to direct expansion air cooler designs or to brine cooling evaporator systems. With the screw compressor a slide valve automatically provides the same unloading feature.

The Halltherm Redicon (REfrigerated DIgital CONtrol) system has been developed to combine a number of simultaneous functions associated primarily with temperature control and measurement. The versatility of this system is exceptional. The console assembly embodies a digital display, audible warning device and, if required, data print-out equipment, all in association with a number of control modules. These are available in various standard designs, each appropriate to the particular plant function being controlled or monitored. Normally a pair of modules are used for each control

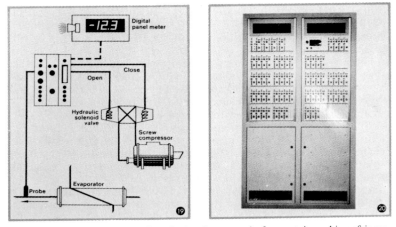

A typical Halltherm Redicon installation for control of a container ship refrigeration system.

loop. The input module, connected to a remote platinum distance thermometer, provides means for indicating the actual temperature in the digital display together with control point setting and alarms, both visual and audible. The second module generates the output pulses for operational purposes and incorporates both automatic and manual facilities. Halltherm Redicon can readily incorporate modules accepting alternative inputs such as pressure or flow using an appropriate transducer.

The success of Halltherm Redicon in the various marine applications for which it has been supplied, has led to a general extension of its use to a number of major land and brewery refrigeration installations. With an accuracy in temperature indication of ±0·15°C and temperature control possible to ±0·25°C its use has been approved by leading classification societies.

In addition to Halltherm Redicon, many other types of accurate temperature indicating and recording equipment for shipboard cargo plants are supplied. For many installations, the manually operated electrical distance thermometer meets all requirements; however, with the modern tendency towards automation and minimal watch keeping, many shipowners prefer to install the strip-chart temperature recorder or even more comprehensive data logging equipment. Normally, such items supplied by Hall-Thermotank International fully conform to classification society, U.S.D.A. and other requirements.

Compressors

The refrigerating compressor is in more senses than one the heart of the refrigerating system. Since J. & E. Hall Ltd., the forebears of Hall-Thermotank International Limited, developed the cold air machine in the 1880s, great importance has been given to the development and testing of all designs of compressor before their use on board ship.

The 50 year reign of the Hall CO_2 machines with their associated brine cooling systems is an example of the Company's high standard of marine design. It will be remembered that the reliability and safety of these machines was a major factor in the establishment of the worldwide carriage of perishable foodstuffs during the early part of the century.

This era was followed by the introduction and development of slow and, later, high speed reciprocating machines for use with the various Halogen refrigerants and Ammonia. The last 20 years has seen the marine use of the company's centrifugal and screw compressors, with the latter becoming increasingly popular for larger marine applications.

Unlike land installations where more stable ambient and storage temperatures usually apply, the marine requirement necessitates a compressor design that will withstand the variation in operating conditions associated with a ship trading in all climates with refrigerated cargoes at differing temperatures.

With restricted headroom a normal feature of refrigeration machinery spaces on board ship, the high speed multi-cylinder range of Veebloc compressors manufactured at the Dartford Hall-Thermotank complex has proved ideal for both small and large cargo ship installations. Based on over 25 years use in both marine and land applications throughout the world, the new V127 (Mark 4) compressor epitomizes the company's reputation for sound marine refrigeration design; more compact than its predecessors it is capable of working at higher speeds and at greater efficiency, with improved ratio of heat extraction to horsepower absorbed.

Veebloc compressors are available with 3, 4, 6 and 8 cylinders per compressor and with four basic sizes of piston bore and stroke. Automatic or manual cylinder unloading is available for capacity control and compound, two-stage, designs are provided for ultra-low temperature applications. Such compressors are in general use with refrigerants R12, R22, R502 and Ammonia (R717).

The current series of these Veebloc machines extends from a swept volume of 24–1665 m^3/h corresponding to a heat extraction rate, at standard conditions of $-15°C$ ($+5°F$) evaporation and $30°C$ ($86°F$) condensation, ranging from 6100–650000 Kcal/h.

With over twenty standard compressor designs it can be seen that there is ample choice to select the appropriate size for the great majority of marine refrigeration systems.

For the larger cargo installations, the rotary screw compressor with its progressive design improvements is becoming increasingly popular. The Halltherm Seascrew packaged marine refrigeration sets have been specially manufactured to incorporate in a low silhouette assembly the latest design of oil injected screw compressor. Such compressors are ideally suited to the present requirement for high capacity at low suction temperatures. The injection of oil into the screws at the suction gas entry provides both the sealing of the rotors and a reduction of discharge gas temperature; this allows the Howden/HTI range of screw compressors to operate at a greater suction/delivery pressure differential than could be achieved with the single stage reciprocating compressor. Other advantages include the reduction in moving parts, general design simplicity and the inclusion of a built-in sliding control valve permitting infinitely variable capacity unloading down to 10 per cent of specified duty. Screw compressor sets are at present being utilized with refrigerant R22 in capacities ranging from 360 300–1 217 600 Kcal/h (1 455 500–4 851 600 Btu/h).

In recent years prefabrication has been a major factor associated with efficient shipbuilding and the company had devoted much attention to the design of composite machine unit assemblies; each unit includes where appropriate condenser, oil separator and electrical control panel in addition to compressor and driving motor.

To facilitate servicing on board ship every consideration is given to the accessability of components and the provision of isolating valves. Comprehensive pressure gauges, operational and protective controls, sight glasses and thermometers are included where necessary to assist the ship's engineers with correct operation of the plant.

With its own specialist engineers experienced in solving sound and vibration problems, the company can include in its designs anti-vibration mountings and other features to minimize the generation of noise and the transmission of vibrations via baseplate or connecting pipework.

In addition to meeting the full inspection requirements of Lloyds or other relevant classification society during the various manufacturing processes, comprehensive factory tests are carried out prior to despatch.

Air Coolers and Ancillary Equipment
Mention has already been made of the historical development of the plain pipe grid into the extended surface air cooling battery of current marine refrigeration practice. With the great technical and manufacturing experience of the Dartford complex, the company has for many years given special consideration to the individual design of air coolers to suit the needs of each refrigerated space. Using other specialist manufacturers where appropriate, a wide variety of brine cooled and direct expansion air coolers can be supplied. These may be arranged with horizontal or vertical air flow and with circuitry, external finning and defrosting arrangements most suited to the particular application.

Each is dimensionally designed for maximum efficiency in association with the fan, air circulation system and the need to maximize cargo carrying capacity. For ships fitted with secondary refrigerant (i.e. brine) cooling systems it was the practice for many years to utilize plain pipe air coolers of all steel construction, hot dipped galvanized after manufacture. Of recent years the size of cooler has been reduced by the introduction of extended surface coolers using spirally wound or plate fins, with spacing appropriate to the type and temperature of the cargo and to the provision of efficient defrosting arrangements. Halltherm coolers of this type are fitted with individual valves for each cooler circuit, drainage trays with defrosting coil and flanged airtight casings for connection to ductwork and fan plenums.

For direct expansion systems, air coolers generally incorporate copper coils with fins of aluminium or copper depending on the environment and owner's requirements. The pitching of fins is varied to suit the application using electric or, in certain cases, hot gas defrosting. The refrigerant circuits are specially arranged for maximum efficiency with liquid distributor at coil inlet and suction header at outlet to ensure balanced cooling with minimal liquid carryover and efficient oil return to the compressor. Each cooler assembly is contained in a galvanized steel casing with heated drip tray as above.

Grids using brine or direct expansion cooling are now rarely used except in special applications where a forced air cooling system would be inadvisable. These include small cargo spaces where an air cooler would restrict storage capacity to an undue extent, cargo lockers for horticultural produce where air movement may damage blooms etc. and fish holds or similar spaces where grids are preferred for a variety of reasons.

It should be more than evident that efficient cargo refrigerating plant is dependent on the proper design and functioning of many other items than the main components previously described. Hall-Thermotank International Ltd. attaches great importance to the suitability of even the smallest component in a Halltherm refrigeration system. Mention has already been made of the continued analysis that is made of equipment available from the world's specialist manufacturers. This ensures that the Company's clients quickly benefit from the technical developments both at the Dartford Hall-Thermotank complex and from the specialist sub-contractors with whom the Company is associated.

The design of fans for cargo space and container ship applications is a good example. In the earlier air circulation systems for cargo spaces it was usual for one, or possibly two, special purpose axial flow fans to be manufactured and fitted in each refrigerated space. Whilst design flexibility enabled the ideal fan to be provided for each installation, problems of interchangeability and quick replacement were evident as well as high production costs. By designing its cargo space air circulation and ducting arrangements in association with one or more fans coupled to each air cooler, greater standardization and simpler spares replacement facilities can be provided. For refrigerated cargo systems, the latest high efficiency marine type aerofoil fans are now generally used. However, in container ships the fan design must prove adequate for wide variation in container loading both as regards the quantity coupled to the cooling system and also to the many types of cargo and its method of loading within each container. After much research, a range of mixed flow fans of high efficiency, have been developed. With non-stalling characteristics and suitability for high pressure application, these fans are extremely reliable, easy to service and flexible in operation.

Other examples of important components receiving similar considerations include electric motors for compressors, pumps and fans, group starterboards for the above, pumps of all types, delivery oil separators, brine heaters and temperature indication/recording equipment. It should be appreciated that, in order to meet classification society requirements temperature data logging and recording facilities must also be kept independent of alternative temperature indicating systems, the Halltherm Redicon unit provides this standby facility, as well as carrying out its many operational functions.

Reefer containers which have individual refrigerating units can be carried on deck in ships without refrigerated holds. They are supplied with electric power, by cable, to run their own machinery.

'I' UNITIZED CARGOES

Containerization implies the practice of grouping loads of cargo together. The creation of this change in method is aimed at cargo being handled physically as little as possible and by mechanical means as much as possible, both in the ship and on shore. This is lessening the need for the conventional derrick, but promoting ship craneage, as already mentioned. It is also promoting greater use of conveyor systems.

In the context of container carriage the following aspects are of importance.

Movement Damage. The conventional systems of cargo handling frequently resulted in damage from handling, dropping, impact, crushing and slinging and also from broken stowage.

In the container, less units are being stowed at one time and by more sophisticated methods, while the number of handling procedures are less, reducing all the above-mentioned damage possibilities.

On the other hand, solidarity of stowage within the container is essential by conventional dunnaging or cushioning material since not only must damage to the goods be avoided but also to the container itself. Indeed, with a standard-size container—20 ft × 8 ft × 8 ft (6·096 × 2·438 × 2·438 m) or indeed with those of 40 ft (1920 m) length, goods should be selected by packaging size to have a solid relationship to the interior volume of the container so that movement within cannot take place. In some containers fittings are available from which lashings can be fixed and for relatively heavy cargo units this is desirable.

Crushing can be avoided by height separation in quasi-decking fashion, using material such as hardboard. It is not unusual to find container operators using air-filled dunnage bags or blocks of expanded polystyrene for separation and blocking purposes.

It is also important that the distribution of cargo within the container is balanced. That is to say that the centre of gravity of the container is indeed central. Without this precaution, and with unsuitable lifting, the container may 'slew' with probable movement of cargo within it. (See paragraph on Lifting.)

From the ship officer point of view the more general use of containers will prevent the attentions referred to earlier, since the unit will arrive at the ship sealed and ready for loading. There will, however, be occasions where the container is stowed, or 'stuffed', as is the term applied, at the berth in which case the officer must apply the attentions necessary. Irrespective of system, however, the lifting precautions do apply.

Ventilation. While climatic conditions are paramount in ventilation precautions with conventional cargo carriage, i.e. rain, temperature and humidity, in the case of the container 'humidity' calls for the greater attention.

Since the container is virtually a closed box, care must be taken with goods placed into it at temperatures likely to change considerably during passage.

Sweat can be present in containers as in a ship's hold, resulting from the metal of the container itself or from the moisture-laden goods within it. As changes of air, as from ventilators or air-conditioning are not available, cargoes susceptible to damage from sweat and condensation must be protected in conventional fashion.

Above-Deck Carriage of Containers. Containers stowed above deck are subject to all climatic conditions as with any other type of deck cargo. Water, however, is the greatest hazard and, in the absence of extremely efficient safeguards, only those containers in good condition should be accepted for 'on deck' stowage.

Lifting Containers. A container is designed to be lifted by fitted attachments at its four top corners.

Any other form of lifting imposes strain or may indeed cause the container to overbalance.

For this reason the ideal system is by properly designed container gantry cranes, now provided by ports equipped to receive container vessels or with some ships of such design as to carry their own fitted facilities.

In cases where conditions preclude these arrangements, such as in lesser ports handling containers by the 'lift on/lift off' systems, the same principles of four top-corner attachments must apply.

Containers are, however, loaded into 'roll on/roll off' vessels. In such cases, where the size of the vessel permits, straddle carriers are used having the correct lifting devices. In others, and notably on some short sea routes to the continent, the container is lifted on to mobile carriers by gantry crane from the land vehicle, and these carriers are then drawn into the ship for stowage. The reverse procedure takes place on discharge.

Principles of Loading/Discharging. Container loading/discharging can be either a separate or simultaneous operation. It is frequently the latter with vessels specifically designed (the cellular ship).

Cellular Container Vessel. A construction which permits of containers placed into, and taken from, the ship by vertical movement through guides forming, basically, cells.

Twenty-five containers per hour is not an exceptional figure. Indeed, large-size deep-sea container ships have the capacity to work 20 000 tons (20 321 metric tons) of containers by two gantry cranes per day. Compared otherwise, this could be 2000–2500 containers worked simultaneously, loading/discharging in a matter of 36–48 hours, possibly only 3–5 minutes for the complete operation of moving a container unit into, or from a vessel. On deck stowage, one-third of the total container load may well apply and when the load factor of from 15–20 tons (15·24–20·32 metric tons) per container may apply, this method of working to speed, both within the vessel and on deck, considerably affects stability conditions.

Against this, container vessels are much broader in beam than conventional ships in relation to draft [150 ft (45·72 m) is not unusual].

Attention is, therefore, drawn to the principles of stability, viz. the draft/beam relationship in maintaining positive stability throughout a loading/discharging operation in order that a satisfactory metacentric height applies, suitable to both normal dockside working conditions and to the weather conditions likely to be encountered on voyage. (See *The Principles of Ship Stability*, by the same author and publishers.)

Refrigerated Cellular Container Carriage. Holds cooled by air circulation which is passed directly into and from each container, each of which is connected to the system by pneumo-mechanical means.

Some Notes on Containers

Containers are classed as:

(a) *Standard*—normal steel construction, usually 20 ft × 8 ft × 8 ft (6·096 × 2·438 × 2·438 m) used for normal stowage and of about 1000 cu ft (30 865·5 d/m³) capacity.

(b) *Standard*—(insulated) similar to the above but with internal insulation of polyurethane type fitted between a plywood lining and the outer skin.

(c) *Top Loader*—of similar size to the standard with a roof aperture opening. Capacity of the order of 1050 cu ft (29 732·6 d/m³).

(d) *Half Heights*—usually 20 ft × 8 ft but of 4 ft height and completely open. Sides can be completely flush with wood or by slat battens. Capacity of the order of 400 cu ft (11 326·8 d/m³).

(e) While standard size is of 20 ft length, containers are in use of 40 ft.

The use of containers is international and their construction likewise. Variations in design and application can therefore be expected.

In this respect detailed information is available through a body known as 'The International Standards Organization' (I.S.O.) which organization is mainly responsible for setting standards in respect of construction, durability, fixtures and attachments and for methods of handling, lifting and slinging of containers.

The Codes of Practice issued by I.S.O. are detailed, with a complexity not relevant to a book of this nature. However, the practices are of such importance that reference to the I.S.O. Container standards and recommendations should undoubtedly exercise the mind of a ship officer. Information in this respect can be obtained from The British Standards Institution, 2 Park Street, London, W.1. Notice should also be taken of the fact that some countries have established their own practices.

Where officers find themselves serving on vessels in particular container trades it is necessary that they should become familiar with any such practices should they differ from the I.S.O. recommendations.

Hazards with Containers. The use of containers does introduce a hazard not in itself outwardly apparent. This is the use of these carrying units on an international basis and their exchange as between one country and another. The I.S.O. recommend standards of safety in use and also standards of construction, while it also lays down sensible methods of slinging and movements of these units but as yet these recommendations are not universally adopted.

Care is therefore necessary when transferring container units of such unknown strength and durability in ensuring that margins of safety are more than reasonable.

THIRD GENERATION—G3—CONTAINER/
ROLL ON-ROLL OFF VESSELS

The care, handling and carriage of cargoes by Container and Roll on/Roll off systems has, of recent years, been a developing and progressive exercise and ship design has met the trading requirements accordingly, aware, also, of the need of ship owners to have a vessel by which the economics of its use benefit from the influences upon it, such as types of 'cargoes' to be handled, services with which it will have to work such as ports and associated transportation facilities. Above all else, its own economic capability will depend upon the degree to which it can 'get in and out' of ports, so avoiding excessive port dues costings and labour demands, and its attractiveness in moving 'cargoes' to the satisfaction of shippers.

In the area of container and roll on/roll off systems, all of the foregoing is of paramount importance.

A new concept has now therefore been introduced, known as the 'Third Generation—G3' vessels, doubtless more adaptable than hitherto.

It is interesting, and indeed useful therefore, to consider the now further particularly sophisticated modern developments which the concept of these vessels promote and the duties and responsibilities with which officers—and other personnel—serving in these vessels will be involved.

Doubtless, over the years, G3 vessels will be trading widely for numerous shipping organizations, but the outline guide lines notes which follow are based upon operations appropriate to vessels within The Atlantic Container Lines Consortium. These are included by the kind permission of Atlantic Container Line Services Limited, to whom grateful appreciation is extended.

Design and Type of Vessel (*See Frontispiece illustration*)

The ACL G3 vessels are of multi-purpose design, appropriate to simultaneous cargo working in the carriage and handling of containers, wheeled vehicular heavy loads, including cars and blocked general cargo. The stowage arrangements include weather deck containers of 40 and 20 feet, in fixed and movable cell guides—and to heights of four; internal under deck container holds with cell guides and roll on/roll off provisions, including hoistable car decks, access being through a wide angled starboard quarter ramp.

Dimensionally, these vessels have an overall length of 249·36 m, with that between perpendiculars of 233·6 m. The moulded breadth and depth is 32·26 m and 20·24 m, respectively. They can work at maximum drafts of 10·89 m, at a service speed of 18 knots.

By weight, the deadweight tonnage is 36 500 tons; the gross and net weight tonnages being 25 362 tons and 12 969 tons, respectively.

The container capacity, as such, is Weather Deck 1008; Cellular Holds 424; Ro/Ro Decks 725. In total 2157 T.E.Us.

Whereas the roll on/roll off provisions are more widely adaptable in respect of space provision than in previously designed vessels, the wide angled ramp on the starboard quarter, leading to internal ramping to various ro/ro car decks; to hoistable decks, to garage decks and to arrangements for container stowage, as well as for heavy load trailer traffic, provide for effective 'stowage' planning over a wide consignment requirement capable of simultaneous working methods.

For container stowage, as such, apart from the five under deck cellular holds, the new conception is fixed and movable cell guides to the weather deck, so constructed as to allow height loading of four containers (40 and/or 20 foot units) in safe and unrestricted weight arrangement.

Security of Loads

Security of cargo has always been an overriding problem—whatever the type of cargo—and particularly with 'deck' cargoes.

Notably is evidence available of this hazard with containers stowed on deck and, apart from the built-in locking arrangements, additional lashings fitted by manual effort, have not always been satisfactory and have led to the loss of units overboard, in heavy weather.

The fixed cell guides to the weather deck of these G3 vessels are so constructed as to safely contain the units without any need for additional manual 'lashing' security, and devoid of weight restriction in the four high stow. Indeed, weight restriction within the deck cell guide system is not imposed by the guide structure, but at the deck point of loading, thus allowing for containers stowed vertically to be placed freely—regardless of weight, acknowledging however, that for a 20 foot TEU unit the maximum weight must not exceed 25 tons and that for a 40 foot unit 30 tons.

Apart from the sea safety factor, these fixed cell guides allow for lift on/lift off speeds of working to be increased—an important factor in the 'Quick Turn Round' economics philosophy of port working. Their availability lends, also, to more effective pre-planning factors.

Within the roll on/roll off decks, there is a vast arrangement of systems for securing containers, vehicular and trailer loading, with numerous adequately designed lashing/security points, specifically adaptable to the different forms of traffic catered for.

Cargo Care

Ventilation. The provisions for ventilation of cargo has been, and always will be, an important part of cargo handling and care.

The G3 vessel's ventilation provisions are, by reason of the scope and size of the spaces to be used, adequately related to AIR FLOW as will obviate unacceptable levels of exhaust gas emission from cars and handling equipment.

The ventilation requirements are pre-selected and pre-programmed by panel control in the ship's control room, the understanding of which being essential to officers serving in these ships.

Fire control, appropriate to control systems, is also provided.

Ship Stability

An interesting feature of the design of these G3 vessels is the fact that the maximum beam of the ship extends over a major proportion of its length. This, therefore, gives the ship a large waterplane area — fundamental to its stability properties in the position of the Meta-

centre — 'M', (Note the basic formula $BM = \dfrac{I}{V}$

$$\frac{\text{Moment of the inertia of the waterplane. I.}}{\text{Volume of Displacement}}.$$

To the serving officer this feature of design should, enable him to assess the 'handling' qualities of the ship in a seaway.

It will have bearing, also, upon cargo planning and distribution in making technological computerized systems more meaningful.

Indeed, these ships are designed to behave comfortably with a maximum GM (Metacentric Height) of 2·5 % of the beam, i.e. 0·8 m.

Apart from the foregoing, however, these G3 vessels benefit from an inbuilt micro-computer (Loadmaster) system such that calculations of stability desirability, bending moments, shear forces and torsion factors can be readily available and compensating factors taken, if necessary.

Furthermore, the stability of the vessel, as cargo operations proceed and 'tank' conditions are observed, as between ports, can be obtained at any time and transmitted over a sophisticated communications system, as is desirable.

It should be carefully noted that it is not expected that officers can fully understand, nor appreciate, the fullness of computerized systems from book study. That is not the intention of these notes. On the other hand, an acceptance of the principles involved is unquestioned. Book study provides this; attention to specifically directed technological treatise assists and manufacturers data sheets, normally available on request, are invaluable. Above all, however, the field of ability and competence can only come from related training and experience. With the 3rd Generation vessels the operational manuals of the ship(s) in which an officer serves must be thoroughly understood, and observed.

Associated with the area of stability is that which concerns itself with the possibility of ship heeling by reason of unsymmetric cargo distribution, such as can be found with fast moving load/discharge procedures in G3 vessels.

This feature is to be avoided; unaccounted for could well create problems with lift on/lift off mechanization.

The remedy is to be found in an automatic/manual heeling system—activated from 'heeling tanks'.

Cargo Control

In G3 vessels, on which these guide lines are based, the controlling function of cargo handling is through instrumentation and related operational devices, situated in a separate control room built into the superstructure.

In this context, port work/port dues timing is kept under control and not permitted to be at any disadvantage by reason of the simultaneous cargo working systems peculiar to these classes of vessels.

Cargo control, in this fashion, is highly related to the need to support 'Quick Turn Round'.

Communications

Within the G3 fleet of the Atlantic Container Line Consortium, the 'paper work' of the carriage and handling of the cargo(es) is professionally covered by a fully complete transmission system, related to all routes of working throughout Europe and North America.

Overall, this provides for rapid and accurate preparation of manifests, packing lists, freight accounts, stowage plans, etc., etc.

In actuality, the system supercedes the hitherto accepted interpretation of 'paper work' as between ports within a voyage.

In its place there is an international communications network throughout the whole of the ACL Services Limited, which embodies Master and Summary Bay Plans, operated to the benefit of all Terminal Managers on a vessels' schedule, to Ship Masters and also to provide the group with information necessary to the ports loading and on going condition of the vessel. Computerization is involved—Loadmaster programming.

Despite the professional techniques involved, it is useful for the ships' officers to understand the purpose of transmission systems, such as these outlined, since, in major form, they are practically involved in supporting the accuracy and usefulness of the procedures.

Rules, Recommendations and Guide Lines

In the international maritime industry the operation of ships is closely influenced by a varied number of official and semi-official guide lines and rules. In this respect 3rd Generation vessels are not exempted, but when it is remembered that 24 such 'orders' do call for compliance in one way or another, this does point to the growing importance of these types of vessels—and their safe and seaworthy handling.

UNIT LOADING
Other Than Containers

It is important to appreciate that containerization is not the panacea for all cargo handling activities. It is only a part, albeit an important and far-reaching one. Unit loading is probably of greater impact and more applicable to a variety of differently-designed vessels, apart from the cellular container ship. Furthermore, unit loading finds application with a variety of cargoes, particularly small packaged goods and certainly cased and boxed fruit and vegetables.

Unit loading has increased by virtue of similar reasons to those for container stowage and ship design and port facilities have met the need.

Since the make-up of cargoes, cased, boxed, bagged or strapped can be brought together on pallets, loading and discharging is frequently possible without the use of ship or shore cranage gear.

With conventional-type vessels the introduction of side ports for cargo working and the design of wider hatchways of lesser coaming height has encouraged the use of mechanical handling equipment to transfer palletized cargoes to and from the ship, and indeed to place the pallets in position in the hold or 'tween deck.

Since conventional ship design is likely to remain for some years yet, the improvements and specialities of the structure are likely to add support to unit cargo handling well alongside, if not in excess of container systems on some trades. This is becoming evident on the shorter sea routes.

In this context has been the development of the 'roll on/roll off' vessel, with appropriate port facilities permitting traffic to flow from ship to shore, or vice versa, without impediment. Both bow and stern entry/exit arrangements prevail.

For speedy transportation of goods made up into unit loads and of those already containerized or trucked, the 'roll on/roll off' principle is ideal. As with containerization, it embraces the 'through transport function', integrating a number of transport systems as between consignor and consignee. Distances over which these types of vessels are operating are increasing but particularly is this form of cargo carriage and vehicle transport becoming increasingly profitable from the U.K. East Coast ports to Western Europe.

SUMMARY
Cargo Movement by Modern Developments

1. *By Containers*
    (*a*) Suitable for cargoes of high density movement on a regular basis which can be economically packed into a container and left there, from origin to destination.

(b) Acceptable for cargoes which are moved over international borders.

TYPES OF CONTAINERS

(a) Standard size of 10, 20, 30 or 40 ft (3·048, 6·096, 9·144 or 12·192 m) lengths with 8 ft × 8 ft breadth/height relationship. Most common length 20 ft.
(b) Specialized containers for refrigerated cargoes, dry bulk cargoes, chemicals in powder form. Pressurized steel tanks built into a framework of 20 ft × 8 ft × 8 ft (6·096 × 2·438 × 2·438 m) for the carriage of liquids.

2. *By Pallets (Unit Loads)*
Suitable for:

(a) Goods of relatively uneconomical grouping which are for discharge at port of destination.
(b) Trade routes of relatively short distances.
(c) Vessels (long haul) with side-port working facilities and clear decks, additional to conventional methods.
(d) Specialized trades of standardized cargoes on short sea routes, such as fruit and vegetables.

3. *By 'Roll on/Roll off' Vessels*
Suitable to the through transit of goods either containerized, or truck made up, or of private and commercial vehicles moving over both relatively short distances, and also 'long haul'.

4. *Spreaders*
Basically, the lifting of a container is by means of a 'spreader'. These take on numerous forms, from the simple beam spreader to the sophisticated automatic control systems. Whatever the system, safety is the paramount issue with provisions for locking twistlock devices on the box correctly engaged and locking into any lifting arrangements. It is essential that these matters are completely in order before any box is lifted.

Numerous organizations, both in the U.K. and abroad, design and manufacture lifting and locking systems, both for the conventional, relatively slower ship or berth-gear working, and for the high speed operations for specially designed and purpose built cellular container vessels by Transporter/Portainer cranes. See section on Ports Equipment, page 351.

5. *Systems*
Although systems of container handling are mainly dictated by the requirements and joint operational procedures agreed as between the shipping companies using the berth and the ports authorities, normal procedures invariably commence, on discharge, with deck stowage first, followed by first cellular cell. Reloading follows the

converse procedure and the completion of an entire cell is usual before moving the crane to other cells, accepting the premise of possible stability considerations.

Container procedures are greatly influenced by the design of the terminal. It must be such as to expedite the reception of export boxes, distribution within the terminal and the delivery of import containers. Thus rail and road services, predominantly, must have unimpeded and non-congestion areas and approaches.

Additionally, adequate provision must be made for customs examination, comprehensive ship and shore documentation and ship loading/discharging lists information. Normally this latter aspect is centrally situated in and handled by control staff.

It is anticipated that container carriage will lead to vessels able to handle 2500–3000 T.E.U. though more moderately sized ships will continue to carry a large proportion of the trade. Two hundred and fifty to five hundred boxes is a fair general average on normal ocean trades.

Gantry crane container handling can be of the order of anything from 25–40 boxes an hour. Complete loading/discharging cycles with transporter cranes is not unusual at $4-4\frac{1}{2}$ minutes.

6. *Containers . . . Stuffing and Stripping*
While the container trades include the loading and discharging of its boxes at either container depots/stacking and distribution areas of the port or at the premises of the consignor/consignee, there will always be a need to fill a container with part loads, as these arrive from different shippers to the berth or quay. Similarly is the process reversed on discharge.

This is termed, 'stuffing' and 'stripping' the former the loading aspect and the latter concerned with discharge. By its very nature the ship officer should be involved in these procedures in co-ordinated supervision with the berth/quay staff. The function of loading and discharging a container in these circumstances differs only in degree from that of normal ship-cargo handling, with all the attendant responsibilities of the ship towards safe stowage and damage controls. But not always is the labour force allocated to stuffing and stripping duties of the best, and may well be less adaptable than when normally employed on ship work. It is not unreasonable in these circumstances to be on the look out for less care and attention being given to the job.

Stuffing and stripping a container need not necessarily be labour intensive; indeed, more secure and effective distribution of the total load can frequently be obtained by judicious and sensible use of fork lift trucks. But the ship officer must insist that the container load meets all the requirements of safe and undamaged cargo.

The practice of 'stuffing' is common in Far Eastern ports where feeder services bring 'small' consignments for container transportation on liner routes.

PALLETIZATION

A revolutionary introduction to cargo handling is the increasing popularity of shipment by pallets.

In brief, the system is one of packing the goods, whether cased or of 'piece good' design, on to wooden or metal pallets (or trays) in the warehouse and/or sheds and loading the whole into the vessel, there to remain in stowage until it is discharged at the other end. By so doing, handling is reduced to a minimum, damage from cargo hooks, manual handling and broken stowage is of almost negligible proportion, if at all, and loading and discharging rates are less in time.

In its simplest form the standard pallet . . .known as the shipper's pallet, as distinct from the factory pallet normally retained by the consignor, is no more than two wooden slatted deck surfaces of about 35 mm thick, separated by three square timber bearers placed at intervals to allow space for the injection of forks by fork lift truck carriage. By virtue of the heavy useage to which a pallet is put, its construction must be robust and durable and conforming to British Standard Specifications, BS 2629, 1967.

The 'four way entry' pallet is considered to be the more preferable for ship work, as illustrated in Figure 4.14.

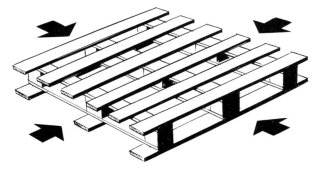

Fig. 4.14 'four way entry' pallet.
By kind permission of National Association of Port Employers, Great Britain

Modern cargo space design, with flush 'tween deck hatch covers and a more 'square' arrangement of lower hold construction permits pallets of cargo to be stowed tightly and compactly such that shifting of the contents of the pallet is unlikely. Much less dunnage is required than with conventional stowage, that which is used should be of even size and thickness so that compactness is not destroyed while maintaining ventilation.

'Palletized' cargo handling lends itself to a wide variety of cargoes, some of which having been successfully carried are boxes of fish; bagged commodities; cartons and cased goods; drums of liquids and bales or rolls of paper.

The introduction of mechanical handling devices such as fork lift trucks; cranes as opposed to derricks, and conveyors have stimulated this form of carriage in that such can be used to place the pallets in any part and height of the cargo compartment. Compact stowage—an important aspect of supervision on the part of ships' officers—is of an advantageous nature, experience proving that very favourable comparison exists between the cubic capacities afforded by the conventional 'grain and bale' space and the newer pallet system.

Not only does the pallet, however, lend itself to fork lift truck movement, but it can be slung by metal stirrups fitted and clamped to its ends. It can, also, if need be, be lifted, in total, by a net sling encompassing both the pallet and its load.

A feature of cargo carriage by palletization is also the introduction of 'balloon' containers. These are collapsible units of synthetic material into which is loaded commodities such as all kinds of powders and similar bulk materials, including food products. They have the advantage of being both air-tight and water-tight and are invaluable as a means of prevention against pests and other forms of contamination often present in ships' holds.

A British invention lending itself to a form of palletization is the aluminium container of some 500 cu ft capacity and of dimension applicable to normal 'tween deck space as well as hold stowage. These containers are light in weight yet durable in strength to withstand all normal usage and permit bulk stowage both in themselves and for a variety of cargoes for which they have been designed. For perishable goods on short sea passages these containers have a high economic value.

Palletization is particularly economic on short sea routes though it is reasonable to expect a growing application to all cargo liner trades. It obviates the growing cost of heavy packaging; it reduces handling; it increases speed of loading and discharge and thus reduces the 'turn round' factor with the associated saving in port dues.

Although there is as yet not complete standardization on the most efficient size of pallet, the recommendation of an international working group which met in Amsterdam in late 1957, suggest a plan size of 48 in × 64 in and 48 in × 72 in and it is likely that these sizes will best apply to economic loads.

Solidarity of stowage is essential with palletized loads. The load itself, on the pallet, must be solid and secure and evenly distributed while the pallet, with its load, solidly secured, chocked off on a level base.

Tea is now carried as palletized loads enabling the chests to be sorted to marks on the quayside for direct load to road vehicles.

It promotes less costs of handling and speedy delivery, assisted by quay crane discharge and fork lift truck movement.

Palletized tea cargoes is a growing trade from India.

Rates of discharge can be 70 000 chests in two to three days; 2400 chests per gang. Indeed rates of handling time is twice as fast as with normally stowed tea cargoes.

Tea, also palletized, is now also carried in containers.

SOME NOTES ON THE CONCEPTS OF UNITIZED CARGOES

The Concept. The concept of unitization is to assist the process of cargo handling by reducing the number of occasions whereby a piece of cargo has need to be handled, and, in creating this situation, also reducing manual handling by the replacement of mechanical means.

In this respect particularly, does unitization have relevance to the making up of a number of 'small-sized' items into one unit of standard size, but the term is not confined only to small-sized cargoes; pieces of mechanical units, sometimes relatively large, can be packed together into one frame carrier or box and thus be easier to stow than individually and be adaptable to 'easier' mechanical means of handling.

The traditional aspect of general cargo changes in concept when the parts of which it is composed can be standardized in size and unit form. It then becomes a form of unit carriage. Indeed, a container is a unit but not the only form of unitization.

Pre-slinging and palletization are equally applicable as is also a loaded lorry or trailer run into and out of a roll on/roll off vessel. Packaged timber is also a form of unit carriage.

Taken to the extreme 'indivisible' loads—generators, chemical extractors and other fabricated heavy mechanical/electrical equipment, such as pressure vessels, which are shipped direct from manufacturer to customer are specially loaded into roll on/roll off ships by custom-built, low-level trailers or by means of floating cranes or sheerlegs to other types of vessels. Loads of this nature can have tonnages of 300–400 tons and are estimated to increase to the 1000 tons range. Two examples prove the point . . . a 640 ton module for a North Sea gas rig, loaded in two sections of 260 and 380 tons on to a supply vessel by means of high powered jacking over steel runners, and a 680 ton prefabricated accommodation unit, loaded by a 400 ton floating crane, for a North Sea oil rig.

Indivisible loads may also be shipped by vessels having appropriate heavy derricks and equipment. This is particularly convenient where loading and discharging is at ports not having adequate lifting facilities for these loads. Here again, it is a unit of carriage.

The Staff 20—Modern Multi-Purpose Cargo Vessel

The Approach. From the point of view of the ship's officer the concept will show itself in a number of different ways according to the type of vessel in which he will be serving, with handling responsibilities varying accordingly.

In the 'Conventional' accepted type of cargo vessel—and this class is unlikely to disappear from the maritime scene for some considerable time—his association with unitized cargo will most likely be only a part of cargo-handling care, since break bulk cargoes will continue to remain a large part of trading patterns and more so where these are related to trades serving the less-developed countries, and ports. In these circumstances part of the deadweight tonnage booked may well be pre-slinged or palletized.

In these situations ship preparation in terms of space provision and accessibility must be such as to avoid overstowing; damage from contact with break bulk cargo and easy access for discharge, since one of the objects of unitization is speedy distribution. In the latter case arrangements for the use of fork lift trucks—frequently slung into the decks or hold to pick up unitized or palletized cargoes direct—will require careful attention to port markings, particularly where loading has been for a number of different ports of discharge. To be completely economical fork lift loading or discharging must move relatively quickly. Manifest and tallying attention is therefore important.

Where conventional vessels have side ports included in their construction it is probable that cargo plan arrangements for loading may well concentrate unitized cargoes in the holds so served by the side ports, stability aspects of course being taken into account. In such cases the cargo space takes on the form of a 'warehouse' or 'transit area' and thus requires to be marked out in such a way as to promote effective reception and discharge of the unit loads.

The development of the conventional cargo carrier to the 'Multi-Purpose' vessel encourages a wider use of unitization, including containers.

The multi-purpose vessel by definition is one designed and constructed to carry a multi-cargo load of varying types in specially-designed compartments with hold, deck, craneage and/or derricks arrangements, with side ports also, such as to permit the loading and discharging of the total cargo load for a port simultaneously.

Multi-purpose vessels can be both relatively small and large in tonnage. On the European/North Atlantic and the developing Far East trades, both from Europe and Australia this type of vessel is outstandingly composite in construction. Roll on/roll off facilities through the stern add to the cargo movement and handling factors into main holds and on deck. The smaller vessl, notably serving the shorter routes, can have similar construction but be less in capacity or facilities. Other types of multi-purpose ships are, primarily, of conventional hull design, but the improvements over the accepted conventional vessel are mainly those of wide hatch openings with low coamings, if any, in 'tween decks; side ports; craneage as distinct from derricks, except for heavy loads and internal capacity in holds/compartments designed for containers, pallets, general break bulk cargo and refrigerated space.

By virtue of this design the multi-purpose vessel can load and discharge a number of different cargoes simultaneously and ports services are appropriately provided.

Cargo-plan arrangements are much more complex; distribution of total load within the vessel requires attention to the full or optimum use of capacity, both by measurement and tonnage since where a concentration of vehicular cargo is loaded, space utilization is important, and safety precautions in securing the units vital. Furthermore, apart from the normal responsibilities of care in stowing, separation and prevention of contamination, the specialisms of container handling other than in a cellular compartment will call for attention to safe lifting procedures for safe stowage and solid distribution; normal unitized loads will doubtless utilize a large measure of mechanical lifting and transportation units (fork lift trucks), hence attention to fast-moving factors; refrigerated part cargo will call for the normal temperature control and, particularly where a number of ports are served on the trade attention to avoidance of overstowage and overcarriage takes on an increasing importance with multi-working of the vessel.

Apart from all of the above, a new dimension enters into the duties of the ship's officer in these types of vessels and that is close liaison with ports services in respect of equipment utilization and labour gang deployment with simultaneous working at all holds.

Within the 'multi-type' of vessel concept, involvement with unit cargoes embraces much wider duties in roll on/roll off vessels but of a more specialized character. These vessels are designed to accommodate all forms of unitization from palletized loads to vehicular traffic of all descriptions, including containers on trailers or lorries, and also forms of break bulk. Their versatility is the ability to load all types of goods through bow and/or stern approaches. Some are devoted to cargo alone; others to cargo and passengers. Considerable tonnages are carried in these vessels and the tendency is for current figures to increase over the envisaged future, particularly on the short sea routes and notably so within Europe.

No longer, however, is the roll on/roll off vessel confined to the short sea routes; distances of 2000 miles or more are not now unusual with ship sizes appropriately related. Certainly considerable services operate within the greater European area, but this type of ship is profitable, for example, on the New Zealand–Japan services and also over the North Atlantic coast ports.

The roll on/roll off vessel works particularly closely with ports services which are designed to provide 'fast movement' facilities of link span berthing; lift on/lift off craneage and vehicular-handling equipment of sophisticated content with fork lift trucks, trailers, etc. The distribution aspect is important with these types of vessels; one of the contiguous objects of their introduction is the ability of the shipper to move his goods quickly from source to destination. In this connection alone there is need for the ship's officer to become familiar with the systems of ports services provided and to work closely with the port in the reception, stowing and securing of the units and later, with the discharging delivery, relative to the quickness with which these vessels must work. Time in port is a vital factor.

With some of the more 'modern' roll on/roll off vessels the construction embraces mechanical/hydraulic systems of binding normal unitized loads in block safety units against movement, and also chain and block arrangements serve to prevent vehicular loads moving, but this does not absolve the ship's officer from supervising these arrangements.

The relatively smaller roll on/roll off vessel, trading on short sea routes and of possibly lesser sophisticated design completes its load with a more varied mixture of general cargo, unit loads and vehicular traffic. In these cases the speed of working calls for particular care in the supervision of safe and solid stowage, and of the stability aspect. Cases are on record of cargo shifting, with consequent damage as a result of heavy weather *en route*, where neglect in this matter has arisen. The responsibility in these directions is no less with any type of roll on/roll off vessel, but takes on a wider dimension with the smaller types.

Specialist Types of Vessels
Possibly the more direct form of unitization is that where most, if not all of the cargo-handling availability is in ships specially designed to cater for unit loading. Five such types of classification are worthy of mention.

(*a*) The 'full pallet' ship, with internal capacity served by side ports and pallet elevators between the decks.
   Attention here must be related to fast-moving loading and discharging systems by mechanical means and careful regard to blocking and securing the pallets.
(*b*) The modern 'banana carrier', with highly-sophisticated cooling systems and elevator methods of loading and discharging the boxes of bananas in unit form.
   Predominantly here is the need for exact control of temperature, which implies not only ship-care, but also supervision of the state of the fruit at loading and conformity to shippers specifications *en route*.
(*c*) The container 'cellular' vessel. See pages 254, 269.
(*d*) The 'barge-carrying' vessel. Attention here is in the super-

vision of the systems of loading, securing and discharging the barges from the carrying vessel.

(e) Heavy lifts 'indivisible loads'. The care and handling aspect is obviously primarily related to lifting safety and ship construction safeguards.

(f) Lifting should be 'plumb' of the derrick(s) with gear in first class condition; speed of movement appropriate and steady and ship stability 'correct'. Loading can be either on deck or in the hold but in either case there is need to stow safely and securely and to ensure that the 'deck' is adequately strengthened by good under-based foundations. (See also note on Indivisible Loads, pages 265, 359).

(Detailed aspects of Ship Types and their applications to unitized cargo handling is given in Section 4.)

'J' MISCELLANEOUS AND CONVENTIONAL CARGOES

The Preparation of Holds and Spaces

A general cargo requires that the holds and spaces are well swept out and any residue of a previous cargo sent up on deck. Precautions should be taken to ensure that the space is well ventilated and dry and to this end windsails may be rigged and hatch covers opened, albeit weather conditions accepted. Liberal supplies of clean and unstained dunnaging material should be available, together with separation cloths and mats. Dunnage can be of wood form or synthetic materials.

Particular care in preparation is necessary with a bagged cargo. Solidarity of stow is essential with clean, wide board dunnage in order to avoid the bags sagging and splitting. Modern carriage of bulk commodities, previously bagged, are now increasingly packed into what are termed 'Intermediate Bulk Carriers' (see Bulk— General). Nonetheless, some trades do still continue to provide bagged cargo.

A Bale or General Cargo may be dunnaged efficiently with almost any types of wooden boards or battens provided they fulfil the requirements of cleanliness. The boards or battens, however, should be selected in accordance with the sizes of the packages or bales necessary for a compact stow.

Appropriate wooden dunnage may be laid prior to the commencement of loading a bagged cargo, for, with most bagged cargoes a complete tier is first laid over the floor of the space. General cargo however, by virtue of different shapes and sizes, will break up and misplace any previously laid dunnage. It is better, therefore, to have a liberal supply of dunnage available in the compartment and use it as required when stowing the packages.

Double dunnage should always be laid. The first tier is arranged athwartships in order to provide water courses toward the bilges, and the upper tier, fore and aft.

Sugar Cargo. Sugar cargoes must be completely free from dampness or contact with iron and steel (condensation problems). Sugar can also be carried in intermediate bulk carriers and by reason of the greater protective features of these, atmospheric conditions do not present so great a problem. But it can also be shipped in bags.

Sugar is said to be either 'dry' or 'green', the former being almost free of syrupy content; the latter of a raw or wet nature. Dampness with green sugar will result in considerable drainage in the form of syrup which is not only damaging to the remainder of the cargo but conducive to causing the bags (if this is the stow) to stick together in the form of a solid block as they settle down. Wet syrup. in contact with iron and steel will cause corrosion.

'Dry' and 'green' sugar should not be stowed together. 'Tween deck stowage is preferable for 'dry' sugar whilst lower holds can be efficiently prepared for 'green' sugar. In both cases, irrespective of the form of carriage, plenty of wide wood boards should be available for dunnage. The bulkheads and sides of the space should be draped with separation cloths and the whole of the bottom layer of dunnage (double) covered with clean separation cloths. Considerable quantities of mats should be handy, to use as a protection against bare ironwork.

A Cotton Cargo. Cotton, shipped in tightly pressed bales is a cargo which is accompanied by fire risk. The preparation of a hold or compartment for this cargo is primarily directed towards lessening the risk of fire. This cargo is liable to produce heat and is also (though this is still a matter of opinion) subject to spontaneous combustion. Outside elements which may cause extra fire risks must be considered.

It is imperative that any space in which cotton is to be stowed should be perfectly dry, well aired, and absolutely free from any oily or greasy stains. The previous cargo will determine the amount of cleaning necessary. Following a clean general cargo, efficient sweeping and airing will suffice, but it must be appreciated that, following a coal cargo, for example, it is necessary to wash the space down, due attention being given to the drying. Following the discharge of oily or greasy cargoes, an amount of deposit on decks and ceiling will be certain. Lime may then be sprinkled and left awhile, in order to absorb the deposit and permit satisfactory sweeping and cleaning. Windsails should be rigged to improve drying.

Precautions Necessary when Loading Cotton

1. All bales should be perfectly dry, clean and free from any stains particularly those of an oily or greasy nature.

   Dampness in bales of cotton is not readily apparent, because the climate of those countries from which cotton is shipped causes quick drying of the outside of the bales. The lower layers of cotton may be wet, perhaps from tropical rain squalls. Considerable vigilance is necessary in this direction, particularly with transhipment cargo and that loaded from lighters.

   Reject any bales suspected under any of the above conditions.

2. Reject any loosely packed bales or any with broken bands. Such bales permit air circulation between the fibres and are more easily fired.

3. Do not load cotton into any space which has recently been painted. The heat produced by the cotton might possibly cause ignition of the paint vapours.

4. Pains should be taken to ensure that the port marks of the bales are not obliterated. With large consignments, obliteration results in considerable delay to consignees apart from hindering discharge.

5. Be aware of the need to quickly cover hatch openings in inclement weather (e.g. heavy rain squalls), whatever the system of hatch coverings to the ship.

6. Strict rules must be enforced against smoking in and around the compartments. All fire fighting equipment must be ready for immediate use.

   All previous wooden dunnage should be sent up on deck and only that dunnage which is absolutely clean, dry and free from any stains, retained for use with the cotton. This selection also applies to any mats and separation cloths. Fresh dunnage should be well seasoned and clean to the above standard.

   Hatch covers to all decks should be complete and in good condition, with at least one tarpaulin available at each of the lower decks. The battening down of each space after completion of loading, restricts fire spreading. Inspection should be made of all fire extinguishing apparatus which serves cargo compartments; these should be in efficient working condition. All ventilator cowls must be covered with a thickness of wire gauze.

A Rice Cargo. This cargo calls for a very elaborate and efficient system of ventilation, for two reasons. Firstly, rice evolves a certain amount of carbonic acid gas, and secondly, its moisture content, at the beginning of the season particularly, leads to the sweating of the hold. Condensation will therefore drip on the cargo from certain points, unless adequate precautions are taken.

The cargo is liable to heat fairly quickly, and this fact, associated with loss of moisture, explains the losses of weight in transit varying from 1–3 per cent.

The bags are filled with a mixture of rice (80 per cent) and paddy

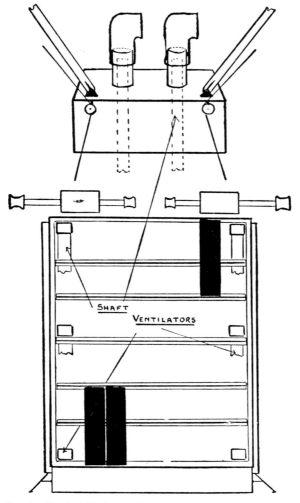

Fig. 4.15 Showing Vertical Shaft Ventilators Leading into Hatchway and also into Permanent Ventilators.

(rice with husks) (20 per cent). The latter prevents the rice grains forming an aggregate which is impervious to ventilation air currents. Without this addition of paddy, the bags would stow in a solid block, thus preventing the passage of air through the bags.

The floor of the hold should be covered with 3 in × 3 in battens, laid athwartships, and 11 in × $1\frac{1}{2}$ in boards fore and aft, laid with a space of 4 in between boards. This will ensure efficient air passages without causing the bottom bags to split, a result which would certainly occur if the boards were spaced too far apart. Special attention should be paid to limbers and cement chocks, where moisture would accumulate.

Spar ceiling should be covered with bamboos, arranged either vertically or in criss-cross fashion, and all other ironwork covered with bamboo mats. The whole of the bottom dunnage should also be covered with bamboo mats.

Temporary vertical box ventilators are fitted in position as follows: one at each corner of the hatchway and one at the middle of the hatchcoaming on each side, making six in all for the hatchway. Two are fitted at each end of the hold, one to port and one to starboard, the last mentioned leading to permanent ventilator shafts (see diagram).

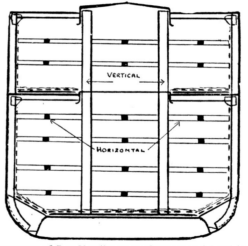

Fig. 4.16 Arrangement of Box Ventilators to Connect and Lead into the Vertical Shaft Ventilators.

Two or three tiers of bags are laid to cover the bottom of the hold, followed by a system of box frame wooden ventilators laid in positions with a five bag horizontal interspace. These are arranged so as to interconnect and also lead the air current into the vertical ventilators.

The system of box frame ventilators is repeated with every three tier of bags. (See diagram of Box Frame Ventilator.)

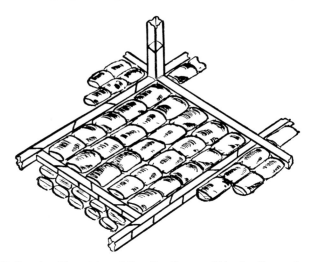

Fig. 4.17 Showing Disposition of Box Ventilators within the Cargo. Arranged at every Third Tier with a Five Bag Spacing.

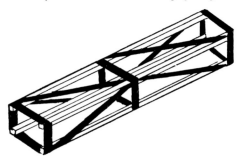

Fig. 4.18 Suggested Form of Box Ventilator. 3 in × 3 in Battens supported by Wooden Straps. Size 8 in × 12 in Square.

The Stowage of Barrels

Bottom stowage is preferable in order that leakage may find access to the bilges without fear of damage to other cargo.

Bearing in mind the 'run' of a vessel, it is the general practice to commence the stow of a forward hold at the after end of the hold and work forward and of an after hold at the forward end of the hold and work aft.

Stout wooden scantlings is the type of dunnage required. A pair of these scantlings is laid athwartships across the fore and aft middle line of the hold and the first pair of barrels is stowed close together, fore and aft, one on either side of the middle line. The scantlings are laid sufficiently far apart to permit the quarters of the barrels to rest upon them. Quoins in the form of soft wooden chocks are placed as shown in the diagram to wedge the barrels in place.

The second pair of barrels is then stowed, one on either side of the first pair and so on in pairs until the row across is completed.

Fig. 4.19 Barrel Stowage.

The barrels rest on their quarters on the scantlings because that is the strongest part of a barrel and it is very important to ensure that the scantlings are of sufficient thickness to keep the bilge of the barrel clear of the tank top or ceiling. Leakage is liable to occur as a result of pressure against the bilge of a barrel.

As each barrel is stowed care must be taken to see that the bung is uppermost (on top). The rivets which secure the hoops of a barrel are always in line with the bung—this knowledge is useful when stowing barrels in a light which is not too good or when the barrels are dirty or stained.

When the barrel is stowed 'bung up' the joints in the boards which form the ends of the barrel are vertical; therefore, if any weight is placed on top of the barrel, the ends are not likely to burst out.

At the turn of the bilge of the vessel liberal supplies of cord wood or soft wooden dunnage should be used to fill in and block off the spaces formed between the line of barrels and the ship's side.

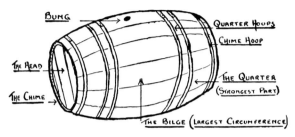

Fig. 4.20 The Parts of a Barrel.

When the first tier of barrels is completed, the upper tier is stowed in such a manner as to permit each upper barrel to line in the cantlines of the four barrels below, as shown in the diagram. In this way the bilge of each barrel in each tier remains 'free'.

It is usual to limit the height to which barrels may be stowed to eight tiers. In some trades, particularly with barrels of oil, only seven are allowed, but it is not a wise procedure to stow higher than this for the weight of the upper tiers may cause the bottom tiers to collapse.

When a hold is to be completely filled with barrels it is necessary to build a platform over the eighth tier. This platform should be suitably secured and supported from below.

Full cargoes of barrels have been successfully carried by building a platform successively over the first two sets of tiers. In this manner the strength of the bottom tiers is more evenly distributed and are thus able to bear the weight of the upper barrels.

Careful watch should be made of all barrels delivered to a ship for loading. Badly coopered and leaky barrels should be rejected and any which have their hoops missing should be put on one side until such have been replaced or new ones fitted.

Casks of Cement. Modern carriage will tend to ship cement in intermediate bulk carriers, rather than casks; indeed large consignments of cement, apart from bulk carriage as such, are so shipped.

Where this is not the case due regard must be given to the strength of casks since these are not as strong as casks or barrels which contain liquids. New casks present less difficulty but recoopered or old casks, require special care to avoid crushing. Stowage may be similar to that adopted for barrels.

Small consignments, stowed either in the lower hold or 'tween decks may be stowed on their ends instead of 'bilge and cantline' fashion. Stowed thus it is preferable to lay wide boards across the top of each tier, each board resting on the chimes of two adjacent casks, with the casks immediately above each other.

Drums of Oil. Quantities of mineral oils still are shipped in drums, particularly lubricating oils which can be conveniently carried and stowed with safety.

Drums are stowed on their ends, tightly packed and chocked off with soft wood to prevent movement. In order to obtain even distribution of weight each tier should be covered with liberal amounts of wide timber boards.

Damage from chaffing is very likely if the drums are loosely stowed. This chaffing is increased by the strengthening bands fitted to some drums or by the two corrugated sections of others and is only prevented by chocking off. Considerable leakage and consequent claims may arise if this precaution is neglected.

Stowage of Motor Cars

The conventional method of car stowage has for years been by cased packaging. To some extent disadvantages have accompanied this form of transport in that the use of unseasoned wood in the construction of the cases has resulted in rust formation on the cars and component parts, through internal condensation.

While this aspect has not been of major portent as to prove an uneconomic form of transport any improvement in carriage which prevents likely damage is to be encouraged.

Of recent years, there has been an increasing trade in the carriage of unpacked cars. Apart from the considerations mentioned above, a feature of economic and profitable car exportation is the ability to deliver off the ship—ready for use.

Normal carriage and stowage requires careful packing and securing while considerable broken stowage is unavoidable.

A new feature of car stowage is the building of false decks in the hold by the use of tubular scaffolding to which wooden decking is clamped.

Three to four tiers are possible and can be quickly erected or dismantled, while the scaffolding provides additional security of lashings.

Complete car stowage thus becomes possible in lower holds where, previously, it was the 'tween decks which were considered only suitable.

Current carriage of motor cars requires large marshalling areas at points of loading and discharging.

Examples of the trade include exports from the U.K. to U.S.A.

Modern Multi-Deck Car Carrier

Pacific ports and to West Africa, by drive on/drive off ship facilities and also cased cars, known as C.K.D. . . . completely knocked down . . . to South Africa, and handled by craneage.

The total number of cars is extensive and, in the course of a year exceeds 20 000–30 000 from one port alone.

Imports, from Japan, for example are as high as 25 000 per year and this trade to the U.K. includes, in one well known port, 700 cars can be unloaded in 6 hours by quay cranes and 1000 cars in 4 hours by roll on/roll off systems. An average of 200–240 per hour is not unusual.

Specially constructed vessels, with internal decks, permit the speedy drive on/drive off procedures.

When not in use these car decks are stowed against the under-side of the deck head immediately above and secured by suspension wires through sheave block to security fastenings on the tank top.

It is essential that this gear is always in first class condition and attention must be given in order to ensure that positive means of securing portable car decks is fitted, and maintained.

Specialized Auto Carriers of 20 000 gross tonnage now operate in the Japanese, Middle East and European trades.

These vessels have 12 car decks, having a capacity of some $5\frac{1}{2}$ thousand plus, cars and car trucks.

The 'cargo' can be loaded/discharged via deck ramps to either stern quarter or ship side ramps through ro/ro procedures.

Not only can these vessels handle cars, as such, but also other vehicular traffic.

DECK CARGOES

Vessels which are engaged on trades which normally provide cargoes for deck stowage are usually broad of beam in relation to their load draft. This provides them with a reasonably high position of M, the metacentre, which usually allows for possible high positions of the centre of gravity and prevents negative metacentric height on all occasions.

Vessels specially constructed for the carriage of timber are required to have subdivision in their double-bottom tanks. This reduces any possible free surface effect. Further, with vessels of this category, rules are published which set out both the minimum amounts of deck timber that can be carried and the maximum heights to which it may be stowed. The extent, efficiency and methods of securing the lashings are also regulated by definite rules. (D.T. Shipping Notice M687.)

The object of these rules is to provide further measures of safety over and above those which a well-found vessel would normally provide, for it must be remembered that apart from the reduction of metacentric height inseparable from the loading of such cargoes, the bulks themselves are exposed to all kinds of weather conditions.

With vessels engaged on such normal trades the question of loading should not present to the officer any undue worry provided he bears in mind the fundamental rule that here, perhaps more than in any other case, a measure of stiffness is desirable.

Reasonable initial stiffness is very necessary when loading deck cargoes and with ordinary vessels which may have occasion to carry such a load it should be the guiding principle of loading.

In all cases the position of the centre of gravity will be high. The consumption of fuel and stores will probably cause G to rise during the voyage, and the possibility of the deck cargo getting wet, becoming heavier as a result and thereby causing further rise of G must always be borne in mind.

The amount of deck cargo to be loaded should be such that, with all the above points taken into consideration, the vessel shall at all times retain positive metacentric height.

The position of M for the load draft may be obtained from the curve of metacentres and calculation of the position of G above the keel may be recorded throughout the operation of loading.

The probable value of GM in the loaded condition can quite easily be determined when the vessel is about $\frac{3}{4}$ loaded by approximating to data relating to the heights of stowage above the keel of the remaining cargo.

By estimating the probable effect upon the centre of gravity consequent upon fuel consumption during the voyage, it will be apparent what margin of metacentric height is likely to remain.

If this is small, it would seem advisable to fill what double-bottom space is available before loading the deck cargo and so increase the initial metacentric height sufficiently to counteract the likely changes during the voyage.

Efficient lashings, compact stowage and making due provision for protecting and keeping free all scuppers and freeing ports, are essential factors to the loading of deck cargoes.

The Merchant Shipping (Load Lines) Deck Cargo Regulations, 1968, provide specific requirements for the carriage of any cargo on deck. The siting and distribution of all such cargoes must be made with the following points in mind:—

(a) The maximum allowable loading on the deck must be checked so that excessive stress is not set up and cargo having heavy point loading must have arrangements for distribution the load over adjacent parts of the ship's structure

(b) Increase in deck weight, and the consequent effect upon the position of the centre of gravity (KG) may result not only from the absorption of water or accretion of ice, but also from fuel and F.W. consumption which, added to the effect of wind moments on the exposed stow, may seriously affect the vessel's stability and behaviour in bad weather.

(c) Navigation must not be hindered by the height of the stow obstructing forward visibility.

(d) Access to working parts of the ship must not be impeded and a walkway must be provided for the crew over the cargo unless an underdeck passageway exists.

In carrying deck cargoes it is particularly important to ensure the watertight integrity of the ship by securely closing all hatches and openings on the upper deck before the cargo is loaded. (See notes on Access Hatch coverings, pages 65, 70, 469).

Ventilators, air pipes and other structures affording entry to the hull must be carefully protected from damage.

In all of the official publications concerning deck cargoes it is stressed that good seamanship is as much a part of the cargo handling and carrying operation as is knowledge of stowage techniques and ship handling, including alteration of course or reduction of speed in severe weather.

COKE

Its Stowage and Precautions in Carriage

Coke is shipped in bags and in bulk. In the former case it may be satisfactorily stowed below decks, but, being a relatively dirty cargo should be allocated to spaces where it is not likely to damage other cargo.

A 'tween deck provides ideal space for bags of coke, but it may be stowed over a general cargo in a lower hold, in order to fill in space, provided a tarpaulin is spread over the general cargo.

Carried below decks, coke presents little difficulty. It is not suitable as bottom cargo, for it settles quickly, and would promote collapsing of cargo stowed on top, but when carried on deck, in either bags or bulk, certain precautions are necessary.

Since coke is of an absorbent character, care should be taken to see that the vessel is not likely to be overloaded during the voyage. Coke absorbs moisture up to 20 per cent of its weight and when loading a deck cargo, allowance must be made for this possible increase in weight. The deck should be dunnaged with 3 in × 3 in battens, laid diagonally (see diagram), in order to spread the weight across the beams and to provide drainage courses. Wide boarding, closely spaced, is used for the upper layer of dunnage.

For bulk coke, uprights should be fitted along the rail about 10 ft apart, with wire netting of small mesh stretched between.

Extra tarpaulins must be spread to prevent the abrasive action of the coke on the actual hatch tarpaulins, if it is stowed on top of the hatches.

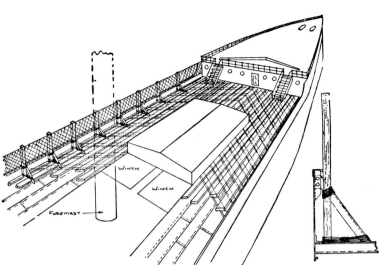

Fig. 4.21 Wire netting may be brought down to deck level or fore and aft planks fitted in order to keep coke clear of scuppers.

Precautions must be taken to ensure that the scuppers and freeing ports are not blocked in any way.

'K' PETROLEUM

In considering this section it should be appreciated that all the organizations concerned with the transportation of petroleum have their own rules and codes of practice for the guidance of personnel. None the less, the notes which follow bear practical relevance.

TANKER FLEETS

The following notes are extracted, and summarize, a section from the earlier established National Ports Council, Great Britain, though now disbanded, Bulletin No. 6 'recent trends in sizes and dimensions of tankers' and inserted with the kind permission of the Council.

A tanker is defined as 'a crude oil carrier'. Up to the years immediately following the Second World War ship sizes had remained stable for quite some time; at the end of the war the largest tanker afloat was about 17 000 dwt.

Subsequently, however, the economics of maritime transport . . . shipbuilding costs, crew costs and voyage length times, etc. . . . . convinced the oil operators that larger vessels were necessary in order to take advantage of the increasing volumes of oil becoming

Shell Tanker S.S. *Latirus.*

available and being needed by industrial growth. Over the past 20 years the situation has changed dramatically.

The late 1950s thus saw the introduction of the 100 000 dwt capacity vessel which later developed into the V.L.C.C. (very large crude carrier) of 200 000–300 000 dwt. By definition, a V.L.C.C. is a vessel with a capacity above an arbitrary size of 150 000 dwt.

In this context the 200 000–300 000 dwt vessels show a preponderance but envisaged design indicates noticeable dw increases on this and it is therefore relevant to consider also the 'other sizes' factors. At the end of 1972 the maximum summer drafts were of the order of 60 ft for vessels of 150 000–200 000 dwt, but only 3–8 ft deeper when the dw increased to 250 000 tons. As the dw increased to around 300 000 tons, drafts became of the order of 72–74 ft, although there are V.L.C.C.s in operation having drafts of around 90 ft, with comparable capacities, a small number however, approaching 500 000 dwt. There are also designs currently available for drafts of over 100 ft for vessels of 700 000–1 000 000 dwt.

The draft factor however, has given rise to the R-D tanker which, indicates the 'Restrictive-Draft' aspect of tanker construction conditioned by the fact that only a very small number of ports/terminals can have sufficient water to handle them.

The length of tanker design has not progressed so vividly; indeed the increase of length/deadweight ratio has been comparatively smoother albeit there has been a noticeable increase of from around 650–1100 ft, overall.

Beam, however, is doubtless the more interesting factor in tanker design. Outwardly they take on a distinctive 'fat' appearance and whereas in 1972 a beam of 80 ft against L650; D36 and DW

25 000 was not uncommon, this has now progressively and steadily increased to 204 ft at a length of 1243 ft, a draft of 92 ft and a dw capacity of 476 000 tons. Proportionate relationships between the beam and the other three dimensions are equally convincing that beam has become the overriding consideration whereby the operator can fully utilize the available ports facilities, consequent upon any other water depth restrictions.

NOTE: Students of stability will appreciate the value of these beam aspects, apart from the economic considerations.

In terms of discharge the V.L.C.C.s of these sizes will be restricted to specialized terminals in deep water harbours or may well off load at single off-shore buoy moorings from which piping installation serves the refineries or part discharge their load into smaller vessels for transhipment from the larger terminals to smaller ports. Second ports of call to discharge part cargoes is also possible.

This is the pattern of the current petroleum trade as refinery capacities increase although it should be pointed out that since tanker construction can increase deadweight capacity from about 280 000–400 000 tons without any increase in draft . . . an increase of about 50 per cent . . . this same design feature could well permit terminals with 45–50 ft of water to handle vessels of 100 000–150 000 dwt. Alongside this trend, however, is the indications of vessels within the 80 000–150 000 dwt range continuing to be ordered.

Reasons for the interest in this size of crude oil carrier seem two-fold. Increasing requirements of imported oil by the U.S.A. is one; this size of vessel being the maximum presently able to use most U.S.A. terminals. The second reason is more speculative in believing that the transshipment of crude oil could become more important, since with the limitations upon the super tankers oil companies need to supply their present refineries many of which are sited at ports with restricted depth of water.

TANKER COMPARTMENTS—CLEANING
with special reference to V.L.C.C.s

The following notes and summaries are included with the kind permission of Esso Europe Inc. with which is associated the Exxon Corporation and Esso Tankers, by whom much research and experimentation has been carried out on the processes of cleaning tanks by crude oil procedures.

V.L.C.C.s . . . very large crude carriers . . . are tank ships of about 160 000 tons or more.

The carriage of crude oil in tanker spaces results, after discharge, in deposits of sediment on the tank bottoms and internal structural parts, while oil film, known as 'clingage' remains on the vertical surfaces. The sediment is made up of waxy and asphaltic composition, detrimental, in some part, to corrosive action upon the structure but primarily can it cause impediment of drainage systems, apart from its effect upon the necessity of having the cargo tanks completely clean prior to a voyage in ballast. Furthermore, the longer the time that crude oil is in tanks, particularly with V.L.C.C. tonnage, allowing the asphaltines to settle, the more severe is the sediment problem. The build up of sludge is not such a problem with smaller ships on 4 or 5 day voyages.

To eradicate these deposits it has long been the practice to wash the tanks out after discharge and, traditionally, this has been done by forcing jets of water on to the 'oily' surfaces. Unquestioned as this practice has been, and still remains, modern experiments and tests results now introduce a new procedure, that of washing the tanks out by the use of the crude oil cargo itself, known as 'crude oil washing' since crude oil has a sizeable fraction of light components which have solvent properties.

Many large tankers, particularly V.L.C.C.s, now use this method and are accordingly fitted outwith appropriate apparatus and piping systems by which the crude oil cargo can be circulated through the tank in its cleaning processes. There are numerous reasons for the adoption of the method of crude oil washing, a summary of which is as follows.

A.   *Generalities*

   (*a*) The cleaning equipment is fitted within the tanks thus avoiding the need to have open apertures in deck openings, through which any gaseous vapours could escape or indeed loss of cargo through broken portable hose connections. These are fitted permanent parts of the system.

   (*b*) The total, broken up, sediment is discharged with the cargo bulk, and is refinable.

   (*c*) It adds to the prevention of pollution by reason of the 'load on top' procedure (L.O.T.) . . . see later notes in section 'Details' . . . whereas with water washing emulsive mixtures result as between the water and the oil and have to be retained until separated. By example, conventional water washing can leave anything up to 2000 tons of sludge, whereas crude washing may leave no more than 300 tons, or so, from a 220 000 dwt tanker.

   It also has safety measures repelling the possibilities of explosion, see section on Safety 'B'.

   (*d*) Economically, the capacity to load further cargo is advanced by the retention of this lesser amount of sludge/sediment, whereas, also by reason of being able to discharge this with the cargo (which is refinable), 'input on loading' and 'output on discharge' figures are favourably comparable.

(*e*) Less time is involved in crude oil washing: it has a superiority over water as a washing medium; risk of pollution to personnel is minimized; it becomes part of normal duties for the crew, rather than a specialized activity, albeit they must be adequately trained. Entry and work within a V.L.C.C. tank, some 90 ft from deck to tank bottom, presents hazardous and difficult problems where personnel have to be engaged in removing sludge manually, as is necessary with the conventional, less solvent, water washing methods.

B. Safety

The use of high speed water jets as a washing medium can, with oil, build up an electrically-charged mist, with dangerous ignition possibilities in an inflammable atmosphere. The use of crude oil is considered to be safer in this respect although the risk is also present with crude oil passing through a jet at high pressure. In this connection 'inert gasiation' is promoted into the tanks before crude oil washing proceeds . . . see later notes in section 'Details'. The system, however, calls for continuous monitoring during the operation and testing for any leaks, while any water which may have settled in the bottom of the tanks beforehand, should be withdrawn. Particularly, precautions must be observed to ensure no oil, through leakage, extends into the engine room, if the system passes through it.

Since crude oil washing is carried out while the cargo is being discharged, there must be complete liaison with port authorities/terminals beforehand.

C. Detail

Two systems can be used. Either while the bulk is being discharged or when it has been emptied from the tanks. The systems of operation are similar.

A tank fitted in cleaning machine, operated by a conventional cargo pump having suction and discharge piping, the latter fitted with a header which recycles the bulk cargo back from the tanks through the cleaning machine, produces jets of crude oil for washing the tank structure.

The number of machines depends upon the number of tanks and their structural configuration. Sixty to ninety machines is not unusual with a V.L.C.C. The capacity range of these machines is of the order of 100–150 tons per hour.

An essential to crude oil washing is that the atmosphere must be safe. As such, it is made inert by checking the oxygen level in the tanks in order to achieve a secure 'gas blanket' and freedom from flammable range. The oxygen level must not exceed 8 per cent and this requires frequent checking, both in the supply lines and in the tank. During crude oil washing the splashing of oil within and on to the structure of the tank generates hydrocarbon gas. Positive inert gas, supplied from the main boiler, or from a gas generator in diesel engined vessels, activates against this in the prevention of cargo tank explosions. Inert gas is a substance with insufficient oxygen to support combustion. The procedure of 'inerting' arises to a large extent from explosions in 1969 within the tanks of three V.L.C.C.s, each in ballast and washing tanks.

Automatic reading gauges are fitted to the system by which the crew/personnel can be aware, at any time, of the level of the oil in the tank.

Finally, when the vessel has left the terminal, tanks are given a light rinse with water to remove the final traces of oil, in preparation for clean ballast, or entry into dry docking.

After crude oil washing it is essential that the tanks are gas freed, by ventilation and water washing. No entry to a tank before this has been achieved should be permitted, unless special full precautions have been taken.

POLLUTION

Operational discharge from large tankers has been, and is, a major source of concern, albeit accidents causing pollution arise more from collisions and groundings, than from inadvertant discharge of 'dirty cargo remains'. Crude oil washing is emerging as an effective abatement measure with inerted crude oil carriers, not the least factor being the adoption of the L.O.T. . . . load on top . . . procedure, although in itself it is not a new concept, being first introduced in 1960, by the oil industry.

Operational pollution by tankers of all sizes results from deballasting, the oil remaining aboard after discharge, mixing with the sea water ballast.

If unrestrained, considerable quantities, representing roughly one-half of 1 per cent of a ship's capacity, i.e. 1250 tons per voyage for a 250 000 ton tanker, would find its way into the sea and be washed up, all or in part, on to the shores, apart from its damaging effect upon marine life.

L.O.T. decreases the amount of oil discharged with ballast. Most of the world's tanker fleets practice it.

L.O.T. allows the oil-water combination in cargo tanks to settle, causing the oil to rise and lie on top of the water, which is then discharged from beneath the oil. The remaining oil can then be combined with the next cargo.

The problem of pollution has been considered on an international basis, resulting in three conventions known as MARPOL 1973; SOLAS 1978 (in force May 1981) and MARPOL 1978 (in force October 1983).

The purpose of these conventions is to introduce, progressively, requirements for the fitting of separate ballast arrangements. The nature of the arrangements depends on whether the vessel is a new building or an existing ship at the effective date of the conventions, and whether it is a crude or a products carrier, so that the ballast system may include any of the following features:—

1. Segregated Ballast Tanks ... sufficient tank capacity must be provided for water ballast to the extent that under ordinary circumstances no water at all is carried in the cargo tanks.
2. Protective Location . . . where the segregated ballast tanks are placed in selected parts of the ship so as to provide a degree of protection in the event of grounding or collision. Examples of protective location of S.B.T.s are shown in the sketch diagram ... page 319.
3. Clean Ballast Tanks. . . . For existing ships, cargo tanks dedicated to water ballast may be allowed as an interim measure. The difference between these and the S.B.T.s is that they do not require an entirely separate pipeline and pumping system.

It follows that if water and oil are to be kept separate, any tank washing must be with crude oil and the old routine of water-washing will cease to operate, except for a final rinse before dry docking or maintenance inspection. Furthermore, the cessation of oily slops should result in a dramatic reduction in pollution.

The siting of the ballast tanks may follow a number of options. Ideally the location should be at the vessel's sides and bottoms, even to the extent as for dry-cargo ships, or, alternatively, a double-sided design giving protection throughout.

Less favoured would be ballast tanks on the centre line only, or concentrated in the fore end of the ship.

The conventions aim to discourage designs which provide for ballast on the centre line only, or where the ballast tanks are arranged in the far end of the ship only.

With regard to the double skin, this arrangement reflects the requirements of the Bulk Liquid Chemicals Code, where protection against spillage of the cargo, in the event of collision or grounding, is provided by the double hull.

GENERAL OBSERVATIONS ON PETROLEUM CARRIAGE

The production of crude and refined oil is one of the world's major industries. Modern industrial and commercial undertakings rely so much upon the petroleum industry that intensive effort is devoted to realizing every potential value of crude oil.

In particular, currently, the Middle East production areas have considerable influence upon world economic and financial development. Crude oil, and its derived products, enter into the economic life of every nation, and the requirements of modern industrial and commercial undertakings, apart from the growth, in itself, of vehicular transportation, both industrial and domestic, has led to the continuing increase in the shipment and marketing of mineral oils.

Furthermore, the development of refinery installations at the 'point of discharge' has stimulated the considerable increase in crude oil shipments from the sources of production, and the growth of large carriers, including the V.L.C.C.s, pointedly indicating 'very large crude carriers'. While the length and breadth of a 200 000 ton tanker is only about twice that of a 20 000 ton vessel, it carries more than 10 times as much oil. Nor is the difference in operating costs singularly out of proportion.

Oil cargoes, however, do have classification, and may be:

(a) Light . . . various spirits such as gasolines, white spirit, alcohol, various kerosenes, light gas oil.
(b) Heavy . . . crude oils, asphalt, creosote, fuel oils, heavy gas oils, diesel oil, lubricating oil.

The cargo officer's interest, primarily limited to the time the cargo is under his care, will be conditioned by the type of oil (and vessel in which it is carried). Crude oils, for example, have hydrocarbon content and call for particular attention, not the least being safety of the ship and risk of contamination of the oceans of the world. (See notes on Tank Washing, pages 285–296). Indeed, considerable research is being carried out internationally to determine the environmental risk to marine life consequent upon the vast quantities of oil now being transported by sea.

Tanker Types
Tanker sizes vary (see page xvi) according to the trades involved and the ports facilities to accommodate them. Both loading and discharging may be direct from wharf or jetty, or by submarine pipe line to, and from, off-shore installations, where water depth introduces relevant restrictions.

In general, tanker design, irrespective of design, follows similar principles . . . the subdivision of the structure into compartments by longitudinal and transverse bulkheads, the spaces so formed being known as tanks, 90 being not unusual in large tankers. In large measure, tankers also now have sophisticated built-in systems covering pumping functions, temperatures and pressures, as well as for the propulsion machinery. Computer techniques are fitted in some large tankers.

The operation of tankers must conform to a series of international and national regulations. The co-ordination of these regulations has been part of the influence of I.M.O. (International Maritime Organization) and includes oil discharges at sea (pollution risk), personnel safety and maritime safety, including loading restrictions, among others. Much of this is related to The International Convention for Safety of Life at Sea; The International Convention on Load Lines; The International Convention for the Prevention of Pollution from Ships and The International Regulations for Preventing Collisions at Sea.

At a national level, the individual governments are charged with enforcing these regulations, as for example, The Department of Trade in Great Britain; The U.S. Coast Guard; and The Maritime Safety Agency, Japan. Additionally, the Classification Societies set standards of construction, maintenance and of equipment which must be met before a tanker can go to sea, apart from the stringent rules laid down by fleet owners themselves.

In this context, one matter alone, deserves the attention of the Cargo Officer, that of oil spills at terminals. It is estimated that some 70 000 tons of oil enter the oceans each year from this source, often caused by faulty equipment, leaking valves and human error.

Loading and Discharging

Oil discharge is by suction pipes from the tanks to pumprooms and hence to delivery pipes at deck level, delivering independently at either side of the vessel, or over the stern. Master valves permit the flow and control of the oil from tank to discharge, as required.

Ventilation is provided by main vent pipes on deck for the whole length of the cargo tanks, with branch pipes leading from the tanks to the main line and thus leading to the expelling of the excess gases into the atmosphere delivery arrangements. In addition to the expelling of excess gas, ventilation may be necessary by the admission of air to the tanks, if shrinkage of volume due to cooling renders this advisable. Normal, ordinary methods of ventilation do not apply on tankers. Most oil cargoes are loaded and discharged in very much the same manner except that more stringent precautions are necessary with cargoes having low flash points. (See terms used in Oil Transportation.)

OIL AND OIL PRODUCTS

Crude oil is a highly complex mixture of compounds, the nature of which is so variable that crude oil drawn from wells even a few hundred yards apart cannot be matched with any other. The basic composition of crude oil can, however, be described and the following table indicates the elements present, together with their percentage of the total mixture.

The term valency indicates the combining power of an atom and the above table shows that the ability to combine the carbon and

Element	% present	Valency bonds	Notes
Carbon	85–90	4	
Hydrogen	10–14	1	
Trace element	trace	–	e.g. Vanadium nickel
Sulphur	2–3	–	
Nitrogen and Oxygen	< 2	–	

hydrogen atoms is one reason for the varying nature of the crude oil and the compounds in it. There are three main groups of compounds present in the crude . . . paraffins, naphthenes and aromatics and the molecular structure of these is such that the carbon atoms are in a straight, or branched chain while the naphthenes and aromatics are in a closed ring, sometimes with branches. Since these primary compounds are not suitable for direct use, the crude oil has to be refined, and in the process of refining the nature of the molecules of each compound determines the refinery processes to be employed and the subsequent treatment of each product prior to sale.

Refinery and Refinery Products

Refinery processes are complex and of a technological character as to be a study of its own, not applicable to only outlines which this section characterizes yet desirable to understand, in principle, when considering the type of vessels and routines through which the transportation of oil is effected.

Basically, there are two stages to be considered . . . distillation of crude oil to extract the primary products and conversion of these to produce the requirements of the customer.

Distillation involves the heating of crude oil in a fractionating tower . . . a tall structure divided into a series of chambers by perforated trays. The lightest and most volatile parts of the oil boil off first but eventually a mixture of vapours rise up the tower separating out and cooling on to the various trays. The distillation process extends throughout the tower, the hot vapours passing through cooler liquids redistilling that portion until each fraction of the crude oil has been separated out. These primary products separate out according to the boiling point, thus the bottom of the tower yields viscous products of bituminous nature; above this the kerosenes and gasolines are drawn off from the top trays.

Due to the relative quantities of primary compounds produced by distillation some means have to be found of breaking down heavier hydrocarbons to produce gasoline . . . a highly needed product and this is achieved, along with the production of innumerable other specialized products in the conversion process . . . known as 'cracking', which involves chemical change. It is here that the molecular structure of the primary is important in that a straight chain paraffin molecule is divided into two entirely new substances, depending on the process used.

Originally the cracking was carried out at high temperature and pressure; more recently catalytic cracking has been adopted which disperses with the need for high pressures. One of the advantages of catalysis is that it can produce gasolines which are more acceptable to modern internal combustion engines, being richer in anti-knock compounds as a result of the chemical change.

Further processes in the refinery are directed to perfecting the final product, such as de-waxing of heavy residue to provide the

TABLE 1

Refinery Products

Product	B.P. Cent	Remarks
Gas and L.P.G.	> 350	Includes methane, ethane, propane, butane. Butane is useable in domestic appliances; the others may be used as fuel for other refinery processes on account of the high calorific value.
Motor spirit	up to 200	Blended to suit the design and performance of the modern car engine.
Aviation fuel	up to 260	AVGAS for piston engine aircraft. High quality gasoline capable of giving smooth running under the widely differing power requirements of take-off and cruising at altitude. AVTUR. Kerosene for commercial airline operations.
Lamp kerosene	150–250	Known as paraffin in the U.K. Used with wick-fed lamps and primus type heating stoves.
Diesel fuels	200–350	High quality 'gas oil' for automotive purposes, i.e. high speed diesel engines. In the U.K. sometimes known as DERV. Marine diesel, usually containing some residual material; suitable for medium/low speed engines, which are not so critical of fuel quality.
Lubricating oils		After the above products have been extracted the waxy residue is further distilled to remove wax and unstable materials which would lead to the formation of deposits on gears and moving parts. The range of lubricating oils is extremely varied, reflecting the varying needs of mechanical gearing.
Fuel oils	> 325	Black oils remaining after distillation has removed the lighter fractions. Usually requires heating in storage prior to use in steam raising plant, either afloat or ashore. Must be relatively sulphur free owing to corrosive effects of sulphur compounds and also because of pollution caused by oxides of sulphur.
Bitumen	—	The 'final' residue consisting of a dark viscous material which has adhesive and waterproofing qualities. Usually in solid at ambient temperatures.

base for lubricating oils, the extraction of toluern and xylene used for such diverse substances as dyes, drugs, saccharine, explosives and the production of bitumen. There is also the problem of removal of impurities, of which sulphur is the more important. Sulphur removal is usually done in the catalytic process by conversion to hydrogen sulphide which is led off to special equipment to be re-converted into sulphur for commercial use. Table 1 gives a list of the more common refinery products.

Bulk Oil Carriers

Ship Cargo Gear and Fittings. With the exception of waxes and bitumen the refinery products are liquids at ambient temperatures and are handled by pipeline. Loading the tanker is effected by connecting the ship's cargo pipeline to the shore system and pumping from the shore. Discharging is carried out using ship's pumps, the equipment having the following features:

1. An appropriate number of loading inlets, according to the size of the vessel, known as the manifold, situated on the main deck, with each inlet capable of being blocked off and controlled by a gate valve.
2. From the manifold a number of cargo lines running directly down to the bottom of the cargo spaces, with a system of branches serving each tank, the actual layout of the cargo lines being described below. There is also the same number of lines connected to the system and leading to the ship's pumproom and, through the pumps, to the manifold. Discharge of the cargo is via these lines.
3. A smaller diameter cargo line, called the stripping line, serves all tanks and is connected via a stripping pump, usually of reciprocating type, to the manifold. The stripping line is designed to remove the last small residue of the cargo below the reach of the main centrifugal pump.
4. A ventilation pipeline, called the gas line, having a branch to each tank, and leading to a position above the deck level (as for example the top of a mast or samsom post), and capped by an equalizing valve, known as a pressure vacuum (P.V.) valve, has the primary purpose of preventing any build up or reduction of pressure in the tanks and assists also in driving off the gas/air mixture as the tanks are filled, when, in this case, the P.V. valve is by-passed.
5. If the vessel has tanks permanently attached for water ballast, a separate ballast line and pump is led to these tanks.

Pipeline Layout. It will be appreciated that every class of tanker may well have a different cargo pipeline system, the design of which being related to the operating company's particular specifications. It is not out of place, however, to consider pipelines in several well defined categories and refer to their characteristics.

(a) *Free Flow System.* For large crude carriers which are designed to operate only on one trade, the loading/discharging lines must be simple, of high capacity and capable of trimming the vessel as loading proceeds. In the free flow layout, incoming oil is fed from the loading manifold on deck down through two direct drops to the lines in the bottom of the tanks. There is a sluice gate in each bulkhead which is lifted to allow oil to flow through to every tank simultaneously as required. Discharging is

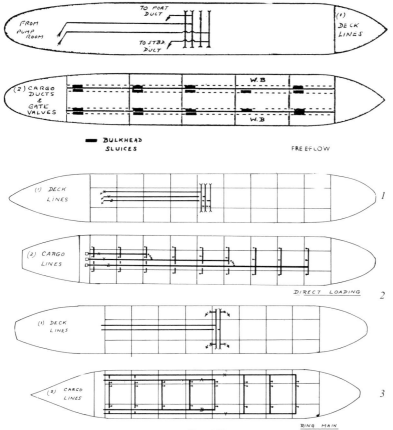

Fig. 4.22

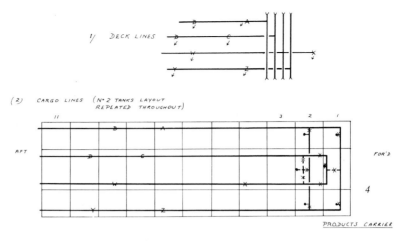

(1) DECK LINES

(2) CARGO LINES (N° 2 TANKS LAYOUT REPEATED THROUGHOUT)

AFT   FOR'D

4

PRODUCTS CARRIER

from the bottom lines, via the pumproom, up to the deck lines and to the manifold.

(b) *Direct Loading System.* Where there is a possibility that the ship will be employed in different trades, the pipelines must have isolating facility for several grades of cargo. The direct loading layout provides for three independent lines which can be linked by crossovers when one grade is carried. Each tank can be isolated so the only limitation on the number of grades is the need to prevent contamination, via the lines. It will be noted that each line serves approximately one-third of the tanks.

(c) *Ring Main System.* Here the lines run from the pumproom in a continuous ring serving one-half of the tanks, with a crossover connection to make both rings common. This form was the forerunner of the free flow in crude carriers of smaller size, but does not have the loading capacity of the former.

(d) *Products Carrier Layout.* Where tankers are designed for the carriage of oil products the primary requirement is for a line layout giving maximum segregation possibilities. One such layout is indicated in Figure 4.

It should be pointed out that it is not size which governs the line system, in that the free flow is in use on vessels of 60 000 tons, as well as on V.L.C.C.s over 200 000 tons.

The Cleaning of Tanks. The state of cleanliness of a tank will depend upon the type of oil to be loaded and the grade carried on the previous voyage. The carriage of 'clean oils' . . . benzine, naphtha, aviation spirit and lubricating oils, for example, requires high standards of cleanliness. The 'black oils' such as fuel oil, creosote and bitumen do not call for such high standards although crude oil carriers reach high levels of tank cleanliness through crude oil washing, and to which attention is drawn on page 285.

Conventional tank cleaning utilizes high velocity steam injection into a tank for at least 6–8 hours, followed by hose washing and adequate ventilation to remove gaseous vapours. Where hot water is available, and this is usually the case, the residue will loosen more quickly, and easily. Further steaming for 2–4 hours, with a final washing down will then usually suffice a clean tank.

Careful attention to ballast strums, valves and ballast pumping is essential during the whole of these operations, as is also the precautionary measures to avoid structural damage to the tanks by excessive steam pressures, usually through freeing the tank openings/ullage pipes.

The Measurement of the Cargo. Under modern arrangements it is not the practice to compute oil capacities from figures supplied by the vessel, but from measurements taken at the shore installation.

It should be noted that this method leads to greater accuracy in practice, although there is no obvious reason why this should be so. (See Terms used in Oil Transportation.)

Careful measurements by ship's officers of their tanks and the oil loaded into them, can lead to a high degree of accuracy and it therefore behoves an officer to give due attention to all the requirements associated with measurement.

Errors in computation from ship's tables are the result of inability to read instruments with sufficient accuracy and to lack of care in taking temperatures, specific gravities and ullages.

However, each ship should be in a position to check up immediately on any unusual or untoward discrepancy between shore and ship measurements.

The Taking of Ullages. The practice in shore installations is to measure the actual depth of oil in the tank by 'dipping', that is, lowering a steel tape into the tank and reading the depth of the oil.

Since ships' tanks are nearly full after loading and before discharge, it is simpler to measure the 'ullage' or space remaining between the top of the oil and the tank top.

Ullages are measured by either a 'T' square or a 'dip tape'. In the former case the 'T' square is inserted into the dip port or ullage pipe or plug, its top resting squarely on the top of the pipe or plug hole.

The 'T' square is graduated in inches and quarter inches, so that such a degree of accuracy may be achieved.

The 'dip tape' consists of a wire or linen tape, on the end of which is a 6 in brass weight, graduated in inches, reading from top to bottom whilst the tape is graduated from the zero at its junction with the weight.

The ullage having been taken, the ship's tables are consulted and the cubic feet or *water tons* ascertained.

See notes on 'Ullage Taking', page 297.

Water. At the time of taking the ullages it is necessary to determine the amount of water present in the tank. This is obtained by the use of a 'water finder', a graduated rod, some 12 in long, to which is attached water-finding litmus paper or paste.

The presence of water in the tank causes discolouration of the paper or paste, and again by the use of the ship's tables, the volume corresponding to the depth of the water can be obtained.

The difference between the total volume of liquid and the volume of water then gives the net volume of oil in the tank.

Temperatures. The correct taking of temperatures is most important in view of the fact that varying temperatures cause variations in the volume of the oil.

Special thermometers are provided by the principal oil companies and these should always be used in preference to any obtained otherwise.

It is usual to take temperatures at the same time as 'sampling' in view of the fact that sampling permits quantities of oil to be taken from all the depths of the tank. Temperatures corresponding to the various depths can be averaged to produce a mean value for the whole tank. Not less than three temperatures should be taken.

Specific Gravities. The specific gravity is determined, usually by the hydrometer, from samples taken from the ship's tanks.

It is important to bear in mind the higher degree of accuracy possible if temperatures are taken and specific gravities determined at the same time and from the same sample.

The hydrometer indication will be affected by any disturbance of the oil surface caused by the wind and also by any sudden changes of temperature.

It is better to place the sample in a hydrometer jar, then to take it to a sheltered part of the vessel and immerse the hydrometer in the liquid.

Effect of Temperature upon specific Gravity. Changes in temperature affect the volume of a liquid, causing expansion or contraction.

Increase in volume, due to a rising temperature, causes a decrease in the S.G., whilst a falling temperature, with the consequent contraction of volume, increases the S.G.

The amount by which the S.G., increases or decreases, per one degree change in temperature is known as 'the specific gravity correction coefficient'.

These coefficients vary with the type of oil and their use is necessary in view of the fact that oil is bought or sold by volume at some agreed temperature.

Any difference from the agreed temperature necessitates a correction to determine the volume of oil.

Special tables are provided by all oil companies, setting out the specific gravity correction coefficients, and they are worthy of close attention by all officers desirous of making accurate computations of oil quantities.

The data necessary for computing the weight of an oil cargo may be stated as:

(a) Volume of oil in tanks.
(b) Hydrometer readings of samples.
(c) Temperatures at the depth from which samples were taken.

Terms Used in Oil Transportation

Ullage. The space left between the tank top and the surface of the oil to allow for expansion of the cargo subsequent upon any rise of temperature.

Ullage usually amounts to about 2 per cent of the tank capacity.

Flash Point. The temperature at which a combustible liquid gives off a vapour which will fire or explode if mixed with air and exposed momentarily to a naked light.

Low Flash Oil. Oil having a flash point *below* the statutory minimum (73°F for U.K.).

Dangerous Oils. Oils having flash points *less* than 73°F.

Ordinary Oils. Oils having flash points between 73°F and 150°F.

Non-Dangerous Oils. Oils having flash points over 150°F.

Ignition Point of an oil is the lowest temperature to which it must be raised so that the vapour is evolved at that rate which permits *continuous burning* when a flame is momentarily applied. The surface of the oil is then considered to be alight, i.e. *the oil is ignited.*

Calibration of Tanks is the process of measuring tanks with a view to determining their capacity.

Viscosity is a property possessed by all fluids whereby they exhibit resistance to internal flow. When a liquid is flowing, the layers do not slide unimpeded over each other. The greater the viscosity, the more difficult the flow. Some 'solids' which exhibit slow flow at certain temperatures, e.g. pitch, are regarded as supercooled liquids.

Viscosity can be measured in terms of C.G.S., units by finding the force in dynes required to move a plane of area 1 sq cm, situated

1 cm from an identical plane, through a distance of 1 cm in one second relative to that identical plane.

Back Pressure. Cargo pipelines, both on the ship and in the shore installation are constructed to withstand a certain pressure. If this pressure is exceeded it is quite likely that the pipelines may burst.

When discharging an oil cargo by the ship's pumps, the pumps are invariably working against a pressure, the reasons for which may be stated as follows.

The oil in the ship usually has to be pumped through considerable lengths of piping to the shore tanks and then through a valve at the bottom of the tank. The ship's pumps therefore have to overcome the pressure caused by the oil already in the shore tank forcing itself on to the valve and also the frictional resistance between the oil and the inside of the pipelines.

If there are many right-angled bends in the pipelines this will increase the resistance and build up more pressure which the pumps will have to overcome.

The sum total of all these pressures are registered on a gauge in the pumproom as soon as the pump starts to work and is known as 'back pressure'.

Sampling. Samples of the oil loaded into each tank in the ship are taken before the vessel leaves the loading berth. These samples are usually taken by the shore staff to the installation.

Two or three small samples are taken from each tank and put into tins or bottles and sealed.

The samples are labelled with the name of the ship, the number of the tank from which the sample was taken, and the type and grade of oil. They are then taken to the installation laboratory for testing. When this testing has been satisfactorily completed two or three of the samples are relabelled and sealed and sent back to the ship for delivery at the discharging port.

On arrival at the port of discharge, samples are again taken from the ship's tanks and compared with the sealed samples.

Degree of Accuracy when Measuring. Upon completion of the measurement of the cargo by both the ship's officers and representatives of the shore installation, the quantity of cargo in the ships is computed independently by both parties.

THE CARE, HANDLING AND CARRIAGE OF PETROLEUM PRODUCTS

Guide Lines for Tanker Personnel

The following notes are included following discussions with and advice from Shell Tankers (U.K.) Limited, and appreciation is recorded herewith in the assistance so helpfully given. The photograph of the V.L.C.C. *Latirus* 280 000 dwt included is also with the kind permission of Shell Tankers.

The growth of petroleum carriage and the wide international involvement in this trade indicates clearly that operating procedures may differ considerably as between different companies. Even so, by reason of the nature of the product, certain basic principles and practices will show similarities, even if only with respect to the risks attached to oil cargoes, albeit, with modern construction and careful and sensible handling, these can be minimal. More widely, however, does the need for tanker operations to conform to international and national regulations, impose practices which will apply, irrespective of ship, or its country of origin.

The following notes cover guide lines to which all officers concerned with the carriage of oil should pay attention, and absorb as background knowledge. Thereafter, it is essential, when appointed to a ship, that the officer should make himself completely familiar with the rules and practices which the operating company impose, and which are invariably contained in 'operating manuals'.

General Applications

Statutory Regulations are detailed and precise.

In the U.K., for example, the Factory Act, in so far as it applies to tankers is enforceable by law. It covers, among other things, the need for adequate supervision over all tanker loading and discharging functions, and particularly so with hatches and tank openings in that risk of gas effects apply in these areas. Tanker companies themselves will have precise rules concerning the attention to be given to any form of opening to a tank. Furthermore, all gear and lifting equipment used in handling operations must conform to statutory requirements.

The Clean Air Act, in the U.K., requires that air pollution from smoke and other injurious elements must be strictly controlled, while pollution through oil contamination of water is prohibited by the Oil Pollution Acts.

Tanker officers must at all times be alert to any contravention of these statutory requirements, the neglect of which can result in heavy fines levied on the ship and owners.

Risk Aspects. Ignition is a prominent risk with tankers—probably the greatest. Rigid attention to *smoking and the use of naked lights* is of paramount importance, both in port and at sea. Most, if not all operating companies will have detailed rules on these matters, imposed by the Master, according to the specific requirements of a particular ship. Obviously it is the duty of all personnel to observe these rules but particularly is it the responsibility of officers to ensure they are being respected. Generally, 'approved places' will be designated where smoking may be permitted and these may well vary according to whether or not volatile or non-volatile cargoes are working, or having been carried, where the tanks are not, as yet, gas free.

Other risks in this area include portable electric equipment, torches, safety lamps and domestic appliances and care must be exercised to ensure that their use meets both rules and instructions supporting the utmost safety.

Ship Contacts. There is a risk, avoidable, where tanker vessels may find themselves lying alongside another. Except where special precautionary provisions are made there is a high risk (since no officer can supervise other than his own ship) and particularly so when handling volatile cargoes or the vessels not being gas free from previous loads. This is a hazard which only exceptional circumstances would ignore, and then only with strict preventative measures.

Hoses. Risk of obtuse and undefined stray electrical current can be prevalent with hose connections as between ship and berth. To avoid these possibilities earthing arrangements are adhered to and ship officers should make themselves familiar with the systems applicable to the circumstances in which their ship may be involved. Furthermore, flexible hose connections in themselves constitute dangers, if not risks, as such.

There is need for constant supervision of all connections when oil is flowing through a line in that bolts or clamps, by which the hoses are joined, must be secure against coming adrift. An interesting feature here is that with sub-marine line hoses the connections are invariably 'clamped' in order that quick release is possible, in the event of inclement weather/tidal influence.

An obvious collary to the above is instant instructions to 'stop' and 'shut off valves'.

Pumping Speeds. Care and attention to hoses and hose connections is tied up with pumping speeds, of which, in petroleum handling, there are minimum and maximum rates, the former being that to which greater attention is needed.

Oil velocity through a pipeline sets up an explosive air/vapour mixture above the liquid surface, and thus constituting possible danger to the ship, which, on loading is minimized by an initial low rate of flow (about 1 m per sec) until the depth of the cargo in the tank has reached that which is considered to be 'safe' (about 2 ft . . . 610 mm) or thereabouts, with the steel longitudinal girders covered.

Normal pumping speeds are usually agreed with shore installation officials, when it is considered to be safe to meet a required rate.

On discharging this risk is related to the shore installation/tanks and the same precautions, as for loading, must be observed.

'Velocity risk' is higher with clean volatile cargoes; crude oils do not constitute anything nearly so dangerous.

Opening and Closing Tanks. With volatile cargoes it must always be borne in mind that gaseous vapour surrounds any opening, thus encouraging an explosive risk. The same is true with tank cleaning or ballasting after such cargoes. In this connection there is need for extreme care when opening *any line* of access to a tank and, also, to be assured that all the venting systems are functioning correctly.

Ullaging and Sampling. The taking of ullages, and providing samples of the cargo, are functions of petroleum carriage which are constantly used, be it for checking on load capacity, while loading or discharging; at sea to check against any volume change or to assess the capacity before immediate discharge. Modern practice rejects the use of metal ullage tapes or rods, or metal cans for sampling with volatile clean oils, but to substitute by non-conduction materials, which will not attract static sparking from the surface of the oil. These risks are not apparent with crude oil or non-volatile petroleum and thus do not call for similar precautions as indicated above.

Weather Conditions. It is useful to bear in mind that where moving air is not apparent concentrations of gas may prevail in and around the deck and superstructure. In extreme cases it may be necessary to stop working. In the same context, the possible presence of thunderous conditions must be carefully monitored in that any lightning factors may well be conducive to hazards.

Routine Functions

Ship Care—Stresses. While it should be clear that all types of vessels are subject to structural stress through cargo load distribution, the aspect is more prominent . . . particularly longitudinal structural stress . . . with concentrated bulk liquid loads, and more so with large tankers of modern dimensions. In most operating companies this fact is highly observed by automatic recording devices and appropriate action taken where indications suggest this to be desirable.

Similarly, attention is given to *The Trim and Stability Particulars Book*, now supplied to all vessels, of all types, by the Department of Trade and Industry. Masters and officers are required to give due attention to the contents and instructions in so far as they relate to the avoidance of stress through inadvisable load distribution.

Loading and Distribution of Cargo. Petroleum carriers differ from other types of vessels in the manner of loading and distribution, by the paramount reason of avoiding any mixture of the types of oils they may be carrying, or handling on loading or discharging.

Vessels which are to carry composite cargoes draw up loading programmes and stowage plans, and liaison with shore installation personnel is necessary. Tanker officers should make themselves familiar with the systems pertaining to composite cargo segregation, in the ships to which they are appointed, be these oil, as such, or product carriers.

Doubtless the condition of the tanks must be acceptable to the types of cargoes to be loaded.

Broadly, the loading and discharging of multi-cargoes is a matter of 'valve' familiarity and 'crossovers'. It also concerns itself with 'grade distribution' it being more advisable to place, for example, kerosine adjacent to gasoline, tank for tank, rather than to a gas oil. It is unwise to load volatile oils direct through tank hatches; only non-volatile oils might be so loaded and then only if the tanks are gas free. Better to utilize the normal ship piping loading arrangements.

The Stowage Plan should indicate the valve arrangements and their settings; this will be an accepted routine procedure, the determination of which dependent upon the type of vessel and the operational customs in being.

The Loading Programme will highlight the need for sample taking, which includes S.G.s and Temps., in order to ensure that the correct grade of oil is being loaded, and ullage procedures in order to check the rate of loading.

Loading rates will vary with the size and type of vessel, with varying requirements as between crude and volatile/non-volatile white oils. Again, these must be determined by the tanker officer from operating manuals.

Finally, on completion of loading, all tanks openings must be secured and the ventilation system arranged for the type of cargo and voyage conditions expected.

Discharging the Cargo. As with loading, it is desirable to have a discharging plan, which is acceptable to, and understandable by the shore authorities.

Ullages, specific gravities and temperatures will have ascertained the quantity and condition of the cargo to be discharged.

The rate of discharge will be that acceptable to the receiving installation, albeit all the necessary safety, local and pollution requirements having been met.

After discharge, the tanks must be properly drained which doubtless will involve vessel trim, particularly if ballasting immediately, in which context it is essential that all tanker officers are familiar with the pumping systems covering cargo and ballasting handling.

TANKER FITTINGS AND EQUIPMENT

It will be appreciated that the degree of care and handling of an oil cargo will depend upon the extent to which an officer is familiar with the constructional fittings on his vessel, the manner of their operation and the reasons for their placement.

In this respect the following notes indicate generalities; the specifics will depend upon the type of ship and the accepted principles associated with its working but, in the main, differences in principle will be minimal, if at all.

No priorities are intended by the following outlines; each fitting has its own importance; all have some inter-relationship to safe handling. As in most matters, it is a case of firstly becoming aware of the probable arrangements relative to oil carriers and, later, from experience, acquiring the knowledge of application. To ignore the former destroys any effectiveness of the latter.

Valves. Valves vary according to their purpose, be they for cargo or ballast. Sea valves have special importance in that they have direct influence upon the safety of the ship and in the prevention of any oil or contaminated water passing through them, the latter a serious matter. On all occasions of working cargo, the sea valves must be closed.

Cargo valves have to be tested from time to time, to ensure they meet certain pressure requirements, the period factor depending upon the types, or types of cargo the vessel is trading in. Composite cargoes call for more frequent testing of valves than for homogeneous cargoes.

The programming of testing will be set by 'standing orders' and the attention they may need laid down by both manufacturers' instructions and the ship procedures.

Flexible Hoses and their Attachments. At all times these must be in perfect working order. As far as the ship, itself, is concerned, it is to be expected that all hose connections will be safe from electrical charge but where any shore attachments, for any reason, have to be used, these must be tested for any possible electrical continuity and earthed, before attachment to the ship manifold. Methods of earthing will be laid down in operating manuals.

Tank Hatch Sighting Openings. These should be securely locked in place after cargo has been loaded into a tank nor subsequently opened, for any reason, without supervision. It is normal for sighting ports . . . to which the openings may be referred . . . to have pressure points which automatically provide release should the pressure in the tanks exceed atmospheric pressure.

Ullage Points. These are fitted for the purpose of taking ullages and samples. Normally there are two such points for each tank, one for use on first loading and the other as the tank continues to fill and also for 'voyage ullage readings'. The taking of ullages and samples must have regard to the gas venting systems being open.

Explosive Prevention. To prevent any possibility of flash back into any openings in the cargo system there are fitted protective screens, known as 'Flash Arresters'. These must always be in good and clean condition. When taking ullages it could well be that gauze plugs are available, for fitting into the openings when fulfilling these duties.

Ventilation. It is necessary to have a means of allowing gas to be expelled from the tanks to the atmosphere. This is especially important when loading or ballasting and these are fitted at safe positions in the deck structure. They are to be found on the main gas lines from the tanks, leading to an upriser, or as a separate lead for each individual compartment.

Pressure Valves and their Operation. Different procedures apply according to whether the vessel is loading, discharging or ballasting, homogeneous or composite cargoes, or on passage with either. The systems will apply according to the type of vessel and reference to the company/ship operating manual is the only safe guide. In the trade these fittings are known as P.V. valves.

Pressure valves are fitted into the ventilating system to prevent any possibility of structural damage arising from excessive pressure or vacuum. They differ in design and manufacturers handbooks will indicate the care and attention they need; likewise, the procedures of venting will depend upon their type. Pressure valves can be completely 'open' to allow the free passage of air or gas without restriction or they can be set to meet certain pressures.

Heating Coils. These are necessary with certain black oils and are extremely important fittings demanding a high standard of maintenance and useage, particularly when a vessel may change from carrying black/white oils.

With cargoes which require heating . . . a black oil cargo . . . relevant instructions must be followed to ensure appropriate temperatures on loading and discharging, and to prevent undue evaporation. A 'required temperature' *at loading* calls for periodic checking to avoid pressure damage to the structure [usually 82°C (180°F) is quoted]. On *discharging* the temperature affects the viscosity of the liquid and if this is incorrect 'out turn' can be inappropriate.

The extent of heating must follow the instructions relevant to the type of cargo, both for loading and to be maintained during the voyage. Temperatures should be checked at least twice daily; overheating and/or rapid changes in temperature can produce dangerous gas concentrations damage to the cargo or loss of the light fractions contained in the bulk.

Crude oil cargoes need to be maintained at a constant temperature during the whole voyage, in order to prevent loss of the light fractions and also to prevent the wax component to precipitate.

Heating of viscous cargoes assists in the draining of tanks and also obviates the retention of sludge in the tanks, which would restrict efficient cleaning.

It must be emphasized that where oils require heating, instructions as to temperatures must be rigidly observed.

PRODUCT CARRIERS—SPECIAL CARGOES

Cargoes such as bitumen, chemicals and lubricating oils call for special consideration in that they contain properties subject to deterioration without particular care. Inattention will damage not only their qualities but may also cause undue stress and pressure upon the ship structure, viz chemical reaction. In general, the carriage of these products must conform to shippers' instructions, regarding heating availability, temperature control during loading and the ambient weather conditions during passage. Where cargoes of high specific gravity are concerned, notably those of chemical composition such as sulphuric acid SG 1·8 or caustic soda SG 1·2, the loading and disposition calls for capacities as will not cause excessive pressures upon the structure, whereas those cargoes of a sticky nature, with possibly high viscosity, involves particular care with heating arrangements.

Bitumen, for example, is a cargo which requires to be of the correct temperature on arrival for discharge [104°C (220°F)]. Adequate heating capacity is therefore necessary; frequent and regular temperature checking by fitted tank thermometers must be maintained during the voyage and the quantity of steam through the heating coils controlled.

Crude wax and *slack wax* tend to solidify with only marginal falls in temperature, unlike other forms of ordinary oils. This gives rise to the term 'pour point' . . . the lowest temperature at which they remain liquid. This point, rather than the actual viscosity quality, influences the heating arrangements.

Other special bulk cargoes include sulphur dioxide constituents, high pressure vapours, aviation fuel and lubricating oils.

With all of these 'special cargoes' conformity to shipping instructions and ship operating procedures is necessary.

(End of 'Shell' notes.)

Guide Lines on the Handling of Bulk Oil Cargoes

Because of the risks attendant upon the handling of bulk oil cargoes the loading and discharging operations are strictly controlled and depend upon a carefully prepared series of routines and precautions, and on close co-operation between ship and terminal.

The major oil companies and terminals have developed their own schemes and procedures . . . nevertheless a summary may be useful.

The standard official guidebook is that published jointly by The International Chamber of Shipping and The Oil Companies International Marine Forum, entitled 'International Safety Guide for Oil Tankers and Terminals'.

In general terms The Tanker International Safety Guide advises:—

1. Conformity to the International Safety Guide for Tankers and Terminals.
2. Attention to official operating manuals issued by tanker companies themselves.

The former is a detailed exposition of 21 chapters and appendices covering 'all' functions, hazards, emergencies and technical information relevant to the handling of bulk oil. The latter will be the rules of procedure by which tanker personnel will be expected to follow.

As such, 1 and 2 are closely related. It is essential that personnel are familiar with both, be it relative to the tanker or to the terminal in which she may be working.

While nothing can replace such a careful and detailed study of the publication, the following summary outlines the major features attendant upon the handling of bulk oil cargoes.

LOADING AND DISCHARGING OPERATIONS

A Summary

(A) *SHIP/SHORE TRANSFER*
The stages to be considered are:—

1. Preparation for arrival, including berthing.
2. Safety requirements and pollution prevention.
3. Liaison between ship and terminal.
4. Cargo handling procedures.
5. Emergencies.

1. (*a*) *Exchange of information*:—the following are sent from ship to shore:—Draft, trim, whether I.G. or not, tank cleaning requirements, C.O.W. or not, manifold sizes and position, whether cathodic protection or not. Repairs required (i.e. hot work).

    In return, information is returned from shore to ship:— Depth of berth, moorings required, whether mooring craft available, impact speed, pipe details, any specified requirements for positioning, etc.

    (*b*) *Ship preparations*:—All compartments closed (peak tanks etc.).

    Mooring lines adequate for berth requirements.

    Self tensioning winches not usually suitable in automatic for mooring system. Fire wires ready.

2. Safety requirements and pollution prevention.

Openings in superstructure—all closed, especially those facing or leading to tank deck. If stern loading or other special circumstances exist all openings to be shut. Doors required to be kept closed to be marked (colour code system of priorities for this). Vents covered or closed.

Air conditioning on recirculate.

Window-fixed fans to be shut off.

Pumproom—Inspection to check for leaks, missing or loose inspection plates. Test trip and low level alarms.

Tank openings—Tank lids closed, S.B. tank lids closed. P/V valves and I.G. system set for loading or discharging. Ullage ports closed except when being used.

Cargo hoses—check for condition, ensure flanges are properly bolted tight, inspect during operations.

Lighting—safe and adequate at all times.

Weather—Wind direction/force affects gas dispersal. Electrical storms—shut down and stop cargo.

Fittings—Overside discharge valves shut and lashed. Scuppers plugged. Drain off water if necessary then replace plugs. Drip trays at manifold (usually permanent fittings). Pipelines etc. not in use, to be secured closed and checked for seepage.

Miscellaneous—No unauthorized persons on deck or on board. Smoking in nominated places, if at all. No unauthorized craft alongside.

Personnel safety—precautions for enclosed places, rescue team and apparatus ready.

Galley equipment off.

3. Liaison between ship and shore terminal.

From terminal (loading)
Cargo specification(s)
Quantities and order of loading preferred
Loading rate
Number of loading arms for each grade
(Discharging)
Acceptable order of discharge
Discharging rate and maximum pressure in shore lines.

From ship (loading)
State of tanks (gas free, inerted etc.)
Maximum loading rate
Preferred order of loading and distribution
Venting arrangements
Disposal of slops
Ballast quantities and condition, whether S.B.T. or C.B.T.
(Discharging)

Cargo specifications
Distribution and quantities of cargo
Preferred order of discharge
Maximum discharging rates/pressure
Whether C.O.W. to be used
Whether I.G. in use or not
Ballasting requirements and rates.

In all cases: Agreed communications for each pumping order, especially emergency stops, etc.

4. Cargo handling procedures.
    (a) *Check list* to be completed to ensure preliminary inspection etc. has been completed.
    (b) *Agreed loading/discharging plan*, taking into account the following:—
        (i) Change over between tanks
        (ii) Avoidance of contamination between grades
        (iii) Avoidance of pollution by spillage
        (iv) Clearance of pipelines
        (v) Stress and trim during cargo transfer
        (vi) Loading/discharging rates
        (vii) Weather conditions leading to interruption of work
        (viii) Allowance for C.O.W. if carried out.
    (c) *Formal agreement* that ship and terminal are ready to work (after safety checks, etc.).
        Check that, after pumping commences, oil is only entering right tank.
        Regular checks of hose/pipeline pressure. Any drop may indicate spillage. Manifold connection is most vulnerable part for pressure surges when nearing final ullage, open next tank valve first to slow rate to the first tank. Ullage carefully to avoid gas. Stand at right angles to wind, keep head well away from emerging gas.
        Commence loading at slow rate until correct cargo flow is verified.
    (d) *Topping off*
        As each tank nears final ullage, valve to next tank is cracked open, increasing until first tank is full. Check ullages from time to time to verify that valves to full tanks have been properly closed. Observe precautions (below) when dipping tanks when full.
        Precautions
        Static accumulation in following oils—Gasoline, Kerosene, air gas, jet fuel, most other clean oils—is a hazard until surface of oil has settled and charge disperses. Therefore:—No dipping, sampling etc. with metal tape or cans for 30 mins after loading ceases.
        Non conducting dipsticks may be used.

Natural fibre ropes only on sampling cans, etc.
Check P/V valves in cold weather.

Loading/Discharging of clean oils
Generally flow rate to be less than 1 m/s in the pipe
until level of oil rises above line inlet, when splashing
and turbulence cease.
Where I.G. is used, risk of sparks exists at tank openings
unless sampling and ullaging gear is earthed to hull.
Most of these oils have a high vapour pressure, therefore:—avoid loading in still weather, low initial and
topping-off rates, avoid venting off at deck level if possible,
if oil is hot, avoid loading or ensure that venting is to
pipe well above superstructure.

Discharging
Particular attention to moorings.
When shore installation ready to receive, open suction
and gate valves and start pump, watching back pressure
in case any obstruction in shore lines.

5. Emergencies
    (*a*) *Terminal* should have comprehensive *emergency plan.*
        This will include control, communications, liaison with
        shore authorities, etc.
    (*b*) *Ship's emergency plan* should be prepared in the usual
        way.
        Particularly important:—
        Condition and availability of FFAs
        Training and drills
        Instruction of crew.
    Dealing with fires:
        Large spillage on deck—dry powder, foam then water
        fog. Cool adjacent structures
        In accommodation—water spray, close space and air
        conditioning. B/A necessary.
        Ullage ports—dry powder, foam, spray across the open-
        ing until possible to close it.
        Mast riser—inject CO_2 or steam into gas line and cut
        off (isolate) riser from rest of gas line or tank.

B. *SHIP TO SHIP TRANSFER*
Where lightening a VLCC into smaller vessel, equally stringent precautions must be taken. The operation will generally be controlled
by the smaller vessel receiving cargo.

1. General precautions as in A(1)(*b*), A(2) above. For 'liaison
   between ship and terminal' A(3) above, read 'liaison between
   masters'.

2. Additional points regarding general safety:—
Site for the transfer will generally have been selected well in advance, with assent of coastal authority.
T.T.T. message for other shipping.
Main engines ready. Bridge manned.
International Code signals hoisted.
Anchor bearings checked frequently.
Fenders (usually on barge—purpose built).
Moorings by fibre ropes.
If gas accumulates on deck, suspend operations. Careful emergency planning involving the action party.
If emergency arises:—
Alert both crews.
Stop pumping.
Emergency stations including mooring parties.
Clear hoses then disconnect.
Unmoor.

3. Cargo Handling Procedures:
Agree transfer routines and rates. One vessel in charge. Commences at low rate. Check line up to first tank is correct. Sufficient personnel on deck, at manifold and at P/R. Tank openings shut. If closed loading is not possible. Gauzes to be fitted on openings.
Ballast—only clean to be discharged. Other retained or transferred to S.T.B.L.
Check length of hoses to allow for differences in freeboard. Drain hoses to lower ship. Ensure drip trays are positioned before uncoupling hoses.

ORE/BULK/OIL CARRIERS

Loading and Discharging Oil

Ore/Bulk/Oil carriers are invariably of large dead weight tonnage, 100 000 tons not being unusual, and attract particular hazards connected with the loading and ballasting functions.

Primarily these are related to stability situations, on the one hand and oil pollution on the other, where loss of positive stability can give rise to unacceptable list or triem, and thus oil spillage.

It is essential with these types of vessels that strict adherence to the ship's stability booklet is maintained and the required procedures covering loading, ballasting and the possibility of free surface in partly filled ballast tanks are correctly followed.

Specialised vessels of this type must be handled to a planned sequence of loading or discharging operations, as laid down in the Stability Booklet and Loading Manual.

In this context, reference to the Department of Transport Merchant Shipping Notice No. 1046 is a priority requirement.

LIQUEFIED NATURAL GAS

(This section has been compiled by reference to information and guidance generously supplied by Shell Tankers (UK) Limited and The British Gas Corporation.)

Introduction

The transportation of Liquefied Natural Gas (LNG) is a complex specialized business. High capital investment conditions its commercial development, the design and construction of the (sea) vessels employed is extremely technical and severely controlled by international rules, regulations and recommendations; the equipment used intensely sophisticated, while the quantity of expertise needed in loading, carriage and discharge of the gas must be to a high standard of competence.

The handling of Liquefied Natural Gas, however, is no more difficult nor hazardous than handling a normal petroleum cargo. What is required is a full understanding of the systems and methods employed, to which end operating companies will have their own procedures by which officers are trained in familiarization techniques and, also, will provide Codes of Practice and Operating Manuals, to which staff must comply.

While methods, systems and procedures will have a degree of similarity as between different companies and carriers, the overriding requirement is that an officer, appointed to any one class of vessel, must become familiar with the local 'routine' with which he will be associated.

In the context of the above, this section, intentionally, is not concerned with technical detail but to provide general guidelines covering The Properties of LNG; Its Carriage; Its Handling and Its Care—the safety aspects.

Properties of Liquefied Natural Gas

LNG is obtained from gaseous minerals, present in crude oil fields, through a system of liquefaction. Primarily it is a mixture of hydrocarbons, the main constituent being Methane, 75–95 % by volume. Smaller concentrations of Ethane, Propane and Butane are present, together with smaller quantities of Nitrogen.

The Methane constituent is that to which prime attention must be given.

Methane has an atmospheric boiling point of $-161 \cdot 5°C$. It is this fact which predominantly governs the care and attention required in the transportation of LNG. Methane, also, has a very low specific gravity—$0 \cdot 424$. Its gas volume ratio to liquid volume is 632, which means that one cubic metre of liquid methane turns into 632 cubic metres of gas, subject to temperature and pressure conditions. This feature determines its profitability in transportation since, by cooling the gas down to a temperature of at least $-162°C$, it becomes a

colourless transparent liquid, reduced in volume to approximately
0·16 % of its original volume.

Methane also has high calorific value; it is pollution free and also
has a high auto-ignition temperature of 650°C, the highest of the
hydrocarbons, the practical significance of which is the more favourable less probability of ignition than with other hydrocarbons.

Methane is also lighter than air, though influenced by temperature,
such that any gas vented to the atmosphere will rise and dissipate.

Carriage of LNG (Ship Transportation)

Currently there are in service LNG carriers of the order of 125 000–
150 000 cu. m. capacity. 50 000 cu. m. vessels were available around
1970/71 whereas in the early 1960s purpose-built carriers were
available of 27/28 000 cu. m. capacity. Prior to the 1960s converted
freighters supported experimental work in the carriage of liquefied
natural gas. It will be appreciated, therefore, that considerable
development and progress has been made in a relatively short period
of time.

Within these ship sizes and designs, LNG is transported in tanks,
but these are of particular design and construction, and give rise to
the term 'containment', being a type of tank. These can be known
as 'free-standing prismatic', 'free-standing spherical', 'free-standing
cylindrical', 'membrane' and 'semi-membrane'. (Figure 4.24 illustrates in outline profile three types of containment.)

Whatever the type, the tanks are constructed of materials capable
of withstanding 'cryogenic', (very low) temperatures. They are also
insulated to prevent heat entering the tanks and also to prevent the
extreme cold within the tanks coming in contact with the normal
carbon steel ship construction which, if not so protected, could cause
structural metal fracture.

Materials capable of withstanding these low temperatures can be
aluminium, low carbon stainless steel or 'Invar' (a nickel iron low
expansion alloy) now more commonly used to contain the gas in the
form of a membrane to the tank facing. A modern form of tank
membrane construction is that of stainless steel. It is said to give a
higher safety measure with the hazardous Liquid Natural Gas.

Free Standing Tanks have their own internal stiffening and are
built into and keyed to the ship structure. Membrane tanks are
separated from each other by transverse cofferdams and from the
ship's outer hull by wing tanks, ballast spaces and double bottoms.

In all the tank systems there are a number of different designs,
developed by different builders, from whom they take their names,
viz. 'Conch Free Standing Prismatic', 'PDM/Gas Transport Free
Standing Cylindrical', 'Technigas Membrane Containment' and
others.

The insulation between the tank and the hull structure is also a
matter of specific constructional detail, and can be formed by

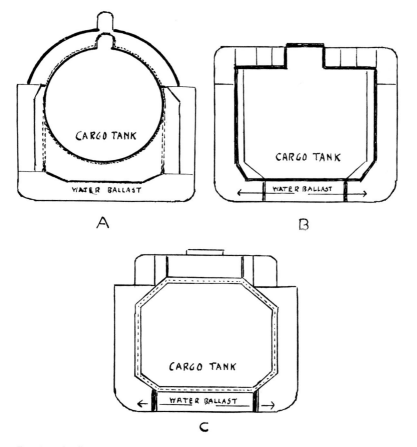

Fig. 4.24 Outline Midship Profiles of LNG Containment Systems. A—Free standing spherical, B—Free standing prismatic, C—Membrane.

plywood, balsa wood, perlite, fibrous glass and other materials. Continuing research aims to produce the more suitable and effective insulation material. (Figure 4.25 illustrates the insulation barrier in a membrane tank.)

Nitrogen is injected into a tank as an inert gas, to maintain the insulation space at a small positive pressure. This prevents air (oxygen) leaking in, so lessening the possibility of an explosive mixture forming.

During active service LNG tanks are maintained at cryogenic temperatures.

Handling LNG

The handling of Methane liquid, or gas, promotes a basic principle—
THE GAS AND AIR IS NEVER ALLOWED TO MIX. This prevents the formation of explosive mixtures.

Provided the tanks in which the substance is carried are filled with

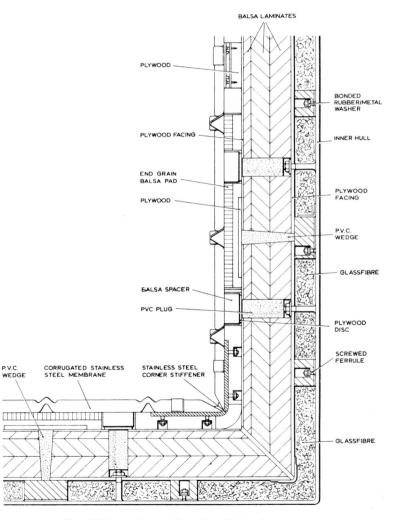

Fig. 4.25 Insulation and Secondary Barrier Construction.

100 % methane gas, or liquid and gas, there can be no oxygen present and hence no explosive. This gives rise to the term 'closed cycle system' by which the cargo tanks and the pipe lines are never open to the atmosphere.

As LNG is loaded from the shore plane, it replaces gas present in the tanks and this is pumped back to the shore by means of compressors on board. This waste gas can be burned off, well clear of the vessel, but by reason of its high economic value, it can also be subject to re-liquefaction. When discharging to the shore, gas is pumped back on board by compressors in the plant, to replace the liquid in the ship's tanks. This ensures that the tank atmosphere remains 100 % methane.

Liquefied Natural Gas is continuously boiling, at or near atmospheric pressure. It is from this fact that the term 'BOIL OFF' arises and has relevance to ventilation procedures. The vapour from any boil off must be ventilated; to neglect this would cause a build up of pressure within the tanks. Experimentation with methods of ventilation is a continuing exercise, in effort to obtain the more satisfactory method. It should also be borne in mind, however, that some ports have strict controlling rules insofar as ventilation is permitted, or, indeed for gas disposal.

'Boil Off' (or evaporation) can arise at sea. In point of fact, in service at sea there is always an amount of boil off with LNG cargoes. This cannot be avoided by reason of sea and ambient temperatures affecting the hull and seeping through the insulation barriers such that the temperature of the gas rises, to prompt boil off. Normally the amount is relatively small.

This loss of gas, for such it is, could be reliquefied and pumped back but since this is a measure requiring expensive sophisticated equipment and supervision, it is fed into the boilers, as fuel.

The greatest risk to a LNG vessel is at the time of 'cargo handling' procedures. Little risk is likely at sea since the cargo is within a sealed system. Loading and discharging embraces the use and application of all systems whereby gas passes to or from ship to shore. All the factors of gas containment, all the possibilities of faults, mechanical, electrical or human, all aspects of spillage, leakage or accident, are more prone at these times and call for particular relevant precaution.

Nitrogen is a fundamental requirement with the handling of LNG. It serves a number of important/vital issues, including:

1. Maintaining a dry atmosphere in the interbarrier insulating spaces.
2. Purging and extinguishing fires.
3. Purging gas lines to the engine room.
4. Sealing compressor glands.

Storage tanks for nitrogen are carried on board, suitably constructed and insulated. The storage must be adequate in content to need and, at all times, maintained as such. Furthermore, should any repairs be necessary to a tank, nitrogen would be used for inerting purposes.

LNG is loaded into the bottom of a tank. This reduces the creation of static charges which could build up from liquid splashing. It also lessens mechanical heat input.

Care with LNG (Safety Aspects)

The predominant safety factor with a LNG carrier is that all personnel involved are familiar with, and understand the ship, its equipment and the nature of the gas being handled. Obviously degrees of familiarity will differ, as between staffing levels, which places a particular onus on officers to ensure no lack of knowledge arises.

In this context INSTRUMENTATION IS ALL IMPORTANT.

A complete understanding of what the instrumentation systems are indicating, and why such an indication arises, permits the handling and carriage of liquefied natural gas to be free of perplexing and untoward problems, all other aspects of the containment being, of course, completely satisfactory.

It is contended that THREE MAIN HAZARDS arise with the carriage of LNG, prompting relevant safety procedures.

(*a*) The brittle fracture possibility as a result of the gas coming in contact with untreated carbon steel, not only the main structure but also to deck fittings.

(*b*) LNG contact with water, which would cause instantaneous freezing and, by reason of resulting expansion, may give rise to reactions of an explosive nature or, perhaps more indicative, a shattering of the built up frozen substance. This can be referred to as 'flameless explosion'.

(*c*) Leakage or spillage from which vapour will seep to form an explosive 'cloud', the need to prevent possibilities of ignition is therefore vital.

In the content of the foregoing attention is drawn to the CONTROL ROOM in LNG carriers. This is an essential detail in the construction of the vessel.

Within the control room the instrumentation devices are reflected, as for example, to name but a few, Gas Detection—a continuous aspect of observation; Humidity Checking—to test the soundness of the insulation and 'the important aspect of pumping "pumps" operations and control'.

Company operating manuals will indicate the extent and purpose of the control room and the degree of attention to be given to its provisions.

Fire Methane fires should not be dealt with by WATER, as such. Spray is preferable and more effective. Dry Powder Chemical

(Sodium or Potassium Bicarbonate) is the best way of dealing with LNG fires. Reference to the Company Fire Manual is essential.

Cargo Spillage This could arise from manifold loading or discharge, cargo piping joints or jettisoning of cargo. Safety systems are built in. None the less, awareness is essential.

Minor leakages can be contained in stainless steel drip trays and the drain lines closed. Loading, for obvious reasons, may promote greater leakage possibilities.

LNG spillage, which will contain methane vapour, can be potentially dangerous. Apart from the fire risk, there is the frost burns issue and in dealing with spillage adequate protective clothing must be worn.

Ship Stability Stability considerations arise with LNG carriers, no less than for any other type of vessel but in this instance there is the prominent factor of 'free surface effect' and its influence upon the reduction of metacentric height and the lessening of the righting lever. The most critical condition is while the vessel is loading/discharging and, simultaneously ballasting.

Reference to 'trim information' (for the vessel) relative to both cargo handling and sea conditions, is essential.

Free surface can give rise to the application of the term 'slosh/liquid sloshing', a feature of this being the surging or sloshing of the liquid in heavy pitching or rolling, which could give rise to structural damage.

In such circumstances, reduction of speed is desirable.

Emergency Shut Down This is a procedure related to loading operations and the systems employed are integrated with the shore loading pump. Reference to the Company Ship's Operating Manual will indicate the procedures to be adopted but sufficient to say that it is an important function, to be carried out in the minimum of time, FOR THE PROTECTION OF THE VESSEL.

Figure 4.26 (in pocket) is a fore and aft outline of a LNG carrier, showing deck zone/areas of particular hazard, within which no equipment other than that intrinsically safe is permitted.

SECTION 5

SHIP AND QUAY...SHORE FACILITIES

The Economics of Cargo Carriage
The integration between ship and quay procedures; the overall transportation mode; cargo patterns; ship types . . . ports facilities.

The conventional, container, roll on/roll off, lash, multi-purpose

Floating Crane Transferring Ore from Bulk Carrier into Barge.

General View—Bulk Shiploaders.

General View—Shiploading Plant—Ore.

Ship Loaders—Phosphate Imports; Potash Exports.

and bulk carrier vessels . . . general descriptions and applications of each type.
Container Stowage . . . modern considerations.
Container Stowage . . . modern practical stability loading computations.
Containers . . . the carriage of dangerous goods.

View of Pier Head with Fertilizer Factory in Background.

Deck Cranes with Four-Rope Grabs and Hook Tackle. Suitable for both Bulk and Unit Loads.

The Modern Seaport. Large Size Complex.

Bulk Vessels
Bulk loading and discharging systems and illustrations of installations.

Ports Cargo Handling Equipment and Facilities
Range of mechanical handling equipment available . . . fork lift trucks, straddle carriers, transporter cranes, low loaders. Unitization services.

Craneage Systems
Conventional craneage . . . jibs, portal and mobile. Heavy lift cranes, gantry cranes.

The Organization of a Port
Ports organization . . . organizational and administrative structure. Types of ports. Ship/port liaison functions. Port associations and their influence upon ship working. Ports and traffic/ship cargo handling. Berth utilization. Influence of ships on port organization.
The effect of trade patterns on port organization.

The Economics of Cargo Carriage

(See also The Management of Marine Cargo Transportation, pp. 375–388.)
All forms of current transportation show increasing cost factors and current tendencies indicate this to continue to be an inflationary process. In this context it is desirable for the ship officer to be aware

of the implications since he is now more closely integrated with other types of personnel engaged in cargo handling; in no way is he isolated.

In terms of 'ship cargo handling' time on berth is a major factor of transportation costs, albeit the introduction of unitization and mechanical handling aims to reduce the total 'cost per ton' in loading and discharging.

An analysis of the services available to the ship, however, indicates its place in the overall cost considerations. These include:

- (a) The cost of capital equipment provided and used, i.e. ships, ports facilities, distribution transportation units.
- (b) Stevedoring activities.
- (c) Labour and staff at berth.
- (d) Labour and staff in general transportation to and from berth.
- (e) General organizational and administrative costs.

Surrounding all of the foregoing is the cost of the ship time in port, the most expensive part of the total voyage cycle since a ship only earns money (freight) when it is at sea. It follows therefore that 'quick turn round' is basic to cost reduction and in terms of marine personnel supervision, this must take account of the services with which the ship is involved when on berth, and these will differ according to the class of vessel and its cargoes.

In Section 1 it has been pointed out that cargo handling, as a ship operation, is only part of the overall transportation mode . . . a link in the chain of events covering a variety of 'handling' procedures and techniques, all having different applications.

Both at loading and discharging these influences become evident and provide the practical examples of cost factors referred to in (a) to (e) above, and the extent to which the whole operation of cargo handling is interdependent upon extraneous functions of one kind and another. At loading the cargo officer has particular concern at the quality of goods he is being asked to accept; he must interpret correctly and follow judiciously any particular instructions which may accompany the cargo and he has need to give careful attention to the increasingly complex documentary procedures which now accompany the transport of goods. On discharging indications will always be evident as to the extent to which proper regard has been given to the influences at the time of loading and the care maintained during the voyage.

It follows therefore that the complex responsibilities surrounding the duties of cargo care can have meaningful assistance and be less open to suspect and unnecessary criticism if attention is drawn to the areas over and in which some of the more usually recurring cargo handling applications have their influence, but which can be, unintentionally disregarded in a busy working environment.

One such area is that concerned with the safe packing and marking of cargo, to which end an admirable and useful booklet has been made available by The National Association of Port Employers, Commonwealth House, 1–19 New Oxford Street, London WC1A 1DZ, England and, by whom, kind permission has been given to make reference to the contents. The title of this booklet is *Recommendations for Safe Packing and Marking of Cargo*; the introduction states:

'This booklet is designed to assist those concerned with the packaging and marking of goods for shipment so that they have as much information as possible on the various factors relating to packing and marking which, if not properly taken into account, may give rise to accidents during the transportation of those goods . . . accidents which can result in injury to people and damage to the goods themselves. It is not always appreciated what can happen to goods being shipped during the normal chain of transportation.'

The introduction goes on to place emphasis on the earlier paragraphs . . .

'At the port the cargo will have to be handled manually or by some form of mechanical appliance . . . it will have to be manoeuvred within easy reach of a crane . . . hoisted into the air and then lowered into the ship's hold . . . at which point further manual or mechanical handling takes place . . . and, possibly, further cargo may be stowed on top of it, or it may even be walked upon.

The lifting machinery used in the port must comply with legal requirements of safe working load . . . it is important therefore to know the weight of packages being loaded in order to avoid overloading of the lifting gear . . . at sea, water movement can also subject goods to strain . . . it is important that certain basic points are borne in mind.'

As a check list of routine procedure the N.A.P.E. booklet has high usefulness and cargo officers would be advised to obtain a copy. Although it covers all forms of cargo carriage it highlights the similarity with each by which attention needs to be given as between manual and mechanically handled cargo; damage precautionary measures; strains upon the cargo from transportation movement and vibration; packaging methods to provide security of load; slinging facilities and marking systems of self explanatory and directive usefulness. In clear and concise form the booklet confirms the fact that cargo work is now primarily seen as a co-ordinated activity between 'the ship and the quay', and by modern interpretation the term has its connotation. The design and type of ship in which goods are carried not only provides space availability and equipment but also does it influence the facilities of loading and discharging which a port may provide.

Particular notes on the handling of cargo, extracted from The National Association of Port Employer's Handbook . . . *Safe Packing and Marking of Cargo*.

Conventional General Cargo
 1. Packaging must always be strong enough to take other cargo stowed on top.

2. Apart from port marks, etc., the correct weight should be indicated on all loads.
3. Slinging points should, where applicable, by clearly evident.
4. Where possible, general cargo should be consolidated into unit loads.

Unit Cargo
1. Cargo, on pallets, should be stowed in a bonded fashion and evenly distributed.
2. Cargo should be secured both independently and on to the pallet.
3. 'Four way entry' pallets are preferable for unit loads.
4. Unit loads, other than palletized, should clearly indicate the method of lifting to be used.

Pre-Slung Loads
1. Pre-slung loads should be made up so that the load is held together as one unit.

Containers
1. Cargo stowed into a container, as for example, stuffing, must be stowed tightly and be adequately secured.
2. Where containers are part loaded adequate chocking off must be provided.
3. The weight of goods in a container must be evenly distributed over the floor with lighter cargo generally stowed on top of the heavier.

Dangerous Goods
1. Must be properly marked, conforming to appropriate regulations.
2. Handling must conform to any special precautions and/or instructions.

Attention is therefore drawn to the references in this section to 'ship types' in so far as they lend themselves to cargo handling techniques and the manner by which ports organize their operating facilities to meet these types. In this context, the following notes apply:

Conventional Cargo, by which is generally understood to mean miscellaneous loads of varying type, content and weight, intended to be handled individually, is likely to remain for quite some years, albeit any decline will be noticeable by reason of multi-purpose and bulk carriage. It is not unreasonable, however, to consider conventional cargo to develop in size, types and bulk to become more adaptable to mechanical handling.

Break bulk patterns, akin to conventional traffic, will remain attractive to developing countries where labour is more plentiful and less costly and where investment in specialized handling equipment is a long-term matter.

By reason of the above, many ports will continue to retain 'common user berths' . . . usually the prerogative of the conventional vessel. As such, cargo officers should give attention to Section 1 of this book, which deals with the basic principles of cargo handling.

The Conventional Type of Vessel, handling mixed cargoes in break bulk fashion, is highly labour intensive. Its effective time on berth calls for realistic care and attention. The bottleneck in conventional handling is the time factor of slow port turn round, coupled with high (labour) stevedoring costs. By reason of this aspect, a different attitude of supervisory approach is necessary according to the type, attitude and experience of the stevedoring labour.

The Pallet Ship is defined as one designed and constructed with some side ports and side hatches, or purpose-built with side ports and hatches served by automatic elevators and roll systems, utilizing mechanical cargo handling procedures and thus, quantatively, lessening the labour intensity. Qualitatively, however, care and attention to the manner in which the mechanical facilities are used is of extreme importance. Greater skill is required than with normal break bulk operations but tendencies to be careless are not uncommon among the labour gangs which, apart from damage considerations, can cause delay.

With palletized loads care is needed in accepting the differentiation between 'shippers packed pallets' and pallets made up at berth. The former is considered to be the more favourable method of shipment in that the pallet is made up at the shipper's premises and, if correctly secured, can well survive the rigours of international transport. Pallets made up at berth can well suffer from haste and inexperience and, in the absence of ship officer supervision, result in damage aspects in subsequent transport.

The Container System by its very nature provides for quicker turn round in that the minimum of labour intensity is required, although it is more specialized. But the capital costs of the equipment are high.

It is for this reason that the container function has so rapidly increased in size and operations and the vessels involved, in size and speeds. Comparatively less officer involvement applies with direct handling procedures since most of this is either the prerogative of the port authority itself or of the shipping, operating, company, except that where lesser numbers of containers are carried on quasi-conventional ships, these may well be handled by ships gear. See Sections 4 and 5.

There are, nonetheless, certain responsibilities incumbent upon the ship officer in ensuring effective time stowage prior to leaving the berth, notably in the areas of 'loading/discharging stability' and in the securing and lashing requirements of the container stow. See Section 2. Particularly is this the case where containers are part loaded, both below and on deck, as can be the case with vessels other than cellular container ships.

The container vessel has evolved to meet a trading pattern but a differentiation applies as between the 'carriage of containers' and the 'cellular container vessel'. Indeed, there are both 'large' and 'small' tonnages in both types, the former for world wide trades and the latter for short sea and feeder service routes. Irrespective of type however, similar ports services are necessary; the extent and size differing only in degree.

Container berths are expensive to equip and maintain but, in effect, are considered to be 5–6 times more effective than in the handling of break bulk cargo and thus, ton for ton, are less expensive . . . provided the consistency of trade volume applies.

Container vessels require the services of transporter/portainer crane, of which there are many types of this specialized lifting equipment; van or straddle carriers for the reception and distribution of the boxes and mobile tractor/trailers for feeding the cranes. Of recent years the side loader has also become prominent as a moving/loader unit for containers, as indeed has also the heavy duty mobile crane.

Container vessels also require extensive reception and marshalling areas adjacent to the berth since fast working and quick turn round is endemic to their service.

In the large container ports 'systems' of operation, as distinct from methods, apply, even to the extent of computerization. These differ as between ports and the shipping companies using the berths. Frequently, the users requirements dictate the system and officers serving on established container vessels doubtless will become involved with the procedures applicable.

The Roll on/Roll off Systems promote wide and comprehensive forms of unit carriage, from palletization in basic form to heavy vehicular traffic, including containers. Mechanization is highly developed with mobile forms of handling continually increasing in adaptability, and ship design forms provide for entry and exit of cargoes in a variety of fashions. Cost factors with the roll on/roll off systems are primarily related to 'quick turn round'. Without this the value of the system is destroyed, but with efficient integration of all the services involved, it is less costly, comparatively, per ton of cargo. Labour costs can be high, more so where loads are handled 'berth to berth', as distinct from being through-routed from consignor to consignee (door to door), and particularly so in the developed industrial countries. Supervision of operations must be carefully promoted to encourage the smooth flow of handling procedures.

Fig. 5.1 Roll on/Roll off Distribution Area

While it is of the utmost importance that all types of vessels should have cargo stowage solid and secure, the aspect takes on greater importance with the fast-moving activities of the roll on/roll off systems, and becomes more so, by degrees, as the voyage distance becomes longer (i.e. securing and lashing). The problem lies not with vehicular loads, for which constructional arrangements for securing are built into the vessel, but it could be a matter of concern with 'loose' or palletized loads fitted in to use up all available space, since the necessity for quick turn round provides a temptation to be 'careless', albeit the attention required in such cases can be time consuming and likely to cause delay.

The roll on/roll off vessel requires a terminal specially constructed and adequately supplied with road and/or rail access, together with extensive adjacent land area for marshalling purposes (see Fig. 5.1).

Link span/ramp construction permits of cargo entering either by bow and/or stern design. In some cases ramp working systems permit of side loading/discharging, an outstanding example being the M.V. *Laurentian Forest*, built in 1973, for the carriage of forest products, including paper by-products, to the U.K. and Europe and motor cars on other trades. This vessel is a dual purpose sophisticated type of roll on/roll off design with large vertical opening patent 'Autocleat' side doors and internal decking arrangements providing for paper rolls and other units of general cargo load to be transported into the vessel by fork lift trucks and then moved on to appropriate decks by hydraulic powered elevators.

On discharge of this cargo four car decks are lowered from stowed positions for the carriage of cars, which are driven off and on via ramp access to the different levels. Specially designed 'Tidebridge' ramp provisions allows of access to the vessel/quay irrespective of the tidal state. All of the equipment necessary for this type of design was provided by Cargospeed Equipment Limited of Govan, Glasgow.

Roll on/Roll off developments. Roll on/Roll off vessels now operate with either or a combination of bow, stern, quarter or slewing ramps, which increases their versatility. Related to these forms of ship construction are interesting facts concerning the ship to shore interface.

Considerable attention has been given to research and study related to the construction of shore ramps (link spans), taking into account water depths and tidal effect at point of loading/discharging, apropos the class and design of the vessel to be berthed.

Heights, slope, inclination and overall dimensions also take into account the 'types of cargoes' likely to be handled. There are some ramps (link spans) which can service double decks.

In this context the cargo officer should be aware of the suitability of the lifting and conveying units, tractor units, trailers, low loaders and fork lift trucks, to be used in handling cargo units, bearing in mind that each type has 'permissible' load factors.

Roll on/Roll off carriage is no longer a 'small ship' operation. A case in point is a 32 000 dwt vessel, equipped with heavily constructed angled loading and discharging ramps at the stern, designed for high capacity car shipments, heavy loads (500/600 tons) and T.E.U. boxes of up to 1700 plus in number. These vessels are to be seen on the European/Australian/New Zealand trades.

The developments within the ro/ro ferry field are now such that some vessels operate at L.O.A. 160 m, Breath moulded of 20·5 m and Draft moulded of 6·25 m.

These ships have four decks and are constructed to serve the carriage of trailers, cars and containers. The decks are strengthened to safely carry axle loads of 55 tons with vehicular traffic.

Loading and discharging can be either alongside to quay or to the stern, by ramp provisions.

The Multi-Purpose System is that provided by a type of vessel prominent in facilities for the carriage of mixed cargoes. The term 'multi-purpose' is one of variation. In basic form it is a general cargo carrier with holds and decks clear of obstructions, wider hatch openings and lower (if any) coamings, a combination of ship craneage and/or derricks and with side ports for direct loading and discharging by mechanical means. Size is equally variable, there being relatively small vessels operating on the short sea routes as a regular service, and those which can meet the needs of broad trading patterns on deep sea routes. Fifteen to twenty-five thousand tons deadweight is not uncommon with drafts of up to 30–35 ft (10–12 m).

The multi-purpose design presupposes, with justification, that its future position as a cargo carrier will be similarly acceptable to that previously enjoyed by the earlier (1930–40) shelter/'tween deck and lower hold conventional vessel. That design, in itself, has been subject to improvement over the years, notably in the fitting of side port doors for vehicular loading and discharging and other easier adaptable working facilities, but the multi-purpose vessel goes even further, and may be said to have overriding advantages in that it lends itself admirably to the now established and continuing development in unitized cargoes, with the resulting faster loading/discharging techniques of mechanical handling.

Cargo handling with the multi-purpose design requires, however, 'multi-purpose ports' facilities; no longer is the one isolated from the other. Wide quay space and aprons between shed and ship are necessary in order to provide for the fast movement of mechanical handling equipment; clear and 'open plan' transit sheds are desirable for the reception and distribution of a variety of types of cargoes which these vessels can work simultaneously, while specialized lifting equipment, craneage on quay and/or craneage/derricks on ship is essential. In particular cases stern and/or bow link span ramps are provided, where cargo working uses bow and/or stern entry additional to conventional procedures. In these cases vehicular traffic is progressed to the interior of the vessel via ramps and inclines to an appropriate deck. There is a distinction between this type of multi-purpose vessel and the roll on/roll off ship, albeit a subtle one.

Furthermore, the documentation of cargo movement with multi-purpose transportation is more complex.

Not all of the ports of the world can handle these vessels but the number is increasing and where this is the case, their working calls for an understanding between ship and port personnel to promote the necessary co-ordination and co-operation involved.

Four types of multi-purpose vessels are worthy of note.

The General Trader, in which classification is there an interesting example of a multi-purpose vessel designed to meet the exigencies of the increasing competitive maritime transportation market. This is the 'Staff 20' (see illustration, page 266) built by Cammell Laird Shipbuilders of Birkenhead, U.K., with whose kind permission the following brief outline notes are included.

THE 'STAFF 20'

1. Is able to handle most, if not all forms of general, unitized and bulk cargoes with easily operated cargo handling gear, over either a four or five hold arrangement.

2. It is of a size and draft as permits its trading to 90 per cent of the world's ports on a deadweight design capacity of around 20 000 tonnes, plus, at drafts of 8·6–9·9 m. Its beam is 26·75 m which ensures adequate stability when carrying containers on deck. Its overall length is 176·70 m and length B.P. 167·80 m. Speed is designed to be of the order of $18\frac{1}{2}$–$19\frac{1}{2}$ knots.

3. The cargo spaces are proportioned such that difficulties are diminished in the handling of heavy and awkward cargo sizes. Hatch openings have clear and unobstructed sides which might, otherwise, foul unloading grabs; the holds are of clear space and with pillars arranged as to permit free passage of fork lift trucks. Both general and/or bulk cargo can be carried either in or on holds or 'tween decks; containers can be stowed both under and on deck. The midship holds have an inner skin which provides for extra ballast capacity when working bulk cargo at a 'fast' terminal. The overall hold and 'tween deck spaces are clear of obstructions which would create broken stowage problems.

4. The cargo gear comprises swinging derricks cranes of normal 22 tonnes capacity but with additional 35 tonne units at midship holds where the likelihood of heavier cargo arises. These can be combined to handle 60 tonne loads, when necessary.

5. The swinging derrick cranes (Velle type) are activated by hoisting, luffing and slewing winches centrally controlled (see pages 32, 97, 98) and their design permits the fitting of container spreaders, bulk cargo grabs, timber grapples and other specialized lifting aids.

6. Power operated steel hatch covers serve both main upper and 'tween deck areas which permits quick coverage in the event of inclement weather, and these are strengthened to take the weight of container stow and, also, fork lift traffic.

7. A particular feature is twin hatches which open up to clear the total hold area and so minimizes the awkward operations of 'understow' normally prevalent in conventional design. This adds to the increase in speed of cargo working.

8. The general design is such that construction can also provide for refrigerated cargo, both by normal stowage or in refrigerated containers. Provision can also be made for liquid vegetable oil tanks. Additionally, cargo cranes, as distinct from derricks can be fitted, as also a Stuelcken heavy derrick. Where cargo cranes are fitted these are of electro-hydraulic design, with capacities of between 3–25 tonnes.

9. Cargo handling cycle times range from under 2 minutes to $7\frac{1}{2}$ minutes as between light $6\frac{1}{4}$ tonne to heavier 35 tonne

loads, respectively, on the 35 tonne derrick and between under 2 minutes to 6 minutes with load ranges of from 4–22 tonnes on the 22 tonne derrick.

Output with the heavier derrick is of the order of 280 tonnes per hour with a 35 tonne load and 106 tonnes per hour with a light load of $6\frac{1}{2}$ tonnes. The lighter, 22 tonne derrick, can handle 264 tonnes per hour.

NOTE: Cargo officers are encouraged to study the layout of 'Staff 20' in that it exemplifies the adaptability of multi-purpose cargo handling procedures likely to be the future pattern.

The Specialized Types. The Atlantic Container Line (ACL) have operated a vessel of approximately 700 ft in length on the U.K./Continental/North American routes, designed to carry up to 700, 20 and 40 ft containers in 5 cellular holds, and on deck, together with internal decks of different heights providing for the stowage of 950 cars and also trucks, lorries and other vehicular traffic. The latter type of cargo is moved into the vessel through link span ramps and this introduces a heavy and busy concentration of roll on/roll off operations.

On the short sea, intercontinental routes the 'Washbay Line' of West Germany has operated a multi-purpose vessel of 67·20 m, length, 12 m beam and 3·9 m draft, carrying normal conventional and unitized loads; containers by the lift on/lift off method and vehicular traffic through the stern by the roll on/roll off systems (see illustration, page 333).

A 6000 tonne deadweight vessel, the *Zaida*, operates on the New Zealand/Japanese trade, designed to carry over 2000 I.S.O. pallets

'Small' type Multi-Purpose Roll on/Roll off Vessel.

in the holds; over 50 standard containers on deck, handled by a 25 tonne ship crane and side ports and elevator provisions for fork lift truck working. Additionally there is provisions for refrigerated space.

Multi-purpose vessels have space and facilities to carry general break bulk, general unitized, heavy loads, refrigerated produce and containers. The very large vessels can carry a considerable container load in cellular compartments, and on deck, together with a variety of vehicular traffic on internal decks from either or both stern and bow ramp entry. The effectiveness of a multi-purpose vessel is the facility of simultaneous working from any or all of the holds or compartments, and this is possible by the combination of vessel craneage, mechanical loading systems . . . fork lift trucks and straddle carriers . . . conveyor belts and, indeed portainer cranes, dependent upon the particular design of the vessel. It is, therefore, 'fast moving', which is one of its characteristics, and calls for positive planning, operating and supervisory handling procedures, the neglect of which could cause bottlenecks, berth congestion and ineffective use of labour and machines, all of which would add up to delay.

The L.A.S.H. vessel development of barge carrying, of which the L.A.S.H. (Lighter Aboard Ship) and the SeeBEE are two types, has not shown similar impetus as has been the case with container and roll on/roll off ships, although earlier reservations as to their usefulness are lessening. They are ideally suitable to coastwise trades where waterway systems inland connect and lead to industrial areas, since they permit of a variety of cargoes being loaded into barges to be transported on the parent ship direct to and from production and manufacturing centres, which is attractive to firms and organizations wishing to move relatively small loads at any one time and not be dependent upon rigid time cycles.

A feature of these vessels is that of barge versatility, there being virtually no constraint upon the type of cargo loaded into them, and the method of handling is unique in that the lifting on and off is by constructional gantry design, replacing the conventional cranes or derricks.

This type of vessel is not entirely restricted to coastwise traffic, there being established routes from the U.S. Gulf ports to Europe, and others developing acceptable trades between the U.S. East Coast ports and the Mediterranean. The ships, and the trades are particular and require of personnel serving in them to be familiar with the constructional design and handling systems.

BULK VESSELS

Loading

Bulk cargo carriage is now of such high tonnage and encompasses a wide variety of commodities that the ports services required are highly specialized. By comparison, perhaps this is more noticeable, and more important, in bulk loading than in discharging . . . a matter accentuated by the opening up of new sources of raw materials where extensively sophisticated loading systems apply. Nonetheless, high capital investment has been devoted to discharging systems and in both loading and discharging, specially equipped berthing arrangements are necessary to the handling of the sizes of bulk carriers now operating. In the areas of ferrous and phosphate minerals, and to a lesser extent non-ferrous commodities these facilities are notably the case and are to be seen in heavy duty belt conveyor systems applying to most forms of solid bulk cargoes, although some forms of ore are transported in slurry form and give rise to piping arrangements in their handling.

By virtue of the sizes of bulk carriers and the distances over which they trade, their costs of operation call for 'quick turn round'. The highly sophisticated, usually electro-mechanical plants, together with open and deep water berths, are designed to this end. It follows therefore that ship preparation, prior to loading or discharging, requires of cargo staff appropriate attention.

The following notes indicate some of the techniques and procedures now operating at ports for both bulk and bagged cargo handling.

The notes illustrate systems handling potash, iron ore and urea and are included with the kind permission of British Ropeway Engineering Co. Ltd. (Breco) of Sevenoaks, Kent, England, members of the Glover Group, which embodies wire rope manufacturers, engineering and plastics companies. Breco design and supply bulk and bag shiploading machines, pneumatic ship-unloaders and onboard ship drag scraper self discharge systems, conveyor plants and aerial ropeway transport systems, their plants to be found in the Far East, Australasia, Asia, Middle East, Africa, Europe and the Americas.

The carriage and distribution of bulk cargoes has become a major aspect of cargo handling and has long passed out of any perfunctory approach. Considerable attention is now given to the wide variety of materials carried, to their care and to the environmental needs from dust and odour in and around the distribution terminals. Plants of the nature referred to are illustrative of facilities with which cargo officers will be involved.

A. *Potash Exports*

Tees Dock Terminal, Cleveland, England.
Annual export capability 1 million tons/year.

The installation comprises conveyors and shiploading machines. The potash, bulk density 70 lbs/cu ft, is transported from a large storage building to one of two shiploaders. Both machines are capable of loading at 1000 tons/hour, however, one machine is designed to load ships of up to 6000 dwt while the second and considerably larger machine can load up to 30 000 dwt vessels.

The two machines are equipped with vertical telescopic chutes and shuttle conveyors arranged to cope with both vessels of varying beam and local tidal variations from 3–23 ft.

The potash is a very fine powder and control of dust was important for reasons of both local amenities and avoiding the loss of a valuable product. Accordingly, comprehensive dust extraction equipment is fitted to the shiploaders and conveyor transfer points.

The complete unit is a highly sophisticated piece of electro-mechanical engineering, serving the comprehensive functions necessary to the movement of the bulk material from the shore to the ship. Operation of the loading and positioning function is controlled by one operator from an elevated visibility clear cabin such that speeds and rates can be adjusted to meet the loading patterns required by the ship.

B. *Iron Ore Exports*
   Rande, Vigo, Spain.

High quality iron ore mined in the Northern Province of Spain and shipped to the industrial ports of Europe in vessels ranging from 5000–42 000 tonnes capacity.

To meet this trading pattern a loading terminal at Vigo, operated by The Compania Minero-Siderrugica de Ponferrada SA and installed by Breco is capable of handling ore at a rate of 2000 tons per hour.

The ore from the mines is reclaimed from stockpiles adjacent to the terminal, to which it is brought in rail cars, by heavy duty belt reclaiming conveyors and passed on to a main trunk conveyor which leads to the jetty, and to the jetty conveyor.

From the jetty conveyor the ore travels to the loading transporter which delivers it into the ship's hold, at belt speeds of approximately 2–3 m per sec, by means of telescopic chute fitted with a revolving mouthpiece to assist trimming.

The loading transporter is mobile in that it is arranged to travel on tracks along the jetty foundations and all the operations are controlled from an elevated operators cabin.

Automatic arrangements provide for the measuring and recording of the amount of ore being shipped.

The loading procedures with cargoes involves attention being given to:

1. The density of the material insofar as this will affect ship capacity factors. Densities of bulk material differ greatly.
2. The moisture content in that ventilation behaviour must be to avoid deterioration, undue dampness or gaseous build up.
3. Temperature requirements during passage.
4. The angle of repose of the material insofar as this can affect

stability considerations. Forty degrees, for example, is not out of place for iron ore cargoes.

C. *Urea Export*
  Umm Said, Qatar, Arabian Gulf.
Urea prills, a fertilizer produced as a by-product in the petrochemical industry, is exported in either 50 kg bags or loose as bulk cargo.

Conveyors feed two shiploaders, each capable of loading vessels up to 40 000 dwt. One machine designed solely for loading bags, the other designed for the dual purpose of either bag or bulk loading.

The loading of bulk has been covered with illustrations of potash and iron ore, bag loading however requires a different treatment as the bags must be lowered into the hold.

This may be mechanized to a high rate by use of either a spiral chute or sandwich belt attached to the end of the shiploader boom conveyor.

Breco prefer the sandwich belt technique, which by holding the bags between spring loaded vertical belts offers a controlled rate of descent minimizing bag damage.

The operation can be controlled from both an elevated operators cabin on the shiploader structure and a man equipped with a remote control hand unit in the ship's hold.

At the foot of the sandwich belts is a short rotatable horizontal conveyor, which delivers the bags at shoulder level for men to stack in the hold and on 'tween decks in such cases. The loading capacity is therefore determined by the ability of the men placing the bags. Internationally this is found to be an average of approximately 1800–2000 bags/hour, with short peak capacity of about 2400 bags/hour.

Summary
In order to adequately cover the various sizes of ships holds and the number of hatches without resorting to warping ships the modern shiploaders at the world's ports will either be mounted on rails to facilitate tracking along the jetty, alternatively mounted on a slewing ring, or a combination of both. Similarly the boom conveyor to achieve outreach over the vessel will either telescope (shuttle) luff up and down or comprise both. For stowing behind the edge of the jetty to permit ship movements, the machines will either luff up or slew to the stowed position.

In the cases of loading loose bulk materials the machines will frequently be found equipped with a telescopic vertical chute to minimize dust emission and assist in accurate ship trimming.

Breco—Bag Handling: New Sandwich-type Conveyor
Two companies, British Ropeway Engineering Co. Ltd. of Sevenoaks, U.K., and Tempo of Woudenberg, Netherlands, have

worked together to develop a sandwich-type bag conveying ship-loader. They regard the machine as an alternative to the spiral chute for loading into a ship's hold. Breco generally specializes in the handling of bulk material, while Tempo's equipment designs specialize in the handling of bags. Because of this the companies decided their business aspects were complementary in the develop-ment of the new machine.

Unlike the simple 'free fall' principle common to nearly all bulk shiploaders the bag shiploader requires a descending system to lower the bags safely into the hold. Lowering perhaps constitutes the main part of the operation, but for efficient handling the

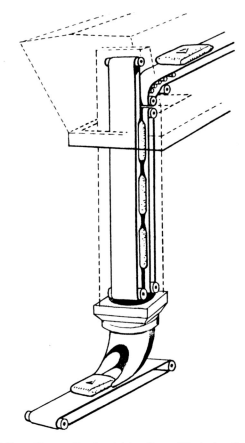

Fig. 5.2 Breco/Tempo Bag Loader has Reversible Action Potential.

descending unit must be equipped with a horizontal distributor so that the bags can be conveyed to any part of the hold.

According to the manufacturers, an excellent and well-proven method of meeting these requirements is achieved by suspending a vertical sandwich-type belt conveyor from the boom of the ship-loading gantry which discharges on to a revolving, horizontal, telescopic conveyor.

Vertical lowering by powered belts is said to guarantee positive conveying at a controlled speed independent of the bag material or climatic conditions. Bags of 25, 50 or 100 kg can be accommodated.

The manufacturers claim that owing to the absence of a long chute, sliding is virtually eliminated, making the damage to bags— and the printing on them—negligible. The sturdy nature of the open box-type structure has good damage resistance and the machine can be converted for the loading of bulk products with the installation of a descending pipe.

Conveyors and bags, it is said, are well protected from the weather as the structure can be enclosed by hinged steel doors but at the same time the dimensions of the unit are small enough to permit loading into small holds and even deep tanks.

Breco and Tempo point out that the rigidity of the box frame makes it possible to vary the discharge attachments. A turntable and short fixed conveyor, apart from the telescopic conveyor, can be used as well as a long-range telescopic conveyor of up to 12 m length complete with the facility for sloping the unit down-wards between 15 and 30 degrees. For loading bulk a thrower-belt conveyor with by-pass chute can be attached.

Sandwich Belt. The sandwich-type belt conveyor consists essentially of two ordinary belt conveyors running at exactly the same speed, both being accommodated within the box steel boom. One con-veyor has idler brackets bolted direct to the structure, the other has idlers fastened in spring-loaded levers which cause them to press parts of the belt against the 'fixed' conveyor. The squeezing action of the unit permits the bags to be lowered between the two belts. Depending on sturdiness of construction, other unit loads may also be handled.

Manufacturers state that the sandwich belt will also carry bags upwards, and that experience with a ship unloading installation has proved that this return system works equally well if the design satisfies certain basic criteria. For loading, the bags pass through a short stainless steel chute at the lower end of the unit on to a telescopic conveyor. The chute and telescopic conveyor are housed in a steel frame suspended from a slewing rim so that the whole unit can revolve horizontally through a preset angle of variable degree.

The chute is designed so that the bags are correctly transferred onto the telescopic conveyor, placed flat and straight, regardless of the conveyor's position.

The capacity of the conveyor is more than sufficient to supply an operating crew in the hold of a vessel. In practice, however, it has been proved that 1900 50 kg bags can be handled per hour over a long period, say the manufacturers, providing the hold is clear of obstacles. A peak figure of 2400 bags/hour has been achieved, but not maintained.

Breco and Tempo point out that at such high capacities the provision of an accumulating device would be pointless because of the lack of free time to clear the accumulation. Also, apart from the complications of accumulation equipment, it is much simpler to provide an immediate start/stop electric system for all conveyors.

Immediate Start/Stop. This system is different to the commonly used step-by-step starting system which requires extra time after a halt before all conveyors become operational again (it is said that time and throughput will always be lost with the step-by-step system as any conveyor will only start to run as the preceeding unit reaches full speed).

Unlike large conveyor systems where excessive power consumption prevents simultaneous starting, low-powered bag conveyors seldom require more than 100, and generally use only 50 hp. If one conveyor fails to reach its proper speed within a few seconds an automatic cut-out halts the preceding units. The two companies state that there are no uncertainties in the new system and it does not require manual assistance to resolve accumulation problems which can reduce throughput capacities in other units. They feel that their machine provides the most efficient and least expensive answer to the needs of high capacity bag handling, shiploading operations.

Aware that a spiral chute could still provide the best solution for some applications, Breco and Tempo make a study of every alternative system before making recommendations.

Discharging

A. *Seabourne*
The increasing size of bulk carriers has conditioned the need for ports authorities to consider new arrangements whereby such vessels can load and unload where water depths restrict the berthing at shore installations.

In these cases it is not unusual for the vessels to be partly unloaded outside the harbour, in deep water, until the reduced draft allows them to berth inside. A favourable, and effective method of so doing is with self-propelled floating cranes, having grabs for the transhipment of the bulk cargo. The stability features of these cranes are such that working capacities can be of the order of 100 tons at 16 m outreach; 50 tons at 28 m or 45 tons at 30 m, while the crane can heel to a maximum of $4\frac{1}{2}°$ without disturbing effects.

Apart from the floating cranes, grabs are prominent with bulk discharge and vessels are fitted with deck craneage, having four rope grabs, providing for lifts of 8–16 tons (grab plus payload). Hook tackle can be readily substituted for the grabs, making the cranes also adaptable for handling unit loads. An interesting feature of these types of cranes is the fitting of portal structures or carriageways for athwartship or fore and aft travel, on the vessel.

An illustration of a floating crane transferring ore from a bulk carrier to barge is shown on page 320 and the illustration on page 322 shows ship deck cranes, with two cranes fixed and two arranged to move athwartships. Both of these illustrations, and the information on which the above notes are based is by the kind permission of M.A.N. Maschinenfabrik-Augsberg, Nurnburg, West Germany.

B. *Shore Installations*

A modern example of installation discharge of bulk (ore) cargoes is that operating at Port Talbot, South Wales, by Associated British Ports, where bulk ore vessels of 100 000 dw tons, and over, discharge over specialized conveyor equipment direct from berth, virtually adjacent to the steel works near at hand.

The digging rate of the unloaders averages about 1800 tons per hour and a 100 000 ton carrier can be unloaded in $2\frac{1}{2}$ days.

The conveyor system consists of 11 600 ft of belting and the grabs of the unloaders feed this continuous belt. The first section, 2000 ft in length terminates in a transfer station at the landward end of the approach road to the jetty.

The third section of the conveyor belt in the main stock yards feeds a boom stacker which distributes the ore where desired. From the stock yard appropriate blends of ore are removed by another conveyor belt to the crushing plant and the sinter plant where they are prepared for the blast furnace.

By modern comparisons, the grab is now in 'competition' with continuous bucket unloaders . . . highly sophisticated electro-mechanical semi-gantry units which, by reason of arm extensions, can 'dig' into the ship bulk in the holds and elevator transport the bulk either to stock piles or to shore carriage transportation. The system is applicable to ore and coal commodities.

Within the range of bulk carriers, some of which are, conventionally, of the order of 100 000 dwt and of L 250 m and draft 15 m, with a beam of 40 m, a shallower draft design is emerging for the Japanese Coal Trades. (See page 171).

The type is directed to greater use in otherwise lesser depths of ports water availability, which could have restrictive features for deeper load draft vessels, as distinct from the normal 60 000 ton bulk coal carrier.

Tonnage availability is also a consideration, by reason of their beam which also adds to stability advantages.

Structurally these vessels have 'split sterns' which, with twin controllable pitch screws, and two rudders, provides excellent manoeuvrability.

Profitably, not only is this reflected in anticipated running costs but also relatively larger cargo loads.

SEA GOING DREDGERS
Sand and Gravel

Sand and gravel is a cargo which has increased in capacity by reason of the increasing demand for sea dredged sand for civil construction work, in consequence of which there has been a development of suitably constructed vessels of appropriate dredging and discharging design, ranging from some of the earlier 1100 tons capacity to the modern dredger of 3500–4250 tons capacity, with discharging rates increasing from 200–250 tons per hour to 1000–1500 tons per hour. The need of the industry is fast discharging rates.

Even so, the trend is for larger vessels with discharge rates as high as 200 tons, or more, the intention being that the dredgers, which work in the gravel beds around the U.K. coasts can unload, and be away, on one tide.

Within this form of ship construction 'Breco' . . . British Ropeway Engineering Co. Ltd., of Sevenoaks, Kent (part of the Glover Group) has been prominent in designing and installing sophisticated drag scraper and discharging plant . . . known as The Drag Scraper System . . . and by whose kind permission these brief explanatory notes are included. (See also Breco plant for Bulk Cargo Working, pages 337, 338.)

Two such examples are as follows:

1. M.V. *Bowherald*. Overall length 99 m, beam 18 m, capacity 3500 tons of dredged aggregates, the cargo being loaded at the rate of 1750 tons per hour and discharged within $2\frac{1}{2}$ hours.

The cargo is loaded by either trail or deep sea stationary dredging, with an electrically driven sand and gravel pump extracting material at a depth of 75 ft, although when deep dredging the vessel can, with jet pump assistance, achieve a maximum operating depth of 150 ft.

Screening equipment distributes the aggregate into the hold by means of rotary and luffing chutes and the reject water and fine sand is collected by flumes beneath the screens and deposited, via chutes, over the ship side.

The discharge equipment is of twin 12 cu yd scraping buckets operating side by side to discharge material weighing 18–22 cu ft per ton into a transverse hopper situated at the after end of the hold,

M.V. *Bowherald* Showing Housed Overside Conveyors and Main Hold.

from which correct feed passes on to a belt feed conveyor, running athwartships. The cross feeder conveyor discharges either to 'port' or 'starboard' on to either of two overside boom conveyors, the feed being controlled by adjustable gates at each end of the discharging hopper.

Both of the overside conveyors are able to slew through 180° and can give an overside coverage of 104°. The whole installation is controlled from a console mounted on the ship bridge, including starting and stopping, and luffing and slewing of the overside conveyors.

2. M.V. *Cambrae*. This is a self discharging gravel dredger, discharging at both ends simultaneously, handling materials of screened sand and/or gravel at, generally, minus 3 in, of weight 90–130 lbs per cu ft and density of 25–17 cu ft per ton. The nominal discharge rate is 1950–2800 tons per hour.

Two 7·5 cu yd scrapers are used at each end of the ship, scraping, material from the hold up fore and aft ramps to the discharge hoppers above the feed belt conveyor, which extracts the material through a variable flow gate, set to give the correct feed for the on shore conveyor system.

With this system each end of the ship can discharge sand and gravel at over 1000 tons per hour, covering a cargo of 4250 tons in 2 hours.

For the majority of the time the vessel is discharging, the controls

M.V. *Cambrae* with Starboard Side Boom Conveyor Extended.

are set so that each bucket is interlocked to give the minimum of manual control; the buckets move backward and forward to predetermined positions in the hold. At the end of discharge only one end of the ship is used for removing the last of the cargo; one pair of buckets . . . either forward or aft . . . are parked on the hopper while the pair of buckets at the other end of the ship are used to long scrape the whole length of the hold for cleaning out purposes. This facility can be used to discharge the whole cargo at one end of the ship, like a conventional two scraper discharge system, if there is a breakdown in the opposite end system.

The cleaning out operation requires the buckets to be moved across the hold to get behind the ridges and mounds of materials on the hold bottom.

Two operating stations control the discharge; one on the bridge to control the aft buckets and conveyors and the other at the forward end to give local control to the forward equipment.

Both the feeder conveyors below the hoppers are of the flat belt type, travelling at 120 ft per minute, either to port or starboard, depending on the requirement of the land installation. The conveyor can be elevated to discharge at 25° above horizontal, or lowered below horizontal for the discharge into barges or low installations.

During discharge, the luffing and slewing of each boom conveyor can be controlled by the operator at the operating console, enabling him to position the boom conveyor correctly as the ship is discharged.

UNITIZATION SERVICES

Summary

The economics of cargo handling are closely related to the procedures adopted by the ports to meet trading patterns and ship types. Indeed, these necessary arrangements condition the loading and discharging functions no less than the design of the ship, and its cargo-handling facilities, and influences the layout of the ports and berths.

'Systems', rather than specific and individual cargo-handling methods, are now the more prominent in determining the probable ship-time in port, and a study of the principles involved is useful to any cargo officer. Notably is this desirable with the roll on/roll off and the container services, if for no other reasons than the following:

1. Roll on/roll off services can substantially increase the volume of traffic moving over a berth in a given period of time, but considerable backing/stacking space and clear accessibility to and from the berth is essential. To this end the planning of operations is highly important, in which context any relevant or particular stowage information which can be provided by the ship officer to the port authorities is desirable.
2. The container trades patterns are subject to intense economic pressures and are highly competitive. Container handling is very much a procedure of 'systems', be it in the planning for trade involvement or in the activities at loading and/or discharging. Its purpose of promoting a safe and speedy through transport mode embraces a number of associated functions to which the various methods of loading and discharging, and in distribution, have relevance.
3. Mobile mechanical-handling equipment is now a major factor in cargo-handling methods, and it will grow. As with ships, it only earns money when it has a load in motion, and working. As the size of the equipment increases this aspect of economic use takes on a greater importance.

1. *Short Sea Routes*

Certain particular features of unitization have relevance to the shorter sea routes. Notably is this so on the North Sea/English Channel and North European ports, and calls for special regard from ship personnel. The trades are highly competitive, and the vessels engaged in them will only remain if the user is satisfied with the services he expects.

The services referred to include:

(*a*) Roll on/roll off vessels of small, moderate and large size, with facilities for all forms of palletization, containers on wheeled transport and vehicular traffic, domestic and industrial, as such.

(b) Multi-purpose vessels of moderate size carrying break bulk, together with heavy lifts, palletized and container loads.

(c) Train ferries, with facilities for full train loads.

Considerable development in both tonnage and capacity is envisaged to be the future pattern, with all three of the services indicated, and providing greatly improved facilities for wide ranges of goods in unitized form. Where these short sea routes can be completely integrated with the distribution transportation mode, then they are likely to be highly profitable and economic.

In terms of container movement by these services, opinion differs as to which is preferable . . . lift on/lift off or roll on/roll off systems. The latter is faster, but since the containers are moved on wheeled transport, a problem is apparent with effective space utilization arising from the vehicle and/or wheeled carrier design. This presents problems of blocking and securing where other sizeable goods or packages, or indeed other vehicles are stowed in the same space area.

The lift on/lift off system provides for more effective utilization of space, but imposes problems of secure stowage and ship stability, the latter particularly so if working with ship-lifting gear and endeavouring to meet a tight sailing schedule.

NOTE: In both of the above illustrations, see the Section on Securing and Lashing.

The carriage of containers on short sea routes is promoting the design and construction of what are known as 'Deckships'. These are vessels of about 4000 tons dw, the term indicating the carriage of all containers on deck, as distinct from underdeck, with the loading and discharging carried out by a shipboard 30-ton container crane. These vessels serve a useful purpose on inter-island trades where applicable handling facilities are not available on shore. They also have very practical application as feeder ships to the larger-size container vessels.

On balance, trade statistics point to an increasing impetus of container traffic by the roll on/roll off services, and it would seem that by virtue of numbers alone, this must be the methods most applicable to the Northern European trades.

2. Container Traffic

The development of container traffic has been accompanied with consideration for the type of material used in the construction of the 'boxes'. Since this has a bearing upon the 'safe keeping' of the contents stowed in the container, it is necessary for the ship officer to be aware of any relevant matters consequent upon the constructional material

In terms of overall construction, the yardstick of opinion is based on the premise of 'suitability to the product carried and the purpose for which used'.

Within this wide specification there are the conventionally constructed and tested containers of carbon steel, those with steel frames and corner castings but aluminium external side sheeting interlined with plyboard and floors of laminated hardboard. Such types of containers have been in use with highly respected successful container operators since the advent of the trades, and maintaining a record of dependability and reliability. A development on from the 'conventional' build, however, is the use of stainless steel, and this is quickly gaining favour. Though costly, stainless steel is used in the construction of reefer boxes.

All containers must meet I.S.O. and Classification Societies' design and constructional requirements.

It is interesting to note the experiments being made with plywood construction; indeed such types are, in fact, in use, particularly in the proverbial 'fruit areas' of South Africa, the Antipodes and in the West Indian trades, where refrigerated and insulated traffic is increasingly adapted to plywood containers.

Such containers are made of veneer ply sheets coated with a form of strengthening, such as glass-fibre plastic. The frames and supports are, understandably, of steel. The construction claims robustness of form with a minimum tendency to distort; easy to clean and with no retention of smell or odour. Compared with steel, it is said that there is less condensation with plywood containers, resulting in possible less damage in transit. The plywood material also offers higher insulation properties than steel, since the thermal conductivity is low. This is an important issue in as much as a major problem with container useage is the ability, or inability to control climatic condition repercussions within it due to the lack of ventilation facilities. With tinned, canned or mixed cargoes this can raise problems.

Fire risk within the container is claimed to be considerably less in plywood boxes than in those of different construction. The lower thermal conductivity factor; the minimal distortion quality both, it is claimed, improve airtightness to the extent of preventing oxygen content, so that any fire which may arise is more likely to disperse, or be more safely contained, thus allowing action to be taken in preventing damage to contents by the normal extinguishing systems available, or to adjacent boxes through heat conduction.

3. *Size and Stowage of Containers*

The loading of containers is related to the depth of the ship's hull. Earlier construction centred around the 20 ft × 8 ft containers, stacked up to 6 ft high. Modern constructional features, both to the boxes and to the ship, have introduced new dimensional factors, weight loaded being one and the introduction of 40 ft × 8½ ft, length and height measurements for containers.

Stacking heights are influenced by I.S.O. recommendations ... the boxes must be strong enough to withstand stacking heights, such that there are now variations between 6 and 9 ft. Modern container ships are designed around a $8\frac{1}{2}$ ft module, which permits a mix of 8 ft and $9\frac{1}{2}$ ft containers to be stowed as well.

But it is essential for ship's officers to be familiar with the recommendations.

Stowing box shaped containers in a ship hold does result in losing cargo space in the curvature parts of the holds. Much of this volume can be regained by stowing on deck such that containers can be supported on the modern designed hatch covers of 2, 3 or 4 tiers, depending upon the stability of the vessel.

In general terms considerations of container stowage are related to:—

1. Effective overall centre of gravity (KG) in acceptable ship stability.
2. Loaded within permissible limits.
3. Containers not overstowed as would present difficulties for different ports.
4. Correct separation of special containers carrying, for example, refrigerated or hazardous cargoes.

Pre-planning is necessary with all forms of 'general' and unitized cargoes. It is even more important for container stowage especially in ensuring that the heavier boxes are at the bottom of a stack.

It is also important not to lose sight of the stresses upon a ship arising from the dynamic forces to which it can be subjected through rolling and/or pitching. These forces become transferred to the whole of the container stow. They call for the accurate positioning of a container, corner to corner, and to accurate securing and lashing procedures. Not only is this important with deck stowage but also to avoid or reduce to a minimum any structural stress upon the frames which form the cell guides. (See pages 19, 20, Vibratory Stress).

A Modern Approach

In the context of the foregoing the notes which follow have been put together following useful discussions with The Atlantic Container Line, to whom we are indebted for their interest and assistance.

In this modern age the handling of container consignments has become highly sophisticated and technological. Particularly is this the case with large associated shipping groups where, in the course of a 'voyage' the ships involved may be loading/discharging at a number of ports before completion of the total load and where the vessels, also, are constructed to carry not only containers lo/lo but also in ro/ro compartments.

In view of this the formation of Cargo Plans is important.

Since the trades involved demand 'quick turn round' at each of a number of ports time does not allow nor permit this to be done by ship personnel, as was customary with normal conventional cargoes.

A procedure has developed therefore with large prominent shipping groups, where central services departments have been set up, to which relevant loading detail and particulars can be transmitted by specialized communication systems, from which 'master' cargo plans can be drawn up, setting out the cargo distributions, weights and stability conditions, related to first and subsequent loading ports, from which, in the final analysis the acceptable safe load condition of the vessel can be determined.

All of this information is then programmed and computerized to provide 'print outs' necessary and useful to the Master of the vessel and to terminals at which the vessel will be discharging. It is a highly complex system, in the hands of specialized professional capable operators such that whereas ship's officers will be aware of the ramifications, and confident of the outcome, they will not be physically a part of it, albeit the Master of the vessel, by virtue of his position in law can question any part of the system if indeed he has any apprehensions, or where any changes in stow arise, seldom does he do so. All such information, if this is necessary, can quickly be transmitted to him by expensive satellite procedures.

It is also interesting to be aware that containers now are not exclusively used for unitized or block cargo of the normally understood nature. Considerable quantities of hazardous commodities are now carried in containers, calling for special and particular precautionary measures.

These are contained in the I.M.O. (International Maritime Organization) 'Emergency Procedures for Ships Carrying Dangerous Cargoes' which is a detailed publication setting out the wide variety of hazardous dangerous goods, by name, content, effect and allowable stowage, above and below deck, with colour markings denoting the degrees of danger and the precautionary measures to be taken.

A copy of this publication (which could be said to be the 'Ship's Bible') is in every ship. As a further precaution, however, its contents are duplicated by the shipping organization, regularly updated such that it can reject any shipment with which it is dissatisfied, as indeed can the Master, also.

With regard to the *stability* of such vessels . . . an outstanding aspect of these container vessels with their loads both totally heavy and widely distributed both below and above deck, detailed programming and computerization is carried out by the central department earlier referred to.

This is based upon the B.S.R.A. (British Ship Research Association) and Classification Rules, which set standards and limits as to how a ship can be 'used' . . . i.e. weight loads and their distribution, draft limits, structural stress moments, heeling and trimming moments, etc. all of which is part of a prepared disc by the B.S.R.A.

From this disc, programmed into a computer, with information from the 'master plan' detail is available on all the necessary features of stability requirement including limits allowable for KGs, GMs, righting moments, bending moments, free surface moments, tonnage distributions, both cargo and ballast and oil, and at each station or section of the vessel.

The print out thus available indicates, apart from the final GM (Metacentric Height) all other information necessary to the Master in safely maintaining his ship during the voyage.

By way of example, on which these notes are based, for a vessel of 32 000 tonnes displacement and deadweight of 18 000 tonnes, the final GM was 0.79 m . . . a comfortable ship. (Note:—Relative to the foregoing notes, see also page 256).

It will be appreciated that not all groups of shipping organizations may maintain similar procedures but since stability with container loading is outstandingly important the guide lines indicated are worthy of note.

A further aspect of container loading is the lashings necessary to deck stowage. Forms and types of lashing facilities are built into the ship structure, but they must be continually maintained and/or renewed where necessary. Lashings are vital attributes.

4. 'Tank' Containers

Tank container transportation is a developing form of cargo carriage and handling and has the advantages of easier handling, completely adaptable to integrated transport systems, more effective useage of volume loading and adaptable to 'return loads' apart from being, in the long-term, less expensive than using drums.

In the carriage of dangerous chemicals, of corrosive, inflammable and toxic agencies, the danger risk is brought within minimal limits, as distinct from situations arising from leakage in standard cylindrical drums.

The tank container, usually of stainless steel and of size and capacity 8 ft × 8 ft × 10 ft, 4000 litres, and suitably framed is an acceptable form of carriage bringing handling, always a source of danger and risk, to minimum requirements.

Regulations covering the transportation of 'chemicals' in tank containers suffer some variance throughout the world but, in general I.S.O. and T.I.R. approval is a necessary requisite. Throughout Europe in particular, stringent regulations serve to satisfy all the participants in the transport mode . . . rail, road, and sea. In the U.S.A. and in Australia similar rigid requirements apply.

Apart from their use for dangerous chemicals and gases, oil and petroleum products, vegetable oils, wines, spirits and beers, bulk powders (cement, charcoal, etc.), granular products and edible fruit juices are some of the many commodities being routed by tank-containers.

In the sense of unitization, the tank container is no different from the ordinary 'box', and can be lifted or transported in similar fashion. The overriding issue with the dangerous chemicals is safe handling and adherence to regulations.

Palletization . . . Cost Factors

A dominating factor of cost reduction in cargo handling is that contained in palletization, of which there are many forms. Primarily it is concerned with the making up of a load into a unit and placing it upon a pallet, with the converse of breaking down, on discharge. (See Pallet Ships.)

Palletization lends itself to a wide variety of homogeneous cargoes which hitherto were shipped loose or in bags, but are now unit-packed for carriage, and can include covered bulk loads (bags, drums, etc.), boxes, cartons, crates . . . indeed most commodities which will pack into a self-contained unit. Palletization, and pre-slinging which, as the term implies, is the arranging of the load with its sling attachments some time prior to it being required, reduces at all stages the labour-intensive factor in cargo handling. Additionally, it assists in rates of tonnage handled per hour . . . an important cost factor. Pre-slinging of palletized cargo can promote handling rates as high as 700–800 tons per hour.

PORTS CARGO HANDLING EQUIPMENT

Mechanical Appliances

The range of mechanical handling equipment available in port operations is wide and comprehensive, leading, as it does, to speedier distributive transportation . . . which assists 'quick turn round'; less manual handling, thus lessening the possibilities of damage; more effective solidarity of stow; quantitatively labour saving though qualitatively improving this and assisting in the promotion of integrated useage as between the ship, sheds and quays as well as with the various supporting transport services.

Primarily, by reason of the unitization of cargoes, the development of fork lift trucks, as a feature of mechanical handling, has, of recent years, been remarkably progressive. There is little, or near nothing in cargo handling, other than specific bulks, which cannot have application through some means of appropriately designed mechanically operated handling equipment, in which the fork lift truck has prominence, be this for warehouse, dock face or shipboard procedures.

In the latter context application has relevance to the palletization of loads, to specific units capable of being lifted, to bales and cases and also to specialized loads such as can be found in the forest products trades, i.e. newsprint reels . . . see page 114. Indeed the range of usage is extremely wide.

Roll on/Roll off procedures are high in the list as is con-

tainerization in all its facets, including container stuffing and stripping
while the use of 'trucks' finds broad application within ship spaces
for loading, discharging and distribution.

It would be invidious, with the proliferation of equipment
available throughout the world to differentiate over the qualities
and applications of this wide area of types and/or facilities.
Sufficient to say that each has its own virtues and all are, or has
been, subject to research and design by the numerous manufacturers
in the market such that they serve a purpose for which they are best
suited.

Generalizing, ports equipment includes gantry/transporter/por-
tainer cranes for container lifting/loading/discharging; straddle
carriers for container transportation on berth; tractors and
trailers/semi-trailers for back up transportation and movement
within a terminal area; stacker cranes and side loaders to assist in
cargo handling; low loaders for heavy indivisible loads and other
bulk heavy units, and fork lift trucks (F.L.T.s) for general purpose
work, of which there are various designs with numerous applications applicable to different forms of loads; indeed, doubtless the
introduction of the F.L.T. has possibly made the greatest impression. Towering over all of this area of equipment is the jib and jib
luffing cranes.

Not all of the 'pieces of equipment' are likely to involve the
practical attention of ship cargo officers, nor will some be evident
in all ports, albeit they should provide a source of interest which
can usefully be widened by reference to informative brochures
produced by the manufacturers.

By way of example, the following notes cover some of the
appliances more likely to assist the cargo officer in his planning
and supervisory duties. These are included with the kind permission
of the manufacturers referred to.

Lansing Bagnall Ltd. of Basingstoke, Hampshire, England, from
whom kind permission has been given to make reference to its wide
range, manufacture numerous related fork lift truck applications.

Of those having particular relevance to maritime cargo handling,
the small number illustrated are pertinent.

(a) Fork lift truck for inboard ship use.
(b) Fork lift truck for container handling.
(c) Fork lift truck for container loading.
(d) Fork lift truck for container stuffing/stripping.
(e) Fork lift truck for roll on/roll off operations.

Also The Rubery Own Conveyancer, Limited of Warrington,
England, a subsidiary of the Rubery Owen Holdings Limited,
cover a wide range of mechanical handling equipment which
includes:

Fork Lift Trucks
Within this range the following warrant attention. E2C and E22C

four-wheel types having capacities of 907 kg (2000 lbs) and 1016 kg (2240 lbs) respectively.

These are battery electric power units with lift heights of up to 3302 mm by fork dimensions of 914 mm in length and tilting availabilities of between $2\frac{1}{2}$–10°.

The performance speeds of travel are 8.1/8.85 Km/h and they can turn on an inner and outer radii of 127 and 1600 mm respectively.

The Stability provisions conform to I.S.O. standards.

The mast arrangements permit appropriate attachments for the handling of different kinds of loads. As such they are highly versitile working in and out of sheds, on the quay and in the decks of vessels, via roll on/roll off provisions.

E3C and E25C range has similar characteristics though with higher capacities of 1306 (3000 lbs) and 1136 Kg (2500 lbs) respectively.

A particular feature of the E3C truck is its compactness providing easy operating where space and headroom is restricted, as would be the case with the loading (stuffing) of containers, apart from other adaptabilities.

In such cases a low silhouette lift truck is necessary, having the ability to enter a container with a load, side shift it to make full use of the space available and to be manoeuverable over a small turning circle.

Rubery Owen Conveyancer Limited also manufacture a fork lift truck which can be easily and quickly main parts assembled in the 'tween decks where lifting facilities on the quay would be inadequate on hoisting from the quayside to on oard the ship. Available also is a lift truck, known as the 'Conve ancer Defiant' which with a capacity of 10 tonnes and a 106 b.h.p diesel engine, can be used for the movement of empty containers.

> Note: F.L.T.s can be of Petrol, Diesel, L. P. Gas or Electric/ Battery power. Certain precautions pertain with petrol and diesel units, particularly in confined spaces and where there is any fire risk.

The effectiveness of fork lift trucks, whatever their type, size or purpose, depend entirely upon the competence of the handler (driver) and the overriding supervision of the collective operations.

In this latter aspect . . . collective operations . . . the ship cargo officer(s) will have specific responsibilities, albeit it is to be expected that the handler (driver) of a F.L.T. is fully aware of the essential needs on the safe handling of this type of equipment.

Stability of the truck is of vital importance where loads are moved in vertical upward and downward directions. When stationary the build in stability should take care of this factor, but travel speeds to and from the cargo positioning calls for especial care and must be given prudent attention.

While manufacturers write into the specifications of F.L.T.s all the aspects of their manoeuvrability, none the less it is wise to remember that a F.L.T. is prone to stability problems, should it become unbalanced, and, as a result, likely to overturn.

This is a vital 'safety aspect' in the use of fork lift trucks.

With the 'smaller' types of F.L.T.s, used for inboard ship work, where speed of operations is often dictated by sailing schedules, an *unladen* travel speed of 7·5 mph/12·1 km/h and a *laden* travel speed of 6·5 mph/10·5 km/h, is recommended.

It should also be remembered that a F.L.T. is steered through its rear wheels . . . the fore wheels must be fixed to allow for steady horizontal positioning of the truck masts/arms/clamps, viz./viz. the load it is handling.

As such, provision must always be made for sufficient clearance at the rear of the F.L.T. in order not to impede its swinging clearance.

In order to determine comprehensive information on fork lift trucks, there is no better way than to obtain from manufacturers copies of their illustrated specifications. The types and applications of the mechanical handling units vary greatly with the kind of work they are designed to do. It would be foolish to assume capabilities and applications.

However, certain aspects of F.L.T.s (and the terms used in relation to their construction) find reasonable comparability. For the purpose of a Cargo Officer's involvement the following could be useful.

Tonnage capacities can be of the order of $1\frac{1}{2}$, 3, 25 and 28 tons be the machines for inboard ship use, dock face activity or for, the handling of containers.

The steering of a F.L.T. can be by Hydrostatic Power Systems, to the rear wheels

The driving power is to the front wheels . . . i.e. drive axles, with hydraulically air operated cam brakes or by electric braking.

The leverage functions incorporated into a F.L.T. can be by hydraulic control to the components.

Lifting power can be by Lift Rams or Lift Chains.

Tilting power (to the masts) can be by jacking and of the order of 2, 5 and 10°, forward and backward. (Tilting will be necessary if working on inclined surfaces in order to place the load in a horizontal plane.)

Overlift is the stacking above and behind an existing load (this can allow two rows of pallets to be stacked from a single aisle).

An important function in servicing ships containing palletized cargoes is the ability to extract the goods from comparatively inaccessible parts of the ship . . . notably 'tween decks where headroom is limited. For this kind of work F.L.T.s of from $1\frac{1}{2}$ to 3 ton capacities are suitable.

With container work the time factor is important in the loading and discharging of goods into and out of a container (stuffing and stripping).

F.L.T.s to be used have relatively low mast units (77″ with a full-free lift of $49\frac{1}{2}''$). This allows the truck to enter the container and double stack or remove pallet loads without difficulty.

Some of these F.L.T.s are fitted with a side shifting unit . . . horizontal movement, either side of the centre line of the masts. This enables palletized loads to be tightly stacked without undue manoeuvring. (It should be remembered that Cargo Officers have responsibility to ensure that a container being 'stuffed' is receiving the same care and attention as is given to normal loading procedures.)

In all forms of fork lift truck working it is necessary to be aware of the *Braking Power* available to the units. Braking can be by Foot Brake, hydraulically operated and by a handbrake independent of the foot brake. The controls will be in the 'cab'.

Maintenance

With ships which carry fork lift trucks as part of their own cargo handling equipment . . . and this is evident in a number of trades . . . it is desirable that Cargo Officers are familiar with the requirements of maintenance to these units, should the occasion arise, albeit the work involved would, understandably, be with the engineering personnel of the vessel. None the less it is desirable that the fork lift trucks should always be in usable working order.

In this context access to the working parts of a F.L.T. are usually easy, through hinged covers.

Points of maintenance should include attention to:—

(a) the engine unit.
(b) the transmission hydraulics.
(c) the battery . . . where electric power is the operative force.
(d) the main electric panel.
(e) the airbrake tanks and circuits.
(f) the air cleaners.

The Straddle Carrier

It is a well known, proven fact that the safest way of handling a laden container is by its corner castings, a four point pick up. Of all the machinery to pick up containers, one that will straddle the container (i.e. pick it up within its own confines) the straddle carrier is the most efficient.

Such a machine is the Karricon.

Available as either the 3042 and the 3043, these ISO container handling straddle carriers have the ability to stack up to 40 ft long containers either 2 high or 3 high respectively.

The carriers are all British designed and manufactured and incorporate a telescopic spreader which, at the touch of a button, can accommodate any standard length of container. Traction is

Fig. 5.3 E3C Type

achieved by hydrostatic motors and each machine is powered by two Perkins engines.

Apart from the steering (which is fully powered)—the brake pedal and the swash pedal, all other controls are push button. Complete interlocks, visually indicated in the cab, prevent wrong handling of containers and stop in the fail safe condition.

Power assisted braking and steering are applied to all four wheels.

Karrilift Handling
Whilst the Karricon range of straddle carriers is ideal for the storage and stacking of containers, it is also possible to unload/load road transport with this versatile range of machines. However, the question of operating within a stack or at a railhead needs special consideration.

It is here that the Karrlift 90 mobile gantry crane becomes the

Fig. 5.4 E22 Type

logical tool for multi-lane handling, such as may be found at rail/road heads.

The Karrilift has a capacity of 30 tonnes, whilst the R.O.C. patented telescopic spreader is able to manipulate containers up to 40 ft in length. Without the telescopic spreaders the capacity is 40 tonnes whilst for lesser industrial applications the Karrilift 65 of 30 tonnes capacity is available.

See illustration Straddle Carriers, pages 358–359.

Stothert & Pitt Limited of Bath, England design and manufacture a wide range of ports equipment, cranes and deck machinery which will be found in many ports of the world and on numerous ships.

In the field of ports craneage reference is here made to:

The Goliath Crane used to handle containers exrail transport to terminal. This is a wide span cantilever type of crane, rail mounted

Fig. 5.5 Karricon 304 Series.

and operationally capable of working a 15 wagon freightliner train over a distance of 1200 ft. See illustration page 360.

The Transporter Crane of 30 tonne capacity is used for ship container handling. This is mounted on 14 rail wheels for travel along the quay and is of a rope operated cross traverse trolley type on a 'bridge' structure, all of which is electrically activated.

Transporter cranes—which can be known by various trade names—i.e. the Portainer—are generally designed to meet the specific requirements of container ship design and ports operations —viz/viz any peculiarities of loading/discharging which may apply.

The Transporter, illustrated on page 24 is a good example of modern design and application.

The Spreader Beam is the critical link in the handling operations with containers in order that the box can be safely lifted at its four corner castings by twist lock securing devices.

The Mk III Spreader, illustrated on page 361 has automatic telescopic beam arrangements adjustable to the handling of 20, 30 or 40 foot boxes, be they in or out of cell stowage, or where space limitations apply. This is included by the kind permission of Stothert & Pitt Limited, of Bath, England.

Low Loaders
The increase in exceptionally heavy loads of large size, termed indivisible loads, has led to the introduction and use of heavy construction multi axle mobile platform units of the order of 40 feet long × 10 feet wide, on to which heavy cargo units can be placed and

Fig. 5.6 Karrilift 90 Series.

Goliath Crane.

towed into a vessel, via roll on/roll off provisions, for internal securing.

The design of these units—by reason of their classification— has low centre of gravity, with adequate stability.

The upward trend is for heavy loads to be of the order of 400/500 tons and where these are of large size—pressure vessels, turbo generators, transformers and the like—specifically adequate lifting gear must be provided by the ports in the form of either shore based floating cranes or by sheer legs.

Where these are not available the low loader comes into its own, either for roll on/roll off transportation in total, or by shipment for transit at a port where facilities for lifting on to applicable ship carriage is available. Indivisible loads can be up to 1000 tons, for which a low loader would be indispensible; 500/800 tons are not unusual; 60/100 tons common place. See Section—Heavy Lifts, and Section—Bulk handling by roll on/roll off systems.

Craneage
It would be beyond the scope of a book of this nature to deal comprehensively with the vast range of craneage equipment and facilities in the ports of the world. The crane manufacturing industry is international and organizations within it are continually examining the trade pattern trends in an endeavour to produce a piece of craneage equipment which can anticipate cargo handling needs for

the near immediate future, let alone any long term planning. Craneage is a capital investment in a fast changing and developing area; design for obsolescence cannot apply.

The ship cargo officer is therefore likely to come in contact with many different types of cranes but, in general terms, each will be of a design and application appropriate to the current and envisaged trade of the port in which it is erected and operated.

On that basis, attention is drawn to the following—the list is by no means exhaustive:

General Conventional and Unitized Cargoes
Jib Cranes of capacities up to 50 tons capacity.
Jib Luffing cranes of up to 35 tons capacity.

Spreader Beam.

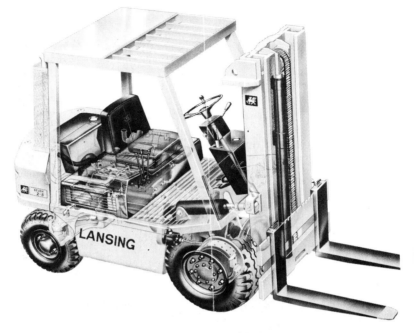

Fork Lift Truck—General Layout.

Double Luffing cranes of up to 50/60 tons capacity.
Portal cranes of ranges 3 to 50 tons capacity.

Heavy Lifts
Derrick cranes of up to 180 tons capacity.
Floating slewing cranes with 50 ton hoists.
Floating cranes of 400 tons capacity.
Diesel-Electric and Diesel-hydraulic mobile cranes with ranges capable of 250 ton loads.

General Mobile handling
Mobile dock cranes of anything from 3 to 50 tons capacity.

Bulk Cargo
Luffing cranes with grab attachments.
Grabbing units attachments to Velle Derrick cranes suitable for 12 tons S.W.L. loads.
Gantry cranes for Forest products—Logs (as can be seen in Amsterdam).

Fork Lift Truck —Roll on/Roll off use.

Container Cargo
Transporter Gantry cranes.

The gantry crane, particularly those of double action type, capable of simultaneous working, ship and shore, with capacities of 50 tons, are likely to become more evident in the larger container terminals, since they are considered to be more inducive to speedier working, which is essential with large size container vessels requiring quick turn round.

Twin lift transporter container cranes can work either single 40 ft boxes or double 20 ft boxes.

Front Lift mobile telescopic spreader lift hook cranes, the 'Defiant' Rubery Own Conveyancer Limited a case in point, is designed for single container movement and stacking. It is useful in smaller ports where minimal container traffic applies.

(For continued, up to date information on craneage developments, the reader is referred to appropriate maritime technical trade journals.)

Fork Lift Truck —Container Handling.

THE ORGANIZATION OF A PORT

Ports structure is now a matter of technological/modernizational change, highly evident in the industrial areas but quickly becoming increasingly noticeable in the 'so called' developing countries.

Whatever the structure however, any one port will differ in degree from another according to the trades it attracts—there is no one, hard and fast rule or standard for port organization and administration, although similarities show up, be it in a large or small port.

None the less, the powers of ports authorities to fashion their functions and activities are to be found in legislative acts of national policy and within those guide lines ports design and implement their administration relative to the organization which legislation suggests. In Great Britain much of this is contained in the Transport Act of 1962; the Harbours Act of 1964 and The Docks and Harbours Act of 1966—acknowledgeing that such legislation is subject to change or modification according to the prevailing political climate. Foreign ports have similar comparable legislative requirements.

In Great Britain ports are classified as Major Ports, which are highly complex and available for all forms of traffic and Small Ports which, by virtue of size, have restricted availability though, in their fashion, can be as effective as the larger undertakings. Particular classification covers Tanker Ports, Ferry Ports and Fishing Ports, although invariably these are part of a larger port connurbation and retain title only from historical interest.

In countries other than Great Britain equally varied arrangements apply, with State, Municipal and Private ownership.

'Free Ports' remain part of ports organization, though mostly confined to the European areas where facilities for the discharge and warehousing of cargo, such as for transit, avoids customs jurisdiction.

Within itself, a port is a complex undertaking embracing a multitudinous collection of functions, procedures and techniques necessary to the reception, loading and discharging of ships. In the

Fork Lift Truck —Container Stuffing/Stripping.

smaller ports these procedures are more easily definable and work-able but in the larger connurbations the complexity of operations are dictated by the need for dynamic and flexible approach, not the least of which is in the area of planning and forecasting maritime and economic behaviour.

The earlier definition of a port being 'a place to which ships resort to load and discharge cargoes' is now an over simplification of term. The new dimension is that of an industrial unit closely tied to business and commerce over the 'catchment area' which it serves and, as such, is part of the total overall local, area and national economic policy to which its position and effectiveness subscribes. Notably is this evident where industrial units develop within and adjacent to the port estate, known as M.I.D.A.S., Maritime Industrial Development Areas, with facilities available by which ships berth and discharge directly into the consignee sites. Particularly can this be seen with bulk commodities which are then processed and distributed to a consumer market direct from the point of bulk delivery.

Furthermore, ports now primarily devote their attention to 'classes of ships'—not just ships.

Ports, therefore, have basic individual requirements, supported, mainly among others, by:

1. Suitable and adequate equipment and services.
2. Appropriate operational activities.
3. Supporting financial, commercial and economic services, the latter involve marketing.
4. A flexible labour policy, both quantitatively and qualita-tively.
5. Integrated association with agencies which use the port and promote the distribution functions, such as transport under-takings, forwarding agents, customs, etc.
6. Association with shipping companies which use the port, either on contract or common user berth arrangements.

A ship, when it enters an environment so influenced, attracts, by the very nature of things, contiguous influences upon itself. These will only react to the benefit of the ship according to the extent to which its personnel—notably the cargo staff—understand and appreciate the implications involved. Both the ship and the port are 'service industries' within the wider overall transportation mode and, as such, neither can be fully effective unless its own services integrate with those of the other. A high degree of liaison need therefore arises.

Liaison functions
By way of illustration, the Cargo Officer, in general terms, is likely to be more frequently associated with:

(a) Ports/Docks Management and Superintendents.
(b) Harbour Masters and Berthing Officers.
(c) Operational Management and Supervision.
(d) Cargo and Cargo Shed Supervision.
(e) Traffic Supervision.

In lesser degree he will become aware of the engineering functions of the port, particularly where these are concerned with equipment maintenance.

Backing up all of the foregoing are the functions of:
Financial and Commercial Control.
Personnel and Industrial Relations.
Marketing.
Research and Development.
Legal Procedures.
Conservancy.
Public Relations.
Management Services/Administration.
Estate Control.

The above list is not exhaustive but all those referred to will impinge upon the position of the ship while it is in the port, although the direct association of the Cargo Officer with any one is likely to be minimal, if at all.

Ports Associations

In British ports much of development and application derives from associations formally established. Of these the major bodies are The British Ports Association; The National Association of Ports Employers; The National Dock Labour Board; The International Cargo Handling Co-ordinating Association.

Each, and to some extent collectively, these bodies are representative of both the national and ports interests. As such their work and purpose has considerable influence upon the acceptance, handling and despatch of a ship. Detail of their activities is contained in published annual reports and in interim bulletins.

Foreign ports have similar associations, carrying out work of like character among which can be mentioned The American Association of Port Authorities; The South Atlantic and Caribbean Ports Association and The Shipping Association (North and South) which are representative of most employers in the ports of Amsterdam and Rotterdam.

External Associations

Of a number of external bodies influencing the maritime transportation area, the Cargo Officer's attention is drawn to two:

1. The International Maritime Organization (I.M.O.) which is a specialized agency of the United Nations with the objectives of facilitating co-operation among governments on technical matters affecting most, if not all aspects of shipping, in order to achieve the

highest practical standards of maritime safety and efficiency in navigation.

In terms of cargo work I.M.O. is responsible for international agreements covering the Transport of dangerous goods by Sea; The safe practice for Bulk Cargoes; The carriage of Liquid Chemicals in Bulk and the Carriage of Bulk Grain. (See Official Shipping Notices which refer.)

2. The international Association of Ports and Harbours, which represents ports throughout the world and disseminates information from members aimed at improving the efficiency of ports and their functions.

The organization, administration and general management of a port therefore, is a highly complex business exercise in no way straightforward by reason of the numerous unpredictable factors to which it can be subject, as a service industry in a mobile transportation environment. It sets out to serve its customers . . . the ships. Where these can effectively respond the more effective becomes the port. It is in the area of responding that much responsibility of knowledge and action falls on the shoulders of ship personnel, not the least being the cargo officer. To understand the peculiarities and needs of the port and to adapt the ship to meet these is truly professional.

(For detailed information on 'Seaports, their place and purpose, the reader is referred to the publication of that title, by the same author and publishers.)

The Ports and Traffic/SHIP/Cargo handling

The dominant factor influencing ports development is the ship. As such, its demands upon the facilities necessary to the cargoes it carries, condition effective, as distinct from satisfactory, handling procedures.

Port traffic may be divided into two broad categories—bulk and general cargoes. The term 'general cargo' covers a wide range of commodities and although containerization has gone far towards converting general cargo into a bulk handling operation it is, none the less, classified within the 'general' concept. Bulk cargoes are those of high tonnage capacities in themselves, the more outstanding being the Ores, Grains, Chemicals, Fertilizers and Petroleum.

Cargo Handling require applicable berthing facilities and these can be termed as:

  (a) UNIT LOAD BERTHS comprising lift-on container berths, i.e. those at which containers are loaded and unloaded by crane and roll on/roll off berths, which require drive on/drive off services for all types of vehicular traffic.
  (b) SPECIALIZED BERTHS are berths which have particular facilities used for handling some commodities classed as

general cargo but frequently handled in bulk, such as chemicals, iron and steel and forest products.

(Container berths can be classified as specialist but these are dealt with more fully in Section 4.)

(c) BREAKBULK BERTHS are berths handling general cargoes shipped by traditional methods, although these may include many of the modernized handling functions.

Of the three, unit load penetration is having the greatest impact—the break bulk berth now requires considerable modernized techniques of operation.

A container berth requires large storage area and highly specialized handling equipment; roll on/roll off berths depend

Break-bulk cargo stowed in the tween-deck of a modern twin hatch ship

largely upon storage capacity and 'holding time' space. Each of these two types of berths can be of 'common user' or 'single user' function. The latter is usually a part of an operators' overall transport chain, the former is provided by the ports, albeit on a speculative basis.

Handling Development. Until the mid 1960s general cargo was handled in 'BITS'. Unitization has changed this into a standardized form, more particularly so when the bits can be stuffed into 'BOXES'. As a result much more is being handled for less effort, but the term 'much more' means 'higher cargo handling rates', 'greater throughput' and 'bigger ships'. The main effect of this development has been the improvement in vessel turn round time.

Conventional general cargo vessels can spend up to 70% of their time in port with throughputs of from 30–100 000 tons a year with one Docker for every 750/1000 tons of break bulk throughout a year. Highly mechanized purpose built terminals have high capital costs but because of their higher throughput have reduced handling costs, per ton. Both container and Ro/Ro berths are capable of 500 000 to 1 million tons a year and the serving ships, though much larger, are more economically attractive. In terms of labour, 1 Docker can handle 5000–10 000 tons per year.

Roll on/roll off is particularly important in the short sea and on the inter-European routes but indications are clearly evident that deep sea traffic is becoming prominent with roll on/roll off ships becoming general purpose vessels, operating into any port and at any berth.

Although the deep sea container vessel can carry limited heavy loads, within the capacity of shore cranes, the roll on/roll off ship is far more versatile in its ability to carry non-unitized cargoes, such as vehicles, machinery, forest products and awkward/heavy loads without, in many cases, the need for shore cranage facilities.

Looking Ahead. Modern port facilities are expensive. A new deep sea general cargo berth could cost £5 million; a specialized type of berth considerably more.

From a national point of view port capacity must be sufficient to accommodate all the nations' traffic, which presupposes and accepts peaks and lows over yearly economic circumstances. In terms of the U.K. for example, foreign trade may well decline up to 1980, by reason of the envisaged reductions in crude oil imports following the development of the U.K. off-shore oilfields. Beyond 1980, however, growth should resume to an increase of about 335 million tons by 1985, half of which will be accounted for by fuels. The rate of growth of non fuel traffic is expected to be 2·2% up to 1980 and 3·2% between 1980 and 1985. Exports of high value non bulk cargoes are forecast to grow by about 3·9% annually up to 1980 and imports growing only 2·4%. In the years

1980/85 exports should grow by 5·9% a year compared with 2·9% for imports.

Generalizations. In less than ten years 62% of the U.K. general cargo trade with Europe and Ireland and 26% of the deep sea trade has been unitized, but this expression comprehends not only containers.

This poses problems for the ports in the creation and location of new facilities, with loss of traffic to some ports to the benefit of others. The advent of new ship types and the developments in other transport units—road and rail—has influenced considerable development in materials handling and on a simple level, alone, any port is now likely to have such general purpose tools as fork lift trucks of all shapes and weights, more specialized tools such as straddle carriers, trailers, conveyor belts, container cranes and other necessary equipment.

Apart from the petroleum carriage (see Section 4) developments are well advanced on solid pipe lines, as for example a slurry of mixed water and iron ore, handled as a liquid through a pipe line. Slurry applications lends itself to other solids, while sulphur, solid at normal temperature, can be liquified by heat and handled by 'pipe form', replacing mechanical handling equipment and labour.

Slurried iron and sand is loaded through a single point off shore mooring buoy off the coast of North Island, New Zealand, at an average rate of over 1200 tonnes per hour.

The barge carrier (L.A.S.H.) discharges not cargo, but barges, to be towed to some convenient point perhaps many miles distant.

Communications. The elaborations of concentrated carriage and handling systems has resulted in highly sophisticated communication procedures adopted by shipper and operators such that their marketing and distribution requirements can quickly meet any particular needs—the timber trade is a case in point. In these arrangements ships can more freely be re-routed, temporarily or permanently, and these shifts place heavy planning and forecasting responsibilities on ports. Notably is this so within the infrastructure of the major European ports.

Summary. It should therefore be clear as to the extent the needs of the ship influences the organization and operations of the port. The contrast between the 'big' and the 'small medium' port is not, necessarily one of area nor has this general bearing upon the cargo handling practices involved; it is the throughput of capacity which can be handled according to the trading developments in which the port is involved and the technological facilities of investment necessary and desirable to the ship types. Some of the conventional large ports of the U.K. for example, are no longer as large as hitherto yet this does not reflect any unattractiveness to shipping, albeit the number in the port at any one time is, statistically, less numerically. The reduction has been overtaken by more effective facilities in the remaining modernized sections, as for example in London, Liverpool, Southampton and Hull. The same is true for the smaller/medium ports. Dover, geographically, is a small/medium size port yet it is the most important passenger port in the country and is 'tooled' up to meet this challenge, apart from its high reputation for handling unitized cargo.

THE EFFECT OF TRADE PATTERNS ON PORT ORGANIZATION

Ports are about ships and they exist, develop or decline according to the manner by which ships can meet the requirements of different trading patterns and adjust their involvement accordingly. Particularly, in this age are they affected by ship technology and, in turn, endeavour to provide services to meet this.

For example, only 20 years ago the biggest tanker afloat was of the order of about 17 000 dwt; a V.L.C.C. (Very large crude carrier) now equates with 200/300 000 dwt. and requires specialized reception, significantly illustrated by the natural deep water harbour of Milford Haven, from which pipe lines serve the refinery installations at Swansea. Swansea, therefore, does not develop to handle deep draught tankers but the environment surrounding it does not suffer by reason of the facilities provided, inter alia Milford Haven. Similarly, refineries in Antwerp are fed by pipe line from Rotterdam, and the Stanlow refinery from oil discharged into and fed by pipe line from an off shore mooring, off Anglesea. As such, this off shore mooring becomes a 'port', in effect. On the North Sea coast of Great Britain, the off shore oil fields either pump by pipe line to the Grangemouth refineries, or ship their oil by smaller tankers to coastal ports unable to handle the larger tonnages. Types of oil ports, therefore, develop according to the types of ships transporting the product.

A similar situation can be seen with bulk carriage, other than fuel, where the quantities of ore being transported, and the sizes of the ships involved, require specialized ports and installations to handle them.

Container traffic patterns have also influenced the development of some ports, with noticeable concentrations at the expense of others, while the roll on/roll off patterns have made considerable impact, but, in this case, on numerous ports and harbours, since these types of ships vary in size from 'small' to 'moderately high' tonnages, acceptable as a result to wider choice of ports providing quick access to wide geographical areas.

The overall unitization of cargoes, and the technical design of ships to handle these with minimal effort, has influenced the growth of mechanical handling devices in all types of ports in order to meet the technological changes in ships procedures.

Apart from these established trading patterns, albeit the increase in size, the shipment of slurries, i.e. solids mixed with water, is conditioning the loading and discharging by pipe line and will require installations to cover these. Furthermore, communications in transportation patterns, with data processing and recording systems, has produced far reaching traffic consequences for ports. Producers and shippers can easily, and effectively, now adapt their transport systems to meet particular requirements and permit the 'large' consignees to plan their operations and distribution on a country, if not international, wide base, from which traffic, hitherto established with a port, can quickly expect new routings. These shifts of traffic can promote all kinds of difficulties for ports and raises the question as to the extent ports in a country should compete against each other.

Transhipment, once a well established part of cargo carriage, has now taken on a much different relationship and is conditioning a pattern of being restricted to particular ports, serving particular, and wider geographical areas. In Great Britain transhipment cargo overall, is now only small in proportion to its total trade, though for import goods, it still remains high. Rotterdam, on the other hand, is by definition a transhipment port serving the vast hinterland of Northern Europe, from which the extensive barge traffic on the Rhine enjoys its profitability.

Grain remains a transhipment cargo of some account, but is more dominant on the continent than in the U.K. As such, the larger grain vessels will be justified for continental ports, albeit transhipment of grain remains important to the U.K.

Transhipment of 'Ore' cargoes to the U.K. will inevitably cease when all the envisaged deep water terminals are fully operational and since the trading patterns encourage the growth of the 300,000 d.w.t. ore carrier, ports and installations must be provided to handle them having regard to the accessibility of the industrial areas to which the ores need to be sent.

Containers, on the other hand, are likely to be high transhipment cargoes since they readily lend themselves to Ro/Ro and ferry traffic, not only within the profitable E.E.C. areas but in any country where geographical situations encourage large/small ports inter-relationships.

Berthing arrangements and contiguous facilities, likewise are influenced by ship technological development, albeit throughput is the cost criteria. Single berths, particularly with bulk trades, have high capacity, although capital costs are high. The modern general cargo berth, equipped for container traffic has high tonnage through-put but is expensive to develop and maintain, whereas the 'multi' used berth is more profitable than a normal break bulk berth. But the roll on/roll off berth is the most effective in terms of cost ratios with throughput and labour utilization. Doubtless the reason for the upsurge in their availability, in all ports of the world, is their flexibility and reliability, attractive to shippers wishing to move goods expeditiously and having a system which can be served by a wide range of vessels, in many cases by reason of their design, unaffected by tidal restrictions.

Cost factors in berth arrangements however, have interesting influences upon ports in other directions. Notably is this with V.L.C.Cs discharging part of their cargoes into smaller tankers for delivery to smaller ports—singularly a 'transhipment function'.

Terminals within ports, i.e. locked in, also handle high capacities with ferry services which may not be tied to a rigid turn round schedule measured in 'hours', without the need for extensive high cost cranage systems, as exemplified by the North Sea Ferries operating out of Hull to the Continent.

'Small ports' have also served useful purpose resulting from the developing patterns of moving heavy, bulky loads, increasingly difficult to move by road or rail. Both in the U.K. and on the Continent small ships can move heavy boiler units and mechanical/ electrical fittings from source of manufacture by sea to ports near or adjacent to point of installation, loading and discharging by either ramps or high capacity (200 ton) cranes. Indeed there is no short sea restriction and some interesting designs in ship development of these sizes are to be seen; ports—harbours capable of handling them have benefited accordingly. A case of particular interest in this pattern is the movement of a 1000 ton unit from Europe to the Persian Gulf, in a vessel of only 3000 d.w. tons.

It is also interesting to note that the rapidly developing trade pattern with forest products, and the high tonnage vessels engaged, with their own handling equipment, can discharge at timber terminals having little high capital cost equipment, other than mobile traction, thus influencing this form of port terminal facility.

Lastly, the barge carrier—the L.A.S.H. or SEABEE ship must not be forgotten, where barges of cargo of various types are off loaded from the parent ship—off shore and conveyed by towage to a port too small to handle the bulk carrier, but capable of benefiting from the trade. Examples of this can be seen in the Medway, U.K. and in the Southern states of the U.S.A. Even so, the barge carrier is increasing in size to meet appropriate traffic from the U.S.A. to Europe.

In short, ports do not necessarily need to be very large in size, but all, irrespective, should be modern in equipment and design, with a high working capacity for each and any category of cargo. As such, they make sense of any policy of ports dispersion for a trading country.

The foregoing notes are included by kind permission of The National Ports Council, G.B. and taken from its 1976 Bulletin No. 9, 'Port Perspectives 1976'.

SECTION 6

THE MANAGEMENT OF MARINE CARGO TRANSPORTATION

(Aspects of study relative to a Cargo Officer's professional duties)

A. Introduction

The management of ships' cargo operations is part of the wider marine cargo transportation function, albeit a very important part. Alone, there could be temptation to consider the aspect all important, but this is not the case.

On reflection it is clear that no management process can expect to be fully effective without regard to other functions which impinge upon it, particularly where influences are very direct and closely related to the subject to which management attention is being given.

In the matter being dealt with, the impingement is 'Ports and Ships'; as such the study becomes one of Shipboard Operations.

The text which follows is designed to show the Cargo Officer how he fits into the picture and how best to develop his capacity for managing the movement and handling of cargoes in ships in which he may be serving. This is Cargo Handling in the widest sense.

For the detail involved see Contents, page 386.

Each text in the above references is basic to the process of handling cargo; in total they set the pattern for the study outline which follows.

B. General Outline

Management is the art of Organization and Administration, no less appropriate for ships than for any other business activity. Both functions condition all forms of behaviour embracing people, materials and equipment.

There is no hard and fast rule, no set pattern, though principles and basic procedures govern the manner of application, some of which are conditioned by inherent rules, recommendations and regulations and can have scientific, physical, technical, mathematical and social background. Others grow out of experience, developing from tradition and custom, tuned by progressive behaviour, and are said to be 'practical' functions.

Much depends upon the objective being pursued and the standards which this demands.

All forms of 'business' develop this way, some in very sophisticated form, others more clearly defined. Much depends upon the attitude of mind of individuals and their ability to PLAN, FORECAST, CO-ORDINATE and MOTIVATE.

The practicalities of any management activity are conditioned by four basic elements.

1. WHY is the procedure to be covered necessary.
2. HOW can it be achieved, how should it be done.
3. WHEN is it preferable or profitable to carry it out.
4. WHERE should it be applied.

These approaches are fundamental and the manner by which they take form gives rise to what is termed 'a style of management'. No two people can expect to have identical styles though similarities will be apparent according to the emphasis placed upon the foregoing elements. Indeed, the overall operation or activity will demand a form of style and, largely, the effectiveness of the job to be done, the coordination of services and the cooperation of people will invariably reflect the style of management being practised. In this context 'the manager' (used in the descriptive term) must be aware of the environment in which he is working and its attendant influences and, also, the extent to which that environment permits him to apply each or all of the basic fundamentals.

The environment surrounding any activity has major influence and needs to be looked at the more deeply, be it with strong theoretical/technical connotations or essentially practical. It is fundamental to the complete approach. Some environments are highly diverse and complex and contain detailed elements of organization which calls for equally detailed administration techniques. This is evident in the specialized nature of modern shipping operations.

Others, less broad, can be seen in similar fashion but are easier to understand while the relatively small undertaking can be of such apparent simplicity that its organizational and administrative features seem, on the surface, indistinguishable, but they are there, none the less. In this latter category can be placed the ship.

Irrespective, it cannot be said that any one is more efficient than the other. Efficiency is relative and needs comparable likes for analysis measurement. A ship, therefore, can aim for comparable efficiency and effectiveness by reason of becoming involved with similar environments and similar demands. Change the environment, differ the demands and the organization and administration functions, of necessity, must change also, although, in basic principle, the approach will be the same. But it does not follow that on another occasion, with a different ship and in a different port, with dissimilar cargoes, the identification may appear so straightforward. The differences will be only a matter of degree, because the environment has changed. Given, however, that familiarity with the ship is reasonably founded and sufficient experience supports this, then practical analysis of management requirements can quickly unfold, provided the officer has given thought to the factors of organization and administration, and where these differ, as indeed they do. By comparison the ship itself can be treated as a 'small undertaking' since, in size, the impingements upon it and the demands can be identifiable.

The matter here being considered is the environment of the ship within the wider trading conurbation. The material is the cargo, the equipment, the gear being employed, the people, both ship personnel and others, those attached to areas in which the ship may be at any one time. Each fact must be looked at from the point of view of its dependence upon another. In simple terms it is 'Knowing Ones' SHIP' and what it, and those who serve in it, are expected to do—receive, carry and deliver cargo, for such is the practice of cargo handling.

C. The Management Practice

Management practice can have short, medium and long term objectives. The detail in the first must be specific and positive; with the other two broader considerations pertain. Ex Ship, loading and/or discharging, the first takes prominence since the work to be done has to be completed in a relatively short time. Medium and long term behaviour is more of a career development, of foreseeable requirements, in that a study of transportation by sea, i.e. patterns of trade and their ramifications, provides a wide continuous picture, more time for analysis and detailed requirements showing up, in more meaningful fashion such that, when faced with short term needs, those of prominent importance can be planned beforehand. In coming to these decisions good management discards what may appear to be unimportant at the time and retains that which must remain of high priority. In this context it is the experience of cargo handling, from junior to senior level, which ultimately trains the officer's mind to distinguish the Whys, Hows, Whens and Wheres of the job which he has chosen, or is charged to do.

D. Organization and Administration

1. *Organization*

On the preceding premises the cargo officer considers his ORGANIZA-TIONAL responsibilities.

Organization, in itself, prompts managerial skills and is centred upon, in this study, the handling of cargoes and the associations with people involved. Its breadth will depend largely upon the shipping company of which the ship is a part, i.e. company practice and also upon the trade(s) in which it is employed. The skills which become needful will cover technical and social areas, embracing sound levels of communication and coordination, alongside professional competence related to the job in hand.

Primarily, the organizational approach is for the cargo officer to 'set out his stall', to have equipment of the right kind and in good order and condition, to have space adequate and appropriate for the cargoes he is to carry, to have correct systems of working, conforming to rules, regulations and codes of practice and to have staff to whom he can delegate with confidence. In short, to make the ship attractive to the markets in which it trades and acceptable, in economic terms, to the shipping community which may consider using it. Given the right design, the cargo officer can do a great deal to ensure the ship has acceptable reputation, that its cargo handling reflects effective methods and that, as an economic unit, contribution to the overall costs of his shipping company is salutary. In this competitive age no ship has a divine right to be always employed.

Nor, any longer, is a ship in isolation, no longer can cargo handling be a function exclusive to itself.

In the long term it should be borne in mind that statistical information on cargo handling techniques, according to types of cargoes and patterns of trade, are promoted through international agencies, the aim being that technical development may, in the future, be increasingly comparable. This form of evaluation is seen in the manner by which shipowners programme their building investment and choice of trading services requirements, such that their ships have ability to handle cargoes as rapidly and effectively as possible and be suitable for transfer to other trades, as circumstances may dictate, i.e. shipping consortiums.

This is another reason why ports are no longer interested in ships, as such, but in classes of vessels (see page 366).

A cargo officer cannot be dismissed from these procedures nor he to lose sight of their effect upon his career in the long term and his current duties. What is required of the ship prompts the manner by which he endeavours to make it acceptable; how it is to be organized to meet the requirements of the environment in which it will be working.

2. *Administration*

Administration involves the ability to determine policy implementation, to evaluate problems and to be able to solve them, to make decisions and to communicate. Its motivating premise is both self developing as well as towards a group; indeed the former is probably the more important since the confidence inspired into the individual can then more easily and effectively be promulgated towards inter-group behaviour. There is need for flexibility in administrative techniques—good management is never irreparably rigid.

The cargo officer's administrative responsibilities aim to ensure that. organizational preparations 'work' and meet the demands imposed. In large degree this involves 'people' both ship personnel and shore contacts. It is also concerned with ship servicing facilities and their disposition when and where required.

Ship personnel efficiency will depend upon the standards set by the Cargo Officer and these will be reflected by the manner in which he promotes his own communications, is aware of his accountability and authority and thus exercises his demands.

Shore contacts, ports and agencies, will react according to the extent to which there is mutual understanding of each other's activities. This is the team effort, embracing coordination and not a little motivating. Services provisions will depend upon the cargoes involved and their movement requirements.

These administrative functions will be conditioned by much of legislation, nationally and internationally, which set out standards to which forms of loading, carriage and discharge must comply and to which the behaviour of all parties must conform. Notably, The Department of Transport 'Code of Safe Working Practice for Merchant Seamen' looms high in this regard. Also, I.M.O. (International Maritime Organization) Codes of Practice and the I.C.S. (International Chamber of Shipping) regulations and recommendations cover a wide range of cargo handling requirements, as also do the Department of Transport 'M' notices. Foreign governments also have local regulations. Alongside, 'company practice' codes of practice will govern much that a cargo officer can, or be expected to do.

Regard for all of these guidelines will determine the extent of administrative practice, and its quality.

It must not be forgotten, neither, that the characteristics and properties of different forms and types of cargoes condition the care and handling they require and 'WHY' the respective methods must apply. Administration benefits or suffers, very strongly from the attitude of mind of the person charged with promoting it.

The administration of cargo handling is also heavily influenced by The Business of Shipping (see pages ix, xiii, 379, 386, 465). Among other things it is responsible for the wide and increasingly changing systems of cargo documentation, the liaison with customs and agencies, freight aspects and the noticeable differences in the working of ports all over the world. Shipping conferences also have wide effect upon the trading patterns to which ships are subjected.

Doubtless it can therefore be understandable that ships' personnel may well find their duties a mixture of clarity and confusion, but it would be undesirable to neglect the implications since, by so doing, planning and forecasting (i.e. the why) would become meaningless, issues, as they arose, without foundation and creative ability, upon which much of management expertise depends, nigh non existent. To look at these matters in any other way could be a waste of time for they are a part of the industry environment. Certainly they have a long term value as equally important to efficient cargo handling management study as to the actual job ability. Indeed, the former strengthens the latter.

It can, of course, be argued that this approach is common to all forms of management, and is not restricted to ships. This is true and successful managers practise it.

E. Practicalities

The more practical feature of cargo handling management is related to the 'HOW', 'WHEN' and 'WHERE' factors.

How cargo is to be handled must conform to reality; there can be no experimentation. Its type is the fundamental issue.

Apart from its properties, which will govern its packaging and therefore how it is to be lifted and stowed, much of regulation controls specific methods of movement and thus inhibits systems, as distinct from methods, as such, into which a working ship finds itself. It is as well to become familiar with systems developed in some of the larger port authorities.

However, shipwise, adequate and suitable space provision also determines systems, as for example the planning and allocation of hold and space(s) availability, particularly where cargo separation necessity aims to fully utilize equipment and labour. How cargo plans are interpreted has wide bearing upon the effectiveness of systems, peculiar to the facilities available.

'How' involves cooperation with port authorities. In the larger ports it can be likely that all the stevedoring is carried out by port labour and equipment or, indeed by the use of ship gear as well. In the smaller ports the use of ship facilities may dominate, may even be necessary. Ship preparation will depend upon whichever pertains. Cooperation and coordination with ports authorities involves a time factor. Time, in port, from the shipowner's point of view is unproductive and unprofitable. Hence the philosophy of 'Quick Turn Round'.

Unproductive time could result from lack of attention to:

(*a*) The systems and methods of handling, customarily related to a particular port.

(*b*) The availability of appropriate equipment of all kinds, be this part of port or ship gear and the advantages of using one or the other, or both.

(*c*) The availability of labour insofar as this affects quay working or 'in hold' disposition.

Liaison with port authorities is an important feature in the management of cargo handling. Sadly, this could be stronger.

F. Ports Liaison

Ports are about ships and ships about ports. Doubtless an over-simplification since each is also concerned with many other functions of diverse character. But in the process of moving a 'piece of cargo' from consignor to consignee, in the shortest possible time and in the most effective manner, together, the port and the ship make up the largest link in the Integrated Transportation Mode.

It thus follows that there is high desirability for both ship and port to be aware of the characteristics of either and, for the ship, in managing its cargo handling facilities, to be more than politely interested in those ports which, particularly, it uses regularly and, more generally, those to which its visits are less frequent. Such an attitude assists in the formation of background knowledge, an adjunct of fundamental value in any management approach.

Some questions to ask can include the following; doubtless there are many others:

(a) Is it a large, medium or small port to which my ship is destined? Definitive classification can be misleading since it does not follow that any one type of port, within the above range, will be any more effective than the other or present exceptional or insuperable services. Some ports have, and build up reputations for handling specific types of cargoes, others have wide facilities catering for any class of vessel. Developing ports may require extensive ship assistance in moving cargo. It is as well to be aware of these differences.

(b) Super ports—the Rotterdam, Antwerp and Le Havre conurbations—are noted for their Maritime Industrial Development Areas where ships discharge directly into production units, ex quay. Bulk cargoes, in such circumstances, may only require the minimum of ship servicing.

(c) Timber and forest products now attract the widest association of both ship and port gear and equipment. At what stage of working will either be used?

(d) At what stage must temperature levels with refrigerated cargo meet the facilities available in a port, notably important with refrigerated containers.

(e) In the carriage of containers will the ship be responsible for lashing security (deck loads) or does the port provide professional facilities.

(f) What depths of water will the ship have in loading or discharging 'heavy loads' (stability considerations).

(g) At what stage will unitized cargo employ the use of port or ship mechanical handling aids. Unitization has increased the importance of stringent supervision. To what extent must the ship be aware of this.

(h) What experience is at hand as to the efficiency and care with cargoes loaded/discharged in fast working roll on/roll off services. Are these acceptable.

(i) What are the systems and their extent, in the large container ports. What are they looking to in the processes of reception, storage, utilization of equipment and distribution.

(j) Relative to (i) how do these considerations apply with roll on/roll off systems.

None of the above is intended to create doubt about a port's effectiveness, on the contrary. They are no more than a check list in a cargo officer's own personal reactions to circumstances with which he may be faced such that his responsibilities and duties can be put to the best use.

Insofar as a ship is an economic unit within a shipping company or a group, the time factor spent in port conditions a further aspect of cargo handling management, of benefit to overall shipping costs. Ports devote time and effort investigating and analysing related problems within their total operations, in some instances employing time study procedures of new and changing methods of reception and distribution, for both existing and envisaged possible future developments in cargo handling functions.

In the lesser sized and/or (possibly) in the developing ports these techniques are not so evident, perhaps non existent. None the less, technical cooperation between ship and port is now more desirable such that a cargo officer, to advantage, could well give thought to similar approaches as far as his own ship handling facilities are appropriate. With this kind of promotion more effective technical cooperation between ship and port could result, apart from the savings in possible unnecessary handling procedures. Time in port represents a substantial part of transportation costs on which the efficiency of a ship could be judged. Furthermore, the aspect adds technical colour to organization and administration, now more necessary in shipboard operations.

In this context it should be borne in mind that opinion in the shipping world envisages an increase in technological activity with cargo carriage over the next decade, which will be seen in increasing tonnages of dry cargo being carried in specialist vessels, roll on/roll off and container ships, with the 'so called' general cargo carrier less involved. Indeed, cargo movement to and from the industrialized areas—and with those others quickly developing—is estimated to become more unitized than is currently the case. Seaports, in keeping, are likely to show increasing specialization, to meet the ship developments.

These changes will promote handling requirements of greater flexibility insofar as both ship and port equipment and gear will demand wider technical, as distinct from physical care and attention. The cargo officer's outlook will, of necessity, need also to be more flexible.

Ports liaison requires strict coordinating procedures, taking on a dual role—ship cargo handling personnel and port shore gangs.

The ship management approach, though authoritative as far as the ship is concerned, should take on a discriminative form with port personnel, bearing in mind the differences between port and ship industry relations. None the less, tuned to tactfulness, it must be emphatic and purposeful and devoid of suspect. It must always be remembered that in the ultimate it is the Ship Master who is responsible for the safe loading of his ship and to whom blame lies for any irregularities.

G. Cargoes Control

Apropos the preceding section, with discharging (liquid cargoes excepted) there can be less urgency than with loading, though each is equally important. Whereas tight associations with port working systems may in these cases be less demanding, loading and stowage always requires strict attention to methods employed and safeguards respected. The faster the operations are carried out the more is this the case.

With liquid cargoes—bulk petroleum, natural gas and chemicals— the 'HOW' factor is highly important at all times. Cooperation and coordination with shore personnel is paramount while, also, during carriage the requirements of temperature, pressure, ventilation and ullage controls involves close working with other branches of ship personnel—engineers and electricians, to name but two, apart from the restrictions and constraints placed upon the whole of the ship's company, in the interests of safety.

Apart from the sincerity of the cargo officer himself, much, if not all of these functions will be promulgated in shipowner codes of practice.

Refrigerated cargoes demand similar attention, vegetable cargoes also. Check lists relating to temperature and ventilation control will be contained in shipping documentation. It follows therefore that cargo handling management embraces technical as well as practical considerations.

'WHEN' cargo is to be worked involves many aspects of administration. To illustrate a few, the following is pertinent:

Its availability, currently alongside on quay or in warehouses, or its estimated arrival, ex quay will affect space dispositions and their working. Port Markings and optional cargo will determine when to accept the cargoes on board. Blocking off requirements will indicate the more favourable loads to use. Dangerous cargoes will dictate their own special requirements, as also special cargo. Special cargoes, such as fruit and other edibles, will call for considerations of timing, relative to temperature needs. Indeed this will apply to discharge also—particularly where refrigerated containers must have their temperatures related to the provisions for maintaining temperature provided by the port of discharge.

Although an unavoidable or often unpredictable hazard, weather can have far reaching influence upon planned working schedules, calling for rearrangement of equipment and labour time tables. Indeed, any unforeseen or unpredictable delay will have repercussions far beyond the ship itself, extending even as far as consignee marketing.

Discharging presents lesser problems of timing at final port of unloading but at intermediate ports it is essential that the cargo plan has been intelligently prepared and clearly interpretable and that supervision is arranged so that overcarriage can be avoided. The cargo plan, together with other related documentation, preferably transmitted to the final port beforehand, as is quite normal, will lessen any difficulties which may arise when contact is made with ports operating personnel and so lead to more effective and profitable discussions which may then be necessary.

Above all else however, is the importance of attention which must always be given to the condition of the vessel when moving loads around. In this context 'WHEN' to load or discharge 'heavy loads' is a paramount stability consideration, bearing in mind the 'critical' moments, the place of the load apropos other cargo, the draft condition of the vessel and its metacentric height.

Stability considerations are always present when moving loads into and from different spaces, notably when these are either low down in the vessel or comprising deck stowage. This feature has particular relevance with multi-purpose vessels and where 'large' numbers of containers are carried as 'part cargo'. Modern container vessels, as such, are assisted in these matters by sophisticated computerized information with which, doubtless, the cargo officer is familiar. Even so, in all cases with the movement of heavy loads cooperation and coordination with ship engineering personnel is necessary, *vis-à-vis* water ballast control, as well as with the labour force concerned with the loading and discharging of the boxes. Furthermore, shipping documentation may well indicate specialized times of working some forms of cargo. This can be seen in the design of related documentation, much of which, as referred to earlier, is processed and forwarded between ports in advance. In effect this is helpful to forward planning. Indeed it suggests the design of cargo flow charts, in support of cargo plans. These can be very helpful, not only with a 'full ship' working sequence, loading or discharging, but also where more than one port is involved.

Two other features of the 'when' factor come to mind.

When might it be necessary to request additional gangs, if the vessel has a sailing time to meet.

When is the supervision aspect the more concerning. Stevedoring can encourage lack of care and when a ship may be busy, all spaces working, some cargoes may call for particular supervisory attention. To ignore this could have far reaching implications—damaged cargo, noted on discharge can involve insurance matters in the apportionment of blame. Ports do have reputations, no less than ships. It is as well to be aware of this.

It should be clear, therefore, that the 'when' factor is strongly related to coordination and cooperation, at varying levels.

'WHERE' cargo is to be worked is the more straightforward and uninhibited of the four basic approaches.

The other three will have reference but cargo, general, specific or particular can, by and large, only be placed where space is appropriate, acceptable, having working equipment suitable and procedures applicable to and approved by the numerous codes of practice and regulations. It cannot be emphasized too strongly that a cargo officer must be fully conversant with these provisions. For example, bulk cargoes, timber, ores, grains, deck cargoes, mineral products, wood pulp are some cases in point where restriction and constraint may apply. The awareness involved is a strong administrative function.

Where cargo is to be discharged will relate to Bills of Lading, T.I.R. documents and Cargo Plan(s) indication, Shipping Notes and documentation coverage, as for example with dangerous goods. Local regulations may also affect the issue, should it be, for example, the practice to move a vessel from its initial berth for the purpose of specialized discharge, i.e. dangerous cargoes.

The Intermodal Aspect

The transportation of cargo is an intermodal affair, involving a chain—acceptance, carriage and distribution. A number of bodies and functions are involved.

The patterns of trade dictate the manner by which goods move and the optimum method of its carriage. The ship is charged with looking after the cargo, often for the longest period in the chain factor, the port authorities with accommodating it and the supporting services, road, rail and water being concerned with its distribution. Any break or constraint in the chain affects the effectiveness of the overall operation, having repercussions far beyond the ship and its cargo.

For this reason, if for no other, it is desirable that ship personnel are familiar with the environmental orbit in which they serve to carry cargoes entrusted to them. Working with ports, though only one aspect, is a vitally important feature. Where unforeseen delays occur or where relevant information is denied them, cooperation and co-ordination becomes unsatisfactory. Where ships do not attract respect for their services equally are the disadvantages apparent.

Organizing and administrating the functions which befall the lot of a cargo officer, and his staff, patterns the manner by which the why, how, when and where become meaningful, and salutary to effort.

The essence of marine cargo transportation is to know the capabilities of the ship in which an officer is serving and the extent to which he is able to promote these to advantage in cargo care. The management of cargo handling is fundamental to this endeavour, it is broader than vocational ability, it adds much to its competence. In this modern age, and, more so for the future, it is a necessary factor.

Knowledge of cargo properties and characteristics, acceptable and suitable methods and systems in their movement and a full understanding of 'guide lines' are paramount requirements together with a professional acceptance of the environment in which cargo movement takes place.

Given that acceptance, distinguishing between organization and administration and respecting attitudes of mind, places the cargo officer in the position of professionally practising management to a degree of formality whereas, previously, his practical behaviour did, in fact, cover it, though without understanding.

Thus, decisions can be made, objectively—the essence of sound management.

THE MANAGEMENT OF SHIP'S CARGO OPERATIONS

The Management of Marine Cargo Transportation
A study of the professional duties of the Cargo Officer.

Commercial Practice
Marine commercial procedures, contracts of carriage, chartering, definitions, documentation, practical guidelines.

Reception, Delivery and Checking
Tallying, Cargo Plans.

Cargo Space and Measurement
Capacity factors, Mate's Log Book.

Port Speed
Loading Lists, Stowage Factors, On Board Distribution.

Stability
Practical applications to loading/discharging and safety.

Cargo Calculations
Distribution of Cargo, measurement computation, Cargo Gear safety factors, Displacement and Tons per Inch.

Cargo and Safety
The Code of Safe Working Practices for Merchant Seamen.

Shipboard Management in Practice
An exercise in the involvement of ship personnel with Shipping Company Operating Procedures.

Department of Transport
Appropriate D.o.T. notices relative to cargo operations.

General Questions on Cargo Handling.

Reception, Delivery and Checking

Tallying. To tally is to 'check' or 'keep a record' of all cargo loaded into and/or discharged from a vessel. It is an essential part of cargo work in order to prevent claims, sometimes illegitimate, upon the ship for short discharge. However efficient the system of tallying instituted by a port/dock authority, officers should realize that any short delivery of cargo will result in claims upon the ship.

As is often the case, so many are the channels through which consignments have to pass before they eventually reach the ship for loading, or eventually reach the consignee after discharge, that much confusion and worry can be saved if the ship safeguards its own interests.

The tallying of cargo should be made in alphabetically indexed books, one for each hatch and each port of discharge and loading and should consist of records of all marks and numbers of the goods, description, quantity and disposition of stow within a compartment.

As a ship's responsibility does not begin nor end until the cargo crosses the rail, tallying should be made on board the vessel and not, as often happens, ashore in the warehouse or on the wharf.

It is sometimes customary for the shipper and/or consignee to provide his own tally clerks, particularly with cargoes of a straight nature, such as bags, bales etc., whereas it is frequently the practice for the warehouse/shed authorities to provide their own clerks when handling a general cargo. Whatever the system, comparison should always be made at the end of the day between the ship tally and the shore tally and any differences immediately investigated. It may even be necessary to retally a consignment if any discrepancy is large.

Upon an efficient system of tallying depends the ability of the Chief Cargo Officer to give proper receipts and, in the case of discharge, allows the ship to check against the Bill of Lading when it is proffered. It also assists in the preparation of a cargo plan and loading list.

Not all tally books are similar in design; much depends upon the practices required by the shipping company.

Tallying a general cargo results in greater effectiveness by doing so in the compartment where the sling is 'broken open'. By so doing it is comparatively easy to obtain all marks and numbers; to supervise and note the disposition of stowage and to ensure correct handling, according to any particular instructions applying to the goods. Tallying and checking is a major component of cargo documentation which, in modern transportation, has become a complex undertaking. With a bagged cargo the slings should each contain the same number of bags in order that each sling can be checked as it crosses the rail. The same system should apply with a bale cargo.

Unitized Cargo. Unitization of cargoes has increased the importance of stringent supervision with the reception and delivery of cargo. Pre-slinging, palletizing, mixed unit loads and mechanical transportation—fork lift trucks—in fast working and moving conditions increases the difficulties of tallying and checking. By the very nature of things it also accentuates the problems of theft and pilferage. There is thus need for greater attention in these circumstances and with well trained and reliable people required for these duties.

Containers. Checking container reception and delivery has its own problems, many of which, by reason of loading/discharging systems, are beyond the control of ship's officers. Where, however, small consignments are stowed in a hold space, or on deck, care should be exercised to ensure that the box seals are secure or have not been tampered with. It is not beyond the wit of determined people to gain unobserved entry to an ineffectively sealed container during loading and/or discharging procedures which can distract attention elsewhere. In this context, periodic unobtrusive visual examination during working can have restraining results. Containers slung aboard in ineffective condition should be rejected and any found tampered with before discharge, reported upon.

Practical Guide Lines

Some of the practicalities of cargo handling are assisted by documentary provisions, shipboard customary practices, national and international 'industry' requirements, official regulations and recommendations and Codes of Practice.

Not all ships have similar documentary provisions although the implications will have common application. Some guide lines will have historical pretence, though progressively updated.

Where regulations and recommendations are concerned, updating is a progressive feature; no book of this nature can therefore expect not to avoid some omissions.

The matters which follow are general examples.

COMMERCIAL PRACTICE

Relating to the Carriage of Goods (Cargoes)

Goods are carried by sea under a contract of carriage between the *shipper* (usually the manufacturer or producer of the goods) and the shipowner.

The shipper may employ a *forwarding agent* whose duties are:

to ascertain a suitable ship, i.e. one that is sailing at a time convenient to the shipper;
to book space on the ship and complete all the necessary documentation;
to arrange for the goods to be delivered to the ship;
to arrange payment of dues and charges on the goods, including arrangements for Customs clearance.

The shipowners may employ a *loading broker* to control the allocation of space and advertise the service, to fill the ship in the best paying way, i.e. by space or deadweight and to make the loading arrangements and prepare documents on the shipowner's behalf.

Payment for the carriage of the goods is termed FREIGHT.

Where there is no provision to the contrary, Freight is paid *On*

Delivery of the goods, i.e. the reward is for delivering goods at their destination. More usually, by current practice, *Advance Freight* is payable, usually in exchange for the signed Bill of Lading and this is payable even if the vessel is lost and the cargo never delivered. If the shipper has options to have the cargo discharged in a choice of ports *Pro-Rata Freight* is payable in proportion to the part of the voyage completed. The term *Lump-Sum Freight* indicates that the full amount is payable even though the entire cargo may not be delivered.

When delivery at the port of destination is not possible for reasons beyond the control of the Master, the cargo may be on-carried or returned. Extra payment for this is termed *Back Freight*.

For vessels under voyage charter, the empty space or capacity represents a loss of income to the shipowner and this can lead to a claim for *Dead Freight* from the charterer.

The contract of carriage is distinct from the sales transaction between the shipper and the consignee. The Sales contract, broadly speaking, can be of two types:

CIF Contract (Cost, Insurance and Freight) where the seller contracts to deliver the goods to the place of destination having paid the insurance on the goods in transit and the cost of shipment (the freight); or

FOB Contract (Free on Board) where the buyer must pay insurance, freight and other charges during transit (i.e. the goods are at buyer's risk).

Sometimes a buyer may wish to hire a ship:

1. for a fixed time — —TIME CHARTER;
2. for a certain voyage—VOYAGE CHARTER;
3. and operate it himself—DEMISE CHARTER.

He may ship his own goods in the chartered vessel or offer space on a speculative basis. The agreement between the owner of the ship and the shipper, referred to as the *charterer* of the vessel is called a *charter party*. The conditions of carriage may be affected by the existence of the charter party insofar as the role of the Bill of Lading is affected.

If the charterer is also the shipper, the Bill of Lading is merely a receipt and a document of title, but cannot alter the conditions in the charter party unless there is a specific clause to the contrary or if the charterer offers space to other shippers the Bill of Lading has its normal function (i.e. between shipper and shipowner) from the moment at which the bill regulates the conditions between carrier and holder.

The relationship between the ship and the stevedoring firm is that the latter is the agent of the shipowner and cannot be sued by the cargo owner. This gives the Master the right, and duty, to control the stevedores where the safety of the ship is concerned.

CARGO DOCUMENTS

1. A shipping note is completed for the consignment by the shipper and forwarded to the shipowner or his agent. The note is a multi-part set, the top copy of which carries the words 'Please receive for shipment the goods described below, subject to your published regulations and conditions'. The goods are briefly described in the appropriate square.

2. The loading broker compiles a list of cargo (booking list) intended for shipment. This is sent to the ship to enable the Master to plan the stow and to the stevedore to arrange the loading. The broker also issues a 'calling forward notice' to the shipper, advising him of the time and place at which he is to deliver the goods alongside.

3 and 4. When a consignment of cargo is delivered to a ship a receipt for that cargo must be given when the goods are on board. If it is a small consignment, one receipt will probably cover it but with large consignments many 'parcels' will be delivered to the ship before the total consignment is finally on board. Each parcel is accompanied by the appropriate 'advice' known as the 'Boat Note', whether or not the cargo is delivered by lighter or by lorry. In some trades it is the practice for the Chief, or Chief Cargo Officer, to sign this boat note and retain a duplicate when he is satisfied, by reference to the tally, that the cargo is on

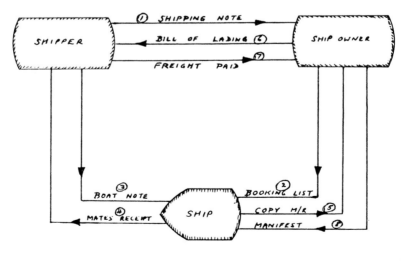

BASIC DOCUMENTATION

board. The boat note then automatically becomes the 'MATE'S RECEIPT'.

With many shipping companies it is the practice for the Chief Cargo Officer to give the official mate's receipt irrespective of the fact that a boat note may be provided by the shipper. A Mate's Receipt may be issued in triplicate— one copy being apportioned to each interested party— shipper, agent, ship.

Modern practice is to present a copy of the Standard Shipping Note as the Boat Note which, when endorsed by the Mate or the wharfinger, becomes the Mate's Receipt.

5. The copy Mate's Receipt, or its equivalent, is returned to the shipowner. It is important to note that the Mate's Receipt acknowledges that the goods have been loaded and have been properly and carefully handled, loaded and stowed. Care must be taken to ensure that any damage to goods before loading is properly recorded on the receipt, for example:

   (a) If goods have minor damage, usually in the packaging, they will be repaired on the quay at the shipper's own expense. The Mate's Receipt should therefore be countersigned with comment, such as 'bags resewn, cases repaired and secured'.
   (b) The usual condition of goods may necessitate an endorsement on the Receipt, for example 'crated motor car, paintwork scratched on front o/s door' or 'steel plating, patches of light surface rust'. If damage is severe the goods should not be loaded and the shipper contacted to enable him to take action by replacing the damaged item(s).

These endorsements on the Mate's Receipt are essential. A clean receipt must only be given if there is no apparent lack of condition of the goods.

The reason for this is that all the particulars and clauses/ endorsements are transferred to the Bill of Lading and since the goods are ship's responsibility once they are on board, the shipper will claim against the shipowner unless the defects are noted. The Bill of Lading acknowledges that the goods have been 'shipped in apparent good order and condition'.

6 and 7. The Bill of Lading is properly completed by the shipowner from detail on the Mate's Receipt. The shipper exchanges his copy of the latter for the Bill of Lading, and, as referred to earlier, the freight may be paid at this time.

8. The complete list of cargo loaded, as compiled from the Bills of Lading form the MANIFEST, copies of which are delivered to the ship before sailing.

Customs regulations at most ports require at least one copy of the Manifest and copies are also required for stevedores at discharging ports.

The Manifest is a comprehensive record of all the cargo in the vessel. It permits checking of the cargo during discharge and thereby overcarriage can be avoided. Its value to stevedoring agencies, among other things, is in the planning of equipment and services required for a ship.

Manifests also provide the material for the compilation of statistics of a nation's trade, viz. its imports/exports.

The Role of the Bill of Lading must be appreciated by Cargo Officers. This document is the primary feature of maritime commercial transactions involving the carriage of goods. It serves three distinct purposes:

1. A receipt for the goods, as outlined in the foregoing.

There is a distinction between a 'shipped' Bill of Lading where the goods are admitted to be on board the ship and a 'received for shipment' Bill, where the wharfinger has custody of the goods until loading takes place. The former is almost invariably required in view of the negotiable nature of the Bill (see 3 below) but a 'received for shipment' Bill can be converted by inserting the ship's name and loading date as an endorsement.

2. Evidence of the contract of carriage.

The principal terms may be printed on the Bill of Lading for the guidance of the shipper. Formerly the reverse of the Bill of Lading was reserved for this purpose but the tendency now is for a Short Form Bill of Lading to be issued, on which terms do not appear. Reference to Maritime Law text books will indicate the complete treatment of interpretation of Bill of Lading terms. In the context of this book it is sufficient to point out that, as for any contract, either party may take proceedings for breach of contract terms. In most maritime nations Bills of Lading must incorporate the provisions of the Hague Rules, enacted in the United Kingdom in the Carriage of Goods by Sea Act, 1971, so that omission of the material conditions from the Bill of Lading is less important than hitherto.

3. Document of Title.

For most commercial transactions the possession of a properly completed Bill of Lading is equivalent to possession of the goods. The original owner may sell goods which are in transit merely by endorsing the Bill over to the purchaser (for the sale price), the latter being then entitled to delivery of the goods on the ship's arrival. The Master has a duty to deliver the goods to the person who first presents the Bill of Lading on which freight has been paid and is of good title. Because of the negotiability of the Bill any clauses relating to damage or loss of condition are looked on with disfavour by shippers, diminishing the market value of the goods and thus the possibility of sale. Sometimes the shipowner will issue a 'clean' Bill when, though the goods are not in good condition, on the understanding that the shipper will indemnify him against any claim by subsequent holders (e.g. a purchaser of the goods) of the Bill.

This may be a commercial convenience but it invalidates any claim owing to the fact that the Bill contains a false statement and the terms cannot be enforced. Neither can the shipowner press for the indemnity which is based on a falsity.

It is not unknown for shippers to approach the Cargo Officer for a clean Mate's Receipt for goods which both know to be damaged. In no circumstances should a clean receipt be issued and the matter should be referred to the shipowner.

Bills of Lading can differ in application as between conventional, container and roll on/roll off through traffic. It is argued that the abolition of the Bill of Lading, as such, would facilitate trade procedures, to be replaced by a more comprehensive document of wider adoption, such as a form of combined transport document, embracing all forms of 'carriage' to which a piece of cargo may be subject, from consignor to consignee. Indeed, such a form of documentation does pertain with the T.B.L. (Through Bill of Lading) on the European and Inter-continental services.

Even so, the legality of the document possibly accounts for the retention of the formal Bill of Lading, albeit the modern conception of cargo carriage being strongly related to an integrated mode—a piece of cargo passing through a number of services in its total transit—does make sense of 'through bills'.

The Waybill

There are difficulties associated with the negotiable nature of the Bill of Lading. Apart from the fact that the Bill cannot be issued until the goods are loaded, there is always the possibility of indeted loss, or theft, which could delay delivery of the goods until the consignee obtains indemnity or guarantee, usually from a Bank. These problems can be dealt with by the issue of a non negotiable receipt, termed a Waybill. This is of the same form as a Bill of Lading but expressly declared to be a simple receipt. It also forms an instruction to the carrier to deliver the goods to the person named on it, at the port of destination. Thus, only that person can take delivery, on identifying himself to the carrier or his agents. Waybills are also used when there is no intention of changing the ownership of the goods, as is the case with mail or personal effects.

Dangerous Goods List

The Merchant Shipping (Dangerous Goods) Rules 1978 make it unlawful to ship goods of any category described in the rules unless the following requirements are observed:

1. The shipper must declare to the Master of the ship that the consignment is properly marked, labelled and packed and carry

Outline method indicating layout for a CARGO STOWAGE PLAN. Figure represents No. 2 Hold of a 4 Hatch two-deck vessel. Refer to detail plan in Jacket.

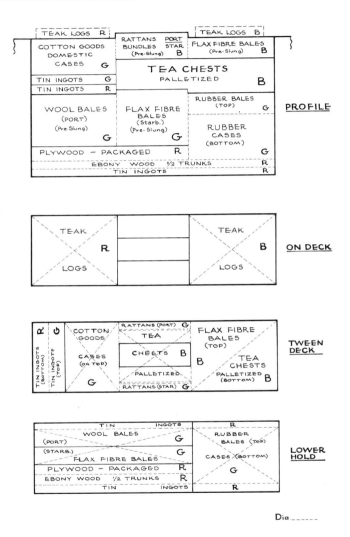

Plan is concerned with a Far East–U.S.A. voyage. Alphabetical designations for discharging ports colouring—1. Boston, B blue; 2. New York, G green; 3. Baltimore, R red.

M.V. Facsimile actual final loading/stowage plan (as prepared by cargo officers)

CONTAINERS ON DECK
LIV × S 2 × 20' Shoes 10T LIV × S 1 × 20' Shoes 5T LIV × S 2 × 20' Shoes 10T LIV × S 1 × 20' Denim 15T
LIV × P Drums lub oil LIV × S 3 × 20' Textiles 45T LIV × P 1 × 20' Textile 6T DOB × S 1 × 20' Denim 15T
DUB × P 2 × 20' Tiles 40T DUB × P 1 × 20' Reefer 3T DUB × P 6 × 20' Tiles 120T

Ports of loading—Porto Alegre, PA; Itajaj, I; Paranagua, P; Santos, S; Rio. R

With reference to figures on previous pages (Final Loading/Stowage Plan) the compilation of such a plan depends, for its effectiveness, very much upon knowledge of the trade involved and the 'peculiarities' of the ports of loading.

Differences can be considerable, some presenting problems, other wide consistences, not least being maintaining an open mind as between any pre-stowage plan, drawn up from prior load(s) information, particularly in regard to tonnages, capacities and possible overbooking.

Knowledge of the dock(s) labour situation is also valuable . . . reputations should be treated seriously; efficiency and effectiveness between ports can vary. Possible limitations of ports equipment must be borne in mind.

Any pre-stowage plan can therefore be treated only as a guide . . . albeit an important one . . . since it provides the Cargo Officer with a degree of flexibility as he plans in 'retrospect' the more favourable use of his available space, from first to final loading port.

In this context, the smaller the number of discharging ports, the less is the problem.

---

the correct technical name of the goods and the class to which they belong. For goods stowed in a freight container there must also be a declaration that the goods are stowed, packed and secured in a container suitable for the purpose, the container being marked with the appropriate I.M.D.G. label at both ends.

2. The Master must compile a list, plan or manifest stating details of all dangerous goods on board, and their location in the stow. Their correct technical name, classification and weight or quantity must also be stated. This Dangerous Goods List is often identified by coloured edging to the paper and, in the case of the shipping note, red printing is invariably used.

Failure to observe these requirements is an offence for which prosecution of the shipper, or the Master, as the case may be, will result.

Other documentary factors affecting cargo movement include the following:—

Export Licences. Required by governments for certain types of cargoes.

Certificates of Origin. To check on duties having been paid.

Shipping Bills. For customs clearance.

Dock Dues Bill. For covering the payment of ports/docks charges.

Consignment Notes. For producing authority for hauliers to move goods.

Contract of Sale. The formal arrangement between exporter and purchaser.

Warehouse Charge. The dues covering goods passing through a warehouse.

Wharfage Charge. The costs/dues covering dock/quay cargo handling.

'Grain Space' and 'Bale Space'. The internal volume of a vessel is measured in two ways.

Firstly . . . the total internal volume, measured from shell plating
to shell plating, and from tank top to under deck is considered to
be 'grain space'.

This space is not only associated with the carriage of grain, as
such, but with any form of bulk cargo which would stow similarly,
that is to say, completely filling the space.

Secondly . . . the internal volume of a compartment measured
from the inner edges of the frames and from tank top to the lower
edge of the beams is considered as 'Bale Space'.

It is obvious that a solid cargo can be stowed only up to the limit
of the frames and beams; therefore, when measuring for general
cargo, it is the bale space which is taken into consideration. This
is not to say that measuring up for the reception of cargo is a
routine job for the cargo officer since the general arrangement plans
and specifications will contain this information in specified form,
and thus can be extracted as required. However, the following
diagrams illustrate the basic methods adopted in 'measuring up' the

HOLD CAPACITIES

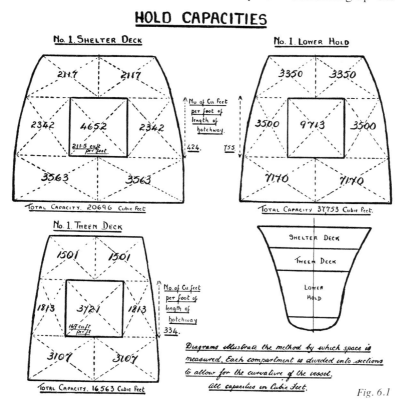

Fig. 6.1

cargo spaces of a vessel. They show the necessity of bearing in mind the curvature of the ship and the fact that usually only in the middle length holds and deck spaces do the sides approach more or less to the upright.

It is good practical procedure to have, in a cargo officer's note book, reference to the space availability in the holds and spaces since it then becomes a comparatively easy matter to keep a check on the space being used while actually in the hold/space supervising the work in hand.

'MEASUREMENT CARGO' AND 'DEADWEIGHT CARGO'

It has been the custom for a considerable number of years to set two standards by which cargo is measured and freight is charged. This is in order to avoid excessive freight charges which might be out of proportion to the space occupied by a particular consignment and to protect the ship from loss of freight *commensurate* with the amount of space used.

Large bulky packages, such as cases of fragile goods or crates of machinery parts require a relatively large volume of space for stowage whilst heavy cargo will most probably require much less in proportion.

Obviously then, it is neither fair nor remunerative to charge freight on the same basis for both types of cargo, for the one uses up more ship space than the other.

Cargo which measures 40 cubic feet or more per ton of weight, is classed as 'Measurement Cargo' whilst cargo which measures less than 40 cubic feet per ton of weight, is classed as deadweight cargo.

THE MATE'S LOG BOOK

The mate's log is a record of everything appertaining to the working of the ship, whether the vessel be at sea or in port. No item is of insufficient importance to record, for, should claims arise respecting damage to ship, crew or cargo, the log book will have to be produced for inspection should the claims be contested.

It is essential that concise and correct entries be made during the time the vessel is working cargo and the following are some of the more important items of loading and discharging which require entry.

1. The times of commencing and completion of work each day, particular note being made of any stoppages due to weather, fault of cargo gear or other causes.

   This is of particular importance if the vessel is on charter, for she is allowed under contract a specified number of days for discharging or loading. This time limit is known as 'Lay Days' and any further extension of time required, other than that allowed for, calls for payment by the ship of money, known as Demurrage.

2. The numbers of the hatches working and the number of gangs of stevedores employed.

This is necessary in order that the vessel may have a check when the bill for stevedoring is tendered.

3. The draught of the vessel at the beginning and end of the day and an entry computed by comparison of two successive days' draught, of the approximate tonnage loaded or discharged.

This can be obtained from the displacement scale which gives the value of the displacement for each draught.

4. When the vessel is at sea, entries regarding the trimming of the ventilators are important.

Ventilation is an outstanding factor in cargo work inasmuch as cargo can be considerably impaired by bad ventilation (see section on ventilation).

Records of the state of weather prevailing, and the precautions taken with the trimming of the ventilators provide data whereby claims for damage arising during transit are met or repudiated. Entries in this respect are also necessary whilst the vessel is in port.

Should any hatch covers be removed during the voyage to assist ventilation, this fact should be recorded in the mate's log book.

The state of the weather prevailing, particularly when at sea, is an important log book entry. Heavy weather and seas—i.e. rolling and pitching—should be specifically recorded. Since these could affect the solidarity of the cargo stow, to which reference would be made in the event of cargo shifting.

PORT SPEED
The Essential Features associated with Port Speed and the Importance of its Successful Accomplishment

Each day that a vessel remains unnecessarily in port results in a reduction of the ship's earning capacity. At the completion of a voyage, the accounts appertaining to the business of the vessel are rendered by the company. The necessary debits are balanced against the credits and the final figure represents the profit made by the vessel on that particular voyage. This is known as determining the earning capacity of the vessel.

Perhaps the outstanding credit item is the 'freight earned' whilst 'dock and wharfage charges' constitute a major debit item.

It is toward reduction of this latter item that 'port speed' is directed, and it is most important to the successful completion of a voyage.

Unnecessary delays in port increase the port dues and allied costs, and invariably the fault can be traced to inefficient distribution of cargo within the vessel. This leads to fewer or unsuitable facilities for speedy loading or discharging, whereas a little forethought would have enabled more gangs to have been employed.

Lack of care in measuring space may result in incorrect information being forwarded to an agent at a subsequent loading port, whose duty it is to book cargo for the vessel. On arrival it may be found that the ship cannot accommodate the particular consignment booked. A knowledge of the trade is essential to any cargo officer in order that he may reserve space for that cargo which he has every reason to believe will be available. It is possible that a considerable tonnage may have to be shifted from one space to another in order to accommodate further cargo, if care is not taken with the measurement of available space.

Within the limits of the space available, consignments of a like nature should be stowed together. Small packages should not be mixed with bulky packages, nor drums with cases; neither should fragile goods be stowed with stronger packages, neglect of which precautions will result in unnecessary delay to transport from the ship, as for example, to the lighters or lorries.

The minimizing of all extraneous costs will reflect substantial credit upon the officer concerned.

STOWAGE FACTORS

For successful loading, a vessel must utilize every cubic foot of space to the best advantage, with due regard to the necessary care and attention to conditions of stowage. Thus the freight earning capability of the vessel is kept at a maximum.

All vessels are provided with capacity plans, which set out the volume content of each compartment and it is important to arrive at a computation of the space which any particular consignment will require and thus be able to determine the remaining space which is available for further cargo.

To do this it is necessary to know the amount of space which each ton of a commodity will require.

This will differ widely with different goods according to their 'light' or 'heavy' nature.

The figure which expresses the amount of space in cubic feet which a ton of any particular cargo will require is known as its 'Stowage Factor'.

The figure does not express the actual measurement of a ton of cargo, but takes into consideration the necessity for dunnage and the form and design of the packages. It is, in fact, the gross amount of space needed for the actual stowage of a ton of the particular cargo in question.

It is unreasonable to expect the stowage factor to apply with equal success to subsequent voyages. Latitude must be allowed in order to cope with the variable factors always possible and generally present. These include the structural design of the compartments, the fact that some cargoes are irregular or nonuniform in size with various shipments, the manner in which a commodity is packed and, in the case of bagged cargo, whether the bags are slack or tightly filled.

Experience is the best guide as to the stowage factor of a commodity and on general trades it is the policy of a cargo officer to check the spaces required for particular goods and so be able to tabulate a reliable list of stowage factors. Most lists given in books are based upon experience and the necessity for 'latitude' explains the reason why a commodity may be given a variable stowage factor; for example, from 69 to 75 cubic feet per ton.

An intelligent knowledge of the use of stowage factors is necessary to all cargo officers in order that they may make economic use of each available space unit.

STOWAGE FACTORS

Commodity	Packages	Cubic feet per ton	Number per ton
Antimony	Cases	17	10 cases
Asphalt	Barrels	42–55	
Beans, green	Bags	57	226–229
Beans, white	Bags	55	lbs per bag
Cassia	Bales	120	30 bales
Gum copal	Baskets	122	14 baskets
Coconut oil	Barrels	68	
Coconut oil	Bulk	39	
Copal	Bags	77	11 bags
Cotton	Bales	65–130	
Essential oils	Cases	56	
Ginger	Casks	60	8 casks
Ginger	Cases	70	20 cases
Hemp	Bales	116	8 bales
Hides	Bales	70–83	
Jelatong	Cases	$49\frac{1}{2}$	$5\frac{1}{2}$ cases
Jute	Bales	48–55	
Kapok	Bales	190	9–10 bales
Latex	Drums	50	$4\frac{1}{2}$ drums
Latex	Cases	60	
Pepper (black)	Bags	93–95	
Pepper (white)	Bags	72–80	
Rubber	Cases	65	9 cases
Rubber	Bales	66	11 bales
Rattans	Bundles	200 (approx.)	28 bundles
Sago flour	Bags	54	13–14 bags
Sugar	Bags	45–52	12–16 bags
Sisal fibre	Bales	70 (Manila)	5 bales
Sisal fibre	Bales	60 (D.E.I.)	4 bales
Tapioca flour	Bags	60	10 bags
Tea (China)	$\frac{1}{2}$ Chests	120–130	30 — $\frac{1}{2}$ chests
Tea (D.E.I.)	$\frac{1}{2}$ Chests	120	20–40
Tea (India & Ceylon)	Cases	90	11 cases
Wool	Bales	60	
Tin	Ingots	10–11	22 ingots

On trades which involve a number of loading ports and from which cargo booked is advised before arrival it is imperative, if cargo is not to be refused, that an officer should use his available space and leave sufficient for this future cargo. This cannot be successfully achieved without a knowledge of the cargo's stowage factor.

Attention is drawn to the diagrams on page 394 illustrating the capacity of each section of a compartment and the amount of space per foot of length. The diagrams were compiled under working conditions on the Far Eastern trade and illustrate the economic use of the stowage factor.

The list of stowage factors on page 400–402 is representative of actual loading conditions.

ON BOARD DISTRIBUTION

The distribution of cargo covers not only its movement to and from a ship but also its place within the vessel, this aspect involving the safety of ship and crew, the effective utilization of space, the assessments of standards desirable in the use of equipment and the conformity to regulations.

It calls for planning, forecasting, co-ordinating and controlling and, as such, involves the four basics in management practice.

In large measure this part of cargo handling is prominent in the examinations for certificates of competency, to which end the text which follows should be studied. It includes factors of:

1. The safety of ship and crew . . . STABILITY . . . insofar as the basics of structural stress, the metacentre, the centre of gravity, righting moments, equilibrium, heavy weights and loading lists apply.
2. Cargo calculations . . . relating to space distribution, safety factors, cargo gear, composition and resolution of forces, curves of displacement and tons per inch, fresh water allowances and cargo routine apply.
3. Shipping notices . . . the ministry notices of The Department of Transport.
4. Shipboard management in practice . . . an experiment carried out by a shipping company.

CARGO PLANNING AND MONITORING

The determination of an acceptable safe and proper cargo load distribution is vital to effective and efficient cargo handling.

Conventionally, appropriate results are invariably manually obtained through the process of preparing Cargo Plans. The modern approach is to utilize computerization. The former includes basic principles; the latter technological analysis.

In this modern age a ship is far more than a 'box' into which goods are placed to be moved from one place to another. It is a piece of technically designed equipment . . . ships are now designed into classes rather than types and are, in the main, appropriate to the trades on which they will operate and the cargoes they will carry. As such, the handling of their purpose must conform to a practice which is not only 'sound' in itself, but also which conforms to rules, regulations and recommendations aimed at the safety of the ship, its cargoes and its personnel.

It would be wrong to discard the conventional basic methods; it would be unwise to ignore the modern approach.

A. Conventional Cargo (Stowage) Planning

Cargo Plans. The Department of Transport, Merchant Shipping Notice M624, draws particular attention to the importance of compiling accurate loading or stowage plans, showing the distribution of weight and capacities, for all types of cargoes both below and above deck.

In general terms however, and in some trades cargo plans are known as stowage plans and may be described as a plan of the stowage of the cargo in the vessel. The outline of a cargo plan shows the vessel in profile and the various decks in plan formation, so that it is possible to show the general distribution of the cargo within the vessel and, also, by means of the deck plans, its actual disposition.

Cargo plans are compiled from the data which each cargo officer should enter in his cargo note book and from the detailed information contained in the mate's receipts or boat notes.

The method and manner in which a cargo plan is compiled depends, to a very large extent, upon the individual ideas of the responsible officer. There is no standard profile, or arrangement; much will depend upon the ingenuity of the officer preparing the plan. 'Different ships, different long splices' is a very true expression and although different shipping companies may stress their own ideas, the essential feature common to all, is that of making it possible to discharge the cargo with as little delay as possible.

A cargo plan, in its simplest term, is a diagrammatic picture of the distribution of cargo within the holds/spaces of a ship . . . picture being the operative term. It serves to show the distribution of the cargo loads, i.e. their own placing and the relationship/proximity to other loads. It has, however, a useful ancillary purpose . . . the compiling of a 'Master Plan' whilst the loading is proceeding . . . such that the Cargo Officer can supervise the loading having regard to space available and the type of cargo 'in situ' available for loading or further consignments yet to arrive, ex ship, or to be picked up at a further port of loading.

The cargo plan need not necessarily be to scale; on the other hand it should not be put together carelessly, for if this was so the 'picture' to be aimed for would be difficult of interpretation. There should be a degree of accuracy in showing the place of the loads . . . preferably with weights and capacities if possible . . . relative to the holds/spaces structure and any obstructions or restrictions therein.

The main purpose of the cargo plan is to assist discharging of cargo, to prevent delay (viz. quick turn round) and to influence correct and appropriate:—

(a) labour and equipment for discharging.
(b) suitable and adequate distribution facilities (warehouse, road, rail or water).
(c) any particular requirements for 'specialist' cargoes.

Systems of stowage relative to the different consignments should be indicated, as for example, in bulk; unitized; fork lift trucks; palletized, preslung, optional discharge and for containers . . . their sizes and contents.

It is usual to adopt a distinctive colour for each port of discharge so that the disposition of the cargo may be easily distinguished in relation to its respective port of discharge. In this manner different consignments may be seen at a glance and the possibility of over-carriage thereby lessened and short delivery avoided. Overcarriage of cargo results in a loss of freight to the ship, for when it is subsequently found, probably at a later port, the ship is responsible for its return to its proper destination.

A copy, or copies of the cargo plan are sent on ahead of the ship, to each port of discharge, so that previous arrangements may be made as to the type of discharging equipment required, the number of gangs to handle the cargo and the proper methods of disposal arranged.

Obviously, considerable time is saved by this arrangement, but it is worthwhile to bear in mind that where a number of copies are to be made from the 'main plan' they will not, if photostat copies are made, reproduce the colours used.

In these circumstances it is useful to add to the plan a schedule list denoting the colours designated for particular ports of discharge.

B. The Modern Approach (Micro Computerization)

Every owner expects a vessel's capacity to be used to the fullest every time she is loaded. It is also expected that loading and discharging shall be carried out as quickly and rationally as possible (port speed and quick turn round) without endangering the structural strength and stability of the ship.

It is also essential, by reason of maritime operational costs, for a ship to have its cargo stowed in the right sequence, in terms of its destination and that, also, the stowage conforms to rules, regulations and recommendations of authorities responsible for ensuring the maritime safety of cargoes, ships and personnel.

The demand for safer and more efficient cargo handling aboard ships is now a prominent requirement. It is no longer a matter of comparison between manual and instrumentation methods but a choice of which systems better suits the circumstances, bearing in mind the technical factors involved, the reliability and ease of handling and the economics of operation.

This can involve lengthy and detailed planning and co-ordination between ship owner/charterer, working (ports) authorities and ship personnel. To effectively promote these functions and to meet the demands of sophisticated cargo distribution, conventional systems are now quickly being replaced by high performance micro computers, albeit some of these systems have now been in operation for quite some time.

One area in which computerization systems have benefited from some considerable research is that which takes the name of 'LOADMASTERS' . . . the parent child of The Kockumation Organization, Box 1044, S 212-10, Malmo, Sweden, to whom we are indebted for its kind permission to include the following notes:—

The systems comprise of three components . . . a computer for processing information relative 'to a ship' (programming); a video terminal for communication with the computer and a print out that provides 'print outs' i.e. results and/or actions to be taken.

Various 'pictures' within the systems provide phases of cargo planning be it for general pre-planning or for more appropriate detailed planning as would be necessary for the specialized container or roll on/roll off vessels, for example, apart from the particular requirements of grain, liquid and dangerous cargoes transportation.

The layout pictures will embrace desirable/necessary weights, vertical centres of gravity (V, C, G) for all cargo decks and spaces, heeling moments, warning limits of distribution, apropos hull stresses and, also, weight destination information for particular loadings. The picture coverage can be wide, in which case the programmes fed into a Loadmaster calculator, by reason of micro computerization, are relative to 'the ship' its design and capacity features. This is important to bear in mind since the resulting print outs can document various cargo distribution alternatives. (It should be emphasized that the programming methods for a ship are those approved by the Classification Societies (or similar official bodies— B.S.R.A. for example) and are covered by approval certificates.)

Cargo planning and monitoring involves Load Types and their distribution, Loading Sequences, Stress Considerations in all classes of vessels, Container and Ro/Ro compartments and, with liquid cargoes predictions for ongoing loading, discharging and simulation, to name but a few major aspects. Stability considerations are paramount.

Every change in the weight and position of cargo results in a different distribution of hull stress . . . the computer processes are such that from appropriate progressing the magnitude of the stresses

... and the permissible limits, can be calculated instantaneously and shown on the video display.

Some particular examples are as follows:—

(a) *Dry Cargoes.* Dry cargo vessel's stability is an important consideration. Programming in a Loadmaster can contain specific Vertical Centres of Gravity for each compartment as well as indications of maximum and minimum values of G.M. recommended by I.M.O. for the ship.

For example . . . the vessel is ready to leave. A last minute request to take on a further load, say 500 tons, is made. Computer programming will provide the answer immediately, taking into account the effects of the overall cargo, ballast, fuel, load type and stress conditions.

(b) *Grain Cargoes.* Computerized information becomes invaluable in order to correctly determine the 'Grain Stability Position' in accordance with I.M.O. recommendations and/or those of other 'international' loading areas relative to the vessel's GM at any time.

Furthermore, grain calculations determine, apart from draft, trim and stability requirements, the need to be aware of Volumetric Moments and Specific Gravities. These are important 'inputs' to the Loadmaster.

Also, I.M.O. recommendations affecting stress factors can be quickly determined to avoid departure from permissible limits.

(c) *Container Cargoes.* (See also pages 408, 424). Information is available covering the light ship condition, i.e. any restrictions to loading/discharging arrangements . . . any limits imposed, as well as desirable loading sequences into decks, bays, cells, tiers, all of which will be related to the load input relative to tanks and stability conditions. Sheer forces, bending moments and torsional influence arising from load distribution, both at sea and in harbour, are also informatively provided, in so far as the Classification Societies allowable limits apply. (Note . . . Hull stress, bending forces and torsional effect are problems applicable to all large vessels with extensive loads, and must always be taken into account.)

(d) Roll on/Roll off vessels . . . much the same will apply as indicated in (c).

(e) *Liquid Cargoes.* Frequently different grades of liquid (petroleum) cargoes are loaded. The specifc gravities will be different and so affect the weight. A situation could arise where four different grades are to be loaded, one for each port of destination. Essential requirements will include water depth at ports of destination, ship trim conditions and bunker consumption. The cargo planning can be prepared quickly and accurately and conditions for each part of the voyage can be pre-calculated.

Simulation and prediction is particularly appropriate to tanker operations. Simulation provides for following the entire loading/discharging procedures, permitting, where necessary, adjustments of flow so that loading or discharging of a number of tanks can be completed at the same time.

Prediction results from computer information predicting the loading/discharging situations at a future point in time.

(f) *Chemical Cargoes.* (i.e. dangerous cargoes). The programming of chemical cargo transportation takes into account the various strict regulations and restrictions that must be obeyed for carrying chemicals in bulk.

Loadmaster applications provide information on:—

1. the proper name of the product and its density.
2. the classification of dangerous good, as per the United Nations reference number.
3. the reactivity grouping.
4. the pollution category.

together with the temperature and type of water to be used for tank cleaning.

The importance of 'care and attention' to chemical cargoes is highly exemplified by the information which can be provided through the micro computer piece of equipment.

Indeed, the 'print out' is a valuable collection of detailed instruction and guide lines, to which ships must follow when engaged in this trade.

(g) *Stability.* Cargo distribution relative to stability is an important responsibility at all times, for 'those concerned with cargo work' but particularly so with a ship at sea.

Circumstances can alter and these will call for continuous and quick analysis. Conventional manual calculations, by their very nature, can be laborious and, possibly, inaccurate. This will have an effect upon safety and, indeed, the desirable stability of the vessel.

Electronic calculators can prevent this. Loadmasters, programmed for the ship, show immediately information on Metacentric Heights, Draft, Trim and Deadweight, as must conform to I.M.O. stability requirements. Particularly is this advantageous in order to conform to the SOLAS-74 Grain stability recommendations.

Information can also be available in determining heeling arising from asymmetrical loading or heavy crane lifts.

Kockumation Marketing Department produce a wide range of informative and technical instruction manuals covering the whole range of Loadmaster equipment, from whom copies may be obtained. If desirable, reference to the organization can be made direct in Malmo or to the U.K. Agents . . . The Energy Marine Co. Ltd., 4 Bridge Street, Leighton Buzzard, Beds. LU7 7AL.

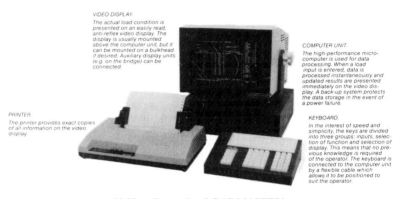

VIDEO DISPLAY.
The actual load condition is presented on an easily read, anti-reflex video display. The display is usually mounted above the computer unit, but it can be mounted on a bulkhead if desired. Auxiliary display units (e.g. on the bridge) can be connected.

COMPUTER UNIT.
The high-performance micro-computer is used for data processing. When a load input is entered, data is processed instantaneously and updated results are presented immediately on the video display. A back-up system protects the data storage in the event of a power failure.

PRINTER.
The printer provides exact copies of all information on the video display.

KEYBOARD.
In the interest of speed and simplicity, the keys are divided into three groups: inputs, selection of function and selection of display. This means that no previous knowledge is required of the operator. The keyboard is connected to the computer unit by a flexible cable which allows it to be positioned to suit the operator.

'A New Generation LOADMASTER'
(by kind permission of Kockumation)

Cargo Planning by Satellite

Whereas telex links, via satellite, has previously been available for container operations, as between ports, it is now available for ro/ro and mixed cargoes, providing rapid advance information on shipments, programming and space availability.

STABILITY

The Principles involved when Loading and Carrying Cargoes

When a ship is built her structural design will affect very largely her stability qualities. A ship is said to be 'stiff' or 'tender' according to whether she is difficult or easy to incline and the extent of one or the other of these characteristics is the result of collaboration between the naval architect and builder in the design and build of the vessel. Considerations of trade and cargoes likely to be carried will affect the design of a vessel to no small extent. Ships are now much larger than hitherto for similar previous trades; engine room design is now much more related to the stern of the vessel than amidships, leaving clearer and wider space for cargo capacity; tankers of large deadweight have beam dimensions far in excess of earlier designs for similar lengths . . . notably is this fact dominant with V.L.C.C.s . . . while timber vessels need to be broad in relation to draught.

General traders require a more normal appropriate design and vessels built for the passenger trades, particularly with both short sea and deep sea roll on/roll off ferries, are built to a special design.

In every case, however, the vessel is built as to be subject to minimum stresses and seaworthy in normal conditions . . . allowing for extraneous circumstances.

Officers have little, if any, influence on design but they should be able to appreciate the likely stability qualities of their vessels, which, in point of fact are included in the *Stability handbook for the ship*, and this more especially because they are held responsible for the behaviour of their vessels at sea. In no manner is this more so than in the distribution of cargo loading.

Structural and local stresses can be considerably increased or decreased by the manner in which a vessel is loaded and her seaworthiness much influenced by the distribution of the deadweight load.

The object of this section is not to teach the subject of stability but to show how necessary is a knowledge of this most important matter in keeping ship stresses within normal limits, thereby causing any vessel to be adjudged a 'comfortable ship'. Cargo work is thus closely related to the question of ship stability and the stresses involved.

The Stresses of Loading. Although the total weight of the ship afloat equals the total buoyancy, the distribution of that weight is not constant throughout the ship's length nor is the upward buoyancy the same, particularly when the ship is among waves.

If the vessel is supported on a wave crest amidships, the deficiency of buoyancy at the ends produces a tendency for the latter to droop, a condition known as 'hogging'. Similarly, a trough amidships would produce a tendency for the middle to droop, known as 'sagging'. In between these extreme conditions there will be varying tension or compression stresses at the top and bottom parts of the hull, which are known as 'bending stresses'. Bending stresses are present even in still water but in these cases the distribution of weight in the hull is the responsible factor. (See Fig. 6.2.)

If the weight distribution is not uniform along the length (and this is invariably so since machinery spaces and cargo placing offer infinite variety of possibilities) then there will be points at which the difference of vertical forces upward and downward will constitute what is known as a 'sheering force' which tends to distort the hull. The distribution of cargo is the critical factor here, particularly if the load consists of small high-density items.

In practice, the calculation of shear force and bending moments is carried out as part of the 'loading pre planning'. Maximum operational bending moments are specified as part of the ship's

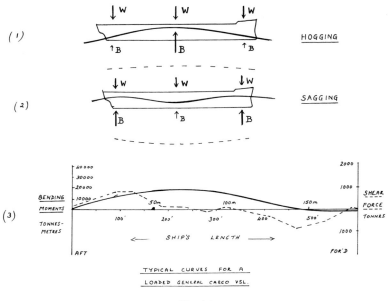

Fig. 6.2

stability information and are incorporated in the stability handbook for the ship.

Formerly it was the general practice to work on rule of thumb such as the distribution of 60 per cent of weight amidships and 40 per cent at the ends or on the basis for vertical distribution of 35 per cent in the 'tween decks and 65 per cent in the lower holds. Modern practice, however, considers these approximations to be too uncertain, taking into account the complexity of modern ships and specialization of their design. (See Fig. 6.2.)

None the less, it is not out of place to remember that the fore and aft distribution of weight affects the pitching of the vessel. With a slow pitching movement there is a strong tendency for a vessel to bury her forward end and consequently ship heavy water. Apart from the additional weight thus involved and its effect upon local structural stress, there is the danger of damage to deck fittings. A vessel with a moderately quick fore and aft motion is less likely to experience such effects and, in general, from the point of view of safety of life at sea, the quicker fore and aft motion is desirable and this is largely obtained by a greater part of the load distribution towards the middle of the vessel, albeit large bulk carriers and container vessels cannot always achieve this end, irrespective of the bulbous bow design.

The Stability of the Ship. Stability of a vessel may be defined as the power of a vessel to return to the upright when inclined from the vertical by an external force. Stability is dependent upon the interaction of two forces, viz. weight and buoyancy, and to a slightly lesser extent, on the position of what is known as the metacentre. In designing a vessel, the naval architect is able to determine the position of the centre of buoyancy and the metacentre. The former item will depend upon the shape of the underwater form and the respective draughts to which the vessel is to be loaded.

A vessel built to the highest standard of specification and with a high degree of structural stability, can be entirely altered in stability behaviour, if an officer fails to realize the importance of the centre of gravity position.

It is essential for the Master and officers to study the behaviour of their vessel under all conditions and at every stage of loading, in order to achieve the most satisfactory positions of *BM* and *G*.

In order that a vessel may remain at rest in still water, these positions will be situated as shown in Figs. 6.3–6.4. The forces of buoyancy have a resultant which acts vertically upwards through *B*, and, similarly, the weight resultant acts vertically downward through *G*. These resultants are equal and opposite and flotation is the result.

When a vessel is heeled over as a result of external force, the centre of gravity remains in the same position relative to the ship,

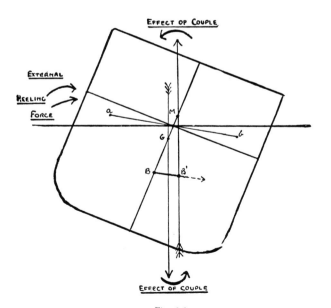

Fig. 6.3.

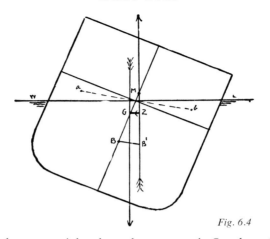

Fig. 6.4

provided that no weights have been moved. On the other hand, the centre of buoyancy will move its position owing to change of underwater form.

The change of underwater form is effected by the two wedges of emmersion and immersion, whose respective centres of gravity are 'a' and 'b'. As the centre of buoyancy must always take up a position at the centre of the underwater form, it moves out along a line parallel to the line joining the centres 'a' and 'b' of the wedges, and for a distance which bears the same ratio to *ab* as the volume of the wedge bears to the volume of displacement of the vessel. Taking an example: If the volume of the wedge is equivalent to 500 tons, and the displacement of the vessel 5000 tons, then if *ab* is 40 feet, *B* will move out $\dfrac{500}{5000} \times \dfrac{40}{1} = 4$ feet.

So long as the vessel does not heel to angles of more than 12 to 15 degrees, the resultant buoyancy line acting upwards through the new position *B*, will pass through the structural position of *M*. Up to such angles of heel, *M* may be considered a fixed point, and for normal weather conditions may be accepted as such without undue trouble, but for larger angles of heel *M* will move in relation to the new positions of *B*. The vessel thus inclined is now under the influence of a 'couple' caused by the weight resultant acting downwards through *G* and that of the buoyancy acting upwards through B_1, with a horizontal distance between their directions. Upon this horizontal separation depends the whole condition of stability of the vessel, for like all heeled bodies, the vessel will endeavour to return to the position in which the two forces act in vertical opposition, viz. upright.

The forces of buoyancy and weight endeavour to bring the vessel back to the upright by reducing the horizontal separation to zero.

These forces will influence the turning of the vessel at the balancing point *G*, and can be said to act at right angles on the lever *GZ*. The moment necessary to right the vessel is therefore the product of the force of buoyancy and the length of the lever *GZ*.

The measure of this product is known as the Moment of Statical Stability or Righting Moment, and gives rise to the formula.

Force of Buoyancy × Horizontal Separation of *G* and *B* = Moment of Statical Stability. This is often stated as:

Displacement × *GZ* (Righting Lever) = Righting Moment.

Since the displacement of a vessel will remain the same for any particular state of loading, it follows that the length of *GZ* will be the determining factor. This length will in turn be influenced by the position of *G* within the vessel, and reference to the preceding diagrams will show how the stability of the vessel is affected by altering the position of *G*. (i.e. Fig. 6.5).

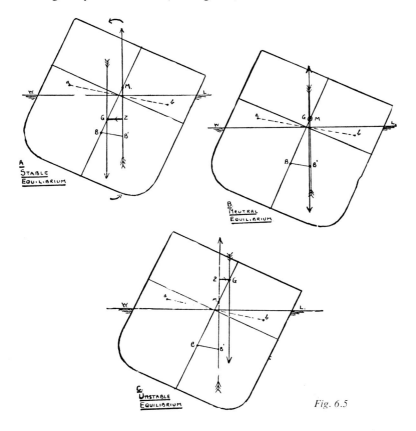

Fig. 6.5

Stable Equilibrium. (a) This diagram illustrates a vessel so loaded that *G* lies well below *M*. The lever *GZ* is therefore comparatively large and the resulting couple is such that the vessel will return to the upright after removal of the inclining force.

Neutral Equilibrium. (b) In this case the vessel has been loaded with a preponderance of weight in the upper parts of the structure. *G* is therefore high in the vessel and may take up a position co incident with that of *M*. There is now no horizontal separation of *G* and *B*, and therefore no couple or righting lever *GZ*. Consequently there is no tendency for the vessel to move one way or the other. *She certainly will not return to the upright.*

Unstable Equilibrium. (c) Extremely bad loading has brought *G* very high in the vessel, so high that it lies *above M*. It will be noted that there is a horizontal separation of *G* and *B*, but, instead of a righting couple, an upsetting couple is produced. The position of the lever *GZ* is such that the vessel is liable to heel farther, and will be in danger of capsizing.

It should be obvious from the foregoing observations, that distribution of cargo, in affecting the position of *G*, is a very important consideration. An officer aware of the position of *M* in his vessel should arrange his loading so that the *GZ* lever never rises above *M*. Should this happen the vessel would lose positive stability. Consecutive voyages will enable an officer who keeps records of data, to determine the most satisfactory position of *G* below *M* for any state of loading.

Many companies require their officers to keep stability data records, and have standing orders to the effect that information concerned with the relative positions of *G* and *M* shall be sent to the head office on completion of loading. Although this entails a little extra work, it is valuable, instructive and worth while, and in addition, serves to emphasise the relationship between strict attention to stability and efficiency in the case of a cargo officer's work.

The distance of *G* below (or above) *M* is known as the Metacentric Height *GM*, and besides governing the length of the righting lever and the ability of the vessel to return to the upright, is responsible for the power or force with which the vessel returns to the upright or has a tendency to roll. No vessel can return from an inclined position and stop directly the upright position is attained; it must move in a manner analogous to that of a pendulum, gradually lessening its extent of movement or roll. If the lever is exceptionally large, the initial power to resist heeling will be large, but when once inclined, the power to roll will be correspondingly large and the movement of the ship will be heavy and quick. The converse is the case when the lever is small, and the two conditions are related to what are termed *Stiff and Tender vessels.*

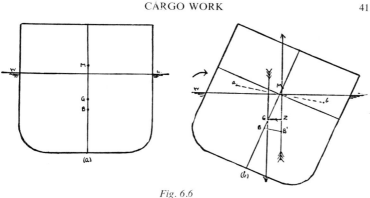

Fig. 6.6

The distribution of weight within the vessel is solely responsible for either of these conditions, inasmuch as it affects the position of G, and therefore the Metacentric Height and the lever GZ.

Fig. 6.6a is a vessel floating upright at the water line w*l*, with B, M, and G shown in their respective positions. Note the large distance of G below M, probably due to the greater weight of the cargo being loaded in the lower holds.

Fig. 6.6b is the same vessel heeled over as from the application of external force. Note the length of the horizontal separation between G and B and consequently the length of the lever GZ. Trigonometrical calculations are omitted for simplicity, but let us assume that the length of this lever is 3 feet, for a vessel having at this draught a displacement of 6000 tons.

The measure of the power with which this vessel returns to the upright is:

Force of Buoyancy × Horizontal Separation (GZ)
= Displacement × GZ.
= 6000 tons × 3 feet.
= 18 000 foot-tons.

All this energy has to be expended before the vessel finally comes to rest and she will have to roll from side to side, each time lessening the period, until this is achieved. Should the wave motion be responsible for the heeling of the ship as is usually the case, a vessel so loaded will roll heavily, for, as she moves from side to side under the influence of the waves, she will be first storing up energy and then releasing same. If the maximum angle of heel is as shown in diagram, the energy will be 18 000 foot-tons as she begins to move from port towards starboard, or vice versa. In the endeavour to expend this energy completely and remain upright, the vessel will probably roll heavily and jerkily, and though not in danger of capsizing, will sustain damage to the structure and may cause the cargo to shift.

It will consequently be realised how dangerous this might be.

Conditions of loading such as would result in a large Metacentric Height, and thus a 'Stiff Ship', do not suggest ideal stability qualities and it behoves a cargo officer to bear in mind the position of M whilst supervising the loading.

With vessels of moderately large beam, M will have a high position in the vessel $\left(\text{see formula } BM = \dfrac{I}{V} \right)$ and, thus, in order to achieve a moderately satisfactory Metacentric Height, a certain amount of the heavy cargo will have to be given upper stowage in order to raise G. Vessels of different class and design will require different values of GM, and no definite value can be stated until experience has shown how a vessel reacts to a particular Metacentric Height. As a guide, it is worthy of note that a 10 000-ton shelter deck type of cargo liner, fully loaded in Far Eastern ports, with a draft 28 ft, behaved remarkably well when crossing the Indian and Atlantic Oceans, her Metacentric Height being 1 ft 8 in.

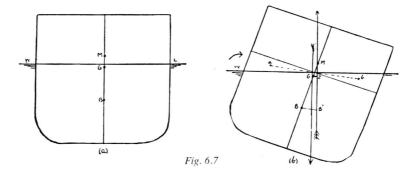

Fig. 6.7

Fig. 6.7a and b represents the same vessel as shown in Fig. 6.6 with the same displacement as before, floating at the same draught. The distribution of weight, however, is such that G is high in the vessel, giving rise to a small Metacentric Height. This is probably due to the greater part of the cargo being loaded (erroneously) in the upper parts of the vessel. When the vessel suffers inclination, the horizontal separation between G and B will be considerably less than was the case with the stiff vessel. Comparing the two sets of diagrams, let us assume this separation to be 9 in for a similar angle of heel as before.

The measure of the power by which this vessel returns to the upright is:

Force of buoyancy × Horizontal separation
= Displacement × GZ.
= 6000 tons × 0·75 ft.
= 4500 ft-tons.

This represents considerably less power than that appertaining to the stiff vessel. The ability of the vessel to oppose rolling is considerably less, and the manner of rolling is entirely different. Bearing in mind the observation concerning the movement of the stiff vessel as being the effect of wave motion, it will follow that a tender vessel will heel very easily and when once heeled, will exhibit no apparent power to return quickly. Her rolling period will be long, slow, and sluggish.

Though there is less stress upon the structure and little chance of cargo shifting provided it is well stowed, the vessel will tend to ship much water, and if in a long heavy swell, there is the possibility of synchronism which might lead to ultimate capsizing. Synchronism is, however, a possibility with stiff vessels also, under certain circumstances.

The disadvantage of a tender vessel lies in the fact that due to consumption of bottom bunkers, G may approach too near M or even above it, thereby reducing the righting moment to a small or even negative quantity. It will be apparent that neither a stiff vessel nor a tender one is conducive to satisfactory seaworthiness, and therefore the loading of cargo must be arranged to achieve a happy medium.

Synchronism. The movement of water, in the form of waves, takes up an orbital movement similar to that of a revolving wheel.

As the wave moves along, each successive crest will pass a stationary object at almost equal intervals of time. This is known as 'The period of the wave'.

Should the oscillation of the ship be less than half this wave period, the rolling of the ship will be 'with' the movement of the wave. This can have disastrous results if the vessel is badly loaded as to have unsuitable stability, for she may continue to roll with the waves, gradually increasing her rolling period until she is liable to turn completely over.

This is known as 'Synchronising' and is common to extremely stiff vessels as well as to very tender ones.

VESSEL WITH A DECK LOAD OF TIMBER

The observations relating to tender vessels must be carefully borne in mind when considering a vessel loaded with a deck load of timber. Due to the weight of the cargo on deck, the centre of gravity of the vessel will be high in the vessel, and a small Metacentric Height will result. During the voyage the deck load of timber will most probably become heavier due to absorption of water from rain and spray. This will cause a further rise in a position of G and unless precautions have been taken to counteract this rise of G, it may move to above M. The vessel will then have negative stability and will be in a condition of unstable equilibrium. This is usually the cause of timber-laden vessels taking a list.

An interesting point arises here, for as the vessel moves over, the change in the underwater form causes a change in the position of *B*. Although it was pointed out that *M* may be considered a fixed point, in actual practice it is always moving, depending upon the change of *B*. It is very likely therefore that the outward movement of *B* may permit the upward buoyancy force acting through the new position of *B*, to cause a slight rise in *M* sufficient to raise it above *G* and thereby produce a slight positive stability. This would prevent any further increase in the angle of list. It is advisable to ensure that there is a certain proportion of bottom weight available either in the form of cargo or ballast tanks filled, before the vessel commences to load the timber on deck.

LOADING AND DISCHARGING HEAVY WEIGHTS

'*Critical Moment*'. Attention is drawn to the remarks contained in the section on Cargo Gear.

The 'critical moment' factor must not be looked at in isolation; that is to say it is not an aspect having relevance to a 'heavy weight' interpreted literally. It has application with any form of excessive load which is being loaded or discharged, at the time when the vessel is light and, perhaps, with only a small or neutral metacentric height.

A moderate degree of stiffness when working cargo is always advantageous but particularly so when first loading 'heavy bottom' weight or discharging 'heavy loads' following the completion of the rest of the cargo. In this latter case, immediately the load clears the bottom of the hold its weight is transferred to the derrick head. This distance could be considerable and on the premise of the stability formula ... Movement of the Ship Centre of Gravity is the result of ...

$$\frac{\text{the weight} \times \text{its distance moved}}{\text{vessel's displacement}}$$ there could be disadvantage effect

upon the vessel's metacentric height and a diminishing of positive stability.

Among other things, this could cause the vessel to list, which is far from desirable when working cargo at this stage.

Cases are on record of cargo remaining in the hold . . . as yet undischarged . . . shifting or slipping . . . giving rise to accidents to those engaged in the unloading procedures, while a listing vessel is unhelpful in containing the proper use of cargo gear . . . particularly derricks.

A feature of this probability is the fact that while the load remains vertically in line with it's upward movement the problem may not arise, but as soon as the derrick 'swings' the load to the quayside, the problem arises. Another feature of this hazard is the fact that some ships can be liable to listing in the light condition ... a constructional feature ... which prompts the point that 'ship's officers should know their own ship'.

This is the practical interpretation of the 'Critical Moment' to which due attention must be given . . . i.e. adding bottom weight (ballast) to offset any rise in the ship's centre of gravity.

Associated with the foregoing is the question of 'free surface' of water or liquid in bottom tanks. This must be avoided.

Free surfaces reduces metacentric height as a vessel lists. It is a stability consideration. (See 'Principles and Practices of Ship Stability' same author and publisher.) The critical moment is a cargo working factor.

As has been mentioned previously, a cargo officer is in a position to affect materially the stability of his vessel. It is hoped that this section will serve to illustrate some of the more important points worthy of consideration. It is strongly recommended that every young officer should acquire a text-book on Stability, and co-ordinate its study with the practical experience he is gaining in this important subject. This part of sea education cannot be commenced too early.

PRACTICAL CARGO STABILITY

Individual methods of applying the study of stability to cargo work vary somewhat with the company in which an officer may be serving. Most of the larger companies issue very definite instructions concerning the stability of their ships during loading and discharging.

Briefly, the following points should be kept in mind when considering practical cargo stability.

1. The ship should be loaded to a moderate value of GM.
2. In achieving this, distribution of cargo should avoid tenderness or stiffness.
3. In the early stages of loading a tendency to stiffness is probably an advantage for it ensures a steady and upright ship during loading.
4. The movement of the centre of gravity, during loading, should be carefully watched in order to prudently arrange for the distribution of later cargo arrivals.
5. It should be possible to calculate the GM before leaving an intermediate port in order to facilitate the booking of suitable cargo at later ports.
6. Similar calculations should be easily possible in order to arrange each succeeding day's distribution of cargo.
7. It should always be possible for a cargo officer to discuss distribution of water or fuel with the engineers without undue concern for the effect upon the stability of his ship.
8. When loading 'Heavy Cargo' an officer must be sure of the

stability of his ship, bearing in mind the disturbing factors at work under such conditions.

9. A cargo officer should always be aware of any slack tanks and take this into consideration when computing the GM.

10. A cargo officer should take into consideration the weather likely to be experienced on the ensuing voyage and load his ship in such a manner that draught and trim will reasonably ensure a comfortable voyage.

With the above general points in mind it is necessary for a cargo officer to make himself familiar with those tables and plans issued to a ship upon completion.

These include:
'Deadweight and Displacement Tables'.
'Tons per Inch Tables'.
'Tables showing the Value of the Inch Trim Moment'.
'Tables showing the Vertical position of the Metacentric for any draught'.

During the actual loading, and with the question of a co-ordinate check upon the stability, a cargo officer should keep, in his cargo notebook, a record of the distribution of each parcel or consignment, its weight and the position of its centre of gravity above the keel.

Summarized Aspects of Practical Cargo Stability Considerations

1. Reference to the stability handbook (the trim and stability particulars) is essential in cargo working.

2. Attention to Codes of Practice and Merchant Shipping Notices . . . inter alia stability needs is essential.

3. A moderate GM (Metacentric Height) is preferable for a loaded vessel, avoiding neither stiffness nor tenderness, while at the earlier stages of loading a degree of stiffness is advantageous.

4. GM . . . Metacentric Heights . . . Calculations should be determined from the cargo handbook at the end of each day's work and certainly before leaving final or intermediate port's loading or discharging. (This is part of cargo work planning and has particular relevance to multi-purpose ship working.

5. Attention to the critical moment factor, when moving 'heavy weights or loads' at the time of a vessel having a 'small' GM, is essential.

Synchronism is a condition of movement in a vessel arising out of its stability which may well be influenced by the loading and distribution of the cargo.

In synchronism the vessel tends to roll with the waves, or 'keeps time' with them and with such conditions existing may well receive an added impulse at the extremity of a roll, the consequences of which could cause the vessel to lurch heavily if the statical forces were small. It is such a state of affairs that promotes cargo shifting.

To prevent or minimise the possibility of synchronism, it is preferable to obtain a reasonable metacentric height by bottom weight distribution but, in the distribution of 'upper deck' stowage, weights should be 'winged out'.

NOTE: Students are recommended to study the associate publication to this volume, namely *The Principles and Practices of Ship Stability*, which deals with those principles of stability affecting the design of a vessel and the proper loading and carriage of cargoes in consequence thereof.

Cargo work and stability cannot be separated; they are two very essential associated subjects and no ship can be properly handled without applying each function with the other.

Increasing importance is being paid by The Ministry of Transport to the question of stability in ships and it is thus important young officers should appreciate that the efficient and judicious loading of their vessel affects considerably its stability qualities and, as a result, its safety at sea.

LOAD STRESS IN LARGE VESSELS

Of recent years a number of vessels have been 'lost'—for unexplainable reasons and some 'breaking up' while loading/unloading, in equally disturbing circumstances.

Some V.L.C.C.s in the petroleum business have been prone to these considerations (or have been thought to have been), though the examples can equally be shown with other heavy bulk load ships.

In the case of V.L.C.C.s the trouble is considered to be a matter of internal structural weakening, as a result of age (10 years) brought about by uneven loading, with little evidence by which ship officers could be aware of the problem, though it should not be thought that 'age' is the only factor.

As a result of the foregoing, a report on the circumstances has been prepared by a well known reputable firm of British Naval Architects, an outline of which was recently published in the magazine *Lloyds Ship Manager*. We are indebted to the editor for permission to refer to this outline, and attention is drawn to the points which follow:

(a)   One aspect appears to be the practice of multiporting where vessels move from one port to another to pick up different cargoes of crude, such that they become loaded with grades of oil having variations in specific gravity as much as 10%. On discharge these vessels may do so at a number of different oil terminals.

(b)   Another feature is the insidious corrosion effect upon V.L.C.C.s as they become 'aged' and suggestion exists that incorrect

LOADING LIST

S.S. .... Voyage ....

Date	Loading Port	Cargo	Stowage	Weight Tons	KG Feet	Moment (Foot Tons)	Load K.G.	Mean Draft	K.M.	G.M. Feet
6/4/35	Hong Kong Light Ship (incl. fuel & water)	—	—	7350	28·2	207 270	—	13 ft 2 in	32·6 ft	+4·4
		Rattans	No. 4 L.H.	70	8·0	560				
		Tin	No. 2 L.H.	80	5·0	400				
6/4/35	Sailed to Manila			7500		208 230	27·7 ft	13 ft 6 in	32·2 ft	+4·5
5 days		Fuel Consumption	2, 3 & 6 Tank	−120	2·0	240				
		Water		−8	30·0	240				
11/4/35	Manila	Sugar	No. 2 L.H.	7372	10·0	207 750	28·2 ft	13 ft 3 in	32·5 ft	+4·3
		Veg. & Oil	Deep Tank	350	10·0	3 500				
		Sugar	No. 6 L.H.	1300	12·0	13 000				
		Coconut Oil	No. 3 T.D.	480	23·5	5 760				
		Sisal	2 & 5 S.D.K.	10	31·0	235				
				140		4 340				
		Domestic	4 Tank	9652	2·0	234 585	24·3 ft	18 ft 0 in	25·2 ft	+0·9 ft
		Water		120		240				
14/4/35	Sailed for Macassar			9772		234 825	24·0 ft	18 ft 3 in	25·1 ft	+1·1 ft

Loading List continued ——

Date		Fuel Const. & water	1 & 7 Tank	60	2·0	120	24·2 ft	18 ft 1 in	25·2 ft	+1·0 ft
16/4/35	Macassar			9712		234 705				
		Tapioca Flour	No. 2 L.H.	420	9·0	3 780				
		Rubber	No. 2 L.H.	570	12·0	6 840				
		Tapioca Flour	No. 5 L.H.	600	11·0	6 600				
		Gum	2 & 5 T.D.K.	100	24·0	2 400				
17/4/35	Sailed for Batavia			11 402		254 325	22·3 ft	21 ft 7 in	24·0 ft	+1·7 ft
		Fuel & water consumption	2 & 5 Tank	60	2·0	120				
19/4/35	Batavia			11 342		254 205	22·4 ft	21 ft 5 in	23·8 ft	+1·4 ft
		Pepper	3, 5 & 6 S.D.K.	250	31·0	7 750				
		Rubber	No. 5 L.H.	530	14·0	7 420				
		Kapok	S T.D.K.	30	22·0	660				
		Gum	2 & 3 T.D.K.	170	24·0	4 080				
21/4/35	Sailed for Singapore			12 322		274 115	22·2 ft	23 ft 5 in	23·8 ft	+1·6 ft

Remarks: Load Lower Hold Cargo and increase this G.M.

Remarks: Lift all available deadweight Singapore with general distribution to achieve $G.M.$ of $+2$ ft, thus allowing for Upper Deck completion at Penang for $G.M.$ of $+1·8$ ft.

loading sequences result in the failure of structural longitudinals through cracking and buckling. (By no means should
this feature be exclusive to tankers.)

(c)   The report refers to the methods of stress measuring by
classification societies, and others, while these large vessels are
building, but points out that, by reason of their great length,
absolute determination is extremely difficult to assess.

(d)   Part of the answer, it is contended, is wider informative
training of ship personnel, not only in the appreciation of
stress resulting from uneven and thoughtless load planning
and distribution, but also in the use of specialized equipment
such as LOADMETERS (or LOADMASTERS). This latter
fact is now becoming more universal in the maritime world.

Note: The I.M.O. (1981) Bulk Cargo Code draws attention to
the foregoing, with bulk cargoes—'Structural damage due to improper distribution of cargo (see page 211) and points out that,
in general, high density cargoes should be loaded in lower hold
spaces rather than in tween deck cargo spaces. Where this may be
unavoidable, particular attention must be given to the stability
qualities of the vessel and in conformity with the guide lines laid
down in the stability information booklet supplied to the ship.

Heavy density cargoes give rise to 'stiff vessels' and an excessive
GM, resulting in violent movement in a seaway, which, in itself, can
lead to structural stress.

CARGO CALCULATIONS

Distribution of Cargo. Safety Factors. Parallelogram of Forces,
(Stresses and Strains). Disposal of Cargo. Freight. 'Displacement'
and 'Tons per Inch' Curves. Allowance for Density.

The successful carriage of cargo is not entirely the result of careful
loading, handling, stowage and discharge. A considerable amount of
calculation enters into the operation and in the course of service a
cargo officer will become increasingly aware of the necessity to
measure and compute space accurately; to determine correctly the
safety factor with regard to blocks and tackles and to be always
aware of the fact that the ship must never be overloaded.

The use of 'displacement' and 'tons per inch' curves are very
closely allied to the work of all cargo officers. This is especially so
when a vessel is loading or discharging under charter and care has
to be exercised as to the proper tonnage worked per day, whilst both
types of curves serve useful and necessary purposes with regard to
cargo distribution and the stability of the vessel.

Although the freight earning capability of a ship is primarily the
concern of the ship owner or agent, occasions do arise, as for
example, in out of the way ports, when the Master or Officers are
called upon to compute the freight on small consignments of cargo.

Apart from this, however, cargo officers should be familiar with the elementary principles of freight computation in so far as it affects the weight or measurement of the cargo.

It can be appreciated that the carriage of cargo is a complex and vast operation and does not lend itself to isolated examples of cargo calculations.

The purpose of this Section is to illustrate a few of the more general and practical types likely to be encountered in general cargo carriage.

The Measurement and Computation of Spaces, both used and available. This type of problem considers the space available in a cargo compartment at the beginning of loading or discharging and the final space or tonnage in hand on completion.

It is necessary to know the dimensions of a compartment, the tonnage and stowage factor of cargo available and the allowances, if any, for broken stowage.

Calculations involving available space are very practical, for they permit officers to compute the tonnage and amount of further cargo that it is possible to load into an already partly filled compartment.

The Safety Factor as regards Cargo Gear. Various and many are the types of cargo blocks, wires and ropes available for cargo work.

Every wire, rope, and block has a specified safe working load, which varies with the size and class. The safe working loads are given in the section on cargo gear, but these refer to the use of the gear as a single unit.

When rove as tackles ropes and wires will safely lift greater loads than when used singly. This is in conformity with the general principles of mechanics in so far as use is made of 'Velocity ratios' and mechanical advantage.

By increasing the number of times that a wire or rope is rove through multiple sheave blocks greater purchase or lifting power is obtained for a lesser amount of power or force required. It is because of this that derricks and winches, of normal size and power, can be used to lift relatively heavy loads.

To obtain 100 per cent efficiency when working cargo tackles, the blocks, wires and ropes should work together without resistance. This is obviously impossible, for friction is always present and tends to restrict the efficiency of a tackle. Under normal working conditions one tenth of the weight being lifted may be allocated as frictional resistance per sheave. With heavy derrick tackle some opinions favour friction being considered as low as 2 per cent.

Attention is drawn to the desirability of studying the theory of pulleys and machines, as a branch of mechanics. Many books, both elementary and advanced, are available on this subject, and it will soon be realised how large is the influence of this subject upon cargo gear and its use.

DISTRIBUTION OF CARGO

It frequently happens that a ship is chartered to carry cargoes of a bulk nature with only two commodities to fill the vessel.

The cargo officer is therefore obliged to determine the actual space and tonnage available and distribute this cargo so that the vessel is fully loaded; in a reasonable state of trim and has satisfactory stability qualities.

The type of problem is best appreciated by reference to the following example.

A ship of 3520 tons deadweight has on board 420 tons of stores and bunkers and 70 tons of water. Stow timber (at 35 cubic feet per ton) and Rolls of Paper (at 120 cubic feet per ton) so as to fill the ship. The hold capacities are: No. 1. 55 100 cu ft, No. 2. 55 970 cu ft, No. 3. 44 100 cu ft, No. 4. 35 900 cu ft.

It will be necessary first to find out how many tons of each commodity can be placed in the ship, and afterwards divide such amounts among the holds in proportion to their sizes. The first can be done by solving a simultaneous equation as shown below, and the distribution can be made by means of the ratio the cubic capacity of each hold bears to the cubic capacity of the whole ship.

1. First, to find the deadweight available for cargo:

Stores	420 tons	Total deadweight	3520
Water	70 tons	Stores and water	490
Total	490 tons	Cargo	3030

2. To find the amount of each commodity that can be loaded in the ship.

Let x = the number of tons of timber and y = the number of tons of paper.

Then $x + y = 3030$ (1st equation).

Hold capacities	No. 1.	55 100 cu ft
	No. 2.	55 970 cu ft
	No. 3.	44 100 cu ft
	No. 4.	35 900 cu ft
	Total	191 070 cu ft

Then $35x + 120y = 191\,070$ (2nd equation).

The equations are solved by the elimination of either x or y, and finding the other unknown.

Suppose we decide to eliminate x. To do this multiply the 1st equation by 35.

Then $35x + 35y = 106\,050$ and $35x + 120y = 191\,070$ (2nd equation).

Subtracting the smaller: $85y = 85\,020$

$$y = \frac{85\,020}{85} = 1000 \text{ (nearly).}$$

The total number of tons of Paper will thus be 1000 and of Timber $3030 - 1000 = 2030$.

3. To distribute the commodities pro rata amongst the holds.

This can be done by simple proportion:
Total cubic capacity of ship : Capacity of particular hold : :
Number of tons in the ship : Number of tons in particular hold.

To find the number of tons of Timber in No. 1 hold.

$191\,070 : 55\,100 : : 2030 : x$

$$x = \frac{2030 \times 55\,100}{191\,070}$$

2030 log 3·307496
55 100 log 4·741152

8·048648
191 070 log 5·281191

x log 2·767457

$x = 585\cdot4$ tons.

To find the number of tons of Paper in No. 1 hold.

$191\,070 : 55\,100 : : 1000 : y$

$$y = \frac{55\,100 \times 1000}{191\,070}$$

1000 log 3·000000
55 100 log 4·741152

7·741152
191 070 log 5·281191

log 2·459961

$y = 288\cdot4$

In No. 1 hold therefore we have 585·4 tons Timber and 288·4 tons Paper.

The amounts for the other holds can be found in the same way.

EXAMPLES FOR EXERCISE

1. Loading bales of wool (at 110 cubic ft per ton) and bricks (at 15 cubic ft per ton) in 4 holds. Deadweight 3500 tons, 60 tons of water and 420 tons of fuel and other stores on board. Dispose of the cargo, supposing hold capacities are as follows: No. 1, 55 100 cubic ft; No. 2, 55 930 cubic ft; No. 3, 44 100 cubic ft; No. 4, 35 900 cubic ft.

2. A vessel's deadweight is 3300 tons and she has on board 440 tons of coal stores and water. The capacities of the holds are: No. 1, 45 300 cubic ft; No. 2, 50 600 cubic ft; No. 3, 55 750 cubic ft; No. 4, 48 550 cubic ft. Stow the following

consignments of cotton at 70 cubic ft to the ton: 900 Manchester, 1000 tons optional Manchester–Liverpool, and the remainder for Liverpool. Vessel must be down to her marks.

ANSWERS (IN TONS)

	No. 1	No. 2	No. 3	No. 4
1. Wool	442·5	449·1	354·1	288·3
Bricks	428·6	435·1	343·1	279·3
2. Manchester	203·6	227·5	250·6	218·3
Optional	226·3	252·7	278·5	242·5
Liverpool	217·3	242·6	267·3	232·8

Curves of 'Displacement' and 'Tons per Inch'. In every ship there will be found curves of 'displacement' and 'tons per inch'. They form part of the stability information issued by the naval architect when the vessel is handed over to the owners.

Their use is very varied, from enabling an officer to compute tonnage on board at any instant to determining the amount of tonnage necessary to complete a predetermined state of loading.

Large, comprehensive curves are usually found displayed either in the chart room or the officers' accommodation and much useful information can be obtained by careful perusal of same.

Curves of displacement have a particular value in enabling an officer to determine the amount of cargo loaded or discharged during a given interval of time, even though, during that same interval, stores, water, or fuel have been placed on board.

This is because with ships of normal design the change of displacement is regular and always consistent with the change of draught.

The curve also shows the number of tons necessary to alter the draft any required amount, and it is interesting to note from the accompanying diagram that whereas 2000 tons of cargo are necessary to change the draft from 10 to 13 ft, only 800 tons are required for a similar change of 3 ft at loaded drafts of 23 ft to 26 ft. This is worth-while information when deciding how much more cargo may be accepted.

The value of the tons per inch curve is directed more towards ascertaining the exact number of tons of cargo that may be loaded when the vessel is within a few inches of her required draft. No vessel must ever be overloaded, and though the question is not of such importance at intermediate drafts, it is of extreme importance when the vessel is nearing the load draft.

The accompanying diagram illustrates the point in question.

Metrication Computation. Tons per inch; inch trim moment and fresh water allowance.

The introduction of metrication has influenced an alternative method of computing the above values.

Tons per inch is referred to as *metric tons per cm immersion* indicated as 'T'.

The working formula to obtain this value is:

(a) In fresh water, $\dfrac{A}{10^2}$

(b) In salt water, $\dfrac{41A}{4000}$

where A is the area of the water plane in sq. m.

Inch trim moment is referred to as *moment in tonnes/m to change trim 1 cm* indicated as M.C.T. 1 cm.

The working formula to obtain this value is:

(a) Ship shape body, $\dfrac{41}{4000} \times \dfrac{I}{L}$

where L is the length of the vessel in metres, and I is the second moment of area about a transverse axis.

Change of draught due to change of density is now determined on the basis of a working formula covering passing from salt water to fresh water, as follows:

$$\text{F.W.A.} \ \frac{W}{4T} \ \text{mm}$$

where W is the displacement in tonnes, and T the metric tons per cm immersion.

The metric tonne is 2205 lb; 1 m is 39·37 in; 1 in is 2·54 cm; 1 imperial ton is 1·016 metric tons; 1 m is 100 cm.

LOADING (Load Lines)

The overriding restriction on the loading of ships is that imposed by the 1967 Load Line Act, giving effect to the 1966 International Convention on Load Lines, and a copy of the Regulations must be carried aboard every ship. Under the rules a vessel must carry the appropriate marks indicating maximum loading in various seasonal zones, or, more precisely, the minimum freeboard appropriate to those zones. The marks are shown on the diagram below, Fig. 6.8. The maximum deadweight available for any given voyage is that which will bring the vessel to a freeboard not less than that indicated by the appropriate mark on first entering the zone, taking into consideration increased freeboard due to consumption of fuel, water and stores, where the vessel passes through a zone requiring greater freeboard than the zone of departure.

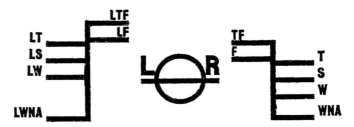

Fig. 6.8. Load Line markings for ocean going vessels, including the markings for vessels loading to timber (L) load lines. Dimensions of the marks are detailed in the Load Line Act, the distance between each mark being computed with reference to the Summer Draught of the vessel.

Where a vessel is loading to maximum deadweight, zone allowance must be made as part of the normal tonnage calculations and, of course, this will apply to any type of vessel. The following example illustrates the calculations needed:

A vessel having tropical summer and winter displacements of 20 695, 20 530 and 20 365 tonnes respectively is loading in Freetown for a voyage to U.K. in December. If the daily consumption of fuel is 60 tonnes and of water and stores 35 tonnes, what maximum tonnage of cargo may be loaded?

Reference must be made to the chart of load line zones of the world to ascertain the zones through which the vessel will pass. In this case she will enter the North Atlantic seasonal winter zone off Cape Torinaña, having entered the summer zone at 30°N. Freetown lies in the tropical zone. Thus the limiting factors are the displacement on arrival in the winter zone and summer zones respectively, the departure (tropical) displacement and the steaming times of the summer and winter zone boundaries respectively.

Departure displacement	20 695
less, consumptions to summer zone (3 days at 95 t.p.d.)	285
Summer zone displacement	20 410
less, additional consumption to winter zone (2 days at 95 t.p.d.)	190
Displacement arriving at winter zone	20 220

The vessel is under the maximum displacement for both zones. A greater weight of cargo cannot be lifted at Freetown because of the limit of the tropical zone line figures above. Careful attention to the fuel and water figures must now be made. The steaming distances to the zones and the fuel consumption will be carefully checked and if necessary, the F.W. tonnage reduced if the maximum cargo is to be loaded.

Loading in dock water requires the usual allowance to be made in determining departure freeboard and draught.

CARGO AND SAFETY

Cargo handling, by the very nature of its activities, contains a high degree of occupational hazard. To minimize this it is necessary to maintain vigilance in many different spheres, not the least being 'within and about the vessel' while working cargo. There is thus a 'management', as distinct from a 'professional' responsibility upon the cargo officer in that it is in the manner of organizing and administering the daily programme of cargo handling activities that the hazards can exist.

Occupational safety regulations apply and are provided for in most responsible ports and by shipping/maritime organizations. To a large extent the 'ship' is expected to comply with local safety regulations and requirements, notably, among others, in the manner by which it uses the equipment and labour provided by the port and also in the application of ship's gear to cargo handling procedures. There is thus a **safety factor** in cargo handling, the effectiveness of which being largely a personal responsibility.

'Safety' is ever present and it would be invidious to draw any distinction between one area or another. In terms of cargo handling, however, certain features take on a more noticeable degree of prominence, some of which are enumerated below, and to which the cargo officer's attention is drawn.

Before so doing, however, particular attention is drawn to The Code of Safe Working Practices for the Safety of Merchant Seamen, an outline of which is as follows:

The Code of Safe Working Practices for Merchant Seamen

Published by The Department of Transport

Of all the guide lines available to the Cargo Officer none has such impact as the above named Code. All other publications have their rightful place and make important contributions, but this Code of Practice highlights the ship as containing danger hazards and concentrates on all shipboard functions, drawing attention to systems and methods aimed at reducing, if not eliminating, the hazard. Cargo Handling functions and their involvement are broadly included and warrant serious attention. The Code was initially produced in 1978 under the supervision of an expert committee comprising representatives of all sides of the shipping industry, professional officers of the

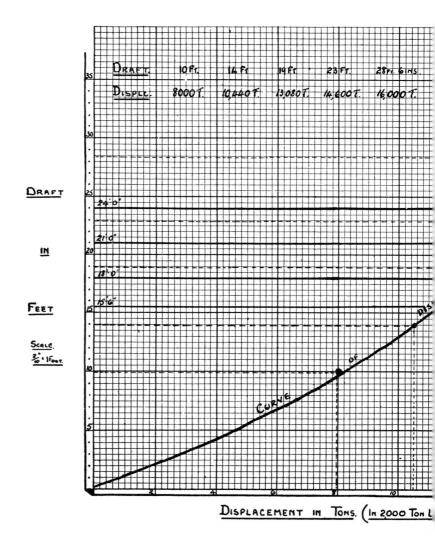

DRAFT	10 FT.	14 FT	19 FT	23 FT.	28 FT. 6 INS.
DISPL.	8000 T.	10,440 T.	13,080 T.	14,600 T.	16,000 T.

DRAFT

IN

FEET

SCALE.
$\frac{3}{10}'' = 1$ FOOT.

24' 0"

21' 0"

18' 0"

15' 6"

CURVE OF DIS

DISPLACEMENT IN TONS. (IN 2000 TON L

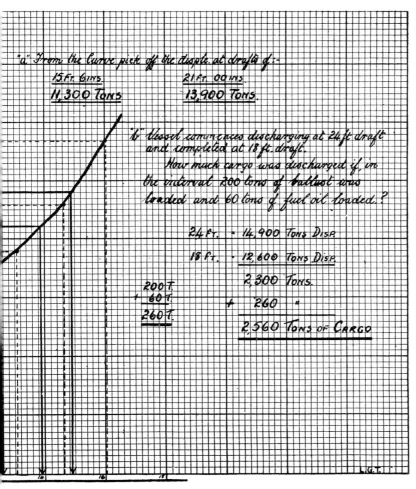

"a" From the Curve pick off the disple. at drafts of :-

15 Ft. 6ins   21 Ft. 00 ins
11,300 Tons   13,900 Tons.

"b" Vessel commences discharging at 24 ft draft
and completed at 18 ft. draft.
    How much cargo was discharged if, in
the interval 200 tons of ballast was
loaded and 60 tons of fuel oil loaded.?

24 Ft. - 14,900 Tons Disp.
18 Ft. - 12,600 Tons Disp.
            2,300 Tons.
200 T.
+ 60 T.   +   260   "
260 T.
            2,560 Tons of Cargo

L.G.T.

Scale, ½" · 200 Tons

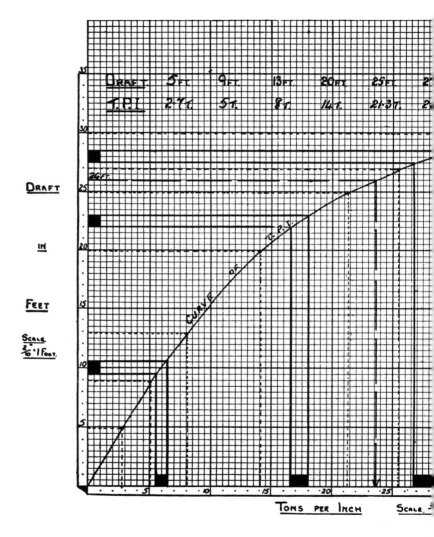

DRAFT.	5 FT.	9 FT.	13 FT.	20 FT.	25 FT.	2
T.P.I.	2.7 T.	5 T.	8 T.	14 T.	21.3 T.	2

DRAFT

IN

FEET

Scale
$\frac{3}{16}$ 1 Foot.

26 FT.

T. P. I.

CURVE OF

TONS PER INCH   Scale

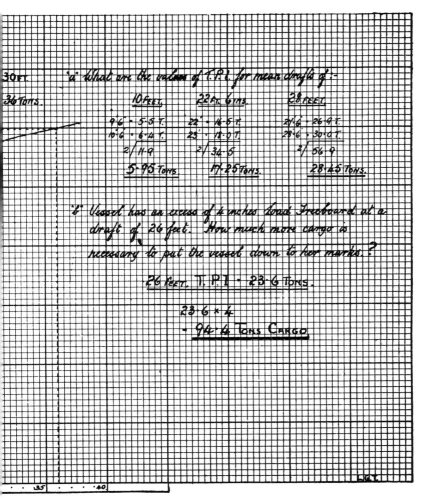

"a" What are the values of T.P.I. for mean drafts of :-

10 FEET.	22 FT. 6 INS.	28 FEET
9·6 · 5·5 T.	22· · 16·5 T.	27·6 · 26·9 T.
10·6 · 6·4 T.	23· · 18·0 T.	28·6 · 30·0 T.
2 / 11·9	2 / 34·5	2 / 56·9
5·95 TONS	17·25 TONS.	28·45 TONS.

"b" Vessel has an excess of 4 inches Load Freeboard at a
draft of 26 feet. How much more cargo is
necessary to put the vessel down to her marks ?

26 FEET. T.P.I. · 23·6 TONS.

23·6 × 4
· 94·4 TONS CARGO

Department of Transport and other expert advisers. Latterly, 1979, it has been revised and updated.

The purpose of the code is to provide authoritative guidance to be followed in operations aboard ship in order to ensure the safety of those concerned and to reduce the number of accidents and injuries affecting seafarers . . . such is the depth of concern to which the code is directed.

In terms of this book there is broad relevance to cargo handling, as such, with sections included detailing functions and procedures as these affect the particular duties and responsibilities of owners, Masters, deck officers and deck ratings, where cargo handling is concerned. As such the code supports much of the detail coverage of handling and stowage procedures covered in this text, and should be studied accordingly.

Other sections of the code have 'indirect' as distinct from 'direct' association with cargo handling and should be regarded accordingly. For example, detail on gangways and means of access; opening and closing of hatchways; methods of slinging and lifting in safe fashion; handling of working gear; visibility and lighting in cargo spaces and safe protection in and around hatchways and care and attention with mechanical hatch covers.

The code is an authoritative guide; it has not the force of law, as such, but suffers no detraction of importance as a result. No experienced seaman would question the practicality of its contents, indeed many of the recommendations, err on the generous side so that their interpretation provides for greater safety margins than might otherwise apply. It covers all departments of a ship and the kinds of work and duties each requires; it is, in fact a *safety guide* which, in the particular context of cargo handling, draws attention to its hazards.

Copies of the code are available in all British merchant ships.

In the above context, and with no priorities intended, care should be exercised in the following directions:

1. In general terms order and cleanliness are essential needs. Untidy and neglected handling equipment and dirty environment are not conducive to good working habits.
2. Good lighting and illumination is essential to the prevention of accidents. Not only is this obviously necessary during night working but applies also in spaces where cargo disposition can obliterate a sufficiency of light.
3. The fire hazard in enclosed spaces is always present with cargo handling. All the normal procedures of prevention and inspection of equipment should be of major routine application.
4. Access to the vessel, and to the spaces in which cargo handling is being carried out must meet all the required

safety provisions covering ladders, gangways, fencing of open areas, such as would be necessary in the protection of hatchways, the access to holds and the clearance of obstructions on hatchcoamings which might interfere with the 'clear and clean' slinging of loads.

5. Working spaces must have 'clear vision' to crane and derrick operations and this can differ as between working in a lower hold, a 'tween deck or with a deck cargo. Care and attention to this need must be given with each change of procedure in a cargo handling programme.

6. With cargo to be loaded on to a hatch cover, be this 'tween or upper deck, there is a first essential in ensuring that the covers are properly secure before working commences. Equally important is it to ensure that the loads being worked are not in excess of the S.W.L. factor on the hatch covers.

7. Routine attention to the maintenance of working equipment, such as cranes, winches, standing and running rigging and all loose gear necessary to cargo work, together with adherence to the safe working load limits, is given. Routine should ensure that all gear within the title of 'loose' conforms to statutory requirements of both proof and S.W.L. standards.

8. The setting up of derricks in the loading and unloading of cargo calls for care in calculating the related stresses on the different parts of the derrick and the rigging, in order to ensure the loads to be handled can safely be covered. Derrick rigging stresses differ according to the angle at which the derrick is set, lifts, luffs or slews in the operation of loading and/or unloading.

9. Safety is maintained by careful and continued attention to the tensions upon the guys and rigging of derricks. The ideal is to ensure a uniform distribution of load on all parts of the gear contributing to the movement of the cargo.

10. Crane safety is largely a matter of attention to the pre-cautionary measures with the electric supply, cables, connections, conductors, switches and breakers must always be in first class condition. Only continuous supervision can ensure this.

11. At all stages of cargo handling care must be exercised with hatch coverings in that those parts remaining in situ during working are safely secured; the stacking of beams and hatch covers are in safe positions so that the slinging arrangements for beam and hatches are suitable. Where power operated hatch coverings are fitted, especially safety precaustions apply and these are linked to merchant shipping notices (No. M992, see page 448).

12. Container and bulk carriage raise their own particular safey aspects. See Section 4 (containers) and Section 4 (bulk

cargoes). Primarily, with container handling, the safety aspect is that concerned with the secure lifting and slinging of the box. With bulk cargo it is related to the avoidance of accidents to personnel from automatic grab working in a hold or space.

13. Some highly dangerous hazards arise with some goods classified as 'dangerous' and attention is drawn to Section 4, page 154 on this aspect.

Some further points are worthy of consideration (no priorities intended).

In general cargo ships the code draws attention to 'tween deck' loading and the desirability of reasonable space between stowed cargo and the hatch coaming at the sides and ends. Within the 'tween deck' area 1 metre is recommended.

Safety provisions with deck cargoes are dealt with, providing access of movement clear of hatchcoamings and, also, the need to avoid blocking out hold ladders should they be needed, at sea.

Dangerous substances find more than passing reference. There is reminder that the 'Blue Book'—Report of the D.o.T. Standing Advisory Committee on the Carriage of Dangerous Goods in Ships—is the regulation coverage insofar as substances, regarded as dangerous, should be classified, packed, labelled and stowed.

With regard to actual working of cargo the code deals with the care and attention consequent upon moving, lifting and handling of goods. It is concerned with safety aspects of slinging and hoisting and with controlling signals. Loads of heavy weight and awkward shape are highlighted. This part of the code is specific and factual, leaving no doubt as to the safe working procedures to be observed.

Containers receive attention in the manner of their lifting, avoiding uneven balance. Distribution of goods, even and safe stowing within the boxes is dealt with. Lashing and securing of containers on deck, and the attendant provisions for personnel engaged in this activity, is widely considered. Stowage of containers in ships not especially constructed should be fore and aft.

Tankers, and Bulk product carriers (Oil and Bulk/Oil construction) are covered from the point of view of fire, explosion and contamination risk.

Liquefied Gas and Chemical carriers attract attention in regard to avoiding suffocation from pungent odour and also danger from 'cold burns' by contact with intensely cold pipes.

References are made to appropriate official safety guides but attention is drawn to the necessity for all concerned with the loading and carriage of these volatile cargoes to be familiar with their nature and characteristics.

Chapter 17 of the Code provides lengthy and detailed guide lines on lifting and on mechanical handling appliances and draws attention to the hazards to be prevented/avoided. This is helpful, since a number of ships now in service carry their own mechanical handling appliances, with which the seamen become involved.

Derrick 'set up' is dealt with, rigging suitabilities indicated in the avoidance of undue tension and stress.

Roll on/Roll off Ferries and Car Carrier services receive attention, relating to the impact the increasing size of the vessels employed are having upon safety measures. It is important to remember, for example, the hazards which can arise from slippery decks in these ships. The fore and aft stowage of vehicular traffic is recommended as adding to 'stowage safety'.

With portable car decks there is reminder that the uniquely designed type of vessel, with internal car stowage arrangements, calls for a high standard of care and attention with those working on board.

Vehicular cargo, in general, is referred to from the point of view of lashing and security attachments.

Dangerous goods, carried in vehicular portable tanks, calls for especial safety provisions.

Officers and others are strongly advised to obtain a copy of the Code—H.M. Stationery Office. It is worth pointing out that this is one document with which D.o.T. Examiners for Masters and Mates expect candidates to be completely familiar.

In regards to the foregoing the attention of cargo officers is drawn to a comprehensive informative booklet published by The International Labour Office, Geneva, entitled *Guide to Safety and Health in Dock Work*.

International Applications to Safety with Cargo Handling

Reference to the International Labour Office
'Guide to Safety and Health in Dock Work'

Since cargo handling is an international activity methods and procedures, while in numerous ways indicating common backgrounds, there are, none the less, systems peculiar to different countries and their practices . . . custom and tradition plays a large part. Numerous parties are involved, not only the 'ships' but also servicing agencies within the transportation field and, of obvious necessity, the ports to and from which ships of different classes trade.

Dominant areas of cargo work procedures no longer are the prime prerogative of the Western industrialized nations, albeit they have much of the background to support desirable example and considerable experience on which to base and promote modern development. But the growing industrialization of the so called 'Third World' and, perhaps particularly so, the Middle and Far Eastern countries, are fast approaching comparable behaviour and may well become, rightly so, increasingly competitive. Considerable cargo tonnages of all types now make up the trading strengths of those countries within which the ships employed frequently carry the appropriate related 'flag'.

In the practice of cargo handling ship's officers of all nations have reason to be familiar with the practices in all of the ports to which modern trading patterns direct their vessels, and be aware of regulations and recommendations which bind together international, national and local requirements.

In this context it is salutary that there should be documentation which aims to promote a fair measure of international co-operation and co-ordination, to which end Cargo Officers' attention is drawn to the I.L.O (International Labour Office, Geneva) 'Guide to Safety and Health in Dock Work', which is fully supported by the United Nations.

In general terms the guide is concerned with SAFETY and thus relates to the desirable environment layout of ports, quays and wharves and within those areas emphasizes the place of ships, the fitments on board of ships and the working practices in and on them, in so far as the word SAFETY within the guide encompasses the work of all those engaged in, and responsible for, the loading and unloading of cargoes. As such the guide is widely adhered to by most maritime nations in establishing good and safe methods of sound maritime practice. It is fast becoming the basis for international agreements. It should be studied by all officers concerned with cargo handling; there is much of detail to digest which can only be completely effective by so doing.

(This book aims to encourage that approach with relevant detail appropriate to most forms of cargo work to which the guide refers. The summary which follows is intended to draw attention to those areas needful of consideration.)

1. In the first instance the desirability, and necessity of co-ordination and co-operation between the ship owner (ship's officers) and the employer of dock labour is stressed. It points out that many accidents can occur by neglect of this approach. Indeed, much can be seen as ineffective cargo handling as a result of haste, excessive speeds of operation, over zealousness and, most of all, from the neglect to involve all parties in the overall supervision of working practices.

   Particularly is this necessary at the times of first approach to loading plans and, more so, at the times of approaching the completion of unloading holds and spaces, when bad practices are likely to be more prevalent.

2. The guide is also concerned with GOOD LIGHTING EN-VIRONMENT. Where natural light is diffused methods of artificial light should always be used to the full. In modern vessels spaces are likely to be so covered by construction but this does not preclude the use of additional means.

Not only is this requirement related to personnel safety in the avoidance of accidents but also towards the care of the cargo. Loading and discharging calls for the prevention of mistakes in identification . . . see pages 180–181 on cargo marking . . . as to the correct placing of loads; the avoidance of 'over carriage' when discharging and the avoidance, also, of claims for damage to the goods.

In this context portable flood lamps will play a part but, in doing so, the guide draws attention to the fact that these pieces of equipment meets national requirements of safety.

3. FIRE. Fire is always a hazard on a ship, be it at sea or in port. In the latter case the cargo handling factor must always be of high priority, apart from the effect upon the ship and to the environment surrounding it. It is essential that the ship fire fighting equipment conforms to the local systems.

Furthermore, the use of extinguishers, though doubtless adequately available, must be used correctly. Not all extinguishers serve the same purpose; some may be of a type where their content might, with some cargoes, cause an acceleration of fire, if not poisoning or asphyxiation. The use of extinguishers calls for special care in confined spaces with cargo handling. Attention to the use of fire fighting equipment is paramount with cargo handling and the guide has much to direct the cargo officer correctly.

4. There is much of worthwhile in the guide relating to HATCHWAYS PROTECTION. (See also text on hatchways . . . pages 65–67.) Accidents from falling are not uncommon.

In so far as modern ship construction provides acceptable means of hatchway provision, and access to holds and spaces, not always will this be comparable on older ships. It is therefore essential that all means of safety provision in and around hatchways, between intermediate decks and the fitting and unfitting of hatchway covers and hatch beams are fully secure.

Working into a 'tween deck' raises a particular hazard; the tween deck hatchway covers (over a possible empty or partly filled lower hold must be absolutely secure.

Even the normally accepted practice of 'covering up' or 'uncovering' a hatchway calls for care. Covering up should always work from the sides towards the middle. Uncovering conversely.

The stowage of heavy loads . . . those over 1 ton . . . on to hatch covers should, preferably, be avoided. Also, with the increasing use of fork lift trucks in loading and unloading within the ship, the hatch covering surfaces over which the trucks will travel, must be not only secure, but in good condition.

5. **LOADING AND UNLOADING EQUIPMENT** calls for continued attention, both as a maintenance function and also within the working/handling cargo procedures. This involves winches, cranes, derricks, blocks, hooks, chains, wires, falls, rigging, loose gear, including slings etc. The list is almost inexhaustible. There is much in the guide on this matter which deserves attention.

Especially is there need to be aware of the different systems of 'power' by which equipment is activated and the methods of its control, viz. braking to winches and cranes.

There is need also to be aware of and conversant with the different settings of derrick rigging for different loading/unloading procedures in so far as this has bearing upon the stresses on derrick rigging and on the falls. (See also pages 48–54).

6. **METHODS OF SLINGING** loads of cargo can raise hazards. These procedures are also dealt with in the guide. Not only is it a case of the condition of the slings, be they rope, wire, chain, nets or metal frames, important as these methods are. The guide also relates to the methods and styles used to sling different loads, frequently often dictated by the custom and practice of the port in which the ship is working and certainly to whether the cargo is homogeneous or of a non-homogeneous nature. This is an area where the cargo officer must exercise 'judicious' observation over the practices being used by the port's stevedoring personnel.

Slinging can be conventional, as for cargoes termed non-homogeneous and can include bags, casks, bales and similar make ups, either on the quay or in the hold, with variable sizes and content, in which case the slinging should suit the shape and weight of each load.

For other forms of cargo the slinging must suit the hazard involved. Cases can be slung by looped slinging, evenly distributed over the case, or by spiked clamps. Drums and barrels are more safely slung by hooks.

Palletized cargo loads call for the arrangement of the sling to provide 'all over' support to the cargo on the pallet. An additional safety factor is to add to the slinging an enclosing net, to provide restriction of possible displacement of any part of the load while it is in transit.

Specialized forms of cargo require particular methods of slinging, i.e. . . . rolls of paper (see page 108), steel bars or solids in bulk (by grabs), the range is wide. Loads of irregular shape, having sharp corners require slinging in such a way that the cargo edges do not damage the sling.

Modern ship construction now embraces fixed, built in loading/unloading slinging equipment, as for example forest product carriers and automobile carriers, which obviates the need for normal slinging, while mechanization, appropriate to the unitization of cargoes, be it by container or roll off/roll on procedures has lessened, if not eradicated conventional slinging. Container slinging is particularly specialized . . . it is a special study, (see pages 252–254), albeit the guide contains informative references.

Vertical and transverse movement of cargo creates its own hazards . . . the guide highlights these, by text and diagrams.

7. (a) Mechanical movement . . . (transversely) of cargo in bulk form can utilize continuous methods by conveyors or pneumatic systems. From a safety point of view these have preferable advantages but preventative measures in the avoidance of accidents with conveyor belt systems include clear space around the working parts, with these suitably fenced or guarded.

Unloading bulk cargo by pneumatic systems has advantages over grabs but the guide points out that if men have to work in a hold with solid bulk, they should be held by safety belts to prevent their being caught into the unloading equipment.

(b) Horizontal Transportation of cargo in this modern age finds considerable usage, be it by fork lift trucks, trailers or low loaders, or indeed by bigger vehicular movement. (See page 67.)

With F.L.T.s (fork lift trucks) the guide draws attention to particular hazards, especially where they are used 'in' the spaces of a ship and particularly so where these may be confined. By the very reason that the work is involved 'in the ship' the Cargo Officer has especial 'care' responsibility.

Fork lift trucks can be power motivated by electric batteries, by diesel or internal combustion units. Internal combustion units can give off odours of toxic effect to personnel and/or damaging influence upon some types of cargoes. Inside of a ship electric powered F.L.T.s are preferable.

There are, also, other precautions necessary in the use of F.L.T.s which the Cargo Officer must ensure. Clearance of the load in carriage should always be available and clear of restriction, thus avoiding damage to the cargo or even the upsetting of the truck with its load, which could affect personnel in the vicinity.

When a F.L.T. is not in movement its 'lifting gear' and the attachments should be lowered; when it is at rest its brakes should always be on. Notably is this precaution if the truck is working on inclined surfaces. It also has sense when the truck is stacking cargo or breaking out from a stack.

The speed of travel of a fork lift truck within a cargo space calls for supervisory attention, (see pages 18, 352) though the I.L.O. recommends no more than 25 km/h.

On occasions horizontal transportation of cargo viz./ viz. the employment of F.L.T.s utilizes the build of a platform within the space on to which the slinged load can be landed, with the F.L.T. picking up the load for placing in the 'space'. These platforms can be of wood or metal construction and be properly designed to bear the loaded/landed cargo weight and also permitting safe movement of men working on and around the platform.

Cargo Officers should pay attention to this aspect, particularly in respect of the dynamic load force which arises from impact when the load meets the platform, raising the hazard of platform collapse.

(Note . . . Mechanical handling of cargo is highly prevalent in modern ships; it is an element of 'quick turn round'. By its very nature it induces hazards. Cargo Officers therefore must determine a balance between effective loading/discharging while not neglecting the hazard/safety factor.)

Hence the attention to which the guide gives to this aspect of cargo handling.

8. On the question of GENERAL LOADING AND UN-LOADING PROCEDURES the guide contains important features to be noted, all of which have bearing upon hazards and safety affecting both personnel and cargo, in which context particular attention in this summary relates to STACKING AND PILING. Leaving aside the essential need for effective dunnage and blocking, and the shoring of cargo, stacking and piling introduces additional requirements, particularly where the design construction of a vessel causes restriction of space. This can well be the case at the 'turn of the bilge' (or at frame brackets where the tank top of a lower hold is continuous) and where platforms are built to receive part of the cargo. It can also be desirable at the ends of the forward and after holds.

Cargoes which lend themselves to this arrangement include 'drums' or reels of 'newsprint paper' to name but two . . . there can be others.

While it is essential that the platform is adequate in size and strength to accommodate 'the pieces of cargo' it is also important that cargo so PILED i.e. standing on its ends, is provided with means by which it can be adequately and effectively STRAPPED OR LASHED, or held by netting, be it from means (cleats or rings) fitted to the structure or by manual arrangements.

This ensures solidarity in the stow and lessens (hopefully

prevents) a hazard of the load moving or shifting during a sea passage, the result of which might well become a factor leading to personnel accident when the loads are being broken down at the time of discharge.

Indeed, both the I.L.O. and the I.M.O. (International Maritime Organization) recommend such provisions where any cargo is stowed in the vicinity of and above any space below it. There is relevance here with cargo piled up to the edge of a 'tween deck' above a lower hold/space opening.

DANGEROUS CARGOES, as such, present their own hazards and safety provisions. These are dealt with in Section 4, page 154.

Conclusions

If for no other purpose than to draw attention to SAFETY in the working of a ship with cargo, the I.L.O. Guide to Safety and Health in Dock Work implies a pattern of behaviour which can only be truly effective by full co-operation and co-ordination as between ship personnel and ports personnel. In this respect the same goes for every activity covering the movement of cargoes, into and out of a ship.

As pointed out elsewhere in this book, the integration of transportation activities is very much a matter of necessity. Ships in ports are no exception. This booklet clearly outlines the attitudes which should be adopted to procedures of loading and unloading where the safety of personnel becomes a matter of concern and importance between ship and shore working functions. It could, of course, be argued that the measures take on even greater importance when working in countries where the development of dock labour is not so highly organized as in the industrial nations.

The booklet is obtainable from I.L.O. offices or direct from the I.L.O. Geneva, Switzerland.

Safety in Ships, and precautionary measures are also widely and usefully promulgated through various other publications.

In this context attention is drawn to:

(a) I.M.O. (International Maritime Organization), 'Maritime Dangerous Goods Guide'.
(b) 'Code of Practice for the Safe Carriage of Dangerous Goods in Freight Containers' (General Council of British Shipping, 30/32 St. Mary Axe, London EC3A 8ET).
(c) 'Tanker Safety Guides—Chemicals, Liquefied Gas, Oils' (The International Chamber of Shipping—I.C.S., 30/32 St. Mary Axe, London EC3A 8ET).

SHIPBOARD MANAGEMENT IN PRACTICE

As indicated earlier in this book, the economics of transportation and the influences of trade patterns upon the movement of goods, reflects both on and from the manner in which a ship is operated. Not the least aspect of this reflection is the approach to cargo handling and the effect its efficiency and effectiveness has upon the ability of a ship to usefully contribute to acceptable economic standards of ship management.

To do so fully requires an understanding of the whole integrated transportation mode, of which the ship is a part, but it also calls for an appreciation of basic management practices.

The intention of this book has been to cover, mainly, the former; the latter is illustrated by an interesting experiment tested and put into action by DFDS. Shipping Organization of Denmark, by whose kind permission the following Press Release is reproduced.

The object of the procedure is to subject the ship officer, and crew, to their responsibilities as part of the total organization such that effective co-ordination exists between the policies of ship operations and the practicalities of running them.

In this modern age the ultimate requires this ability from Ship Masters . . . the position to which all good officers should aspire.

Shipboard Management a Success for DFDS

One of the major reasons given by DFDS A/S for their substantial increase in profits in 1975 was the application of the company's shipboard management technique. Shipboard management places much greater responsibilities on the Captain and crew of each ship, which is considered as an independent floating subsidiary company. The Captain becomes the managing director, with his officers as the executives.

The land-based central organization is effectively reduced and primarily they look after the income side, finance and control accounting. In addition a central service organization is available for advice or to deal with specific requests from ships.

Shipboard management gives the ship's officers and crew greater operational freedom and this in turn develops their capabilities to the maximum extent. This delegation of authority also leads to a greater degree of job satisfaction as well as producing an improved economic result.

To a large extent ships prepare their own operational budgets with little interference from ashore. An examination of the 1976 budgets, which are based on one year's experience, showed that the ships were doing a more thorough job of budgeting than the average company ashore and were very much more cost conscious.

The liaison between ship and shore is an operational inspector or ship manager. His main function is to serve the ships and to maintain contact with top management ashore. One inspector can easily service five or six cargo vessels or a smaller number of passenger ships. DFDS have five operational inspectors, plus a few people in purchasing and personnel, and in addition a very small group of experts whose services can be drawn on as necessary.

Before the shipboard management system was applied, DFDS established preventive maintenance programmes, lubricating systems and spare parts systems. A policy was established covering crewing and leaves. All ships were sent copies of invoices, price lists, stevedoring contracts, etc., in order to foster cost consciousness. Seminars of one to three day's duration were held on a subject-by-subject basis. Later seminars were held on shipboard management and these were focussed on management techniques.

Mr. Erik Heirung, chief executive of DFDS A/S, speaking at the Arab Shipping and Trade Conference at Kuwait has said: 'In DFDS . . . as far as we can see shipboard management is the only management style which can ensure the survival of our company. . . . Our experience is that we have never had a better operation than we have today.'

The success of the shipboard management project has aroused the interest of other shipowners both in Denmark and elsewhere. As a result DFDS has now established a department called Dana Consult which offers the company's expertise to other shipping lines. Dana Consult is already working on contracts while others are under negotiation.

DEPARTMENT OF TRANSPORT

Shipping Notices relating to Cargo Loading and Stowage

The Department of Transport publish, from time to time, its booklet of merchant shipping notices, the contents of which relate to a variety of subjects affecting the safe handling of ships and cargoes, and the safety of personnel. The information, usually referred to as 'M' notices, and regularly issued as circumstances dictate, is of such importance that all officers are recommended to make themselves familiar with the guidance contained therein and, indeed, the instructions which, in some cases, these notices lay down. In many cases the contents of the notices stem from actual practical issues of accidents and danger hazards which have arisen from non-observance of normal precautions or from regulations.

From the examination point of view, for certificates of competency, it is important that officers should be reasonably familiar with the implications of these 'M' notices.

The following summary relates to 'M' notices referred to in the text of this book. An outline of each is given, together with page references in which detail can be seen.

Summary of Department of Transport Shipping Notices

(Related to Cargo Work)

Tank Vehicles for the Carriage of Dangerous Goods.
Earlier Notice 807. Page Ref. 178.

992   *Hatchways and Hatchcovers.* The need to ensure these being properly closed and secure before proceeding to sea. The safety aspect of personnel working in proximity to hatchcovers. Page Ref. 65–67.

1051   *Wood Pulp.* Precautions to be taken to avoid wetness and/or saturation of pulp in bags consequent upon the tendency for these to swell and expand, so causing structural stress. Page Ref. 189.

1045   *Carriage of Dangerous Chemicals in Bulk.* Precautions to avoid the dangers of asphyxiation and toxic vapours in tanks and closed spaces. Page Ref. 177.

1046   *Carriage of Liquefied Gases in Bulk.* The issue of fitness as to the suitability of ships to carry such gases. Page Ref. 313.

1110   *Loading of Timber Deck Cargoes.* Care to be exercised in ensuring the correct type of slip hook is used. Page Ref. 189.

1032
1082   } *Dangerous Cargoes.* Page Ref. 172 + .
1124

970 and   *Safe Carriage of Coal Cargoes* . . . precautions against
971   liquefaction of coal slurry, duffs, small coals and coke, and also the emission of flammable gases and spontaneous combustion. Page Ref. 172.

Attention is drawn to the fact that Department of Transport Shipping Notices are periodically revised, amended or even withdrawn, for further issue. As such, continued need arises to be aware of these possibilities.

CARGO HANDLING CLAIMS
The Place of the Cargo Officer

(Notes for Guidance)

Claims arising out of the processes of Cargo Handling can be varied, some simple and straightforward, others complicated and some encompassed by elements of doubt. All are open to questioning. Within this orbit it is not improbable that a Cargo Officer could find. within his career span, involvement with 'cases'.

These could be, mainly, of two circumstances . . . his own involvement with the features surrounding a claim, i.e. the presentation of facts, or by 'invitation' to assist either the claimant or the defendant on the reasons for or rejecting a claim by expressing an 'opinion'.

Claims within Cargo Handling can include damage to the cargo, from a variety of causes, damage to the ship or 'damage' to personnel by reason of safety hazards. Whatever the circumstances the matters can be subject to litigation involving the law, be it civil or maritime. It is therefore quite wrong to assume or to adopt an approach of assumption.

It follows, therefore, that the possibilities of becoming involved in 'claims' cases is a matter to which an officer should give serious thought and acquaint himself with an understanding of basic procedures, so that, should the situation arise, he will not find himself acting out of ignorance. This is not to say that he should be completely familiar with the details of law, as will undoubtedly surround a case . . . these should be left to solicitors or counsels . . . but that he is knowledgeable of codes of practice within which his responsibilities to cargo work are determined and that he is satisfied that his experience conforms to accepted maritime practices. Furthermore, he should be aware of rules and regulations, national and international, which surround the types of cargoes, and their handling, with which he is familiar.

A good beginning is to become familiar with a responsible career book of the type and title of 'Shipmaster's Business, accepted and reliable data on cargo handling and a complete understanding of guide lines issued by the company(ies) in which he is or has served, in so far as effective cargo handling duties are expected of him.

In any case of being a 'WITNESS' two aspects will be prominent.

1. Professional qualification and competence.
2. Experience.

Both of these must be guarded; not only are they sacrosanct to the officer himself but also of vital importance to the 'body' for whom he may be testifying. Both will be subject to close examination by both sides, directly and in cross-examination. On these will he be judged and accepted.

What, therefore, is important?

Above all else respect for facts. These must either reflect experienced knowledge of what may have given rise to the damage, by reason of observing or by direct contact with the circumstances, or they must reflect opinions with qualification, competence or experience suggests to be realistic and leading to a point of view.

Of the two, OPINION is the more difficult by which to make impression. It is personal and therefore can be expected to attract opposing personal view. It can encourage argument and herein lies a danger.

If a witness is called upon to pronounce opinion, there are a number of aspects to which attention should be given.

(a) Careful preliminary discussion with the solicitors/counsels by whom he will be 'called', clearing and clarifying aspects along which they propose to base their case.

(b) Spending some considerable time studying and digesting informative detail on the 'damage', examining other people's evidence or view, assessing the environment(s) surrounding the alleged damage and being satisfied that there are no irregularities or inconsistences in what, at this stage, may have been put into print.

(Need relating to the foregoing can well be necessary where the case is a retrial and/or when depositions have been taken from earlier witnesses of opposing sides . . . all will be in official documentation, to read.)

(c) Assessing the said cause of the damage against his own experienced view. Was it reasonable, unreasonable, realistic or unrealistic? Was it by neglect? Some countries set high importance to neglect. It is important to be sure how high in opinion does this rate. Did it, or did it not, conform to accepted maritime practice?

(d) Being satisfied that the 'job' he is being invited to do is within his own capabilities and concerned with subject matter of which he is fully aware. He must be absolutely true to his own convictions.

(e) Leave no doubt that the evidence is that of 'opinion' and that alone. Avoiding any doubt in this direction strengthens his credibility . . . highly important in this kind of exercise.

None of the issues outlined above are unnecessary. Nor should they be treated lightly . . . certainly not ignored. In the process of so doing conclusions will be drawn, the picture will unfold, to be supported or debased by personal experience. Satisfied that the conclusions are realistic . . . an opinion (or opinions) will be formed.

These must be of a positive character, remembering that opinions being put forward can well be challenged by opposing equally competent view and challenged by counsel as to show all the attributes of searching ruthlessness. This is where care must be taken to avoid being drawn into argument.

It is he, the witness, who is the 'expert'. It is on that basis he is being used. It is not for others to question that validity . . . though doubtless they will. Furthermore, those who want to argue a point are not always sure of themselves.

However, being satisfied with his conclusions, believing he is right, the witness forms his opinion(s) and states them without reservation allowing nothing to cause any deviation. But it will not be easy.

Being an 'opinion' witness can be very frustrating. There will be times when he may well begin to doubt himself. By the very nature of human reaction he will find himself being nigh to becoming disgusted with opposing view, foreign to his own background. Much will depend upon the extent to which his 'own' counsel supports him.

The strength and influence of opinion witnessing cannot be known until the case is over and judgement given. This may well become time consuming and in the meantime that interim period can well raise doubts of authenticity.

A 'WITNESS OF FACT' to coin a phrase is more likely to be the situation where the position of the officer has been related to the procedures in which the damage or hazard has occurred. This calls for considerable attention to facts which the opposing solicitors or counsels will seek to question. Furthermore, such an involvement will doubtless be challenged by an OPINION witness for the 'other side' and in that case the issue becomes, more often than not, a matter of professional challenge . . . not to be disregarded.

Two features of important note arise. Primarily qualification and accepted competence must support experience, while responsibility to one's employers/owners is paramount. The first involves personal credibility, the second integrity.

Both can be challenged, the former because it would be expected that a qualified officer would be in a position to prevent or minimize any possible damage or hazard and to use his judgement accordingly. The latter can induce searching examination of his loyalty.

On examination such a witness of fact must give his evidence in a manner as to leave no doubts that he is, and was, capable of taking a course of action which could, and was intended to have prevented or minimized the damage or hazard for which the 'case' is being raised. He must prove, to accepted level, that his behaviour was in the best traditions of good maritime practice, and that his actions were conditioned by knowledgeable observance of all the appropriate codes of practice and shipping regulations and recommendations. Good 'seamanship' is as much a part of efficient cargo handling as is the physical contact with it.

While it is unlikely that damage to cargo would be in question before the vessel commenced its voyage (such damaged cargo would have been rejected beforehand) there are, however, numerous factors that can arise before the cargo is ultimately discharged or, indeed, unexpected hazards to arise.

Efficient and effective stowage can be questioned; the stability of the ship correct for the envisaged passage; the state of the weather encountered . . . which could have influenced a shift of cargo leading to damage and the proper supervision of all aspects of discharge in the avoidance of damage to the cargo or hazards arising from which personnel working the discharging could suffer.

A qualified officer should be capable of dealing with all and each of the foregoing to such a degree that his competence cannot be in doubt. He should know not only the cargoes he had on board and their peculiarities, if any, which would have to have dictated 'en voyage' care, but he would also be expected to 'know his ship' and how she is likely to behave in anticipated weather in certain stages of stability and what precautions it would be necessary to take. He must also be seen to be of suitable personality as to impress his ability to use authority in ensuring that his subordinate officers behave correctly in all matters of 'ship keeping' and in supervision, on his behalf, when the cargo is being discharged. He must remember that until the last piece of cargo has been successfully cleared from the ship he (the ship) is responsible for it and for those who work it (irrespective of the presence of shore dockers) albeit considerable importance is attached to close effective co-operation with 'dock labour'.

Any weaknesses in any of the aforementioned links will be seen as aspects of neglect and strongly challenged as indications of inferior competence to that expected, while the manner in which his testimony is given will be looked at in depth.

Much, of course, will depend upon the type and extent of the damage or of the result of an hazard, conditioning the extent of a claim.

Whatever, however, if such a qualified experienced officer can be faulted the likelihood of the case is in jeopardy.

As has already been stated, a 'fact' witness must remember that his evidence will, most likely be challenged by opinion from the 'other side' from a number of sources. His cross examination will test this to the full. Much of ultimate decision will depend upon his reactions, bearing in mind that the 'expert opinion witness' may be equally or better qualified than he himself and, doubtless have anticipated the views he will himself have put forward, thus acting from an advantageous point of view.

————

Cases of the type to which these introductory notes relate ... as in most if not all courts' proceedings ... are subject to 'examination' and 'cross examination'. The former can tend to be less disturbing since the witness will be led by his own counsel, whereas in the latter case the others counsel will, understandably, be using all his powers of rhetoric to confuse.

It should be appreciated also that the notes are intended to be no more than 'guide lines' it frequently being the case that the care, handling and carriage of cargoes forgets that a Cargo Officer by virtue of his position, can make valuable contribution of advantage to his ship, his owners, to those affected by 'damage' and, most of all, to his own full appreciation of his professionalism.

GENERAL QUESTIONS ON CARGO HANDLING

The following questions cover all of the text in this book and range over basic principles to modern developments. Some are directed towards, and intended for general study and information; many may well find place in examinations; all have application to the carriage of cargoes. They should be considered accordingly.

1. A hatch has two derricks and two winches. Make a sketch, naming all the gear and giving the probable sizes, of the derricks rigged to discharge a general cargo.
2. A vessel's draught is F.23 ft 8 in and A.24 ft 10 in. Her load draught is 24 ft 9 in. How many tons of cargo can be loaded if the T.P.I. is 48?
3. A ship has a capacity of 396 400 cubic ft. Equal weights of two commodities, which have stowage factors of 38 and 54 cubic ft per ton, respectively, fill the ship. Find the weights and space occupied by each.
4. What is a tally book and what entries are made therein? Where would you tally a general cargo?
5. Why is it necessary to know the density of the dock water when loading?
6. Define:
    (a) Flash point.
    (b) Ignition point.
    (c) Ullage.
7. For what purpose is it usual to fit a strong room into the cargo space of a vessel?
8. Discuss briefly the distribution of cargo in order to have the minimum structural stress on the vessel and the most efficient condition of stability.
9. Enumerate the duties of a junior officer when working cargo.
10. What precautions should be adopted to prevent damage from crushing when loading a general cargo?
11. Two shackles are available; one of 10 tons S.W.L. and the other of 5 tons S.W.L. It is required to attach a block to the derrick head and a cargo hook to the end of the runner. Give your reasons for your choice of shackle for each attachment.
12. The deadweight of a vessel in salt water is 171 tons more than in fresh water, floating at the same draught.
    If a hydrometer shows 15 how much more cargo can be loaded than in fresh water?
    (F.W. 1000 oz per cubic ft, S.W. 1025 oz per cubic ft.)
13. What precautions should be taken to avoid 'sweat' in cargo compartments? Under what conditions and with which cargoes is 'sweat' likely to be present?
14. Discuss the preparations necessary for the reception of a refrigerated cargo.

15. What type of slings would you use for the following cargoes?
    (*a*) Small packages.
    (*b*) Rod iron.
    (*c*) Grain in bags.
    (*d*) Patent fuel.
    (*e*) Heavy log timber.
    (*f*) Barrels.
16. Give a diagram showing a heavy derrick rigged to lift a load of 35 tons. What precautions would you adopt previous to and during the operation?
17. Define:
    (*a*) Broken stowage.
    (*b*) Stowage factor.
    (*c*) Measurement cargo.
    (*d*) Bale space.
18. Discuss the procedure relevant to the inspection of cargo spaces prior to the reception of cargo.
19. What are the requirements covering the inspection and overhauling of cargo gear?
20. Discuss the procedure governing the reception, preparation of spaces, tallying and discharge of a bagged cargo. Would you advise 'bleeding' with such a cargo?
21. Prepare a compartment and stow a full consignment of barrels.
22. Give a specimen of a page from a tally book, showing the usual entries you would expect to find covering reception and discharge of cargo.
23. Quote the more important regulations covering the loading of grain in British ships.
24. What precautions should be observed in order to avoid damage by crushing in a general cargo?
25. Discuss the salient points to be borne in mind when emptying and filling tanks during working of cargo.
26. Differentiate between permanent and portable dunnage.
27. Describe the preparation of compartments and the loading of a rice cargo.
28. What precautions should be observed in order to minimize the risk of fire in coal cargoes? Quote the official requirements in regard to the ventilation of a coal cargo for a long voyage.
29. What points would you look to when overhauling a tanker's pipe lines in dry dock?
30. How is a tank, in a bulk oil carrier, ventilated?
31. Write short notes on the cleaning of a tank, particularly when preparing for clean oil, following the carriage of dirty oil.
32. Describe the difference between 'dead-weight cargo' and

'measurement cargo' and between 'grain space' and 'bale space'.

33. What entries are made in the mate's log when loading?
34. What is meant by the term 'sweat'? What precautions would you take in the case of a cargo liable to sweat?
35. What precautions must be taken when loading inflammable cargoes?
36. The fresh water allowance of a ship is 8 in. How much could the load line be submerged in water of density 1010?
     Ans. 4·8 in.
37. A vessel's fresh water allowance is $5\frac{3}{4}$ in and when loading in a certain dock the authorities allow $2\frac{1}{2}$ in submersion. Find the density of the dock water.
     Ans. 1014·1 oz per cubic ft.
38. Enumerate and briefly describe the different approaches necessary with checking and tallying a unitized cargo.
39. What are the particular uses of a Bill of Lading? How would you define this document?
40. What is the relationship between a manifest and a cargo plan? What particular values has the latter?
41. For what reasons would you consider the mate's log book to be important?
42. What features make port speed so important?
43. How, and why, do stowage factors differ?
44. Briefly describe the purpose of The Code of Safe Working Practice for Merchant Seamen.
45. Why does container and bulk carriage promote particular safety considerations?
46. Briefly describe the effect of trade patterns on cargo handling procedures.
47. To what extent does a cargo officer's involvement in cargo handling assist in the business of shipping?
48. Enumerate the types of vessels in maritime transportation and the cargoes with which they could be concerned.
49. Why is cargo handling an organizational and administrative function and in what manner is the cargo officer concerned with this?
50. What difference, if any, would you consider there to be in the routine duties of a 'senior' as distinct from a 'junior' cargo officer?
51. What is 'stuffing' and 'stripping'?
52. What major considerations enter into the distribution of a cargo load into a vessel?
53. Enumerate some of the main causes of damage to cargo:
     (*a*) At loading.
     (*b*) In carriage.
     (*c*) On discharge.
54. What is palletization and pre-slinging?

55. Why is it important that a cargo officer should be familiar with the different systems of marking of goods offered for shipment?

56. Describe the more usual systems of dunnaging and the materials used.

57. What is an 'optional' port of discharge?

58. What precautions, and why, would you adopt with fork lift trucks working cargo in a hold or space?

59. Describe the types of sweat involved with cargo carriage and the effects of each.

60. What are 'hygroscopic' and 'non-hygroscopic' cargoes?

61. Why is 'dew point' so important in cargo ventilation?

62. Define 'air conditioning' in terms of cargo spaces.

63. Describe briefly the features connected with general ventilation and how, in modern methods, this is achieved.

64. Describe briefly the main arrangements concerned with the basics of ventilation and their uses.

65. What do you understand by 'The safe packing and marking of cargo'?

66. What, briefly, are the main features of: conventional, pallet, container, roll on/roll off, multi-purpose and lash vessels?

67. Outline the characteristics of a container as a suitable conveyance for cargo.

68. In terms of handling cargo in a port or dock, enumerate the main items of mechanical equipment available. Comment upon the particular applications of each.

69. What is a 'low loader'?

70. What is an 'indivisible load'?

71. Explain, briefly, the different characteristics of:
    (a) Unit load berths.
    (b) Specialized berths.
    (c) Break bulk berths.

72. Why does a ship influence the type and extent of development in a port or dock?

73. What are the dominant factors necessary to the correct rigging of derricks?

74. What do you understand by the 'raise', 'traverse', and 'lower' terms use in cargo handling?

75. How would you ensure stability in the processes of derrick/crane working, irrespective of type?

76. Summarize the Docks Regulations, 1934.

77. What is understood by a 'heavy derrick'? How do different types apply to different tonnage loads?

78. What do you understand by 'stresses upon cargo gear'? How can these be minimized?

79. Enumerate some types of slings used in cargo handling and the cargoes for which they are suitable.

80. What are the particular precautions to be observed where

mechanical patent power operated rolling hatch covers are fitted?

81. What is a 'Velle' derrick/crane? What is meant by load stabilization?
82. Define 'heavy lift' in terms of the load ranges involved.
83. Enumerate briefly some of the characteristics of the Stuelcken mast and derrick.
84. Briefly describe some of the major precautionary measures to be adopted in the use of the 'Velle', 'Hallen', and 'Stuelcken' derricks.
85. Compare the derrick with the crane and indicate the advantages and disadvantages of each.
86. What is understood by the 'master and slave' arrangements with derrick/crane rigging? Indicate a particular type of load for which you would use this method.
87. Outline the precautions necessary when working deck cranes.
88. Describe some of the procedures in the handling of forest products. Indicate your understanding of the term and any special methods applicable to different cargoes.
89. What is the concept of securing and lashing? What kinds of attention do different forms of cargo require?
90. Where, and why, does the centre of gravity of a load influence securing and lashing?
91. What is understood by 'in lanes' with the loading of vehicular traffic on a roll on/roll off vessel?
92. The carriage of containers calls for particular securing and lashing requirements, and M.S.N.s refer to these. Discuss the need for these.
93. What is an 'intermediate bulk carrier'? Outline some of its advantages.
94. Outline some of the main precautionary measures with an iron and steel cargo, carried in bulk loads. Indicate your understanding of the types of loads which would fall into this category.
95. Outline the precautions necessary with iron and steel swarf.
96. Outline the main precautions with a coal cargo.
97. What is coal slurry?
98. What is 'The Blue Book'?
99. Outline the main features of marking with dangerous goods.
100. What is a dangerous cargo?
101. Summarize, briefly, 'The Code of Practice for Ships carrying Timber Deck Cargoes'.
102. To what extent does 'stability' enter into the carriage of timber?
103. Compare the carriage of 'loose' and 'packaged' timber and give your understanding of the development of the latter.

104. Under what regulations is the carriage of grain covered? What are the main features?
105. Indicate the provisions of stability in the loading and carriage of grain.
106. How would you ventilate a grain cargo?
107. Discuss the development in the carriage of ores and similar derivatives.
108. Summarize/outline the main provisions of The Code of Practice for Bulk Cargoes.
109. What is 'ore concentrates' and what particular precautions are necessary with its carriage?
110. What is:
    (*a*) Angle of repose.
    (*b*) Flow moisture point.
    (*c*) Moisture content.
111. Describe the general precautions desirable prior to the loading of a bulk cargo.
112. Compare cargoes carried in insulated containers and in non-insulated holds. To which forms of cargo can each apply and what care and attention is required with each system?
113. Define:
    (*a*) 'Reefer container'.
    (*b*) 'Port hole' container.
114. What is 'brine circuit' in refrigeration?
115. What refrigeration considerations are necessary with:
    (*a*) Bananas.
    (*b*) Citrus fruits.
    (*c*) Deciduous fruits.
116. Briefly outline the refrigeration system of a container vessel.
117. Describe a system of refrigeration control.
118. What are the main differences in the carriage of 'frozen' and 'chilled' refrigerated products?
119. Explain the 'concept of unitization'.
120. What is a 'spreader'? For what purpose is it used and why is it considered to be an important item of cargo handling equipment?
121. What is understood by a 'system' in container handling?
122. What is understood by palletization? Describe the form and purpose of pallets and the precautions with their use.
123. Describe some of the systems applicable to the carriage of motor cars and outline the precautions against hazards with motor car 'decks'.
124. Define a 'tanker'.
125. What is 'restrictive draft', as applied to tankers?
126. Define a V.L.C.C.
127. Discuss the advantages of crude oil washing of tanks.
128. What is 'clingage'?

129. What is 'inert gas' and how is this applicable to tank cleaning?
130. Why are precautions necessary with high speed water or oil jets in the washing of tanks?
131. Under what conditions would you fit locking bars after, otherwise, correctly battening down a hatchway?
132. Enumerate the types of lashing/securing devices used for containers and vehicular cargoes and indicate the methods of ensuring correct tension and security.
133. Quote the fundamental rule relating to the stability provisions for ships carrying grain in bulk.
134. What is the stability information booklet and how does it affect the duties of cargo officers?
135. How does the density of bulk cargoes relate to void spaces in holds and what precautions are necessary in this matter?
136. What are the three major hazards appropriate to bulk cargoes?
137. What particular precautions are necessary with a cargo of wood pulp bales?
138. How would you plan for the loading of a multi-purpose vessel, as distinct from a conventional general carrier and what particular types of gear would you expect to either have on hand or be involved with? What particular matters would you expect to deal with, and supervise?
139. For what reason is it recommended that where cargo is stowed in a 'tween deck reasonable space should be left between the edge of the stow and the hatch coaming? What is this recommended space?
140. Describe, briefly, the system of manifolds, inlets and cargo lines in tanker construction.
141. What is the purpose and application of the following:
    (a) Free flow system.
    (b) Direct loading system.
    (c) Ring main system.
    (d) Products carrier layout.
142. What is the purpose of a P.V. valve in tanker construction?
143. In what manner does The British Standards Institution influence the working of Cargo Gear?
144. In what manner does the I.M.O. (1981) Bulk Cargo Code influence the permissible tonnage loaded into a cargo space?
145. To what degree does the I.M.O. (1981) Bulk Cargo Code differ from previous recommendations?
146. What is the basic safety principle with the handling of Liquefied Natural Gas?
147. Which gas compound has the 'greater' influence upon L.N.G. and to what extent must the fact be appreciated?
148. What is understood by the term 'containment' with Liquefied Natural Gas carriage?

149. What is 'Boil Off'?
150. Which aspect of L.N.G. handling presents the 'greatest' risk? What precautions can contain this?
151. It is considered that 'Three Main Hazards' can arise with the handling of Liquefied Natural Gas, in its carriage. Enumerate these and indicate pointers of precaution.
152. What documents—primarily—should govern a ship's officer's behaviour in the carriage and handling of L.N.G.?
153. Outline, briefly, the major aspects of Organization and Administration in Marine Cargo Transportation.
154. Why are Ports more interested in 'classes' of ships, as distinct from 'types' of ships?
155. Identify short, medium and long term objectives in Marine Cargo Management practice.
156. How is Marine Cargo Management practice related to The Business of Shipping?
157. What features of Ports facilities should exercise the mind of a Cargo Officer?
158. How do you see the 'How', 'When', 'Why' and 'Where' factors in Marine Cargo Management practice?
159. What is understood by 'The Intermodal' aspect?
160. Define... Freight Aspects.
Chartering Aspects.
161. What is:
    (a) A Booking List.
    (b) A Way Bill.
    (c) Document of Title.
    (d) Contract of Carriage.
162. What is 'C.I.F.'. 'F.O.B.'?
163. What functions influence Planning and Monitoring of Cargo Handling?
164. To what extent can computerized systems assist in minimizing the Load Stresses in Large Vessels?
165. Develop a brief thesis on the essentials of The Code of Safe Working Practice for Merchant Seamen.
166. What is a Hazardous Zone?
167. What is understood by 'Cargo Access Systems'?
168. In what manner can 'Vibratory Stress' on a ship affect cargo stowage?
169. What is a 'geared' and/or a 'gearless' ship?
170. What documentary 'codes' influence the safety aspect of cargo handling?
171. Where 'systems' are employed in Ports Cargo Handling procedures, what does this imply?
172. What is understood by Vibratory Stresses on a ship? How can these affect cargo stowage?
173. What are the main considerations in drawing up a Cargo Plan?

174. What precautions are necessary in the stowing and handling of Newsprint paper reels?
175. What is meant by Fork Lift Truck 'Clamping' with reels of paper?
176. What is a tiltable mast on a Fork Lift Truck?
177. Enumerate some of the main documentation factors affecting the movement of cargo, and their purpose.
178. What precautions are necessary with the working of a Fork Lift Truck, either on quay or in ship?
179. Why is a Fork Lift Truck steered by the rear wheels?
180. Outline the major points of maintenance with a Fork Lift Truck.
181. In. what respect does the term 'Cargo Access Equipment' differ from 'hatch covers'?
182. Enumerate some of the more prominent modern means of hatch coverings and the types of ships to which they can be applicable.
183. What 'regulation' influences Cargo Access Equipment?
184. How would you stow reels of paper (newsprint)
      1. On platforms.   2. By modern systems.
185. What features or factors have bearing upon the design and fitting of a piece of access equipment for a ship?
186. Outline, briefly, the main features of the I.L.O. Guides to Safety & Health. (1) In Docks and (2) In Ships in so far as these affect cargo handling.
187. Enumerate some of the features of Modern Forest Products Carriers.
188. What are the main forest products consignments? How are they packed, slung, loaded and distributed?
189. Define, briefly, the term 'Forest Products'.
190. Outline, briefly, the I.S.O. Recommendations relating to the carriage of Containers.
191. Outline your views on the modern systems of determining the Stability condition of a loaded and of a loading container vessel.
192. What are the recommendations covering the problem of Pollution with ships?
193. What is 'pond coal'?
194. What is the safety temperature for the carriage of coal?
195. What is the preferable method of stowing and trimming coal?
196. What are 'general arrangements' in respect of ship design? How can they assist cargo handling?

THE PRINCIPLES OF AND BACKGROUND TO CARGO HANDLING

(Guide Lines and Check Lists)

(The notes which follow supports all of the relevant text treated in detail in this book)

First Principles

The transportation of cargo is, primarily, related to two functions ... to carry raw materials for the use and development of a nation's industries and to move manufactured and processed goods according to the needs of a nation's current and envisaged expanding economy. Both are interwoven and of advantage to all countries, those established and those developing.

In brief this is known as PATTERNS OF TRADE.

To carry out the foregoing carriers, in the maritime orbit, are of specific types and classes, each and all appropriate to the commodities available for transportation. Each type, or class of carrier, to meet these demands, is designed, and built, to effectively and safely be able to deal with the "peculiarities" and requirements of the different cargoes which the patterns of trade promote.

In general terms this is known is STOWAGE.

Stowage is a matter of planning and co-operation/co-ordination between a wide area of interests and applications which make up a "TRANSPORTATION MODE". This evolves within the BUSINESS OF SHIPPING.

The largest unit within this area is THE SHIP and, for it to be profitable, stowage is very much a case of "WHY" ... "HOW" "WHEN" and "WHERE". The process of meeting these requirements is known as CARGO HANDLING, towards which those responsible for the part played by the ship is of major importance.

Cargo handling is not just the ensurance that a ship is correctly stowed. It calls, also for a knowledge and understanding of the properties of cargoes and the rules, regulations, recommendations and Codes of Practice which surround and support acceptable procedures.

Cargo handling takes into account the care and safety of the ship (indeed "safety" ranks high in modern cargo carriage), the effective use of equipment and services available in working the cargoes, and the most acceptable placing of the goods comprising the cargoes, in order to ensure their effective acceptance and distribution. It is also highly related to the practice of STABILITY ... cargo stowage and stability are inter-related ... they cannot be otherwise.

As an agent in the acceptance, carriage and distribution of the goods comprising the cargoes, nothing is decisive in itself ... the operations and procedures can be influenced by international custom and tradition . . . practices can show differences in different ports. As such, the ship and its personnel must always be open to improvisation as circumstances dictate . . . accepting, without any doubt whatever, that there is no deviation from safety standards.

There is a "language" in cargo handling much of which has universal acceptance. This is known as TERMS, all having meaningful definitions. In themselves, terms are guide lines. (Which see).

In this modern age, however, the transportation mode is continually becoming increasingly influenced by technological/scientific aspects, including computerized systems. The ship, no less than other supporting areas, is involved, with methods of cargo working so assisted, while THE PORTS, to which the ships trade, are now more involved in SYSTEMS of cargo handling, as distinct from methods.

There is therefore, a need for a balanced approach using both the old (basic), and the new, each to assist the other. This it is and continuation as such will remain the order of things. It is a progressive function and alongside there must be a demand for well, broadly trained and knowledgeable officers. By the very nature of things this cannot be otherwise and in the process fundamental basics should not be ignored but applied such as to make the more sophisticated procedures increasingly meaningful.

To build up an intelligent background approach to all of the foregoing, and to be capable of effective application, is to understand THE ART OF CARGO WORK, in which context the study of a Cargo Officer's professional discipline must now contain a wider concern than hitherto was applied when cargo matters were less complex.

The Environmental Influences

Whereas hitherto the movement of goods followed, more or less, established patterns, no longer do such restrictions apply, nor are ships so consistent in their habits.

As markets develop ships follow to benefit from the trade available. Conversely, shipping is equally reactive to unprofitable markets with ships, in the ultimate, disappearing from routes previously used, to show up elsewhere. This pattern of behaviour has grown out of new areas where more and newer raw materials have become available and where financial investment in the economy of developing countries has enabled them to compete more widely and require goods and equipment to support their economic progression, and their standards of living.

Alongside, the established highly commercialized countries expand their marketing and develop their "industry" to meet the needs of nations less able to maintain similar standards (or are in the process of aiming to such directions) promote their results accordingly. Not only is this to be seen as between industrialized and non-industrialized countries, the same considerations apply inter-continentally where there is evidence of considerable trading patterns.

All of the foregoing has led, and continues to lead, to especially adaptable ships.

A trade pattern is not a static involvement nor in any way is it an insular matter . . . on the contrary it is continually changing though it could be said to be only an extension of the past. The difference now is that it is more "world" influenced and has to be interpreted accordingly. It is, however, basic to cargo handling . . . and its development. Its study, in reasonable depth, is not only desirable but essential to the position of an effective cargo officer.

While he would not be expected to practise professionally in this aspect of the Business of Shipping, none the less he does make a contribution by reason of the extent of influence by which the ship for which he is responsible, must be a profitable unit.

Alongside the developing and current trade patterns is the area which aims to serve them . . . namely The Business of Shipping. This arena is at all times conscious of, and endeavouring to anticipate cycles of prosperity in the movement of trade. Since these cycles are dependant upon the fluctuations in world trade, ships can be affected by reason of becoming both over and under employed, both in the short and long term, thus creating instability in the business of running ships. The Business of Shipping therefore contains a high degree of careful judicious planning and by balancing facilities available in the employment of its ships. Only by employing and using the right type and class of ship can it aim to alleviate what otherwise might be a slump period.

The ship itself, therefore, whatever its type or class, and its cargoes, is very much a part of the Business of Shipping . . . indeed it is the activist, and towards the Patterns of Trade also.

The former is highly financially orientated . . . the latter intensely influenced by international economic and political considerations.

It is not, therefore, out of place to coin a phrase . . . "the romance has now gone out of shipping" to be replaced by hard financial practicality. "Small" in as much as a ship may be, in the wider spectrum and in relation to the overall activities of its owning company, it is a "capital cost" both in building and in operating and thus must, like any other part of a group to which it belongs, "pay its way" . . . i.e. obtain revenue.

The manner and effectiveness with which it carries and handles its cargoes is a major factor as to whether or not it is acceptable to the shipping community (buyers . . . sellers . . . importers . . . exporters). If it is, it will remain of viable advantage, maintaining acceptable reputation, from which its owners will feel justified in keeping it in service. If the contrary is the case it may be switched to other trades, laid up or even sold within the second hand ship market. Whichever may be the case, the result can be traumatic for its personnel. Sentimental considerations no longer can be justified in the maritime world albeit their absence raises wide implications in the maintenance of a healthy shipping community.

It behoves ship officers, therefore, to be familiar and understanding of the ramifications of The Patterns of Trade and of The Business of Shipping. Each carries deep influences and establishes the reasons for effective cargo handling. It is not out of place that, in this modern age, career progression is not necessarily now a matter of one ship, from Mate to Master but a case of broad experience, qualification and understanding in order to be adaptable, come what may be the opportunities. This is so, be it within the general carriers or in the specialized vessels.

Relative to the foregoing, effectiveness stems from efficiency, the latter resulting from sound knowledge acquired from study, research, examination and, not the least, wide experience and application. Effectiveness in cargo handling is the sound realistic approach to the "Why ... How ... Where and When" aspects. There is an answer to each of these. Why does a cargo need to be handled in a particular way ... how should that cargo be handled ... where should it be stowed ... when should it be loaded, or discharged?

All of the above is a co-ordinated and co-operative matter as between the care and safety of the ship, the care and safety of the cargo(es), the care and safety of personnel, the right use of proper equipment and facilities and the profitable association with others equally interested in that ship and its cargo, notably consignees, consignors, forwarding agents, other forms of transportation and, most of all, the organization of the port(s) with which the ship becomes concerned.

This is known as The Management of Cargo Control.

Organization and Administration

Cargo handling, no less than in any other area involving men, materials and equipment, is subject to organization and administration.

There is need for systematic control and those responsible for employing such systems have numerous related functions directed towards ensuring that their own abilities and actions and those also with whom their work processes impinge, can be identifiable and meaningful.

In this context, the Cargo Officer's responsibility has a first call in "setting out his stall" (his ship) in such a manner as to make it attractive and acceptable to the markets it serves. That is to say ... its facilities and equipment, and the knowledge of its personnel, are adequately available and in sound order to be appropriate to the types and cargoes it is going to carry.

Administratively, the Cargo Officer has responsibility to ensure that all the organizational framework ... "work" ... that he has a policy of behaviour understood by all personnel (ship company) whose duties are related to the ability of the ship to carry and work its cargo when, and how required.

Much of a Cargo Officer's administrative ability will stem from his knowledge and understanding of "legislative procedures" upon which the handling of cargo is controlled and, above all else, the practices within the "policy directions" of the company which he, and the ship, serves.

SOME PRACTICALITIES ... DESIRABLE AND/OR ESSENTIAL FUNCTIONS

(*No precedence of interpretation is intended by this layout*)

Ideally, ships should be full to capacity each time they are loaded.

Loading and discharging should be carried out rationally and as quickly as possible ... commensurate with the safety of the vessel.

Loading and discharging must have recourse to appropriate rules, regulations and recommendations.

Co-ordinated and co-operative planning is essential.

The technical/scientific features of ships ... and of their "ports" is of vital understanding.

Dangerous goods now make up a vast area of cargo carriage ... demanding strict attention to legislation.

Cargo Plans are essential to effective cargo handling but their formation must be free from any form of misinterpretation.

Mechanical handling now forms a wide area of cargo handling ... with little, if any restrictions upon types of cargoes. Careful attention to the methods is essential.

Ship behaviour in seaways is a prerequisite of cargo stowage methods ... re vibratory and torsional stresses.

Bulk cargoes ... particularly the very heavy deadweight commodities ... impose particular attentions to stowage and to the safety (stability) of the ship.

Combination carriers ... ore/oil, ore/bulk/oil call for especial attention to "cleaning" procedures ... particularly relevant to pollution.

Container handling is a matter of "load planning".

Roll on/Roll off vessels call for attention in speeds of working, the safeguarding of loads, the solidarity of stow and the stability of the vessel.

Reefer vessels highlights temperature control.

Safety and Health in Dock work involves and affects the ship as well.

Haste, excessive speeds of operation and over zealousness ... apart from neglect, are the main causes of hazards arising in cargo handling.

Modern access equipment (hatch coverings) etc. raise their own hazards, albeit, with sensible handling, they are efficient attributes to cargo work.

The combination of a variety of mechanical/electrical forms of equipment in ships raises the question of strict adherance to maintenance.

Slinging, including pre-slinging, is very much a part of cargo handling which frequently involves "custom and tradition". Care is needed.

Cargo Handling calls for strict attention to the ship Stability Handbook . . . the trim and stability particulars and to the various Codes of Practice.

The carriage of chemical cargoes calls for particular care.

An essential feature of Cargo Handling is "To know your own ship".

A coal cargo calls for especial care re types of coal and voyages.

Container stacking is influenced by I.S.O. recommendations.

The success of a refrigerated voyage is measured by the condition in which the cargo arrives at the port of discharge.

Unitization, with its broad applications, contains major aspects of ship responsibility, notably those related to safe packing, handling and movement. Particularly is this so where palletization is involved.

General cargo carriage imposes strict attention to the "condition" of spaces to be used and to effective stowage planning in the avoidance of incorrect discharge, distribution and overcarriage.

Barrels should, preferably, be given "bottom" stowage and well chocked to give solidarity of stow.

Deck cargo, whatever its form, must comply with appropriate "rules".

The carriage of petroleum is of a character which imposes hazards. Strict attention to "company" rules and manuals is imperative.

Ore/Bulk/Oil carriers (specialist carriers) usually of large deadweight tonnage, call for strict planning sequences in loading and discharging apropos the Ship Stability Handbook.

Liquefied Natural Gas (L.N.G.) cargoes, though if properly handled need not be any more difficult nor hazardous than a normal petroleum cargo, call for strict attention to Codes of Practice and "company" operating manuals.

Ship cargo handling time "on berth" is a major factor of transportation costs. A ship does not earn money (freight) unless it is at sea. on normal business.

CARGO HANDLING TERMS...A GLOSSARY

(Terms used in cargo handling are wide in application and will frequently relate to traditional customs in different areas and ports ... and indeed with different countries. It is nigh impossible to try to include all possibilities or probabilities; the following is a representative list covering a reasonable sphere of Cargo Work. Detail information relating to any one of these terms is included in the main text of this book.)

A.

Access Equipment...the modern term relating to hatch covering and other systems of access and egress with cargo movement.

Angle of Repose...the angle of a bulk load as between its "cone shape" and the horizontal plane surface on which it is stowed.

Asymmetrical Loading...the peculiarity of container working which gives rise to torsional moments.

Average...the term relating to maritime ship insurance cover, where a ship, or its cargo, is lost or damaged.

B.

Bale Clamp...automatic lifting arrangement for Bales of paper pulp.

Bareboat Charter...where an operator hires a vessel to cover all his trading requirements.

Barge Ships...vessels especially designed to carry standard size barges, loaded on to and from them.

Barrels...specially constructed wooden carriers for liquids, needful of being stowed in a particular manner.

Bay Level...computerized stowage information for containers loaded into bays.

Bill of Lading...the receipt for goods (cargoes) ... the document of title.

Bill of Lading...T.B.L....a through bill of lading finding application in the European/continental through services.

Blue Book...Report of Department of Trade & Industry (U.K.) Advisory Committee on the carriage of dangerous goods in ships.

B.M....Distance of Metacentre from the Centre of Buoyancy.

Body Damage...relative to paper reels.

Boil Off...an evaporation feature of L.N.G. (Liquid Natural Gas).

Break Bulk Cargo...commodities of different types and sizes making up a "general cargo".

Broaching...the pilferage of cargo.

Broken Stowage...space lost in a compartment due mainly to the variable sizes/shapes of goods to be loaded.

Bulk Cargo...that classified as of a bulk nature . . . covers many forms of commodities.

C.

Cargo Plan...a diagramatic "picture" of the distribution of cargo within the hold/spaces of a ship

Cargo Runner...the wire from the winch, through sheaves, to the derrick head (or cargo block).

Certificate of Origin...documentation certifying duties having been paid.

Charter Party...the document covering the conditions of chartering.

Chartering . . . the hiring or lending of a ship by its owners, to another operator, for a period of time.

Chop Mark...an identification marking on the outside of a unit of cargo.

C.I.F....cost, insurance, freight...the costs involvent indicated in a contract of carriage.

Claims...action against damage, injury or carriage faults to cargo or personnel with which the cargo officer may be involved as witness.

Clamping force...the pressure (or force) to enable a clamp to correctly and safely lift, place or move a reel of paper.

Clamps...attachments to clamp trucks...fixed, rotating and tippling, in the handling of paper reels.

Coal slurry...fine particles of coal containing a large proportion of moisture and mineral matter.

Codes of Practice...guide lines relative to the safe, handling and carriage of goods. Wide and substansive, carrying rules, recommendations and regulations officially issued and to be followed.

Combi Ships...combination carriers...bulk, conventional etc ...i.e. multi-purpose. Sometimes referred to as Combination carriers.

Concentrates...a bulk cargo having undergone purification or physical separation of undesirable ingredients.

Consignment Notes...authorization for hauliers to move goods.

Container Level...overall computerized information of essential "working data" in loading and discharging containers.

Container Module...the "open" design factor having relevance to modern (multi-purpose) cargo liners.

Container Ship...the cellular "open" deck vessel.

Containers...the "boxes"..."TEUs" for the stowage of cargo

which, mainly can be of three types...standard, toploader or half heights, available for a wide variety of cargoes.

Containment System . . . space provisions for Liquid Natural Gas.

Contract of Sale . . . arrangements between exporters and purchasers of goods.

Conventional Break Bulk...term applied to cargo liners.

Core Probe...an arrangement for lifting paper reels.

Cranston Unit...a specialized...vessel fitted crane for Forest Product handling.

Critical Moment...a stability function related to the effect upon vessels with a "small" GM when moving heavy weights.

Cyrogenic...very low temperature.

D.

Dangerous Cargoes...those which by reason of their inflammable or explosive nature are liable to spontaneous combustion, and which are covered by special requirements in their carriage.

Dangerous Oils...those having flash points less than 73°F.

Deck Cargo...that cargo suitable for and desirable to be stowed above deck.

Demurrage...money paid to the shipowner when a vessel on charter exceeds its agreed lay days.

Despatch...a financial imbursement paid by a shipowner to a charterer when the vessel on charter uses less than the agreed lay days to complete loading/discharging.

Direct Loading System...a method of pipe line layout in oil tankers.

Dock Dues Bill...documentation covering the payment of Ports/Docks charges.

Driving Power (Fork Lift Trucks)...by front drive axles.

Dunnage...the use of material...frequently loose wood but can be other materials, to assist in the solidarity and protection of cargo.

Dwell Time...unnecessary time spent in port.

E.

Edge Damage...relative to paper reels caused by unusual striking or pressure to the edge of the reel.

Emergency Shut Down...a vital precautionary measure written into Oil Company's Operating Manual.

Environmental Damage...that arising to cargo from water or excessive moisture. It could be also the failure of a refrigerated unit in a reefer container.

Equilibrium (Stability)...sometimes referred to as Stable Stability, with the loading of a vessel or distribution of weight, that she has a moderate amount of metacentric height. (M above G).

Export Licences...documentation requirements of Governments for certain types of cargoes.

F.

Flash Point...the temperature at which a combustible liquid gives off vapour which will fire or explode if mixed with air and exposed momentarily to a naked light.

Flow Moisture Point...the moisture content at which a fluid state could occur. Important in assessing the safety factor in the carriage of such cargoes.

F.O.B. . . . Free on Board. (re Contracts of Carriage).

Forest Product Carriers...specially designed vessels to handle various types of forest products.

Forest Products...wide varieties of "prepared" timber or the by-products of timber.

Fork Lift Trucks . . . Steering . . . by the stern, wheel axle.

Free Flow System...a method of pipe line layout in oil tankers.

Free Surface...unfilled tanks/spaces of water or liquid which, when in movement has effect upon the CG–GM metacentric height, in reducing its amount.

Freight . . . the charge levied for carrying goods . . . cargoes.

F.W.A....Fresh Water Allowance. A factor to be allowed for when loading in, or passing into or out of Fresh Water.

G.

Gantry Cranes...back up handling equipment for lift on/lift off container work.

Gas Detection...a continuous aspect of observation with L.N.G. (Liquid Natural Gas) carriage.

Gearless Vessel...ship designed such that the handling of its cargo is dependant upon shore gear entirely...notably in the bulk trades.

General Arrangements...a detailed plan of the design and building provisions of a ship, issued by the shipbuilders. Invaluable in providing guide lines for the safe loading and handling of cargoes.

General Average ... maritime insurance cover for the general benefit of parties interested in damage to ship or cargo.

G.M. ... the metacentric height of a vessel as a result of weight distribution.

Grain Space . . . the internal volume space to the limit of the ship side plating re holds and cargo spaces.

Gravity Loading ... bulks loaded into a vessel from overhead chutes.

H.

Hatch Covers ... coverings to the hatchways of holds and spaces ... now more usually referred to as access equipment.

Head Damage ... relative to paper reels ... indentations to the ends of the reel.

Headroom ... the clear distance from the top of a hatchway to the joint of two runners/or the cargo hook.

Heavy Derrick ... a derrick specially designed, or rigged, to handle over average weights.

Heavy Lifts ... cargo loaded above average weights which normally requires special derrick or crane design, adapted rigging to normal derricks or special mechanical equipment.

High Quality Coal ... of high methane content ... likely, in the absence of care, to induce explosive reaction.

Homogeneous Cargoes ... cargo of similar/like types.

Horizontal Movement ... or transportation ... cargo movement by mechanical handling equipment.

Hot Coal ... coal with a high water content and unfree from a sulphur condition. Likely to develop high temperatures on long voyages (sometimes known as "Pond Coal") which see.

Humidity Checking ... testing the soundness of insulation features in L.N.G. Carriers.

Hydrodynamic Forces ... caused by "sloshing" liquid cargo within a hold against the hatch covers.

Hydrostatic Forces ... with particular reference to liquid cargoes the intermittent pressure of the liquid, with the ship rolling or pitching, against the internal surfaces of the hatch covers.

Hygroscopic Cargoes ... those mainly of vegetable origin affected by the humidity of the atmosphere, giving off and retaining atmosphere, leading to ship sweat.

I.

Ignition Point ... the lowest temperature to which oil must be raised so that the vapour evolves at a rate which permits continuous burning when a flame is momentarily applied.

I.L.O. ... International Labour Office notably concerned with Health and Safety in ports and with ship working.

I.M.O. ... International Maritime Organization (responsible for a variety of Codes of Practice)

Inboard Boom ... a derrick positioned over the hatchway.

Indivisible Loads ... cargo of exceptional weight and design calling for especial means of handling (not to be confused with "heavy weights").

Infestation ... damage to cargo from insects and mites.

Infrastructure ... the areas surrounding a port from which, and into which, trading patterns and movement of goods relate.

Intermediate Bulk Carriers ... (I.B.C.s) a "bag type" mini bulk carrier ... differing sizes ... used for adaptable forms of bulk carriage with loads larger than conventional bags.

Intermodal ... the "chain" in the transportation of cargo ... acceptance, carriage, distribution.

International Load Line Convention ... rules which govern the fitting of access equipment to ships.

I.S.O. ... International Standards Organization ... body responsible in respect of containers and their handling.

I.T.M. ... Inch Trim Moment, force related to the fore and aft trimming factor in loading and discharging.

I/V ... formula derivation for Moment of Inertia of Waterplane.

L.

Lashing of Cargo ... securing cargo from movement by forms of strapping.

Lay Days ... time allocated for a vessel on charter to load and/or discharge.

L.C.G. ... Longitudinal Centre of Gravity.

L.N.G. ... Liquid Natural Gas (cargoes).

Loadmaster ... computerized digital calculation equipment used for preplanning and distribution of all types of cargoes aboard ships, or for cargo operations in port or for checking hull stresses.

L.O.T. ... a term, related to Tankers ... Load on Top ... concerned with tank cleaning procedures.

Low Flash Oil ... having a flash point below the statutory minimum (73°F, U.K.).

Low Grade Coal ... less porous, losing any gas content quickly.

M.

Management Practice . . . Ship Shore . . . co-ordination/co-operation between ship and shore, in the working of cargo . . . Codes of Practice issued by The International Chamber of Shipping and The International Shipping Federation.

Manifest ... the complete list of all cargo carried in a ship ... per voyage.

Marpol ... International convention proposals covering the prevention of pollution.

Master and Slave ... a twinning arrangement with two electric/electric hydraulic cranes, situated at opposite ends of a hatch opening.

Master Plan ... the compilation of a "running" plan whilst the vessel is loading, from and by which planning and replanning of the final stow can be achieved.

Mate's Receipt ... the ship's receipt ... signed by the Mate/Chief Officer for cargo received on board.

Measurement Space ... that volume of internal hold space up to the inner edge of the spar ceiling.

Measurement Tonnage ... cargo on which the freight charged is based upon volume per ton, either $40\,\mathrm{ft}^3$ or $36\,\mathrm{m}^3$.

Mechanical Damage .. damage to cargo from breakage, scraping, scratching and other forms of physical deformation generally resulting from improper packaging, improper stowing and rough handling.

Mechanical Movement of Cargo ... that by conveyors or pneumatic systems transversely for bulk cargo.

Membrane ... the insulation fitment materials to tanks holding L.N.G.

Methane ... the main constituent of L.N.G. (Liquid Natural Gas) to which precise attention must be given.

Microbiological Spoilage ... damage to cargo from bacteria and mould.

"M" Notices ... Published rules, regulations and recommendations by the (U.K.) Department of Transport covering acceptable (and necessary) procedures in the handling of cargoes and the safety of ships.

Moisture Content ... the percentage of water/liquid in a bulk cargo.

Moisture Migration ... the transfer of moisture through a stowed cargo during the voyage.

Multi Grab ... mechanical-hydraulic clam arrangement for the handling of tape or wired bound bales of paper pulp, in multiple units.

Munck Transporter Crane . . . specialized (vessel fitted) crane for forest products.

N.

Neutral Stability ... the loading of a vessel or distribution of weight that she has no metacentric height. G & M coincident. Unfavourable condition.

Non Dangerous Oils ... having flash points above 150°F.

Non Homogeneous Cargo . . . cargo of variable sizes and content.

Non Hygroscopic Cargoes . . . materials of "solid" nature (steel, canned goods, machinery, earthenware etc., which can be damaged from cargo sweat.

O.

Optional Cargo ... cargo loaded when, at the time, its exact port of discharge is unknown but may be indicated later (on voyage). Calls for special stowage.

Ordinary Oils ... having flash between 73°F and 150°F.

Out of Roundness . . . relative to paper reels . . . the affect upon these by incorrect pressure clamp handling, incorrect gripping, accidental dropping, unevenly landing or excessive pressure if stowed horizontally.

Outward Boom ... derrick positioned outboard, to either side of the ship.

Overlift ... re Fork Lift Trucks ... stacking above and behind an existing load.

P.

Packaged Timber ... that made up into standard units.

Palletized Cargo ... that loaded on to pallets.

Pallets ... wood or metal "trays" on to which units of cargo can be packaged and handled into larger individual units.

Panamax Vessel . . . a bulk ship designed to have the greatest possible deadweight capacity consistent with constraints set upon it by water depths and locks of the Panama Canal.

P & I Insurance ... a specific form of insurance cover through Protection and Indemnity Clubs, covering a variety of claims outside of the established "average" systems.

Piling ... cargo standing on its ends ... notably relevant to "circular" items ... drums or paper reels, for example.

Pond Coal ... that left over from earlier mining and dumped into "ponds" later to be reclaimed and shipped. See Hot Coal.

Port Marking ... a system, usually coloured indexes for different ports (Circles, Triangles etc) stamped on to the outside of a cargo unit to assist stowage and discharge.

Port Speed ... cargo working as quickly and as rationally possible.

Port Time ... time spent in port loading and/or discharging. High ship cost factor.

Ports facilities ... cargo handling systems, services, methods and costs in ports.

Prediction ... planning "future" requirements in cargo/load working from computerized simulation.

Pre-Plan Stowage ... the term relating to forward planning of cargo space utilization.

Pre-Slinging ... cargo made up into "slinged" loads on quay or in warehouse, prior to it being loaded into the ship.

Print Outs ... tabulated data results covering computerized elements of cargo working.

Probe Clamp ... an arrangement for the lifting of paper reels.

Pumping Speeds ... re Tankers ... minimum and maximum rates, to which attention has to be given.

Q.

Quick Turn Round ... utilizing all cargo handling facilities to get a ship in, and out of a port in the minimum amount of time, consistent with all effective and safety measures.

R.

Ramps . . . means of transporting or transferring cargo units from one position to another, either between ship and quay or between ship internal decks.

Reefers ... a specialized vessel (or a container) for the carriage of refrigerated products.

Registration ... ships ... the classification of a vessel by an appropriate authority ... a classification society ... as to its suitability for the "work" it is intended to do.

Ring Main Systems ... a method of pipe line layout in oil tankers.

Roto Loaders ... equipment for moving cargo loads between decks.

S.

Seaworthiness ... explicit in British Common Law is that "Cargo Worthiness" is an essential element of seaworthiness.

Securing of Cargo ... the prevention of cargo from movement ... variety of appropriate system. While there is no mandatory or other specific regulations covering the fastening of cargoes, the British Carriage of Goods by Sea Act ... and equivalent legislation in other maritime countries, are implicit in the requirements to secure cargo against all movement.

Semi-Submersible ... vessels capable of being submerged horizontally to load and/or discharge very heavy floated objects.

Ship Measurement ... Gross or Net.

Shipping Bills ... for Customs clearance.

Shipping Note ... documentary evidence covering the shipment of goods which is forwarded by the shipper to the shipowner.

Side Shifters ... loads accepted on to platforms and slewed inboard.

Simulation ... the use of, and practical application of, detail afforded by computerized ship loading/discharging.

Slewing Guy ... that derrick guy for placing or altering the position of the derrick.

Slinging ... the handling and movement of cargoes by rope, wire, chain nets or metal frame slings.

Span Blocks ... those blocks which carry the wire leads affording the span (or positioning) of a derrick.

Specialized Cargo ... especial types such as containers, palletized loads, heavy indivisible, cars, paper, etc.

Specie Cargo . . . vulnerable (valuable) cargo calling for special safety and loading requirements.

Spillage ... leakage from manifold loading or discharging points in L.N.G. carriers. Awareness essential ... potentially dangerous.

Stability Handbook ... detailed information relating to a ship's stability qualities and its requirements in the loading/discharging/handling of cargoes.

Stacking ... cargo fitted into load height and cubic arrangements.

Stacking Heights ... containers ... influenced by I.S.O. recommendations according to sizes of containers and their weights.

Standing Guy ... that guy used to hold a derrick in its required position.

Steering ... fork lift truck ... by the rear axles.

Steulken Mast & Derrick ... specialized mast/derrick design arrangement for the handling of "heavy weight loads".

Stiff Ship ... vessel loaded with weight distribution such that she has a "large" metacentric height likely to make her uncomfortable in a seaway.

Stowage Factor ... the amount of space which a "parcel" of cargo will require.

Stowage Order ... the consideration of the character, sizes, contents and ports of discharge in planning the order of effective stowage.

Straddle Carrier ... mechanical handling/movement large equipment for containers.

Strapping ... securing cargo from movement by forms of lashings.

Stripping ... unloading a container ex quay or distribution area.

Stuffing ... loading a container ex quay or at a collection area prior to ship acceptance.

Sweat ... the condensation which forms on all surfaces and on all goods in a hold or a compartment, due to the inability of cooled air to hold in suspension as much water vapour as warm air. (Sweat can be considered as ship or cargo sweat).

Sweepings ... the residue from torn or broken bag cargoes left in a space after the main "load" is discharged. Sweepings are part of the load, to be discharged and passed to the consignee.

S.W.L. ... Safe Working Load.

Synchronism . . . a ship "rolling" with the waves . . . a stability factor.

Systems ... methods of loading and discharging vessels which have regard to numerous technical/sophisticated arrangements leading to reliability, ease of handling and economies of operation. (Notably present in large modern ports).

T.

Tallying ... checking ... keeping a record ... of cargo loaded or discharged.

Tanker International Safety Guide . . . a detailed exposition covering all functions, hazards, emergencies and technical information relative to the handling of bulk oil.

Tender Ship ... a vessel with a "small" metacentric height.

Tilt Angle ... the angle at which fork lift truck mast can be tilted from the vertical, to allow symmetrical load placing in or from a stack. Usually 2–5–10 degrees.

Time Charter ... vessel hired from its owner for a specific period of time.

T.I.R. ... "Transports internationaux routiers". The system within European countries which permits the passage of cargo loads, underseal, without custom examination.

Total Container System ... the control of container cargo from point of collection to point of discharge ... computerized communications.

T.P.I. ... Tons per inch ... the weight requirement per tons to alter the draft one inch, according to displacement. Obtainable from "curves".

Transport Mode ... the complete integration of all services involved in the movement of cargo from first source to final destination.

Transportable Moisture Limit ... the limitation of a cargo, subject to moisture content, at which it can be safely carried.

Travel Speed ... F.L.T.s ... the optimum safe travelling speed when carrying loads.

Trimming ... distributing and levelling bulk cargo to promote a solidarity of load. Also referred to in respect of ventilator cowl direction.

U.

Ullage ... the practice of measuring depth of oil (in tanks) by dipping, i.e. the space left between the tank top and the surface of the oil.

Union Purchase ... a pair of derricks used in combination.

Unitization ... the concept of handling cargo ... by reason of its "sizes" by reducing the number of occasions whereby it needs to be handled.

Unstable Stability ...

V.

Vacuum Clamp ... an arrangement for the lifting of paper reels.

V.C.G. ... Vertical Centre of Gravity.

Velle (and Hallen) Derricks ... derricks with specialized attachments giving versatility in swinging and in the lifting/lowering of weights.

Vertical Movement ... the lifting and handling of cargo in vertical up and down direction.

Vibratory Stresses ... stresses which build up throughout the whole of a ship structure from heavy and excessive rolling and pitching. Incorrectly stowed cargo is likely to show damage from vibratory stress.

Viscosity ... properties of liquids whereby they exhibit resistance to internal flow.

V.L.C.C. ... Very Large Crude Carriers.

Voyage Charter ... a vessel hired from its owner for one voyage only.

W.

Way Bill ... a "qualified" Bill of Lading. Non Negotiable.

Wrapper Damage ... relative to paper reels resulting from rough handling by a clamp truck.

Warehouse Charges . . . dues covering goods passed through a warehouse.

Wharfage Charge ... costs covering dock and quay cargo handling.

APPENDIX A.

CONTAINERIZATION

Types of Containers and Their Application

The following notes are included by reason of the interest, helpfulness and guidance of:—

P & O CONTAINERS LIMITED, of LONDON, ENGLAND.

They include detail to inform ship's officers and other maritime personnel how the differation of container types have influence upon Cargo Handling.

General Purpose Containers are "closed" units suitable for the carriage of all types of general cargo. They are, basically, of a steel framework with steel cladding. In all cases the floors are either hardwood timber planked, or plywood sheeting.
Access for loading or unloading is through full width doors.
Sizes can be 20ft. × 8ft. × 8ft. 6in. or 40ft. × 8ft. × 8ft. 6in.

Open Top Containers are containers with a top loading facility designed for the carriage of heavy and awkward cargoes, and those cargoes with height in excess of that which can be stowed in a general purpose container.
Sizes are similar.

Fantainers are identical to a general purpose container, with similar internal dimensions but with the added ability to be easily converted into a Fantainer. This is achieved by the introduction and fittings which allow the electric extraction fans to operate, so to permit an air duct under the cargo, which is stowed upon pallets.
The aim is to remove any respiratory heat developed by the cargo and to balance the internal temperature of the container, plus the cargo, with that of the varying ambients outside, in order to prevent the formation of condensation.

Flat Rack Containers are containers designed to facilitate the carriage of cargo in excess of the dimensions of either General Purpose or Open Top Containers.

They consist of a flat bed with fixed ends, the external dimensions conforming to I-S-O (International Standards Organization) requirements.

(Uncontainerable Cargo ... A combination of 2 or more Flat Rack containers can be used to form a temporary "tween deck space" for uncontainerable cargo moved on a "port to port" basis).

Insulated Containers. These are containers which are insulated against heat loss or gain and are used in conjunction with a blown air refrigeration system, to convey perishable, or other cargo, which needs to be carried under temperature control. These containers can be, and are used, for the carriage of fresh, decidious and citrus fruit.

Refrigerated Containers. These containers are designed to operate independently of a blown air refrigerated system and are fitted with their own refrigeration units, which require an electrical power supply for operation. This can be either 200/220 Volts or 380/440 Volts.

Each container is capable of being set at its own individual carriage temperature.

Cargo should not be stowed to the full height of the container, but an air gap of approximately 75 mm. should be left at the top.

Sizes can be 20ft. $\times$ 8ft. $\times$ 8ft. 6in. or 40ft. $\times$ 8ft. $\times$ 8ft. 6in.

Bulk Containers. These containers are designed for the carriage of dry powders and granulated substances in bulk.

To facilitate top loading, three circular hatches (500 mm. diameter) are fitted in the roof. For discharge a hatch is fitted in the right hand door of the container.

Tank Containers. The tanks conform to I.M.O. requirements, i.e. they are suitable for carrying a considerable variety of goods. They are constructed of stainless steel and maintained to "food quality status" and are primarily dedicated to the carriage of potable spirits, although they may be used for the transport of other liquids. The stainless steel tanks are suspended in 20ft. frameworks.

Open Sided Containers. A type of container designed to accommodate the carriage of special commodiities such as plywood from the Far East, certain perishable commodities and the carriage of livestock.

Ventilated Containers. Primarily designed for the coffee trade. They are of steel construction and to all intents and purposes are the same as General Purpose Containers, except for the inclusion of full length ventilation galleries, allowing for the passive ventilation of the cargo.

Loading Containers.
There is no especial method of handling and packaging containers, except to say that:—

(a) Safe container transport depends chiefly on a correct and immovable stow, and an even "weight distribution".

The containers must be stowed tightly so that lateral and longitudinal movement of the cargo within it is impossible, or the cargo must be restrained.

(b) Stowage must be tight.

(c) There should be "restraint" on the cargo such as to present a collapse of the stow while packing, unpacking, or during transit. There must be "stoppage" of any movement during transit of part loads or of single heavy items.

Prevention of the "face" of the stow collapsing and leaning against the container doors.

(d) There must be methods of securing the cargo, i.e. from shoring, lashing or locking. This can be done by the use of bars and struts, ropes, wires, chains. Wedging takes the form of wooden distance pieces or pads of synthetic material.

There is no simple formula when securing cargo. Each stow must be treated on its own merits.

(e) Restraining certain types of cargoes.
1. Top heavy articles should be wedged, shored and lashed, to prevent toppling.
2. Heavy weights should be secured — i.e. chain, wire or bottle screws to lashing rings sited in the floors, plus shoring with timber.
3. Wheeled vehicles should be chocked and lashed.
4. Resilent loads can cause lashings to slacken — this may be overcome by introducing elasticity, (i.e. rubber rope) into the lashing pattern.

(f) Securing the face of the stow near container doors.
It is not unusual to finds a space remaining between the face of the cargo and the container doors.
1. This can be made secure by the use of suitably positioned lashing points, with wire, rope strapping, etc.
2. The build up of a wooden gate for any wider gaps and/or heavier cargo.
3. Filter pieces of paper pads, polystyrene, wood, wool pads etc.

(g) Fall out ... Care must be taken to ensure that there is no "fall out" when the container doors are opened.

(h) Heavy loads should be loaded according to their shape, dimensions and weight. Their distribution must be over the entire width of the container and a fair distribution of dunnaging should be laid to avoid extra stress upon the container floor.

(*i*) In the loading of dynamic loads consideration must be given to the type, and use, of mechanical handling devices, such as Fork Lift Trucks, Pallet Trucks and special Roller Systems.

In doing so any unavoidable gaps in the stow should be along the centre of the container, and not at the sides.

CARGO HANDLING EQUIPMENT — Generalities.

A. This can be varied and care must be taken to use that method which gives the best efficiency, with economy.

These methods include the Fork Lift Truck, The Side-Shift Mechanism, Extension Forks, Drum Handlers, Push Pull attachments, Barrel Handles, Lift Trucks and Pallet Transporters, Crane Jibs and Squeeze Clamps.

Each of the foregoing, in their useage, is intended to load and place the load in its best position.

Specialities.
(*a*) Portable Hydraulic Rollers . . . capable of loading/unloading any size or weight, up to the maximum dimensions and weight capacity of the container.
(*b*) Cantilever Jib Cranes . . . mobile cranes with a suitable cantilever jib suitable for placing awkward loads into a trailer mounted container.
(*c*) Overhead Cranes . . . of all types are extremely efficient in loading trailer-mounted open top containers.
(*d*) Cranes of the correct capacity may be used for dismounting and remounting containers, provided they are fitted with approved lifting gear . . . i.e. Container Spreaders.
(*e*) Mobile Gantries . . . Electro/Hydraulic and operated with self-adjusting rams to ensure even lifting of containers.

Bulk Handling.
1. Solids. Solid bulk commodities may be loaded into General Purpose Containers suitably fitted with bulkheads at the door end of the container.
2. Liquids. Certain non-hazardous liquids can be transported in General Purpose Containers, fitted with special flexible tanks.

Abbreviations.

C/B. Containerbase . . . one of a group of UK Container Freight Stations.
CFS. Container Freight Station. Place for packing or unpacking small loads.

CFC. Container Safety Convention. International Convention for Safe Containers.

CY. Container Yard Collection and Distribution point for FCL containers.

FCL. Full Container Load. The utilization of all the space in a container.

LCL. Less than Container Load. A parcel of goods too small to fill a container.

LO/LO. Lift-on/Lift-off. A containership on to which and from which containers are lifted by crane.

MT. An Empty Container.

OW. Overwidth. A container with goods protruding beyond its sides.

Slot. Space on board a vessel occupied by a container.

Stuffing/Stripping. The action of packing/unpacking a container.

Terminal. Port at which containers are loaded/unloaded on to/from container vessels.

UNCON. Uncontainerable Goods. Goods which, because of their dimensions, cannot be containerised and which are therefore carried other than in a container.

BOX. Colloquial name for a Container.

OH. Overheight. A container with goods protruding above the top of the corner posts.

OOG. Out of Gauge. Goods whose dimensions exceed those of the container in which they are packed.

REEFER. Refrigerated.

APPENDIX B.

EXAMPLES OF
MODERN SHIPPING AND CARGO MOVEMENT

GENERAL KNOWLEDGE

Aberdeen is a port developing modern applications, to which ship's officers could well take note.

Cargo handled at Aberdeen in 1990 averaged almost 4 million tons, comprising imports and exports, including general cargoes, containers, forest products, cereals, fishing . . . and oil cargoes.

Grain exports are high. Steel pipes cover a healthy import/export trade.

The port has a new operational multi-user quay, providing two berths for a range of ships, covering increasing traffic handled by the port.

Le Havre remains a major continental port having handled 53 million tons in 1989, covering all types of cargoes, including 12 million tons of general cargo and 9 million tons of containers. The port has a multi-purpose bulk centre to accommodate foodstuff products through a new provision of conveyor belts.

Hong Kong. Some 130,000 (plus) ocean going ships move in and out of Hong Kong each year, with a large proportion of this number computerised.

Of the 130,000 ships this figure is made up of 16 million passengers and 86 million tons of cargo, much of which is covered by 4-5 million TEUs handled by the container port.

Hong Kong also has a refrigerated container depot. The port is, in fact, classified as a major container environment, in which sense it can be realistically compared with Singapore. It has wide areas of container stacking and modern transporter loading/discharging craneage units. Trade wise Hong Kong attracts wide tonnages and it berths large tonnage container ships.

Liverpool has, over recent years, doubled its traffic tonnage to almost 20 million tons, of which cargo handling remains dominant. Oil transportation accounted for 9 million tons. Containers cover almost 148,000 TEUs while timber handling has been of the order of approximately 500,000 plus tons.

China is developing its shipbuilding tonnage and is planning vessels of 850,000 tons during the next decade.

A Japanese building organization has developed a system by which, with the attention of maritime officers, the time needed for developing an optimum oil loading plan will assist in the scheduling of tankers and prompt decision making in the purchasing of crude oil.

Container Ships are forecast during the next generation, to have capacities of up to 6,000 TEUs.

The development of container vessels has introduced "hatch coverless" systems.

The dispensation of hatch covers makes container handling, and port turn round, considerably reduced.

Ship handling of containers varies from 28 per hour to 50 per hour, within a wide range of container cranes.

Modern container vessels can have capacities of 3,600 plus TEUs.

Containers vary in size; normally they can be 20 feet, 40 feet or 48 feet lengthwise. There are, also, refrigerated containers.

(See Appendix A).

China Clay is exported through the South Coast UK ports of Par and Fowey. Indeed it is one of the UK's largest bulk exports. It is for use in the paper industry and is exported for use in that industry through the ports of Finland, Sweden, West Germany and Italy.

Argentina has recently developed its meat market. Most of its exports are in the form of special cuts boxed in 20/25 kilogrammes and chilled or frozen. The cargo is shipped in Reefer Containers.

Rotterdam serves a highly industrialised hinterland, handling some 200/300 million tons of cargo per year. The port is said to be the largest in the world. General cargo and containers show the most consistent increase.

Antwerp is the principal seaport of Belgium — competing with Rotterdam to be a leading maritime gateway into Europe.

Forest Products. The shipping of Forest Products is largely a commercial and technical matter, since there is a variety of forest products which call for shipping services.

North America, Canada and Scandinavia are leading export environments.

Basically there are three groups of Forest Products ... bulk products (sawn timber), woodpulp and kraftliner, produced to meet customer requirements, neobulk products such as newsprint, and customer products such as printing and writing paper, and some plywood products. Central Europe is interested in high value special printing paper. Japan has high requirements for Forest Products. The North American markets are stable.

Shipping is benefiting from the expansion of the Brazilian forest industry.

Ferries — Safety Measures.

A series of measures to improve the safety of passenger ships, especially the Ro/Ro ferries, came into force internationally in April 1990.

After loading, and before departure, the ship's Master must determine the ship's trim and stability, and also ascertain, and record, that the ship is complying with stability criteria.

Cargo loading doors are to be closed, and locked, before the ship proceeds on any voyage. Where the door cannot be opened, or closed at a berth, the rules make provision for the doors to be opened, or closed, while the ship is approaching, or leaving, a berth.

Tanker loading.

A new technological system has been developed in Japan, which assists ships' officers, and shore loading personnel, to correctly plan the optimum time necessary to load a tanker, and scheduling its trading systems.

As tankers frequently load several kinds of crude oil, from different ports, the stowage aspects, which affect the balance of a ship and the strength of the hull, are important factors for a safe voyage, to be decided by the ship's chief officer. This is time consuming.

There is, however, a relatively new system — a "planning export system" which plans optimum oil loading of tankers.

This is a technological system, developed by the Japanese.

L.N.G. Carriers . . . their design.

Over the immediate future years . . . up to 1993 . . . the changes in ship design, and cargo carriage, is intended to be formidable.

For the stowage of L.N.G. there is to be 4 spherical tanks, as distinct from the usual 5/6 tanks in existing L.N.G. carriers, albeit in comparative size the 4 tanks are larger than those in the 5/6 tank ships.

These new L.N.G. carriers will have fewer cargo pumps, less instrumentatious equipment, and simplified pipe arrangements.

In size these ships are larger with a wider hull, and a shallower draught. They are longer, producing a smaller length/breadth ratio (an important aspect in the characteristics of any ship). On average these ships are to be length 272 m., breadth 48 m., depth 27 m., and draught of 11 m. They will have a gross tonnage of approximately 1,050, a deadweight of 67,000, with a cargo capacity, at —163c of 128,000 m³.

The ships are being built in Japan.

Types of L.N.G. include propane, butane, propane/butane mixture, propylene, butylene, butadiene, antrydrous, ammonia and naptha.

Currently L.N.G. (Liquid Natural Gas) is carried in large tankers, of high tonnage and capacities.

British Shipping is now, to a great extent, owned by companies, which form part of larger commercial groupings.

The Port of Singapore is said to be the world's busiest port. It is also an important bunkering port and a large container port. It is also an oil refining centre. In terms of "Cargo Handling" this can be in the region of 170+ million tons, for a year. It is also recorded as having, these present years, handled 4/5 million TEUs (which is of the order of handling approximately 38/40 containers every hour a vessel is alongside a berth).

In these circumstances, ship "turn round" can be of 10-12 hours.

Singapore has vast areas of stacking for containers, which permits the units to be stacked up to five high.

Apropos the handling of containers, Singapore also handles a wide variety of "general cargo", and "bulks". Its services are worldwide, as well as a wide concentrated Middle and Far Eastern trades.

In this context it is practical to comment that with such a dynamic approach, Singapore can well attract shipping organizations, and ships, to use the port. Singapore is thus a "cargo handling" port.

Organization and Administration is of high order, such that a variety of cargoes, apart from containers, are quickly and effectively loaded, and discharged. Singapore is effectively computerized by which the planning of its operations are technically operated. In this context there is the "Teleport" arrangement by which there is electronic linkage with other ports, such as Bremen in West Germany and Le Havre in France.

In these arrangements shipping and cargoes information can be effectively exchanged, almost immediately.

Melbourne is said to be the largest container port in the Southern Hemisphere, having high volumes of general cargo. Primarily the largest growth in trade comes from the South East Asia and the Pacific Rim, albeit trade with Great Britain, Hong Kong, New Zealand Japan, the United States and South Korea has kept Melbourne busy.

Fremantle ... Australia, is the third largest general cargo port in Australia, after Melbourne and Sydney, In 1990 it handled 500 million tons of cargo, including that discharged from containerships.

Hamburg is West Germany's largest seaport. It offers services to over 300 export/import business houses and this covers conventional, containerised, heavy lifts, dry and liquid bulk, chemicals, Ro/Ro services, reefers and barges etc. cargoes.

New York (U.S.A.) is considered to be the most dynamic seaport in the world.

Shipping World Tonnage. Tankers over 10,000 tons d.w. form the largest shipping group, to the extent of some 240 million tons d.w.

Dry bulk carriers make up the second group with a total of approximately 200 million tons d.w. and general cargo ships take up some 66 million tons d.w.

Of these figures combined carriers account for 35 million tons d.w., containerships 26 million tons d.w. and L.P.G. carriers 3 million tons d.w.

Cargo Handling Lift Trucks.

While the traditional general purpose fork lift trucks still "work" within ports and transporter centres, there are now available engine powered lift trucks, suitable for lifting tonnages of from 3 tons to 42 tons, the latter useable as container handlers, as well as for heavy materials handling.

Not only are these truck developments designed for vertical lifting or lowering, but hydrostatic sideloaders are also available. These assist Ro/Ro traffic.

The worldwide increase in the use of containers for transporting goods has resulted in the need for reliable and efficient machines designed and built to handle 20, 30, 35 and 40 foot containers on forks, fixed side lift, fixed end lift or telescopic side lift attachments.

Containers can be stacked 2, 3, 4 or 5 high.

The preceeding notes are included by the kind permission of LANSING LINDE LTD. of Basingstoke, Hampshire, England. This organization provides among other things, extensive and informative illustrated documentary material.

Southampton.

Southampton can be said to be a port of versatile qualities.

It has geographical advantages in that, by reason of natural causes it has the helpfulness of maximum tidal flow by which this is only two knots. This "double" tide promotes the world's largest vessels unrestricted access during 17 hours of rising and high water in every 24 hours. Thus it has the advantages for vessels of all sizes.

Handling bulk cargoes is a growing and influential business for Southampton. It is a leading U.K. grain exporting centre, as also are the trades of timber, wine, fruit, vegetables, aggregates and cement. It is also an important oil port.

The timber trade includes softwood and panel products, such as plywood, chipboard and hardboard. Timber products are imported from the Far East, Canada, U.S.S.R., Finland and Sweden.

Considerable tonnages of Bulk Wine are stored, bottled and distributed through the port. Regular shipments of palletised vegetables arrive from the Canary Islands and the Jaffa trades. Southampton has a deepwater bulk cement importation facility.

Due to its marine and geographical advantages and cargo landing facilities the port is one of the busiest vehicle-handling centres, covering cars and other vehicles by foreign and U.K. manufacturers, as well as heavy wheeled Ro/Ro cargo, such as excavators, trucks, diggers and tractors. In 1989 over 240,000 vehicles for import and export requirements were handled within the port.

Ships are involved which are the largest and most modern Ro/Ro vessels in the world.

Container operations are an integral part of Southampton's trade, involving high standards of cargo handling. Indeed, by reason of its tidal advantage, the biggest container ships can gain almost unlimited access.

In these respects the port has a 40 ton gantry crane with an outreach of 148 feet, a back reach of 52 feet and an operational lifting height of 100 feet. It can handle both 20 and 40 foot boxes.

Operations at the Southampton container terminal are highly automated. (see separate notes). The majority of container handling is provided by a multi-national trio consortium, operating, between Europe and the Far East and Southern Africa.

Cargo handling facilities in Southampton (as with other U.K. ports) is covered by the emergence of the independent stevedoring companies, which took over in the U.K. following the end of the Dock Labour Scheme. These independent stevedoring companies are able to concentrate on the needs of customers. These arrangements can deal with a wide variety of ships and cargoes — car carriers, large Ro/Ro vessels, military cargo vessels and ships carrying Lo/Lo (load on/load off) cargo to be handled with conventional gear.

Southampton Container Terminals.

Southampton has its own Container Terminal, albeit this, in itself, is a private limited company operating within the overall Southampton Dock area. The terminal covers some 95 acres and has 930 metres of quays. It has three deep water berths which can handle the world's largest container vessels.

The annual throughput of the terminal is in excess of a quarter of a million containers a year.

Advance information systems are a feature of the terminal, which has its own computer installation. This provide a complete terminal management and control system.

Operationally, the terminal provides a 24 hour a day, seven days a week service, with concurrent shipside and landside activities. This permits the continuous receipt and delivery of cargo.

The operations of the terminal are based on the use of six quay cranes and a fleet of 32 straddle carriers. The stacking area consists of some 5,500 TEU ground slots, giving a capacity for 8,000 TEUs.

Containers are stacked up to 3 high for exports, 2 high for imports. For dangerous goods this is 1 high.

All containers are inspected on receipt and delivery at the gatehouse (the point of entry). The terminal is said to manage and operate one of the largest and most modern complexes in the U.K.

Initial input consists of information about each container, which is stored until the container physically arrives, either by road or rail. Containers entering the terminal are categorised by an automatic system according to voyage, port, weight, size, and a directive given for the placement of each container. After loading has been completed, and the ship's tanks have been considered, the complete ship stability is calculated by the operating system. Southampton Container Terminal has become the U.K.'s main choice for handling Far East traffic, the ports involved containing Jeddah, Singapore, Hong Kong, Kelung, Busan, Kobe, Nagoya and Tokyo.

THE HUMBER PORTS

Hull, Immingham, Grimsby, Goole.

Within the Humber Ports environment, Hull, as a major port, dominates cargo handling and its services. In this context Roll on/Roll off services are very effective while the varied facilities offered at Hull are ideal for shippers to take advantage of the port's location between the industrial heart of Britain and its continental partners ... hence the increase in Ro/Ro traffic in recent years.

Hull has five modern, purpose built Ro/Ro berths. Apart from British ships, Baltic shipping offers frequent Ro/Ro services. Import traffic includes high numbers of cars, together with horticultural glass ware. Exports include chemicals, tin, machinery and electrodes, general cargo and spirits. Finanglia Ferries use Hull for weekly sailings to Helsinki, Rauma and Turku.

Forest products from paper to packaged timber are regular imports, using both Sto/Ro (Stow off/Roll off) to traditional handling methods.

The D.S.R. England line offers a regular weekly service to Rostock with cargoes including Acetate, bagged chemicals, furniture and basket-ware, making up a wide range of manufactured goods . . . and containers.

Hull also has a groupage depot available for all services, including the stuffing, stripping and consolidation of cargo. It also has 3 heavy lift Scotch Derrick Cranes available for Lo/Lo lifts up to 35 tons. The shoreside activity is bolstered by 2 fixed jig gantries, 2 Ferranti straddle carriers and a fleet of fork lift trucks with maximum capacity of 42 tons.

Cement is another cargo, transported into the port by bulk carriers and then transferred into storage facilities.

Hull is also engaged in container traffic within a Container Terminal, with 3 gantry cranes. The port is also active in the timber trade with imports of softwoods from Scandinavia and the Baltic. Hardwood and plywood is imported from the Far East. Additionally there are shipments of lumber from the east coast of Canada and hardwood logs from West Africa.

Immingham handles more than 35 million tons of cargo a year, with emphasis on dry and liquid bulk commodities, together with the "general" field, utilising Ro/Ro and Lo/Lo services.

The port has a spectacular growth in grain exports.

Five specialised river terminals handle much of Immingham's bulk traffic.

Goole is located on the River Ouse, 80 kilometres from the open sea but close to the M62 and M18 motorways. As such, at the heart of Goole is the Boothferry Container Terminal, the container throughput covering 20,000 TEUs.

A bulk cement terminal, with self discharge techniques has a silo capacity of 6,000 tons, imported from Poland.

Goole, also, has berthing facilities to handle predominantly bulk traffic, with services including 3 grabbing cranes, front loading shovels and skid steer loaders, all designed for high speed operations.

Grain cargoes move within the port of Goole, while heavy lift cargoes are a regular feature of the port's traffic.

Liner services, with emphasis on containers and unit loads, serve Sweden, Finland, West Germany, Holland, Spain and North Africa.

Additionally, solid fuel, timber, iron and steel, fertilisers, minerals, grain and animal food, move on a regular basis in charter vessels.

South Wales (Barry).

The port traffic of Barry includes materials for the construction industry, foodstuffs, solid fuels, scrap, general cargo, chemicals and petroleum products. It has considerable experience in handling fruit and vegetable cargoes and has long been involved in the importing of bananas from the Windward Islands. Geest Line imports some 200,000 tons of bananas a year through Barry . . . on the return journey the trades cover a variety of consumer goods.

In general terms Barry can be said to be a general cargo port, together with bulk cargoes. Dry bulks include scrap metal for export, as well as coal and coke.

Kings Lynn (Norfolk).

In this modern age it is difficult to differentiate between large, medium and small ports. Large ports have clear distinctions, but the difference between medium and small ports can be questionable. Kings Lynn can be placed within the two, medium and small ports.

The port handles a wide range of traffic embracing a variety of cargoes. It has wide arrangements with Ro/Ro Lo/Lo cargoes. Import and export steel are traditional traffics, utilising 20/25 ton craneage and high capacity fork lifts.

Timber is a major commodity from the Russian and Baltic ports.

Other cargoes in palletised and mini-bulk form pass through the port, as does a wide range of dry bulks.

The Port of Baltimore (U.S.A.)

The Maryland (U.S.A.) Port Administration has marketing responsibilities insofar as it encourages the movement of cargoes . . . general, bulk, Roll on/Roll off and Containerised . . . throughout the Maryland marine terminals and for export requirements.

Within the environment the Port of Baltimore is prominent and attractive to shipship lines and shippers around the world. Baltimore(s) modern terminal, known as the Seagirt Marine Terminal, has been developed to primarily "work" containers, be they for import or exports to the extent of 150,000 containers annually. The Seagirt Terminal is one of the most modern terminals in the world. It is a 265 acre environment, including a 100 acre container storage area, having high technology cargo handling systems, including modern dual hoist cranes and computerised controls. The dual hoist cranes can move 55 containers per hour.

The long established Dundalk Marine Terminal, which is, currently being fully modernised, is, in fact, the largest marine terminal in the Port of Baltimore and is sufficiently versatile. It is capable of handling containers, breakbulk and Roll on/Roll off cargoes. It has 6 general cargo berths and 7 container berths, with 10 40-ton container cranes and 2 60-ton gantry cranes handling general and container cargoes.

The Port of Baltimore(s) inland position permits of quick distribution of goods to the U.S. Midwest areas. It is also an exporting gateway to Europe, the Far East, the Mediterranean and South America.

Apart from containers, cargoes which find movement through Baltimore include bulks, coal, steel products, forest products, "cars", molasses, latex, asphalt and grain.

Baltimore is said to be one of the most modern and busiest ports in the United States.

INDEX

Note—In the use of this index attention is drawn to pages 463–8 "Principles of and Background to Cargo Handling" and pages 469–79 "Cargo Handling Terms—A Glossary". Both of these inclusions support the overall index by reason of their specific detail.

LIST OF DIAGRAMS

LIST OF ILLUSTRATIONS

CODES OF PRACTICE

ACKNOWLEDGEMENTS

The practicality of a book of this nature could not be produced without the interest, association and guidance from many organizations and individuals We record here our thanks and appreciation for all that has been willingly and helpfully given, the following list being indicative of that generosity.

Atlantic Container Line Services Limited (ACL)
Associated British Ports
Austin and Pickerskill Limited
British Standards Institution
Blohm & Voss, A.G., Hamburg
British Gas Corporation
British Ports Association
British Ropeway Engineering Ltd (Breco)
Cargospeed Equipment Limited
Coubro & Scrutton (M&I) Ltd
Cammel Laird Shipbuilders Ltd
Hagglunds AB, Hagglund & Soner, Sweden
Handford Photography
Hall Thermotank International Limited
International Maritime Organization
MacGregor Zaire International Group
MacMillan Bloedel Meyer Organization, British Columbia
Lansing Bagnall Limited
Kockumation Organization, Malmo, Sweden
National Association of Port Employers
Overland Freight Forwarders Ltd
Pertwee Industrial Limited
Prince Line ... Furness Withy Group
Rubery Owen Conveyance Ltd
Starman Shipping
Stothert & Pitt Limited
Shell Tankers (UK) Limited
Esso Tankers
Blue Star Line
P & O Containers Limited
Associated British Ports
Southampton Container Terminals Limited
The Port of Baltimore

H.M. Stationery Office for permission to refer to Ministry of Transport Merchant Shipping Notices and also to ex-colleagues and associates in the nautical world, who have made comments on previous editions.